ADVANCES
IN THE PSYCHOLOGY
OF HUMAN INTELLIGENCE

Volume 1

ADVANCES
IN THE PSYCHOLOGY
OF HUMAN INTELLIGENCE
Volume 1

Edited by

Robert J. Sternberg
Yale University

LEA LAWRENCE ERLBAUM ASSOCIATES, PUBLISHERS
1982 Hillsdale, New Jersey   London

Lawrence Erlbaum Associates, Inc., Publishers
365 Broadway
Hillsdale, New Jersey 07642

ISBN   0-89859-163 5
ISSN   0278-2359

Printed in the United States of America

10   9   8   7   6   5   4   3   2   1

Contents

Preface

During the past decade, we have witnessed a remarkable resurgence of interest in the psychology of human intelligence. In the late 1960s, research in the field of intelligence seemed to have gone into at least a partial remission. But today a large number of investigators are pursuing active research programs concerning human intelligence.

The rapid expansion of the field of intelligence convinced me of the need for a *Handbook of Human Intelligence*—a volume that would help guide research on intelligence during the next decade or so. But a handbook cannot keep up with a rapidly advancing field, and it was for this reason that I decided that there was also a need for a series of volumes to complement the handbook—in essence, to continue the work that I hope the handbook initiates. This series of volumes will mark significant advances in the psychology of human intelligence.

Advances in the Psychology of Human Intelligence, to be published biannually, contains articles by leaders in the field that document the progress that is being made toward understanding human intelligence. This series does not attempt to achieve the encyclopedic coverage of a handbook, but it can keep up with, and, I hope, lead the field in a way that no single, one-time volume could. Thus, the Advances series complements the handbook in its documentation and guidance of developments in research on human intelligence.

The present volume is the first in the series, and contributors were asked to address the following questions in their chapters (as well as any others that might be of particular concern to them):

1. What notion of intelligence motivates the research program to be described?

2. How does the research build upon and clarify this notion of intelligence?
3. What theoretical or practical questions about intelligence does the research address?
4. What are the particular advantages and disadvantages of the proposed approach to intelligence?
5. How, if at all, does this research tie in with previous and current research by others in the field of intelligence?
6. What are the major findings of the research program, and what is their significance for the understanding of intelligence?
7. What directions is the research likely to follow in the next 5 to 10 years?

The concept of intelligence explored in this and subsequent volumes is broadly conceived. All volumes include contributions both by individuals whose research is clearly identified with the mainstream of research on intelligence and by individuals whose research may not be so identified but yet has an important bearing on our understanding of intelligence. Although contributors always represent a diversity of substantive and methodological foci, they share a seriousness of commitment and contribution to research on intelligence, broadly defined.

The present volume reflects the diversity of approaches and substantive concerns that will characterize future volumes. It includes chapters dealing primarily with attention (Hunt & Lansman), choice reaction time (Jensen), reading (Frederiksen), spatial visualization (Cooper; Pellegrino & Kail), number (Gelman), reasoning (Sternberg), and complex problem solving (Chi, Glaser, & Rees; Polson & Jeffries). All of the chapters deal with intelligent behavior, broadly conceived, and illustrate the diversity of research topics currently being pursued under the general rubric of research on intelligence.

Robert J. Sternberg

ADVANCES IN THE PSYCHOLOGY OF HUMAN INTELLIGENCE

Volume 1

Introduction

Robert J. Sternberg
Yale University

Until the second half of the 20th century, two theoretical questions seemed to predominate in the literature on intelligence: (1) what is the structure of intelligence? and (2) to what extent is intelligence determined by inheritance and to what extent is it determined by environment? With the advent of the information-processing approach to studying intelligence, these two questions became less central, and a multiplicity of other questions arose that had received relatively little consideration in earlier work. Many of these new questions are dealt with in the present volume.

To the extent that the selection of authors and topics in this book is biased, it is unabashedly biased toward the information-processing approach to intelligence and the kinds of theoretical questions this approach generates. In order to introduce these questions and the chapters that address them, I have chosen a single key theoretical question that I believe each chapter addresses in a particularly apt way. I raise each of these questions here and discuss briefly how each given chapter addresses the questions I have selected. I wish to emphasize that the choice of questions is mine and that the authors of the chapters might not view their own contributions in the same light that I do. Nevertheless, I believe that my own perspective might provide at least a minimal unifying backdrop for the contributions of the various authors in the volume.

1. To What Extent Should Research on Intelligence Focus on Process and to What Extent Should It Focus on Product? The psychometric approach to intelligence was characterized by its emphasis on the products of intelligent performance. In the information-processing revolution, emphasis shifted to the processes of intelligent behavior. Psychometricians were criticized for their inatten-

1

tion to the processes that give rise to the products measured by the tests. Indeed, information-processing methods are especially well suited to the identification and examination of the processes constituting intelligent performance.

Recently, some information-processing psychologists have begun to question whether information-processing researchers have not been too extreme in their shift from product to process. But these psychologists are not advocating a shift back to the emphasis on observable products that characterized many psychometric investigations. Rather, they are suggesting that more attention be paid to mental products, in particular, the knowledge base that is generated by the processes of intelligent performance. Their goal is the formulation of a knowledge-based theory of intelligence, or at least a theory that gives knowledge the prominence these psychologists believe it deserves. Chi, Glaser, and Rees, in their review of others' and their own research on "Expertise in Problem Solving," propose an outline for the development of a knowledge-based theory of intelligence. They argue that differences between expert and novice performance in the solution of physics problems (and other types of problems as well) are heavily knowledge-dependent. To the extent that one wishes to view individual differences in intelligence as reflecting differing levels of expertise in varying kinds of problem-solving performance, the findings of the studies they review on complex problem solving are relevant for understanding individual differences in human intelligence.

2. To What Extent Can Individual Differences in Intelligence Be Understood in Terms of Discrete Differences in Cognitive Styles in Strategic Behavior? During the mid-20th century, research on cognitive styles in intelligent behavior flourished. People seemed to be potentially characterizable as field independent or field dependent, as levelers or sharpeners, as reflective or impulsive, and as tolerant or intolerant of ambiguity, to name just a few of the constructs that were investigated. But research on cognitive styles began to peter out during the late 1960s and early 1970s. Research of this kind was not discontinued altogether, but the number of investigations and the attention attracted by this kind of investigation almost certainly decreased. There seem to have been several reasons for this decrease in the salience of cognitive-styles research: questions regarding the distinguishability of some of the styles from general intelligence; questions about the cross-situational consistency of some of the styles; questions about whether the styles really represented discrete types of performance or rather merely represented ends of various continua; and questions about where such research was heading.

Cooper accidentally stumbled onto what appeared to be a cognitive-style difference in visual comparisons. In her early research on mental rotation and comparison, she found what appeared to be two discrete strategies for solving rotation and comparison problems. Individuals seemed to be characterized by the use of either one strategy or the other. In Chapter 2, Cooper reviews her program of research on holistic and analytic processors in visual processing. Because she is especially sensitive to the problems of cognitive-style research, her chapter on "Strategies for Visual Comparison and Representation: Individual Differences" in some respects provides a model for how cognitive-styles research (or, as I prefer to call her work, "neocognitive-styles" research) can remain viable in the 1980s.

3. Can the Factor Model of Differential Psychology and the Component Model of Information-Processing Psychology Be Integrated in a Way That Maximally Exploits the Potential of Each, with Neither Subservient to the Other? In the enthusiasm that accompanied the information-processing revolution in research on intelligence, there was an unfortunate tendency to dismiss the factor model out of hand or, at best, to give it short shrift. Factor analysis provided a convenient whipping boy, especially because research using the factor model seemed to be foundering on the shores of what appeared to some to be insuperable problems. Some information-processing investigators continued to use factor analysis in their research, but such analysis was relegated to a relatively minor role. The idea was not to dispense with factor analysis altogether, but somehow to "put it in its place."

Many of the criticisms that were directed against factor analysis centered around its relative inefficacy in hypothesis testing (as opposed to hypothesis generation). But at the same time that these criticisms were being made, powerful new methods based on the factor-analytic model were being developed that made factor analysis a potentially valuable tool in confirmatory as well as exploratory studies. One of these confirmatory methods, analysis of covariance structures, has been used by Frederiksen in the studies that have led to the development of "A Componential Theory of Reading Skills and Their Interactions." Frederiksen combines differential and experimental-cognitive methods in an extremely powerful way. Both correlational and subtractive logics play indispensable roles in his research. I believe Frederiksen's methodology to be as elegant as any in showing the power that the two kinds of logics can provide when truly integrated, rather than when simply used side-by-side as has been true in much earlier research seeking to "combine" the two kinds of logics and methods.

4. Can a Substantial Base of Theory and Data Be Constructed for Understanding What Young ("Preoperational") Children Can Do, as Well as for What They Cannot Do? The work of Piaget provided a monumental base of theory and data for understanding children's cognitive development. Unfortunately, children in one age bracket—that from roughly 3 or 4 to roughly 7 or 8 years of age—often seemed to be characterized more by what they could not do than by what they could do. Typically, it might be shown what concrete-operational children could do (e.g., conservation of quantity, volume, number, or whatever) that preoperational children could not do. In her research program on "Basic

Numerical Abilities," Gelman has gone a long way toward helping us understand what young children *can* do in the domain of numerical information processing. She has used a set of ingenious experimental techniques to show that young children have surprisingly sophisticated understandings of number concepts and that they already possess the basic counting principles needed for later quantitative skills development. At the same time, she has shown how experimental methods can be used to address in a rigorous way some of the theoretical problems that Piaget and his disciples have in many cases addressed only through observational techniques. Sophisticated experimental techniques, such as those employed by Gelman, when used in combination with observational techniques, show that children demonstrate strikingly high levels of numerical competence. Their competence may be less readily visible when it is studied solely by observational techniques.

5. What Role, if Any, Should an Account of the Distribution of Attentional Resources Play in a Theory of Intelligence?   Ideal conditions for the testing of intelligence, either in school or in laboratory settings, are usually considered to be a silent, well-lighted room in which distractions of any kind are minimized. But people rarely function in such a rarified environment. Typically, there are many demands on their attentional resources, and they may find themselves trying to behave intelligently in two or more ways at once, while at the same time filtering out various distractions that threaten to prevent them from performing any of the tasks in an intelligent way.

Hunt and Lansman have proposed a model of "Individual Differences in Attention" that takes at least one step toward remedying the relative inattention theorists of intelligence have paid to attentional variables. In particular, they have tried to account for how people distribute their attention when they do two things at once. Although these theorists have not integrated their model of attentional resource distribution with their own or others' models of intelligence, such an integration would seem to be a possible next step in a future research program. To the extent that the only moderate predictive validities of intelligence tests might be due to the lack of ecological realism on the part of these tests, a test that manipulates situational variables, such as the amount of attention that can be devoted to a given task, might provide something of a breakthrough in our understanding of intelligent performance in real-world situations.

6. What Role, if Any, Should the Measurement of Very Basic Information Processing, Such as Simple and Choice Reaction Time, Play in Theorizing About and Research on Intelligence?   In his very early work on individual differences in intelligence, Sir Francis Galton measured intelligence through the use of a wide variety of simple physical and psychophysical tasks. The Galtonian tradition was carried over to the United States by James McKeen Cattell, but it was aborted by Wissler's findings that relatively simple psychophysical measurements were neither very much correlated with each other nor with performance in school. The relatively greater success of the more complex judgmental tasks used by Binet and his disciples led to a tradition of intelligence research that had little use for the simple tasks advocated by Galton, Cattell, and their disciples.

In the past few years, Jensen has been one of a number of psychologists who have claimed that we were too quick to dispense with measurements made in the Galtonian tradition—that whereas the more physical kinds of tasks used by Galton may indeed have been off base, the simple and choice reaction-time tasks may not have been; that with more refined and sophisticated measurement of basic information processing, it may be possible to identify the bases for the more complex kinds of information processing measured by the judgmental tasks studied by Binet and his successors. In his chapter on "The Chronometry of Intelligence," Jensen reviews evidence from his own and others' laboratories suggesting that speed to perform basic processes, such as visual and memory scanning, is at least moderately correlated with psychometric test performance. Moreover, when several information-processing predictors are combined into a single predictive equation, quite substantial prediction of psychometric test performance can be obtained. Theorizing about the reasons for this relationship is still in early stages; Jensen proposes a first-pass theory of intelligence that attempts to account for intelligent behavior as at least partially derivative from mental speed. Whether or not this theory ultimately proves viable, it is clear that theorists (such as myself) who prefer to understand intelligence in terms of more complex forms of information processing will eventually have to deal with the correlational data Jensen and others of his persuasion have to offer.

7. Can "Cognitive Components" Analysis Be Applied Beyond the Domains of Inductive and Deductive Reasoning? During the mid- and late 1970s, an approach to research on intelligence called "componential analysis" or "cognitive components" analysis became fairly salient in the literature. In this approach, the investigator takes a complex task, often one found on actual IQ tests, and decomposes performance on the task into elementary information-processing components. The approach has been quite successful in accounting for variation in the difficulty of stimulus items and in accounting for individual differences in componential terms. But a disproportionate number of componential analyses seemed to deal with reasoning tasks, and the question inevitably arose as to whether componential analysis could be applied to tasks in domains other than that of reasoning. Research in the early 1970s by Shepard, Cooper, and their associates suggested the possible feasibility of componential analyses of spatial tasks, and in Chapter 7, "Process Analyses of Spatial Aptitude," Pellegrino and Kail have shown beyond any doubt the usefulness of componential analysis as a way of understanding spatial abilities and their development. The program of research has thus served a dual function, providing us with both a rather comprehensive view of the nature of spatial abilities and a demonstration of the applicability of componential analysis in a domain quite different from that of reasoning behavior.

8. Does Human Performance on Problem-Solving Tasks Show the Same Kinds of Communalities That Have Been Shown in the Reasoning Tasks Most Often Used to Measure General Intelligence?   Tests of general intelligence, or *g*, have tended to emphasize various kinds of inductive reasoning tasks, such as analogies, classifications, and series-completion problems. Information-processing analyses of these tasks have suggested that the appearance of a general factor when these tasks are factor analyzed may be accounted for at least in part by communalities in the information-processing components used to perform the tasks. Although at least some IQ tests, such as the Stanford-Binet, have also used "transformation problems" (e.g., the water-jugs problem) as one basis for assessing intelligence, for some reason, performance on these has not been much studied in the context of research on process generality in human intelligence. Although Newell, Simon, and others have shown that a single computer program can solve various kinds of transformation problems, there has been a dearth of evidence to suggest that human beings actually solve various types of transformation problems in a similar way. In their chapter on "Problem Solving as Search and Understanding," Polson and Jeffries review evidence from their laboratory suggesting that a common model, with suitable adjustments, can account for performance on at least two transformation tasks—water jugs and missionaries and cannibals—and on variants of these two tasks. This demonstration is an important one because it provides a basis for selecting components of problem-solving performance that might be related in subsequent investigations to psychometric intelligence test performance and to performance on other information-processing tasks. In particular, one might ask whether there is a *g* for problem-solving tasks, whether this *g* is the same one that has been identified in factor-analytic and information-processing investigations of intelligence, and if not, why not.

9. Are Sources of Individual Differences in Intelligence the Same Within and Across Age Levels?   A recurrent, but as yet unanswered, question is that of whether the sources of differences in intelligent performance are the same within and across age levels. I address this question in my chapter describing "A Componential Approach to Intellectual Development," where I propose that the sources of differences in performance are largely the same. I take my previously proposed componential framework for understanding adult intelligence and attempt to show how it can be applied to the understanding of intellectual development from childhood through old age.

In conclusion, the chapters in this book represent a diversity of problems and perspectives within the information-processing framework. I believe they do indeed describe significant "advances in the psychology of human intelligence" as studied from a multiplicity of viewpoints.

1 Expertise in Problem Solving

Michelene T. H. Chi, Robert Glaser, Ernest Rees
University of Pittsburgh

INTRODUCTION

At first glance, it may seem anomalous for a chapter on expert performance to appear in a volume on intelligence. But an accumulation of scientific events indicates that the analysis of expertise in semantically rich knowledge domains is quite relevant to understanding the nature of intelligence. These events have occurred in a number of disciplines, particularly cognitive psychology and artificial intelligence. The first part of this chapter briefly outlines work in these fields. The common theme is the increasing emphasis on the structure of knowledge as a significant influence on intelligence and high-level cognitive performance. The latter part of the chapter describes, as an illustration of this, investigations of high and low competence in a knowledge-rich domain, namely, problem solving in physics.

Intelligence has been studied by contrasting individual differences, age differences, differences between the retarded and the gifted, and between fast and slow learners. These dimensions of difference are well represented by the past research of the contributors to this volume, including ourselves. What have we learned by investigating intelligent performance along these dimensions? If we consider speed of processing, memory span, and the use of complex strategies as three straightforward measures of cognitive performance, the following picture emerges. More intelligent individuals have faster processing speed, longer memory span, and use more sophisticated strategies than less intelligent persons (Belmont & Butterfield, 1971; Hunt, Lunneborg, & Lewis, 1975; Jensen, 1981). This is also true of older versus younger children (Chi, 1976) and fast as compared with slow learners. For example, good readers can encode words faster and have a longer memory span for words than poor readers (Perfetti & Hogaboam, 1975). Thus, over these demensions of comparison, measured intelligence correlates positively with faster processing, more complex encoding and recall, and the use of sophisticated strategies.

Although this pattern of results occurs reliably, we still do not understand what the underlying mechanisms are and whether similar mechanisms are operative in various disciplines and areas of knowledge. This is one reason the analysis of expertise has emerged as an interesting area of investigation. The study of expertise forces us to focus on a new dimension of difference between more and less intelligent individuals—the dimension of knowledge—because expertise is, by definition, the possession of a large body of knowledge and procedural skill. The central thesis of this chapter is that a major component of intelligence is the possession of a large body of accessible and usable knowledge. In the following section, we briefly outline the literature in two related disciplines that have gradually come to the same conclusion.

THE FOCUS ON KNOWLEDGE

Cognitive Psychology

Memory Skills

In cognitive psychology, the effects of knowledge on complex skilled performance were first explored in the seminal work of de Groot (1966) and Chase and Simon (1973a, 1973b) in their studies of chess skill. In an attempt to discover what constitutes skill in chess, de Groot (1966) found that differences in skill were not reflected in the number of moves the players considered during their search for a good move, nor in the depth of their search. Both the master and the novice did not search any further ahead than five moves. Both experts and novices used the same search strategies, that is, depth first with progressive deepening. In order to capture the essence of skill differences in chess, de Groot resorted to a different type of task—memory for chess positions. He found that when masters were shown a chess position for a very brief duration (5 seconds), they were able to remember the position far better than novice players. This difference could not be attributed to superior visual short-term memory on the part of the masters because, when random board positions were used, recall was equally poor for masters and novices (Chase & Simon, 1973b).

In order to understand the chess masters' recall superiority, Chase and Simon attempted to uncover the structures of chess knowledge that the masters possessed. Using "chunks" as a defining unit of knowledge structure, Chase and Simon set out to identify experimentally the structure and size of chunks in the knowledge base of masters and novices. They used two procedures. One was to record the placement of chess pieces on the chessboard during the recall of positions and use 2-second pauses during recall to segment the chunks. A second procedure was to ask the chess player to copy a position and use head turns from board to board to partition the chunks. The theoretical rationale underlying both the pause and the head-turn procedure was the notion that chunks are closely knit units of knowledge structure. Hence, retrieval of one item of information within a chunk would lead to retrieval of another in quick succession.

Both master and novice did retrieve pieces in chunks—bursts followed by pauses—and they reproduced chess positions pattern by pattern, with a glance (or head turn) for each pattern. These were familiar and highly stereotypic patterns that chess players see daily, such as a castled-king position or a pawn chain, or they were highly circumscribed clusters of pieces, often of the same color and located in very close proximity. The difference between the novice and the expert chess player was the size of the chunks. The master's patterns were larger, containing three to six pieces, whereas the novice's patterns contained single pieces. If one counted by chunks rather than pieces, the novice and the master were recalling the same number of chunks from the board position.

There are limitations with the procedure of identifying chunks by a 2-second pause and/or a head turn. One limitation is that it does not provide a description of the complex structure of the chunk, for example, the overlapping nature of chunks (Reitman, 1976). A more serious limitation is that it does not allow for the identification of higher-order chunks. The pause procedure permits only the identification of "local" chunks, that is, chunks that are spatially close and defined by such relations as next to, color identity, piece identity, etc. (Chase & Chi, 1981).

The existence of higher-order chunks is evidenced in the master's recall for sequences of moves (Chase & Simon, 1973a). That is, after viewing all the moves of a game, a master's recall of move sequences shows clustering of move sequences represented by pauses that is similar to the clustering of pieces in the board-recall task. This says that a given board position generates a sequence of stereotypic moves. Data from eye-movement studies clearly show that chess players fixate predominantly on the pieces interrelated by attack and defense strategy (Simon & Barenfeld, 1969) and that these pieces are typically not proximally related, as are the local chunk pieces.

The study of expert–novice differences in the use of complex knowledge in other domains has also revealed higher-order chunk structures. In electronics, Egan and Schwartz (1979) found that skilled technicians reconstructing symbolic drawings of circuit diagrams do so according to the functional nature of the elements in the circuit such as amplifiers, rectifiers, and filters. Novice technicians, however, produce chunks based more upon the spatial proximity of the elements. In architecture, Akin (1980) found that during recall of building plans by architects, several levels of patterns were produced. First, local patterns consisting of wall segments and doors are recalled, then rooms and other areas, and then clusters of rooms or areas. The hierarchical nature of chunks also has been illustrated in the recall of baseball events. High-knowledge individuals can recall entire sequences of baseball events much better than low-knowledge individuals (Chiesi, Spilich, & Voss, 1979).

Like the chess results, the expert in several diverse domains is able to remember "sequences of moves" much more rapidly than the novice. Also, we see a similarity between chess patterns, circuit diagrams, and architectural patterns in that functional properties are more important at higher levels, whereas structural properties (such as proximity and identity in color and form) are more important at lower levels. And with increasing skill more higher-order chunks are developed.

In sum, one aspect of cognitive psychology research has clearly identified the superior memory capacity of skilled individuals, as exhibited in the large pattern of chunks, whether they are adult chess players, child chess players (Chi, 1978), Go players (Reitman, 1976), Gomoku players (Eisenstadt & Kareev, 1975), bridge players (Charness, 1979), musicians (Sloboda, 1976), baseball fans (Chiesi et al., 1979), computer programmers (Jeffries, Turner, Polson, & Atwood, 1981; McKeithen, Reitman, Rueter & Hirtle, 1981), or electronic technicians (Egan & Schwartz, 1979). Although a number of these studies have uncovered the hierarchical nature of the patterns (Akin, 1980; Chiesi et al., 1979; Egan & Schwartz, 1979), no work to date has explicitly related the knowledge and chunk structures of these skilled individuals to the complex skill that they are able to perform.

Problem-Solving Skills

A currently prominent area of research in cognitive psychology is problem solving. Problem-solving research was revolutionized in the 1960s when researchers turned from studying the conditions under which solutions are reached to the processes of problem solving. Following the contribution of Newell and Simon's (1972) theory, problem-solving research proceeded to model search behavior and to verify that humans indeed solve problems according to means–ends analyses. Numerous puzzlelike problems were investigated, all of which indicated that human subjects do solve problems according to means–ends analyses to some degree (Greeno, 1978).

In puzzle problems, sometimes known as MOVE problems, the knowledge involved in solving the problems is minimal. All the knowledge one needs to solve the problems is given: the initial state, the number and function of operators, and the final goal state. Solution requires that a set of operators be applied to transform one state of knowledge to another, so that eventually the goal state can be reached. A variety of puzzle problems have been investigated: the water-jug problem (Atwood, Masson, & Polson, 1980; Atwood & Polson, 1976; Polson & Jeffries, Chapter 8, this volume), hobbits and orcs (Greeno, 1974; Thomas, 1974), missionaries and cannibals (Simon & Reed, 1976), and Tower of Hanoi (Egan & Greeno, 1974; Simon, 1975).

The research on puzzle problems, however, offered limited insights into learning. Because learning in real-world subject matters requires the acquisition of large bodies of domain-specific knowledge, cognitive scientists turned their attention from knowledge-free problems, like puzzles, to knowledge-filled domains like geometry (Greeno, 1978), physics (Simon & Simon, 1978), thermodynamics (Bhaskar & Simon, 1977), programming (Jeffries, Turner, Polson, & Atwood, 1981), understanding electronic circuits (Brown, Collins, & Harris, 1978), and recently, political science (Voss & Tyler, 1981).

Solving real-world problems presents new obstacles that were not encountered previously in puzzlelike problems. Basically, the exact operators to be used are usually not given, the goal state is sometimes not well defined, and more importantly, search in a large knowledge space becomes a serious problem. (The research on artificial intelligence programs in chess, to be mentioned in the next section, gives the flavor of this difficulty.) Solving real-world problems with large knowledge bases also provides a glimpse of the power of the human cognitive system to use a large knowledge system in an efficient and automatic manner—in ways that minimize heuristic search. In general, current studies of high levels of competence by cognitive psychologists appear to support the recommendation that a significant focus for understanding expertise is investigation of the characteristics and influence of organized, hierarchical knowledge structures that are acquired over years of learning and experience.

Artificial Intelligence

The goal of artificial-intelligence (AI) research is to make a machine act intelligently. In this area, the problem of understanding intelligence has become increasingly focused on the large structure of domain-specific knowledge that is characteristic of experts. This is in contrast to the early years of the field, when the creation of intelligent programs was identified with finding "pure" problem-solving techniques to guide a search, for any problem, through the problem space to a solution, as in the General Problem Solver (Newell, Shaw, & Simon, 1960). The techniques elucidated, such as means–ends analysis, are clearly part of the picture, but it was apparent early on that in realistically complex domains such techniques must engage a highly organized structure of specific knowledge. This shift in AI is characterized by Minsky and Papert (cited in Goldstein & Papert, 1977) as a change from a power-based strategy for achieving intelligence to a knowledge-based emphasis. They write as follows:

> The *Power* strategy seeks a generalized increase in computational power. It may look toward new kinds of computers ("parallel" or "fuzzy" or "associative" or whatever) or it may look toward extensions of deductive generality, or information retrieval, or search algorithms. . . . In each case the improvement sought is intended to be "uniform"—independent of the particular data base.

The *Knowledge* strategy sees progress as coming from better ways to express, recognize, and use diverse and particular forms of knowledge. This theory sees the problem as epistemological rather than as a matter of computational power or mathematical generality. It supposes, for example, that when a scientist solves a new problem, he engages a highly organized structure of especially appropriate facts, models, analogies, planning mechanisms, self-discipline procedures, etc. To be sure, he also engages "general" problem-solving schemata but it is by no means obvious that very smart people are that way directly because of the superior power of their general methods—as compared with average people. Indirectly, perhaps, but that is another matter: A very intelligent person might be that way because of specific local features of his knowledge-organizing knowledge rather than because of global qualities of his "thinking" which, except for the effects of his self-applied knowledge, might be little different from a child's [p. 86].

We can now elaborate on this transition in AI research from building programs that emphasized heuristic search to knowledge-based programs, using chess programs as examples. The chess problem space can be pictured as a game tree. Figure 1.1 shows a very simple example of such a tree. Each node represents a possible position (of all the pieces) during a game, and each link leading from a node represents a possible move. At first glance, the problem might seem fairly simple: Start at the top of the tree and find a set of paths that force the opponent into checkmate. However, as Shannon (1950) pointed out, at any given point a player has approximately 30 legal moves available, so the number of nodes at successive levels of the tree increases dramatically. In an entire game, each player makes an average of 40 moves (giving the tree 80 levels), and the number of possible paths to the bottom of the tree total about 10^{120}. Even the fastest computer could not search such a tree exhaustively, so intelligent choices must be made to limit the exploration severely. There are two basic limitations that can be applied: limiting the number of moves considered from each node (width of search) and limiting the number of successive moves that will be considered on each path (depth of search). Both of these methods require the use of some chess knowledge if they are to be applied successfully. In the case of depth of search, inasmuch as positions reached are not final (won or lost), they must be evaluated to determine if they are advantageous or not. In addition, simply cutting off the search at a specified depth can cause problems (e.g., the cutoff may be in the middle of an exchange of pieces), so some analysis is required to determine if the search should be deepened.

Full-Width Search

Two general search-based approaches have been followed in attempts to create chess-playing programs: full-width (brute force) search and selective search. Both limit the depth of search, but in a full-width program, the width of search is not limited at all, as the name implies. To date, a modification of this approach has been the most successful. It uses a mathematical algorithm that

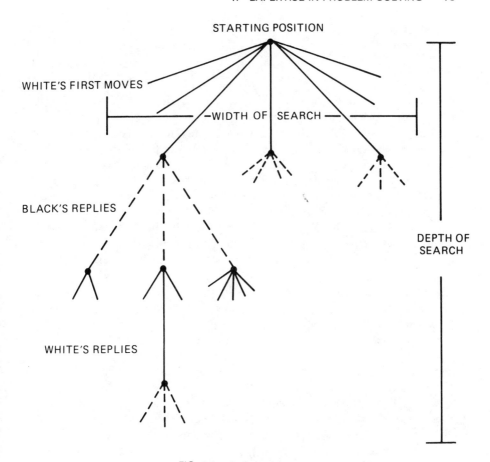

FIG. 1.1.   A chess game tree.

eliminates from consideration moves by the opponent that are worse than the best move already found (based on the evaluation of the positions to which they lead) because it must be assumed that one will make the best possible move. The 1980 world computer chess champion, BELLE by Thompson and Condon at Bell Labs, and a former champion, CHESS 4.6 by Slate and Atkin at Northwestern, are both of this type. These programs, and others like them, have a bare minimum of chess knowledge but make use of a computer's speed and memory to do vast amounts of searching. Although these programs can now beat practically all human players, they cannot beat the top ranked experts (grand masters). Estimates of 10 more years of work to reach this level are not uncommon. The main reason for such slow progress is probably the explosive branching of the game tree. Each level contains about 30 times as many nodes as the level above, so a large increase in computational power is needed for a very small increase in depth of search.

Selective Search

Clearly, grand masters do not play better chess because they outsearch a computer. The limited size of short-term memory and the amount of time required to fixate items in long-term memory limit humans to very tiny tree searches. In fact, de Groot (1965) and Newell and Simon (1972) have shown through protocol analysis that expert players tend to choose good moves without any search at all and then conduct a limited search to test their choices. This approach is an example of the second programming method—selective search. The Greenblatt program (Greenblatt, Eastlake, & Crocker, 1967), the first to make a respectable showing in human tournament competition, provides an example of how this approach has been implemented. His program selects moves for consideration on the basis of "plausibility." It first generates all of the legal moves available from the present position. A plausibility score is then calculated for each move on the basis of a subset of 50 heuristics (not all are applicable to a given situation). These heuristics are simply "rules of thumb" taken from chess lore for selecting a good move, which have been roughly quantified to allow for calculating a numerical score. The moves are then ranked in order of decreasing plausibility, and only the first few are considered. In addition, all of the continuations used to evaluate a move are generated in the same way. Because only a handful of the possible moves is considered at each node, the game tree is significantly reduced in size. The size of the search must be reduced still further, however, so the mathematical algorithm mentioned before is used to "prune" more branches from the tree. The depth of search is also limited.

Although expert players do choose a few plausible moves for consideration, they do not do it through computation and evaluation as does the Greenblatt program. Rather, they respond intuitively to patterns on the board. As mentioned earlier, de Groot (1965) has shown that grand masters can reproduce complicated positions almost exactly after seeing them for only 5 seconds. Apparently, the years of practice necessary to become a chess expert result in a very large knowledge base of patterns of pieces and probably patterns of moves as well. When experts look at the board and "see" good moves, they are engaging in pattern recognition. Thus, an obvious direction for chess-program design is to build production systems that can recognize and respond as human players do (Simon, 1976).

Knowledge-Based Chess

There is more to human play than just recognizing a possible next move, however. The moves of a good player advance toward some goal; they fit into a plan that looks at least a few moves ahead. An early attempt to give chess programs simple goals is the Newell, Shaw, and Simon program (1958), which has a series of independent goal modules. Each module can recognize appropriate situations on the board and generate moves with specific purposes, such as king safety, center control, etc. The purpose of these goals, however, is only to select a few reasonable candidates for the next move in order to limit the search tree; there is no overall plan.

A program called PARADISE (Wilkins, 1980) contains the factors we have discussed that seem to give expert chess players an edge over even the best search programs. It uses an extensive knowledge of chessboard patterns, embodied in production rules, to establish goals, which are then elaborated into more concrete plans. Search is used only to check the validity of the plans.

PARADISE does not play an entire game; it plays "tactically sharp" positions from the middle game. Tactically sharp simply means that success can be achieved by winning material from the opponent—a common situation in chess. The knowledge base consists of some 200 production rules, each with a general pattern of relationships among pieces as its condition. Most of these rules are organized around general higher-level concepts necessary for effective play, such as looking for a THREAT to the opponent's pieces, looking for a way to make a square SAFE to move a piece to it, trying to DECOY an opponent's piece out of the way, etc. The effect of applying the production rules to a given position is to suggest a plan or plans with the overall goal of winning material. A given plan may include calls back to the knowledge base to produce plans to accomplish subgoals of the original plan (if such a subplan cannot be found, then the overall plan is scrapped). Plans are thus hierarchically expanded until they are ready for use. Each plan contains an initial move plus a series of alternative future moves depending on the types of replies by the opponent. Each plan also contains information about why it was produced by the knowledge base in the first place. The plan and its associated information are then used to guide a very small tree search to determine if the plan is feasible.

Productions in the knowledge base are used to generate the defensive moves used in the search. Calls for additional planning and analysis to expand the original plan can also be generated by the search. The depth of search is not artificially limited in this program; instead, analyses are conducted (using the knowledge base) at the ends of lines suggested by the plans to determine if termination of the search is proper. Inasmuch as the plans limit the number of alternatives considered at each node to only a few, the search can go much deeper than in other programs. Because all of the analysis, planning, and searching is guided by the knowledge base, altering or improving the play of PARADISE consists of simply modifying or adding individual production rules. Such a system seems to have great potential for playing expert chess, if the requisite knowledge can be determined and coded into the knowledge base or if a self-learning system can be designed to modify its own base.

In sum, the example of chess programs illustrates the general tendency in AI toward knowledge-based programming. Even though computers have great advantages over humans in speed and memory, it seems that knowledge provides an edge, which pure power can only overcome at great cost, if at all.

PHYSICS PROBLEM SOLVING AND EXPERTISE

In this section, we review what is known about how physics problems are solved and, in particular, how expert physicists solve them as compared to novices. The first subsection reviews the available empirical evidence, and the second reviews the resulting theoretical models simulating the way experts and novices solve physics problems.

Empirical Findings

In the relatively small amount of work done in this area, there are basically three types of empirical investigation. One examines the knowledge structures of physics concepts. Shavelson (1974; Shavelson & Stanton, 1975), for instance, has investigated methods for determining this "cognitive structure." He delineates three methods that may be used singly or in conjunction: word association, card sorting, and graph building. Of the three, word association is the most venerable and widely used. Using this method, Shavelson (1974) has shown that students' physics concepts become more interrelated and that their cognitive structures become more like the course "content structure" (as determined by a structural analysis of the instructional materials) at the end of the course than at the beginning. Thro (1978) has found similar results using the instructors' cognitive structure as the content structure.

A second type of empirical research is investigation of subjects' prior conception of the physical world, with a view toward how that preconception might affect one's learning of physics. For example, McCloskey, Caramazza, and Green (1980) have shown that a sizable number of students who have had no physics courses, as well as some who have had one or more college courses, believe that an object once set in curvilinear motion (e.g., through a spiral tube) will maintain that motion in the absence of any further external forces. Also, Champagne, Klopfer, and Anderson (1980) have constructed the Demonstration, Observation, and Explanation of Motion Test (DOE) to test students' ideas of motion due to gravity. They have found, similarly, that a sizable number of students entering a college mechanics course have erroneous ideas about motion (and that students who had taken high school physics did no better than those who had not). They also found, however, that results on the DOE alone were of little predictive value in determining success in the mechanics courses.

The third type of empirical evidence relates specifically to problem solving and is usually gathered in the context of solution protocols. Careful analyses of protocols have indicated significant differences between the expert and novice. The only obvious similarities between them are in the macroprocesses they use in solving physics problems. According to Simon and Simon (1978), both expert and novice proceed to solution by evoking the appropriate physics equations and then solving them. The expert often does this in one step, however, simply stating results without explicitly mentioning the formula being used, whereas the novice typically states the formula, puts it into the appropriate form, and substitutes the values of the variables in discrete steps. McDermott and Larkin (1978) include another two "stages" prior to the evoking and instantiating of equations, postulating that solution proceeds in at least four episodes: the first stage is simply the written problem statement; the second involves drawing a sketch of the situation; and the third is a "qualitative analysis" of the problem, which results in a representation containing abstract physics entities. Generating the equations is the fourth stage. According to Larkin (in press), experts seem to perform all four processes, whereas the novice may skip the qualitative analysis stage. Beyond this gross similarity lie much more subtle and salient differences between the expert and novice protocols, which can now be elaborated.

Quantitative Differences

There are three major differences between the novice and the expert physicist that are easily quantifiable. The most obvious is time to solution. The speed with which a problem can be solved depends a great deal on the skill of the individual. Simon and Simon (1978) noted a 4:1 difference between their expert and novice. Larkin (1981) also reported a similar difference between her experts and novices. This difference is not unlike the speed difference found in chess-playing ability of the master versus beginner. This is to be expected if we postulate that experts in general are more efficient at searching their solution space.

Related to solution time is another quantifiable difference: the pause times between retrieving successive equations or chunks of equations. Larkin (1979) has claimed that a number of physics equations are retrieved by the experts in succession, with very small interresponse intervals, followed by a longer pause. Her novice did not seem to exhibit this pattern of pause times in equation retrieval. This is interpreted as suggesting that experts group their equations in chunks so that the eliciting of one equation perhaps activates another related equation, and thus it can be retrieved faster. (There is also some evidence that the chunk is associated with a "fundamental principle" of physics, such as Newton's Second Law or Conservation of Energy.) Additional evidence for the rapidity of equation retrieval by the experts was demonstrated by Larkin (1981) when she found that experts were four times faster than novices in accessing and applying equations during problem solving. This suggests to Larkin (1979) that, for the experts, physics equations are stored in chunks or related configurations so that accessing one principle leads to accessing another principle. This result is appealing because it is reminiscent of the chess results, where chess pieces were found to be chunked when the interpiece pause times during recall of a chess position were examined.

Another interesting aspect of novice problem solving is not only that they commit more errors than experts but that, even when they do solve a physics problem correctly, their approach is quite different. It is this difference that we want to understand, as well as why they commit errors. Likewise, it is also interesting to understand the circumstances under which experts make errors.

Qualitative Differences

Qualitative differences between an expert and novice problem solver are harder to define operationally, especially in empirical studies. However, it is the qualitative differences that distinguish expertise most noticeably. One prominent yet elusive difference between the expert and novice is that expert physicists, as noted before, seem to apply a "qualitative analysis" (Larkin, 1977a, Larkin, 1980; McDermott & Larkin, 1978) or "physical intuition" (Simon & Simon, 1978) to the problem, prior to the actual retrieval of physics equations. There are several possible interpretations of what constitutes qualitative analysis. One interpretation is that qualitative analysis, occurring usually in the beginning phase of problem solving, is the construction of a physical representation (i.e., a representation that has some external, concrete physical referents). This ability to represent the problem physically in terms of real-world mechanisms was first noted over a decade ago, although not in the context of the expert–novice distinction. Paige and Simon (1966) observed that when algebra word problems that corresponded to physically unrealizable situations were presented to subjects, a few of them immediately perceived the "incongruity" in the problem, whereas others proceeded to evoke equations before realizing that the solution was meaningless (e.g., a negative quantity for the length of a board). The former solvers apparently imagined the physical referents of the objects mentioned.

In physics problem solving, the construction of a physical representation may be helpful, or even necessary, for several reasons. First, Simon and Simon (1978) suggested that physical representation provides a basis for generating the physics equations. Second, physical representation provides a situation that can be used to check one's errors (Larkin, 1977a; Simon & Simon, 1978). Third, the physical representation provides a concise and global description of the problem and its important features. And finally, we conjecture that the physical representation permits direct inferences to be drawn about certain features and their relations that are not explicit in the problem statement but can be deduced once a representation is constructed.

However, there is also reason to think that what occurs during qualitative analysis is more than the construction of a physical representation, because the often complex physical configuration and intuition deriving from what happens in a physical situation may not necessarily lead to correct inferences. As the aforementioned work of Champagne, Klopfer, and Anderson (1980) and McCloskey et al. (1980) have indicated, naive problem solvers must not always rely on their physical intuition for constructing a representation. However, inasmuch as it is predominantly the experts who construct an elaborate representation, we postulate that this representation need not correspond directly to a physical representation, but may be more abstract.

A second qualitative difference between the expert and the novice observed by Simon and Simon (1978) is in the number of "metastatements." Metastatements are comments made by the subjects about the problem-solving processes. On the average, their expert made only one metastatement per problem, whereas the novice made an average of five. They were usually observations of errors made, comments on the physical meaning of an equation, statements of plans and intentions, self-evaluations, and so on.

There are several possible explanations for why their expert made fewer metastatements. First, the expert might be better at recognizing the correctness of a solution, and thus need not voice any uncertainties, etc. Second, the expert may have multiple ways to solve a problem (Simon & Simon, 1978), so that the solution can easily be doublechecked. Finally, the expert might have a well-structured representation of the problem to check results against.

Another blatant qualitative difference between the solution processes of experts and novices lies in their solution paths (sequence and order of equations generated) (Simon & Simon, 1978). The important distinction between the expert and the novice is that the expert uses a "working-forward" strategy, whereas the novice uses a "working-backward" strategy. The expert's strategy is simply to work from the variables given in the problem, successively generating the equations that can be solved from the given information. The novice, on the other hand, starts with an equation containing the unknown of the problem. If it contains a variable that is not among the givens, then the novice selects another equation to solve for it, and so on. (These processes and models based on them are explained more fully later.)

This interpretation of the novice's performance initially seems counterintuitive; that is, the novice's strategy appears to be more goal oriented and sophisticated. One interpretation of this difference is that experts know that they can achieve the goal simply by direct calculations of the unknowns from the givens. Another intepretation is that experts do not require complex planning for simple problems. They probably have existing routines or production systems that they can apply directly to the problems. This simple forward-working strategy of the expert does change, however, to a very sophisticated means–ends analysis of the goals and planning when the problems become more difficult (Larkin, 1977b).

A puzzling question concerning the difference between the two strategies is how people change from one to the other. Why is it that the expert can develop a more efficient system? One possible answer is that over the years the expert has built up and stored several fundamental sets of subroutines that can solve several types of basic problems. In this case, solving a problem becomes a matter of categorizing the problem into one or more problem types and applying the existing subroutines. As we describe later, this ability to categorize the problem quickly is faciltitated by a powerful parsing mechanism that translates key words in the problem statement—words such as "at the moment," "catch-up," etc.—into problem types.

The second question is how can the expert construct a more efficient subroutine, if one does not already exist for solving a complex problem? We think that this facility lies in the rich internal representation that the expert has generated, a representation that permits many appropriate inferences to be drawn so that the problem can be simplified and reduced.

In sum, the analysis of the qualitative aspect of protocol data raises a number of important questions: Why is the initial "qualitative analysis" of the problem important? What kind of representation of a problem is constructed during this initial stage of analysis? Why are the sequences of equations generated by experts and novices different? What enables an expert to generate a sequence of equations that is more efficient? The quantitative analysis of the protocol data simply confirms a number of intuitions that we already have but cannot explain: Experts commit fewer errors, they can solve problems faster, and they seem to store related equations in closely knit chunk structures. Moreover, not one of these quantitative findings provides any answers to the qualitative questions. Nor do they answer our questions posed earlier, namely, why are novices less successful at solving physics problems, and why are their procedures somewhat different, even when they are successful? Answering these questions is the focus of our own experimental program, which is described in the latter part of this chapter. These questions also drive current research and theory; we now turn to considering the current state of theory.

Theoretical Models of Physics Problem Solving

There has been a great deal more theoretical than empirical work done on problem solving in physics. In this section, we review all of the existing models. They are of two types: psychological models that explicitly attempt to simulate human performance and artificial-intelligence models that do not (although they may contain components that are similar to human performance). Both types of model are written in the form of computer programs.

Psychological Models

The majority of psychological models discussed here have several things in common. First, the behaviors they simulate are generally think-aloud protocols gathered while a person solves a physics problem. Second, except for one case, most of them solve mechanics problems taken from a first course in physics. Although these problems are straightforward, they are by no means simple. They do require some thought and usually take at least 2 minutes to solve. Third, the aspects of protocols that the models attempt to simulate are generally the sequences of equations generated by the solver. Hence, the qualitative aspects of the protocols (such as the initial analysis of the problem, the metastatements, and so on) are usually ignored. Finally, the simulation usually takes the form of a production system.

To be more specific, the core of several of these models is a symbol-driven process. The variables representing the knowns and unknown(s) (the answer) in the problem are simply compared to the variables appearing in the various formulas that the model has in its possession. Two very simple selection criteria can be applied to produce two different behaviors. On the one hand, a formula can be selected in which all variables but one are knowns. That one unknown variable can then be asserted to be known (tagged as solvable, without any actual algebraic or arithmetic computation), and the process can be repeated until the new known is the answer to the problem. This is a working-forward strategy typical of experts. On the other hand, a formula can be selected because it contains the desired unknown. If all the other variables in the formula are known, then the problem is solved. If not, the unknown variable (the models discussed here generally discard a formula if it has two or more unknowns) becomes a new desired variable, and the process is repeated. This is the working-backward strategy characteristic of novices.

To make these two strategies more concrete, consider the following very simple example: There are two formulas available, one relating the variables a, b, and e, and the other relating d, c, and e:

$$e = f(a, b) \tag{1.1}$$

$$d = f(c, e) \tag{1.2}$$

Suppose a problem is proposed such that a, b, and c are given (the knowns) and d is the desired answer (the unknown). The forward-working method chooses Equation 1.1 first because a and b are known, allowing the calculation of e. Inasmuch as c and e are now both known, Equation 1.2 can be selected and used to find d. By contrast, the working-backward method chooses Equation 1.2 first because it involves the desired unknown d. Since e is unknown, it becomes the intermediately desired unknown, and Equation 1.1 is then chosen. Equation 1.1 can now be solved for e, which is substituted into Equation 1.2 to find d.

Simon and Simon Models.   The first models to be discussed use the two strategies just described—working forward and backward. In the Simon and Simon (1978) models, the behaviors of two subjects—one novice and one expert—working a series of kinematics problems (describing motion in a straight line without any consideration for the causes of that motion) are simulated by two very simple production systems. The available formulas are represented in the conditions of the productions as lists of the variables they contain. The problem itself is presented as a list of the known and desired variables it contains. As explained earlier, the expert productions match the knowns in the problem with the independent variables in the formulas, whereas the novice productions match the desired unknown against the independent variable and the knowns against the dependent variables. The productions are listed in different orders, reflecting the fact that the two subjects sometimes used different formulas where both strategies might be expected to choose the same one. These two versions of the model simulate the equation-selection behavior of the subjects quite well.

In this theory, there is no need to postulate any differences in the mechanism by which equations were produced; it is only necessary to specify a difference in the order in which they were generated. Nor is skill difference attributable to trivial differences such as the lack of certain formulas. Both the expert and novice systems contain basically the same set of equations.

Knowledge Development and Means–ends Models.   Two related models are described in Larkin, McDermott, Simon, and Simon (1980). One is referred to as the Knowledge Development model, which simulates the expert behavior, and the other is the Means–Ends model, simulating novice behavior. These models expand and improve on the Simon and Simon models in several ways to reflect more accurately human information-processing capacities and the behavior of the subjects. Three separate memories are present: Long-term memory (LM), working (short-term) memory (WM), and external memory (EM). Long-term memory consists of the productions themselves, which contain the necessary physics and procedural knowledge. Working memory is a small memory limited to about 20 elements, and it is the contents of this memory that the condition sides of the productions are matched against. External memory represents the pencil and paper used by a problem solver. The complete problem statement resides in this EM, and elements can be periodically transferred back and forth between EM and WM by the actions of certain productions to simulate the changing focus of attention of a problem solver and the process of recording intermediate results on paper.

The solution process begins with the problem statement in a coded form that specifies the objects involved, their attributes and points of contact, instants and intervals of time, and the desired unknown(s). (The complex problem of natural language understanding is avoided.) Both models have productions that assign variables to the necessary elements of the problem so that the appropriate formulas may be selected. As before, the two basic selection strategies—forward and backward—are employed, but they are more elaborate to simulate behavior more closely.

The differences between the current and the previous Simon and Simon models are the most marked in the selection of a formula in the Means–Ends novice model because novices are observed to do this in several discrete stages, first selecting a formula, then relating its variables to items in the problem, and then using it. A formula is originally selected for consideration if it merely contains a desired quantity. In cases where more than one formula contains the desired quantity, selectors tailored to represent observed novice preferences pick one. This model produces the same backward chain of equations as the earlier model. It then "solves" them by chaining forward, marking each previously unknown variable as known until the originally desired variable becomes "known." (Neither of these models has any actual algebraic manipulation ability.)

The Knowledge Development model is more similar to the previous Simon and Simon expert model. This is because experts generally do not exhibit the step by step behavior of stating an equation and then connecting it to variables in the problem. Thus, as before, the selectors choose a formula on the basis of the unknowns and assert that the dependent variable is now known in one step. This situation can be viewed as a "collapsed" or overlearned version of the novice model. (This becomes clearer shortly when other models are discussed.) The main new feature of the model is that when more than one formula can be selected based on the knowns, information from the problem is used to decide among them. For instance if a (acceleration) and t (time) are knowns, then both $x = \frac{1}{2}at^2$ and $v = at$ could be selected. If the problem contains an object falling or rolling from rest, the first is selected. In all other instances, the second is selected, corresponding to the observed expert preferences. It is in this sense that the knowledge about the problem is used.

In addition to these differences, the Larkin et al. (1980) models have the ability to solve more kinds of problems than the previous ones, which were confined to kinematics. They solve dynamics problems (describing the motion of a body by considering the forces causing or influencing that motion) using two basic methods for solving such problems—Forces and Energies—and because they contain more than one solution method, they have an attention focusing mechanism. If a model is solving a problem using Energies, it should not try a Force equation halfway through the solution, nor should it select an equation when it is not through writing a previous one. To accomplish this focusing, goal elements are included in the conditions of many of the productions. At the beginning of a solution process, a goal is set (placed in WM and EM) so that only productions related to that goal can execute.

Able Models. The Able models of Larkin (1981) address a different issue than strictly simulating the problem-solving processes. Instead, they attempt to simulate the learning processes, (i.e., how a novice might become an expert). In the model's "naive" state, it is called the Barely Able model; after substantial learning, it is called More Able. The learning process is modeled by a mechanism for adding procedures that is generally used in adaptive production systems (Waterman, 1975).

Barely Able starts with a list of equations that can be used in the Forces or Energy methods and operates with a general means–ends strategy for applying them that is similar to the previous Means–Ends model. The learning process itself is quite straightforward: Whenever a production succeeds in applying an equation to derive a new known value, it creates a new production that has the previous knowns on the condition side and an assertion of the new known on the action side. For example, if Barely Able solves the equation $V = V_0 + at$ for a, then the new production will check to see if V_0, V, and t are known and, if so, assert that a is known. Psychologically, this means that the procedure for finding the right equation and solving for the unknown becomes automated once the initial production has been executed. Thus, as Able solves more and more problems, it looks more and more like the Knowledge Development model mentioned earlier—it becomes forward-working because all the backward-working steps become automated.

There are two limitations to the Able model. The first is that the learning takes place in one trial. This is psychologically unrealistic, and a more complicated learning function probably needs to be built in which some aspects of learning take place faster than others. The second limitation is that the model does not provide the capability to concatenate series of productions into one (Neves & Anderson, 1981). Such a mechanism would allow two or more formulas to be combined into a single step, as experts are often observed to do.

Model PH632. A model labeled PH632, developed by McDermott and Larkin (1978), has a somewhat different focus than those previously described. Its purpose is to examine and model in a general way the use of problem representations by an expert solver but not to exhibit a detailed psychological model of the process. It is, again, a production system with external, working, and long-term memories. The condition sides of the productions can contain goal elements that keep attention focused on the specific task at hand and that allow the productions to be organized hierarchically.

A series of four representational stages of a problem is postulated: verbal, naive, scientific, and mathematical (see also Larkin, 1980). The model assumes that a problem solver progresses through these stages as a problem is solved. However, the detailed description of the model (McDermott & Larkin, 1978) starts with the naive representation. The naive representation is a sketch depicting the components of the problem and their relationships and is implemented as a data structure that encodes this information. The scientific representation contains abstract physics concepts such as forces, momenta, and energies (which must generally be inferred by the problem solver) and is usually depicted as a free-body diagram. The mathematical representation consists of the equations relating the variables in the problem that must be solved to produce the final answer.

Once PH632 has a naive representation, it tries one of the two solution methods mentioned earlier—Forces and Energies. If both are adequate, the one chosen may simply be the first one tried. Once a particular method is chosen, its productions give the model the ability to scan the sketch qualitatively to determine where the objects and systems of interest are, whether they are familiar or unfamiliar, and how they are related. If a system is familiar (e.g., a hanging block), PH632 can use its knowledge to build a production describing it. If the system is unfamiliar, an extended analysis is conducted to produce an encoded version of a free-body diagram. This difference in representation corresponds to an expert's tendency not to draw an explicit free-body diagram of a familiar system. The model makes qualitative checks as it proceeds to determine whether its representation seems correct and whether its approach is working. For instance, in a statics problem (one with no motion), it checks to make sure all of the forces are balanced by at least one opposing force. It can also test whether all of the entities generated in the scientific representation (e.g., forces) can be related to the quantities given in the problem statement so the equations can be generated.

Once assurance is gained that the model is on the right track, it can write the equations for the mathematical representation. Because all of the forces have already been located and resolved into components in construction of the scientific representation, this step is relatively simple. Unlike the previous models, PH632 can perform the algebraic and arithmetic operations necessary to produce the answer.

Atwood.   Larkin's (1980) latest program, Atwood, concentrates on the verbal representation stage, an area generally ignored by the previous models. Considering the difficulties and complexities encountered by artificial-intelligence researchers in building language understanders, Atwood accomplishes its task in a surprisingly simple and straightforward way. Because mechanics problems in general contain a rather small set of basic objects attributes, and relationships, it can simply ignore most of the words in a typical problem statement and concentrate on the key words.

Basically, Atwood contains a set of schemata that tell it what words to attend to and what situations those words may indicate. Thus, it knows that the word *rod* is important and that there should be one and only one length associated with it. *Pulley* is another key word, and Atwood's schema tells it that there will be a rope passed over this object and that the rope should have objects connected to each end.

Using some rudimentary knowledge of English syntax, Atwood processes the problem statement word by word, creating nodes for each physics object it recognizes and connecting these nodes into a semantic net with the help of the knowledge of their legal relationships contained in the schemata. When tested on a set of 22 of the problems collected by Chi, Feltovich, and Glaser (1981), Atwood was able to build correct nets for 15 of them, while ignoring roughly two thirds of the words they contain.

Summary and Discussion of the Psychological Models.   The psychological models so far developed focus their attention on the different approaches that experts and novices take in terms of the sequence of equations they generate—forward-working versus backward-working. In these models, it is assumed that experts are forward working because their initial backward solution procedure becomes automated with learning. The question of initial problem representation is generally avoided in these models, perhaps primarily because it is difficult to obtain empirical information on this process solely through the usual forms of protocol analysis. As we describe later, other techniques are required for this purpose.

An alternative theoretical framework is to suggest that novices are data driven. They treat the unknown and known variables as literal symbols and plug them into equations in their repertoire. Experts, on the other hand, are schemata driven in the sense that their representation of a probem accesses a repertoire of solution methods. Hence, for the expert, solving a problem begins with the identification of the right solution schema, and then the exact solution procedure involves instantiation of the relevant pieces of information as specified in the schema. This is particularly likely because mechanics problems are overlearned for the experts, especially experts who have spent a great deal of their time teaching. Another interpretation is to postulate that novices also solve problems in a schemata-driven way, except that their schemata of problem types are more incomplete, incoherent, and at a level hierarchically lower than those possessed by the experts. In our opinion, the development of psychological models should proceed in this particular direction, building knowledge structures in the forms of schemata, in order to capture the problem-solving processes of experts and novices. Some empirical evidence for the validity of this interpretation is presented later.

Artificial Intelligence (AI) Models

Artificial intelligence programs, unlike those previously discussed, are not specifically intended to model observed behavior or to take into account theories of human cognitive architecture. Their general aim is to solve physics problems successfully by any means possible. However, they do contain elements that are very similar to both human behavior and the previous psychological models.

One of the main issues addressed by the AI models is representation—how to represent the knowledge that the program needs in order to form a representation of the problem and solve it. Indeed, the current recognition in psychology of the importance of representation probably derives from the early recognition of its importance in AI and computer science in general. The question of how physics knowledge is represented is a major research problem, as the rudimentary state of such representations in the psychological models indicates.

The first phase of a problem solution is reading and understanding (or translating) the verbal problem statement. Much work has been done on the general problem of natural language understanding in AI, and two of the programs to be described put considerable emphasis on this stage. Both are more detailed and complex than the simple Atwood (Larkin, 1980) translator because they aim for a complete translation utilizing all of the information in the problem statement. Thus, both use esoteric translation processes and have extensive knowledge bases of syntactic and semantic information, including specific physics knowledge in a well-organized form to allow a correct physical interpretation of a problem. Once translation is complete, some kind of language-free, internal computer model of the problem exists, which can be compared to a naive representation.

Issac.   Issac (Novak, 1977) is a program that can read the problem statement. It does this for statics problems only. The key feature is the representation of objects as idealized physics entities. For instance, in a problem that has a man standing on a ladder, the properties that are important to the solution are his mass and location on the ladder. He can therefore be represented as a "point mass." But if he is holding up one end of the ladder, only the point on the ladder he is holding is important, and he becomes a "pivot." This idealization is accomplished in Issac by using Canonical Object Frames (schemata) from the knowledge base. Each one contains the knowledge necessary to abstract the proper characteristics from the "real-life" object and to use the idealized object properly in the solution of the problem. This idealization process corresponds only partially to the formation of scientific representation because no attempt is made to represent or analyze qualitatively the other essential physics entities in a statics problem—the forces. Instead, all possible balance-of-forces equations are written at each point of contact between objects, resulting in many more equations than are actually needed for a solution. This illustrates the problems that can arise if the representation of a problem does not generate an efficient solution.

Newton.   Newton (de Kleer, 1977) does not have any language-translation facility. It solves roller-coaster problems (blocks sliding on curved surfaces), and they are best represented as a picture of the track, which is provided in a symbolic form. The key feature of this program is a process of qualitative analysis referred to as envisionment. Newton envisions, as a human solver might, what might happen to the sliding block based only on the general shape of the track. Thus, on an upslope, the block might slow down and slide back, or continue up. At the crest of a hill, the block might be traveling so fast that it flies off into space, or it might slide down the other side. Using a series of production rules that codify such qualitative knowledge, Newton builds a tree of possible paths for the block that guides further processing of the problem. Some simple problems may be solved using only this qualitative reasoning. If this is not possible, then schemata are used that contain knowledge and formulas necessary to analyze each node of the tree (section of the track) mathematically. In cases where the value of a particular variable is needed for the answer, the familiar means–ends process is used to choose the proper formulas.

Mecho.   Another language translator is Mecho (Bundy, Byrd, Luger, Mellish, & Palmer, 1979), which solves problems from kinematics and those with pulleys. It has also been extended (Bundy, 1978; Byrd & Borning, 1980) without translation to solve problems in statics and roller coasters in an attempt to make the problem-solving part as general as possible by encompassing the work of others (e.g., de Kleer, 1977; McDermott & Larkin, 1978; Novak, 1977). The salient feature of this program, and perhaps, the key to its extensibility, is a two-level knowledge organization. On the object (lower) level is the physics knowledge, organized as rules, schemata, and the problem itself. The problem passes through several stages of representation on the way to a solution. For example, the natural language-translation feature produces a symbolic representation specifying the objects in the problem and their properties. Where necessary, schemata describing important objects (e.g., a pulley) are cued in from the knowledge base. Thus, this initial internal representation might be viewed as naive with elements of a scientific representation. The next general step is to produce the mathematical representation, which can then be solved algebraically. This is not a simple step however. The metalevel (upper level) of the knowledge base contains all of the procedural knowledge necessary for the entire solution process, organized as a set of rules and schemata. It includes rules for interpreting the object-level knowledge for use at each step of the process, for making inferences when needed information is not explicitly stated, for deciding on a general solution strategy, for selecting equations (means–ends strategy again), and so on. Although a complete scientific representation is not explicitly formed, the planning and inferencing powers of the metalevel implicitly use the elements of such a representation to plan the solution before equations are actually generated. Thus, in a statics problem, for instance, the planning process eliminates the problem of excess numbers of equations experienced by Issac.

The organization of procedural knowledge into explicit modular form is what is most interesting psychologically about Mecho. Quite often, such knowledge is buried in the structure of a program and the assumptions that went into writing it, making changes difficult and modeling of procedural learning impossible. This two-level organization also allows the declarative knowledge to be present in only one form, which can be interpreted by the metalevel for use at each step of the solution process. By contrast, both Issac and Newton contain separate representations of the same physics knowledge for each step. In a sense, Mecho can learn (though not on its own) and has learned to solve new problems in a fairly realistic way psychologically because all that is necessary is to give it other new pieces of procedural and declarative knowledge.

Summary.   Although, as noted, the purpose of these AI programs is not to model human behavior, it is clear that they contain many psychologically important features and ideas. The question of representation of the problem and the knowledge base is common to both fields, and the proposed solutions—stages of representation, rules, and schemata (often called frames in AI)—are generally similar. However, because AI is not limited by empirical knowledge of behaviors, these programs can venture into areas where psychological model builders have more difficulty simulating, such as natural language translation, qualitative analysis (e.g., envisionment), planning and inferencing processes, and the actual specification of knowledge organization. The importance of these items to the success of AI programs emphasizes the need for much more work to determine empirically how they occur in humans.

EMPIRICAL STUDIES
TOWARD A THEORY OF EXPERTISE

The objective of the series of investigations that we have carried out is to construct a theory of expertise based on empirical description of expert problem-solving abilities in complex knowledge domains. In this case, the knowledge domain is physics, specifically mechanics. There are three basic questions that guide our efforts. First, how does task performance differ between experts and novices? This question has been partially answered in the review of empirical evidence on physics problem solving. To recapitulate, the basic differences found thus far are: (1) the two groups use different strategies for solving problems, forward versus backward; (2) they seem to have different chunking of equations; (3) in an initial phase of problem solving, experts tend to carry out a qualitative analysis of the problem; and (4) experts are faster at solving problems. One of our goals is to describe more extensively these differences between experts and novices.

The second question asks: How are the knowledge bases of skilled and less-skilled individuals differently structured? It is clear that the skilled individual possesses more knowledge, but how is that knowledge organized? Again, some research has already addressed this issue. Simon and Simon (1978) initially postulated a difference in the knowledge base in terms of the conditions of the productions. Larkin (1979) has postulated a difference in the way equations are stored. Experts store them in relation to a high-level principle, but this does not seem to be the case for novices. In our work and in Larkin's (1980) model Atwood, knowledge is postulated to be organized in the forms of schemata.

The third question guiding our work is: How does the organization of the knowledge base contribute to the performance observed in experts and novices? The relation between the structure of the knowledge base and solution processes must be mediated through the quality of the representation of the problem.

A problem representation, as we stated in Chi et al. (1981): "is a cognitive structure corresponding to a problem, constructed by a solver on the basis of his domain-related knowledge and its organization [p. 121–122]." We adopt Greeno's (Riley, Greeno, & Heller, 1981) notion of a representation, which takes: "the form of a semantic network structure, consisting of elements and relations between these elements [p. 23]." Hence, we hypothesize that at the initial stage of problem analysis, the problem solver attempts to "understand" the problem (Greeno, 1977), that is, construct a representational network containing elements specifying the initial state of the problem, the desired goal, the legal problem-solving operators, and their relational structures. From such a structure, new inferences can be deduced. Hence, the quality, completeness, and coherence of an internal representation must necessarily determine the extent and accuracy of derived inferences, which in turn may determine the ease of arriving at a solution and its accuracy. Therefore, the quality of a problem representation is determined not only by the knowledge available to the solver, but by the particular way the knowledge is organized. One way to capture empirically the difference between the representation of the expert and that of the novice has been the amount of qualitative analysis occurring in the beginning of the problem-solving processes.

Because of its apparent overriding influence on problem solution (Hayes & Simon, 1976; Newell & Simon, 1972), we have focused our studies mainly on the representation of a problem. We employ methods of tapping knowledge in ways other than the analyses of problem-solving protocols because, as we see shortly, the analyses of protocols often provide limited information. However, the first study we describe examines the protocols of problem solving to see what kind of information they do provide, as well as the ways they provide a limited glimpse into the knowledge structure. The next set of studies looks at the categorization behavior of problem solvers, and the third set looks at the knowledge available to individuals of different skill levels. Finally, the fourth set of studies examines the features in a problem statement that might elicit the categorization processes—or to put it another way: What are considered to be the relevant features of a problem by experts and novices?

Study 1: Protocols of Problem Solving

In this study, we attempted to characterize and contrast—both quantitatively and qualitatively—the problem-solving processes of experts and novices, beginning with the reading of the problem through to the checking of the solution. To do so, the problem-solving protocols of two experts and two novices solving five mechanics problems were examined. This study (initiated and carried out by Joan Fogarty) had two specific goals: (1) we wanted to describe some quantitative parameters of expert and novice problem-solving processes and compare these data with those existing in the literature; (2) we wanted to contrast some qualitative differences between experts and novices, particularly focusing on the qualitative aspects of problem analyses.

The five mechanics problems were taken from Chapter 5 of Halliday and Resnick (1974). The expert subjects were two professors of physics who had considerable experience teaching introductory physics. The novices were two freshmen physics majors (A students) who had just completed a term of undergraduate physics using Halliday and Resnick (1974) as the textbook, in which mechanics problems of the type used in this study were taught. Each subject was presented with written problems, one at a time, and was instructed to "think aloud" while solving the problems.

Quantitative Results and Discussion

A variety of quantitative measures can be obtained from protocol data, and these are elaborated in the subsections that follow.

Errors.   On the average, the experts made one out of five possible errors, whereas the novices made three out of five (Table 1.1). As anticipated, experts made fewer errors than novices. The fact that one of the experts made two errors suggests that these problems are nontrivial, yet they are problems that a competent novice can solve. Novice K. W., for example, solved 4.5 out of the 5 problems correctly.

Solution Times.   Solution times were determined by timing the length of the protocols. Looking only at the correct solution times for the entire problem (see Table 1.1), the mean solution time for the experts averaged about 8.96 minutes, whereas the average correct solution time for the novices was 4.16 minutes. The magnitude of our solution time for problem-solving protocols is much longer than that obtained by Simon and Simon (1978). Their problems were selected from a high school physics text and were limited to kinematics; such problems can be solved mainly through algebraic manipulation. Our problems were more complex; they were chosen from a college physics text and involved dynamics, which requires that forces be explicitly taken into account. Applying the Force Law requires making some physical inferences before equations can be brought into play.

The novices in this study actually solved problems faster than the experts. However, this seems to be an artifact of the great number of errors made by Novice C. H. That is, Novice C. H.'s only correct solution was problem 1, which in fact took him longer to solve than the rest of the subjects. But, because problem 1 happens to be a short problem and because it was the only problem he solved correctly, his average latency was reduced because it was determined by the speed of solving that particular problem. Novice K. W.'s solution times, on the other hand, are actually comparable (averaging 7.01 minutes) to the experts' (averaging 8.96 minutes).

The only obvious outlier in solution time occurs in problem 2, where Expert R. E. took significantly longer than Novice K. W. Examining the protocols in detail, we see that Expert R. E. in this case sought and calculated a value unnecessarily. When he discovered that the problem was really much simpler than he thought, the actual protocol for the short solution took only about 1.33 minutes.

Hence, barring unusual circumstances, competent novices not only can solve these problems, but they can do so in approximately the same amount of time as experts. However, if the task had emphasized speed, the experts probably could

TABLE 1.1
Solution Time (Sec), Number of Equations Generated, and Number of Diagrams Drawn for Each Subject and Problem

Problems		Problem 1	Problem 2	Problem 3	Problem 4	Problem 5	Mean[a]
(No. of Subparts)		(1)	(2)	(2)	(3)	(2)	
Expert R. E.	Solution Time	225	625	555	590	585	516
	No. of Equations	6	8	12	9	14	9.8
	No. of Diagrams	3	4	4	1	2	2.8
Expert M. V.	Solution Time	(165)	(325)A,B	500	590	590	560
	No. of Equations	3	5	7	12	15	8.4
	No. of Diagrams	1	1	1	2	3	1.6
Novice C. H.	Solution Time	275	(585)A,B	(925)A	(835)A,B,C	(325)A,B[b]	275
	No. of Equations	7	10	12	19	8	11.2
	No. of Diagrams	3	3	5	3	3	3.4
Novice K. W.	Solution Time	200	105	(290)B	655	420	345
	No. of Equations	7	10	12	19	7	11.0
	No. of Diagrams	2	0	2	2	1	1.4

Note: Parentheses around the solution time indicate an incorrect solution. The letter(s) that follow indicate the incorrect part(s) of the problem.

[a] The mean solution time was calculated only for problems solved correctly.

[b] The subject attempted only Part A of this problem.

have solved the problems much faster than the novices. We suggest, however, that protocol data are not a particularly viable way to assess the speed of problem solving.

Number of Quantitative Relations.   Another quantitative parameter that may shed some light on skill differences between experts and novices is the number of quantitative relations generated by the subjects as they solve problems. Table 1.1 also shows the total number of quantitative relations generated by each subject for each problem. A quantitative relation is defined as any mathematical relation among physical entities, and it generally takes the form of an equation. Excluded are algebraic manipulations of already generated equations and instantiations of equations (i.e., substituting values for the variables). In general, there appear to be no systematic differences in the number of quantitative equations generated as a function of skill. There was greater variability in the number of equations generated by a given subject for the different problems than between subjects on the same problem.

"Chunks" of Equations.   As stated earlier, Larkin (1979) has hypothesized that experts store physics equations in tightly connected "chunks," whereas novices store equations individually. To test the "chunking" hypothesis, Larkin (1979) measured the times during the problem-solving process when quantitative relations were generated. Her results showed that the expert generated a great many pairs of equations with short pauses between the equations, whereas the novice generated fewer equations with shorter pauses.

Using the same analysis, we also examined the distribution of generated equations over time. For each subject, the time interval between the generation of each pair of quantitative relations was calculated for each problem. Our data do not discriminate between the generation pattern of experts and novices. If anything, the results indicated that the opposite was true. That is, the novices seemed to have generated a greater number of relations in close succession.

There are substantial individual differences, however. Novice C. H. showed the strongest degree of chunking or generated the largest number of quantitative relations in rapid "bursts." How do we account for the discrepancy between our results and Larkin's? One interpretation is to hypothesize that a burst of equation generation might be an artifact of various problem-solving strategies that subjects may adopt. Our novice subjects, for example, reported that when they get stuck on a problem, they write down as many related equations as they can think of. They then look at the equations they have generated to get some hints about how to proceed. This would produce clusters of equations.

Another strategy, reflecting the style of solution processes of individual subjects, relates to the way equations are generated, which often is all at the same time. Novice C. H., for example, would spend a considerable amount of time generating equations. This pattern of solution processes would necessarily inflate the number of equations generated within a short period of time. Perhaps the generation of equations in bursts may also be the outcome of another artifact, discussed in the next section: the drawing of free-body diagrams.

Even though we did not replicate Larkin's (1979) finding that experts tend to generate equations in clusters, this does not deny the possibility that the storage of equations may indeed be different in the knowledge base of the experts and novices. Our conclusion is that protocol analysis of equation generation will not address this particular issue directly. In order to address the issue of how equations are stored in the knowledge bases of experts and novices, one needs to design a study where experts and novices are asked to generate or freely associate equations outside the context of a problem-solving situation.

Number of Diagrams Generated. Another potentially interesting quantitative measure is the number of free-body diagrams drawn by the subjects. The construction of free-body diagrams appears to form an important component of problem solving. Free-body diagrams are partial figures that depict partial abstractions of the total physical situation. They may be drawn for all or part of the physical situation and utilize directional arrows denoting the forces acting in a physical system.

The number of diagrams, including free-body diagrams, drawn by each subject for each problem is also shown in Table 1.1. Again, there appear to be no systematic skill differences, although there seem to be some individual differences, with Expert R. E. and Novice C. H. drawing the greatest number of free-body diagrams. These two individuals also generated the greatest number of equations and produced the greatest amount of clustering.

Drawing free-body diagrams may inflate the number of equations generated in clusters. Both novices as well as the experts, though to a lesser extent, utilized the strategy of constructing free-body diagrams, which is taught and emphasized in introductory physics courses. By using the free-body diagrams, equations relating the forces can be generated. Hence, the more frequently subjects draw free-body diagrams, the more likely they are to have clusters of equation generation. Therefore, bursts of equation generation may be an artifact of a solver's need to generate many diagrams.

The purpose of generating many free-body diagrams is not clear to us. We speculate that when subjects find a problem difficult, they tend to draw more diagrams. Each drawing may be seen as an attempt to create a meaningful representation of the problem. For example, for problems that took the longest to solve, a large number of diagrams tended to be generated (such as problem 2 for Expert R. E.). Furthermore, problem 2 was the one that Expert R. E. had some difficulty with, having derived a value unnecessarily. Likewise, for Novice C. H., problem 3 took the longest time to solve (which he did incorrectly); he also generated the greatest number of diagrams for that problem. These speculations need to be confirmed, but it seems that drawing free-body diagrams may be a way of helping the subject create a meaningful representation. It may also indicate that the subject is having difficulty going beyond the visual stage of problem representation.

In Study 5 (this chapter), when four experts and four novices were asked to solve a problem, the novices generated four times as many (4.7) diagrams as the experts (1.0 diagrams). The novices had more difficulty solving the problem correctly (three out of four errors) than did the experts (one out of four errors). This provides some additional support for the notion that frequent generation of diagrams is used as an external aid to create a meaningful problem representation, especially when subjects are having difficulties.

Summary of Quantitative Measures. The results of this study indicate that few of the quantitative measures we used meaningfully differentiated the experts from the novices. The quantitative measures obtained from protocols seem to be tenuous measures that are confounded with individual differences and the particular strategies adopted by the problem solver. We now turn to qualitative analyses of the protocols to locate differences that can be attributed to skill.

Qualitative Results and Discussion

For reasons already indicated and because a great deal of attention has been devoted to the equation-generation and manipulation stages of problem solving, we now focus on the initial qualitative analysis stage of problem solving. We assume that during this stage of processing a representation of the problem is constructed, that this occurs primarily during reading of the problem, and that it is completed in the first 30–40 seconds after the problem has been read. We estimate that this stage takes a very short time because it appears to be analogous to the stage of "initial analytical assessment" that Simon and Barenfield (1969) talked about for chess problem solving and the stage of "preconception" that expert musical sight readers engage in prior to the actual playing of a musical piece (Wolf, 1976). The short duration of these initial processes is an important consideration in determining our subsequent experimental procedure.

Figures 1.2 and 1.3 show two samples of protocols, one from Expert R. E. and the other from Novice C. H., both on the first part of problem 5. The protocols have been segmented into four types of episodes: qualitative analysis, drawing diagrams (which may be either the diagrams depicting the main components of the problem or the abstracted free-body diagrams), generating equations, and manipulating equations.

Before proceeding with the discussion of the protocol data, it may be necessary to clarify a few terms and operational definitions. Any statements in the protocols that do not relate to drawing diagrams or generating and manipulating equations were considered to be "qualitative analyses" of the problem. Furthermore, these statements can be a variety of types such as references to planning, checking of the solution, and so on. We focused specifically on those

Taxonomy of Episodes	Physics	Protocols
*Qualitative Analysis (inferences)	Constant velocity ⟶ Frictional force Frictional force opposes force due to weight of block *Friction ⟶ Coefficient of friction ∿ angle φ	"There must be a frictional force retarding the motion because otherwise the block would accelerate down the plane under the action of its own weight...the angle φ must be related to the coefficient of friction somehow."
Drawing Free Body Diagram	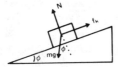	"You would have a normal force perpendicular to the plane, the weight down, and the force of kinetic friction would lie along the plane...the angle between the weight vector and the normal to the plane is also angle φ."
Generate Equations	$mg\sin\phi - f_k = 0$ $N - mg\cos\phi = 0$ $f_k = \mu_k N = \mu_k mg\cos\phi$	"For motion down the plane would be mg times sinφ minus f which is retarding things and that's equal to zero. For motion perpendicular to the plane, you would have the normal force acting upward, but mgcosφ acting downward or into the plane and those two things sum to zero. The only relation you need in addition is that the force of kinetic friction is μ times the normal and is therefore μ times mgcosφ."
Albegraic Manipulation	$mg\sin\phi - \mu mg\cos\phi = 0$ $\mu_k = \tan\phi$	"So substituting that (f = μmgcosφ) into the first equation, which I've circled, you would then have mgsinφ, f which would be μ times mgcosφ, and all of that would be equal to zero, and so what one finds then is that μ, the coefficient of friction must be tanφ."
Reread Question A		
Draw Free Body Diagram	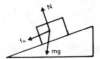	"So let's draw the plane again... the difference is that the frictional force...acts in the other direction."
Qualitative Analysis		"We know the initial speed is Vo...I'm sort of fishing here for a minute, the final speed... is obviously zero."

CONTINUED

EXPERT R. E.
(PROBLEM #5) CONTINUED)

TAXONOMY OF EPISODES	PHYSICS	PROTOCOLS
GENERATE	$V_f^2 - V_o^2 = 2ax$	"We have an expression which relates several things of interest to us...all at the same time."
QUALITATIVE ANALYSIS		"We can easily solve for x providing we know the other things in the equation....We don't know a but that's not hard to find."
GENERATE	$mgsin\phi + \mu_k mgcos\phi = ma$	"This time both mgsinϕ and the frictional force...those two forces act in the same direction."
MANIPULATE	$\cancel{m}gsin\phi + \mu_k\cancel{m}gcos\phi = \cancel{m}a$ $\mu_k = tan\phi = \frac{sin\phi}{cos\phi}$ $a = gsin\phi \times \frac{sin\phi}{cos\phi}gcos\phi$ $= 2gsin\phi$	"The masses cancel everywhere ...we also know $\mu_k...\mu_k$ is the tangent of ϕ... which is the sin of ϕ over the cos of ϕ...the cosϕ's cancel and you're left with the acceleration down the plane of...twice gsinθ.
QUALITATIVE ANALYSIS (INFERENCE) (CHECK ANSWER)	block slides uniformly $\longrightarrow f_k = F_g$ $= mgsin\phi$ f_k now in opposite directions > Total Force $= F_g + f_k = 2mgsin\phi$ $a = \frac{Ftotal}{m} = 2gsin\phi$	"So effectively you have...an acceleration...of twice the weight... I n the first part of the problem...friction... must be exactly equal to gsinϕ and if you have it operating in the opposite direction..."
MANIPULATE	$0 - V_o^2 = 2(-2gsin\phi)x$ $x = V_o^2/4gsin\phi$	"Now let's go ahead and solve for...V Final squared was 0. V initial squared was what it is...so what you end up with for, for x is Vo squared over 4gsinϕ."

FIG. 1.2. Expert R. E.'s protocol on problem 5, segmented into episodes.

qualitative analysis statements that seemed to generate knowledge not explicitly stated in the problem (i.e., inferences). (These qualitative analysis statements are not to be confused with qualitative analysis of the protocol data.)

There are several general remarks that can be made about the initial stage of the protocols. First, contrary to the picture painted earlier, the protocol data indicate that our novices also spent time analyzing the problem qualitatively.

Novice C. H.
(Problem #5)

Taxonomy of Episodes	Physics	Protocols
Draw Diagram		"Let me draw a picture. An inclined plane with slop angle ϕ ...and it's (the block) sliding down the plane with a velocity ...constant velocity."
Qualitative Analysis (Inferences)	Constant velocity ——>$\Sigma F = 0$ ——>friction	"Since it's (the block) sliding down the plane with constant velocity, it means the sum of the forces is zilch so there's a, there's got to be some kind of friction on the thing..."
Draw Free Body Diagram		"I'll draw a free body diagram. There's the weight mg, there's the frictional force, then there's the normal force perpendicular to the plane.
Generate Equations	Force parallel to plane = $mg\sin\phi$ $F_N = mg\cos\phi$ $f = \mu F_N$	"Ok. So I'm going to draw trusty axes and resolve weight into a, into....You've got ϕ there so this $mg\cos\phi$, and this is $mg\sin\phi$...normal force is going to be equal to $mg\cos\phi$ and friction equals, umm...μ times the normal force."
Manipulate	$f = \mu mg\cos\phi$	"So that frictional force is equal to $\mu mg\cos\phi$."
Generate	$v^2 = V_0^2 + 2a(x - x_0)$	"The block is projected up the plane with an initial velocity. So I'm going to use...equation for motion $V^2 = V_0^2 + 2$ times acceleration times change in distance."

CONTINUED

During this stage, some inferences about the problem are drawn. A simple count of the number of propositions that were made, which can be judged to be inferences, shows that experts average 12.75 propositions and novices average 10.58, which is not reliably different. Consistent with our earlier assertion, the initial episode of qualitative analysis is usually short in duration, taking only one paragraph in the protocols.

NOVICE C. H.
(PROBLEM #5) CONTINUED

TAXONOMY OF EPISODES	PHYSICS	PROTOCOLS
MANIPULATE	$x_o = 0$ $V = 0$ $\dfrac{V_o^2}{2a} = x$	"Initial position I'm going to call O...final velocity equals 0 so I get V_o(sic) over 2a is going to equal the x."
*QUALITATIVE ANALYSIS (INFERENCE) DRAW FREE BODY DIAGRAM		"a is going to be acceleration due to the frictional force." (WRONG) "Now we've got a different drawing. We've got mg and the velocity is up the plane so frictional force...is down the plane."
GENERATE	$\Sigma F_x = ma$	"...sum of the forces in my x direction is going to equal mass times acceleration."
MANIPULATE	$mgsin\phi + f = ma$ $mgsin\phi + \mu mgcos = ma$ $a = g(sin\phi + \mu cos\phi)$ $x = \dfrac{V_o^2}{(gsin\phi + \mu cos\phi)}$	"So, you've got $mgsin\phi$ + frictional force equals the mass times acceleration, so frictional force is equal to... μ times the normal force... my m's go out so the acceleration equals g times $sin\phi$ + $\mu cos\phi$. So I substitute back in the other equation." (Leaves out factor of 2)

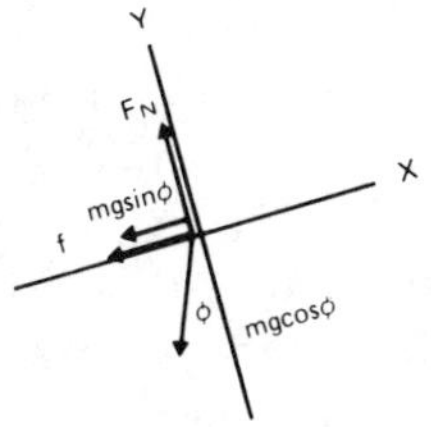

FIG. 1.3.   Novice C. H.'s protocol on problem 5, segmented into episodes.

The second observation is that, unlike what is commonly believed, the qualitative analysis episode often occurs throughout the protocols, not just at the beginning. For example, the inference episode occurs, on the average, $2\frac{1}{2}$ times throughout each problem for the experts and $1\frac{1}{2}$ times for the novices, although this difference is again not significant. Because of this phenomenon, it is difficult to ascertain exactly when the construction of a representation is completed. These protocols lead us to think that a gross representation is initially constructed; refinement, if necessary, can occur later in the protocol.

The third observation is that errors in solution have two sources. One source is trivial computation error resulting either from faulty manipulation or instantiation of equations. An example of a trivial computation error occurs in the last episode of Fig. 1.3. In manipulating the equations, the novice made an error by a factor of 2. The other source of solution errors can be traced to either the generation of wrong inferences or the failure to generate the right inference. The inference episode with an asterisk beside it in Fig. 1.3 indicates an example of a wrong inference. We attribute the source of solution errors in general to these incorrect inferences, even though the incorrect inference in this particular case was not the cause for the problem's incorrect solution. This is because the novice was able to generate all the correct equations. The mistake in this problem arises from the solver's failure to complete the solution by substituting for μ. Incorrect inferences are relatively easy to detect in the protocols. What is more difficult to capture is the solver's failure to generate a necessary inference. This can be captured only by comparing and contrasting the expert's and the novice's protocols in trying to understand a novice's error. Our interpretation is that Novice C. H. did not complete the solution (see the last episode of Fig. 1.3) because he failed to generate the inference that the coefficient of friction μ is somehow related to the angle ϕ, as did the expert (see the first episode of Fig. 1.2). Without setting an explicit goal to relate the two (μ and angle ϕ), Novice C. H. could not solve the problem, even though he had all the necessary equations.

Hence, in general, we would conclude from examination of the inference generating episodes of the protocols that both experts and novices are just as likely to spend time generating tacit knowledge about a problem and that both groups are just as likely to do so iteratively across the entire problem-solving protocols. However, it is the quality of the inferences that matters. Novices are more likely either to generate the wrong inference or fail to generate the necessary inferences. A large number of the novices' errors can be traced to this source.

Studies on the Categorization of Problems

To say that novices either fail to make the appropriate inferences during qualitative analyses, or that they do not generate inferences at all, does not explain the source of incomplete or erroneous inference making. To uncover this limitation of the novices, we have to understand the knowledge structure of both experts and novices and how that knowledge enhances or limits their problem-solving abilities. Analyzing the protocols of problem solving does not appear to provide enough information of this kind. Our research described here, therefore, is concerned with ways of exploring the knowledge of a problem solver through means other than analyzing solution protocols.

We hypothesize that a problem representation is constructed in the context of the knowledge available for a particular type of problem. Further, we make the assumption that the knowledge useful for a particular problem is indexed when a given physics problem is categorized as a specific type. Therefore, expert–novice differences may be related to poorly formed, incomplete, or nonexistent problem categories. Given this hypothesis, we investigated knowledge contained in problem categories. Our first order of business, then, was to determine whether our initial hypothesis is true. That is, are there reliable categories to which problems are typed, and, if so, are these categories different for novices and experts?

Evidence already exists to suggest that solvers represent problems by category and that these categories might direct problem solving. For instance, Hinsely, Hayes, and Simon's (1978) study found that college students can categorize algebra word problems into types and that this categorization occurs very quickly, sometimes even after reading just the first phrase of the problem statement. This ability suggests that "problem schemata" exist and can be viewed as interrelated sets of knowledge that unify superficially disparate problems by some underlying features. We refer to the knowledge associated with a category as a schema. The chess findings of Chase and Simon (1973a, 1973b) can also be interpreted as showing that choosing a chess move results from a direct association between move sequences and a chunked representation of highly stereotyped (or overlearned) chess pieces or patterns. There is also evidence in studies of medical diagnosis that expert diagnosticians represent particular cases of disease by general categories and that these categories facilitate the formation of hypotheses during diagnostic problem solving (Pople, 1977; Wortman, 1972).

Study 2: Sorting Problems

To determine the kinds of categories subjects of different experience impose on problems, we asked eight advanced PhD students from the physics department (experts) and eight undergraduates who had a semester of mechanics (novices) to categorize 24 problems selected from Chapters 5–12 of Halliday and Resnick's (1974) *Fundamentals of Physics*. The subjects' task was simply to sort the problems on the basis of similarities in how they would solve them.

Analysis of Quantitative Results.   Again, no gross quantitative differences between the two skill groups were produced. For example, there were no significant differences in the number of categories produced by each skill group (both averaged about 8.5 categories), and the four largest categories produced by each subject captured the majority (about 77%) of the problems. There was also little difference in the amount of time it took experts and novices to sort the problems, although experts tended to take slightly longer, about 40 seconds per problem (discarding one outlier), whereas novices took about 37 seconds per problem.

The absence of gross quantitative differences in measures such as number of categories, number of largest categories, and time to categorize, confirms the notion that there are no fundamental capacity differences between experts and novices. That is, the novices are not inherently slower, for example, nor do they have limited abilities to discriminate the problems into eight categories. The lack of a general quantitative difference points to the necessity of examining the qualitative differences.

Analysis of Qualitative Results. If we examine the nature of the categories into which experts and novices sorted the problems, they are qualitatively dissimilar. This difference can be seen most dramatically by observing the two pairs of problems that the majority of the subjects of each skill group sorted together. Figure 1.4 shows two pairs of problems that eight out of eight novices grouped together as similar. These problems have noticeably similar "surface structures." By surface structures, we mean either: (1) the objects referred to in the problem (e.g., a spring or an inclined plane); (2) the key words that have meaning in physics (e.g., center of mass or friction); or (3) the physical configuration that involves the interaction of several object components (e.g., a block on an inclined plane).

The suggestion that these surface structures are the bases of the novices' categorization can be further confirmed by examining subjects' verbal justifications for the categories, which are presented in the right-hand column of Fig. 1.4. The novices' explanations indicate that they grouped the top two problems together because they both involved "rotational things" and the bottom two together because they involved "blocks on an inclined plane."

For experts, surface structures do not seem to be the basis for categorization. There is neither a similarity in the key words used in the problem statements nor in the visual appearance of the diagrams for the problems (Fig. 1.5). No similarity is apparent in the equations used for the problems grouped together by the majority of the experts. The similarity underlying the experts' categorization can only be detected by a physicist. It appears that the experts classify according to the major physics principles (or fundamental laws) governing the solution of each problem (sometimes referred to as the solution method). The top two problems in Fig. 1.5 can be solved by the application of the Conservation of Energy Law, and the bottom two are better solved by the application of Newton's Second Law ($F = MA$). The verbal justifications of the subjects confirm this analysis. We might refer to these underlying principles as the "deep structure" of the problem, which is the basis by which experts categorize problems.

In sum, the results of this study uncover several facets of problem solving that were not observable from protocol analyses. First, through a sorting task, it became apparent that categories of problems exist. These categories probably correspond to problem schemata, that is, unified knowledge that can be used to solve a particular type of problem. Second, category membership can be determined rather quickly (between 35–45 seconds). This is the amount of time we initially alloted to the qualitative analysis episodes of problem solving. Third, the results also imply that within 45 seconds the experts, at least, can already perceive the solution method applicable to the problem. The possibility that such categorization processes may occur during problem solving is never evident from the problem-solving protocols because there was never any cause for solvers to mention either the principle underlying a problem or the surface structure of the problem. Only through an alternative task, such as sorting, are we able to detect the presence of categories that may be related to solution methods.

Diagrams Depicted from Problems Categorized by Novices within the Same Groups	Novices' Explanations for Their Similarity Groupings

Problem 10 (11)

Novice 2: "*Angular* velocity, *momentum,* circular things"

Novice 3: "*Rotational* kinematics, *angular* speeds, *angular* velocities"

Novice 6: "Problems that have something *rotating; angular* speed"

Problem 11 (39)

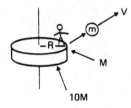

Problem 7 (23)

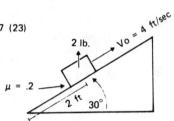

Novice 1: "These deal with blocks on an *incline plane*"

Novice 5: "*Inclined plane* problems, coefficient of *friction*"

Novice 6: "Blocks on *inclined planes* with angles"

Problem 7 (35)

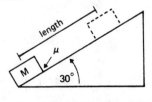

FIG. 1.4. Examples from novices' problem categories. Problem numbers represent chapter and problem number from Halliday and Resnick (1974).

Diagrams Depicted from Problems Catergorized by Experts within the Same Groups

Problem 6 (21)

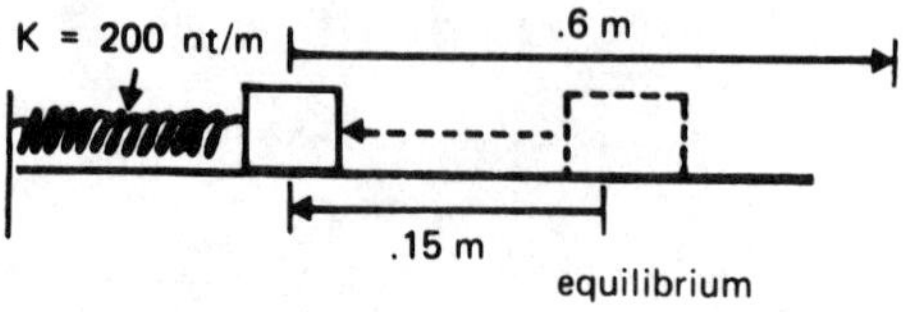

Problem 7 (35)

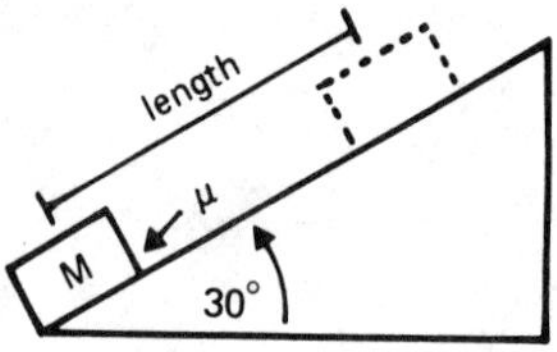

Experts' Explanations for Their Similarity Groupings

Expert 2: "*Conservation of Energy*"

Expert 3: "*Work-Energy Theorem*. They are all straight-forward problems."

Expert 4: "These can be done from energy considerations. Either you should know the *Principle of Conservation of Energy*, or work is lost somewhere."

Problem 5 (39)

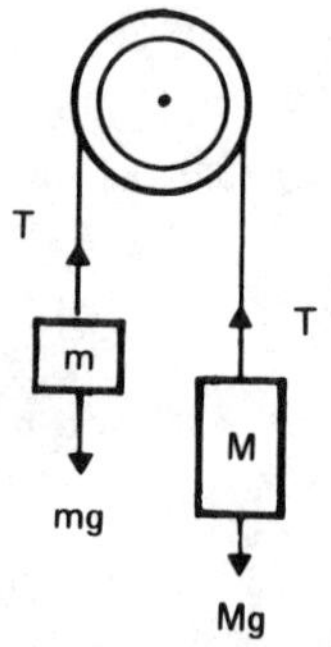

Problem 12 (23)

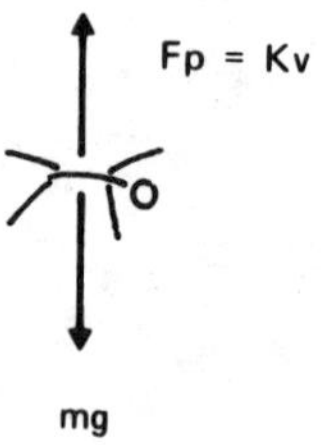

Expert 2: "These can be solved by *Newton's Second Law*"

Expert 3: "F = ma; *Newton's Second Law*"

Expert 4: "Largely use F = ma; *Newton's Second Law*"

FIG. 1.5. Examples from experts' problem categories. Problem numbers represent chapter and problem number from Halliday and Resnick (1974).

Study 3: Sorting Specially Designed Problems

If the interpretation of the previous sorting results is accurate, then one should be able to replicate the findings and, further, to predict how a given subject at a specific skill level might categorize a given problem. In this study, we specially designed a set of 20 problems to test the hypothesis that novices are more dependent on surface features, whereas experts focus more on the underlying principles. Table 1.2 shows the problem numbers and the dimensions on which they were varied. The left column indicates the major objects that were used in the problem; the three right headings are the solution methods (or the basic laws) that can be used to solve them. Figure 1.6 shows an example of a pair of problems (corresponding to problems 11 and 18 in Table 1.2), which contain the same surface structure but different deep structures. In fact, the problems are identical except for the question asked. From the results of Study 2, we predicted that the novices would group together problems with similar surface features, such as the two problems shown in Fig. 1.6, whereas experts would not. Instead, experts would group together problems that have similar deep structures, regardless of the surface features. Intermediate subjects might exhibit some characteristics of each skill group.

TABLE 1.2
Problem Categories

		Principles	
Surface Structure	Forces	Energy	Momentum (Linear or Angular)
Pulley with hanging blocks		20[b]	
	11	19[b]	
	14[a]	3[ab]	
Spring		7	
	18	16	1
			17[c]
		9	6[c]
Inclined plane	14[a]	3[ab]	
		5	
Rotational	15		2
			13
Single hanging block	12		
Block on block	8		
Collisions (bullet-"block" or block-block)			4
			6[c]
			10[c]

[a] Problems with more than one salient surface feature. Listed multiply by feature.

[b] Problems that could be solved using either of two principles, energy or force.

[c] Two-step problems, momentum plus energy.

No. 11 (Force Problem)

A man of mass M_1 lowers himself to the ground from a height X by holding onto a rope passed over a massless frictionless pulley and attached to another block of mass M_2. The mass of the man is greater than the mass of the block. What is the tension on the rope?

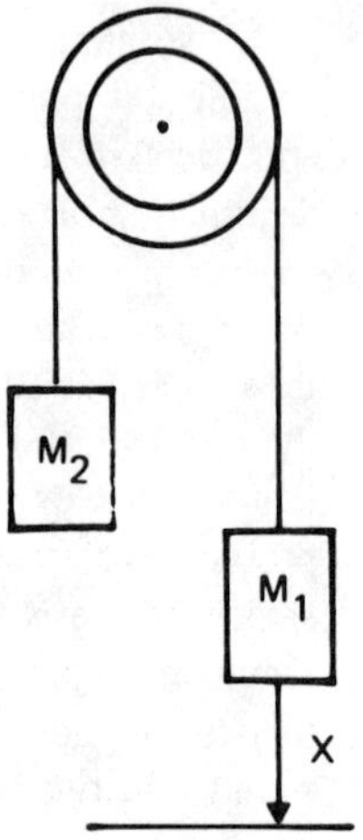

No. 18 (Energy Problem)

A man of mass M_1 lowers himself to the ground from a height X by holding onto a rope passed over a massless frictionless pulley and attached to another block of mass M_2. The mass of the man is greater than the mass of the block. With what speed does the man hit the ground?

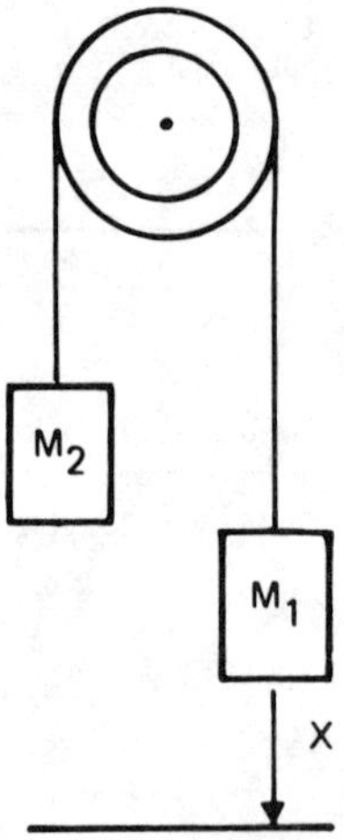

FIG. 1.6. Sample problems.

The results confirmed our previous interpretations. One novice, who had completed a course in mechanics, grouped strictly on the surface structures of the problems. Table 1.3 shows his problem categories and the explanations he provided for his groups. First of all, if one scans only the verbal justification column (far right), it is evident that, except for the fourth group where he mentioned a physics principle ("Conservation of Energy"), the remaining categories were all described by either physics key words (e.g., "velocity problems") or the actual

TABLE 1.3
Problem Categories and Explanations for Novice H. P.

Group 1:	2, 15	"Rotation"
Group 2:	11, 12, 16,[a] 19	"Always a block of some mass hanging down"
Group 3:	4, 10	"Velocity problems" (collisions)
Group 4:	13,[b] 17	"Conservation of Energy"
Group 5:	6, 7, 9, 18	"Spring"
Group 6:	3, 5, 14	"Inclined plane"
Groups 7, 8, 9 were singletons		

[a] Problem discrepant with our prior analysis of surface structure as indicated in Table 1.2.

[b] Problem discrepant with our prior analysis of solution principles as indicated in Table 1.2.

physical components contained in the problem ("spring"). And indeed, he collapsed problems across the physics laws. For example, in Group 5 (Table 1.3), problem 18 is obviously solvable by the Force Law, whereas problem 7 is solvable by the Energy Law (see Table 1.2 again). The only category for which he made any reference to a physics principle is Group 4, which he described as a "Conservation of Energy" category. However, this is to be distinguished from the expert's labeling of "Conservation of Energy" because this novice only labels those problems as "Conservation of Energy" when the term "Energy" is actually mentioned in the problem statements themselves, as was the case here.

In contrast, the expert's classifications are all explained by the underlying principles, such as Conservation of Angular Momentum, Conservation of Energy, etc. (See Table 1.4). Furthermore, as predicted, the expert collapsed problems across the surface similarities. For example, in Group 3, problem 1 is basically a spring problem, and problem 4 is a collision problem.

Table 1.5 shows the groupings of an advanced novice (an intermediate). His categorizations of the problems are characterized by the underlying physics principle in an interesting way. These principles are qualified and constrained by the

TABLE 1.4
Problem Categories and Explanations for Expert V. V.

Group 1:	2, 13	"Conservation of Angular Momentum"
Group 2:	18	"Newton's Third Law"
Group 3:	1, 4	"Conservation of Linear Momentum"
Group 4:	19, 5, 20, 16, 7	"Conservation of Energy"
Group 5:	12, 15, 9,[a] 11, 8, 3, 14	"Application of equations of motion" ($F = MA$)
Group 6:	6, 10, 17	"Two-step problems: Conservation of Linear Momentum plus an energy calculation of some sort"

[a] Problem discrepant with our prior analysis of solution principles as indicated in Table 1.2

TABLE 1.5
Problem Categories and Explanations for Advanced Novice M. H.

Group 1:	*14, 20*	"Pulley"
Group 2:	1, *4, 6, 10, 12*[a]	"Conservation of Momentum" (collision)
Group 3:	*9, 13,*[a] *17, 18*[a]	"Conservation of Energy" (springs)
Group 4:	*19, 11*	"Force problems that involve a massless pulley" (pulley)
Group 5:	*2, 15*[a]	"Conservation of Angular Momentum" (rotation)
Group 6:	*7,*[a] *16*[a]	"Force problems that involve springs" (spring)
Group 7:	*8, 5,*[a] *3*	"Force problems" (inclined plane)

Note: Italic numbers mean that these problems share a similar surface feature, which is indicated in the parentheses, if the feature is not explicitly stated by the subject.

[a] Problems discrepant with our prior analysis of solution principles as indicated in Table 12.

surface components present in the problems. For example, instead of classifying all the force problems together (Groups 4, 6, and 7), as would an expert, he explicitly separated them according to the surface features of the problems. That is, to him there are different varieties of force problems, some containing pulleys, some containing springs, and some containing inclined planes.

To summarize this study, we were able to replicate the initial finding that experts categorize problems by physics laws, whereas novices categorize problems by the literal components. If we assume that such categories reflect knowledge schemata, then our results from the person at the intermediate skill level suggest that, with learning, there is a gradual shift in organization of knowledge—from one centering on the physical components, to one where there is a combined reliance on the physical components and physics laws, and, finally, to one primarily unrelated to the physical components.

Study 4: Hierarchical Sorting

The results of the previous two sorting studies strongly suggest that the problem categories of experts are different from those of novices. That is, we assume that the differences lie not only in the "category labels" that subjects of different skill prefer to use. We assume that problem categories correspond to problem schemata and, theoretically, that schemata can have subschemata embedded in them and be embedded in higher-level or superschemata. Hence, if we can identify some similarity of the contents of schemata at different levels for individuals of different skills, then perhaps we will have converging evidence that the schemata of the novices and experts are indeed different and that their schemata might be the same when different levels are compared.

To test this assumption, a hierarchical sorting task was designed by Christopher Roth. In this task, subjects were first asked to sort the problems in the same manner as in the previous two studies. Then, groups that they had initially sorted were returned, and they were asked to subdivide each group further if they wished. The sorting of each group was conducted in a depth-first manner. When all the discriminations of each group were completed, they were also asked to combine their initial groups until they no longer wished to make any further combinations. Subjects' rationale for each grouping was also recorded.

Sixteen subjects were run. They ranged from graduate students (experts), to fourth-year physics and chemical engineering majors (intermediates), to A–C students (novices) who had taken courses in physics (mechanics, electricity, and magnetism).

The 40 problems used in this study were selected from Chapters 5–12 of Halliday and Resnick (1974), as in Study 2, which is the minimum amount of material typically covered in a first-year mechanics course. There are two aspects of the data to examine: the contents of the groups and the tree structures. We believe that the most naive structures are those generated by the novice C-students (R. R. and J. T.) (Fig. 1.7, top two panels). The circular nodes represent the groups from the initial sort, and the numbers inside the nodes indicate how many problems are in that group. The square nodes beneath the circular nodes are the groups formed when the problems were further discriminated, and the triangular nodes above the circular nodes indicate the combinations. The tree structures of these two novices have three distinct characteristics that none of the other more skilled subjects exhibited. First, the initial groups (circular nodes) have a greater than average number of categories. (Eight categories is the average number derived from Study 2.) The second characteristic is that they either cannot make further discriminations (Novice R. R.), suggesting that their categories are already at the lowest level, or they make such fine discriminations (Novice J. T.) that each problem is in a category by itself. This is reminiscent of the chess results, where beginning chess players have chunks consisting of one or two pieces. The nature of the initial categories is physical configurations, much like what was found in Study 2, such as "gravity," "pulley with weight," etc. When the novice (J. T.) breaks the categories down so that each problem is a category, the descriptions of these categories are very specific and still bound to the physical configuration. For example, one of the initial categories of Novice J. T. is "tension in rope." When that category was further broken down, one subdivision was specified as "tension with two blocks on incline," and another was "tension with two blocks and pulley on incline." The most sophisticated tree structures of the experts are shown in the lower two panels of Fig. 1.7. The initial circular nodes are generally the different varieties of physics principles, much like those uncovered in Study 2. For Expert C. D., one group of circular nodes contains Conservation of Energy, Conservation of Momentum, and Conservation of Angular Momentum, and the other group of three are $F = MA$, $F = MA$ to find the Resultant Force, and Simple Harmonic Motion. Each group of three (circled) categories was further collapsed to two superordinate categories: Conservation Laws and Equations of Motion. The subordinate categories for the same subject are generally discriminations based on physical configurations, such as "tension prob-

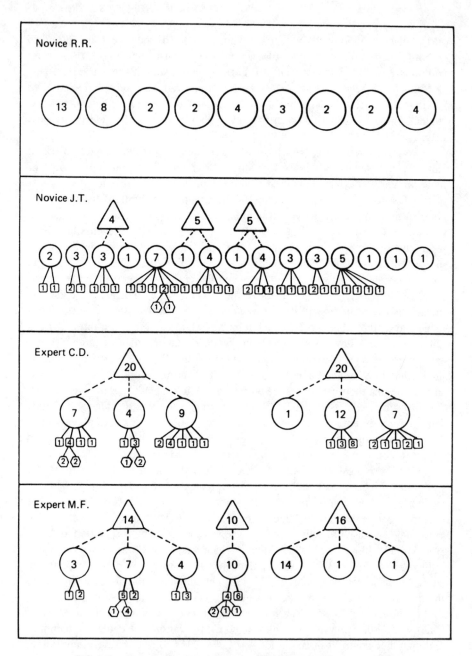

FIG. 1.7. Groupings made by novices and experts on a hierarchical sorting task. Circular nodes are the preliminary groups, squares and hexagons are subsequent discriminations, and triangles are the combinations.

lems.'' Hence, from our limited analyses, we could hypothesize that the subordinate categories of the experts correspond to the initial categories of the novices. Although this study is not definitive in hypothesizing that experts' categories are at a higher level than novices' categories, additional data from Study 5 converge on the same notion.

The results of this study can also be interpreted in the framework proposed by Rosch (1978) of ''basic'' categories. The term basic can be used loosely to mean the preferred or dominant categories into which problems were divided by the subjects. Hence, one could say that the basic categories of the novices correspond to the subordinate categories of the experts.

Studies of the Knowledge Base

If the knowledge bases of the experts are different from those of the novices, in what ways are they organized differently, and in what way does the knowledge of experts and novices enhance and hinder their problem-solving processes? These questions, coupled with the results of the categorization studies, lead us to an examination of the knowledge bases. The categorization studies show that without actually solving the problems, and in less than 45 seconds, experts can encode the problem into a deep level of representation, which enables them to grossly determine the solution method applicable to the problem. We speculate that such encoding skill necessarily reflects the knowledge-base differences between experts and novices. The next set of studies asks to what extent and in what ways are the knowledge bases of the novices less complete and coherent than the experts.

Study 5: Summaries

With these questions in mind, we attempted to capture what subjects knew about physics, independent of a problem-solving context. One simple approach was to ask subjects to summarize a chapter of a physics text. This should reveal the knowledge they have on a particular topic. We selected Chapter 5 on particle dynamics from Halliday and Resnick (1974) because subjects in the first protocol study needed this information to solve the five problems correctly. Furthermore, this chapter introduced Newton's three laws, which could be a common theme that all subjects might mention during their summaries. Hence, we might be able to make some comparisons.

We asked four experts (two college professors, one postdoctoral fellow who had never taught lower division physics, and one fifth-year graduate student who had often taught lower division physics) and four undergraduates (who had just completed the introductory physics course with a B grade, using Halliday & Rensick as a text) to review the chapter for 5 minutes and then summarize out loud its important concepts. Subjects were run individually, and 15 minutes were allotted for the summary. The book was available to them while they summarized, so that any limitation in their summaries could not be attributed to a retrieval problem. (Then they were all asked to solve a single problem taken from Chapter 5. These problem-solving protocols provided the data for discussing the frequency of diagram drawing mentioned in Study 1.)

Again, we began by looking at various quantitative measures such as the length of the summaries, the number of quantitative relations mentioned in the summaries, and so on. Cursory examination of the data suggested once more that there were no skill differences in any of these quantitative measures. We then turned to an examination of the content of the summaries. Since every subject mentioned Newton's three laws of motion, we compared what they said about two of them.

Newton's Third Law appears at the top of Table 1.6, and the bottom of the table shows one possible way of breaking the law into its component parts. Using these subcomponents as a scoring criterion, we analyzed the summaries of the experts and novices to see what proportion of the subcomponents were mentioned by each skill group. The results are shown in Table 1.7. The X's in the table show the subcomponents of the law that were mentioned by each subject. At the bottom of the table are samples of protocols of a novice and an expert. It is clear that experts in general make more complete statements about the physical laws than do novices, even though the textbook was available for them to use.

Table 1.8 represents a similar analysis of Newton's First Law. Again, experts mentioned an average of three subcomponents, whereas novices tended to mention an average of two subcomponents at most. It is also interesting to note that

TABLE 1.6
Newton's Third Law and Its Decomposition

"To every action there is always opposed an equal reaction; or the mutual actions of two bodies upon each other are always equal, and directed to contrary parts."

Components of the Third Law

---

1. The law applies to *two general bodies* (or particles)
   a. Discussion must mention 2 bodies, and
   b. These must be general bodies or particles
      (Particular example bodies *alone* are not sufficient to meet this condition, although example bodies are allowed to be present)
2. Action and reaction refer to *Forces* exerted by each body on the other, where these forces need not be of any particular type
   a. Must be an explicit statement that *each* body (however body is discussed) exerts a "force" on the other; and
   b. "Force" must be in general terms (particular example forces, such as kick, push, alone won't do although such examples are allowed to be present)
3. Reaction (however stated) is *equal in magnitude*
4. Reaction (however stated) is *opposite in direction*
5. Line of action/reaction is in a *straight line between two bodies*

TABLE 1.7
Newton's Third Law Decomposed into Five Components and Two Sample Protocols

	Novice				Expert			
	K.D.	S.B.	J.W.	C.H.	O.G.	M.V.	S.D.	B.P.
Reaction opposite in direction	X	X	X	X	X	X	X	X
Reaction equal in magnitude	X		X	X	X	X	X	X
Action–Reaction involves two general bodies					X	X		X
Action–Reaction are general forces extended by each body on the other					X	X		X
Direction of Action–Reaction is a straight line					X			

Examples of Subjects' Summary Protocol

Novice S.B.	"And his third law states that for every action there's an opposite reaction to it."
Expert O.G.	"The third law . . . states that for every action there is an equal and opposite reaction, or in other words, if Body A exerts a force on Body B, then Body B exerts a force on Body A in a direction which is along the line joining the two points. When you say bodies in this chapter, you mean they are really particles, point masses."

the postdoctoral fellow's performance (S. D. in Table 1.8) is most "novicelike," perhaps because he did not have any experience teaching mechanics.

The summaries of experts and novices on a given chapter from a physics text indicate that experts do have more complete information on physics laws than do novices. This is not surprising in the sense that one would expect experts to know more. On the other hand, it is surprising because the students have been taught this knowledge and had the book available. One would hope that, after instruction, students have mastered at least the declarative knowledge of the laws of physics. However, one obvious deficiency of novices is that they had not. One cannot automatically assume that all students have mastered the prerequisite knowledge needed for solving problems. Nor can we assume that the novices' deficiencies lie mainly in the inadequate strategies or procedural knowledge that improves with experience in solving problems.

Up to this point, our data show that novices are deficient in three aspects of knowledge. First, very good students, as Study 1 shows, make errors in problem solving only when they have either generated the incorrect inferences or failed to generate the correct inference during the initial encoding or representation-generation stage of problem solving. We attribute the generation of the wrong inference to incomplete knowledge in the data base, so that the appropriate inference (the right link between certain nodes in the semantic network; Greeno & Riley, 1981) could not be made. Second, we discovered that whether novices

TABLE 1.8
Components of Newton's First Law

"Every body persists in its state of rest or of uniform motion in a straight line unless it is compelled to change that state by forces acting on it."

	Novice				Expert			
	J.W.	S.B.	K.D.	C.H.	S.D.	O.G.	M.V.	B.P.
No net unbalanced force	X		X	X	X	X	X	X
Rest		X	X					X
Uniform motion				X	X	X	X	X
Straight line						X	X	X

Examples of Subjects' Summary Protocol

Novice J.W.	"The first one is inertia, which is that a body tends to stay in a certain state unless a force acts upon it."
Novice S.B.	"First of all there's, the body wants to stay at rest, the body just, it's resistance toward any other motion."
Expert B.P.	"His first law is a statement that a body is moving in a uniform velocity in a given straight line or statics. It will keep moving or stay where it is unless some external forces are applied."
Expert O.G.	"The first law is called the law of inertia. And it states that a body persists in its motion along a straight line of a uniform rate unless a net unbalanced force acts upon the body."

and experts have the same knowledge base or not, it is organized differently. That is, we can view the knowledge of problem types as schemata, and the experts' schemata center wround the physics principles, whereas the novices' schemata center around the objects. Finally, a third deficiency in the novices' knowledge base, at least for B students, is the lack of a certain fundamental knowledge of physics principles.

These three deficiencies are general in the sense that we do not have a good grasp of exactly what knowledge is missing from the novices' data base (except for the summary study), nor do we have any means for comparing the knowledge bases. And, most importantly, we have tapped only the declarative knowledge that the subjects possess. The next study attempts to be more detailed in assessing the knowledge that subjects do have. It provides a means of comparing the knowledge bases between subjects and begins to look at the use of procedural knowledge, because it is the procedural knowledge that will ultimately determine how well a person can solve a problem.

Study 6: Elaboration Study

In this study, we were interested in the knowledge associated with certain physics concepts. These are concepts generated by the category descriptors provided by the subjects in the sorting studies. We view these concepts as labels designating schemata. Hence, the purpose of this study was to uncover what knowledge is contained in the schemata of experts and novices. From the sorting studies, we concluded that the schemata of the experts are principle oriented, whereas the schemata of the novices are object oriented. But, what we needed to know is how the schemata of the two skill groups differ. Do the schemata of the experts contain more information or a different kind of information? Are the schemata of the novices subschemata of the experts' schemata as we hypothesized in Study 4? This study addressed these issues.

Two experts (M. G. and M. S.) and two novices (H. P. and P. D.) were asked to elaborate on a selected sample of 20 prototypical concepts that subjects in the sorting studies had used to describe their classifications. Figure 1.8 gives a frequency count of those category labels used by the experts and novices in Study 2. The sample of 20 ranged from labels provided by experts (e.g., Force Law) to those provided strictly by novices (e.g., inclined plane). Subjects were presented with each concept individually and given 3 minutes to tell everything they could think of about it, and how a problem involving the concept might be solved.

We use two ways to analyze the contents of these elaboration protocols. One way is to depict the contents of the protocol in terms of a node-link network, where the nodes are simply key terms mentioned by the subjects that are obvious physics concepts. The links are simply unlabeled relations that join the concepts mentioned contiguously. Using this method, the networks of a novice's (H. P.) and an expert's (M. G.) elaboration of the concept "inclined plane" are shown in Figs. 1.9 and 1.10. Since we view each of these concepts as representing a potential schema, the related physics concepts mentioned in the inclined plane protocol can be thought of as the variables (slots) of the schema. For example, in Novice H. P.'s protocol, his inclined plane schema contains numerous variables that can be instantiated, including the angle at which the plane is inclined with respect to the horizontal, whether there is a block resting on the plane, and what are the mass and height of the block. Other variables mentioned by the novice include the surface property of the plane, whether or not it has friction, and, if it does, what the the coefficients of static and kinetic friction. The novice also discussed possible forces that may act on the block, such as possibly having a pulley attached to it. At the end, he also discussed the pertinence of Conservation of Energy, but this was not elicited as an explicit solution procedure that is applicable to a configuration involving an inclined plane, as is seen later in the case with the expert. Hence, in general, one could say that the inclined plane schema that the novice possesses is quite rich. He knows precisely what variables need to be specified, and he also has default values for some of them. For example, if friction was not mentioned, he probably knows that he should ignore friction. Hence, with a simple specification that the problem is one involving an inclined plane, he can deduce fairly accurately what are the key components and entities (i.e., friction) that such a problem would entail.

The casual reference to the underlying physics principle, Conservation of Energy, given by the novice in the previous example, contrasts markedly with

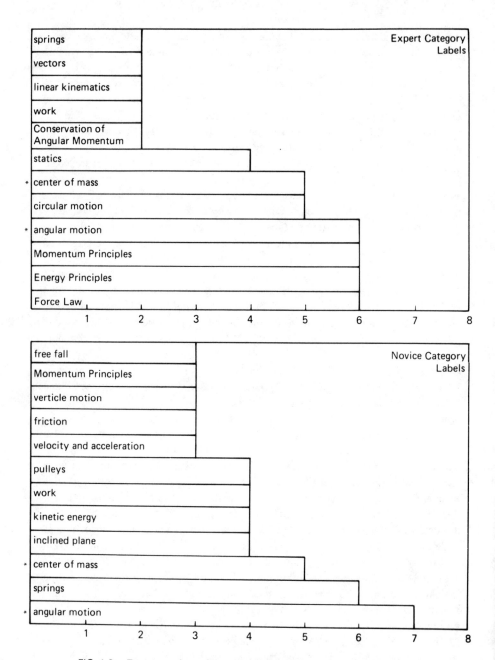

FIG. 1.8. Frequency of use of category labels by eight experts and eight novices. Asterisks indicate labels used by both groups.

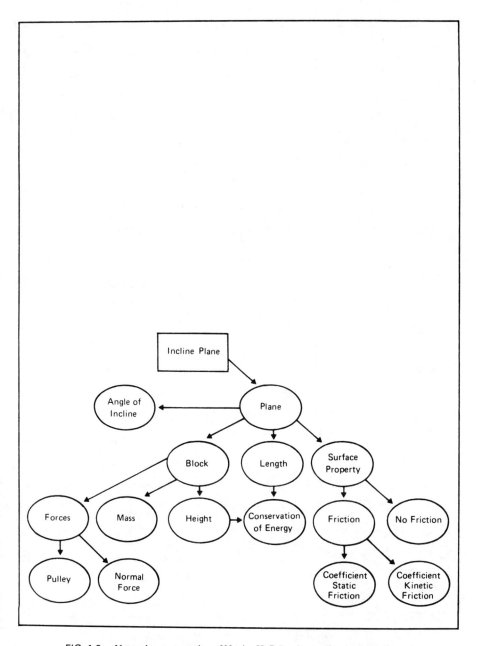

FIG. 1.9.   Network representation of Novice H. P.'s schema of an inclined plane.

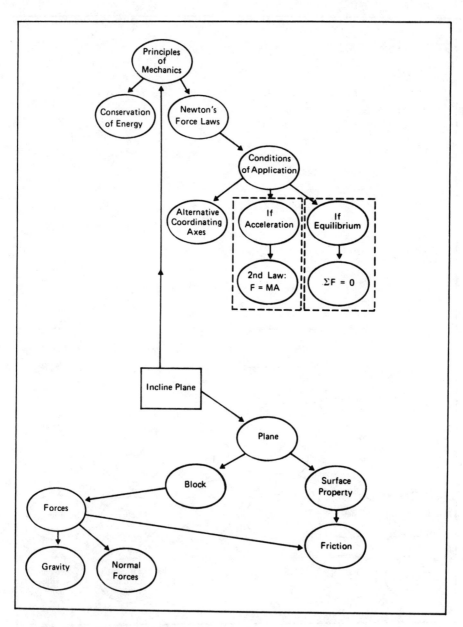

FIG. 1.10. Network representation of Expert M. G.'s schema of an inclined plane.

the expert's protocol in which she immediately makes an explicit call to two principles that take the status of procedures, the Conservation of Energy Principle and the Force Law (Fig. 1.10). (In Greeno & Riley's, 1981, terminology, they would be considered calls to action schemata.) We characterize them as procedures (thus differentiating them from the way the novice mentioned a principle) because the expert, after mentioning the Force Law, continues to elaborate on the condition of applicability of the procedure and then provides explicit formulas for two of the conditions (enclosed in dashed rectangles in Fig. 1.10). (She also explained the conditions of applicability of Conservation of Energy, but did so during other segments of the study.) After her elaboration of the principles and the conditions of applicability of one principle to inclined plane problems (depicted in the top half of Fig. 1.10), Expert M. G. continued her protocol with descriptions of the structural or surface features of inclined plane problems, much like the descriptions provided by Novice H. P. (see Fig. 1.9). Hence, it seems that the knowledge common to subjects of both skill groups pertains to the physical configuration and its properties but that the expert has additional knowledge relevant to the solution procedures based on major physics laws.

Another way of viewing the difference between the novice's and expert's elaborations of inclined plane is to look at the description that Rumelhart (1981) ascribes to schemata of inactive objects. That is, an inclined plane is seen by the novice as an inactive object, so that it specifies not actions or event sequences but rather spatial and functional relationships characteristic of inclined planes. Because novices may view an inclined plane as an object, they thus cite the potential configuration and its properties. Experts, on the other hand, may view an inclined plane in the context of the potential solution procedures; that is, not as an object but more as an entity that may serve a particular function.

An alternative way to analyze the same set of protocols is to convert them directly into "production rules," or "if-then" rules (Newell, 1973). To do so, a simple set of conversion rules can be used, such as when the protocols manifest an if-then, if-when, or when-then structure. This transformation is quite straightforward and covers a majority of the protocol data. Tables 1.9 and 1.10 depict the same set of protocols that were previously analyzed in the form of node-link structures. What is obvious from such an analysis is that the experts' production rules contain explicit solution procedures, such as "use $F = MA$" or "sum all the forces to 0." None of the novices' rules depicted in Table 1.10 contain any actions that are explicit solution procedures. Their actions can be characterized as attempts to find specific unknowns, such as "find mass" (see H. P.'s rule 2 and P. D.'s rule 1 in Table 1.10).

We alluded to an important difference between the way Conservation of Energy was mentioned by novice H. P. versus expert M. G. The present analysis makes this difference more transparent. The difference lies in the observation that the novice's statement of Conservation of Energy (Rule 8 in Table 1.10) was part

TABLE 1.9
Expert Productions Converted from Protocols

M.S.

---

1. IF problem involves an inclined plane
   THEN a. expect something rolling or sliding up or down
        b. use F = MA
        c. use Newton's Third Law
2. IF plane is smooth
   THEN use Conservation of Mechanical Energy
3. IF plane is not smooth
   THEN use work done by friction
4. IF problem involves objects connected by string and one object being pulled by the other
   THEN consider string tension
5. IF string is not taut
   THEN consider objects as independent

M.G.

---

1. (IF problem involves inclined plane)[a]
   THEN a. use Newton's Law
        b. draw force diagram
2. (If problem involves inclined plane)[a]
   THEN can use Energy Conservation
3. IF there is something on plane
   THEN determine if there is friction
4. IF there is friction
   THEN put it in diagram
5. (IF drawing diagram)[a]
   THEN put in all forces—gravity, force up plane, friction, reaction force
6. (IF all forces in diagram)[a]
   THEN write Newton's Laws
7. IF equilibrium problem
   THEN a. $\Sigma F = 0$
        b. decide on coordinate axes
8. IF acceleration is involved
   THEN use F = MA
9. IF "that's done" (drawing diagram, putting in forces, choosing axes)[a]
   THEN sum components of forces

---

[a] Statements in parentheses were not said explicitly by the subjects but are indicated by the context.

of a description of the condition side of a production rule, whereas the statement of this principle by both experts (M. S.'s rule 2 & M. G.'s rule 2 in Table 1.9) is described on the action side of the production rules.

On the elaboration of an inclined plane (Fig. 1.10), we stressed that the expert mentioned the conditions of applicability of the Force Law (the statements in the dashed enclosures). This points to the presence of not only explicit procedures in the experts' repertoires but also of explicit conditions for when a specific proce-

TABLE 1.10
Novice Productions Converted from Protocols

H.P.

---

1. (IF problem involves inclined plane)[a]
   THEN find angle of incline with horizontal
2. IF block resting on plane
   THEN a. find mass of block
        b. determine if plane is frictionless or not
3. IF plane has friction
   THEN determine coefficients of static and kinetic friction
4. IF there are any forces on the block
   THEN . . .
5. IF the block is at rest
   THEN . . .
6. IF the block has an initial speed
   THEN . . .
7. IF the plane is frictionless
   THEN the problem is simplified
8. IF problem would involve Conservation of Energy and height of block, length of plane, height of
   plane are known
   THEN could solve for potential and kinetic energies

P.D.

---

1. (IF problem involves an inclined plane)[a]
   THEN a. figure out what type of device is used
        b. find what masses are given
        c. find outside forces besides force coming from pulley
2. IF pulley involved
   THEN try to neglect it
3. IF trying to find coefficient of friction
   THEN slowly increase angle until block on it starts moving
4. IF two frictionless inclined planes face each other and a ball is rolled from a height on one side
   THEN ball will roll to the same height on other side
5. IF something goes down frictionless surface
   THEN can find acceleration of gravity on the incline using trigonometry
6. IF want to have collision
   THEN can use incline to accelerate one object

---

[a] Statements in parentheses were not said explicitly by the subjects but are indicated by the context.

dure applies. Another analysis supports this difference. We examined all statements made by the two experts and the two novices throughout the protocols of the entire set of 20 concepts and recorded all statements made about Conservation of Energy. Nearly half of each expert's statements (10 out of a total of 22 for M. S.; 9 out of 21 for M. G.) were specifying the conditions under which Conservation of Energy could be used. For example, the following are two quotes, one from each expert:

M. S.: "If the [inclined] plane is smooth, of course then you could use Conservation of Mechanical Energy to solve the problem. If it's not smooth, then you've got to take into account the work done by frictional forces."

M. G.: "Energy conservation can also be used [in a collision problem] but only for an elastic collision because no heat is produced."

The novices, on the other hand, made only one such statement between them (1 out of 22 for H. P.; 0 out of 13 for P. D.).

In sum, this study shows that the contents of the schemata are different for the novices and the experts. First, for an object schema, both experts and novices possess a fundamental knowledge of the configuration and its properties, but the experts possess additional knowledge, which may be viewed as also activating higher level schemata (Rumelhart, 1981) that are relevant to the principle. Second, the schemata of the experts contain more procedural knowledge. That is, they have explicit procedures, which may be thought of as the action side of the productions. Finally, the experts' schemata contain much more knowledge about the explicit conditions of applicability of the major principles underlying a problem. Hence, this study, coupled with the Summary Study, emphasizes the impoverished nature of novices' schemata, which can seriously hinder their problem-solving success.

Studies to Identify the Key Features of Problems

The previous studies have suggested that novices in general have knowledge that is deficient in a variety of ways (perhaps with the exceptions of A students). Hence, it is important to ascertain whether the difficulties novices encounter in problem solving also lie in their inability to identify the relevant cues in the problem, as is the case with poor chess players. The common finding in chess research is that the poor players have great difficulties seeing the meaningful patterns on the chessboard. The ability to perceive the relevant chessboard patterns reflects the organization of the chess knowledge in memory. Hence, we need to determine whether both novice and expert problem solvers have the ability to identify the relevant cues in a problem and, if so, how this ability affects problem solving. From the studies we have already discussed, we speculate that the difficulties experienced by novices derive from their inability to generate the appropriate knowledge from the relevant cues.

Study 7: Basic Approach

In this study (designed and carried out by Paul Feltovich), we were interested in knowing about the features that help a subject decide on a "solution method," which can be interpreted as one of the three major principles (Conservation of Energy, Conservation of Momentum, and Force Law) that can underlie a mechanics problem of the kind we use. Putting it another way, we are attempting to determine the problem features that subjects could have used in eliciting their category schemata, if the solution methods, at least for the experts, may be viewed as their schemata of problem types (see Study 3).

Subjects in this study were asked to do three things. First, they were to read the problem statement and think out loud about the "basic approach" that they would take to solve the problem. Basic approach was not further defined for them. Second, they were asked to restate the basic approach explicitly in one concise phrase. Finally, they were asked to state the problem features that led them to their choice. Here, we focus predominantly on the last aspect of this study (see Chi et al., 1981, for additional details).

The subjects were two physicists (J. L. and V. V.) who had frequently taught introductory mechanics and two novices (P. D. and J. W.) who had completed a basic college course in mechanics with an A grade. The problems were the same 20 (described in Table 1.2) used for the sorting replication study (Study 3).

Table 1.11 summarizes the key features cited by the experts and novices as contributing to their decisions about the basic approach to the solution of the problems. The numbers in the table show the frequency with which each feature was cited. A feature was included for each skill group only if it was mentioned at least twice (across the 20 problems), once by each subject or twice by one subject.

First, analysis of these features shows that there is essentially no overlap in the features mentioned by novices and experts, except for the object "spring." Second, the kinds of features mentioned as relevant by the novices are different from those identified by the experts. Novices, again, mention literal objects and key terms that are explicitly stated in the problem, such as "friction" and "gravity." This is consistent with the results of the categorization studies. Experts, on the other hand, identify features that can be characterized as descriptions of states and conditions of the physical situation, as described implicitly by the problem. In some instances, these are transformed or derived features, such as a "before-and-after situations" or "no external force." Because these features are not explicitly stated in the problem, we refer to these as second-order features (or, as we previously mentioned, generated tacit knowledge).

In sum, the most interesting finding of this study is that the features mentioned as relevant for suggesting a solution method are different for experts and novices. Because the subjects used their own words to describe the features, there is often a lack of consensus concerning relevant features, particularly between the experts. In Table 1.11, for example, in 14 of the 24 features cited, the experts did not refer to the same features, whereas this occurred only once for the novices (see the asterisks). This is consistent with the interpretation that novices must have greater consensus because they refer to the explicit key terms in the problem statement itself. Experts, on the other hand, must necessarily show a great deal of individual difference because they transform the literal surface features into some second-order features based on their individual knowledge bases. However, even

TABLE 1.11
Key Features Cited by Experts and Novices

	Experts	
	V.V.	*J.L.*
Given initial conditions	9	3
Before-and-after situations	3	4
* Spring	0	5
No external force	4	1
Don't need details of motion	4	1
* Given final conditions	5	0
Asked something at an instant in time	4	1
* Asked some characteristics of final condition	4	0
* Interacting objects	0	4
* Speed-distance relation	0	4
* Inelastic collision	2	2
* No initial conditions	4	0
No final conditions	4	0
Energy easy to calculate at two points	1	2
No friction or dissipation	3	1
* Force too complicated	0	3
Momentum easy to calculate at two points	2	1
* Compare initial and final conditions	2	0
* Can compute work done by external force	2	0
Given distance	1	1
* Rotational component	0	2
* Energy yields direct relation	0	2
* No before and after	2	0
* Asked about force	2	0

	Novices	
	P.D.	*J.W.*
Friction	3	5
Gravity	3	3
Pulley	3	3
Inclined plane	3	2
Spring	2	3
Given masses	3	2
Coin on turntable	1	1
Given forces	1	1
* Force-velocity relation	0	2

*Asterisks indicate features mentioned by only one of the two subjects.

with such wide individual differences, there was a distinct characteristic to the experts' cited features that distinguished them from the novices' cited features.

Study 8: Judging Problem Difficulty

Even though the experts cited the abstracted features as the relevant cues in the previous study, it is still possible that the experts transformed the same basic set of key terms as those identified by the novices. A direct way to ascertain whether subjects of different skill consider the same set of words important is to ask them to point out the important words in the problem statements. In this study, we presented six novices (undergraduates averaging grades of B) and six experts (graduate students) the same set of 20 problems used earlier and asked them to judge (using a 1–5 rating) how difficult it was to solve a problem after reading the problem statement. We then asked subjects to circle the key words or phrases that helped them make that judgment. Finally, we asked how those particular key words helped them reach their decision.

The most striking finding is the extensive overlap between the cues that experts and novices identified as important for deciding on the difficulty of a problem. If anything, experts identified fewer cues as important compared with the novices. Table 1.12 presents one of the problems broken down into eight propositions. There were, on the average, seven propositions per problem. The propositions containing words chosen by three or more of the novices and three or more of the experts are indicated by N and E respectively. For 19 of the 20 problems, the experts and the novices circled the same sets of words or phrases in the problem statements, which are embedded in 2.7 propositions, on the average. Only in 7 of the 20 problems did the experts identify additional cues (about 1.6), whereas in 13 of the 20 problems, the novices identified additional cues (2.1) as important. This result suggests, at least, that novices' difficulties in problem solving do not stem from the failure to identify the relevant cues.

TABLE 1.12
Decomposition of a Problem Statement into Propositions

	Problem 8
	1. A block of mass M1
N	2. is put on top of a block of mass M2
NE	3. In order to cause the top block to slip on the bottom one,
NE	4. a horizontal force F1 must be applied to the top block
N	5. Assume a frictionless table
NE	6. Find the maximum horizontal force F2
	7. which can be applied to the lower block
NE	8. so that both blocks will move together.

N = Propositions indicated by three or more of the novices.
E = Propositions indicated by three or more of the experts.

The subjects' responses to both the questions of why these particular cues are important and how they help in making decisions were classified according to the following categories: (1) whether the cues refer to one of the three fundamental principles ("the cues tell me to use Energy Conservation"); (2) whether the cues refer to some surface feature of the problem, much like what novices refer to when they categorize problems (e.g., Fig. 1.8); (3) whether the cues bring their attention to some characteristic of the problem that is not related to physics ("it is difficult to visualize" or "it has many concepts"); or (4) whether the cues elicit some reasons that are unrelated to the specific problem (the problem is difficult "because I have never solved it before" or "because it has a lot of words").

Table 1.13 is a breakdown of experts' and novices' reasons for why a problem was judged difficult or easy, along with samples of quotes. Consistent with our previous findings, experts, much more often than novices, rely on the underlying physics principle when judging the difficulty of a problem (e.g., "compressing spring tells me to think Energy").They both rely equally often on problem characteristics, such as whether a problem involves friction or the center of mass. However, novices are much more likely to rely on superficial nonphysics aspects of a problem to make their judgements (the third category in Table 1.13), such as whether "it is abstractly phrased" and "it has a lot of words." Finally, the

TABLE 1.13
Proportion of Response Types

	Novices	*Experts*
Abstract Principle	9%	30%
"straightforward application of Newton's Second Law"		
"collision problem, use Conservation of Momentum"		
"no friction, no dissipative forces, just apply Energy Conservation"		
Problem Characteristics	33%	35%
"frictionless, problem is simplified"		
"massless spring simplifies problem"		
"pulley introduces difficulty"		
Nonphysics Related Characteristics	40%	28%
"problem is difficult to visualize"		
"easy calculations but hard to understand"		
"many factors to consider, make problem difficult"		
Nonproblem Related Characteristics	18%	7%
"never did problems like this"		
"numbers instead of symbols"[a]		
"must consider units"		
"diagram distracting"		

[a] All our problems used symbols for known quantities rather than actual numerical values.

novices often introduce reasons for why a problem is difficult that are not specific to a given problem, such as "I have never done problems like this before."

When inferences were generated in the protocols of problem solving (Study 1) and when second-order features were identified (Study 7), we speculated that such tacit knowledge was generated from the literal key terms in the problem statement. Now, we can verify some of these speculations directly by examining several of the reasons that subjects gave for how particular key terms that they circled contributed to their judgment of problem difficulty. Table 1.14 presents examples of the kind of statements produced by experts. These statements of reasons can be judged to be inferences generated either directly from the literal terms in the problem, such as "frictionless, use Conservation of Momentum," or the inferences may be generated from a derived cue, such as "no dissipative

TABLE 1.14

Inferences Generated from Literal and Derived Cues

Literal Cue	Derived Cue	Inference
Frictionless		Conservation of Momentum
Frictionless	No dissipative forces	
	No dissipative forces	Conservation of Momentum
	No dissipative system	Conservation of Energy
Frictionless	No dissipative force	Conservation of Energy
Frictionless	No dissipative force	Conservation Laws
	Energy not consumed	Conservation of Momentum then calculate new Energy
Frictionless	Only force is restoring force	Newton's Second Law
Center of mass at rest	No external forces	$\lvert M_1 V_1 \rvert = \lvert M_2 V_2 \rvert$
Center of mass at rest		
Center of mass at rest		Relative Momentum = 0
	Pulley must be taken into account	Newton's Second Law for translation and rotation
Mass and radius of pulley		Consider Rotational Kinetic Energy
	Pulley can't be neglected	Rotational Dynamics
Mass of pulley		Rotational Energy
Massive pulley		Rotational Dynamics
Compressing spring		Think Energy
Motion		Energy Analysis
Slip and force	Friction	
$M_1 + M_2$ collide		Conservation of Energy and Momentum
M_2 stops after distance L		Work-Energy
Speed		Newton's Second Law to Find Acceleration then Equation of Motion
Merry-Go-Round	Rotational motion	Conservation of Angular Momentum

forces.'' These correspond to the second-order features mentioned in the previous study.

Recall that the purpose of this task was to have experts and novices judge problem difficulty. The experts, in general, were more accurate at judging the difficulty of a problem than novices. Accuracy was determined by comparing the ratings of problem difficulties that subjects gave to our own assessment of how difficult a problem actually is to solve. The aforementioned examination of the reasons subjects gave for why a particular problem is difficult, and why those particular key words were helpful in identifying a problem's difficulty (Table 1.13), suggests that novices are less accurate at judging a problem's difficulty because they rely heavily on nonphysics-related or nonproblem-related features. Obviously, these are not the reliable factors to consider when one attempts to solve a physics problem.

In sum, even though the task of this study—requesting sources of problem difficulty—is slightly different from either a problem-solving task or tasks used in the other studies (e.g., sorting), we suspect that the features identified as relevant are the same as those used in other tasks. Basically, the results show that the relevant and important key terms in a physics problem can be identified by novices quite accurately. In this sense, a physics problem is not analogous to a "perceptual" chessboard, in which case the beginner cannot pick out the relevant or important patterns. However, the similarity between a chess expert and a physics expert remains and can be seen in their ability (compared to novices) to abstract the relevant tacit knowledge cued by the external stimuli. The chess master's expertise derives from the ability to abstract or impose a cognitive structure onto the pattern of black and white chess pieces. Although novice chess players are just as capable as experts at perceiving the chess pieces per se, "seeing" the relations among the pieces requires fitting one's schemata to the configuration of chess pieces. Similarly, the novice physicist is just as capable as the expert in identifying the key terms in a problem statement. The difficulty resides in the novice's limited ability to generate inferences and relations not explicitly stated in the problem.

GENERAL DISCUSSION

The goal of this chapter has been to contribute to our understanding of high-level competence in complex domains of human knowledge. Expert individuals in various areas of knowledge perform remarkable intellectual activities, and cognitive psychlogists are on the threshold of understanding these feats of memory retrieval, rapid perception, and complex problem solving. Since intelligence is generally measured through tests that assess skill in acquiring new knowledge in scholastic settings, understanding the nature of the competence attained should shed light on this ability to learn.

Early in this chapter, evidence was provided for the necessity to focus on the organization and structure of knowledge, in both psychological and AI research. This trend toward understanding the influence of knowledge is relatively recent in contrast to the earlier emphasis on search algorithms and other heuristics for deducing and retrieving information. The techniques and theories that evolved, such as means–ends analysis, were intended to be independent of the particular data base and, as such, have proven to be valuable search heuristics that are generalizable across different tasks and knowledge domains.

The turn to a focus on the knowledge base was necessitated in part by the inability of psychological theories to model human capabilities solely on the basis of search heuristics and in part by the limitations discovered in attempting to construct AI programs that would outperform humans, even though the computer's search capabilities are essentially limitless. Hence, the constraints of powerful search techniques, when they did not engage an organized knowledge structure, soon compelled researchers to develop theories and programs that took account of the role of knowledge structure.

The emphasis on the knowledge base has also changed the direction of research. Since knowledge has different degrees of structure depending on an individual's experience, it was intuitively apparent that an important problem was how a particular knowledge base is structured. The obvious choice was to model the expert's knowledge, as was done most dramatically in a number of AI programs. This choice has also led to psychological investigations of developing structure of novices' knowledge, in contrast to the richly organized structure of experts' knowledge.

The research on problem solving generated by this new emphasis has revolved around understanding the processes of arriving at a solution in the context of the knowledge available to a solver. In physics, this has led to the construction of numerous theoretical models that attempt to simulate the processes of problem solving, in particular, the knowledge that is necessary to generate a particular sequence of equations. Other theoretical models constructed by AI researchers have put more emphasis on the representation of the problem in the context of the available knowledge.

The important issue of problem representation has also been recognized in the psychological research. It is conspicuous in protocols of problem solving in the form of "qualitative analysis" of the problem, which usually occurs early in the solution process. Most empirical findings to date have failed to explicate this initial qualitative analysis, although the consensus has been that a representation of the problem, constructed at this point, is a significant factor in driving the solution process. Numerous quantitative differences between the experts and novices have also been identified, such as solution speed, errors, and equation-generation pattern. None of these measures, however, has succeeded in shedding much light on understanding the different problem-solving processes of experts and novices.

The research from our own laboratory has been oriented toward magnifying the representational "stage" of problem solving through techniques other than the analysis of problem-solving protocols. Our findings (Study 1) have emphasized that solution protocols provide limited insights to the processes of representation and, further, produce quantitative measures that are difficult to interpret because they are subject to large individual differences. These individual differences are dictated by a variety of particular strategies that solvers adopt, such as generating a number of equations when one cannot think of a way to proceed. Through the use of a sorting task (Studies 2, 3, and 4), we were able to uncover a potential source of representational difficulty for novices. If we assume that a problem is represented in the context of the available knowledge, then novices will undoubtedly have an incomplete and less coherent representation because of the organization of their knowledge. Their knowledge is organized around dominant objects (e.g., an inclined plane) and physics concepts (e.g., friction) that are mentioned explicitly in the problem statement. Experts, on the other hand, organize their knowledge around fundamental principles of physics (e.g., Conservation of Energy) that derive from tacit knowledge not apparent in the problem statement. An individual's "understanding" of a problem has been explicitly defined as being dictated by knowledge of such principles (Greeno & Riley, 1981). Hence, during qualitative analysis of a problem, experts would understand a problem better than novices because they "see" the underlying principle.

A person's understanding of a principle can be evaluated in several ways (Greeno & Riley, 1981). One way is to have it stated explicitly, as was done by experts in the Summary Study (Study 5) and in the rationale they provided in the Sorting Studies (Studies 2, 3, and 4). Another way is to analyze the nature of the categories into which individuals sort problems; this constitutes an implicit assessment of their understanding of principles. An alternative but consistent interpretation of the Sorting Studies is that experts and novices organize their knowledge in different ways. Experts possess schemata of principles that may subsume schemata of objects, whereas novices may possess only schemata of objects. Some support for this conjecture was provided in both Study 4, on the hierarchical nature of the sorting categories, and in Study 6, on the elaboration of the contents of object and principle schemata. Once the correct schema is activated, knowledge (both procedural and declarative) contained in the schema is used to process the problem further. The declarative knowledge contained in the schema generates potential problem configurations and conditions of applicability for procedures, which are then tested against the information in the problem statement. The procedural knowledge in the schema generates potential solution methods that can be used on the problem. Experts' schemata contain a great deal of procedural knowledge, with explicit conditions for applicability. Novices' schemata may be characterized as containing sufficiently elaborate declarative knowledge about the physical configurations of a potential problem, but they lack abstracted solution methods.

Our hypothesis is that the problem-solving difficulties of novices can be attributed mainly to inadequacies of their knowledge bases and not to limitations in either the architecture of their cognitive systems or processing capabilities (e.g., the inability to use powerful search heuristics or the inability to detect important cues in the problem statement). This conjecture follows from several findings. First, similarity in the architecture of experts' and novices' cognitive systems is probably implied by the fact that there are generally no differences between experts and novices in the number of categories into which they prefer to sort problems, in the latency required to achieve a stable sort, and in a variety of other measures. These quantitative measures point to the invariance in the cognitive architecture of experts and novices. Second, novices do show effective search heuristics when they solve problems using backward-working solutions. Third, in our last set of studies (Studies 7 and 8), we showed that novices are essentially just as competent as experts in identifying the key features in a problem statement. The limitation of the novices derives from their inability to infer further knowledge from the literal cues in the problem statement. In contrast, these inferences necessarily are generated in the context of the relevant knowledge structures that experts possess.

In concluding this chapter, we would like to speculate on the implications of the work and theory reported here for a conception of intelligence. The tests of intelligence in general use today measure the kind of intellectual performance most accurately called "general scholastic ability." Correlational evidence has shown that the abilities tested are predictive of success in school learning. Given this operational fact, these commonly used tests of intelligence are not tests of intelligence in some abstract way. Rather, if we base our conclusions on their predictive validity, we can conclude that they are primarily tests of abilities that are helpful for learning in present-day school situations. More generally, we can assume that these intelligence tests measure the ability to solve problems in school situations, which leads to learning. The problem-solving ability possessed by the expert learner is a result of experience with the domains of knowledge relevant to schooling.

If expertise in learning is the ability for representing and solving school problems, then for a less intelligent learner, a problem representation may be in close correspondence with the literal details of a problem, whereas for a more intelligent learner, the representation contains, in addition, inferences and abstractions derived from knowledge structures acquired in past experiences. As a result of prior experience in various knowledge domains relevant to schooling, the representations required for solving school problems are more enriched and contribute to the ease and efficiency with which learning problems are solved. We speculate further that the knowledge the expert learner brings to a problem would incorporate a good deal of procedural knowledge—how a knowledge structure can be manipulated, the conditions under which it is applicable, and so on. Novice learners, on the other hand, would have sufficient factual and declarative knowledge about a learning problem but would lack procedural skill, and this would weaken their ability to learn from their available knowledge.

A knowledge-based conception of intelligence could have implications for how individuals might be taught to be more effective learners. Such an attempt would de-emphasize the possibility of influencing mental processing skill (i.e., developing better methods for searching memory). Improved ability to learn would be developed through a knowledge strategy in which individuals would be taught ways in which their available knowledge can be recognized and manipulated. Improvement in the skills of learning might take place through the exercise of procedural (problem-solving) knowledge in the context of specific knowledge domains. To date, conceptions of intelligence have been highly process oriented, reminiscent of earlier notions of powers of mind. If, in contrast, one did take a knowledge-emphasis approach to the differences between high and low performers in school learning, then one might begin to conduct investigations of knowledge structure and problem representation in the way that we have begun to do in the expert–novice studies described in this chapter. This orientation might provide new insights into the nature of the expert performance we define as intelligence.

ACKNOWLEDGMENTS

The research reported here was supported in part by Grant N00014-78-C-0375, NR 157-421 from the Office of Naval Research and in part by the Learning Research and Development Center, University of Pittsburgh, which is funded in part by the National Institute of Education. Our research on physics problem solving represents a team effort. The person who took major responsibilities for any single study is recognized as the study is discussed. However, almost everyone worked to some extent on each study. We acknowledge particularly the efforts of our colleague Paul Feltovich. Our thanks also go to Joan Fogarty, Andrew Judkis, Tom Laritz, and Christopher Roth, for data collection and analyses. We are also grateful to the physics professors and graduate students who have generously contributed their time to participate as subjects.

REFERENCES

Akin, O. *Models of architectural knowledge.* London: Pion, 1980.
Atwood, M. E., Masson, M. E. J., & Polson, P. G. Further explorations with a process model for water jug problems. *Memory & Cognition,* 1980, *8,* 189–192.
Atwood, M. E., & Polson, P. G. A process model for water jug problems. *Cognitive Psychology,* 1976, *8,* 191–216.
Belmont, J. M., & Butterfield, E. C. Learning strategies as determinants of memory deficiencies. *Cognitive Psychology,* 1971, *2,* 411–421.

Bhaskar, R., & Simon, H. A. Problem solving in semantically rich domains: An example from engineering thermodynamics. *Cognitive Science,* 1977, *1,* 193–215.

Brown, J. S., Collins, A., & Harris, G. Artificial intelligence and learning strategies. In H. O'Neil (Ed.), *Learning strategies.* New York: Academic Press, 1978.

Bundy, A. Will it reach the top? Prediction in the mechanics world. *Artificial Intelligence,* 1978, *10,* 129–146.

Bundy, A., Byrd, L., Luger, G., Mellish, C., & Palmer, M. Solving mechanics problems using meta-level inference. *Proceedings of the 6th International Joint Conference on Artificial Intelligence,* Tokyo, 1979, 1017–1027.

Byrd, L., & Borning, A. *Extending Mecho to solve statics problems* (Tech. Rep. DAI 137). University of Edinburgh, Department of Artificial Intelligence, 1980.

Champagne, A. B., Klopfer, L. E., & Anderson, J. H. Factors influencing the learning of classical mechanics. *American Journal of Physics,* 1980, *48,* 1074–1079.

Charness, N. Components of skill in bridge. *Canadian Journal of Psychology,* 1979, *33,* 1–50.

Chase, W. G., & Chi, M. T. H. Cognitive skill: Implications for spatial skill in large-scale environments. In J. Harvey (Ed.), *Cognition, social behavior, and the environment.* Hillsdale, N.J.: Lawrence Erlbaum Associates 1981.

Chase, W. G., & Simon, H. A. The mind's eye in chess. In W. G. Chase (Ed.), *Visual information processing.* New York: Academic Press, 1973. (a)

Chase, W. G., & Simon, H. A. Perception in chess. *Cognitive Psychology,* 1973, *4,* 55–81. (b)

Chi, M. T. H. Short-term memory limitations in children: Capacity or processing deficits? *Memory & Cognition,* 1976, *4,* 559–572.

Chi, M. T. H. Knowledge structures and memory development. In R. Siegler (Ed.), *Children's thinking: What develops?* Hillsdale, N.J.: Lawrence Erlbaum Associates, 1978.

Chi, M. T. H., Feltovich, P., & Glaser, R. Categorization and representation of physics problems by experts and novices. *Cognitive Science,* 1981, *5,* 121–152.

Chiesi, H., Spilich, G. J., & Voss, J. F. Acquisition of domain-related information in relation to high and low domain knowledge. *Journal of Verbal Learning and Verbal Behavior,* 1979, *18,* 257–273.

de Groot, A. *Thought and choice in chess.* The Hague: Mouton, 1965.

de Groot, A. Perception and memory versus thought: Some old ideas and recent findings. In B. Kleinmuntz (Ed.), *Problem solving.* New York: Wiley, 1966.

de Kleer, J. Multiple representations of knowledge in a mechanics problem solver. *Proceedings of the 5th International Joint Conference on Artificial Intelligence,* Cambridge, Mass., 1977, 299–304.

Egan, D. E., & Greeno, J. G. Theory of rule induction: Knowledge acquired in concept learning, serial pattern learning, and problem solving. In L. Gregg (Ed.), *Knowledge and cognition.* Hillsdale, N.J.: Lawrence Erlbaum Associates, 1974.

Egan, D. E. & Schwartz, B. Chunking in recall of symbolic drawings. *Memory & Cognition,* 1979, *7,* 149–158.

Eisenstadt, M., & Kareev, Y. Aspects of human problem solving: The use of internal representation. In D. A. Norman & D. E. Rumelhart (Eds.), *Explorations in cognition.* San Francisco: Freeman, 1975.

Goldstein, I. & Papert, S. Artificial intelligence, language, and the study of knowledge. *Cognitive Science,* 1977, *1,* 84–123.

Greenblatt, R. D., Eastlake, D. E., & Crocker, S. D. The Greenblatt chess program. *Proceedings of the Fall Joint Computer Conference,* 1967, *31,* 801–810.

Greeno, J. G. Hobbits and orcs: Acquisition of a sequential concept. *Cognitive Psychology,* 1974, *6,* 270–292.

Greeno, J. G. Process of understanding in problem solving. In N. J. Castellan, D. B. Pisoni, & G. R. Potts (Eds.), *Cognitive theory* (Vol. 2). Hillsdale, N.J.: Lawrence Erlbaum Associates, 1977.

Greeno, J. G. Natures of problem solving abilities. In W. K. Estes (Ed.), *Handbook of learning and cognitive processes* (Vol. 5). Hillsdale, N.J.: Lawrence Erlbaum Associates, 1978.

Greeno, J. G., & Riley, M. S. Processes and development of understanding. In F. E. Weinert & R. Kluwe (Eds.), *Learning by thinking.* Stuttgart, West Germany: Kohlhammer, 1981.

Halliday, D., & Resnick, R. *Fundamentals of physics* (2nd ed.). New York: Wiley, 1974.

Hayes, J. R., & Simon, H. A. The understanding process: Problem isomorphs. *Cognitive Psychology,* 1976, *8,* 165–190.

Hinsley, D. A., Hayes, J. R., & Simon, H. A. From words to equations: Meaning and representation in algebra word problems. In P. A. Carpenter & M. A. Just (Eds.), *Cognitive processes in comprehension.* Hillsdale, N.J.: Lawrence Erlbaum Associates, 1978.

Hunt, E., Lunneborg, C., & Lewis, J. What does it mean to be high verbal? *Cognitive Psychology,* 1975, *7,* 194–227.

Jeffries, R., Turner, A. T., Polson, P. G., & Atwood, M. E. Processes involved in designing software. In J. R. Anderson (Ed.), *Cognitive skills and their acquisition.* Hillsdale, N.J.: Lawrence Erlbaum Associates 1981.

Jensen, A. R. Reaction time and intelligence. In M. Friedman, J. P. Das, & N. O'Connor (Eds.), *Intelligence and learning.* New York: Plenum Press, 1981.

Larkin, J. H. *Problem solving in physics* (Tech. Rep.). Berkeley: University of California, Group in Science and Mathematics Education, 1977. (a)

Larkin, J. H. *Skilled problem solving in physics: A hierarchical planning model.* Unpublished manuscript, University of California at Berkeley, 1977. (b)

Larkin, J. H. Processing information for effective problem solving. *Engineering Education,* 1979, *70*(3), 285–288.

Larkin, J. H. Understanding, problem representations, and skill in physics. In S. F. Chipman, J. W. Segal, & R. Glaser (Eds.), *Thinking and learning skills* (Vol. II). Hillsdale, N.J.: Lawrence Erlbaum Associates, in press.

Larkin, J. H. Enriching formal knowledge: A model for learning to solve textbook physics problems. In J. R. Anderson (Ed.), *Cognitive skills and their acquisition.* Hillsdale, N.J.: Lawrence Erlbaum Associates, 1981.

Larkin, J. H., McDermott, J., Simon, D. P., & Simon, H. A. Models of competence in solving physics problems. *Cognitive Science,* 1980, *4,* 317–345.

McCloskey, M., Caramazza, A., & Green, B. Curvilinear motion in the absence of external forces: Naive beliefs about the motion of objects. *Science,* 1980, *210*(5), 1139–1141.

McDermott, J., & Larkin, J. H. Re-representing textbook physics problems. In *Proceedings of the 2nd National Conference, the Canadian Society for Computational Studies of Intelligence.* Toronto: University of Toronto Press, 1978.

McKeithen, K. B., Reitman, J. S., Rueter, H. H., & Hirtle, S. Knowledge organization and skilled differences in computer programmers. *Cognitive Psychology,* 1981, *13,* 307–325.

Neves, D. M., & Anderson, J. R. Knowledge compilation: Mechanisms for the automatization of cognitive skills. In J. R. Anderson (Ed.), *Cognitive skills and their acquisition.* Hillsdale, N.J.: Lawrence Erlbaum Associates, 1981.

Newell, A. Production systems: Models of control structures. In W. G. Chase (Ed.), *Visual information processing.* New York: Academic Press, 1973.

Newell, A., Shaw, J. C., & Simon, H. A. Chess-playing programs and the problem of complexity. *IBM Journal of Research and Development,* 1958, *2,* 320–335.

Newell, A., Shaw, J. C., & Simon, H. A. Report on a general problem solving program for a computer. In *Information processing: Proceedings of the international conference on information processing.* Paris: UNESCO, 1960.

Newell, A., & Simon, H. A. *Human problem solving.* Englewood Cliffs, N.J.: Prentice-Hall, 1972.

Novak, G. S., Jr. Representations of knowledge in a program for solving physics problems. *Proceedings of the 5th International Joint Conference on Artificial Intelligence,* Cambridge, Mass., 1977, 286–291.

Paige, J. M., & Simon, H. A. Cognitive processes in solving algebra word problems. In B. Klein-muntz (Ed.), *Problem solving*. New York: Wiley, 1966.

Perfetti, C. A., & Hogaboam, T. The relation between single word decoding and reading comprehension skill. *Journal of Educational Psychology,* 1975, *67*(4), 461–469.

Polson, P. G., & Jeffries, R. Problem solving as search and understanding. In R. Sternberg (Ed.), *Advances in the psychology of intelligence* (Vol. 1). Hillsdale, N.J.: Lawrence Erlbaum Associates, 1981.

Pople, H. E. The formation of composite hypotheses in diagnostic problem solving: An exercise in synthetic reasoning. *Proceedings of the 5th International Joint Conference on Artificial Intelligence,* Cambridge, Mass., 1977, 848–855.

Reitman, J. Skilled perception in Go: Deducing memory structures from inter-response times. *Cognitive Psychology,* 1976, *8,* 336–356.

Riley, M. S., Greeno, J. G., & Heller, J. I. Development of children's problem-solving ability in arithmetic. In H. P. Ginsberg (Ed.), *Development of mathematical thinking*. New York: Academic Press, 1981.

Rosch, E. Principles of categorization. In E. Rosch & B. Lloyd (Eds.), *Cognition and categorization*. Hillsdale, N.J.: Lawrence Erlbaum Associates, 1978.

Rumelhart, D. E. Schemata: The building blocks of cognition. In R. Spiro, B. Bruce, & W. Brewer (Eds.), *Theoretical issues in reading comprehension*. Hillsdale, N.J.: Lawrence Erlbaum Associates, 1981.

Shannon, C. E. Programming a digital computer for playing chess. *Philosophy Magazine,* 1950, *41,* 356–375.

Shavelson, R. J. Methods for examining representations of a subject-matter structure in a student's memory. *Journal of Research in Science Teaching,* 1974, *11*(3), 231–249.

Shavelson, R. J., & Stanton, G. C. Construct validation: Methodology and application to three measures of cognitive structure. *Journal of Educational Measurement,* 1975, *12*(2), 67–85.

Simon, H. A., & Reed, S. K. Modeling strategy shifts in a problem solving task. *Cognitive Psychology,* 1976, *8,* 86–97.

Simon, D. P., & Simon, H. A. Individual differences in solving physics problems. In R. Siegler (Ed.), *Children's thinking: What develops?* Hillsdale, N.J.: Lawrence Erlbaum Associates 1978.

Simon, H. A. The functional equivalence of problem solving skills. *Cognitive Psychology,* 1975, *7,* 268–288.

Simon, H. A. The information storage system called "Human Memory." In M. R. Rosenzweig & E. L. Bennett (Eds.), *Neural mechanisms of learning and memory*. Cambridge, Mass.: MIT Press, 1976.

Simon, H. A., & Barenfeld, M. Information processing analysis of perceptual processes in problem solving. *Psychological Review,* 1969, *76,* 473–483.

Sloboda, J. A. Visual perception of musical notation: Registering pitch symbols in memory. *Quarterly Journal of Experimental Psychology,* 1976, *28,* 1–16.

Thomas, J. C., Jr. An analysis of behavior in the hobbits-orcs problems. *Cognitive Psychology,* 1974, *6,* 257–269.

Thro, M. P. Relationships between associative and content structure of physics concepts. *Journal of Educational Psychology,* 1978, *70*(6), 971–978.

Voss, J. F., & Tyler, S. *Problem solving in a social science domain*. Unpublished manuscript, University of Pittsburgh, Learning Research and Development Center, 1981.

Waterman, D. A. Adaptive production systems. *Advance Papers of the 4th International Joint Conference on Artificial Intelligence,* Georgia, USSR, 1975, 296–303.

Wilkins, D. Using patterns and plans in chess. *Artificial Intelligence,* 1980, *14,* 165–203.

Wolf, T. A cognitive model of musical sight reading. *Journal of Psycholinguistic Research,* 1976, *5,* 143–171.

Wortman, P. M. Medical diagnosis: An information processing approach. *Computer and Biomedical Research,* 1972, *5,* 315–328.

2

Strategies for Visual Comparison and Representation: Individual Differences

Lynn A. Cooper
University of Pittsburgh

INTRODUCTION

The objective of this chapter is to provide a description of an ongoing research program studying individual differences in modes of processing visual information. Aspects of the research program have been discussed elsewhere (e.g., Cooper, 1976, 1980a, 1980b; Cooper & Podgorny, 1976), but this chapter represents the first attempt to synthesize the results of the program in its entirety. The research project did not begin as a study of individual differences. Rather, attention was initially directed toward questions concerning the general nature of memory-comparison processes. It soon became clear that individuals differ quite dramatically in performance on visual memory-comparison tasks, so the individual-differences aspect of the research program became its primary emphasis.

The study of individual differences in performance on cognitive tasks—particularly as those differences relate to differences in intelligence or ability—has recently been an area of active research. The research effort has grown as both cognitive and differential psychologists have attempted to provide an information-processing analysis of the cognitive skills that underlie human aptitude (see Carroll, 1976). Pellegrino and Glaser (1979) have distinguished between two approaches to studying individual differences in ability.

In the "cognitive correlates" approach, the goal is to identify particular information-processing skills that are related to levels of aptitude. The work of Hunt and his colleagues (e.g., Hunt, Lunneborg, & Lewis, 1975) provides a good example of this approach. Performance of low-aptitude and high-aptitude subjects are compared on cognitive tasks that have been studied previously and for which information-processing models have been developed. The effort is to find the basic information-processing differences that distinguish high- from low-ability persons. These differences can be thought of as differences in the efficiency with which one or more component processing operations are executed.

In the "cognitive components" approach, the goal is to develop information-processing models of performance on aptitude items themselves. The works of Sternberg (1977) and Mulholland, Pellegrino, and Glaser (1980) provide good examples of this approach. Items on tests of aptitude are recast into versions appropriate for laboratory investigation, and models are developed for performance on these laboratory tasks. The effort is to model the processes underlying task performance and to locate individual differences in one or more of the component processes specified by the model.

The research style that my co-workers and I have adopted differs from both the cognitive correlates and the cognitive components approaches to analyzing individual differences. Our primary concern has been to characterize differences in the sorts of *strategies* that individuals use in solving spatial problems. Our view is that individuals may differ *qualitatively* in the nature of the processes underlying task performance as well as *quantitatively* in the efficiency with which component processing operations are carried out. The goal of our program has been to analyze in detail the nature of these underlying strategies for performance and to understand the conditions under which a certain strategy is most effectively used. We have directed a good deal of the research toward observing the flexibility or responsiveness of strategy selection to manipulations of both task demands and stimulus properties.

This emphasis on the importance of strategies—or methods for approaching a task or solving a problem—is consistent with an emerging view in work on human intelligence. The weakness of the relationships frequently found between ability measures and basic information-processing parameters has led several investigators to argue that global strategy differences may make at least as powerful a contribution to individual differences in intelligence as do differences in the efficiency of basic information-processing skills (e.g., Baron, 1978; Cooper & Regan, in press; Hunt, 1978). Hunt (1974), for example, has analyzed two quite different strategies for solving items on the Raven Progressive Matrices Test of general intelligence. And, experimental demonstrations of the relationship between strategies and abilities have been provided recently by several investigators. MacLeod, Hunt, and Mathews (1978) have shown that selection of a strategy for performing a "sentence-picture" verification task (see Clark & Chase, 1972) is influenced by and predictable from subjects' relative levels of verbal and spatial ability. Sternberg and Weil (1980) have reported a similar finding for the solution of linear syllogisms. Subjects who were identified as using a linguistic strategy for solving these problems showed correlations between solution times and level of verbal ability, but no such correlations emerged with spatial ability. In contrast, subjects identified as using a spatial strategy showed the reverse correlational pattern.

The strategy differences that we have been studying have not yet been related to ability differences. Nonetheless, we view our research program as having implications for studying the relationship between strategy use and individual differences in intelligence for two primary reasons. First, the qualitative differences that we are investigating have emerged in relatively simple visual information-processing situations. To the extent that strategy differences appear in simple information-processing tasks, there is reason to believe that such differences contribute as well to differences in performance on more complex problems—such as items on tests of spatial aptitude. Indeed, a future direction of our research program involves an analysis of the contribution made by strategy selection to performance on such spatial items. Second, our research program provides an example of how individual differences in strategies can be studied experimentally. In particular, our experiments show how natural, preferred strategies can be manipulated by changes in task demands and properties of stimulus structure. Our findings thus have implications for the joint issues of both the nature of strategy selection and the flexibility of a particular strategy user in adopting alternative strategies. We suspect that both of these issues will gain increasing importance in the study of human intelligence.

In this chapter, our program of research on individual differences is presented in detail. An overview of the general experimental methods used is first provided, followed by a discussion of the basic patterns of performance differences that we have obtained. Subsequent phases of the research project are described in three sections. In the first, we present experiments designed to manipulate individual subjects' use of a particular processing strategy. In the second, we present work suggesting that individual subjects may differ in how visual information is represented in memory. In the third, we present our preliminary efforts to relate the strategy differences that we have been studying to other reported sources of individual differences.

THE RESEARCH PROGRAM

General Experimental Method

The overall research strategy that we have adopted is a psychophysical one. That is, relatively few subjects are tested in any one of our experiments, but they are tested for an extended period of time (in the case of most of the studies, between 300 and 600 experimental trials for each individual subject). The goal is to observe patterns of performance at asymptotic and error-free levels. This has resulted in the adoption of various procedural measures, including the elimination of initial practice-session data and the re-presentation of trials on which errors are made at some semirandom point during each experimental session.

The sequence of events that might occur on a trial in a typical experiment is as follows: A subject views an initial or "standard" visual pattern (projected as a slide on a screen or plotted as an outline on an oscilloscope) for a sufficient amount of time to encode the pattern (about 3 seconds). The pattern is removed and, following a 1 to 1½ second blank interstimulus interval, a second visual pattern or "test" pattern is displayed. The subject's task is to indicate as rapidly and accurately as possible, by actuating one of two response buttons, whether the test pattern is the same as the standard or different from the standard according to some prespecified criterion. Both the speed and the accuracy of the discriminative response are dependent variables of interest. Additional procedural details, including variations in stimulus parameters and response criteria, are discussed in the context of the particular experiments to be reported.

An important issue concerns the selection of subjects for these visual comparison experiments. In general, our subjects have been drawn from a relatively homogeneous population consisting of faculty, graduate students, laboratory personnel, and paid undergraduates from various universities. Until recently, we have not been concerned with sampling the entire range of measured spatial or verbal aptitude, although possible relationships between strategy selection and aptitude scores constitute an important part of our current and projected research program. Rather, we have been interested in identifying individuals whose reaction-time and error data conform to one of two basic types to be described later. Our notion is that these two patterns of data correspond to the use of two distinct strategies for comparing a visual memory representation with an external visual object. We have thus chosen to study individuals who clearly exhibit one or the other of the two basic performance patterns. Once we have identified such individuals, we can engage in a within-subject, across-experiment research approach in which we observe the extent to which individuals who are known to prefer a particular comparison strategy will change that strategy as a result of well-defined task and stimulus manipulations imposed in additional experiments. (For another example of this attempt to isolate strategy changes within subjects resulting from task manipulations, see Glushko & Cooper, 1978.) Our claim is not that every individual can be unequivocally characterized as adopting one of the two visual processing modes that we have identified. Our claim is only that the individuals that we have chosen to study quite clearly exhibit one processing mode or the other. It is worth noting, however, that in the majority of our preliminary experiments, most of the subjects could be adequately categorized as using one of the two basic strategies (see, e.g., Cooper, 1976; Cooper & Podgorny, 1976).

Basic Patterns of Individual Differences in Performance

Two distinct and reliable patterns of performance in individual subjects have emerged in our initial series of visual comparison experiments. These experiments have been used to "screen" or to identify subjects as using one processing strategy or another for purposes of inclusion in subsequent experiments. To date, over 50 subjects have been tested using minor variations of this procedure. We now present data from just one illustrative experiment, chosen for discussion because the eight subjects who were tested also participated in a series of subsequent studies.

The stimuli used in this experiment (see also Cooper, 1976; Cooper & Podgorny, 1976) are depicted in Fig. 2.1. The right-hand column shows the initially presented or standard visual patterns, which varied in complexity, and which was defined as the number of points in each shape. Each standard could be followed either by the identical visual pattern, in which case the required response was "same," or by one of the test probes shown in the left-hand columns, in which case the required response was "different." The "different" test probes are random perturbations of the points determining inflections on the perimeter of the standard shapes. They vary in their rated similarity to the standards, with "D1" probes being highly similar to the standards and "D6" probes being highly dissimilar. The particular "different" perturbations shown in Fig. 2.1 were selected from a much larger set on the basis of similarity ratings made by an independent group of subjects. Care was taken to insure as well as possible that similarity between the standards and the test probes decreased monotonically and

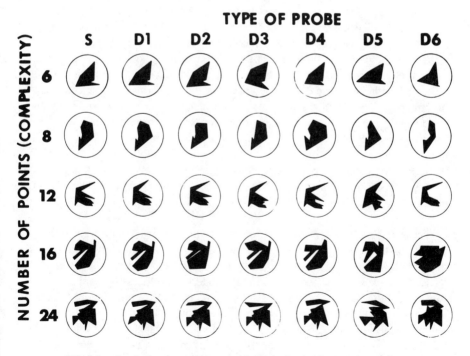

FIG. 2.1.   Standard and test shapes used in the basic visual comparison task or "screening" experiment (adapted from Cooper & Podgorny, 1976).

in approximately equal steps from D1 to D6 perturbations both within and across the various standard shapes.

The reaction-time data from this screening experiment are plotted in Fig. 2.2 as a function of type of test probe. With the exception of subject 4, whose data are plotted individually, reaction times (and, in subsequent figures, error rates as well) have been averaged over individual subjects conforming to each of the two basic patterns of performance. This aggregation of individual subjects' data within each group has been done for clarity of presentation, as the pattern of performance of each individual subject in each of the groups follows the pattern of the average data quite closely. In general, only when a particular subject exhibits patterns that deviate from the group trends (e.g., subject 4 in subsequent experiments) are that subject's data shown individually.

Consider, first, the data of subjects 5, 6, 7, and 8. Three features of the performance of these subjects are important: (1) reaction time to "different" test patterns decreases monotonically with increasing dissimilarity between the standard and the test shape; (2) "same" reaction time is intermediate in speed— slower than the shortest "different" times to highly dissimilar probes but faster than the longest "different" times to similar probes; (3) overall response speed is slow relative to the other subjects shown in Fig. 2.2.

In contrast, subjects 1, 2, 3, and 4 exhibit a considerably different pattern of performance. The salient features of these subjects' data are: (1) reaction time to "different" test patterns is virtually constant, regardless of the similarity between the standard and the test shape; (2) "same" reaction time is faster than "different" reaction time to any type of test probe; (3) overall response time is quite rapid relative to the other group of subjects. Furthermore, these considerable group differences in reaction-time performance are not accompanied by appreciable differences in either the magnitude or pattern of their errors. Figure 2.3 shows percentage of errors as a function of type of test probe for each of the two groups of subjects. It is clear from this figure that, for both groups, error rates decrease monotonically with increasing dissimilarity between the standard and the test shape. Thus, for subjects 5, 6, 7, and 8 reaction time and error rate are positively correlated, whereas for subjects 1, 2, 3, and 4 these measures are not correlated.

These differences between subject groups have proven interesting because they involve patterns of performance rather than simple quantitative differences between individuals. It is difficult to characterize the performance differences in terms of changes in the value of a single underlying processing parameter because an entire set of performance indices—including overall response speed, relative speed of "same" and "different" responses, sensitivity of "different" reaction time to similarity between standard and test patterns, and relationship between accuracy and reaction time—covaries systematically within an individual subject and differs between subject groups.

Still another reason for our interest in these patterns of group differences is the inability of certain simple accounts to explain them. Consider, for example, an

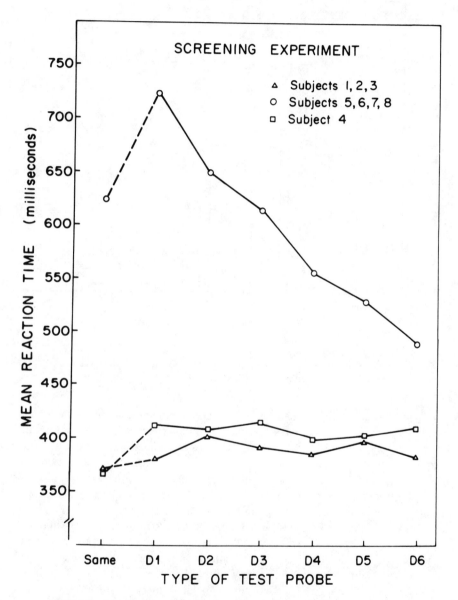

FIG. 2.2.   Mean reaction time plotted as a function of type of test probe for the screening experiment. Subjects 1, 2, 3, and 4 are classified as holistic processors; subjects 5, 6, 7, and 8 are classified as analytic processors (Cooper, 1980b).

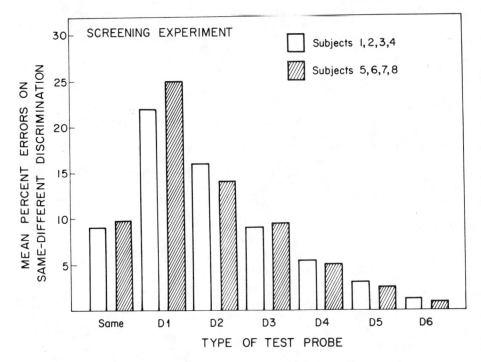

FIG. 2.3.   Mean percentage of errors on the same–different discrimination from the screening experiment. Subjects 1, 2, 3, and 4 are classified as holistic; subjects 5, 6, 7, and 8 are classified as analytic (Cooper 1980b).

account that attributed the pattern of differences to a speed-accuracy trade-off. This account seems unlikely because there is little difference in the error rates of the two groups despite the marked differences in their reaction-time data. The equivalence of error rates also casts doubt on an explanation that attributes the reaction-time differences to some heightened ability of the faster subject group to detect differences between memory representations of visual patterns and externally presented patterns. A final simple account might postulate some sort of "floor effect" on processing speed for the faster group of subjects. Although such a floor effect could explain why this group's response times are unaffected by similarity relations between visual patterns in memory and "different" test probes, it has difficulty explaining why "same" response times should be more rapid than all "different" response times for this subject group.

A more interesting type of explanation—the one on which our research program has been predicated—places the difference between subjects in the nature of the strategies they naturally use for comparing internally represented and externally presented visual information. We now present a sketch of two possible types of spatial comparison processes that could produce the alternative patterns of performance obtained in the initial screening experiments. The central notion is that one pattern of performance results from the use of a "holistic" strategy for processing spatial information, whereas the other pattern derives from adopting a more "analytic" processing mode.

The group of subjects that shows no effect of similarity on "different" response times (along with other features of performance described earlier) could be comparing a memory representation of a visual shape with a test shape in a holistic, parallel fashion seeking to verify that the two representations are the same. This sort of comparison strategy would not involve a search for stimulus differences or for visual features that distinguish the memory representation from the test shape. Instead, the goal of the comparison process would be to achieve a match between the test shape and the corresponding memory representation. If such a match were obtained, then the "same" response could be executed. If such a match were not obtained, then the "different" response could be executed by default. Note that a unitary, holistic comparison process could produce the reaction-time results for this group of subjects. The superior speed of the "same" response would result from the initial attempt to achieve a match between the memory representation and the test shape. The constant additional time for the "different" response would result from its default execution only after the matching process had failed. The insensitivity of "different" response times to similarity between the standard and test shapes is also a natural consequence of this processing strategy because "different" responses are assumed to be made by default rather than on the basis of an analysis of distinguishing visual features. Errors could be produced from this unitary comparison process if complete structural information about the standard shape was on occasion not retained in its corresponding internal representation. On just those occasions, the comparison operation could accept an incorrect match or reject a correct one, and the chances of this occurring would be greater, the more similar the representations of the standard and the test shape.

The group of subjects that exhibits a monotonic decrease in "different" response time with decreasing similarity between the standard shape and the test probe could be using a more analytic comparison process, and/or two different and independent processes could be generating the "same" and the "different" responses. A process specialized for detecting differences could compare the visual features of the memory representation and the test shape. As soon as this process found a feature that distinguished the two representations, the "different" response could be executed. Such a self-terminating difference comparison could explain the monotonic decrease in reaction time with increasing dissimilarity between the standard and the test shape. This is because the greater the dissimilarity between the two visual representations, the earlier a difference will be found and the faster will be the response.

A second process, similar to the single comparison process of the holistic subjects, could operate simultaneously with the difference-detection process and under a time deadline. If a match is achieved before the deadline has been exceeded, then the "same" response could be executed. Note that there are two aspects of this second, holistic comparison process. First, this process cannot lead to the initiation of a "different" response if a match is not found. Second, the particular assumptions made about the value of the time deadline determine the speed of the "same" response relative to "different" responses. Clearly, in order to characterize the data of the analytic subjects shown in Fig. 2.2, the value of the time deadline must be set at an intermediate level.

This analysis of the comparison strategy of the analytic subjects—sometimes called a "dual process" model—has been proposed by others as a general model of same–different visual comparison (e.g., Bamber, 1969; Sternberg, 1977). And other modifications of the processes just outlined are consistent with general theories of perceptual matching (e.g., Krueger, 1978; Tversky, 1969). For example, the analytic group of subjects could begin with a holistic comparison process, but then move to a difference-detecting process on some proportion of the trials on which a match is not found. Under this account, the intermediate speed of the "same" response would result from some "same" decisions occurring immediately after a holistic match and others occurring after the completion of the analytic comparison process.

Regardless of which particular version of a two-process model most adequately describes the behavior of the analytic subjects, we view the central difference between the proposed alternative processing strategies as follows: The holistic strategy involves the rapid, parallel comparison of a memory representation with a visual shape, and little analysis of difference information is performed. The analytic strategy, in contrast, is based on a process specialized for detecting features that differentiate a memory representation from an external visual pattern.[1]

Manipulation of Visual Comparison Strategies

Having identified reliable individual differences in performance on a visual comparison task and having related these to possible strategy differences, the next step in our research program was a more detailed analysis of the underlying strategies, with a particular emphasis on the flexibility or modifiability of strategies within individual subjects. The sorts of questions that we have been addressing include: To what extent are strategies preferred yet optional charac-

---

[1] In previous publications describing earlier aspects of this research (e.g., Cooper, 1976; Cooper & Podgorny, 1976), holistic subjects were referred to as "Type I" subjects, and analytic subjects were termed "Type II" subjects. As these labels have little mnemonic value, an effort has been made to avoid them in this paper. The use of the terms "holistic" and "analytic" is also unfortunate because of the multiple and sometimes conflicting meanings that these terms have acquired. They are used as labels for the processing differences described in this paper for lack of any better terminology.

teristics of an individual subject's performance in visual comparison situations? Stated differently, under what conditions can an individual subject be induced to adopt a strategy different from his or her natural one when those conditions make a particular strategy more efficient? Is one type of strategy (holistic vs. analytic) more responsive to changes in task demands than the other?

The experimental approach that we have adopted has been designed not only to provide information concerning the modifiability of processing strategies but also to provide independent evidence concerning the nature of the strategies themselves. Our goal has been to observe the performance of previously identified holistic and analytic processors on new but related tasks that have been constructed with particular purposes in mind. First, we want a reasonably clear a priori analysis of processing demands imposed by the new tasks. Second, we want these processing demands to draw naturally upon one of the hypothesized strategies used by the two types of subjects. Then, by having both types of subjects perform the new tasks, we hope to observe either differential change in the performance of one type of subject but not the other or change in the performance of both types of subjects but in identifiably different ways.

The new tasks that are described next were not designed simply to increase or decrease overall levels of performance. Instead, we hoped that the demands of the new tasks would cause a change in performance only if the subject has adopted a particular processing strategy. If an alteration in the performance of one type of subject but not the other is observed, then we can draw two conclusions: (1) the demands of the new tasks embody certain aspects of the natural comparison strategy of the subjects whose performance remained unchanged; (2) the subjects whose performance did change are capable of adopting multiple comparison strategies in different situations. This second conclusion is a potentially important one, particularly if we find that the performance of individuals characterized by one visual processing strategy was easier to change than the performance of individuals who naturally used the other processing strategy. On the view advanced earlier that one aspect of intelligent or adaptive behavior might involve the ability to select and execute the strategy most appropriate for a given task, then we might expect that individuals capable of strategy flexibility in this low-level visual processing task would show the same sort of flexibility in solving more complex visual problems such as those found on tests of spatial aptitude. Thus, our research program has revolved around two interrelated goals: the discovery of how modifiable different comparison strategies are both across subject groups and within individual subjects and the use of persistence and change in individual subjects' patterns of performance to provide a deeper understanding of the nature of those underlying strategies.

Detecting Differences: The Quadrant Experiment.   Our initial attempt to manipulate processing strategies was suggested by the introspective report of one of the holistic subjects from the screening experiment. This subject claimed that when she responded "different," she did so without a clear notion of just how the test shape differed from the standard shape in memory. This report is consistent with the foregoing analysis in which the "different" response of holistic processors was attributed to a default decision following the failure of the matching operation. Analytic processors, in contrast, are assumed to search actively for information concerning the location of features that distinguish a memory representation from a test shape in executing the "different" response.

The idea behind this particular experiment was that holistic processors might be forced to adopt the analytic mode if the detection and report of differences were explicitly required by the task. The same eight subjects whose screening data are presented in Figs. 2.2 and 2.3 were tested on this new task, which again required same–different comparison of a memory representation of a standard shape with a test shape. The novel feature of this experimental procedure was that, in addition to the same–different judgment, subjects were required to indicate how a test shape differed from a standard, if they judged the two shapes to be

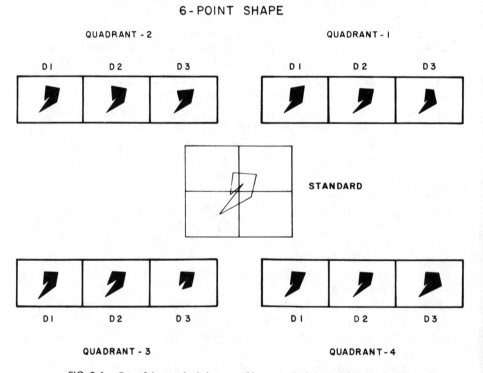

FIG. 2.4. One of the standard shapes—of low complexity—and the corresponding "different" probes used in the quadrant experiment. Each of the four sets of probes corresponds to one of the four quadrants in the standard shape (Cooper, 1980b).

different. We implemented this requirement of difference detection in the following fashion: Random, angular standard shapes were constructed, and "different" test probes were made by applying local perturbations of varying magnitude to points within each of four "quadrants" of each shape. Associated with each quadrant of each standard shape were three "different" probes, which varied in their rated similarity to the standard. Figures 2.4 and 2.5 illustrate two of the standard shapes, divided into quadrants, with all 12 of the corresponding "different" probes for each shape.

Figure 2.6 illustrates the sequence of events on a typical experimental trial. As can be seen, the procedural innovation consisted of presenting lines depicting the four quadrants of a shape, contingent on a response of "different," and requiring the subject to indicate in which of the four quadrants the standard and the test shape differ. This is done by pressing one of four buttons corresponding to each of the four quadrants.

Our hope was to affect the performance of holistic and analytic subjects differentially by adding the new requirement of the detection and report of difference to the basic same–different comparison task. Specifically, we rea-

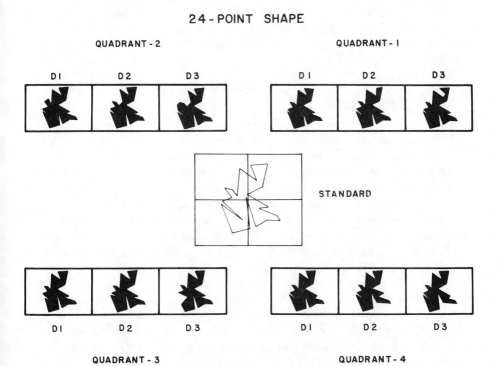

FIG. 2.5.   One of the standard shapes—of high complexity—and the corresponding "different" probes used in the quadrant experiment. Each of the four sets of probes corresponds to one of the four quadrants in the standard shape.

  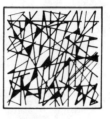 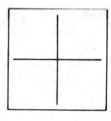

STANDARD SHAPE   TEST SHAPE   NOISE (Masking)   QUADRANT LINES
                                              FIELD

I - Second memory   Same-Different response   Quadrant identification
     interval   (Different)   (Quadrant-I, upper right)

FIG. 2.6. Sequence of events on an experimental trial for which the correct response was "different" in the quadrant experiment. Quadrant lines appeared only when the response "different" was made. (Cooper, 1980b).

soned that analytic subjects should be affected minimally if at all by the additional task demand. For if the chief component of these subjects' natural comparison strategy is an analysis of differences between a memory representation and a test shape, then information concerning the location of a difference found during the same–different comparison should be available for report immediately following the execution of the "different" response.

Holistic subjects, however, should be affected in one of two ways by the addition of the difference detection. If the additional processing requirement causes them to adopt the analytic strategy, then same–different reaction-time performance should change considerably from that obtained in the standard visual comparison task. Specifically, "different" reaction time should decrease monotonically with increasing dissimilarity between standard and test shapes, reflecting the operation of a difference-detecting process. Another possibility is that the addition of the new task requirement is not sufficient to force these subjects to drop their natural holistic matching process in favor of a more analytic comparison strategy. If these subjects persist in using a holistic comparison process instead of searching for differences, then their reaction-time performance should be similar to that obtained in the standard visual comparison task. However, use of this strategy should cause performance on quadrant identification to be substantially poorer than performance by subjects using an analytic strategy. This is because, by hypothesis, the holistic comparison process does not search for information concerning the location of a difference between the standard and test shapes. Hence, this information is not available for report following execution of the "different" response.

The reaction-time data from this experiment are shown in Fig. 2.7. Errors on the same–different discrimination are presented in Fig. 2.8, and errors on quad-

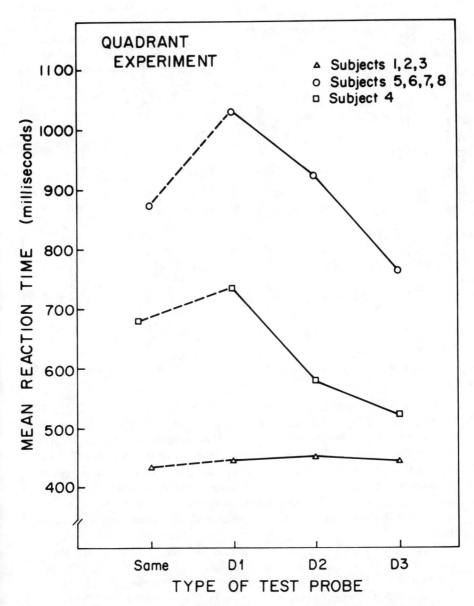

FIG. 2.7. Mean reaction time plotted as a function of type of test probe for the quadrant experiment (Cooper, 1980b).

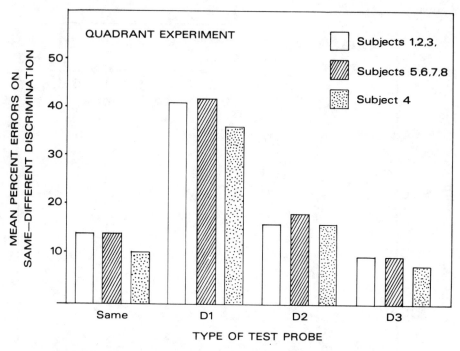

FIG. 2.8.   Mean percentage of errors on the same–different discrimination illustrated for the types of test probes used in the quadrant experiment (Cooper, 1980b).

rant identification following a response of "different" are shown in Fig. 2.9.
Consider, first, the performance of subjects 5, 6, 7, and 8, who were formerly
identified as analytic processors. As expected, the pattern of latencies and errors
is much like that obtained in the basic visual comparison task (cf. Figs. 2.2 and
2.3). Both reaction times and error rates decrease monotonically with increasing
dissimilarity between standard and test shapes, and the "same" response is
intermediate in speed. These findings are consistent with the use of an analytic
comparison strategy, which is just what we should expect from these subjects in
this situation.

Examination of subject 1, 2, and 3's reaction-time performance clearly shows
that, as in the basic visual comparison task (Figs. 2.2 and 2.3), "different"
response times are not affected by similarity between the standard and the test
shapes and that "same" response time is as fast as the fastest "different"
response. These patterns—along with the monotonic decrease in error rate with
increasing dissimilarity—are consistent with the persistence of a holistic comparison strategy, even when the task incorporates the additional demand of
detecting and reporting stimulus differences. As corroboration of this analysis of
a subset of the previously classified holistic processors, subjects 1, 2, and 3 show

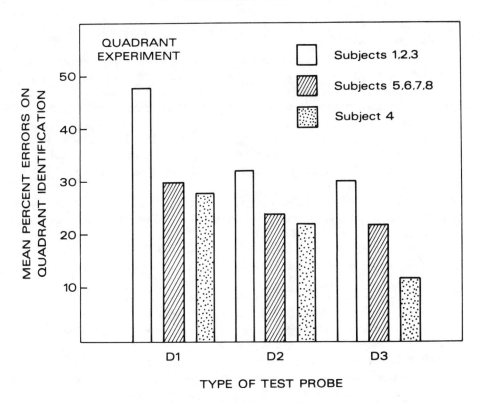

FIG. 2.9.   Mean percentage of errors on identification of the differing quadrant illustrated for the types of test probes used in the quadrant experiment (Cooper, 1980b).

markedly inferior performance on identification of the differing quadrant to that of the previously classified analytic processors (subjects 5, 6, 7, and 8), particularly for test probes highly similar to the standard shapes. Again, this finding is consistent with what we should expect if this subject group was unable to switch to an analytic mode of processing in the face of the new task demand.

Subject 4's performance pattern is particularly revealing. In the basic visual comparison experiment, this subject's "different" reaction times showed the typical holistic pattern (cf. Fig. 2.2), but now reaction-time performance is heavily influenced by the similarity between the standard and the test shape—a characteristic of the analytic processing strategy. Also consistent with this subject's change from holistic to analytic performance are the overall increase in response time and the intermediate speed of the "same" response, which in the previous experiment was faster than all "different" times. Furthermore, subject 4's quadrant-identification performance is at the level of the other analytic subjects (5, 6, 7, and 8) and considerably superior to that of the subjects (1, 2, and 3) who retained the holistic comparison strategy despite the requirement of difference detection.

The constellation of results from this experiment provides some insight into the nature of the two underlying strategies for comparing a visual memory representation with a visual test form. The data for subjects 1, 2, and 3 support the idea that their natural comparison strategy involves a single holistic process. This type of process was predicted to result in "different" responses of constant speed, rapid "same" responses, and relatively poor quadrant identification. This exact pattern was found. The failure of these subjects to switch to an analytic comparison strategy—even under conditions requiring the processing of difference information—suggests that the natural holistic strategy is not terribly flexible. The alteration of subject 4's performance in this task, which specifically required the detection and report of differences, gives information concerning the nature of the analytic comparison strategy. In particular, the performance change suggests that the natural comparison strategy of the previously classified analytic subjects does indeed involve a search for and detection of differences.

Changing the Judgmental Context: The Probability Experiment. In the experiment just reported, persistence and change in individual subject's patterns of performance resulting from a particular type of task demand were used to make inferences concerning both the nature of visual comparison strategies and the modifiability of these strategies. The same approach was used in the present experiment, but instead of imposing additional task demands we explored the responsiveness of spatial processing strategies to manipulations of the judgmental context for making same–different decisions. The particular manipulation selected was the probability—within a given block of trials—that a pair of visual shapes would be identical or different.

The same eight subjects, four previously identified holistic processors and four analytic processors, were tested. The experimental task required a speeded same–different decision, and the stimuli were the same as those used in the quadrant experiment. (No quadrant identifications were required, however.) The major procedural modification was to include three distinct experimental conditions. In one condition, the probability of "same" and "different" stimulus pairs was equal (50% same)—as in previous experiments. In another condition, "same" pairs were considerably more likely than "different" pairs (75% same); in a third condition, "different" pairs predominated (25% same). Subjects were informed in advance of the probability structure of each condition.

The notion behind this experiment is quite straightforward. We reasoned that large changes in the probability structure of a sequence of trials might make one comparison strategy more efficient than the other and thus cause both subject groups to adopt alternative processing modes in response to the probability manipulation. Specifically, when confronted with a situation in which most of the stimulus pairs were different, holistic subjects might find it more efficient to adopt the analytic strategy of search for and detection of difference. When confronted with a situation in which most of the stimulus pairs were identical, the analytic subjects might find it more efficient to switch to a holistic process based on matching for sameness. Our prediction, then, was that the typical group difference in performance patterns would emerge in the 50%-same condition. In the unbalanced conditions, we hoped to induce all subjects to use an analytic strategy when "different" trials predominated and a holistic strategy when "same" trials predominated.

The reaction-time data from this experiment are shown in Fig. 2.10, and error rates are presented in Fig. 2.11. Consider, first, the results from the 50%-same condition. As expected, when the probability structure of the trials is balanced, subjects 1, 2, 3, and 4 exhibit a holistic pattern of performance, and subjects 5, 6, 7, and 8 exhibit an analytic pattern. Of greater interest are the results from the unbalanced conditions. When "same" trials predominate (75%-same condition), subjects 1, 2, 3, and 4 continue to show holistic patterns, which is consistent with our predictions concerning the most efficient mode of visual comparison for this particular condition. However, subjects 5, 6, 7, and 8 show no evidence of

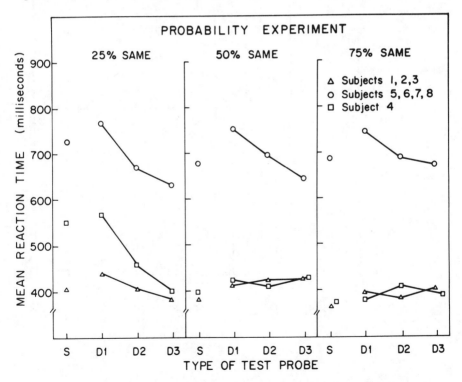

FIG. 2.10.   Mean reaction time plotted as a function of type of test probe for the three experimental conditions in the probability experiment.

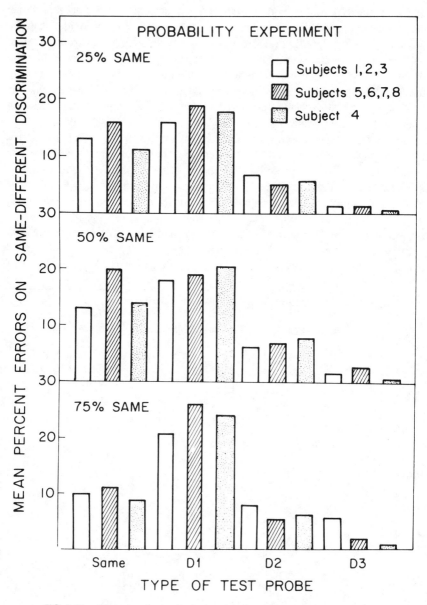

FIG. 2.11. Mean percentage of errors on the same–different discrimination illustrated for the types of test probes and for each of the experimental conditions in the probability experiment.

altering their analytic processing mode to conform to the change in judgmental context. As usual, this group's "different" reaction times decrease with increasing dissimilarity between the standard and the test shape; their "same" response is intermediate in speed.

The condition in which "different" trials predominated (25% same) was much more effective in manipulating processing strategies. As expected, subjects 5, 6, 7, and 8 continued to use their natural analytic strategy. Subject 4's data show evidence of a switch to the analytic mode—with "different" times decreasing with dissimilarity, "same" times increasing relative to the other conditions, and overall response time increasing—and, to a lesser extent, the performance of the other three formerly holistic subjects shows evidence of these trends. Although consistent with the framework provided here, it should be noted that this change in performance—particularly in the case of subject 4—is somewhat surprising because reaction times to "different" pairs actually *increased,* relative to the other conditions, in just the condition in which that type of stimulus pair was most prevalent. One further aspect of the data deserves mention. For all subjects in all conditions, relative error rates appear to be sensitive to the probability manipulation. From Fig. 2.11 it can be seen that when "different" trials predominate, they produce a lower error rate than when they are in the minority, with the 50% condition falling between these two extremes. Similarly, error rates on "same" trials are lowest in the 75%-same condition, intermediate in the 50% condition, and highest in the 25%-same condition.

In summary, the results of this experiment suggest that at least some holistic processors can adopt the analytic comparison strategy in situations for which it is most efficient. Analytic subjects appear unable to adopt the holistic processing mode even though the particular task structure may make this strategy more efficient than their natural comparison operation.

Forcing Analytic Processing Via Stimulus Structure: The Multidimensional Pattern Experiment.   The quadrant experiment and the probability experiment were both partially successful in causing subjects using a holistic processing mode to adopt an analytic strategy as a result of explicit or implicit task demands. In this experiment, a somewhat different manipulation was created in an effort to elicit analytic processing in all subjects. Our idea was that the use of stimulus materials quite obviously composed of discrete, separable dimensions might encourage subjects to base their visual memory comparison on these features or dimensions. That is, such stimuli might prove difficult or impossible to process holistically and thus might require an analytic processing mode.

The same group of eight subjects—four classified as holistic and four as analytic—were tested in this experiment. The stimuli used for the visual comparison task were displays that varied on the three dimensions of size, shape, and color. Two levels of size (large, small), two different shapes (square, circle), and two different colors (blue, red) were used, and these values on the three dimensions were combined in all possible ways to create the stimulus set. On any given trial, the two sequentially presented visual objects could be identical on all three dimensions, or they could differ with respect to values on one, two, or all three. So, on a typical trial a subject might be asked to make a same–different comparison of a small blue circle followed by a small red square (two differing dimensions). The independent variable of "number of differing dimensions" between the first display and the test display was considered analogous to the variable of "dissimilarity between the standard and the test shape" in previous experiments.

The reaction-time data, plotted as a function of number of differing dimensions, are shown in Fig. 2.12. The error data from this experiment are not presented because virtually no errors were made by any of the subjects. It is clear from Fig. 2.12 that the dimensional nature of the visual stimuli was effective in causing all subjects to exhibit the analytic pattern of performance. For all eight subjects, "different" reaction time decreases monotonically with an increase in the number of dimensions on which the two visual patterns differ. Somewhat curiously, "same" responses are as fast as the fastest "different" responses rather than intermediate in speed as is typical of the analytic pattern. This same result has been obtained for group data reported by previous investigators who have performed modifications of this basic type of experiment (Egeth, 1966; Hawkins, 1969; Nickerson, 1967).

One other puzzling feature of these data concerns the overall response speed of the two groups of subjects. Although the difference between the speed of the holistic and analytic processors is considerably smaller in the data shown in Fig. 2.12 than that obtained in previous experiments (cf. Figs. 2.2, 2.7, and 2.10), there is still an overall advantage for the subjects originally classified as holistic. The reason for this finding—which recurs in experiments discussed later—is not apparent. In summary, then, accentuating the discrete dimensional structure of the visual materials used in a memory comparison task appears to force both types of subjects to adopt a processing mode based on an analytic comparison of those dimensions.

Forcing Holistic Processing Via Stimulus Structure: The Faces Experiment. Having identified stimulus variables that can change the holistic processing mode to an analytic one, the question naturally arises whether analogous variables can be found that change the analytic mode to a holistic one. In the probability experiment, modifications of judgmental context were found to affect the holistic mode of processing—but not the analytic one—so our initial expectations concerning the modifiability of analytic processing were somewhat negative. Indeed, in one experiment based on the logic of the multidimensional pattern experiment, these expectations were confirmed. We reasoned by analogy to the multidimensional pattern experiment that a situation in which dimensional or feature-based stimulus structure was absent might encourage holistic processing in all subjects. Accordingly, the eight subjects were required to compare two sequentially presented lines and judge as rapidly as possible whether they were

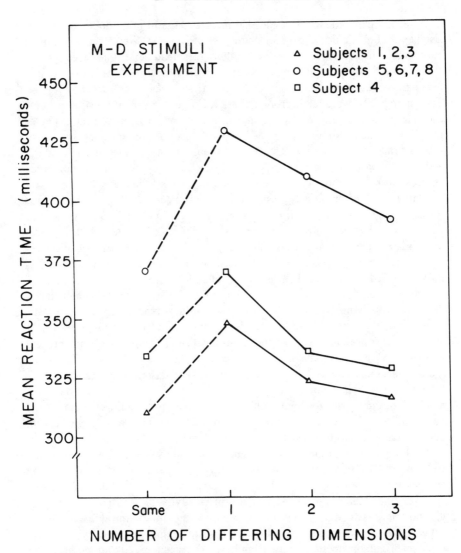

FIG. 2.12. Mean reaction time plotted as a function of number of differing dimensions for the multidimensional pattern experiment (Cooper, 1980b).

the same or different in length. The lines were centered in the visual field, and, if they differed in length, the extent of that difference could have one of four values. This task proved very difficult for all subjects, yielding extremely high error rates. The reaction-time data were difficult to interpret, but they suggested the same sort of group differences found in previous experiments. For the holistic subjects, reaction times were constant over extent of difference in length, but, for the analytic subjects, times decreased as extent of length difference increased.

A second experiment was somewhat more successful in producing data consistent with holistic processing for both types of subjects. We selected as stimuli photographs of human faces in light of the widespread belief that faces possess "configural" properties that make them difficult to analyze in terms of component parts or features (e.g., Carey & Diamond, 1977; Diamond & Carey, 1977). The photographs were taken from a Cornell University sorority yearbook. Five standard photographs were chosen, and associated with each was a set of photographs ranging in similarity to the standard face. An independent group of subjects rated the similarity of each "different" photograph to each standard, and on the basis of these ratings five distractors—representing a monotonic decrease in rated similarity—were selected for each standard face.

Only two of the previously classified holistic subjects and three of the analytic subjects were available for testing in this experiment. In addition, three new subjects who had not participated in the screening task were tested. The procedure was similar to that of the earlier experiments. A standard face was presented, followed by a test face, and subjects were required to judge as rapidly as possible whether the pair of faces was identical or different.

The reaction-time results are presented in Fig. 2.13. Error data are not shown because virtually no errors were made by any subject type to any stimulus pair. Note, first, that overall response times are quite rapid for all three groups of subjects. This was also true in the multidimensional pattern experiment, and undoubtedly, it is attributable in both cases to the fact that sets of faces and multidimensional patterns are considerably more discriminable than the subtly varying random shapes used in other experiments. Note, too, that overall response times are faster for both groups of previously tested subjects than for the new subjects. This difference most likely results from general experience with performing reaction-time tasks.

For both the new group of subjects and the holistic subjects, the reaction-time patterns are consistent with holistic processing. Many features of the data for the analytic subjects are consistent with this pattern as well. In particular, the relative speed of the "same" response and the insensitivity of "different" times to dissimilarity between the standard and the test faces (for D2 through D5 probes) suggest that these subjects have adopted a holistic comparison strategy as a result of the configural properties of the stimuli. The only aberrant datum point, under this account, is the elevated reaction time of analytic subjects to the highly similar D1 category of test probe. The reasons for this elevation are not clear, but we take the overall pattern of results from this experiment as preliminary, if not compelling, evidence that variables of stimulus structure can change analytic processing to the holistic mode.

There is a possible artifactual explanation for the data in Fig. 2.13 that attributes the flat reaction-time functions to a floor effect on the speed of the "different" response. That is, any human face is sufficiently dissimilar from any other human face that our manipulation of rated similarity does not effectively

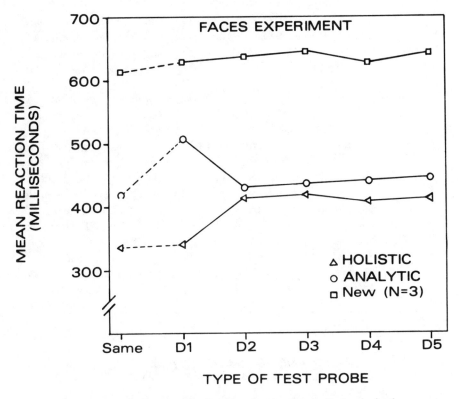

FIG. 2.13.   Mean reaction time plotted as a function of type of test probe for the face-comparison experiment. The function labeled "new" shows the data of subjects who had not been tested in the screening experiment. Functions for holistic and analytic subjects are also shown separately.

achieve a similarity continuum that could affect response times. We are not inclined to favor this explanation for one central reason. In the multidimensional pattern experiment, the test stimuli were also highly dissimilar from the standard patterns at all levels of difference. And in that experiment subjects also responded quite rapidly and with virtually no errors. However, reliable decreases in "different" response times were obtained. The point is that if a floor effect were to operate under the current conditions of high test-probe discriminability, then it should also have operated in the multidimensional pattern experiment.

One final but very tentative finding argues against a floor-effect interpretation of the face-comparison experiment. In a pilot study, we have tested subjects with the same stimuli turned upside down in an effort to destroy the strong configural properties of human faces. In this situation, we appear to be obtaining "different" reaction-time functions that decrease with increasing rated dissimilarity between standard and test faces. Considerably more work is necessary to strengthen this finding, so at present it should be taken only as suggestive. However, the constellation of results from the face-comparison experiment is consistent with the idea that analytic processing can be changed to holistic because of variations in stimulus structure.

Changing Response Criteria: The Identity Versus Similarity Experiment. In all of the aforementioned experiments, the visual comparison tasks involved deciding whether a test shape was identical to a standard or different in any respect. In a recently completed experiment (Cunningham, Cooper, & Reaves, 1980), we have studied the effect on both holistic and analytic processing modes of changing the comparison decision from one of identity versus nonidentity to one of similarity versus nonsimilarity. Specifically, in certain conditions of the experiment, subjects were required to expand their ''same'' response category to include not only pairs of visual patterns that were identical but also pairs that were similar.

The stimuli used in this experiment were the ''free form'' visual patterns originally generated by Shepard and Cermak (1973). A typical set of shapes from our experiment is shown in Fig. 2.14. Briefly, the forms are generated by a

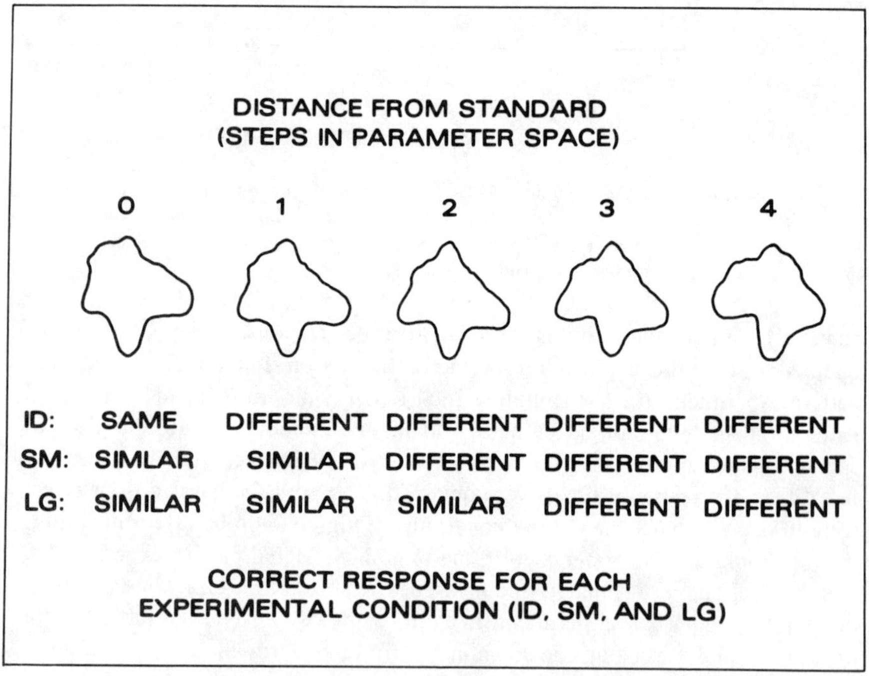

FIG. 2.14. Examples of the stimuli used in the similarity experiment and an explanation of the experimental conditions. For each condition, the correct response is shown under each form, given that the first or standard form presented on the trial was the one labeled ''O.''

mathematical function; by gradually changing the parameters of the function, changes in the shape of the form can be produced. We varied two parameters, using nine levels of each, thus generating 81 different forms. Shepard and Cermak (1973) have demonstrated that as the mathematical parameters of the forms are varied smoothly, the perceived similarity of the forms also varies smoothly. For the shapes in Fig. 2.14, a single parameter is changed step by step to transform the form on the left into the form on the right. The leftmost form in Fig. 2.14 was one of nine standard shapes, and the other four forms can be identified by the number of steps in the parameter space separating each from a given standard. The greater the number of steps separating two forms, the greater will be their dissimilarity in shape. In our experiment, one of the nine standard shapes was presented, followed by a test shape that could either be identical to the standard or could differ from the standard by one, two, three, or four steps in the parameter space.

The basic manipulation concerned the criterion required for deciding that two forms were the same or different. The bottom of Fig. 2.14 depicts how correct response type varied with experimental condition. In one condition, labeled ID ("identity"), the correct response was "same" only if the test form was identical to the standard and "different" otherwise. In the SM ("small difference") condition, the subjects were requested to give a positive or "similar" response if the test form was identical to the standard or if it differed by only one step in the parameter space. If the pair of forms differed by two, three, or four steps, then a response of "different" was considered correct. In condition LG ("large difference"), the correct response was "similar" if the pair of forms differed by two or fewer steps and "different" if the pair differed by three or four steps. Trials were blocked by experimental condition, and three holistic subjects and three analytic subjects were tested.

The purpose of this experiment was twofold. First, we hoped to replicate the essential features of the group-performance differences in the identity condition, which has the same characteristics as earlier visual comparison experiments but uses different stimulus materials. Second, we hoped to observe precisely how the two processing modes would respond to the inclusion of the similarity conditions. One possibility was that the holistic subjects might experience difficulty in adjusting their response cirteria in the similarity conditions because their positive responses are presumed to result from a search for "sameness." The analytic subjects might find the transition easier in that they might be able to abstract some feature defining the similarity sets.

Figure 2.15 presents one depiction of the reaction-time data from this experiment, plotted as a function of distance between the standard and the test form separately for the two subject groups and three experimental conditions. Note, first, that the function labeled ID replicates our earlier visual comparison experiments. For the analytic subjects, "different" reaction time decreases sharply with increasing dissimilarity between the standard and the test shapes, "same" responses (and, indeed overall response times) are rapid, and "different" re-

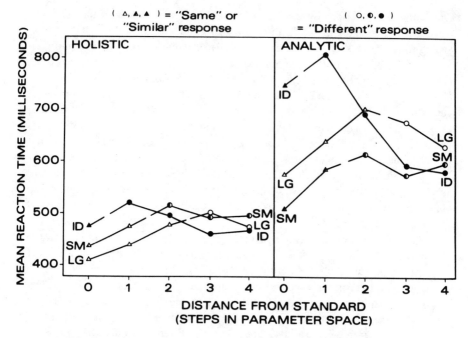

FIG. 2.15.   Mean reaction time plotted as a function of the distance between the standard and the test probe in terms of steps in the parameter space for the similarity experiment. Holistic and analytic processors are shown in the two panels; the three experimental conditions are plotted separately within each panel.

sponses do not vary significantly with increasing dissimilarity (although a slight decrease is apparent). Furthermore, there are considerable group differences in performance in the similarity conditions (SM and LG), but these differences are difficult to interpret.

There is a way of viewing the change produced by experimental conditions that leads to a slight reconceptualization of the underlying visual comparison processes. Consider, first, the holistic subjects. The slight effect produced by variation in experimental conditions (Fig. 2.15) could be interpreted as resulting from a change in the location of the criterion used to distinguish similar forms from dissimilar forms. Under this account, the criterion expressed as steps in the parameter space between a pair of forms would be between zero and one for the identity condition, between one and two for the small difference condition, and between two and three for the large difference condition. If the reaction-time data are replotted as a function of the difference between the criterion and the number of steps separating a pair of forms for each condition and each subject group, then Fig. 2.16 results.

It is clear from Fig. 2.16 that the functions for all three conditions for the holistic subject group are essentially superimposed. These data are consistent

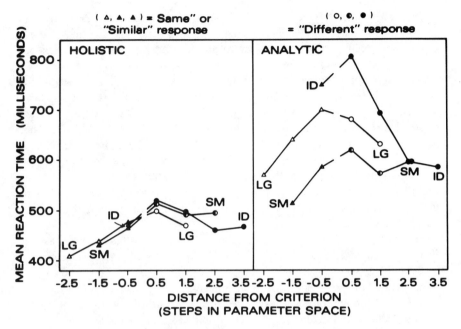

FIG. 2.16.   Mean reaction time plotted as a function of the distance from the criterion for the similarity experiment. Holistic and analytic processors are shown in the two panels; the three experimental conditions are plotted separately within each panel.

with the idea that the holistic subjects are using the same type of comparison process in all experimental conditions. What is changing from condition to condition is the location of the criterion. These data do show a small effect of distance from the criterion and direction of distance from the criterion on both positive ("same" or "similar") and negative ("different" or "dissimilar") response times. Perhaps the output of the holistic comparison process in this situation is some overall measure of discrepancy or similarity between the pair of visual forms. That overall measure must then be compared with some criterion to determine the appropriate response. Some amount of time is needed to make this comparison, and that time might increase as the criterion and the measure become closer in value. Of course, this account is speculative. However, it does explain the main features of the holistic subjects' data in Fig. 2.16, and it retains the important idea that the performance of the holistic subjects is the outcome of a unitary comparison process.

The situation is considerably different for the analytic subjects shown in the right-hand panel of Fig. 2.16. The transition from identity to similarity decisions has a dramatic effect on this group's performance. In particular, overall response time becomes faster when making the similarity decision, and response times are less affected by dissimilarity between the standard and test form than in the case of the identity decision (see Fig. 2.15). It is tempting to interpret these data in the following fashion: In the identity condition, these subjects use their natural difference-detection process in order to achieve the same–different decision. However, when required to make similarity–dissimilarity decisions, analytic difference detection proves to be an ineffective strategy. This is because the analytic process no longer provides information concerning the correct response. That is, even if information concerning the location of differences between the standard and the test shape is found, the correct response could still be either positive ("similar") or negative ("dissimilar"). The suggestion is that these subjects drop the difference-detection process in favor of holistic matching in the similarity conditions. Hence, they show further evidence of processing flexibility. This account is certainly consistent with the similarity of their performance to that of the holistic subjects in both the small difference and large difference conditions.

However, several aspects of the data pose problems for these interpretations. First, the analytic subjects—although showing a *pattern* of performance similar to the holistic subjects in the similarity conditions—never achieve the overall speed of the holistic subjects. Second, it is somewhat paradoxical that the analytic subjects show considerably slower reaction times in the large difference condition than in the small difference condition. Given the account of the holistic subjects' behavior, we should expect these response conditions to be of approximately equal speed.

Figure 2.17 illustrates error rates in this task as a function of the dissimilarity between the standard and test forms, separately for each subject type and each experimental condition. Note that the patterns of errors are approximately the same for both types of subjects and that the error rates in the identity condition replicate those found in earlier visual comparison experiments. Note, too, that the error rates are quite high, suggesting—particularly in the similarity conditions—that this was a difficult task. However, these substantial error rates, especially for the analytic subjects, cast doubt on the floor-effect explanation for their performance in the face-comparison experiment discussed earlier. For even in the presence of high error rates that vary with dissimilarity between stimulus pairs, trends toward reaction-time performance showing a *smaller* influence of these variables were obtained.

In summary, this experiment has provided converging evidence (in the identity condition) concerning the basic patterns of performance that distinguish our two subject groups. In addition, it has provided a wealth of evidence concerning how the two basic strategy types respond to changes in criteria for classifying visual patterns. Our initial expectation that the holistic processing mode would break down under conditions of similarity decisions was not confirmed. Instead, these subjects persisted in using a single comparison process for all conditions. However, analytic subjects appeared to drop their preferred difference-detection strategy when that strategy clearly yielded little information useful for selecting

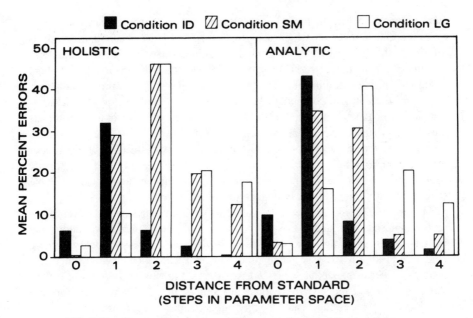

FIG. 2.17.   Mean percentage of errors shown as a function of distance, in terms of steps in the parameter space, between the standard and the test probe for the similarity experiment. Holistic and analytic subjects are shown in the two panels; the three experimental conditions are illustrated separately within each panel.

the appropriate response. Again, persistence and change in patterns of performance have provided useful evidence concerning both the nature of visual comparison strategies and the flexibility of these strategies in the face of task manipulations.

General Comments and Future Directions.   The overall goals of this phase of our research program have been to establish clearly individual differences in natural strategies for performing visual comparisons and to explore the manipulation of these strategies in the face of various task demands and modifications of stimulus structure. The general conclusion is that strategy selection does represent a stable individual difference but that the use of one strategy or another can be influenced by a variety of factors. Specifically, some holistic subjects adopt the analytic mode when explicitly or implicitly requested to search for stimulus differences. They can also easily switch to an analytic strategy when stimulus structure prevents the use of a holistic comparison. The analytic strategy for visual comparison appears to be more difficult to modify. However, some evidence was presented suggesting that configural stimulus structure encourages holistic processing in analytic subjects. In addition, these individuals adopt the holistic mode when an analysis of stimulus differences does not provide sufficient information for making a correct response. Under these conditions, however, the efficiency with which analytic subjects can use the holistic mode is inferior to the efficiency with which holistic subjects use their natural strategy.

This phase of the research program, directed toward questions of strategy modification, is continuing. For example, we are currently examining the possibility that the analytic comparison process serves a nonobligatory "checking" function. The experimental context that we have selected is one in which subjects must make visual comparisons under conditions of time constraint. By examining patterns of speed-accuracy trade-off under a variety of deadlines for responding, we hope to assess: (1) whether or not analytic processors will use a holistic strategy when there is insufficient time for difference detection; and (2) the efficiency with which they can engage in holistic comparisons.

We attribute considerable significance to the fact that stable differences in performance can be found in even the "simple" visual comparison situations that we have been studying. For purposes of developing process models for these cognitive tasks, an analysis of the conditions that lead to changes in individual patterns of performance has provided a powerful tool for furthering our understanding. The existence of individual differences in strategies for performing simple visual processing tasks strongly suggests that the success of efforts to understand performance in solving complex spatial problems will depend critically on an adequate analysis of strategic variation.

Individual Differences
in Visual Memory Representation

In the foregoing experiments, the assumption has been made that the locus of individual differences lies in the nature of the process used to compare an internal representation of a visual pattern with another external visual shape. In this section, we consider the possibility that individuals may also differ in the way in which they encode and represent visual patterns in memory. The specific suggestion we make is that subjects differ in the extent to which they represent patterns in terms of higher-order, organized visual units and how such visual units are used at the time of comparison. It is clear that no single experiment or set of experiments can distinguish aspects of visual memory representation from aspects of the processes that act on such a representation because behavior in any experimental context may result from complex interactions between representational characteristics and processing mechanisms. Indeed, Anderson (1978) has recently argued that behavioral data cannot discriminate among proposed alternative internal representations because in any experiment one is simultaneously testing assumptions about the nature of the processes that operate on the proposed representations to produce the behavioral outcomes. Nonetheless, we believe that results of experiments presented in this section are at least consistent with the notion that subjects differ in the way visual information is organized in memory as well in the way represented information is compared with new visual input.

The general idea motivating these experiments is that individual differences in the selection of visual comparison strategies may result in part from differences in the nature of the memory representations on which the comparison strategies must operate. Consider, first, the analytic comparison mode. The chief characteristic of this strategy is the search for and detection of features that distinguish a memory representation from a visual pattern. Such a comparison operation would operate most efficiently on a memory representation in which visual information was organized in terms of component parts or features of patterns. Such a memory representation might not prove optimal for the operation of the holistic comparison mode. Inasmuch as the holistic strategy does not involve an analysis of differences between parts or features of visual patterns, but rather performs an overall match searching for pattern identities, it may be more efficient for the holistic comparison to operate on a memory representation consisting of a low-level, unstructured specification of a visual pattern. The intended contrast is between a memory representation of the subunits, parts, or features of a visual pattern (with a comparison operation that accesses those component parts) versus a memory representation of all the low-level information in a visual pattern (with a comparison operation that examines such information simultaneously and globally). This view of the possible differences between the way analytic and holistic subjects represent visual information in memory led us to perform an experiment exploring the sensitivity of the two types of processors to organization in visual patterns.

Probing Sensitivity to Visual Structure: The Part-Detection Experiment. The experiment that we conducted to test these ideas was similar to one reported by Palmer (1977), although Palmer's study was not designed to investigate individual differences. The stimuli were visual patterns made up of combinations of six line segments, which varied in their rated "goodness." Figure 2.18 illustrates examples of patterns judged as high, medium, and low in overall goodness. Associated with each six-segment pattern was a set of two-segment probe patterns. The two-segment probes also varied in their rated goodness as parts of the six-segment figures. Examples of high-, medium-, and low-goodness probes for each of three patterns are shown in Fig. 2.19.

The subjects' basic task was to determine as rapidly and as accurately as possible whether or not a particular two-segment probe was contained in a particular six-segment pattern. In one experimental condition, the pattern was presented followed by the test probe. In another condition, the two-segment probe was presented before the six-segment pattern. On half of the trials, the probe was in fact a part of the pattern; on the other half, the probe was not a part of the pattern. If the probe was not contained in the pattern, it could have either no line segments in common with the pattern or one segment in common. Six

FIGURE GOODNESS

HIGH   MEDIUM   LOW

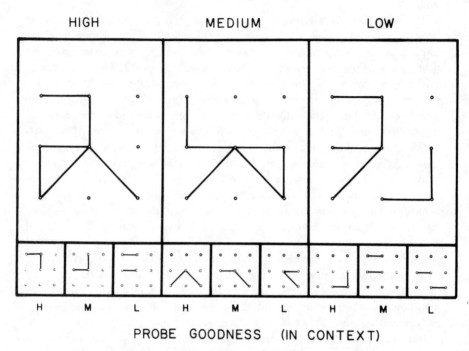

H   M   L   H   M   L   H   M   L

PROBE GOODNESS   (IN CONTEXT)

FIG. 2.18.   Examples of six-segment patterns and corresponding two-segment probes used in the part-detection experiment. Patterns vary in their rated goodness; probes vary in their rated goodness as parts of the appropriate six-segment pattern.

subjects—three who had been previously classified as analytic and three who had been classified as holistic—were tested.

Our basic idea was that certain two-segment probes—those rated as "good" parts of the patterns—would correspond to natural organizational units of the patterns. If a visual pattern were represented in memory in terms of its component features or parts, then those units in the memory representation should contain the good two-segment pieces. (This is essentially the view advanced by Palmer, 1977, for patterns similar to those shown in Fig. 2.18). We hypothesize that the analytic subjects represent visual information in memory in terms of features or part structures and that they use these units as a basis for comparison with other visual patterns. This hypothesis leads to the prediction that, for these subjects, verification of good two-segment probes as being contained in a pattern should be easier and, hence, more rapid than verification of medium or bad two-segment probes. This is because verification of a good probe only requires comparison with a single unit in the memory representation of the pattern, whereas verification of bad probes requires accessing multiple units, 2 which should take more time than the one-unit case. So, for the analytic subjects, part-detection time should increase with increasing probe "badness." An additional prediction is that verification time should be related to figure goodness for this group because it is presumably easier to decompose good figures into their component part structure than bad figures. That is, bad figures may not be easily parsed into features or units. Thus, for the analytic subjects, these figures prove difficult to represent in memory and use for purposes of comparison.

A rather different set of predictions was made for the holistic subjects. We hypothesized that these subjects do not incorporate the component structure of patterns in their memory representations. A low-level, unstructured memory representation of the patterns might consist of six independent line segments with no further internal organization. How would such a memory representation function at the time of comparison? Presumably, each of the individual segments in the representation of the pattern would be equally accessible and available for verification against the probe segments. That is, inasmuch as no structural sub-units larger than individual segments are used for comparison, no set of segments should be more difficult than any other to access from the memory representation. Indeed, this sort of a process—in which all parts of a memory representation function independently, are equally accessible, and are available simultaneously for comparison—is just what we mean by "holistic." This view of the holistic subjects' memory representations and comparison operations leads to the prediction that their verification times should not be affected by probe goodness. Nor should these times be affected by the goodness of the overall six-segment pattern.

The reaction-time results from this experiment are displayed in Figs. 2.19 and 2.20. In Fig. 2.19, mean reaction time is plotted as a function of probe goodness for each of the six subjects and separately for the two experimental conditions. The three holistic subjects are shown in the top panels, and the three analytic subjects are shown in the bottom panels. Consider, first, the results for the probe-after condition in which the six-segment pattern was presented first, followed by the two-segment test probe. Figure 2.19 clearly shows that reaction times for the three analytic subjects (4, 5, and 6) were influenced markedly by the rated goodness of the probe as a part of the pattern. Figure 2.20 shows a similar pattern—verification time increasing monotonically with decreasing part goodness—when times are plotted as a function of figure goodness for the three analytic subjects. Inspection of both figures reveals no such trends for the three holistic subjects (1, 2, and 3). For this group, verification times are virtually constant for all levels of probe and pattern goodness. These results confirm our expectations concerning the sensitivity of holistic and analytic processors to variations in probe and pattern organization.

Of some interest are the results for the "probe-before" condition in which the two-segment part was presented before the six-segment pattern. Overall, reaction times are faster than in the probe-after condition, and neither type of subject

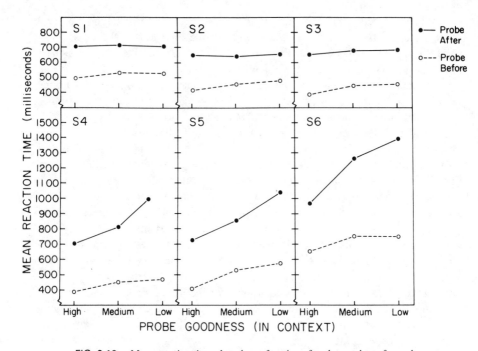

FIG. 2.19.   Mean reaction time plotted as a function of probe goodness for each of the six individual subjects in the part-detection experiment. Subjects 1, 2, and 3 are previously classified holistic processors; subjects 4, 5, and 6 are analytic processors. Conditions in which the probe appeared before and after the six-segment pattern are illustrated separately.

shows much of an effect of either figure or probe goodness on verification latency. (For some analytic subjects these variables affect reaction time, but the effect is attenuated when compared to effects obtained in the probe-after condition.) It makes sense that the effect of structural variables should be reduced in this condition because only the two-segment pattern part need be stored in memory. Unlike the probe-after condition in which the entire six-segment pattern must be represented (for the analytic subjects, in terms of its component structural units), there is no need to process the structure of the pattern in the probe-before condition. Hence, there is no reason to expect that structural variables should affect verification times when the pattern is presented after the two-segment part.

In summary, the data from this experiment are consistent with the idea that holistic and analytic subjects may differ in the way they represent visual information in memory as well as in the nature of their comparison strategies. Our explanation for the pattern of results is that analytic processors represent visual information in memory in terms of natural component parts or units. By hypothesis, our good probes are contained in a single memorial unit, whereas bad

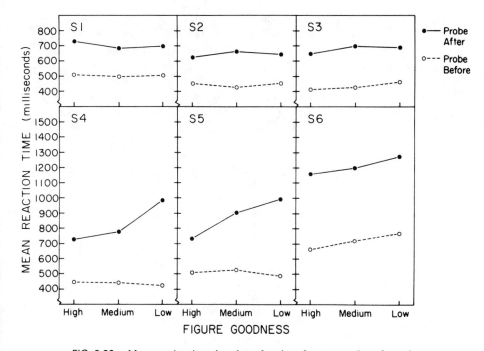

FIG. 2.20.   Mean reaction time plotted as a function of pattern goodness for each of the six individual subjects in the part-detection experiment. Subjects 1, 2, and 3 are previously classified holistic processors; subjects 4, 5, and 6 are analytic processors. Conditions in which the probe appeared before and after the six-segment patterns are illustrated separately.

probes are contained in more than one unit. Thus, information about the good probes is easier to access from the structured memory representations of the analytic subjects than information about the bad probes, which might require the decomposition and analysis of multiple units in the memory representation. For the holistic subjects, who are hypothesized to have memory representations that preserve no pattern structure at a level higher than the individual line segment, all parts of the memory representation are equally available for comparison. Hence, part and pattern goodness have no effect on the time required to perform visual comparisons.

General Comments and Additional Preliminary Results.   In an experiment still in progress, we are trying to assess possible limitations on the ability of holistic subjects to represent in memory all low-level parts of a pattern independently. We have reasoned that as visual patterns begin to approximate the true structure of three-dimensional objects, that structure might become so compelling that even the holistic processors would incorporate structural units in their memory representations of visual materials. Accordingly, we constructed stimuli that are three-dimensional analogues of the two-dimensional patterns used in the previously reported experiment. Examples of these perspective drawings of three-dimensional objects are illustrated in Fig. 2.21. Ratings were obtained of the goodness of two-, three-, and four-line-segment parts of these objects, and we selected for use in the experiment parts that varied in their rated goodness as units of the patterns. Examples of good and bad two- and four-segment parts of

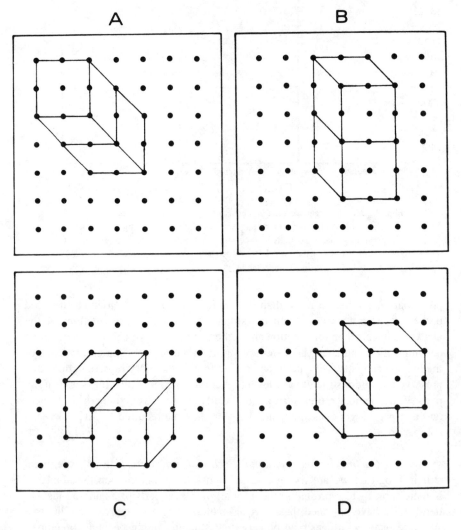

FIG. 2.21.   Examples of standard forms used in the three-dimensional version of the part-detection experiment.

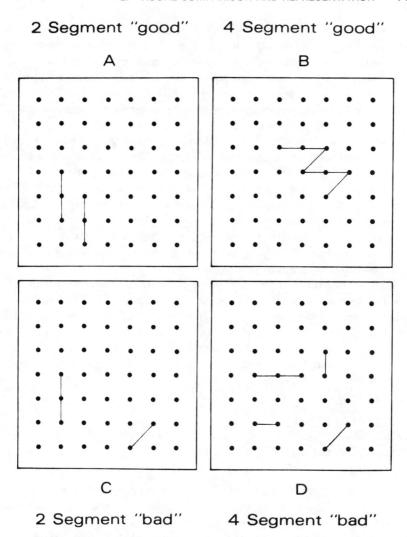

2 Segment "good"   4 Segment "good"

A

B

C

D

2 Segment "bad"   4 Segment "bad"

FIG. 2.22.   Examples of good and bad two- and four-segment probes (corresponding to the patterns shown in Fig. 2.22) from the three-dimensional part-
detection experiment.

the patterns shown in Fig. 2.21 are illustrated in Fig. 2.22. Subjects were shown
one of the perspective drawings of a three-dimensional object followed by a
two-, three-, or four-segment probe. Their task was to determine as rapidly and
accurately as possible whether the probe was contained in the pattern. Probes
contained in the patterns varied in rated goodness as pattern parts, and probes that
were not in the patterns differed from actual pattern parts by either an overall
structural translation or by a change in the placement of one line segment.

Our prediction was that all subjects would be affected by the goodness of the part probes in this situation. We reasoned that even the holistic subjects would incorporate three-dimensional structure in their memory representations of the visual patterns. That is, rather than representing the patterns as independent sets of individual line segments, the portrayed three-dimensionality of the stimuli might force the holistic subjects to represent the patterns as surfaces connected in a particular structural relationship.

Although not all subjects have completed this experiment, preliminary results have not confirmed our expectations. Already, there are clear indications of individual differences, with analytic subjects showing a marked effect of probe goodness on verification latencies and holistic subjects showing little if any effect. There is also some evidence of complex trade-offs between reaction time and accuracy, which we are currently analyzing in detail. However, these preliminary results suggest that holistic subjects persist in representing visual patterns in terms of low-level components rather than structural units, even when those patterns portray three-dimensional objects.

A further question that we are exploring concerns the extent to which initial encoding operations might differ for the two subject types. That is, does the fashion in which visual information is extracted from a pattern constrain both the way that information is represented in memory and how the information is used for subsequent comparison? It is, of course, difficult to separate encoding operations from memory representation and comparison, but we are hoping to gain some information on this issue by observing how the two subject types scan visual patterns that are to be represented in memory.

Relationship of the Holistic-Analytic Strategy Distinction to Other Sources of Processing Differences

Having isolated distinguishable strategies for representing and processing visual information in comparison tasks, it seems natural to ask whether these particular strategy differences are related to other global sorts of individual differences reported in the literature. Although this has not been a major thrust of our research program, two relevant experiments can be briefly described.

An information-processing dichotomy that has received considerable attention during the past decade concerns the hypothesized specialization of activity of the brain's two cerebral hemispheres. Superficially, the terms used to characterize hemispheric functions are quite similar to those applied to the alternative comparison strategies that we have been studying. That is, the left hemisphere of the brain is thought to excel in abstract, analytic processing, whereas the right hemisphere has been described as specialized for holistic, "Gestaltlike" activity (see e.g., Patterson & Bradshaw, 1975). It is possible that the natural strategies selected by our groups of subjects reflect preferred tendencies to rely on one hemisphere or the other in performing spatial comparison tasks.

We addressed this possibility experimentally by presenting visual information briefly to a single half of the visual field. The idea was that presentation of information to the left visual half field might encourage holistic processing because the information would arrive initially to the right hemisphere of the brain. Alternatively, information presented only to the right visual half field might encourage analytic processing because that information would first reach the left hemisphere.

The same eight subjects tested in our original screening experiment participated in this study. The stimuli were the random shapes shown in Fig. 2.1, but only four levels of difference were used. There were three types of test trials, randomly intermixed. On all trials, the initially presented standard shape was shown in the center of the visual field. The test shape that followed could appear in the center of the field, in the left visual half field, or in the right visual half field with equal probability. The test shape was presented for only 125 milliseconds to insure that, under conditions of visual half field presentation, subjects had inadequate time to shift fixation to the test shape. Again, the notion behind the experiment was that if holistic processing (as we have characterized this mode) is mediated by the right hemisphere of the brain, then all subjects should show appropriate holistic patterns under conditions of left visual half field presentation. If our form of analytic processing is mediated by the left hemisphere, then all subjects should show appropriate patterns under conditions of right visual half field presentation. However, the group performance differences that we typically find should emerge under conditions of central presentation of both standard and test shapes.

The reaction-time results, plotted separately for each method of presentation and for each of the subject groups, are shown in Fig. 2.23. Error data, displayed in an analogous fashion, are shown in Fig. 2.24. The results are quite clear. For all three presentation modes, the two subject groups exhibit the reaction-time and error patterns that were originally used to define the difference in their processing strategies. The only difference attributable to presentation method is that analytic subjects have shorter response times when the test shape is presented centrally than for either type of half field presentation. Neither of these findings is particularly surprising because acuity is better in the center of the visual field than in the periphery. Hence, performance should be better under conditions of central presentation. To the extent that this experiment is sensitive enough to pick up potential differences in hemispheric processing, we conclude that there is no obvious relationship between our holistic-analytic distinction and the specialized activity of the cerebral hemispheres.

A second information-processing dichotomy, which superficially seems related to the holistic-analytic distinction in comparison modes, has been proposed

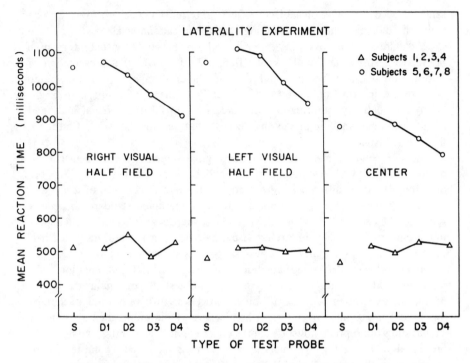

FIG. 2.23.   Mean reaction time plotted as a function of type of test probe for the three different presentation modes in the laterality experiment.

by Hock and his associates (e.g., Hock, 1973; Hock, Gordon, & Gold, 1975; Hock, Gordon, & Marcus, 1974). Hock's research strategy has involved manipulating aspects of stimulus structure in same–different comparison tasks and then determining—for individual subjects—the extent of "same" reaction-time difference that results from the stimulus manipulations. Typical stimulus manipulations might include whether two letters are presented upright or upside down, and whether they are presented in the same or in different cases. The reaction-time differences attributable to stimulus manipulations for each subject are then correlated. Significant positive correlations are used to argue for individual differences in modes of processing visual information. Hock has characterized the differences in processing modes as follows: Subjects whose "same" responses are influenced by stimulus variables are termed "structural" because their times appear to be affected by aspects of stimulus structure. Subjects whose "same" responses are relatively less affected by stimulus variables are termed "analytic."

Hock's experimental methods and techniques of data analysis are sufficiently different from our own to cast doubt on the possibility of a relationship between the holistic-analytic distinction and his proposed structural-analytic processing

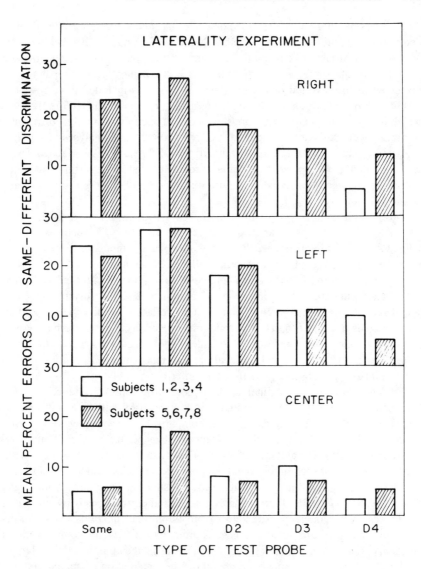

FIG. 2.24.   Mean percentage of errors shown as a function of type of test probe
for the three different presentation modes in the laterality experiment.

difference. In addition, there is reason to believe that Hock's evidence for group
differences is less than compelling. (See Carroll, 1978; Cooper & Regan, in
press, for critical discussions of this evidence for individual differences in visual
information processing.) Nonetheless, we performed an experiment similar to
that reported by Hock et al., (1975), using four analytic and four holistic subjects
in an attempt to find individual differences corresponding to those obtained by

Hock. Pairs of letters were presented on each trial, and subjects were required to determine as rapidly as possible whether they were the same or different in name. The stimulus variables we manipulated were whether the same-name letters were presented in the same or in different cases and whether the letter pairs were presented in the inverted or upright position. We also included three response conditions: one in which a same–different choice response was required; one in which only "same" responses were signaled; and one in which only "different" responses were signaled. The central outcome of statistical analyses of the data showed no individual differences in the effects of the stimulus variables. Thus, we conclude that this experiment did not provide evidence supporting any correspondence between our holistic-analytic distinction and Hock's suggested processing dichotomy.

Other candidates for processing differences that might relate to our holistic-analytic distinction are varieties of "cognitive styles," such as "field independence–field dependence" (Witkin, 1964) and "impulsivity-reflexivity" (Messick, 1976). We have not systematically investigated the possibility of such relationships, but there is reason to believe that the impulsive–reflexive distinction taps something different from our holistic-analytic distinction. The impulsive–reflective dichotomy is thought to reflect a tendency to attend to global versus detailed aspects of visual stimuli. However, the performance patterns that define the two styles involve trade-offs of speed and accuracy in visual processing tasks. And, the holistic-analytic differences in reaction-time patterns are obtained in the absence of differences in errors.

Of considerably greater interest than these processing differences are the implications of holistic-analytic strategy differences for intelligence—in particular, spatial aptitude. The kinds of visual comparisons for which we have found individual differences are certainly a component of performance on items contained in tests of spatial ability. Indeed, process models that have been developed for performance on such items contain operations corresponding to encoding and visual comparison. Furthermore, in his series of studies on spatial aptitude, Egan (1976, 1978, 1979a, 1979b) has consistently found correlations between spatial ability scores and intercept parameters of reaction-time functions, which in his tasks provide measures of the times required to encode and compare visual materials. One avenue that we intend to pursue in the future will involve an analysis of the role of comparison operations in the solution of spatial aptitude items. Of particular interest is the possibility that either the holistic or the analytic processing mode has greater success in solving such items in terms of both speed and accuracy. The pattern of results in our experiments seems to suggest that the holistic mode should be associated with greater success than the analytic mode because holistic subjects perform comparisons more quickly without a sacrifice in terms of error rates.

One form that such an investigation could take would involve correlating parameters of performance on spatial aptitude test items with parameters that define the holistic-analytic processing distinction. This information will be useful, but the central premise of our research program has been the importance of strategy selection, use, and modifiability in processing visual information. In this sense, our research program provides a framework for viewing sources of individual differences, and we intend to apply this framework to the analysis of spatial aptitude. That is, rather than generating models of the processing operations underlying performance on spatial items and then correlating model parameters with ability scores, we prefer to observe high- and low-ability subjects solve the items and then attempt to characterize the strategies associated with ability differences. Our notion is that strategic variation may be at least as potent a source of individual differences in ability as is the efficiency with which any particular processing operation can be executed. So, our projected research approach to the area of spatial aptitude will involve intensive observation of subjects solving a variety of spatial problems and a subsequent attempt to understand differences in underlying strategies. Hopefully, it will then be possible to relate strategy selection and flexibility to both ability differences and problem characteristics. We can then go on to ask the important question of whether strategies can be modified for maximal efficiency in different problem environments. In this sense, our goal in the aptitude area is the same as the goal of the program described in this paper. We will be searching for qualitative individual differences in performance and allowing those differences to generate models for aptitude tasks, rather than assuming a model of the aptitude task and searching for quantitative individual differences in task parameters.

CONCLUDING REMARKS

This chapter has provided a description of our research program on individual differences in visual information processing. The differences between subjects have been characterized as alternative strategies for representing visual information in memory and for comparing a memory representation with external visual information. The central objectives of the research program have been to understand the nature of the strategies underlying differences in patterns of performance and to examine the flexibility of these strategies in the face of changes in task demands and stimulus structure.

It has not yet been demonstrated that the holistic-analytic processing distinction relates to differences in human intelligence. Nonetheless, we view this research program as providing a framework for the study of human ability. It is our contention that strategy selection and adaptability are important aspects of ability. The research program reviewed in this chapter provides an example of how an analysis of strategies can be accomplished. Finally, we see the research program as providing indications of the importance of strategies in an understanding of ability. For the fact that we have found qualitative processing differences in relatively simple task environments suggests that the contribution of strategic variation to individual differences in performance on complex problems may be a substantial one.

ACKNOWLEDGMENTS

I use the pronoun "we" throughout this chapter in describing the research program because of the large number of colleagues, students, and research assistants who have contributed to the work in one way or another. They include: George Campbell, Joyce Farrell, Dale Feuer, Robert Glushko, Eric Gold, Reginald Gougis, Ann J. Gumbinner, Frank Keil, Randy Mumaw, Steve Palmer, Peter Podgorny, Celia Reaves, Gary Sawyers, Roger Shepard, James Staszewski, and Robert Vallone. In particular, I owe an immeasurable debt of gratitude to James P. Cunningham of Cornell University. He has collaborated on aspects of the research reported here, discussed the work with me on numerous occasions, and, perhaps most remarkably, cheerfully participated as a subject in every experiment reported in this chapter. Most of the research described in this chapter was supported by National Science Foundation Grant BNS 76-22079 to the author.

REFERENCES

Anderson, J. R. Arguments concerning representations for mental imagery. *Psychological Review,* 1978, *85,* 249–277.

Bamber D. Reaction times and error rates for "same"–"different" judgments of multidimensional stimuli. *Perception & Psychophysics,* 1969, *6,* 169–174.

Baron, J. Intelligence and general strategies. In G. Underwood (Ed.), *Strategies in information processing.* London: Academic Press, 1978.

Carey, S., & Diamond, R. From piecemeal to configurational representation of faces. *Science,* 1977, *195,* 312–314.

Carroll, J. B. Psychometric tests as cognitive tasks: A new "structure of the intellect?" In L. B. Resnick (Ed.), *The nature of intelligence.* Hillsdale, N.J.: Lawrence Erlbaum Associates, 1976.

Carroll, J. B. How shall we study individual differences in cognitive abilities?—Methodological and theoretical perspectives. *Intelligence,* 1978, *2,* 87–115.

Clark, H. H., & Chase, W. G. On the process of comparing sentences against pictures. *Cognitive Psychology,* 1972, *3,* 472–517.

Cooper, L. A. Individual differences in visual comparison processes. *Perception & Psychophysics,* 1976, *19,* 433–444.

Cooper, L. A. Recent themes in visual information processing. A selected overview. In R. E. Nickerson (Ed.), *Attention and performance* (Vol. VIII). Hillsdale, N.J.: Lawrence Erlbaum Associates, 1980. (a)

Cooper, L. A. Spatial information processing: Strategies for research. In R. Snow, P-A. Federico, & W. E. Montague (Eds.), *Aptitude, learning, and instruction: Cognitive process analyses.* Hillsdale, N.J.: Lawrence Erlbaum Associates, 1980. (b)

Cooper, L. A., & Podgorny, P. Mental transformations and visual comparison processes: Effects of complexity and similarity. *Journal of Experimental Psychology: Human Perception and Performance,* 1976, *2,* 503–514.

Cooper, L. A., & Regan, D. T. Attention, perception, and intelligence. In R. Sternberg (Ed.), *The handbook of human intelligence.* New York: Cambridge University Press, in press.

Cunningham, J. P., Cooper, L. A., & Reaves, C. *Visual comparison processes: Identity vs. similarity decisions.* Paper presented at the annual meeting of the Psychonomic Society, St. Louis, Missouri, November 1980.

Diamond, R., & Carey, S. Developmental changes in the representation of faces. *Journal of Experimental Child Psychology,* 1977, *23,* 1–22.

Egan, D. E. *Accuracy and latency scores as measures of spatial information processing* (Res. Rep. No. 1224). Pensacola, Fl.: Naval Aerospace Medical Research Laboratory, February 1976.

Egan, D. E. *Characterizations of spatial ability: Different mental processes reflected in accuracy and latency scores* (Res. Rep. No. 1250). Pensacola, Fl.: Naval Aerospace Medical Research Laboratory, August 1978.

Egan, D. E. *An analysis of spatial orientation test performance.* Paper presented at the annual meeting of the American Educational Research Association, San Francisco, April 1979. (a)

Egan, D. E. Testing based on understanding: Implications from studies of spatial ability. *Intelligence,* 1979, *3,* 1–15. (b)

Egeth, H. Parallel versus serial processes in multidimensional stimulus discrimination. *Perception & Psychophysics,* 1966, *1,* 245–252.

Glushko, R. J., & Cooper, L. A. Spatial comprehension and comparison processes in verification tasks. *Cognitive Psychology,* 1978, *10,* 391–421.

Hawkins, H. L. Parallel processing in complex visual discrimination. *Perception & Pychophysics,* 1969, *5,* 46–64.

Hock, H. S. The effects of stimulus structure and familiarity on same–different comparison. *Perception & Psychophysics,* 1973, *14,* 413–420.

Hock, H. S., Gordon, G. P., & Gold, L. Individual differences in the verbal coding of familiar visual stimuli. *Memory & Cognition,* 1975, *3,* 257–261.

Hock, H. S., Gordon, G. P., & Marcus, N. Individual differences in the detection of embedded figures. *Perception & Psychophysics,* 1974, *15,* 47–52.

Hunt, E. Quote the Raven? Nevermore! In L. Gregg (Ed.), *Knowledge and cognition.* Hillsdale, N.J.: Lawrence Erlbaum Associates, 1974.

Hunt, E. Mechanics of verbal ability. *Psychological Review,* 1978, *85,* 109–130.

Hunt, E., Lunneborg, C., & Lewis, J. What does it mean to be high verbal? *Cognitive Psychology,* 1975, *7,* 194–227.

Krueger, L. E. A theory of perceptual matching. *Psychological Review,* 1978, *85,* 278–304.

MacLeod, C. M., Hunt, E. B., & Mathews, N. N. Individual differences in the verification of sentence-picture relationships. *Journal of Verbal Learning and Verbal Behavior,* 1978, *17,* 493–508.

Messick, S. B. Reflection-implusivity: A review. *Psychological Bulletin,* 1976, *83,* 1026–1053.

Mulholland, T. M., Pellegrino, J. W., & Glaser, R. Components of geometric analogy solution. *Cognitive Psychology,* 1980, *12,* 252–284.

Nickerson, R. S. "Same"–"different" response times with multi-attribute stimulus differences. *Perceptual and Motor Skills,* 1967, *24,* 543–554.

Palmer, S. E. Hierarchical structure in perceptual representation. *Cognitive Psychology,* 1977, *9,* 441–474.

Patterson, K., & Bradshaw, J. L. Differential hemispheric mediation of nonverbal visual stimuli. *Journal of Experimental Psychology: Human Perception and Performance,* 1975, *1,* 246–252.

Pellegrino, J. W., & Glaser, R. Cognitive correlates and components in the analysis of individual differences. *Intelligence,* 1979, *3,* 187–214.

Shepard, R. N., & Cermak, G. W. Perceptual-cognitive explorations of a toroidal set of free-form stimuli. *Cognitive Psychology,* 1973, *4,* 351–377.

Sternberg, R. J. *Intelligence, information processing and analogical reasoning: The componential analysis of human abilities*. Hillsdale, N.J.: Lawrence Erlbaum Associates, 1977.

Sternberg, R. J., & Weil, E. M. An aptitude x strategy interaction in linear syllogistic reasoning. *Journal of Educational Psychology*, 1980, *62*, 226–236.

Tversky, B. Pictorial and verbal encoding in a short-term memory task. *Perception & Psychophysics*, 1969, *6*, 225–233.

Witkin, H. A. Origins of cognitive style. In C. Scheerer (Ed.), *Cognition: Theory, research, promise*. New York: Harper & Row, 1964.

3 A Componential Theory of Reading Skills and Their Interactions

John R. Frederiksen
Bolt Beranek and Newman Inc.

GENERAL THEORETICAL FRAMEWORK

A componential theory of reading (or of any other complex performance) attempts to identify a set of functionally defined information-processing systems or components, which in interaction with one another accomplish the more complex performance—in this case, reading with comprehension. Component processes are defined by the types of data structures on which they operate (the *domain* or *situation* in which they operate) and by the specific transformations of those data structures that result (the *function* or *action* performed). Components can be thought of as corresponding to the production systems of artificial intelligence, which consist of situation-action pairs (Winston, 1979). Productions (and components) are applied when their triggering situations occur. Their actions alter the internal data structures and therefore set the stage for still other productions. Productions (and components) are, in effect, always available for use and are automatically applied whenever their defining input data structures make an appearance.

An advantage of production-system theories is that no executive control processes need be postulated. Components will be applied in sequences that are determined by their pattern of interaction, as it is determined by their joint effects on a common internal data base. Thus, the controls over component operations reside in the specification of the situations in which they are applied. For example, in the theory of reading, a decoding process is postulated that has, as input, an orthographic array consisting of encoded letters or multiletter units. This process applies grapheme-phoneme correspondence rules and results in a pronunciation for the input array. The process cannot operate until its input situation occurs—namely, until letters and/or multiletter units have been encoded. Thus, there is an automatic sequencing of processes for encoding orthographic units and decoding. However, the encoding of multiletter units and the encoding of individual graphemes both require as input a set of spatially distributed visual features. These two components are, therefore, not sequentially organized.

In a componential theory, readers may be thought of as differing in the degree to which productions (or components) have become automated (cf. Schneider & Shiffrin, 1977; Shiffrin & Schneider, 1977). Automatic processes can operate concurrently with other components, without degrading their efficiency of operation. In contrast, controlled (nonautomatic) processes make demands on general, shared processing resources; when they must operate concurrently with other processes, performance is degraded. A skilled reader possesses many highly automated components, whereas a less-skilled reader has a smaller number of such components, which may be quantitatively less automated. However, the *specific* components that lack automation may vary considerably within the population of poorly skilled, young adult readers. Thus, although readers may be reliably classified along a single dimension of "general reading ability," the actual sources of low tested ability may vary considerably from reader to reader.

Measurement of Components

A definition of a processing component such as the one we have presented has immediate implications for the *measurement,* and thus the identification, of components as determiners of readers' performance. The precise specification of a domain of operation allows: (1) the selection of a task that invokes the component; and (2) the identification of stimulus variables whose manipulation will alter processing difficulty with respect to the designated component. Contrasts among task conditions can then be developed that represent the degree to which performance is degraded as component-specific processing is rendered more difficult. Measures such as these are theory based and are thus susceptible to experimental validation or invalidation. Validity is established by showing that the manipulation of task difficulty has produced the predicted change in performance. Component-specific measures of individual performance are the values of these contrasts obtained for individual subjects.

Example: Encoding Multiletter Units.   Consider, for example, the process of encoding multiletter units. Unit detectors are hypothesized to respond more readily when: (1) units are of high frequency within English orthography; and (2) units are in positions where they are likely to occur normatively (Mason, 1975; Mason & Katz, 1976). Accordingly, an experiment was carried out to test the effects of these variables on a subject's speed in encoding and reporting multiletter units. The display conditions were arranged to insure that efficient perceptual processing would be required for task performance, while at the same time allowing manipulation of these variables. Stimuli were four-letter items, preceded and followed by a 300 msec pattern mask, allowing an exposure duration of 100 msec. On a third of trials, the items were common four-letter English words, but, on the remaining trials, two of the four letters were masked continuously during the exposure, allowing only a single letter pair (a bigram) to be available for encoding. The critical bigrams were either of high or low frequency ($T > 260$ or $T < 75$ in the Mayzner & Tressault, 1965, tables), of high or low positional likelihood (with a priori conditional probabilities of being presented in the tested position, P[Position/Bigram] $> .55$ or $< .10$), and they were presented in either the initial, middle, or final position within the array. The subject's task was to report all letters as soon as possible.

For the least skilled readers (those who scored below the 48th percentile on the Nelson–Denny Reading Test), performance was found to depend on the frequency and positional likelihood of the stimulus bigrams, as had been predicted. For these subjects, high-frequency bigrams were encoded an average of 41 msec faster than were low-frequency bigrams, and initial brgrams were encoded 39 msec faster when they were likely to appear in that position than when they were unlikely to appear there. Comparable figures for a middle group of readers (scoring between the 48th and 77th percentiles) were 35 msec and 20 msec, whereas those for a high-ability group (scoring at or above the 85th percentile) were essentially zero—.3 msec and 4.2 msec. The experimental variables thus had the predicted effects on performance, particularly for those readers who were least likely to have automated perceptual skills for encoding multiletter orthographic units.

When, as in this example, mean performance for the various task conditions has followed the predicted pattern, a second criterion for validation of the component can be applied. This criterion serves the purpose of establishing that individuals differ reliably in measured levels of performance on the given component, even when alternative measurement operations—that are in theory equivalent—are employed. In this next step, two or more contrasts among task conditions are chosen that: (1) are experimentally independent; and (2) produce changes in processing difficulty with respect to the particular component. These contrasts, calculated for the individual subject, constitute alternative indices of component-specific performance. As such, they must show *construct validity;* they must be positively correlated with one another (convergent validity) and, at the same time, show consistent patterns of correlation, or lack of correlation, with measures of other components (discriminant validity). The theory thus generates an explicit hypothesis about the componential complexity or structure for a set of measures, and this hypothesis (termed a *measurement model*) is amenable to statistical evaluation through the use of confirmatory maximum-likelihood factor analysis.

Overview of Component Skills in Reading

The two methods for validation of component-specific measures—verifying effects of task manipulations on task difficulty and analyzing correlations among measures in fitting a measurement model—have been applied to three major processing areas in reading. In Fig. 3.1, these three major processing levels are described and their interrelations represented. The unit of informational analysis is the single fixation, which makes a set of words or phrases available for processing. At the moment of fixation, the reader can apply to the information obtained within the fixation: (1) a set of *word-analysis processes;* (2) a discourse model generated from previous text by *discourse-analysis processes;* and (3) an ability to combine information from word and discourse sources by what we term *integrative processes.* As indicated in the figure, we suggest a set of component processes that constitute each category.

Word-Analysis Processes

Word analysis includes processing components involved in the perception of single-letter and multiletter orthographic units, the translation of orthographic information into a phonological representation, the assignment of appropriate speech patterns (e.g., stress, pitch, contour) to such translated units, and the depth of processing in retrieving lexical categories. Note that the defining characteristics of these word-analysis processes is that they are all limited to processing information available within a single word.

Discourse-Analysis Processes

Discourse-analysis processes are used for analyzing lexical and structural information at a text level (rather than at the word level) for the purpose of constructing a text model that represents the reader's understanding. These component processes include retrieving and integrating word meanings, constructing a propositional base (including analysis of noun groups and establishing case relations), analyzing cohesive relations among sentences or propositions, resolving problems of reference (anaphora and cataphora), constructing inferential elaboration of the text structure, and relating the text structure to prior knowledge of the subject matter.

Integrative Processes

At the moment of visual fixation, the reader has available: (1) perceptual, phonological, and structural information about lexical items included in the fixation; and (2) semantic, conceptual, and pragmatic knowledge resulting from the analysis of prior discourse. Integrative processes permit the reader to combine information from these multiple sources, yielding a set of lexical identifications for the fixated items. The components of the integrative processes are directly related to the sources of available information. They include the extrapo-

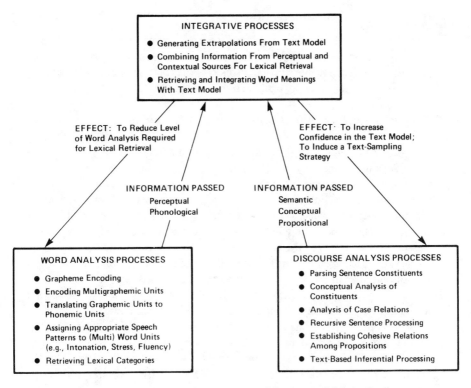

FIG. 3.1.   Categories of reading processes and the nature of their interactions.

lation of the discourse model in terms of generating semantic-syntactic forms, which can be expected to occur in the text that follows, and the utilization of this information—this preactivation of nodes within memory—so as to make lexical identifications more readily. The generative process may, in a skilled reader, resemble the spread of activation postulated by Collins and Loftus (1975). The integrative utilization of perceptual and semantic information requires a mechanism such as the logogen, postulated by Morton (1969).

In Fig. 3.1, we have attempted to show how capability with integrative processing can lead to improved efficiency of processing within both the word-analysis and discourse-analysis categories. For example, by using semantic constraints, the amount of orthographic encoding and analysis required for word recognition could be reduced, and the tendency to encode in phrasal units could be increased. In addition, success in generating hypotheses regarding semantic-syntactic aspects of future text could increase readers' confidence in the text model they have created. This in turn could lead to an increased tendency by readers to use a sampling strategy as well as a decrease in the amount of text required for establishing the adequacy of text analysis.

Forms of Component Interaction

Within or between these processing areas, components can *interact* by virtue of their effects on the common internal data base and their usage of shared processing resources. Together, these mechanisms provide for a number of functionally determined types of component interaction (Table 3.1).

Functionally Determined Component Interactions

Data-Linked Components. Components can interact by virtue of their operating on a common memory store. For example, two components may require common input information structures but may operate independently otherwise. Such components are linked through *correlated input data*. Other components may in their operation construct input data structures that are needed by still other components. Their operation will thus determine the usage of the later-occurring processes, so that together the components form a processing hierarchy. If two processes run concurrently, but the second process improves in efficiency and quality of output as the first process runs further to completion, the processes are called *cascaded processes* (cf. McClelland, 1978). If the operation of the second process depends on data structures created by the first process running to completion (or to some fixed point), the processes are *dependent processes*. Finally, concurrent processes may both operate on a common data store and, if attendant changes in the data store caused by one process facilitate (or otherwise alter) the operation of the other, then the components are *mutually facilitatory*.

TABLE 3.1
Types of Component Interactions

I. Functionally determined interaction
A. Data-lined components
1. Correlated input data
2. Cascaded processes
3. Dependent processes
4. Mutually facilitatory processes
B. Process-linked components
1. Shared subprocesses
2. Shared control processes
C. Resource-linked components
1. Due to general processing capacity
2. Shared memory access/retrieval channels
3. Limited capacity working memory
II. Nonfunctional sources of process intercorrelation
A. Etiologically linked components
1. Reflecting a learning hierarchy
2. Reflecting effectiveness of learning environments
B. Reflecting general, biologically determined ability

Process-Linked Components.   Components can also interact by virtue of their mutual dependence on the operation of other component processes and such components are termed *process-linked components.* For example, two components might require a common or *shared subprocess* for their execution. Alternatively, two components might be invoked by a single, *shared control process.* (This latter case is formally a special case of processes linked through correlated input data; here of course the emphasis is on the third component, which creates the required data structures.)

Resource-Linked Components.   A third form of functional interaction among components occurs when two or more components must compete for common or shared processing resources. Such components are called *resource-linked components.* Shared resources might include use of a limited capacity processor, shared memory access/retrieval channels, or limited capacity working memory (cf. Perfetti & Lesgold, 1977, 1979). When two processes are in competition for resources, increases in the automaticity of one process will free resources for the second process.

Each of these types of functional interaction among components constitutes a possible source of correlation among components. If a componential theory of reading is to be complete, it must delineate these forms of interaction and thus account for correlation among measured components. Theories of component interaction—presented as explicit hypotheses concerning the manner and nature of component interactions within the processing system—can be stated and evaluated by defining a set of structural equations that accounts for the links among components. (Bentler, 1980, has provided a clear account of structural equations and their use in psychological theory.) Estimation of parameters of these equations, as well as a test of goodness of fit, are possible through an application of Jöreskog's Analysis of Covariance Structures (ACOVS) program (Jöreskog, 1970) or LISREL (Jöreskog & Sörbom, 1977).

Nonfunctional Sources of Covariation Among Components

In addition to these functional sources of component interactions, there are nonfunctional sources of intercorrelation among components. These include correlations due to etiological factors—the circumstances under which processing components are acquired—and other, biological factors. For example, component reading skills might be sequenced in instruction. Differential access of pupils to effective learning environments would constitute a second etiological source of intercorrelation among components. A third nonfunctional source of process interaction, and probably the most controversial, is the notion of a general, biologically determined propensity for acquiring certain classes of component processes. Evidence for these etiological sources of reading skill are found in the presence of persistent background correlations among components that remain after specific theoretically hypothesized and functionally determined interactions have been taken into account. The statistical procedures for analysis of covariance structures allow us to verify the presence or absence of such background correlations by permitting us to fit alternative structural models that by hypothesis allow or disallow such background covariation. As with any statistical test, the results permit us to accept or reject the hypothesis of background intercorrelation among components, or they indicate an inconclusive outcome.

STRUCTURAL MODELS AND THE ANALYSIS
OF COVARIANCE STRUCTURES

Components can be correlated due to any of these functional sources of interaction among processes or to other nonfunctional, etiological factors. My purpose here is to show how hypotheses concerning component interactions can be represented as a set of structural equations. These equations can be used to generate, in turn, an hypothesized covariance structure falling within the family of models dealt with in ACOVS (Jöreskog, 1970) or LISREL (Jöreskog & Sörbom, 1977).

Since 1965, I have been intrigued with the possibility of using confirmatory maximum-likelihood factor analysis as a tool for testing theories of human cognition. In particular, I have been interested in developing measurement systems with theoretical underpinnings that thoroughly constrain the parameters of the second-order factor model (e.g., Jöreskog, 1970):

$$\Sigma = \beta \, \Lambda \, \Phi \, \Lambda' \, \beta' + \Theta^2. \tag{3.1}$$

In this equation, Σ denotes the variance-covariance matrix (usually the correlation matrix) for a set of componentially specific measures. β contains parameters of the measurement model. Each row of β represents a single measure, and the columns correspond to components or, in the older language, factors. A nonzero entry in the ith row and jth column of β indicates that the measure i is, by hypothesis, determined at least in part by the level of skill in component j. Matrix θ^2 is a diagonal matrix containing unique (or error) variance associated with each of the measures. If we define

$$\Phi^* = \Lambda \, \Phi \, \Lambda', \tag{3.2}$$

Equation 3.1 can be rewritten as:

$$\Sigma = \beta \, \Phi^* \, \beta' + \Theta^2 \tag{3.3}$$

where Φ^* contains the intercorrelations among the measured components. This equation is that of a first-order factor model and is used in testing an hypothesized measurement model. Equation 3.2 relates intercorrelations among measured components to parameters of the interactive model. The specification of a structural model for component interactions leads to a series of constraints on the matrix Λ. (How this is done is described later.) The matix Φ contains background intercorrelations among components, after removing correlations due to theoretically proscribed component interactions.

In summary, each of the matrices in Equation 3.1 corresponds to a different aspect of our problem: the relation of observed variables to components in a measurement model (β), the forms of component interaction as represented by a set of structural equations (Λ), and the presence of background correlations among components (Φ). By constraining parameters within each of these matrices in the general model, one can test these different aspects of the componential theory.

Evaluating the Measurement Model

Fixing parameters of β, while allowing the factors—measurements of components—to intercorrelate freely (i.e., by regarding all elements of Φ^* to be free parameters), permits us to test a measurement model. Comparative model fitting is accomplished by varying the hypothesized structure of β. No assumptions about component interactions are necessary at this stage.

Testing Structural Models

Measured performance on a component j (η_j) is resolved within the structural equation system into: (1) that which is contributed by measured performance on other components (η_k, $k \neq j$); and (2) that which is contributed by *unique* skill on the jth component itself (ζ_j). These relationships are expressed in a linear structural equation relating performance on component j to each of these contributory sources:

$$\eta_j = \sum_{k \neq j} \delta_{jk} \, \eta_k + \delta_{jj} \, \zeta_j \qquad\qquad 3.4$$

where $\delta_{jk} = 0$ if component k does *not* directly influence performance on component j, and $\delta_{jk} \neq 0$ where specific interactions among components are postulated. After specifying the pattern of component interactions by specifying j equations of form 3.4, the resulting set of equations is rewritten so as to express each of the ζ's (the unique components) as a linear function of the η's (the measured components). These equations can then be combined in a single matrix equation:

$$D \, \zeta = \Delta \, \eta \qquad\qquad 3.5$$

where D is a diagonal matrix whose jth element is δ_{jj}, Δ is a square matrix having diagonal elements 1 and off-diagonal elements $-\delta_{jk}$, and ζ and η are random vectors representing unique and measured components, respectively. Since in the factor model of Equation 3.1, measured components must be expressed as linear combinations of unique components, Equation 3.5 must be solved to give:

$$\eta = \Delta^{-1} D \, \zeta = \Lambda \, \zeta. \qquad\qquad 3.6$$

Thus, the parameters of the structural equation system are related to those of the factor model by the relation $\Lambda = \Delta^{-1} D$. The covariances among the measured components are then given by:

$$E\left(\Lambda \zeta \zeta' \Lambda'\right) = \Lambda E(\zeta \zeta') \Lambda' = \Lambda \Phi \Lambda', \qquad 3.7$$

where Φ contains the covariances among *unique* components.

The structural model for component interactions is identifiable if elements of Δ and D (the δ's) are a computable function of the values in Λ and if there are a sufficient number of fixed parameters in Λ to allow a unique solution. Identifiable models may be tested by appropriately constraining the elements of Λ and using ACOVS (Jöreskog, 1970) to fit Equation 3.1. The estimates of free parameters in Λ are then used to calculate the required values for the δ's.

Testing Background Correlations Among Components

Hypotheses concerning the presence of background correlations among components can be evaluated by comparing a model in which the unique components are uncorrelated ($\Phi = I$) with one in which correlations are allowed ($\Phi \neq I$). In performing these tests, the structures of β and of Λ are, of course, determined by the measurement and structural models. If the model provides an acceptable fit with $\Phi = I$, it may not be necessary to test the alternative.

In the remainder of this chapter, each of the steps we have described is applied to data obtained from our study of the components of reading. First, the measurement tasks developed for each of the three general skill areas are described. For each skill domain, the procedures for testing and fitting a measurement model are presented. The validity of the resulting measurement models is established through comparative model fitting. By testing a series of alternative measurement models, which differ from the hypothesized model in particular features, the critical characteristics of a "correct" model are established. Finally, I describe and apply the procedures for developing and testing structural theories of component interaction. Structural models are first presented for the word-analysis domain and then for the integrative and discourse-analysis domains. The status of "general reading ability" as a construct can be evaluated in light of these structural models.

COMPONENTIAL ANALYSIS OF READING SKILLS

Subjects

Subjects in this study were 48 readers of high school age chosen to represent a wide range of ability. They were recruited from two schools, an inner-city school and a suburban school. Subjects were selected to represent a wide range of reading ability, as measured by percentile ranks on the Nelson–Denny Reading

Test. Each potential subject was administered the entire Nelson–Denny Test: a vocabulary test, a timed reading passage, and a series of comprehension items. Their total score was the sum of the vocabulary and comprehension scores. The final distribution of total scores for four groups of 12 subjects was as follows:

1. Group 1. 11th–47th percentile.
2. Group 2. 48th–77th percentile.
3. Group 3. 85th–97th percentile.
4. Group 4. 98th percentile or greater.

Characteristics of the Reading Components Battery

In the course of eight experiments conducted over the last 3 years (see Frederiksen, 1977, 1979, 1980), a series of computer-administered tasks has been developed, each of which appears to meet the conditions we have set for component-specific measurement: (1) each task clearly involves processing associated with a specified component; (2) its design permits the manipulation of task characteristics in ways that will alter difficulty with respect to the involvement of the particular component; and (3) it has received experimental validation in that mean performance has been shown to vary in the predicted manner with changes in task characteristics. The Reading Components Battery is made up of a subset of the tasks and measures developed in the previous set of experiments. The tasks and measures are grouped under three general skill areas: word analysis, discourse analysis, and context utilization.

The Measurement Model for Word-Analysis Tasks

The experimental tasks used in studying word-analysis components are listed in Table 3.2, along with the measures derived from each task. These measures were chosen for their componential specificity, and the components they represent are also indicated in the table.

Anagram-Identification Task.   Subjects were presented with a briefly exposed four-letter stimulus array, followed by a masking field. Stimuli were high-frequency words (*salt*), pseudowords (*etma*), or unpronounceable nonword anagrams (*rtnu*). Sixteen items of each type were presented at each of five durations, which ranged from 5 to 45 msec. For each exposure, we measured the number of correctly reported letters (the order of report was disregarded). A logit transformation of the number of letters correct N_c, $\log [N_c/N - N_c)]$, when plotted against exposure duration, yielded a linear function. Fitting straight lines to this plot provided two descriptive parameters: a location parameter and a slope parameter. The measure employed in the present analysis was the slope parameter: the rate of increase in letter information encoded during an anagram display, measured in logits per second. Rates of encoding anagrams were found to differ for the four groups of readers. They were 364, 378, 406, and 443 logits/sec,

TABLE 3.2
Reading Components Battery:
Word-Analysis Tasks and Measures

Experimental Task	Derived Measures	Components[a]
A. Anagram Identification: Subjects report letters seen within a briefly presented, masked display containing four-letter anagrams.	1. Rate of letter encoding, inferred from increase in logit (Prob. Correct) per unit increase in exposure duration.	I
B. Posner Letter Matching: Subjects respond same or different on basis of similarity of letter names.	2. RT (Aa) − RT (AA).	I
C. Bigram Encoding: Subjects report letters seen within a briefly presented, masked display containing four-letter words; on critical trials, all letters except a single bigram are simultaneously masked.	3. Increase in RT for low-frequency compared with high-frequency bigrams.	II
	4. Scanning Rate: Increase in RT for each shift (left to right) in bigram position.	I, II
	5. Increase in RT for bigrams having low positional likelihood.	II
D. Pseudoword Pronunciation: Subjects pronounce pseudowords that vary in orthographic structure (in length, syllables, and vowel type).	Increase in vocalization onset latency for:	
	6. Digraph vowels compared with simple vowels.	III
	7. Increase in array length from four to six letters.	II, III
	8. Two syllables compared with one syllable.	III
E. Word Recognition: Subjects pronounce words that vary in frequency and orthograpic structure:	Correlation of pseudoword onset latencies obtained for each of 19 orthographic forms with those for:	
	9. High-frequency words presented in isolation.	IV
	10. Low-frequency words presented in isolation.	IV

[a] I. Letter encoding efficiency.
   II. Perceiving multiletter units.
   III. Decoding or phonological translation.
   IV. Efficiency in word recognition.

respectively, for the four reader groups, ordered from least skilled to most skilled. Inasmuch as the anagrams were random strings of letters, this measure was interpreted as an index of letter encoding efficiency.

Letter-Matching Task.   This task was similar to the letter-matching task of Posner (Posner & Mitchell, 1967). Subjects were presented with 144 pairs of letters that were similar in physical form (e.g., *AA, aa*), similar in name but not form (e.g., *Aa*), or dissimilar (e.g., *ad, AD, Ad*). Letters were presented for 50 msec, and subjects responded by pressing a "same" button when the letters were visually or nominally similar (*AA, Aa*) or a "different" button otherwise. The difference in "same" reaction times (RTs) for nominally and physically similar letter pairs (the "NI-PI" RT) has been interpreted as a measure of time for retrieval of a letter name because in the visually similar case subjects are thought to respond on the basis of a rapid matching of visual features (but, see Carroll, 1980a). This difference was calculated for each of our subjects. The means for each of the four reading groups, again in order of ability, were 130, 114, 122, and 87 msec.

Bigram-Identification Task.   The bigram-identification task has been described earlier in this chapter. In the context of attempting to encode and report the letters making up four-letter English words, subjects were presented displays in which only a single pair of adjacent letters (a bigram) was visible; the other letters were masked by simultaneously presenting an overwriting masking character. On these occasions, subjects reported only the target bigram. Low-frequency bigrams were found to be more difficult to encode than high-frequency bigrams, as measured by the RT in reporting them. Likewise, bigrams presented in unlikely locations within the array took longer to encode than bigrams presented in likely positions. These two measures were interpreted as indicating a reader's efficiency in encoding multiletter units. Large RT differences indicate that the "bandwidth" of frequencies/positional likelihoods over which a reader maintains efficient performance is narrow; small RT differences indicate efficient performance over a wide range of stimulus conditions. Finally, a third measure was calculated; the increase in RT per unit shift in bigram position from left to right. This measure of scanning time is interpreted as potentially representing both components I and II because high rates can in principle be achieved when individual letters and/or multiletter units are rapidly encoded.

Pseudoword-Pronunciation Task.   In this task, subjects were presented 304 pseudowords, which were derived from a like number of words by changing one or more vowels. The pseudowords represent 19 orthographic forms (varying in length [four to six letters], number of syllables [one or two], presence of markers, and vowel type [VV vs. V]). There were 16 examples of each form, two for each of eight initial phenomes. Mean onset latencies for pronouncing pseudowords were measured, along with the experimenter's judgment of response correctness. Three contrasts among orthographic forms were chosen on the basis of their presumed common effect on difficulty of decoding. These were the increases in onset latency brought about by: (1) increasing pseudoword length from four to six letters; (2) increasing the number of syllables from one to two; and (3) replacing a single vowel with a digraph. (In manipulating any one of these variables, items were counterbalanced with respect to the other factors.) The increases in decoding times were typically greatest for the less able readers: For the four groups of readers, length effects were 55, 37, 29, and 13 msec, respectively; syllable effects were 114, 71, 53, and 22 msec; and vowel-complexity effects were 44, 65, 49, and 25 msec. Accordingly, each of these measures is regarded as an index of decoding efficiency.

Word-Recognition Task. This task is similar to the pseudoword-pronunciation task, except for the substitution of 304 words for pseudowords. The stimuli included 152 high-frequency words (SFI > 50; Carroll, Davies, & Richman, 1971) and a like number of low-frequency words (SFI ≤ 50). The 152 words in each group included eight representatives of each of the 19 orthographic forms employed in the pseudoword-pronunciation task, and these eight representatives were matched on initial phoneme with their pseudoword counterparts. We sought to construct a scale-free index of the degree of orthographic decoding in the context of word recognition. It was shown in prior research (Frederiksen, 1976, 1978) that variability in onset latencies for decoding brought about by changes in orthographic form are reliable. This pattern of change in RT for decoding pseudowords can be thought of as a "trace" of the operation of a decoding process. To the extent that similar changes in *word*-recognition latency are found as orthographic form is similarly manipulated, we have evidence for the operation of a decoding process in word recognition. Our measure of depth of decoding in word recognition is, therefore, the correlation (calculated for an individual subject) of mean pseudoword latencies for each of the 19 orthographic forms with those for words that are matched in orthographic form. A high correlation indicates continued operation of the decoding process and, thus, a high depth of orthographic analysis in word recognition. A low or zero correlation indicates low depth of decoding—that words are recognized on the basis of their visual form, per se. This measure of depth of decoding was calculated separately for high- and low-frequency words. There were differences among the four groups of readers in their reliance on decoding processes in word recognition. Mean correlations for high-frequency words were .42, .41, .35, and .22 for the four reader groups; the corresponding measures for low-frequency words were .38, .37, .45, and .35. Thus, the evidence suggests that, for a vocabulary of high-frequency English words, the better readers are able to *reduce* their dependence on decoding processes below the level required for low-frequency words, but the poorer readers are not. These correlations, for high- and low-frequency words, constitute our measures of processing efficiency in word recognition.

Validation of the Measurement Model. The componential interpretations offered for the 10 measures of word analysis detailed in Table 3.2 constitute an explicit hypothesis concerning the form of matrix B in Equation 3.1 and, as such, constitute a measurement model. This hypothesis has been schematically represented in Fig. 3.2. Four components are postulated: (1) letter encoding; (2) encoding multiletter units; (3) decoding; (4) word recognition. The variables $y_1 - y_{10}$ correspond to the numbered measures in Table 3.2. Performance on a measure y_i is determined by the skill level in one or more of the components and

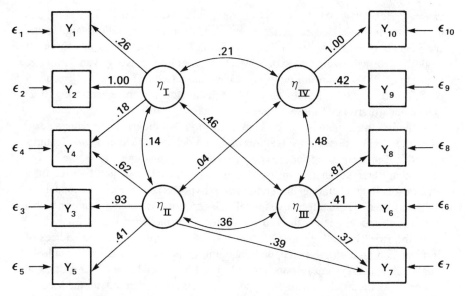

FIG. 3.2. Schematic representation of the measurement model for tasks in the word-analysis domain. The arrows denote the direction of causation in the model; squares denote the observed variables (1–10 in Table 3.2); circles denote the components (η_I – η_{IV}), including: letter encoding (I), encoding multiletter Units (II), decoding (III), and word recognition (IV). The model uses 18 parameters to account for 45 correlations. The test of fit yielded $\chi^2_{27} = 38.3$, $p = .073$. Standard errors of parameters averaged .20.

by a unique or task-specific error factor ϵ_i. In evaluating the measurement model, a free parameter is entered into matrix B for each link between a measure and a component shown in Fig. 3.2. Following this procedure, the hypothesized componential structure is seen as corresponding to the following hypothesized form for the matrix B:

| | Component | | | |
Measure	I	II	III	IV
1	V	Ø	Ø	Ø
2	V	Ø	Ø	Ø
3	Ø	V	Ø	Ø
4	V	V	Ø	Ø
5	Ø	V	Ø	Ø
6	Ø	Ø	V	Ø
7	Ø	V	V	Ø
8	Ø	Ø	V	Ø
9	Ø	Ø	Ø	V
10	Ø	Ø	Ø	V

where V denotes a free parameter or variable to be estimated. In testing this measurement model, no restrictions are placed on the correlations among the components (the matrix Φ^* in Equation 3.2). This hypothesized measurement model was tested, using Jöreskog's ACOVS program (Jöreskog, van Thillo, & Gruvaeus, 1971). The resulting value of chi-square (with 27 degrees of freedom) is 38.3, and $p = .073$. Values of the fitted parameters are presented in Fig. 3.2. (The standard errors of these parameters averaged .20).

Although the hypothesized measurement model is judged to be satisfactory, we wished to investigate what features of the model are critical and what features less critical in accounting for the correlations among measures. Thus, we set out to evaluate three alternative measurement models, each of which focused on a specific distinction among the components hypothesized under the model we have presented. These alternative models are described in Table 3.3, along with a test of each model against the full four-component model of Fig. 3.2.

In the first alternative model, measures $y_1 - y_5$ are regarded as indices of performance on a single perceptual encoding component. Under this model, a single perceptual system responds to individual letters and multiletter units, and readers who are efficient with one type of unit are also efficient with the second. As shown in Table 3.3, this model is rejected, with $\chi^2(4) = 10.83$, $p = .03$. In the second alternative, the parsing of an orthographic array into multiletter units and the rule-based decoding of these units are regarded as two aspects of a single

TABLE 3.3
Comparison Among ACOVS Models for Word-Analysis Components

Alternative Model[a]	Number Components	Number of Parameters	Chi-Square	d.f.	Prob.
1. A single perceptual encoding component; combine components I and II	3	14	10.83	4	.03
2. A single orthographic analysis component; combine components II and III	3	14	17.89	4	.001
3. No distinction drawn between decoding efficiency and decoding depth; combine components III and IV	3	15	9.24	3	.03
4. Test of independence of original four components	4	12	12.62	6	.05
5. Test of independence of components I and II, I and IV, and II and IV	4	15	2.95	3	.83
6. Test of structural model, with links between components I and III, II and III, and II and IV	4	17	1.88	1	.17

[a] Alternatives are each tested against the full four-component model containing 18 parameters.

decoding process. And again, readers who are most capable of encoding multilet-ter units are also most capable of analyzing them. This alternative is also re-jected, with $\chi^2(4) = 17.89$, $p = .001$. The third alternative sought to investigate the distinction between efficiency in decoding and word recognition. In this model, the efficient decoding of pseudowords and recognition of words involve the same process—orthographic decoding of words in the same manner as pseudowords or, perhaps, decoding of pseudowords by analogy with similarly spelled words (Glushko, 1980). Again, the alternative model is rejected, with $\chi^2(3) = 9.24$, $p = .03$.

Our conclusion is that each of the four components hypothesized must be represented in the measurement model. These results do not imply that the components are independent. To test this possibility, a fourth alternative model was fit, which was similar to the model in Fig. 3.2 except for the additional constraint that the components are uncorrelated (i.e., that $\Phi = I$). The test of this hypothesis yielded $\chi^2(6) = 12.62$, with $p = .05$, and again we are led to reject this alternative. In order to focus on where the most important intercomponential correlations are found, we tested a fifth alternative in which the perceptual components (I and II) are independent and correlated with the decoding compo-nent (III) but are independent of the word-recognition component (IV). This model is an acceptable alternative to the original, with $\chi^2(3) = 2.95$, $p = .83$. A more thorough analysis of component interactions, using the technique of build-ing a structural equation system (alternative six) is discussed in a later section of this paper. For the moment, we conclude that: (1) each of the components represents a distinct source of expertise among readers; (2) there are clearly demonstrated correlations among components, indicating the need for a theory of componential interaction.

The Measurement Model
for Discourse-Analysis Processes

Measures related to the processing of discourse are all drawn from an experi-mental study of anaphoric reference (Frederiksen, 1980). The purpose of this experiment was to identify text characteristics that influence a reader's difficulty in resolving problems of, specifically, *pronominal reference*. In the process, we hoped to draw some inferences about the procedures used by readers in searching for antecedents and selecting referents from prior text when encountering a pronoun.

The experimental task required subjects to read a series of test passages, one sentence at a time. To motivate careful reading, subjects were at times probed for, the meaning (referent) associated with a pronoun. This was accomplished by underscoring the probed item. Whenever an underscore appeared, the subject's task was to supply (vocally) the correct referent noun or noun phrase from the preceding text. However, the major focus of the study was not the accuracy of performance in the probe task (the four reader groups did not differ in their accuracy in supplying referents) but rather the time spent in processing sentences containing a pronoun or other referential item. More particularly, we were interested in the changes in reading time that occurred as the difficulty of the reference problem was increased through manipulation of the structure of prior text.

The patterns of reading times obtained under a variety of text conditions supported a model having three distinguishable features:

1. When readers encounter a pronoun, they retrieve from memory the available antecedents (nouns or noun phrases matching the pronoun in gender and number).

2. Readers evaluate those antecedents within the semantic or propositional frame of the sentence containing the pronoun, using those semantic constraints that are present to select the correct referent.

3. Some readers appear to adopt a test strategy of assigning priority to antecedents that have topical status at the time the pronoun is encountered. For example, topical status is higher for noun phrases appearing as the subject of a sentence (particularly the initial sentence of a paragraph) than it is for predicate nouns.

The choice of measures—contrasting sets of text conditions—for use in this study was based on this processing model. We sought measures that, although experimentally independent of one another, would represent each of these three components: automatic assignment of a topicalized antecedent as referent (numbered VII within the final component list); semantic evaluation/integration of antecedents within a current discourse representation (numbered VIII); and exhaustive retrieval of antecedents (numbered IX). These measures are described in Table 3.4.

The influence of topical status of an antecedent on the problem of reference was studied by presenting two-sentence texts in which the initial sentence contained two antecedent noun phrases (NP), which both agreed in gender and number with a pronoun presented as the subject of a second, target sentence. Reading times for the target sentence were longer when the correct antecedent was in the predicate of the initial sentence than when it was the subject (i.e., when it was topicalized). This difference (the first measure in Table 3.4) is therefore interpreted as a measure of readers' sensitivity to topicality in assigning text referents.

In developing our second measure, we were interested in the effect of a prior, consistent use of the pronoun on reading times for a subsequent sentence containing the same pronoun. In particular, we wanted to see if a pronoun, once assigned a referent, would automatically be given the same referent when it was repeated in a subsequent sentence. The initial sentences again contained two antecedents, the first of which was referred to pronominally in the final sentence.

TABLE 3.4
Reading Components Battery:
Discourse-Analysis Tasks and Measures

Experimental Task	Derived Measures	Components[a]
Anaphoric Reference Experiment: Subjects read texts containing pronouns and supply referents for pronouns whenever they are underscored.	Differences in reading times for sentences containing anaphora under contrasting text conditions:	
	1. The correct antecedent is *not topicalized/topicalized* in the initial sentence.	VII
	2. The pronoun appears *in the predicate/as the subject* of a sentence intervening between referent and target.	VII, VIII
	3. The correct antecedent is referred to *collocatively/by lexical repetition* within the timed sentence.	VIII
	4. The correct antecedent is sematically *ambiguous/unambiguous* within the target sentence.	VIII, IX
	5. *Two/only one* antecedent noun phrase(s) agreeing with the pronoun are (is) present in the initial sentence.	IX
	6. An incorrect antecedent noun phrase appearing in sentence 1 *is/is not* repeated as the topic of an intervening sentence, which occurs prior to the target.	VII, VIII

[a] VII. Assignment of topicalized antecedent as referent.
   VIII. Semantic integration/evaluation of antecedents with discourse representation.
   IX. Exhaustive retrieval of antecedents.

The second (intervening) sentence contained the same pronoun, occurring either as subject or within the predicate. The third sentence, as before, began with the pronoun used to refer to the same antecedent. The results of this experiment showed that pronouns are *not* automatically assigned their previous referent when re-encountered in a text. Reading times depended on the position of the pronoun in the intervening sentence. They were longest when the intervening sentence began with an alternative noun phrase and contained the pronoun in the predicate. This manipulation had the effect of reducing the topical status of the antecedent referred to pronominally and introduced a new topic—the subject of the second sentence. Reading times were shortest when the intervening sentence began with the pronoun and thus maintained the topical status of the referent. Hence, the difference in reading times for these conditions is taken as a measure of component VII. It is also thought to involve component VIII because of the need for subjects to evaluate and reject alternative antecedents efficiently when the pronoun is not made topical in sentence two.

When a pronoun (or other referential expression) is encountered, antecedents must be evaluated within the semantic context of the pronoun. One method we have used to measure this process of semantic evaluation has been to compare reading times for sentences containing collocative reference (reference to a previous lexical category, using a different lexical item; Halliday & Hasan, 1976) with sentences in which the problem of reference is made as trivial as possible by simply repeating the lexical item. The former condition requires readers to search their discourse model for lexical categories that are associated with the newly encountered lexical item and to select from among those categories the ones that are semantically acceptable within the semantic context of the current sentence. Reading times for sentences containing collocative references were longer than those for sentences containing lexical repetitions, and we thus use this contrast (measure 3) as an index of skill in component VIII.

A second text manipulation was employed to study the semantic evaluation component. We generated sentences that were ambiguous in that either of two antecedents appearing in the initial sentence would be semantically acceptable. Reading times for such semantically ambiguous sentences were substantially longer than those for unambiguous sentences, reflecting the fact that it is difficult to decide which antecedent should be regarded as the most meaningful in ambiguous sentneces. This difference in reading times (measure 4) is thus taken to be a function of readers' speed in evaluating antecedents. However, it is also thought to be related to another factor—the readers' exhaustiveness in retrieving all available antecedents (our ninth postulated component). The rationale for this interpretation is as follows: If a reader retrieves only a single antecedent from the earlier sentence, it will be found to be semantically acceptable within the current sentence context, and no additional time will be expended in searching for alternative referents. It is only when two or more referents are retrieved that the semantic evaluation of antecedents becomes a difficult problem.

Another text comparison was carried out that focused directly on readers' exhaustiveness in retrieving antecedents. We compared texts in which the initial sentence contained two antecedents with alternative texts having only a single antecedent. In both cases, the correct referent for the pronoun in the second sentence was the subject (topic) of the initial sentence. Here we were comparing a situation in which there was a semantically irrelevant NP agreeing in gender and number with the target pronoun against a situation in which there was no additional NP agreeing with the pronoun. The results showed clearly that reading times for the target sentence were greater when a second potential referent was present in the first sentence. Readers thus do appear to retrieve multiple antecedents. Our fifth measure was therefore interpreted as an index of exhaustiveness in retrieving antecedents for solving problems of pronominal reference.

The final text comparison (measure 6) allowed us to test our componential analysis on a text condition in which one component was expected to contribute to high performance, and a second component was expected to hinder performance. The texts began with a sentence containing two antecedent NPs and ended with a sentence referring pronominally to the topicalized NP in the first sentence. In one set of texts, the incorrect antecedent (the one contained originally in the predicate of the first sentence) was used as the *subject* of a second intervening sentence, but, in the control texts, a neutral sentence was used instead as the intervening sentence. For readers sensitive to the topicality of antecedents, the effect of topicalizing an incorrect antecedent between the referent and pronoun will be to increase reading times. At the same time, readers who are efficient in evaluating antecedents will more quickly reject the inappropriate antecedent and discover the correct referent. We thus predict that measure 6 will be negatively related to component VII and positively related to component VIII.

Validation of the Measurement Model.   The hypothesized componential analysis of the six measures derived from the anaphoric reference experiment is represented schematically in Fig. 3.3. This measurement model provided an acceptable fit to the matrix of intercorrelations among measures, with $\chi^2(3) = 3.17$, $p = .37$. The three components of this model can be regarded as independent because a model constraining the component intercorrelations to be zero could not be rejected ($\chi^2[3] = 1.82$, $p = .61$; see Table 3.5).

Inasmuch as our three-component model provides what appears to be a good fit, we set out to test a series of alternative measurement models in order to determine the critical features of the present model. The results of these alternative analyses are presented in Table 3.5. In the first alternative model, the distinction was dropped between sensitivity to topicality (component VII) and semantic integration (component VIII). We were led to reject this alternative ($\chi^2[4] = 10.01$, $p = .04$) and concluded that these two components must be distinguished in a componential theory for anaphoric reference. In our second alternative, retrieval of multiple antecedents (IX) and semantic integration (VIII) are functionally linked and therefore form a single component. This model could not be rejected when compared with the original three-component model ($\chi^2[3] = 1.97$, $p = .58$). Finally, in the third alternative model, a single component was postulated (combining components VII and IX) that contrasted the automatic assignment of topic as referent (VII) with the exhaustive retrieval of multiple antecedents (IX). This model also could not be rejected when compared with the original three-component model ($\chi^2[2] = 2.04$, $p = .36$).

We are forced to conclude that the available evidence in the intercorrelations among our six measures is insufficient for establishing the separate status of component IX. (This would probably not have been the case if our fifth variable,

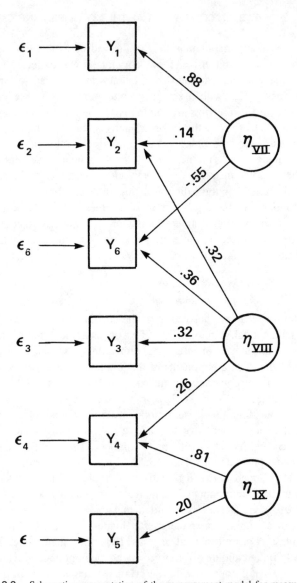

FIG. 3.3. Schematic representation of the measurement model for measures in the discourse-analysis domain. Arrows denote the direction of causation in the model; squares denote the observed variables (1–6 in Table 3.4). η_{VII} – η_{IX} denotes the components: automatic assignment of topicalized antecedent as referent (VII), schematic integration/evaluation of antecedent with discourse representation (VIII), and exhaustive retrieval of antecedents (IX). ϵ_1 – ϵ_6 represent measurement error specific to a single measure. Chi-square (with 3 d.f.) is 3.17, p = .37. A test of independence of the three components yielded χ^2_3 = 1.82, p = .61.

TABLE 3.5
Comparisons Among ACOVS Models for Measures of Discourse Analysis

Alternate Model[a]	Number of Components	Number of Parameters	Chi-Square	d.f.	Prob.
1. No distinction between sensitivity to topicality and semantic integration; combine factors VII and VIII	2	8	10.01	4	.04
2. No distinction between semantic integration and retrieval of multiple antecedents; combine VIII and IX	2	9	1.97	3	.58
3. A single factor contrasting rapid assignment of topic vs. retrieval of multiple antecedents; combine VII and IX	2	10	2.04	2	.36
4. Test of independence of original three factors	3	9	1.82	3	.61

[a] Alternatives are tested against the full three-component model containing 12 parameters.

the one in which we manipulated the number of antecedents, had been a more reliable measure of the exhaustive retrieval component.) Therefore, for present purposes, we adopted the second alternative and accepted the fact that there would be some ambiguity in the resulting measure of semantic integration (VIII), namely, the tendency to retrieve several antecedents that are the subject of such a semantic evaluation.

The Measurement Model
for Context-Utilization (Integrative) Tasks

The integrative skills we have postulated allow a reader to combine information contained in semantic and syntactic constraints associated with a discourse context with information contained in the orthographic code in a system that efficiently recognizes words and phrases. Two components of these context-utilization processes are: (1) activation of semantically related items in memory (the generative use of context); (2) use of contextual information to increase the speed of lexical identifications. The first component (numbered component VI) is intended to contrast readers who are low in generative depth with those who are capable of activating a wide network of nodes in semantic memory, some of which may be strongly related to context and others only moderately so. High skill in this component represents what Guilford (1967) has termed a "divergent production" ability. The second component (numbered component V) is exemplified, at one extreme, by readers who emphasize speed of performance over depth of search when reading in context and, at the other extreme, by readers who emphasize depth of search over processing efficiency.

Word Recognition in Sentence Context.   Measures developed for these context-utilization components are drawn from two experimental tasks described in Table 3.6. The first task is an extension of the pseudoword and word-decoding tasks outlined in Table 3.2. In this task, subjects are asked to pronounce target words that are either tightly or loosely constrained by a prior context sentence. For example, consider the following sentence, in which the final word has been deleted: *I reminded her gently that this was something that she really should not_____.* This sentence frame allows the target word to be any of a number of alternatives—*buy, do, take, see, read, tell,* and so forth. The sentence represents a moderately constraining context. Contrast this with the following sentence: *Grandmother called the children to the sofa because she had quite a story*

TABLE 3.6
Reading Components Battery:
Context-Utilization Tasks and Measures

Experimental Task	*Derived Measures*	*Components*[a]
Word Recognition in Sentence Context: Subjects pronounce words that vary in orthographic form, presented in a high- or low-constraining context.	Correlation of pseudoword onset latencies obtained for each of 19 orthographic forms with those for:	
	1. High-frequency words presented in moderately constraining context.	IV, (−)V
	2. Low-frequency words presented in highly constraining context.	IV, (−)V
	Drop in mean onset latency when words are presented in context rather than in isolation for:	
	3. High-frequency words presented in a moderately constraining context.	V
	4. Low-frequency words presented in a highly constraining context.	V
Reading Phrases in Paragraph Context: Subjects report all words seen within a display containing a phrase that completes the context paragraph.	Increase in Visual Span when context was added for:	
	5. Easy (highly readable) texts.	VI, VIII
	6. Difficult (less readable) texts.	VI, VIII
Word Recognition in Paragraph Context: Subjects report all words seen within a display containing randomly sequenced words derived from a phrase that would complete the context paragraph.	Increase in Visual Span when context was added for:	
	7. Easy (highly readable) texts.	V, VI
	8. Difficult (less readable) texts.	V, VI

[a]   IV.   Efficiency in word recognition.
V.   Speed set in applying context to identify a highly predictable target.
VI.   Extrapolating a representation of discourse context: Activation of semantically related items in memory.
VIII.   Semantic integration of antecedents within a currently formulated discourse representation.

to_____. Here only a few words remain that fit the sentence—*tell, relate, present,* and the like—this frame represents a highly constraining context.

In our experiment, 304 words were selected representing two frequency classes (high and low), 19 orthographic forms, and eight initial phonemes, as before. For each word, two context sentences were created representing high and moderate degrees of constraint, as illustrated in the foregoing examples. The "constraining power" of these context sentences was scaled in a prior experiment (Frederiksen, 1978): Highly constraining contexts allowed an average of 7 words (which was the estimated domain size), whereas moderately constraining contexts allowed an average of 14 words. By comparing subjects' vocalization latencies for words in highly and moderately constraining contexts with those for words and pseudowords presented in isolation, component-specific measures of performance reflecting context utilization were derived. (For a more detailed discussion of the experimental results, see Frederiksen, 1978, 1980.)

The first two measures are the correlations of pseudoword-vocalization latencies obtained for each of 19 orthographic forms with those for high-frequency words presented in moderately constraining context (measure 1) or for low-frequency words presented in highly constraining context. Such correlations, it can be recalled, measure the extent to which orthographic decoding similar to that involved in analyzing pseudowords is operating as subjects process and pronounce English words. In general, the more highly skilled readers (groups 3 and 4) showed lower involvement of orthographic decoding than did the poorer readers (groups 1 and 2). Mean correlations for the former groups were .16 for words in moderately constraining context and .13 for highly constraining contexts. For the less skilled readers, the corresponding means were .25 for the moderately constraining context and .22 for the highly constraining context. The measures we have constructed are hypothesized to represent two components: general efficiency in word recognition (IV) and increase in speed of word recognition with provision of a reliable context (V). These measures do not involve the generative capacity in context utilization (VI) because in each case the target is a likely item for that context. The relations of these measures to component V are negative because a strong emphasis on speed of responding should lead to a lower depth of decoding.

Measures 3 and 4 are the differences in *mean response latencies* for words presented in context and in isolation. Large values of these measures indicate a large drop in processing time when a predictive context is provided; small values indicate a small decrease in speed of word recognition when context is supplied. We found that the mean drop in RT when context is presented varied as a function of reading ability. The mean reduction in RT was 88 msec for readers in group 1, 60 msec for group 2, 49 msec for group 3, and 29 msec for group 4. Apparently, the most highly skilled readers were the least apt to increase their speed of responding when a predictive context was presented. Measures 3 and 4 are interpreted as representing the degree of emphasis placed by subjects on speed in applying context when identifying a highly predictable target (component V).

Measurement of Effective Visual Span. The final experiment conducted within the Reading Components Battery was a study of readers' effective visual span and the amount of information they could encode within a fixation, in the presence and absence of a prior paragraph context. Effective visual span is defined as the distance, in character spaces, from the leftmost to the rightmost character encoded from a phrase presented tachistoscopically. Subjects were presented a passage of text (taken from the Degrees of Reading Power Test, State of New York, 1977), but with the last four to seven words of the final sentence missing. After reading the context passage, readers pressed a response key to receive the final words of the passage, which were presented in a brief (200 msec) exposure. Their task was to report as many words as they saw, in any order. Controls were included to insure that subjects were fixating an indicated spot near the beginning of the test phrase at the time the test words were presented. (The spot changed subtly during the 200-msec interval preceding the target, and subjects had to discriminate those changes successfully by pressing a second response key.)

There were two major variables in the experiment: (1) presence or absence of the prior context passage; (2) order of presentation of the words of the target phrase (normal or scrambled). Thus, contextual effects—the increments in effective visual span occurring when a prior context passage is provided—could be measured separately for the case where the target words were presented in an unpredictable sequence and where the target phrase was presented intact.

There were clear differences among groups of readers in the contextual effects shown under these two test-phrase conditions. Less able readers showed substantial benefits of passage context only when the target words were presented in a meningful sequence. The average effects of context for readers in groups 1, 2, and 3 were 1.20, 1.59, and 2.19 letter positions when the test phrase was intact, but only .32, .84, and .26 letter positions when the test phrase was scrambled. In contrast, readers of high ability showed large contextual effects regardless of the condition of the test words. For the top group of readers, contextual effects were 2.57 letter positions when the target phrase was not scrambled, and 2.01 letter positions when the phrase was scrambled. The similarity in performance under these two conditions suggests that, for highly skilled readers, an automatic spreading-activation process is operating, which renders semantically related concepts within the lexicon more accessible.

We derived four measures from the visual span experiment. Measures 5 and 6 (in Table 3.6) are the increases in visual span that occurred when context was added for the case in which the target words were presented in normal order. The two measures correspond to separate groups of texts—those having high- and low-scaled readability. These measures are thought to depend primarily on the sixth component we have postulated: activation of semantically related concepts in memory (VI). However, because the target phrase is presented in normal word order, we hypothesize that semantic integration within a discourse model (component VIII) may also play a role in determining levels of performance on these measures.

Measures 7 and 8 are also the values of contextual effects, again measured for high- and low-readability tests. Here, however, the target words have been scrambled. Under our interpretation of component VI as an automatic activation process, performance on these measures also depends on the activation of semantically related concepts. However, because in this case target words do not form meaningful sequences, they are processed individually, and speed in recognizing individual items that are contextually constrained is advantageous. The speed factor is not thought to be of importance when the target is a meaningful phrase because, in that case, groups of words are processed together as representatives of concepts. (Additional evidence for this distinction in size of processing units was found: When test phrases were scrambled, there was a strong effect of the number of words within a test phrase on RT. When test phrases were intact, RT was independent of the number of words they happened to contain.)

Validation of the Measurement Model.   The componential interpretation we have offered for each of the context-utilization measures provides a basis for the specification of a measurement model (Fig. 3.4). Subjects performance with regard to these eight measures is hypothesized to be determined by four reading components. Two of these represent the context-utilization skills—speed set in applying a predictive context (V) and extrapolation of discourse context through activation of semantically related items in memory (VI). The other two components represent processes in word analysis and discourse processing drawn from our earlier studies. These are efficiency of processing in word recognition (IV) and semantic integration within a discourse representation (VIII). Two additional measures were selected from our prior analysis to provide unambiguous identification of each of these components. For component IV, measure 9 and 10 were introduced, representing depth of decoding of high- and low-frequency words presented in isolation. Measures 11 and 12 were drawn from our prior analysis of discourse processes in the Anaphoric Reference Experiment. Measure 11 represents the increase in reading time when a sentence containing anaphora is ambiguous with regard to the selection of a referent. Measure 12 represents the increase in reading time for sentences containing a collocative reference to an earlier noun phrase, compared with sentences in which the reference problem is already "solved" for the reader—by simply repeating the antecedent noun phrase.

In Fig. 3.4, hypothesized relations between components and measures are represented by arrows. Efficient word recognition (IV) contributes to low depth of decoding for words of high or low frequency, presented in context (y_1 and y_2)

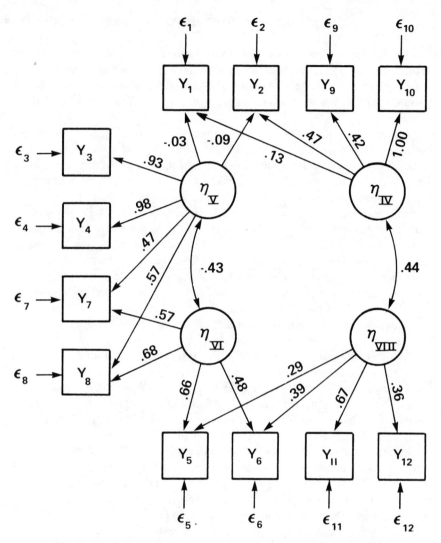

FIG. 3.4. Schematic representation of the measurement model developed for measures of context utilization (integrative skills). Arrows denote the direction of causation in the model; squares denote the observed variables. (Variables 1–8 are those in Table 3.6; variables 9 and 10 correspond to those in Table 3.2—the depth of decoding of high- and low-frequency words presented in isolation; variables 11 and 12 correspond to variables 4 and 3, respectively, in Table 3.4—two measures of time for evaluating antecedents in reading a sentence containing an anaphor.) η_{IV}, η_{V}, η_{VI}, and η_{VIII} denote the components: word recognition (IV), speed set in applying context (V), extrapolation of discourse context (VI), and semantic integration within a discourse representation (VIII). Measures of components IV and VIII were included in order to partial out their involvement in tasks related to the integrative components (V and VI). Chi-square for this measurement model was 45.8, with 42 d.f.; $p = .316$. Standard errors of parameters averaged .17. Only the two significant component intercorrelations are represented in the diagram.

or in isolation (y_9 and y_{10}). Efficiency in semantic integration (VIII) leads to smaller increases in reading time in solving problems of anaphoric reference (y_{11} and y_{12}) and to larger measures of visual span when the target phrase is a meaningful word sequence (y_5 and y_6). Activation of discourse-related items within semantic memory (VI) leads to increases in visual span when prior context is included, regardless of whether the target words are phrases (y_5 and y_6) or scrambled sequences (y_7 and y_8). Finally, speed set in applying context (V) leads to increases in speed of word recognition when words are predictable from context (y_3 and y_4), to increases in visual span when words are scrambled (y_7 and y_8, and to lower depth of decoding when context is provided (y_1 and y_2).

The measurement model presented here was fit using the ACOVS program, with no restrictions on intercorrelations among components. The resulting value of chi-square with 42 d.f. was 45.8, $p = .316$. When the component intercorrelations were restricted to be zero, the statistical test yielded $\chi^2(6) = 11.77$, $p = .07$. Therefore, the possibility of component interactions is considered. To explore which components are correlated, we allowed components IV and VIII and components V and VI to correlate with one another and fixed all other intercorrelations at zero. For this model, $\chi^2(4) = 3.21$, $p = .52$. Parameter estimates for this measurement model are the ones displayed in Fig. 3.4.

Although the measurement model we have hypothesized is clearly acceptable statistically, we again tested several alternative models in order to discover the features of the hypothesized model that are crucial and those that are not. Statistics resulting from this procedure are presented in Table 3.7. In the first alternative model, components VI and VIII are combined into a single semantic analysis factor. This resulted in $\chi^2(5) = 9.25$, $p = .10$. Given the face validity of the measurement operations employed to mark each of these components, we reject this possible alternative. In the second alternative model, components V and VI

TABLE 3.7
Comparisons Among ACOVS Models for Measures of Context Utilization

Alternative Model[a]	Number of Components	Number of Parameters	Chi-Square	d.f.	Prob.
1. Single semantic analysis factor; combine factors VI and VIII	3	19	9.25	5	.10
2. Single context utilization factor; combine factors V and VI	3	19	24.99	5	.0001
3. Test independence of original four components	4	18	11.77	6	.07
4. Test independence of factors IV and V, IV and VI, V and VIII, and VI and VIII	4	20	3.21	4	.52

[a] Alternatives are tested against the full four-component model containing 24 parameters.

were combined in a single context-utilization factor. Here, $\chi^2(5) = 24.99$, $p = .0001$. Thus, the evidence strongly suggests that activation of contextually related items in memory is distinct from the *use* of such constraints in reducing time for analysis of perceptual/orthographic information contained in words. The significant negative correlation between these components $(-.43)$ indicates that readers who show the greatest depth of context-determined activation within semantic memory also show the smallest reductions in word-recognition time when a constraining context is provided. Availability of a large number of activated units in memory would seem to reduce the opportunity for a primarily context-based word recognition because perceptual and orthographic information must be analyzed in order to select among the numerous alternatives. Conversely, if the mechanism for extrapolating context is a serial predictive system that generates only a few, high-probability candidate items, then the opportunity for increasing speed in word recognition (and circumventing time-consuming decoding operations) will be greater.

Estimation of Parameters for the Full Measurement Model

For purposes of studying component interactions, twenty variables were selected from those described in Tables 3.2, 3.4, and 3.6. These variables are listed in Table 3.8. A single measurement model—the combined measurement models developed for the word-analysis, discourse-analysis, and context-utilization domains—was constructed. It is represented by the hypothesized pattern of zeroes and nonzero parameters in the matrix B, which is also given in Table 3.8. This model was fit using ACOVS, with no restrictions on component (factor) intercorrelations. This yielded $\chi^2(133) = 185.35$, $p = .002$. The average standard errors of factor loadings was .16. Note that although the model can be rejected on purely statistical grounds, it contains only 29 nonzero factor loadings in the matrix B (out of a possible 160) and, in all, uses only 57 parameters to account for 190 intercorrelations among variables. Therefore, this is adopted as the standard measurement model to be used in our future studies of interactions among reading components.

Maximum-likelihood estimates of intercorrelations among the eight components are presented in Table 3.9. These correlations are attributable to two sources of covariation among components: functional interactions among components and nonfunctional, etiological factors. In the remainder of this chapter, we first examine the functional sources of correlation among components, as expressed in structural equation systems. After fitting such interactive models, it will then be determined whether residual correlations remain among components that require the postulation of other nonfunctional factors such as "general reading ability."

TABLE 3.8
The Complete ACOVS Model Used in Validity Studies[a]

Measure (Effect)		I	II	III	IV	V	VI	VII	VIII
						Component			
1. ANAG:[b]	Rate of letter encoding	.26	∅	∅	∅	∅	∅	∅	∅
2. LTM:	RT(Aa) − RT(AA)	1.00	∅	∅	∅	∅	∅	∅	∅
3. BG:	Bigram Frequency	∅	1.00	∅	∅	∅	∅	∅	∅
4. BG:	Position	.19	.58	∅	∅	∅	∅	∅	∅
5. BG:	Positional Likelihood	∅	.39	.41	∅	∅	∅	∅	∅
6. PSEU:	Vowel Type	∅	.30	.43	∅	∅	∅	∅	∅
7. PSEU:	Length	∅	∅	.77	∅	∅	∅	∅	∅
8. PSEU:	Syllables	∅	∅	∅	∅	∅	∅	∅	∅
9. CORR:	HFW/NC w/PSEU.	∅	∅	∅	.56	∅	∅	∅	∅
10. CORR:	LFW/HCC w/PSEU.	∅	∅	∅	.91	−.30	∅	∅	∅
11. CONTEXT:	NC-LCC (HFWs)	∅	∅	∅	∅	.91	∅	∅	∅
12. CONTEXT:	NC-HCC (LFWs)	∅	∅	∅	∅	1.00	∅	∅	∅
13. SPAN:	C-NC (Phrases, Easy)	∅	∅	∅	∅	∅	.58	∅	.42
14. SPAN:	C-NC (Phrases, Diff.)	∅	∅	∅	∅	∅	.52	∅	.28
15. SPAN:	C-NC (Words, Easy)	∅	∅	∅	∅	.58	.72	∅	∅
16. SPAN:	C-NC (Words, Diff.)	∅	∅	∅	∅	.58	.62	∅	∅
17. ANAPHOR:	Referent not Topic/Topic	∅	∅	∅	∅	∅	∅	1.00	∅
18. ANAPHOR:	Pred./Subject of Interv. Sen.	∅	∅	∅	∅	∅	∅	.29	.26
19. ANAPHOR:	Amb./Unamb. Reference	∅	∅	∅	∅	∅	∅	∅	.61
20. ANAPHOR:	Foregrnd. NP2/Neut. Interv. sent.	∅	∅	∅	∅	∅	∅	−.33	.46

[a] The average of standard errors is .16.
[b] Variable was reflected in the analysis.

TABLE 3.9
Intercorrelations Among Components in Complete ACOVS Model[a]

Component	I	II	III	IV	V	VI	VII	VIII
I. Letter recognition	1.00							
II. Perceiving multiletter units	.12 ± .15	1.00						
III. Decoding	.49 ± .21	.35 ± .17	1.00					
IV. Word recognition	.25 ± .18	.10 ± .16	.66 ± .16	1.00				
V. Speed set in context utilization	-.09 ± .15	.10 ± .14	.34 ± .16	.32 ± .24	1.00			
VI. Extrapolating context	.20 ± .18	-.15 ± .17	-.42 ± .21	-.44 ± .19	-.51 ± .18	1.00		
VII. Topicality set for locating referents	.19 ± .15	.49 ± .14	.49 ± .17	.49 ± .15	.16 ± .14	.07 ± .18	1.00	
VIII. Semantic integration	.22 ± .20	-.19 ± .20	.87 ± .18	.48 ± .20	.08 ± .21	.16 ± .26	.18 ± .21	1.00

[a] Standard errors are indicated after each correlation.

ANALYSIS OF COMPONENT INTERACTIONS

Adopting the validated measurement models for each processing domain, we tested hypotheses concerning interactions among components. This was accomplished by building a set of structural equations describing the hypothesized interactions among reading components, demonstrating identifiability of parameters, and testing the structural model by use of the ACOVS procedure (Jöreskog, 1970). A chi-square test then allowed us to compare our structural models against the null case where only the measurement model was specified and all components were free to intercorrelate.

Word-Analysis Components

The first application of this procedure concerned the word-analysis domain where, on the basis of intercorrelations of 10 variables, four components have been identified. Components I, II, III, and IV represent: the processes of (1) letter recognition; (2) perceiving multiletter units; (3) decoding; and (4) efficient word recognition (low depth of processing in word recognition). In the interactive model, components I and II are both hypothesized as contributing to efficient, automatic decoding because the decoding process requires orthographic information as input. Furthermore, availability of encoded multiletter units facilitates more efficient decoding because the number of units to be processed will then be reduced. However, components I and II are themselves hypothesized to be independent because the input data structures they require (visual features) are readily available to all readers. The effect of these perceptual components on word recognition (IV) is thought to be indirect, through their effect on decoding. Efficient decoding (III) contributes to efficient word recognition (IV) by accelerating the availability of phonologically encoded units. Word recognition also has a unique component associated with it, which represents the ability to encode words directly on the basis of their visual form. Finally, unique components of decoding and word recognition are assumed to be independent.

The structural model that incorporates these hypotheses concerning component interaction is presented in Fig. 3.5. In addition, Table 3.10 shows the derivation of the factor matrix Λ relating measured components to unique components and the methods for estimating parameters. Inasmuch as there are fewer parameters in D and Δ than unconstrained elements in Λ, the structural model is overdetermined. An estimate of nonfixed values in Λ was obtained using ACOVS. The equations were then used to estimate the parameters. These were in turn used to recalculate values for λ_{41}, λ_{42}, and λ_{43} using (4) in Table 3.10. The ACOVS model was then refit with *fixed* values in Λ to provide a χ^2 value for the fully constrained model. This test yielded $\chi_1^2 = 1.88$, $p = .17$.

In this structural model, the two perceptual components make independent contributions to decoding efficiency. Thus, they indirectly affect word recogni-

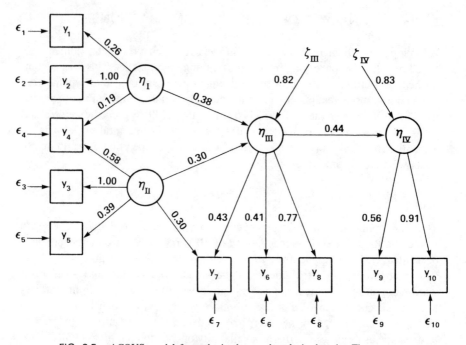

FIG. 3.5.   ACOVS model for tasks in the word-analysis domain. The arrows denote the direction of causation in the model; squares denote the observed variables ($Y_1 - Y_{10}$); circles denote the manifest components. $\eta_I - \eta_{IV}$ denote, respectively, the components: encoding letters (I), encoding multiletter perceptual units (II), phonological decoding (III), and word recognition (IV). ζ_{III} and ζ_{IV} represent unique components; $\epsilon_1 - \epsilon_{10}$ represent measurement-error variance specific to a single measure.

tion. Efficient word recognition is not directly related to the perceptual skills but is strongly related (with $r = .66$) to efficient decoding. However, component-specific individual differences are the most important determiners of decoding and word-recognition efficiency. Note finally that, beyond these hypothesized functional interactions among components, there is no evidence of residual correlations among components.

Interactions with Higher-Level Components

In this section, our problem is that of modeling the relations of the low-level reading components both to components of discourse processing and to those involved in utilizing contextual information in guiding lexical retrieval. The procedure for fitting and testing a structural model of component interaction, with modification, can be used to investigate the relations between high-level components and low-level word-analysis components.

TABLE 3.10
Analysis of Interactions Among Word-Analysis Components

Structural Equations

$\eta_1 = \zeta_1$

$\eta_2 = \zeta_2$

$\eta_2 = \delta_{31}\eta_1 + \delta_{32}\eta_2 + \delta_{33}\zeta_3$

$\eta_4 = \delta_{43}\eta_3 + \delta_{44}\zeta_4$

(1)

Unique Components as Functions of Measured Components

$\zeta_1 = \quad\quad \eta_1$

$\zeta_2 = \quad\quad\quad\quad \eta_2$

$\delta_{33}\zeta_3 = -\delta_{31}\eta_1 - \delta_{32}\eta_2 + \quad \eta_3$

$\delta_{44}\zeta_4 = \quad\quad\quad\quad\quad\quad -\delta_{43}\eta_3 + \eta_4$

(2)

or, in matrix form:

$$
\begin{bmatrix} 1 & 0 & 0 & 0 \\ 0 & 1 & 0 & 0 \\ 0 & 0 & \delta_{33} & 0 \\ 0 & 0 & 0 & \delta_{44} \end{bmatrix}
\begin{bmatrix} \zeta_1 \\ \zeta_2 \\ \zeta_3 \\ \zeta_4 \end{bmatrix}
=
\begin{bmatrix} 1 & 0 & 0 & 0 \\ 0 & 1 & 0 & 0 \\ -\delta_{31} & -\delta_{32} & 1 & 0 \\ 0 & 0 & -\delta_{43} & 1 \end{bmatrix}
\begin{bmatrix} \eta_1 \\ \eta_2 \\ \eta_3 \\ \eta_4 \end{bmatrix}
$$

$$\quad\quad D \quad\quad\quad\quad\quad \zeta \quad = \quad\quad\quad\quad \Delta \quad\quad\quad\quad\quad \eta$$

(3)

Factor Matrix $\Lambda = \Delta^{-1}D$

$$
\begin{bmatrix} 1 & 0 & 0 & 0 \\ 0 & 1 & 0 & 0 \\ \delta_{31} & \delta_{32} & \delta_{33} & 0 \\ (\delta_{43}\delta_{31}) & (\delta_{43}\delta_{32}) & (\delta_{43}\delta_{33}) & \delta_{44} \end{bmatrix}
$$

(4)

Identifiability of Parameters

$\hat{\delta}_{43} = $ Average of $\hat{\lambda}_{41}/\hat{\lambda}_{31}$, $\hat{\lambda}_{42}/\hat{\lambda}_{32}$, and $\hat{\lambda}_{43}/\hat{\lambda}_{33}$.

$\hat{\delta}_{31} = \hat{\lambda}_{31}$

$\hat{\delta}_{32} = \hat{\lambda}_{32}$

$\hat{\delta}_{33} = \hat{\lambda}_{33}$.

(5)

Method of Analysis

Theories of the interaction between high-level components (of context utilization and discourse analysis) and low-level word-analysis components can be stated as systems of structural equations. These equations relate measured performance on particular high-level components to measured performance on: (1)

TABLE 3.11
Analysis of Interactions Involving Higher-Order Components

Structural Equations[a]

$\eta_1 = \zeta_1$

$\eta_2 = \zeta_2$

$\eta_3 = \zeta_3$

$\eta_4 = \zeta_4$

$\eta_5 = \delta_{53}\eta_3 + \delta_{54}\eta_4 + \delta_{55}\zeta_5 + \delta_{56}\eta_6$

$\eta_6 = \delta_{63}\eta_3 + \delta_{64}\eta_4 + \delta_{66}\zeta_6$

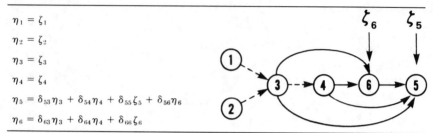

Unique Components as Functions of Measured Components

$\zeta_1 = \eta_1$

$\zeta_2 = \eta_2$

$\zeta_3 = \eta_3$

$\zeta_4 = \eta_4$

$\zeta_5 = -\delta_{53}\eta_3 - \delta_{54}\eta_4 + \eta_5 - \delta_{56}\eta_6$

$\zeta_6 = -\delta_{63}\eta_3 - \delta_{64}\eta_4 + \eta_6$

Factor Matrix $\Lambda = \Delta^{-1}D$

$$
\begin{bmatrix}
1 & \emptyset & \emptyset & \emptyset & \emptyset & \emptyset \\
\emptyset & 1 & \emptyset & \emptyset & \emptyset & \emptyset \\
\emptyset & \emptyset & 1 & \emptyset & \emptyset & \emptyset \\
\emptyset & \emptyset & \emptyset & 1 & \emptyset & \emptyset \\
\emptyset & \emptyset & (\delta_{53} + \delta_{63}\delta_{56}) & (\delta_{54} + \delta_{64}\delta_{56}) & \delta_{55} & (\delta_{55}\delta_{66}) \\
\emptyset & \emptyset & \delta_{63} & \delta_{64} & \emptyset & \delta_{66}
\end{bmatrix}
$$

Identifiability of Parameters

$\hat{\delta}_{56} = \lambda_{56}/\lambda_{66}$,

$\hat{\delta}_{53} = \lambda_{53} - \hat{\delta}_{63} \cdot \hat{\delta}_{56}$,

$\hat{\delta}_{54} = \lambda_{54} - \hat{\delta}_{64} \cdot \hat{\delta}_{56}$,

$\hat{\delta}_{55} = \lambda_{55}, \hat{\delta}_{63} = \lambda_{63}, \hat{\delta}_{64} = \lambda_{64}, \hat{\delta}_{66} = \lambda_{66}$.

---

[a] Components 1–4 are allowed to be freely intercorrelated; the correlation between components 5 and 6 may or may not be constrained, depending on the model. Intercorrelations between components 1–4 and high order components 5 and 6 are assumed to be zero.

other high-level components; (2) the four word-analysis components. As the goal is to estimate the path coefficients (δ_{ij}'s) relating measured components, it is not necessary to simultaneously model the structural relations among the lower-level components. A fairly general structural model, which illustrates the properties of structural models that we actually adopt, is given in Table 3.11. In this hypothetical model, word-analysis components (numbered 1–4) are assumed to be correlated. (This is due, as we have already seen, to component interactions that are indicated by dashed lines in the figure. The present model, however, does not specify these relations.) In the model, performance on high-level components 5 and 6 is determined by levels of skill on components 3 and 4. Performance on high-level component 5 is determined, as well, by performance on another high-level component (6). These two types of assumed relations among components are the types we consider later in building our interactive models.

The structural equation system corresponding to this model is presented in Table 3.11, along with a derivation of the factor matrix Λ expressed in terms of the model parameters—the path coefficients (δ_{ij}'s). Several observations concerning the matrix Λ are helpful. First, consider the factor loadings for component 6, corresponding to the final row of Λ. Performance on this component is determined in the model by performance on lower-level measured components and by a unique component. For this type of variable, the values in Λ give the path coefficients directly. The values of λ_{63} and λ_{64} (corresponding to δ_{63} and δ_{64}) are simply regression coefficients obtained in the regression of component 6 on components 3 and 4, and $\lambda_{66} = \delta_{66}$ is an estimate of the error (or unique) component of variance (if we assume in the model that the unique component is uncorrelated with other components). The relations of the factor loadings for component 5 to underlying model parameters are more complex because this is a case where the high-order variable is related to lower-level components (3 and 4) both directly and indirectly—through the relationship of component 5 to a second high-order component (6). Here, the parameters of Λ are related to the parameters of the structural model by expressions such as $\lambda_{53} = \delta_{53} + \delta_{63}\delta_{56}$, which contains two additive terms: δ_{53} (representing the direct path from component 3 to 5) and $\delta_{63}\delta_{56}$ (representing the indirect path from component 3 to 5 via 6). Likewise, $\lambda_{56} = \delta_{56}\delta_{66}$ represents the path from unique component 6 to 5 via measured component 6. In developing and testing models for the interaction of high-order components and word-analysis components, we encounter each of these situations exemplified by variables 6 and 5 in the foregoing example. Several of the high-order components are simply regressed on the set of word-analysis components, as was variable 6. And one of the high-order components is dependent on both a second high-order component and the word-analysis components, as was the case for variable 5.

Structural Models of Component Interaction

The initial model of component interactions incorporated the following hypotheses:

1. Word-analysis components of decoding efficiency (III) and word-recognition efficiency (IV) are hypothesized to influence context-utilization components (V and VI) directly because early retrieval of lexical categories increases the time available for activation of semantically/syntactically constrained items in memory.

2. The generative component of context utilization (VI) directly (and negatively) influences the speed component (V) because speed is inversely proportional to the number of contextually related alternatives that have been activated.

3. Word-analysis components of perceiving multiletter units (II), decoding efficiency (III), and word-recognition efficiency (IV) are also hypothesized to influence components of discourse processing (VII and VIII). The discourse-analysis processes involved in selecting and evaluating referents in building a propositional representation for a sentence take place *concurrently* with processes of decoding and word recognition and, therefore, must share processing resources with them. High levels of automaticity in word-analysis components reduce the resource demands of those processes and, thus, improve the efficiency of concurrent processes of discourse analysis. (However, the direct relation of component VIII to II was eliminated in the model because the correlation between them was nonsignificant: $r = -.19$, with a standard error of .20.)

The structural equations for high-level components V–VIII corresponding to these hypotheses are then:

$$\eta_5 = \delta_{53}\eta_3 + \delta_{54}\eta_4 + \delta_{55}\zeta_5 + \delta_{56}\eta_6,$$

$$\eta_6 = \delta_{63}\eta_3 + \delta_{64}\eta_4 + \delta_{66}\zeta_6,$$

$$\eta_7 = \delta_{72}\eta_2 + \delta_{73}\eta_3 + \delta_{74}\eta_4 + \delta_{77}\zeta_7, \text{ and}$$

$$\eta_8 = \delta_{83}\eta_3 + \delta_{84}\eta_4 + \delta_{88}\zeta_8.$$

The second-order factor matrix Λ for this model has the hypothesized structure indicated at the top of Table 3.12. The hypothesized structure for Φ is also given in this table. Here, the unique components V–VIII are assumed to be independent.

To evaluate the fit of this structural model, two more general models were constructed. In the first (model 2), the four high-order components were regressed on *all* lower-order components. The nonsignificant chi-square of 12.86 (d.f. = 7) indicates that the restrictions of the original model are supported. To evaluate assumptions concerning the independence of higher-order unique factors, a second alternative model was constructed (model 3). In this model, the

TABLE 3.12
ACOVS Models for Component Interactions
with and without Assumptions of Component Independence

Interactive Model[a]	Fixed and Variable Parameters Resulting from the Structural Model (Λ)	Intercorrelations Among Components (Φ)	Comparisons among Models		
			χ^2	d.f.	p
1. Restricted model for interaction of higher order components and word-analysis components, assuming component independence.	$\begin{bmatrix} I & \emptyset \\ \begin{matrix} \emptyset\emptyset vv \\ \emptyset\emptyset vv \\ \emptyset vvv \\ \emptyset\emptyset vv \end{matrix} & \begin{matrix} vv\emptyset\emptyset \\ \emptyset v\emptyset\emptyset \\ \emptyset\emptyset v\emptyset \\ \emptyset\emptyset\emptyset v \end{matrix} \end{bmatrix}$	$\begin{bmatrix} \Phi_{11} & \emptyset \\ \emptyset & I \end{bmatrix}$	—	—	—
2. Unconstrained regression of higher order components on word-analysis components, assuming component independence.	$\begin{bmatrix} I & \emptyset \\ \begin{matrix} vvvv \\ vvvv \\ vvvv \\ vvvv \end{matrix} & \begin{matrix} vv\emptyset\emptyset \\ \emptyset v\emptyset\emptyset \\ \emptyset\emptyset v\emptyset \\ \emptyset\emptyset\emptyset v \end{matrix} \end{bmatrix}$	$\begin{bmatrix} \Phi_{11} & \emptyset \\ \emptyset & I \end{bmatrix}$	12.86	7	.08[b]
3. Restricted model for interaction of higher order components and word-analysis components, allowing correlation among components.	$\begin{bmatrix} I & \emptyset \\ \begin{matrix} \emptyset\emptyset vv \\ \emptyset\emptyset vv \\ \emptyset vvv \\ \emptyset\emptyset vv \end{matrix} & \begin{matrix} v\ \ \emptyset \\ v\ \ \ \\ \ \ v \\ \emptyset\ \ v \end{matrix} \end{bmatrix}$	$\begin{bmatrix} \Phi_{11} & \emptyset \\ \emptyset & \Phi_{22} \end{bmatrix}$	9.63	5	.09[b]

[a] The general model is $\Sigma = \beta\Lambda\Phi\Lambda'\beta' + \Theta^2$, where β contains the measurement model, Λ and Φ depend on the particular structural model, and Θ^2 contains error variances. The rows and columns of matrices Λ and Φ correspond to the eight components; submatrix Φ_{11} contains intercorrelations among word-analysis components; Φ_{22} contains intercorrelations among the higher order components; and I represents the 4×4 identity matrix. Free parameters, or variables, are denoted by v.

[b] Model 1 is tested first against model 2 and then against model 3.

high-order components are allowed to intercorrelate freely with each another, instead of introducing the explicit relation of dependence between the two context-utilization components V and VI. The obtained chi-square of 9.63 (d.f. = 5) is again nonsignificant, and the assumption of independence of the unique components is supported. Thus, the obtained correlations among high-order measured components can be attributed entirely to their common dependence on levels of automaticity/efficiency of lower-level components and to the specific relation of dependence hypothesized for the context-utilization components.

Summary of Interactions for Discourse-Analysis Components.   The relationships of discourse-processing components to low-level components are illustrated in Fig. 3.6, which contains the estimated path coefficients. Component
VIII represents efficiency in integrating the semantic information associated with
an antecedent lexical item with the semantic representation being formulated by
the reader for the current sentence or phrase. This skill was established, for
example, by comparing reading times for sentences containing an ambiguous
pronominal reference with those for a sentence containing an unambiguous refer-

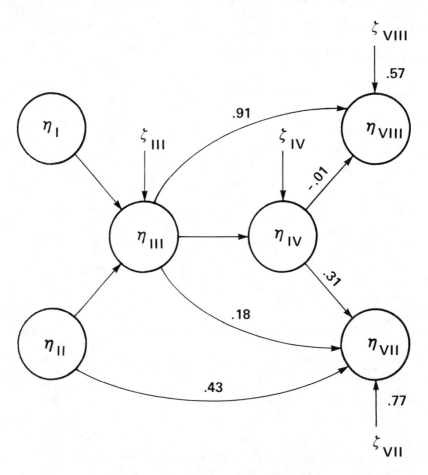

FIG. 3.6.   Causal model relating two components of discourse processing, assignment of topicalized referent (VII) and semantic integration of antecedents
within a discourse representation (VIII), to components of word analysis: letter
recognition (I), Multiletter unit identification (II), decoding, (III), and word recognition (IV). In the model, there are direct structural relations between
perceptual/decoding components and discourse processing components.

ence. Semantic integration is not significantly associated with word recognition (IV), but it is strongly associated with decoding efficiency (III), with $r = .87$ and a regression coefficient of .91. Thus, there is a direct effect of automatic decoding on this discourse-processing component, which can be interpreted as an example of process interaction due to competition for a limited resource (Perfetti & Lesgold, 1977). Perfetti and Lesgold (1979) have subsequently suggested that the resource limitation is in working memory capacity and that inefficient decoding requires space in working memory that would otherwise by utilized for discourse processing. Whatever the nature of the resource limitation, it is clear that efficient decoding has an important, direct impact on discourse processing. And we are led to entertain the hypothesis that training for automatic decoding may have an impact on efficiency of discourse processing.

The remaining discourse processing component we have identified, preference for a topicalized antecedent as a referent (VII), reflects a dependence of the reader on the topical status of antecedents in effecting retrieval from memory. This component was measured, for example, by comparing reading times for sentences containing a pronoun when the referent was topicalized or not topicalized in the first sentence of a paragraph. Component VII is associated with three word-analysis components, suggesting again that automaticity of low-level processes contributes to efficiency in processing at the text level, presumably through lessened demands on the processing resource.

Finally, even though our investigation of discourse-analysis components is still in its infancy, the results obtained thus far suggest that components in this domain may be independent. Training targeted at one component under those circumstances would not be expected to generalize to other components. This expectation does not hold for word-analysis components where increased automaticity could contribute to efficiency in a variety of discourse-related components.

Simplified Model for Interactions of Context-Utilization Components. Several simplifications in the relationships of context-utilization components to lower-level components were introduced and found acceptable. These are models 4 and 5 shown in Table 3.13. The first simplification is based on the feeling that the basic process of context utilization is the generative component (VI). The speed component represents an optional strategy that some subjects employ— that of trading off speed in responding against the possibility of errors in identification that can occur when the amount of orthographic/phonological evidence developed while reading in context is being minimized. In this model, all correlations between the speed component (V) and lower-level components are regarded as attributable solely to dependence on the more basic generative component (VI). The structural equation corresponding to component 5 thus becomes:

$$\eta_5 = \delta_{55}\zeta_5 + \delta_{56}\eta_6.$$

TABLE 3.13
Alternative Structural Models for Context-Utilization Components

Interactive Model[a]	Comparisons with Model 1		
	χ^2	d.f.	p
1.	—	—	—
4.	.61	2	.74
5.	.94	3	.82

[a] In all models, components 7 and 8 are regressed on components 2–4 and 3–4, respectively. Intercorrelations among components are as indicated for model 1 in Table 3.12.

The other structural equations were, of course, unchanged. Comparison of model 4 to the original model yielded $\chi^2(2) = .61$ and thus strongly supported the first simplification.

A further simplification also proved possible. In structural model 5, the direct influence of the decoding component (III) on context utilization (VI) was eliminated. This simplification was motivated by the feeling that the generative use of context is an automatic process—one that is not likely to be in competition for processing resources with an inefficient decoding process. Thus, the influence (correlation) of decoding efficiency with context utilization should be entirely attributable to its effect on efficiency of word retrieval (component IV). Comparison of this model (which included the simplifications of model 4 as well) with the original model yielded $\chi^2(3) = .94$, again providing strong support for the reasoning behind the simplification.

The final pattern of process interactions for the context-utilization components is summarized in Fig. 3.7. Again, components I–IV are the word-recognition components, interrelated as in Fig. 3.2. Generating extrapolations from a discourse representation (VI) and speed set in employing highly predictive context (V) are the two identifiable aspects of context utilization. The generative component (VI) is related directly to word-recognition efficiency (IV) and related

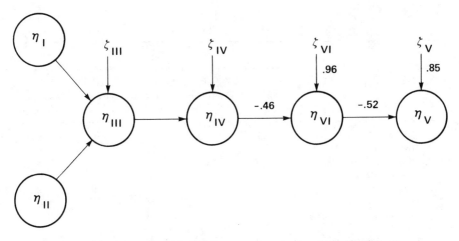

FIG. 3.7. Structural model relating two components of context utilization, extrapolating a discourse representation (VI) and speed set in utilizing highly predictive context (V), to components of word analysis: letter identification (I), multiletter unit identification (II), decoding (III), and word recognition (IV). In this model, there are no direct effects of perceptual/decoding components on higher order components.

indirectly to the other word-analysis components through their effects on word recognition (IV). The path coefficient ($-.46$) is negative because, for the generative component, high values (large increases in visual span with the provision of prior context) indicate efficient performance. (For the other components, low values reflect efficient performance.) The interaction of generative use of context (VI) with word-recognition efficiency is in theory due to the increased time for activation of semantically associated lexical units when words are more rapidly encoded. Speed set in utilizing predictive context (V) is *negatively* related to the generative component (VI), representing a strategy that is most applicable when the generative component yields a small (unitary) set of constrained alternatives. The correlations of the strategic component (V) with other components are all attributable to its relation to the more basic generative component. Note, finally, that the greatest factors contributing to context-utilization components are the unique components, which in this model are mutually independent.

RELATIONSHIP OF READING COMPONENTS TO OTHER COGNITIVE FACTORS

Eleven tests representing five cognitive factors were drawn from the Educational Testing Service kit of reference tests for cognitive factors (French, Ekstrom, & Price, 1963), and these are listed in Table 3.14 for each of the factors. The first three factors represent perceptual skills. Speed of Closure tests require the sub-

TABLE 3.14
ACOVS Model for Cognitive Ability Tests[a]

	Factor				
	A	B	C	D	E
Test Measure	Speed of Closure	Flexibility of Closure	Perceptual Speed	Word Fluency	Fluency of Association
1. Concealed words	.52	∅	∅	∅	∅
2. Gestalt completion	.54	∅	∅	∅	∅
3. Hidden figures (power)	∅	1.00	∅	∅	∅
4. Hidden patterns (speed)	.64	.32	.41	∅	∅
5. Finding As	∅	∅	.36	∅	∅
6. Finding identical pictures	∅	∅	.90	∅	∅
7. Word endings	∅	∅	∅	.69	∅
8. Word beginnings	∅	∅	∅	.79	∅
9. Controlled association	∅	∅	∅	∅	.77
10. Doubly constrained association	∅	∅	∅	∅	.75
11. Simile interpretation	∅	∅	∅	∅	.49

[a] The model uses 23 parameters to account for 55 correlations. The test of fit yielded $\chi^2_{32} = 43.3$, $p = .09$. Standard errors of parameters averaged .21.

ject to identify figures or words on the basis of their overall visual form without the benefit of specific features or details. Flexibility of Closure tests require the reader to maintain in memory a specific figure so as to identify it when it occurs embedded within a larger figural context. Tests of Perceptual Speed measure the rate at which subjects can identify simple figures, or letters, amid an array of distractors.

The last two factors are measures of the accessibility of items in lexical memory when memory is searched for items having particular features of a phonological (orthographic) or semantic nature. Word-Fluency tests measure the number of lexical items having particular phonological/orthographic characteristics that can be retrieved in a fixed time—those that begin or end with a particular set of letters (e.g., begin with pro-, sub-; end with -ay, -ow). Fluency of Association tests measure the number of lexical items bearing semantic/ associative relationships to a given word or words that can be generated within a designated time. In the Controlled Associations test, all words having meanings similar to a given word (e.g., dark) must be supplied. In the Doubly Constrained Associations test, words must be found that are simultaneously associated with two presented words (e.g., jewelry–bell; answer: ring). Finally, the Simile-Interpretation test requires subjects to list as many interpretations for a simile as they can think of within a timed period.

The factor model for this set of measures is also shown in Table 3.14. It reproduces the pattern of factor loadings typically posited for this set of variables with the single exception that measure 4 (Hidden Patterns), which is a highly speeded test, loads on Speed of Closure and Perceptual Speed, as well as on Flexibility of Closure. Correlations among the five factors are given in Table 3.15. Correlations among the perceptual factors are low, but the correlation between the two fluency factors is extremely high (.86). Furthermore, correlations between the fluency factors and perceptual factors are sizable.

Correlations of reading components with cognitive ability factors were obtained by adapting the ACOVS program for performing an interbattery factor analysis. The results generally supported our interpretation of reading components (Table 3.16). Speed of Closure, a factor reflecting the ability to recognize words on the basis of their overall visual characteristics, correlated with each of the word-analysis components except letter-recognition efficiency; it correlated most highly with efficiency in word recognition (component IV). Flexibility of Closure, a measure of the ability to recognize familiar visual forms embedded in a larger context rapidly, was not correlated with any of the reading components. And Perceptual Speed, measured by two tests of visual search (for a target letter or picture), was generally correlated with all components, suggesting that this factor is componentially nonspecific.

Two additional cognitive abilities were included, which are measures of word accessibility via orthographic/phonological structure (Word Fluency) or by semantic features (Fluency of Association). These two fluency factors are highly correlated ($r = .89$). There was a general "background" correlation of $-.30$ to $-.40$ between these factors and the reading components. Beyond this background correlation, it is interesting that, of these two factors, the one measuring word accessibility via orthographic/phonological cues was more highly correlated with decoding efficiency ($-.85$) and word-recognition efficiency ($-.61$). In addition, Fleuncy of Association was more highly correlated with extrapolation of discourse representation (component VI) ($r = .70$), a component that shares with the fluency factor a need to access lexical items on subtle semantic grounds. It is interesting that semantic integration of antecedents (component VIII) is not tapped by either of the fluency measures. This component, we believe, does *not* involve divergent production of semantic relations. Rather, it

TABLE 3.15
Correlations Among Cognitive Ability Factors[a]

	A	B	C	D	E
A. Speed of closure	1.00				
B. Flexibility of closure	$-.11 \pm .22$	1.00			
C. Perceptual speed	*.28 ± .24*	.12 ± .18	1.00		
D. Word fluency	*.60 ± .23*	*.39 ± .29*	*.33 ± .19*	1.00	
E. Fluency of association	*.55 ± .21*	*.32 ± .26*	*.40 ± .18*	*.86 ± .11*	1.00

[a] Correlations having absolute value .25 or greater are in italics.

TABLE 3.16

Correlations of Reading Components with Cognitive Ability Factors
Resulting from the Interbattery Factor Analysis[a]

| | Cognitive Ability Factor | | | | |
Component	Speed of Closure	Flexibility of Closure	Perceptual Speed	Word Fluency	Fluency of Association
I. Letter encoding efficiency	−.05	−.10	−.31	−.45	−.25
II. Perceiving multiletter units	−.28	−.14	−.32	−.39	−.38
III. Decoding efficiency	−.30	−.09	−.44	−.86	−.57
IV. Word-recognition efficiency	−.40	.06	−.56	−.61	−.41
V. Speed in applying context	−.15	.08	−.23	−.41	−.29
VI. Extrapolating a discourse representation	.35	.02	.20	.52	.70
VII. Assignment of topicalized antecedent as referent	−.34	−.08	−.52	−.45	−.22
VIII. Semantic integration of antecedents with a discourse representation	.03	.19	−.33	−.01	.21

[a] Correlations having absolute value .25 or greater are in italics.

involves the specific testing of retrieved antecedents within the semantic frame under construction in working memory.

EXAMINATION OF
THE READING ABILITY CONSTRUCT

Composite Measures of Reading Ability

It is well known that tests of reading ability, comprehension, vocabulary, and general verbal fluency correlate highly with one another (cf. Davis, 1971). When batteries of such tests are factor analyzed, a general factor of "verbal facility" is typically extracted and interpreted as evidence for an underlying aptitude dimension. The question at issue is: How can we reconcile the empirical demonstration of an "ability" dimension, which is easily and reliably measured, with the theoretical view of reading as a collection of interacting, but largely independent, components of skill?

From the standpoint of componential theory, general reading tests are complex, requiring what is potentially a large number of individual component processes for their successful completion. High levels of tested skill are found for readers who have achieved high levels of automaticity in a large proportion of those components, and low levels of performance are found for readers for whom the set of automatic components is more restricted. The model I am advocating here is a *compensatory model* for determining the overall performance of a system of components as it is represented by scores on a composite reading task. Within a compensatory model, high levels of skill in one component can compensate for low levels in another. Performance on the composite task is thus taken to be a linear function of the skill levels on individual components.

It is easy to show that a high correlation between two composite measures of reading is to be expected within the framework of such a compensatory model, even in the case where the underlying reading components are mutually independent. Let $t = \sum_i w_i y_i$ represent performance on one composite reading task, and let $s = \sum_i v_i y_i$ represent performance on a second reading task. Each composite task is a linear combination of performance levels on a set of components, represented by y_i. If we further assume that the variances of the components are 1 and scale the weights (w_i and v_i) so that their sum of squares is 1, then the correlation between the composites t and s is given by:

$$\rho(t, s) = \frac{\sum_i w_i v_i \rho(y_i, y_i') + \sum_{i \neq j}\sum w_i v_i \rho(y_i, y_j)}{\left[1 + \sum_{i \neq j}\sum w_i w_j \rho(y_i, y_j) \right]^{\frac{1}{2}} \left[1 + \sum_{i \neq j}\sum v_i v_j \rho(y_i, y_j) \right]^{\frac{1}{2}}} \qquad 3.8$$

where $\rho(y_i, y_i')$ is the reliability of the ith component, and $\rho(y_i, y_j)$ is the correlation between the two discrete components i and j (Lord & Novick, 1968). If we now introduce the further condition that the components are independent (that $\rho[y_i, y_j] = 0$), Equation 3.8 can be simplified to yield:

$$\rho(t, s) = \sum_i w_i v_i \rho(y_i, y_i'). \qquad 3.9$$

Finally, if actual component automaticities/performance levels are substituted for measures of those quantities, the reliabilities will be 1, and the correlation between the two composites will simply be the correlation between the weightings of the components for the two composite tasks. Thus, two composite measures having similar weighting on a set of component processes will be highly correlated, even if the components operate independently. If the components are not independent (i.e., they interact), the correlation will be less dependent on the similarity of weights for the two composite measures of reading. High correlations among reading tests are therefore to be expected, as long as the tests represent componentially complex composites of individual components and the weightings of components are similar. Hence, the *fact* that batteries of reading tests generally yield a large general factor has no bearing whatsoever on the componential complexity of the reading process represented in the tests. Such a finding only suggests that the composite tests of the battery are making similar demands on a set of underlying reading components. It is only when the individual measures within a test battery are constructed so as to be componentially specific that the high, positive correlation among measures will be eliminated and the pattern of component interactions will become apparent.

Componential Analysis of Reading Tests

Given a set of measures of reading components resulting from the application of the measurement model displayed in Table 3.8, it is possible to study the relation of several composite measures of reading ability to underlying reading components. The correlations of the eight reading components and four criterion measures of reading ability were estimated using the ACOVS program (Table 3.17). The four criterion measures are reading time for context paragraphs in the visual span experiment, the number of lines of text read in the Nelson–Denny timed reading passage, and the Nelson–Denny vocabulary and comprehension subtest scores.

There are consistent relationships between word-analysis components and the four criteria, including the comprehension subtest. Decoding efficiency and word-recognition efficiency both correlate highly with vocabulary and comprehension measures and with the computer-based measure of reading speed. Perceiving multiletter units (component II) is also moderately correlated with three of the criterion measures. The letter-encoding component appears to be of lesser importance for the tests that are specifically reading tasks, but it does correlate $-.31$ with vocabulary. (This value is in close agreement with the one obtained by Hunt, Lunneberg, & Lewis, 1975.) The finding of high correlations of word-analysis components and measures of comprehension is consistent with results of Perfetti and Lesgold (1977; see also, Perfetti & Roth, 1980). Together, these findings provide additional support for the hypothesis advanced in our interactive model: that automaticity of word-analysis skills essentially frees processing resources for the purposes of discourse analysis.

Although the majority of word-analysis components are strongly correlated with criterion measures of reading ability, measures of higher-level components are generally less predictive—at least as reading ability is measured by conventional tests of speed and comprehension. Of the context-utilization components, the most prominent is the generative process of extrapolating a discourse representation in the activation of semantically constrained items in memory (component VI). This component correlates .59 with comprehension and is also highly correlated with the other reading measures. The correlation of this component with the vocabulary test (.47) suggests that general knowledge of word meanings may be one prerequisite for developing skill in the generative use of context.

TABLE 3.17
Validity Coefficients[a]

	Criterion Measure			
Component	Reading Time for Context	Nelson–Denny Speed	Nelson–Denny Vocabulary	Nelson–Denny Comprehension
I. Letter encoding efficiency	.17	−.18	−.31	−.20
II. Perceiving multi-letter units	.20	−.28	−.30	−.29
III. Decoding efficiency	.70	−.48	−.62	−.68
IV. Word-recognition efficiency	.50	−.17	−.35	−.51
V. Speed in applying context	.42	−.03	.00	−.21
VI. Extrapolating a discourse representation	−.51	.37	.47	.59
VII. Assignment of topicalized antecedent as referent	.23	−.17	−.23	−.34
VIII. Semantic integration of antecedents with a discourse representation	.41	−.11	.08	.02
Multi R	.74	.63	.73	.76
F (7, 38)	6.48	3.63	6.08	7.50
Prob.	.000	.000	.000	.000

[a] Correlations of .25 or greater are in italics.

Finally, and surprisingly, neither of the discourse-analysis components is strongly correlated with conventional reading test measures of speed, vocabulary, or comprehension. Influence of topicality in assigning reference relations (component VII) correlates −.34 with comprehension, indicating that good comprehenders are less influenced by the topical status of a referent in analyzing anaphoric relations in a text. Semantic integration (component VIII) appears to be poorly "tapped" by the conventional reading test measures; it correlates highly with only the computer-timed measure of reading speed ($r = .41$). This finding serves to remind us that there are discourse processing skills that would appear to have broad applicability in processing text, but these skills are only poorly represented in conventional tests of reading comprehension.

Status of the Reading Ability Construct
in Componential Theory

Apart from the identification of "reading ability" with performance on a composite test of reading performance, can a role be found for a reading ability construct within componential theory? One possibility is that an explicit, theoretical definition of reading ability as a processing component can be developed. For example, reading ability might be equated with a single component such as "constructing a propositional representation of a text." The problem with this approach is that, in our attempt to be theoretically explicit in defining the component, we are likely to discover that the proposed process is itself multicomponential, with each of the resulting subcomponents probably too specific to qualify as a general reading ability. It is probably the case that any reasonably general processing system is resolvable into a set of more particularized components together with their interactions. Nevertheless, it is possible for components to be grouped in more general systems. For example, even though the decoding component we have studied includes subprocesses for syllabication and for translating digraph vowels, measures of these subcomponents can be regarded as indicators of efficiency of a more general decoding system. The empirical check on the validity of a component as an integrated system of subprocesses is in the convergent and discriminant validity exhibited by the collection of subprocess measures, as they are evaluated in the fitting of a measurement model. Thus, in theory it is possible to identify a system of components that are process-linked and that together performs a type of text analysis that could be considered a primary ability in reading. However, the components of discourse analysis that we have analyzed thus far do not appear to be closely related aspects of a single system for text analysis.

A second possible locus for general reading ability within a componential model lies in the concept of resource or capacity limitation, used to explain interactions between low- and high-level components of reading. Low reading ability might be thought of as a result of restricted processing resources (Kahneman, 1973; Norman & Bobrow, 1975) or, perhaps, restrictions in working memory capacity (Perfetti & Lesgold, 1977). Such an explanatory concept has not been limited to reading, however. For instance, limitations in attentional resources have been proposed to explain age-related deficits in memory (Craik & Simon, 1980; Kinsbourne, 1980). Furthermore, factor analytic studies of resource-sharing measures (e.g., contrasts between performance in a task performed alone or concurrently with a second task) have provided no evidence as yet for a general factor reflecting a common attentional resource component (Sverko, 1977). The only factors that could be extracted in the Sverko study were clearly task specific. Other students of the resource-sharing "ability" (Hawkins, Church, & DeLemos, 1978) have reached similar conclusions. Resource-capacity limitations, if they exist as stable aspects of individuals, are multifaceted and task specific. Thus, it is difficult to see how reading ability could be conceptualized as a general limitation in processing resources. Deficits in reading-related processing resources might, however, contribute to poor performance on composite reading tasks.

A third possible interpretation remains—one that is based on the background environmental and biological factors that condition levels of performance on components. According to this view, these etiological factors enable some individuals to acquire high levels of skill in numerous components, whereas others remain incapable of developing such general expertise. This essentially empirical definition of reading ability is similar to the identification of verbal ability as the general (g) factor underlying a series of verbal tests or the equating of a first principle factor with "general intelligence." There is a difference, however. Here we are dealing with components, not with tests that are composites of components. Given a set of theoretically derived measures of components that have met the two standards of validity we have proposed, empirical evidence for general ability will be found in the presence of background correlations among components that remain after removing any covariation that is attributable to theoretically proscribed interactions among components. Our results so far provide no evidence of such background correlations. Thus, they offer no support for an underlying general factor of reading ability.

DISCUSSION

In this chapter, I have attempted to outline the form of a procedure-based componential theory of reading and develop multiple standards by which the validity of such a theory can be judged.

The first level of validation concerned the ability to predict mean performance on a criterion-measurement task for a set of particular task conditions. These predictions are based on an information-processing theory offered for the criterion task. In the experiments I have reported, separate tasks are generally employed to measure each of the specific reading components under investigation, and the selection of component-specific measures is based on the particular processing model developed and validated for each task. An alternative approach has been used by Sternberg (1977) in his studies of reasoning abilities. Rather than working with a set of experimental tasks, a single criterion task is chosen, which although representing a componentially complex (composite) performance, is susceptible to a variety of parametric variations in task conditions. A multicomponential theory is developed for predicting performance on the criterion task, and a "componential analysis" is advanced stating the theoretical degree of involvement of each component for each of the task conditions. A regression equation is then fit in which mean performance on the criterion task is predicted from the theoretically specified component weights for each of the task conditions. These regression equations can be fit to data for groups of subjects or for individuals. The goodness-of-fit of the componential model is indexed by the multiple correlation obtained in predicting composite performance from the theoretically specified component involvements. And the regression weights are interpreted as measures of the efficiencies of the individual components. These weights are in fact contrasts among the task conditions and, as such, are formally similar to the component-specific measures we have been developing. Carroll (1980b) has shown how these beta weights may serve as variables in further analyses of covariances among components through the use of factor analysis.

Level-one validation can be thought of as equivalent to building and testing a theory of item or task difficulty. Rather than simply scaling item difficulties by applying a standard statistical theory of task performance (e.g., a latent trait theory), an information-processing theory of task performance is fit to the performance records for each individual, and parameters of the theoretical model are taken as the "test" measures. This approach has been explicitly adopted by Brown and Burton (1978), who have shown how, by applying a theory of performance on arithmetic problems, patterns of errors can be used to identify specific conceptual "bugs" within the individual's information-processing system. The hope in adopting such an approach is that a cognitively rich theory of task performance will yield measures of particular features of an individual's processing system. These measures will in theory reveal the status of particular processing components, rather than merely reflect the operation of the overall system as it is performing a composite task.

The second level of validation was concerned with the differences in levels of component-specific performance evidenced by individual subjects over a set of measures that have been found to conform to the level-one standards of validity. We have attempted to show how the componential theory developed for predicting the effects of task manipulations in level-one validation also implies a highly specific measurement model, which relates performance on one measure to that on other measures of similar or dissimilar components. This measurement model can be statistically evaluated using techniques of confirmatory maximum-likelihood factor analysis. I believe that the logical correspondence between theoretically derived hypotheses underlying level-one and level-two validation is a tight one. If two measures share a processing component according to the model developed in level-one validation, then they must be resolvable as functions of the same underlying component in fitting a measurement model. In addition, their correlations with other measures must be proportional to their weights (loadings) on the underlying common component. Any violation of these relationships suggests that there is an unanticipated functional independence between measures and that further theoretical specification will be needed to account for the discrepancy. It is only when a measure is found to be unique—to be uncorrelated with *all* other measures—that there is ambiguity in the theoretical interpretation of the outcome. (Here the measure may represent some theoretically unspecified component, or it may simply be unreliable.) Finally, it should be emphasized that the testing of measurement models underlying the covariances among component-specific measures is not factor analysis in the usual sense because here the factor structure is specified in advance of the analysis.

A componential theory not only specifies the processing components underlying each of the experimental measures introduced; it must also provide for an analysis of component interactions. The procedural view of components provides a means for predicting when components are linked and when they are not. According to this view, components are invoked whenever particular situations—or data structures—occur, and they operate on those data structures in specified ways. Components are thus linked through their operation on a common internal data base and through the joint demands they place on shared processing resources. The specification of a theory of component interaction therefore requires specific knowledge of the attentional demands and levels of automaticity of the components. Particular theories of componential interaction can be stated as systems of structural equations, and the parameters of those equations (the path coefficients) can be estimated (at least for some models) by using maximum-likelihood techniques for the analysis of covariance structures. The alternative to this structural modeling approach is the use of training studies. The results of componentially specific training should transfer to other componentially specific measures, as specified in the theory of componential interaction.

Finally, the componential theory of reading has provided a basis within which I could re-examine the concept of "general ability" in reading. The existence of a large general factor in the analysis of composite reading tests was shown to be an expected outcome, given a compensatory model relating processing components to composite test performance. I believe there is little hope for uncovering component skills in reading by the analysis of correlations among such composite tests. What is needed is a set of theoretically based, componentially specific measures that have met the proposed standards of validity. If a set of such measures is available that covers the broad range of component skills of reading, it should be possible to test for a general, background correlation among reading skills attributable to general ability. Evidence for such a correlation has so far been lacking. However, a stronger and more definitive statement concerning an underlying "verbal ability" must await further evidence and, more particularly, the development of a more articulated componential theory for discourse analysis. Nevertheless, I feel that the approach outlined here might be applied fruitfully in other areas of complex cognitive performance and serve as a means of resolving the ongoing debate concerning the existence and nature of general intelligence.

ACKNOWLEDGMENTS

The research described herein was supported primarily by the Personnel and Training Research Programs, Psychological Sciences Division, Office of Naval Research, under Contract No. N00014-76-C-0461, Contract Authority Identification Number NR-154-386 and also by the National Institute of Education under Contract No. US-NIE-C-400-76-0116.

This work would not have been possible without the sponsorship and encouragement of the Office of Naval Research and the fruitful suggestions and comments offered by Drs. Marshall Farr and Henry Halff, of that office, and Dr. Joseph Young, formerly of that office. The anagram experiment was carried out in collaboration with Dr. Marilyn Adams, who also served as a consultant in the design of the bigram experiment. Most of the software for implementing the research design was the work of Barbara Freeman, to whom I am greatly indebted. Jessica Kurzon supervised the conduct of the experiments and developed a data-management system; she was also a collaborator in the design and analysis of the visual span experiment. Finally, the textual materials used in the context and anaphoric reference experiments were written, to demanding and exacting specifications, by Marina Frederiksen. It is her skill as a writer that made an experimental design based on textual manipulations a real possibility.

REFERENCES

Bentler, P. M. Multivariate analysis with latent variables: Causal modeling. *Annual Review of Psychology*, 1980, *31*, 419–456.

Brown, J. S., & Burton, R. R. Diagnostic models for procedural bugs in basic mathematical skills. *Cognitive Science*, 1978, *2*, 155–192.

Carroll, J. B. *Individual difference relations in psychometric and experimental cognitive tasks* (Report No. 163). Chapel Hill, N.C.: The L. L. Thurstone Psychometric Laboratory, University of North Carolina, April 1980. (a)

Carroll, J. B. Remarks on Sternberg's "Factor theories of intelligence are all right almost." *Educational Researcher*, 1980, *9*(8), 14–18. (b)

Carroll, J. B., Davies, P., & Richman, B. *The American heritage word frequency book*. Boston: Houghton Mifflin, 1971.

Collins, A. M., & Loftus, E. F. A spreading-activation theory of semantic processing. *Psychological Review*, 1975, *82*, 407–428.

Craik, F., & Simon, E. Age difference in memory: The roles of attention and depth of processing. In L. Poon, J. Fozard, L. Cermak, D. Arenberg, & L. Thompson (Eds.), *New directions in memory and aging*. Hillsdale, N.J.: Lawrence Erlbaum Associates, 1980.

Davis, F. B. Psychometric research on comprehension in reading. In M. Kling, F. B. Davis, & J. J. Geyer (Eds.), *The literature of research in reading with emphasis on models*. New Brunswick, N.J.: Graduate School of Education, Rutgers University, Final Report, 1971.

Frederiksen, J. R. *Decoding skills and lexical retrieval*. Paper presented at the annual meeting of the Psychonomic Society, St. Louis, Mo., November 1976.

Frederiksen, J. R. Assessment of perceptual, decoding, and lexical skills and their relation to reading proficiency. In A. M. Lesgold, J. W. Pellegrino, S. Fokkema, & R. Glaser (Eds.), *Cognitive psychology and instruction*. New York: Plenum, 1977.

Frederiksen, J. R. *Word recognition in the presence of semantically constraining context.* Paper presented at the annual meeting of the Psychonomic Society, San Antonio, Tex., November 1978.

Frederiksen, J. R. Component skills in reading: Measurement of individual differences through chronometric analysis. In R. F. Snow, P. A. Federico, & W. E. Montague (Eds.), *Aptitude, learning, and instruction: Cognitive process analysis.* Hillsdale, N.J.: Lawrence Erlbaum Associates, 1979.

Frederiksen, J. R. Sources of process interaction in reading. In A. M. Lesgold & C. A. Perfetti (Eds.) *Interactive processes in reading.* Hillsdale, N.J.: Lawrence Erlbaum Associates, 1980.

Frederiksen, J. R. Understanding anaphora: Rules used by readers in assigning pronominal referents. *Discourse Processes,* in press.

French, J. W., Ekstrom, R. B., & Price, L. A. *Manual for kit of reference tests for cognitive factors* (revised). Princeton, N.J.: Educational Testing Service, 1963.

Glushko, R. Principles for pronouncing print: The psychology of phonography. In A. M. Lesgold & C. A. Perfetti (Eds.), *Interactive processes in reading.* Hillsdale, N.J.: Lawrence Erlbaum Associates, 1980.

Guilford, J. P. *The nature of human intelligence.* New York: McGraw-Hill, 1967.

Halliday, M. A. K., & Hasan, R. *Cohesion in English.* London: Longman, 1976.

Hawkins, H. L., Church, M., & DeLemos, S. *Time-sharing is not a unitary ability* (Tech. Rep. No. 2). Center for Cognitive and Perceptual Research, University of Oregon, 1978.

Hunt, E. B., Lunneborg, C. E., & Lewis, J. What does it mean to be high verbal? *Cognitive Psychology,* 1975, *7,* 194–227.

Jöreskog, K. G. A general method for analysis of covariance structures. *Biometrika,* 1970, *57,* 239–251.

Jöreskog, K. G., & Sörbom, D. Statistical models and methods for analysis of longitudinal data. In D. G. Aigner & A. S. Goldberger (Eds.), *Latent variables in socioeconomic models.* Amsterdam: North-Holland, 1977.

Jöreskog, K. G., van Thillo, M., & Gruvaeus, G. T. *ACOVSM: A general computer program for analysis of covariance structures including generalized manova* (Research Bulletin RB-71-1). Princeton, N.J.: Educational Testing Service, 1971.

Kahneman, D. *Attention and effort.* Englewood Cliffs, N.J.: Prentice-Hall, 1973.

Kinsbourne, M. Attentional dysfunctions and the elderly: Theoretical models and research perspectives. In L. Poon, J. Fozard, L. Cermak, D. Arenberg, & L. Thompson (Eds.), *New directions in memory and aging.* Hillsdale, N.J.: Lawrence Erlbaum Associates, 1980.

Lord, F. M., & Novick, M. R. *Statistical theories of mental test scores.* Reading, Mass.: Addison-Wesley, 1968.

Mason, M. Reading ability and letter search time: Effects of orthographic structure defined by single-letter positional frequency. *Journal of Experimental Psychology: General,* 1975, *104,* 146–166.

Mason, M., & Katz, L. Visual processing of nonlinguistic strings: Redundancy effects in reading ability. *Journal of Experimental Psychology: General,* 1976, *105,* 338–348.

Mayzner, M. S., & Tressault, M. E. Tables of single-letter and diagram frequency counts for various word-length and letter-position combinations. *Psychonomic Mongraph Supplements,* 1965, *1,* 13–22.

McClelland, J. L. *On the time relations of mental processes: A framework for analyzing processes in cascade* (Rep. No. 77). Center for Human Information Processing, University of California, San Diego, La Jolla, California, 1978.

Morton, J. Interaction of information in word recognition. *Psychological Review,* 1969, *76,* 165–178.

Norman, D. A., & Bobrow, D. G. On data-limited and resource-limited processes. *Cognitive Psychology,* 1975, *7,* 44–64.

Perfetti, C. A., & Lesgold, A. M. Discourse comprehension and sources of individual differences. In M. A. Just & P. A. Carpenter (Eds.), *Cognitive processes in comprehension*. Hillsdale, N.J.: Lawrence Erlbaum Associates, 1977.

Perfetti, C. A., & Lesgold, A. M. Coding and comprehension in skilled reading and implications for reading instruction. In L. B. Resnick & P. A. Weaver (Eds.), *Theory and practice of early reading*. Hillsdale, N.J.: Lawrence Erlbaum Associates, 1979.

Perfetti, C. A., & Roth, S. Some of the interactive processes in reading and their role in reading skill. In A. M. Lesgold & C. A. Perfetti (Eds.), *Interactive processes in reading*. Hillsdale, N.J.: Lawrence Erlbaum Associates, 1980.

Posner, M. I., & Mitchell, R. F. Chronometric analysis of classification. *Psychological Review*, 1967, *74*, 392–409.

Schneider, W., & Shiffrin, R. M. Controlled and automatic human information processing: I. Detection, search, and attention. *Psychological Review*, 1977, *84*, 1–66.

Shiffrin, R. M., & Schneider, W. Controlled and automatic human information processing: II. Perceptual learning, automatic attending, and a general theory. *Psychological Review*, 1977, *84*, 127–190.

State of New York, The Board of Regents. *Degrees of reading power test*. Albany, N.Y.: State Education Department, 1977.

Sternberg, R. J. *Intelligence, information processing, and analogical reasoning: The componential analysis of human abilities*. Hillsdale, N.J.: Lawrence Erlbaum Associates, 1977.

Sverko, B. *Individual differences in time-sharing performance. Acta Instituti Psychologici*, 1977, 79, 17–30.

Winston, P. H. *Artificial intelligence*. Reading, Mass.: Addison-Wesley, 1979.

4 Basic Numerical Abilities

Rochel Gelman
University of Pennsylvania

Typically, definitions of human intelligence include some reference to mathematical abilities. Most IQ tests have questions requiring some knowledge of mathematics or arithmetic. Piaget highlighted the role of mathematical-logical knowledge in the development of concrete and formal operations. And, people who are able to do mathematics are thought to be bright—at least in Western cultures. Why the pervasiveness of the assumption that mathematical abilities contribute to intelligence? I think it follows from a general view that "abstract" thinking abilities are fundamentally involved in "intelligent" thinking. By definition, mathematical ideas are abstract. This is even true for our ideas about natural numbers—they are *not* "out there" in the real world waiting to be noticed. Hence, by implication, mathematical ideas represent an advanced level of intellectual ability.

I believe the assumption that mathematical thought is both abstract and intelligent has contributed to our willingness to presume that the concept of number and arithmetic abilities are relatively late on the developmental scale. Be it Piaget (1967), Vygotsky (1962), or Bruner, Olver, and Greenfield (1966) to whom we appeal, the view is that abstract concepts are not available to preschoolers. Against this theoretical backdrop, it is easy to accept the argument that arithmetic concepts likewise are not available to preschoolers. It is common to read that preschoolers count by rote with no understanding of the counting procedure (Piaget, 1952; Saxe, 1979a, 1979b), let alone an accurate concept of number. Piaget's finding (1952) that preschoolers fail the conservation of number task served to buttress the view that number concepts are late in developing. However reasonable such assumptions might seem, they are probably wrong. Recent evidence points to the conclusion that certain mathematical abilities are present during the preschool years. Indeed, it seems that the ability to count and do simple arithmetic problems may be as natural as the ability to speak a language.

In this chapter, I review the findings on the nature of early counting abilities—findings which support the view that very young children have implicit knowledge of counting principles. Next, I consider how implicit knowledge of counting might develop into explicit knowledge, including a beginning understanding of infinity. Then I take up the functions that can be served with this knowledge of the principles. I then marshal the evidence that counting and related abilities involve natural, universal cognitive abilities. I end with a discussion of the limitations of this conclusion.

A DEFINITION OF COUNTING

In order to assess the young child's ability to count, it helps to have a definition of counting as a yardstick against which to compare performance levels. According to Gelman and Gallistel (1978), counting involves the coordinated application of five principles. This list of principles was derived from a consideration of formal definitions, existing psychological models of counting (e.g. Klahr & Wallace, 1976; Schaeffer, Eggleston, & Scott, 1974), and an initial analysis of what looked like counting sequences generated by preschool children. The principles are: (1) the one-one principle; (2) the stable-order principle; (3) the cardinal principle; (4) the abstraction principle; and (5) the order-irrelevance principle.

As Gelman and Gallistel (1978) point out, every known counting model assumes the use of the one-one principle, which involves ticking off the items in an array with distinct tags so that one and only one tag is used for each item in the array. In following this principle, an individual has to coordinate two component processes: *partitioning* and *tagging*. Partitioning involves the step by step maintenance of two categories of items—the to-be-counted and the already-counted categories. Items must be moved (physically or mentally) from the latter category to the former. The partitioning process must be coordinated with the tagging process, which involves the summoning up of distinct tags, one at a time. These are typically the count words, but they need not be. As long as the set of tags is distinct and different from the names of attributes of the to-be-counted items, it can serve the tagging function.

Although counting must involve the one-one principle, the use of this principle by itself does not constitute counting. At the very least, the one-one principle must be applied in coordination with the stable-order principle. That is, the tags used in a count must be arranged or chosen in a stable, repeatable order. The principle requires the availability of a stable list that is at least as long as the to-be-counted number of items requires it to be.

The one-one and stable-order principles involve the selection and application of tags to the items in a set. The cardinal principle captures the fact that the *final* tag in a count sequence has a special status. It, unlike any other tags, represents the number of items in a set. This principle presupposes the first two principles and the ability to pull out the last tag in a sequence for use in indexing the cardinal value represented in an array.

The three foregoing principles together constitute the *how-to-count* procedure of the Gelman and Gallistel model. The fourth principle—the abstraction principle—captures the fact that the counting procedure can be applied to any collection of real and imagined objects. Although not a common practice, we could in principle collect together for a count such disparate items as the letters of the alphabet, all pieces of furniture in a room, and the number of minds in that room. For adults, at least, any set of any combination of discrete things can be counted. This is so obvious that one might question its elevation to the status of a principle. The reason comes from the developmental literature. Many have maintained that young children severely restrict the definition of countables. Ginsburg (1975) wrote that early counting and the concept of number are: "tied to particular concrete contexts, geometric arrangements, activities, people, etc. It is a long time before the young child treats number as abstract [p. 60]." Gast (1957) advanced a similar view and, on the basis of his counting experiments, concluded that only children 7 years of age or older have a fully abstract conception of what can be counted.

Gast shared a widespread view of how a child comes to recognize that any kinds of objects can be put together for a count. To do this, the child must recognize that all objects can be assigned to the common category *things*. By one account of development, this ability is very abstract. This follows from a common theoretical argument about the nature of classification abilities, namely, that they proceed from being extremely concrete to very abstract (cf. Bruner et al., 1966; Vygotsky, 1962; Werner, 1957). The idea is that the ability to classify objects as things is the result of being able to form an extremely elaborate hierarchy of subcategories wherein the superordinate is *thing*. Hence, the view is that children slowly develop a more and more abstract conception of *thingness*. If so, what may be obvious to the adult may not be obvious to the child.

Should it turn out that young children are relatively indifferent to the definition of countables, it is not necessary to conclude that they make use of a complex scheme for constructing hierarchies. One can view the ability to classify the world as things and nonthings as a close derivative of the ability to separate figures from grounds. Following this interpretation, the categorization of things as opposed to nonthings may well be among the earliest mental classifications. Hence, should the data reveal an early ability to classify heterogeneous items together for counting, we have an alternative to the conclusion that this ability implies the use of a hierarchical classification scheme.

The order-irrelevance principle captures a crucial fact about the adult's knowledge of counting. In many respects, it does not matter which tag is assigned to which object. Any object can be tagged with any of the appropriate count words (i.e., those in the stable-order list). Given a linear array showing pictures of a star, a circle, a triangle, a nonsense shape, and so on, it makes no difference which item is tagged as *one*. Furthermore, it is perfectly acceptable to designate the star as *one* on trial *a* and the triangle as *one* on trial *b*. As long as each item is uniquely tagged and the stable-order principle is honored, the order in which items are tagged is irrelevant. The child who recognizes this fact can determine that the cardinal number of a set is the same, no matter which items are tagged *one, two,* etc.

Ginsburg (1977) cites anecdotes of young children who seem to believe that a given number word becomes attached to a given object. Piaget (1952) makes much of a child who was surprised to discover that a set of 10 objects was still a set of 10 objects even if a count was started at a different point in the array. If preschoolers do not recognize that the order in which items are tagged is irrelevant, it would be difficult to conclude that they understand the role of counting in the quantification of a display. Counting represents a set of procedures for generating a numerical representation, a representation that is not a direct perception of things "out there" in the world. A child who insists that the first object is called *one* fails to recognize that much about counting is arbitrary.

Children who honor all the counting principles clearly know how to count. But what about children who make errors? It depends on what kind of errors children make as to whether we grant them implicit knowledge of any one principle or any combination of principles.

EVIDENCE THAT YOUNG CHILDREN DO "KNOW" HOW TO COUNT

A Caveat

It is important to recognize the distinction between an implicit and explicit understanding of principles or rules. Young children are granted implicit knowledge of linquistic structures well before they are granted explicit knowledge (cf. de Villiers & de Villiers, 1972; Gleitman, Gleitman, & Shipley, 1972), which is often characterized as metalinguistic. As we see later, a similar distinction can be made concerning counting principles.

Evidence for Implicit Knowledge of the Three How-To-Count Principles

A child is granted implicit knowledge of the rules of a language on the basis of at least two kinds of data—the systematic production of sentences of given complexity (e.g., Brown, 1973) and overgeneralization errors like *mouses, footses, unthirsty,* etc. that can only be explained by reference to the availability of rules (e.g., Berko, 1958; Brown, 1973; Clark & Clark, 1977). In 1978, Gelman and

Gallistel provided comparable evidence that even some 2-year-olds honor the three how-to-count principles and that many 3-year-olds honor all five counting principles.

The 2½-year-olds.   Perhaps the most compelling evidence that some 2½-year-olds have implicit knowledge of the how-to-count principles is the use of what Gelman and Gallistel call idiosyncratic lists and Fuson (e.g., Fuson & Richards, 1979) calls nonstandard lists. These appear in very young children even when they count larger set sizes. Although the lists are nonstandard, they are nevertheless used systematically. Thus, for example, a 2½-year-old child might say "2-6" when counting a two-item array and "2-6-10" when counting a three-item array (the one-one principle). The same child will use his or her own list over and over again (the stable-order principle) and, when asked how many items are present, repeat the last tag in the list (the cardinal principle). Gelman and Gallistel note that the 2½-year-old who uses an idiosyncratic list is better able to use it in the same order over count trials than one who works with the conventional list. This observation fits with the fact that subjects who impose their own organization on material are better able to recall it (e.g., Mandler & Pearlstone, 1966). The latter argument presupposes that the child is honoring some rule or organization; the stable-order principle is as good a candidate as any we can think of.

The 2½-year-old also reveals some—albeit not a perfect—ability to honor the one-one and cardinal principles. When asked to count the number of items in an array, there is a systematic tendency to use more tags for set sizes 4 and 5 than for set sizes 2 and 3 (Gelman & Gallistel, 1978). Although the numerical relationship between the number of tags and objects is imprecise, it is far from random. Hence, Gelman and Gallistel suggest that 2½-year-olds recognize that counting involves assigning tags to items in an array. They also report that 50% of the 2-year-olds who participated in a counting experiment were able to identify the cardinal numerosity of a two-item array, and all of the same children could count the same number of items when asked. Only 25% of the children could likewise count and then identify the cardinal value of three-item arrays. Gelman and Gallistel conclude that the tendency of very young children to apply the cardinal principle is weaker than the tendency to apply either the stable-order or one-one principle, an observation that finds support in the analysis of the counting abilities of 3- to 5-year-old children.

The Older Preschoolers.   The main evidence for the Gelman and Gallistel claim that 3- to 5-year-olds honor the how-to-count principles came from their study of how well children adhered to each of the separate principles and how well they coordinated the application of all three principles when responding to requests to count heterogeneous set sizes of 2, 3, 4, 5, 11, and 19 items. The design called for a child to count each set size six times (three times for a linear arrangement and three times for a haphazard arrangement of the display). Thus, it was possible to determine if a child used an idiosyncratic or a standard list. (If they did use an idiosyncratic list, it was not held against them.) Each count trial was scored for whether a child used as many tags as there were items (the one-one principle); for whether the list of tags was systematic, by virtue of the fact that the conventional or an idiosyncratic list was used repeatedly over trials (the stable-order principle); and for whether the child indicated the correct cardinal value of an array by repeating the last tag used. Then, summaries of how well a child did on a given set size were analyzed to determine how many children in each age group honored all or some of the how-to-count principles. Error analyses shed light on the sources of difficulty and development involved in the application of the counting procedure.

The evidence regarding the application of the one-one principle was quite good. A crude index of the tendency to honor this principle is whether or not children used as many tags (unique or not) as there were objects to count. If children attempted to count a given set size, they did quite well at applying either N or ($N \pm 1$) tags even for set sizes of 19. The 3-year-olds did make errors. For set sizes of 7, 9, 11, and 19, 73%, 65%, 67%, and 10% of them used either N or $N \pm 1$tags. Still, except for set size 19, these scores are quite creditable.

Error analysis of the application of the one-one principle revealed two major types of errors: (1) the double counting or skipping of an item in the middle of a count; (2) doing the same thing, i.e., double-counting or skipping an item at either the beginning or end of a count. Tagging errors were infrequent, and when they occurred they always involved the repetition of a tag rather than the use of an inappropriate one (e.g., *blue* or a *mouse*). Gelman and Gallistel point out that such results are consistent with a performance-demand hypothesis of the errors. Children have trouble starting and stopping a count (hence, one-too-many or one-too-few tags), and they slip up as they pass between adjacent items, sometimes double counting or skipping an item. They conclude that even 3-year-olds in this experiment did a reasonable job of applying the one-one principle.

More than 90% of the 4- and 5-year-olds and 80% of the 3-year-olds in the Gelman and Gallistel study used the same list on all their trails regardless of set size. Hence, it was concluded that these children honored the stable-order principle. They did not do nearly as well in applying the cardinal principle (see Table 4.1 where the children's tendency to apply all three principles in concert is summarized).

The main reason a child was not scored as having used all three principles was his or her failure to indicate the cardinal value of an array of a given set size. Gelman and Gallistel concluded that the performance demands of counting larger and larger set sizes became too great. Thus, a child forgot to repeat the last tag.

Further Evidence. Some have argued that Gelman and Gallistel granted their subjects too much competence (Siegler, 1979; Sternberg, 1980). But, if

TABLE 4.1
Percentage of Children
Who Used All Three How-to-Count
Principles in the Gelman and Gallistel
Counting Experiment[a]

Set Size	Age		
	3 Years	4 Years	5 Years
2	76	74	93
3	67	79	100
4	57	68	100
5	43	63	86
7	19	47	80
9	0	37	67
11	5	37	47
19	0	16	20

[a] Based on Table 8.10, pp. 128–129, Gelman and Gallistel (1978). These figures included children who applied all principles perfectly and those who were shaky in their adherence to either or both of the one-one and stable order principles. See Chapter 8 of Gelman and Gallistel (1978) for coding information.

preschoolers do "know" the counting principles, they should recognize counting errors. And, if performance demands limit their application of the cardinal principle, experimental manipulations that reduce performance demands should increase their tendency to state the cardinal value of a set. Recent research along both lines lends support to the original Gelman and Gallistel conclusion.

Gelman and Gallistel commented on the ubiquitous tendency of their subjects to self-correct their own counts. It is difficult to explain this without presuming that a child monitored the application of the counting principles and detected an error. And, now there is evidence that preschoolers can detect some kinds of counting errors. Fuson and Richards (1979) refer to the fact that 3-year-olds recognize counting errors, although only older children can describe them. Mierkiewicz and Siegler (1981) find that 3-year-olds are able to recognize some counting errors, especially the skipping of an item (what I call a partitioning error). Four- and five-year-olds recognize a diverse set of counting errors (e.g., omitting or adding an extra tag; double counting an item) moreover, they recognize that it is acceptable to count alternate items of the same kind and then back up to count the remaining items of another kind in a given display. They also recognize that it is acceptable to start a count in the middle of an array. Gelman and Meck (in preparation) find that 3½- and 4-year-old children can indicate whether a puppet's count trials had errors when the errors were violations of the cardinal principle (e.g., the puppet said $x + 1$ rather than x in response to a "how many" question). The children did this even for set sizes to which they themselves failed to apply the cardinal principle (e.g., 15 and 20).

Having a puppet do the counting for a preschooler is one way of reducing the performance demands of the task, and this is presumably why the children did so well in detecting cardinal errors. Gelman and Meck (in preparation) followed this reasoning in their second experiment with 2½- to 3-year-olds. As expected, the children's ability to count with accuracy broke down with set sizes larger than 2 and 3. However, when the experimenter did the counting and then asked the child to indicate "how many," 78% of the subjects were correct on at least one set size beyond that which they could count; 44% were correct on set sizes up to 20.

If 3- to 5-year-olds do not have the cardinal principle available, Markman (1979) should not have been able to increase the preschooler's tendency to report the cardinal value of an array as a function of variations in question type. Yet she did. Markman distinguishes between concepts that are organized as *classes* as opposed to *collections* (Markman, 1979; Markman & Siebert, 1976). To illustrate this distinction, consider the concepts of *trees* and *forests*. Given a particular instance of a tree, one can answer whether or not it is a member of the class *trees*. However, given the same instance of the same tree, one cannot answer whether it is a member of a forest. A tree by itself does not a forest make. There must be other trees nearby (i.e., a tree is a member of a forest only if it is in close proximity to many other trees). Likewise, a particular child is not a member of a *family* unless it has a relationship with other people (e.g., siblings or parents). In contrast, a particular child *is* a member of the class *children*.

Markman (1979) suggests that class terms for a given display have the effect of focusing attention on the particular members of the display and that collection terms have the effect of focusing attention on the overall characteristics of the display. She notes that the cardinal number of a display represents the complete set but not the individuals in that set; a set may be said to represent five items but none of the individual items can be labeled *five*.

When young children are asked to count the number of items in a display and then indicate "how many" are there, they have a strong tendency to recount the display (e.g., Schaeffer et al., 1974). Markman tested 3- and 4-year-old children's ability to apply the cardinal principle when asked collection versus class questions. For example, children in the collection condition were instructed: "Here is a nursery school class. Count the children in the class. How many children are in the class?" Children in the class condition were asked: "Here are some nursery school children. Count the children. How many . . . . ?" Set sizes were 4, 5, or 6. On 86% of their trials, children in the collection group gave the last number in their count list as a response to the final question. In contrast, children in the class group were as likely to recount without repeating the last number as they were simply to repeat the last number. Clearly, a standard counting task underestimates the young child's ability to apply the cardinal principle. When all facts are considered, it seems reasonable to say that young children honor the cardinal principle, but this tendency is restricted to certain conditions. And because their application of the cardinal principle depends on applying the one-one and stable-order principles, they obviously must be using these as well—an assumption confirmed by their ability to detect errors in their application.

Implicit Knowledge of the Abstraction and Order-Irrelevance Principles

Over the years, I have varied the type of item used in an experiment, including two- and three-dimensional displays and homogeneous versus heterogeneous displays. I have seen little, if any, effect of these variations on performance levels. For example, Gelman and Tucker report no differences in the ability of their preschool subjects to make absolute judgments of the set sizes of homogeneous of heterogeneous items. Thus, it seems that young children are indifferent to a wider range of variations in item type than predicted by Klahr and Wallace (1976) or observed by Gast (1957). In addition, the Gast study can be faulted on the grounds that children were first tested on homogeneous arrays, which probably prompted the younger children to count only similar items (Gelman & Tucker, 1975).

Elsewhere, I report on experiments designed to determine the conditions under which 3- and 4-year-olds would be affected by item type (Gelman, 1980). In one such experiment, children were asked to count everything in the room. If children refuse to classify animate and inanimate objects together for a count, they should count items within each category only. Given that young children recognize the difference between animate and inanimate objects (Carey, 1978; Gelman & Spelke, 1981; Keil, 1979), it seemed reasonable to expect them to keep these objects in separate groups when counting. The fact that they did not further supports the conclusion that preschoolers apply the abstraction principle when deciding what can be collected together for purposes of a count. In response to instructions, children typically did one of two things. They spontaneously counted all the objects (i.e., people, tables, chairs, etc.) or they started by counting only animate or inanimate objects. But when asked "what about me and you?" (or "what about the other things in the room?"), they continued their count. That is, they did not start over again from 1 as would be expected had they thought that animates and inanimates could not be grouped together for counting.

Given these findings, I conclude that preschoolers are rather indifferent to item types when it comes to applying the counting procedure. I do believe, however, that conditions that make it more difficult for the young child to apply the one-one principle correctly *will* affect performances. I have also reported (Gelman, 1980) on an experiment where children were asked to count the exact same heterogeneous arrays under two conditions. In one condition, they could touch and move the objects; in the other, they could not because the objects were under a plexiglass dome. The idea was that item type would influence performance when items are presented in a way that interferes with the young child's prevalent tendencies to point to, touch, and move objects—a strategy that I see as being used in the service of the partitioning process requirement of the one-one principle. Results were as expected. Overall performance in the plexiglass condition was worse. An age-by-condition-by-set-size interaction supports the hypothesis that practice at counting a given set size reduces the performance demands and hence increases accuracy (cf. Case & Serlin, 1979).

On the basis of these experiments, I conclude that the main effects of stimulus variables involve performance-demand variables or tendencies of young children to be unduly influenced by context variables. Recent habituation studies show that even an infant's ability to discriminate among two-, three-, and four-item arrays is *not* dependent on item type (Starkey, Spelke, & Gelman, 1980; Strauss & Curtis, 1980). Given this fact, it is hardly surprising that the same is true for preschoolers.

In the counting experiment summarized earlier as well as in a subsequent experiment designed to test for the use of the order-irrelevance principle, Gelman and Gallistel asked children to count repeatedly a given set size of heterogeneous items. In both experiments, there was little, if any, tendency to try to keep assigning the same tag to a given item as it got moved around from trial to trial. The children seemed indifferent to the order in which they tagged particular items. Hence, the conclusion followed that children had implicit knowledge of the order-irrelevance principle. And because the subsequent order-irrelevance experiment (see the following section) revealed explicit knowledge of this principle in almost all 5-year-olds and many younger children, the idea that children of the same age have implicit knowledge of the order-irrelevance principle is reasonable.

The Development of Explicit Knowledge

When children as young as 3 are asked to count a set of a given value, over and over again, they are indifferent as to the order of the items as the items change across trials. Such behavior is what one would expect if the child has an implicit understanding of the order-irrelevance principle. The behavior does not index explicit understanding of this principle. Indeed, explicit understanding is at best weak in the 3-year-old child. However, the development of explicit understanding of this principle is well advanced by 5 years of age. This fact is illustrated in the 5-year-olds' performance on a modified counting task.

The modified counting task required a child first to count a linear display of five heterogeneous items. Almost all children do this by starting at one end or another and thereby setting the stage for the modified counting trials. These trials start with the experimenter pointing to some item in the middle of the array and saying: "Count all these but make this be the 1." Having done that, the child is asked to make the designated item the *2, 3, 4* . . . and $x + 1$. Then the child is asked similar questions about a different object. Five-year-olds are nearly perfect across all the modified counting trials. Further, they try to say something about how movement of the items per se does not affect the tagging process.

The results of the modified counting task provides evidence that most 5-year-olds have explicit knowledge of the order-irrelevance principle. The $x + 1$ trial allows us to reach a similar conclusion about the cardinal principle. This is true because many of the 5-year-olds balked at the $x + 1$ request, often complaining "there are only five" and/or "I need another one." Stated differently, they knew their count was conserved no matter how the items were arranged as long as the same set size was maintained through rearrangements of the objects. I submit that they also knew that number names are temporary tags. Otherwise, they would not have rearranged objects in a row so as to establish a correspondence between the position of that item and the order of tags (Merkin & Gelman, 1975). Nor would they have been able to answer the questions asked at the end of the experiment.

To end the modified counting task, the experimenter first pointed out that, over trials, the child had labeled a given object 1, 2, 3, 4, etc. and then another object 1 and 2. The child was then asked if it was all right to use the same count word for the two different objects. Finally, the child was asked if he or she could reverse the names of the object (e.g., by calling the chair a baby and vice versa). Even most of the 5-year-olds failed the Piagetian nominalism question and insisted that a chair was a chair and a baby was a baby. In contrast, the same 5-year-olds—as well as many 3- and 4-year-olds—showed no inclination to restrict the assignment of a given count work. Indeed, they occasionally were very articulate, as was one 4-year-old who said: "It could be 1 or 2 or any number, like 6, 10, and even 14."

Just as there is development from an implicit to an explicit understanding of the order-irrelevance and cardinal count principles, so there is such a course for the other counting principles. As indicated earlier, 3-year-olds can tell which count sequences have double count, omission, and other errors, but only older children can say why (Fuson & Richards, 1979). Mierkiewicz and Siegler (1981) find that preschoolers are able to recognize a variety of counting errors. But it is not until children reach school age that they are able to say why an errorless count sequence involving the alphabet as tags is a better count trial than one that uses the conventional count words but includes errors (Saxe, 1979a). Thus, we see the development of an understanding of the one-one and stable-order counting principles becoming more explicit.

But, it is not only the explicit understanding of the counting procedure that develops. So does an explicit appreciation of the facts that counting is an iterative process and that there is no largest number. Evans (1982) finds that kindergarten children typically resist the idea that each addition of one item will increase number. Their resistance is highly correlated with their ideas of what constitutes a "big number." These are usually under 100 or made-up combinations like "forty-thirty-a hundred." Apparently, children need some experience with largish numbers before they can induce that counting is iterative. For, at a second level of development, children talk about a 1,000,000 and other large numbers when asked what is a very large number. They then allow that the addition of an item can go on and on. But even this advancement does not guarantee that they think there is no upper limit on the natural numbers. Instead, they maintain that despite the possibility of another, and another, and another larger number with each addition of one, there is nevertheless a largest number. Finally, by 8 or 9 years of age, children recognize and accept the possibility of nonending iteration and state that there is no largest number. There seems to be a progressive bootstrapping of one level of understanding to the next with intermediate plateaus where children assimilate enough examples before achieving, in Piagetian terms, a reflective abstraction of their earlier levels of knowledge as well as a new level of understanding.

RELATED NUMBER CONCEPTS AND ABILITIES

There is an evergrowing body of literature on the nature of addition and subtraction skills in preschool children, and it points to the conclusion that preschoolers know that addition increases set size whereas subtraction decreases set size. Smedslund (1966) had 5- and 6-year-olds indicate whether two arrays of equal value ($N = 16$) were in fact equal; then the arrays were screened. When one of the arrays was transformed by adding or subtracting one object, the children were able to indicate which array contained more elements. The same finding was reported for 4- and 5-year-olds by Brush (1972), and for 3-, 4-, and 5-year-olds by Cooper, Starkey, Blevins, Groth, and Leitner (1978). Also, I (Gelman, 1972a, 1972b, 1977) and Cooper et al. (1978) found that 3-, 4-, and 5-year-olds could infer the occurence of a screened addition or subtraction by comparing the pre- and posttransformation values of arrays.

What does one make of the fact that preschoolers can count *and* do understand the respective consequences of adding and subtracting? I submit it is possible for young children to use counting as an algorithm in simple arithmetic tasks. Stated differently, one consequence of being able to count is the ability to develop early skill at addition and subtraction. I often find that 3- and 4-year-olds spontaneously count when confronted with unexpected changes in set sizes and thereby determine the difference. Groen and Resnick (1977) taught 4½-year-olds to solve simple addition problems by use of a counting algorithm. Their instruction consisted of having children first count out two groups of objects of given set sizes, then combine the groups and count them to achieve an answer to arithmetic problems. Half the children spontaneously employed a more efficient algorithm than they had been taught. This was to count on from the cardinal value of the greater of the to-be-added numbers.

Starkey and Gelman (in press) tested 3-, 4-, and 5-year-olds on a variety of mental addition and subtraction tasks. Each task began with the experimenter asking how many pennies she held in her open hand. The experimenter then closed her hand and thereby screened the array of pennies. She then said: "Now I'm putting x pennies in my hand; how many pennies does this bunch have?" or "Now I'm taking x pennies out..." Thus, the two values to be added or subtracted were never simultaneously visible. Children did quite well in these tasks. For example, the majority of the 5-year-olds could solve problems that began with one to six items and required adding or subtracting one to four items. As expected, many children used a counting algorithm even though the items were screened.

To be sure, the continued use of a counting algorithm as tasks become more complex could present problems for children in school. The larger a set size, the greater the chance of making counting errors. Written problems are easier to negotiate if some number facts are known or if new algorithms are learned. Obviously, children will have to learn in school many things that they do not know about arithmetic and mathematics. What I am suggesting is that the ability to count facilitates an early understanding of addition and subtraction.

I have hinted at another function served by children's tendency to count. This is that they can provide themselves with thought experiments (cf. Kuhn, 1977) about the nature of natural numbers. Children who set the task of counting all the cracks in the sidewalk, the number of telephone polls they drive by, etc., provide themselves with an opportunity to find out—on their own or from someone else—that counting can go on, and on, and on. This must happen frequently, or else it is hard to explain why half of Evan's first and second grade subjects (who were from a lower-middle to middle-middle class community) said that numbers never end and that there is no largest number. They were not taught about such matters in school.

As indicated before, if children can reach an induction about infinity on the basis of experience with counting, they must have ideas about very large numbers. Counting can serve as a source for learning about the existence of a count sequence that can be very long, as well as for learning about the base rules that contribute to the sequence's potential for length. As in the case of inductions about infinity, I suspect that there is more than one path to this knowledge. Children might ask on their own what the next, and the next, and the next number is. And parents and teachers alike provide input about base rules as to how to count in the 100s and 1000s, etc. Whatever the case may be, the ability and motivation to count at young ages supports inductive learning about some properties of the number system.

In sum, young children who count are able to invent counting algorithms to solve arithmetic problems and provide themselves with practice and inputs that in turn support the acquisition of further knowledge about counting and the natural numbers. Such learning requires a supporting environment. Our culture uses a list of count words and base rules for combining natural numbers just as it provides samples of the English language to the young language learner. However, such learning seems not to require structured lesson plans; it is a case of "informal" learning (cf. Ginsburg, 1977). If I am correct, it should be that counting and simple arithmetic skills are universal and that they develop even in cultures without schools.

EVIDENCE FOR UNIVERSAL ABILITIES

Cross-Cultural Findings

Evidence from a variety of sources converges on the conclusion that the kind of arithmetic abilities we grant preschoolers is universal. First, it appears that most cultures use a counting procedure. It was once commonplace to assign "primitive" numerical abilities to those from nonliterate cultures (e.g., Menninger, 1969). Zaslavsky's (1973) work shows that Africans do indeed count and have done so for centuries. It also illustrates the folly of relying on the ability to use conventional count words as evidence for the ability to count.

Many African societies (e.g., the Kinga, Hebe, and Nyatura of east Africa) use finger gestures and hand configurations to represent different set sizes. A failure to recognize that gestures may be used as tags in enumeration would necessarily lead to an underestimation of the extent to which members of such a society could count. Similarly, a failure to take into account the possibility that number-word sequences need not derive from a base-10 system could lead to the same underestimation of ability. There is a Bushman language that combines the words for 1 and 2 to get the words for 3 and 4. The comparable English count-words sequence for 1 through 4 would read "1, 2, 1-2, 2-2." If we failed to realize that the Bushmen were using a binary concatenation rule, we might conclude they could only count up to 2 and that they had a "one-two-many" conception of differences in set size. Indeed, this is much like the conclusion Menninger (1969) reached. He argued that an ability to count required the use of a count sequence that went beyond the use of 1 and 2: "The number sequence begins at three; three, four, five, . . . etc. When a tribe of South Sea Islanders counts by twos-urapan, okasa, okasa urapan, okasa okasa, okasa okasa urapan (i.e., 1, 2 2'1, 2'2, 2'2'1), we distinctly feel that they have not taken the step from two to three [p. 17]."

Perhaps the best evidence that counting need not be done with a conventional string of words comes from Saxe's (1979a) work in Papua, New Guinea. He reports that people there use the names of their fingers and successive parts of their arms and upper torso as counting tags. The system is illustrated in Fig. 4.1.

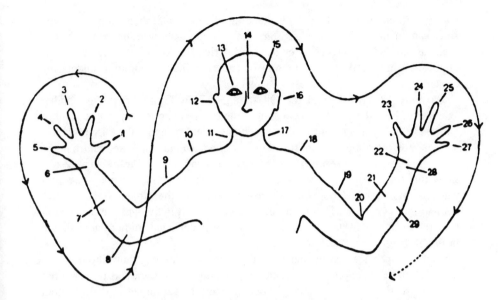

FIG. 4.1.   Illustration of the use of body parts to correspond to number words by a group in Papua, New Guinea. Adapted from Saxe (1979a).

Ginsburg and his colleagues lend further support to Zaslavsky's conclusion that Africans do count. They also find that unschooled children in two West African groups—the Dioula and the Baoule—know informal mathematics at about the same level as preschoolers in American culture. For example, they understand the operations of arithmetic and use counting strategies with concrete objects to solve simple arithmetic problems (Posner, 1978). In both communities, children (7–8 years) are able to accomplish such tasks, whether they are in school or not. An effect of a school-nonschooled variable is observed with the Baoule but not the Dioula children. This is because all of the Dioula children are at ceiling on these tasks before they even start school. Posner (1978) attributes this to what she refers to as the informal mathematics in the Dioula culture.

The Dioula are Muslims who have spread throughout the Ivory Coast. Traditionally, they have engaged in commerce and have a well-developed number system (Zaslavsky, 1973). Hence, theirs is a culture wherein informal mathematical notions are indigenous, much like our own. In contrast, the Baoule culture does not emphasize mathematical thinking and thereby provides a less supportive environment for the arithmetic competence of a child to develop. Thus, schooling becomes a significant variable for the Baoule children's performance levels on even simple mathematical tasks.

Ginsburg's (1979) work with inner-city children in the Baltimore and Washington, D.C. areas supports his view that there are "natural" arithmetic abilities that develop without the support of a school environment. When tested with tasks that assessed their understanding of *more,* and their ability to count and to add using a counting algorithm, these children showed the same kinds of errors as did middle-class children here and African children in West Africa. The implication here is that a common error pattern reflects a common underlying capacity.

Saxe's (1980) work with the Oksapmia of New Guinea provides another example of how the presence of a supporting environment enhances the level of arithmetic ability in an culture without schools. Until recently, the Oksapmia had no money. Now some men are flown to work on a tea plantation and return home with money. Some have even opened small trading stores. Preliminary results show that those who have had the greatest interaction with currency have developed, on their own, more efficient calculation algorithms than those who have not had the interaction. Furthermore, the most skilled individuals are beginning to introduce a base system that is not present in the original count system shown in Fig. 4.1.

I must emphasize that neither I nor Ginsburg are claiming that schooling has no effect on the development of mathematical abilities. Our view is that children bring a great deal of knowledge about numbers and arithmetic to the school setting because counting and simple notions of addition, subtraction, equivalence, and nonequivalence reflect natural, universal abilities. These develop in a supporting environment.

The Effect of Retardation

From the evidence in the previous section, one might conclude that there are limited individual differences in the abilities to learn to count and use counting to solve simple arithmetic tasks. Similar lines of evidence are often cited to support the conclusion that there are limited effects of individual differences in the ability to acquire a first language. In the case of language acquisition there are, however, effects of an extreme variation in individual differences. Retarded individuals are often delayed in the start of language acquisition (Lenneberg, 1966) and, in some cases, lag far behind their Mental Age (M.A.) controls. Fowler, Gelman, and Gleitman (1980) find very limited syntactic abilities in some Down's syndrome teen-agers. Still, many of their abilities are indistinguishable from those of a control group. For example, when teen-age retardates with an average mean length of utterance (MLU) of about three words are compared to normal 2½- to 3-year-olds with the same MLU, we find no differences in the kinds of grammatical morphemes and syntactic structures used.

Reasoning by analogy from the language-acquisition data, I thought it possible that retarded children would show a comparable delay in the acquisition of their ability to count and hence to solve the kind of simple arithmetic tasks considered in this chapter. To find out, Gelman, Haberstedtt, and Hungerford (In preparation) assessed the counting ability of a sample of retarded children. Then,

Starkey and Gelman (in preparation) assessed the ability of some of these children to solve the same arithmetic problems that we had given to normal preschoolers. Children came from three class rooms at a parochial school. The median ages of the groups were 7, 11, and 13 years, respectively, and their median M.A.s were 4 years, 3.5 months; 5 years 9 months; and 7 years 6 months. Half of the two younger groups and one individual from the oldest group were Down's syndrome children. All children in each group were seen in the counting study, and then a sample of the older children was selected for the arithmetic study.

One condition in the counting study was run in much the same way as the initial Gelman and Gallistel experiment—a second demonstration condition was run after the basic condition. In pilot work, I noted a limited tendency for the retarded children to point at and move objects. Hence, we added the *demonstration* condition, wherein the experimenter asked the children to count as she did (i.e., "to touch each toy and count out loud—just like this"). Both sessions were recorded for later scoring according to the Gelman and Gallistel code.

In Fig. 4.2, the results of a composite counting analysis are shown as a function of set size, M.A. group, condition, and criterion strength. The left-hand panels show the percentage of children who used all three how-to-count principles on at least one of the three test trials; the right-hand panels show the percentage who counted perfectly. Inasmuch as no child used systematic non-conventional lists, these percentages reflect tendencies to count correctly with the standard count sequence.

There is a clear effect of M.A. Children in the youngest group with an M.A. of 4 years 3 months are not able—under any conditions—to count even set sizes of 2 and 3 accurately. When left on their own (i.e., the no-demonstration condition), around 30%, 20%, and 0% of these children consistently count set sizes of 2, 3 and 5. The comparable figures reported by Gelman and Gallistel for normal preschoolers were better. For 3-year-olds, they were 76%, 67%, and 58%; for 4-year-olds, they were 74%, 79%, and 68%. Furthermore, some normal 3-year-olds could count set sizes of 7, and some 4-year-olds could succeed on set sizes of 7 through 19. In terms of developmental level, the retardates were behind what I expect of normal 3- and 4-year-olds. The tendency toward a larger developmental lag than expected according to M.A. level persists throughout the groups.

The group data represent individual children who seem unable to count at all and children who are quite excellent counters. Principle-by-principle analyses of the data revealed that retarded children who failed our counting criteria produced error types that I have not see in normal preschoolers. We failed to observe the use of *any* idiosyncratic lists, either within repeated trials on the same set size or across trials. Further, we observed the repeated use of a given count word (a tagging error in the use of the one-one principle), some labeling of objects by name (another tagging error), and a ubiquitous tendency to tag items repeatedly

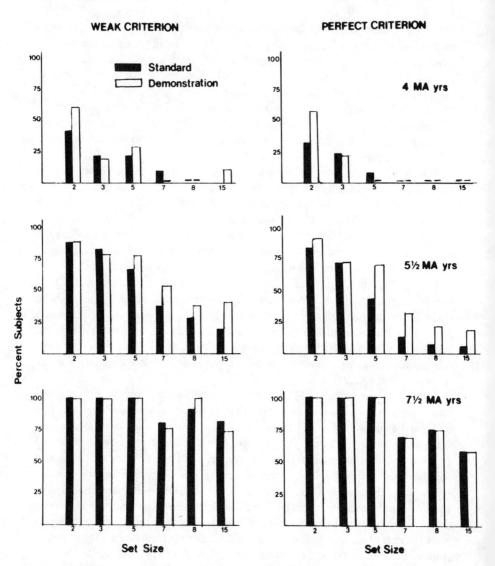

FIG. 4.2.   The ability of retarded children to apply all three how-to-count principles as a function of M.A. level, set size, and experimental condition.

that had already been tagged. When asked "how many" items there were in an
array, children had a strong tendency to keep saying the same number (usually 1
or 2) across different set sizes. Occasionally, a child even used the name or an
attribute of an object.

   In order to determine whether the ability to count is related to the ability to
solve simple arithmetic problems, we assigned an overall grade of "poor,"

"shaky," or "very good" to each child. Eighteen children, six within each grade, were then seen in conditions much like those used by Starkey and Gelman (in press) with normal preschoolers. As we wanted to use some additional tasks, we also ran groups of normal 3-, 4-, and 5-year-olds for comparison with the retardates.

The poor counters (median M.A. = 6 yrs.; median C.A. = 12 yrs.) in the arithmetic study simply could not count set sizes larger than 5. And only one of them was able to indicate the cardinal number for all three of the smaller set sizes (2, 3, 5). Furthermore, their lists of count words were often random beyond 5, similar to what Fuson and Richards (1979) call "spews." Shaky counters (median M.A. = 6 yrs. 6 mos.; median C.A. = 13 yrs.) used the conventional sequence most of the time. However, as set sizes increased beyond 5, they often used the wrong number of tags and hence were scored as weak in their application of the one-one principle; they typically failed on the cardinal principle. Very good counters (median M.A. = 8 yrs. 3 mos.; median C.A. = 13 yrs. 3 mos.) were able to use all three how-to-count principles for all set sizes. Except for one or two error trials on the larger set sizes, these principles were applied consistently. When I watch these children count, the qualitative impression is that the poor group counts by rote, the shaky group is catching on, and the good group is just that. Performance differences on simple arithmetic tasks confirm these impressions.

Here I summarize the data for only the simple arithmetic tasks and some repeated iteration tasks. These involved initial arrays of one to six pennies, which were transformed by adding or subtracting one to five pennies. The initial arrays were screened before addition or subtraction took place.

For both normal preschoolers and retarded children, the difficulty of the simple addition and subtraction problems increased as a function of set size, and success was related to counting ability. Actually, the retarded children did somewhat better than the normal younger children. Thus, 3-year-olds were correct on 31% and 35% of their addition and subtraction tasks, and the respective pairs of percentage correct scores for the 4- and 5-year-olds were 64% versus 52% and 83% versus 71%. In contrast, the poor retarded counters were correct on 64% and 40% of the subtraction problems, shaky counters on 72% and 49%, and good counters on 97% and 97%.

I suspect that many of the differences between the results for normal 3-year-olds and the poor counters reflected the use of different solutions. The 3-year-olds counted and did about as well as expected, given that their skill at counting breaks down around 3. The poor counters in the retardate sample, unlike the normal 3-year-olds, had the benefit of drill in school on similar arithmetic tasks and had memorized some number facts. The suggestion that different solution types were used is confirmed by error analyses.

No matter what their answers, normal preschoolers at every level gave a larger number than the augend on addition trials and a smaller number than the minuend on subtraction trials. This was not true for the retarded poor counters who often gave addition answers for subtraction problems. As an example, they might say the answer to a $4 - 2$ problem is 6. Furthermore, iteration addition tasks (e.g., $x + 1 + 1$) were easier than control items (e.g., $x + 2$) for all preschoolers. This would be expected if solutions were reached via a counting algorithm and not by the retrieval of memorized number facts. Inasmuch as there was such an advantage on the iteration task for the shaky counters but not for the poor counters, the influence that the poor counters did not use a counting strategy is supported.

In sum, as expected, we are finding differences in the ability to count as a function of M.A. in a retarded population. And the hypothesis that these in turn reflect differences in the understanding and solution types used on simple mental arithmetic tasks is supported. On the basis of some pilot work, I venture to guess that the retardate's problems with money are, (e.g., they have terrible problems shopping or buying tickets,) likewise related to a failure to understand the counting principles. Indeed, Thurlow and Turnure (1977) suggest that special education programs probably fail in teaching money concepts because the programs assume the ability to count. In the context of the present chapter, I find Thurlow and Turnure's (1977) speculation that "most [normal] children are apparently able to pick up much of their knowledge about time and money from casual or incidental exposure to the concepts [p. 203]" intriguing because it suggests that these abilities are also candidates for natural and universal abilities. At least with regard to money, Saxe's and Zaslavsky's work would support this conjecture.

Counting in Babies? Probably

Studies of infant's abilities to abstract the numerical value of arrays lend further support to the view that number is a natural domain of competence. Starkey and Cooper (1980) showed infants aged 4 through 6 months linear arrays of dots of white light. In the first phase of their experiment, infants were repeatedly shown a given set size in arrays that varied in length and density over habituation trials. Infants dishabituated to changes in numerosity from two to three or three to two but not changes in length on density. In a subsequent study, Starkey and Cooper (1980) found that 6- through 8-month-old infants habituated to displays of three (or four) items and dishabituated when shown displays of four (or three) dots.

Recovery of habituation is often taken as an index of infants' ability to discriminate between the display they habituate to and the subsequent display. A follow-up to the Starkey and Cooper work confirms the assumption made by these investigators that the reported discriminations were based on numerical judgments. Starkey, Gelman, and Spelke (1980) tested 6- to 8-month-old babies with heterogeneous displays. The displays were photographs of common household items (e.g., comb, pipe, lemon, scissors, corkscrew, etc.) selected to include a variety of colors, shapes, sizes, and surface textures. Each array contained either two or three objects, and no two objects in any array were the same.

Further, the spatial arrangement of the objects was unique from trial to trial. In short, the only common characteristic of the set of three-item and two-item displays was the numerical value. Half of the babies in the experiment viewed either a set of two-item or three-item displays. When their tendency to look at these arrays habituated, they were given a set of posthabituation trials. Both the two-item and three-item groups were shown two-object and three-object arrays presented in alternation. We predicted that infants who habituated to two-item arrays during phase one of the experiment would look longer at the three-item array during posthabituation trials. Conversely, infants habituated to three-item arrays should look longer at the two-item arrays.

As predicted, during the recovery phase, infants looked longer at *their* different-number arrays than at their same-number arrays. Strauss and Curtis (1980) have reported a similar result. In addition, they found that female infants habituate to the class of three (or four) objects and then recover to a change to four (or three) objects. The conclusion I reach about such findings is that infants can attend to the number of objects in a display and abstract a numerical invariant over changes in displays. Inasmuch as we intentionally varied item types and item positions, it is hard to imagine what else they could have been responding to.

In further studies, Starkey, Spelke, and I have determined that infants can also to respond intermodally to numerical information. One study used a procedure devised by Spelke (1976) to investigate infants' knowledge of an auditory-visual relationship. An infant is shown two films side by side while, between them, a loudspeaker plays the sound track that goes with one of the movies. Because infants look at the appropriate movie (i.e., the one that corresponds to the sound track), Spelke has been able to investigate the nature and development of inter-modal perception in infants (e.g., Spelke, 1979). In our study, infants were shown two-item and three-item heterogeneous displays placed side by side. The loudspeaker between the displays emitted either two or three taps on each trial. I confess being surprised to find that babies had a significant tendency to look at the two-item display when two taps were sounded and at the three-item display when three taps were sounded. Thus, it is not only that babies attend to the numerical value represented in a visual display; they can also match visual and auditory modes of presentation on the basis of number. To do this, they must not only be able to abstract number but also be able to use a rudimentary form of nonverbal counting. For what other procedure can be used to compare visual and auditory presentations?

I said I was surprised by the intermodal results. To be sure, they lend strong support to the thesis I advance here. But even if I wanted to say that the full-blown ability to count is innate (and I do not), I need not expect infants to attend to and use number. The human ability to walk upright is largely innate; yet, no one expects a 6-month-old to walk. Hence, I'm puzzled by the fact that 6-month-old infants are interested enough in number to succeed on our tasks. In any event, the research with infants lends support to the idea that the ability to abstract numerical values of displays, and do so by something akin to counting, is natural.

FINAL COMMENTARY

I have argued that the abilities to count and to do simple arithmetic tasks are natural, universal abilities. The preschooler's acquisition of counting is guided by a set of counting principles. Babies can match a numerical abstraction of small sets in the visual mode with one in the auditory mode. As best as we can tell, normal people in all cultures are able to count. And even in environments without schools, there is evidence that the people can solve simple arithmetic tasks. Finally, the ability to count is diagnostic with regard to retarded children's ability to solve simple mental arithmetic problems.

I have repeatedly used the phrase "simple arithmetic" tasks and have done so on purpose. I do not want people to reach the conclusion that rich mathematical abilities can develop irrespective of the environment. Even if I am correct in assuming that there are universal arithmetic abilities, it does not follow that the teaching of mathematics is unimportant. To illustrate why, I consider another natural universal ability—the understanding and production of speech.

Every normal child can and does acquire his or her mother tongue. Language learning, although dependent on a supporting environment, seems to be able to proceed without structured lesson plans (e.g., Newport, Gleitman, & Gleitman, 1977). Still, grammar is taught in schools. This, I submit, is because educators recognize a basic distinction between the ability to converse and the ability to access the structure of the spoken language. Grammar lessons are geared to teaching children the rules that govern their language. However, mastery of these rules does not guarantee that one can do linguistics. This is the task of professional linguists who have studied long and hard to achieve their special abilities. Similar considerations apply to the acquisition of mathematical prowess. The child who invents a counting algorithm is unlikely to discover, on his or her own, the formal properties of a group. Like linguists, mathematicians need to study and master a great deal of mathematics before they are able to do mathematics. And as compared with the ability to learn to count, there are tremendous individual differences in mathematical ability. It remains an open question as to how and whether early arithmetic abilities are related to the ability to learn mathematics in school.

ACKNOWLEDGMENTS

Some of the research and the preparation of this chapter was supported by NSF Grants BNS-770327 and BNS-80-04881 and NICHD Grant 1 PO-HD-10965.

REFERENCES

Berko, J. The child's learning of English morphology. *Word*, 1958, *14*, 150–177.

Brown, R. *A first language: The early stages*. Cambridge, Mass.: Harvard University Press, 1973.

Bruner, J. S., Olver, R. R., & Greenfield, P. M. *Studies in cognitive growth*. New York: Wiley, 1966.

Brush, L. R. *Children's conceptions of addition and subtraction: the relation of formal and informal notions*. Unpublished doctoral dissertation, Cornell University, 1972.

Carey, S. *The child's concept of animal*. Paper presented at the annual meeting of the Psychonomic Society, San Antonio, Texas, November 1978.

Case, R., & Serlin, R. A new process model for predicting performance on Pascual-Leone's test of M-space. *Cognitive Psychology*, 1979, *11*, 308–326.

Clark, H. H., & Clark, E. V. *Psychology and language: An introduction to psycholinquistics*. New York: Harcourt Brace Jovanovich, 1977.

Cooper, R., Starkey, P., Blevins, B., Goth, P., & Leitner, E. *Number development: Addition and subtraction*. Paper presented at the meeting of the Jean Piaget Society, Philadelphia, May 1978.

de Villiers, J. G., & de Villiers, P. A. A cross-sectional study of the development of semantic and syntactic acceptability by children. *Journal of Psycholinguistic Research*, 1972, *1*, 299–310.

Evans, D. *Development of the understanding of concepts of zero, infinity, and negative numbers*. Unpublished doctoral dissertation, University of Pennsylvania, 1982.

Fowler, A., Gelman, R., & Gleitman, L. R. *A comparison of language in normal and retarded children equated for mean length of utterance*. Paper presented at the Fifth Annual Boston Child Language Conference, Boston, Mass., October, 1980.

Fuson, K. C., & Richards, J. *Children's construction of the counting numbers: From a spew to a bidirectional chain*. Northwestern University, July 1979.

Gast, H. Der Umgang mit zahlgebilden in der Furhen Kindeit. *Zeitschrift Fur Psychologie*, 1957, *161*, 1–90.

Gelman, R. The nature and development of early number concepts. In H. W. Reese (Ed.), *Advances in child development and behavior* (Vol. 7). New York: Academic Press, 1972. (a)

Gelman, R. Logical capacity of very young children: Number invariance rules. *Child Development*, 1972, *43*, 371–383. (b)

Gelman, R. How young children reason about small numbers. In N. J. Castellan, D. B. Pisoni, & G. R. Potts (Eds.), *Cognitive theory* (Vol. 2). Hillsdale, N.J.: Lawrence Erlbaum Associates, 1977.

Gelman, R. What young children know about numbers. *The Educational Psychologist*, 1980, *15*, 54–68.

Gelman, R., & Galisstel, C. R. *The child's understanding of number*. Cambridge, Mass.: Harvard University Press, 1978.

Gelman, R., Haberstett, L., & Hungerford, B. *The nature of counting abilities in retardates*. In preparation.

Gelman, R., & Meck, E. *Further evidence on the preschoolers' use of the cardinal principle*. In preparation.

Gelman, R., & Spelke, E. The development of thoughts about animates and inanimates: Some implications for research on the nature and development of social cognition. In J. H. Flavell & L. Ross (Eds.), *Social cognitive development: Frontiers and possible futures*. Cabmridge, England: Cambridge University Press, 1981. 43–66.

Gelman, R., & Tucker, M. F. Further investigations of the young child's conception of number. *Child Development*, 1975, *46*, 167–175.

Ginsburg, H. *Young children's informal knowledge of mathematics*. Unpublished manuscript, Cornell University, 1975.

Ginsburg, H. *Children's arithmetic*. New York: Van Nostrand, 1977.

Ginsburg, H. *Mathematical thinking in inner city black preschool children.* Paper presented at the meeting of the Society for Research in Child Development, San Francisco, April, 1979.

Gleitman, L. R., Gleitman, H., & Shipley, E. F. The emergence of the child as grammarian. *Cognition,* 1972, *1,* 137-164.

Groen, G., & Resnick, L. B. Can preschool children invent addition algorithms? *Journal of Educational Psychology,* 1977, *69,* 645-652.

Keil, F. *Semantic and conceptual development.* Cambridge, Mass.: Harvard University Press, 1979.

Klahr, D., & Wallace, J. G. *Cognitive development; an information processing view.* Hillsdale, N.J.: Lawrence Erlbaum Associates, 1976.

Kuhn, T. S. A function for thought experiments. In P. N. Johnson-Laird & P. C. Wason (Eds.), *Thinking: Readings in cognitive science.* Cambridge, England: Cambridge University Press, 1977.

Lenneberg, E. H. *Biological foundations of language.* New York: Wiley, 1966.

Mandler, G., & Pearlstone, Z. Free and constrained concept learning and subsequent recall. *Journal of Verbal Learning and Verbal Behavior,* 1966, *5,* 126-131.

Markman, E. M. Classes and collections: Conceptual organization and numerical abilities. *Cognitive Psychology,* 1979, *11,* 395-411.

Markman, E., & Siebert, J. Classes and collections: Internal organization and resulting holistic properties. *Cognitive Psychology,* 1976, *8,* 561-577.

Menninger, K. *Number words and number symbols.* Cambridge, Mass.: MIT Press, 1969.

Merkin, S., & Gelman, R. *Strategic behavior in preschoolers who are tested with a modified counting task.* Unpublished manuscript. University of Pennsylvania, 1975.

Mierkiewicz, D. B., & Siegler, R. S. Preschoolers' ability to recognize counting errors. Paper read at a symposium: *Children's Early Number Knowledge.* Society for Research on Child Development, Boston, April, 1981.

Newport, E. L., Gleitman, H., & Gleitman, L. R. Mother, I'd rather do it myself: Some effects and non-effects of maternal speech style. In C. E. Snow & C. A. Ferguson (Eds), *Talking to children: Language input and acquisition.* Cambridge, England: Cambridge University Press, 1977.

Piaget, J. *The child's conception of number.* London: Routledge and Kegan Paul, 1952.

Piaget, J. *Six psychological studies.* New York: Random House, 1967.

Posner, J. K. *The development of mathematical knowledge among Baoule and Dioula children in the Ivory Coast.* Unpublished doctoral dissertation, Cornell University, 1978.

Posner, J., & Ginsburg, H. *Mathematical competence in two west African societies.* Paper presented at annual meeting of the American Anthropological Association 1978.

Saxe, G.B. Children's counting: The early formation of numerical symbols. *New direction for child development: Early Symbolization,* 1979, *3,* 73-84. (a)

Saxe, G. B. *Numerals as body parts: A developmental analysis of numeration among a village population in Papua, New Guinea.* Paper presented at the meeting of the Society for Research in Child Development, San Francisco, Ca., April 1979. (b)

Saxe, G. B. *The changing form of numerical thought as a function of contact with currency among the Okasapmin of Papua New Guinea.* Unpublished manuscript, The Graduate Center of the City University of New York, 1980.

Schaeffer, B., Eggleston, V. H., & Scott, J. L. Number development in young children. *Cognitive Psychology,* 6, 357-379, 1974.

Siegler, R. S. What young children do know. *Contempory Psychology,* 1979, *24,* 614-615.

Smedslund, J. Microanalysis of concrete reasoning. I. The difficulty of some combinations of addition and subtraction of one unit. *Scandanavian Journal of Psychology,* 1966, *1,* 145-156.

Spelke, E. Infants' intermodal perception of events. *Cognitive Psychology,* 1976, *8,* 53-60.

Spelke, E. Perceiving bimodally specified events in infancy. *Developmental Psychology,* 1979, *15,* 626-636.

Starkey, P., & Cooper, R. G. Numerosity perception in human infants. *Science,* 1980, *210,* 1033–1035.

Starkey, P., & Gelman, R. *Arithmetic abilities of retarded children.* In preparation.

Starkey, P., & Gelman, R. The development of addition and subtraction abilities prior to formal schooling. In J. P. Carpenter, J. M. Moser & T. A. Romberg (Eds.), *Addition and subtraction: A developmental perspective.* Hillsdale, N.J.: Lawrence Erlbaum Associates, in press.

Starkey, P. Spelke, E. & Gelman, R. *Number competence in infants: sensitivity to numeric invariance and numeric change.* Paper presented at the meeting of the International Conference on Infant Studies, New Haven, Conn., April 1980.

Sternberg, R. J. Capacity of young children. *Science,* 1980, *208,* 47–48.

Strauss, M. S., & Curtis, L. *Infant perception of numerosity.* Paper presented at the meeting of the International Conference on Infant Studies, New Haven, Conn., April 1980.

Thurlow, M. L., & Turnure, J. E. Children's knowledge of time and money: Effective instruction for the mentally retarded. *Education and Training of the Mentally Retarded,* 1977, 203–212.

Vygotsky, L. S. *Thought and language.* Cambridge, Mass.: MIT Press, 1962.

Werner, H. *The comparative psychology of mental development* (2nd ed.). New York: International Universities Press, 1957.

Zaslavsky, C. *Africa counts.* Boston, Mass.: Prindle, Weber & Schmidt, 1973.

5 Individual Differences in Attention

Earl Hunt
Marcy Lansman
University of Washington

People seldom concentrate their attention on a single activity. Drivers allow their minds to wander without crashing into walls. The executive talking on three telephones at once may be fictional, but the airline traveler who reads while listening for flight announcements is real. Thinking about more than one thing at a time is a complex and important aspect of daily life.

When asked to explain complex behaviors, psychologists often try to break them down into their constituent elements. In factor analysis, performance on a complex test is depicted as a linear combination of basic abilities. Similar reasoning motivates Sternberg's (1977, 1979) technique of componential analysis. Sternberg's approach is to break complex problem-solving behavior into stages and to measure the processes involved in each stage. Problem solving, from this point of view, can be compared to the execution of a complex program with many subroutines. The program is to be understood by isolating the subroutines and measuring their capacities. A similar logic appears in our own research (Hunt, Frost, & Lunneborg, 1973; Hunt, Lunneborg, & Lewis, 1975), where we utilized what Pellegrino and Glaser (1979) have called the "cognitive correlates" approach. The basic idea behind this work is that human thought, as a form of information processing, must involve some basic information-processing functions, analogous to the machine level operations (not the subroutines) of a digital computer (Hunt & Poltrock, 1974). Pure measures of these functions should be related to complex performance.

The assumption that has pervaded our work and that of others is that tasks done in isolation place the same demands on the information-processing system as tasks done concurrently. This is the assumption we wish to question here because it not only pervades the way we analyze data, but also the way we collect it. We take great care to present people with just one problem at a time. But by concentrating on the ability to do things singly, we may miss a dimension of human behavior that is associated with the execution of concurrent tasks. The point has been made eloquently by H. A. Simon (1969) in his book *The Science of the Artificial*. Simon observed that complex systems are often made up of simple subsystems. The complexity arises not from properties of the subsystems, but from their interaction. Hence, we cannot hope to understand the operation of the large system simply by an analysis of the subsystems in isolation.

In this chapter, we look at a very simple model of dual task execution—a model in which each task is seen as competing for a general attentional resource. In such a model, the phrase "pay attention" is taken quite literally. The concept of an allocatable mental resource has received considerable attention in experimental psychology, but little formal effort has been made to apply the concept to individual-differences research or to discover how patterns of individual differences could be used to test models of resource allocation.

This chapter is divided into four sections. The first contains a discussion of the concept of attentional resources as it has been developed by experimental psychologists. The second presents a formal model of the role of attentional resources in determining individual performance. The third reports experimental results that pertain to this model. The closing section deals with further implications of these basic ideas.

THE RESOURCE-COMPETITION MODEL

Theory

According to the resource-competition model, attention is akin to an energy resource in that it can be parceled out over concurrently executed tasks. The proposal has a long history in psychology. Posner (1978) cited relevant papers from the 19th century. Even Spearman's (1927) writings on the nature of general intelligence can be interpreted in terms of a general attentional resource. Kahneman (1973) has written the most comprehensive modern treatment, and we generally follow his analysis.

Consider any information-processing task. By definition, the task involves the manipulation of signals being transmitted through the central nervous system. The manipulations must be carried out by specific structures. What happens when an information-processing system executes two logically independent tasks concurrently? If the tasks require access to the same information-processing structures, then the two tasks will interfere with each other. This is called *structural interference*.

Structural interference is obvious in many situations that require external sensors and effectors. We cannot look to the left and right simultaneously. Nor can we jump east and west. If the "structures" involved are central rather than peripheral, the interpretation is less obvious. For example, Baddeley and Hitch (1974) conducted a series of experiments in which people first memorized a list of digits, then attempted to comprehend sentences, and finally recited the digits. They found that digit memorization interfered with sentence comprehension. Baddeley and Hitch's interpretation was that the two tasks competed for space in a working memory structure. There is no way that such a structure can be observed directly.

Other cases of intertask interference are harder to explain in terms of competition for a structure because it is not clear what structure is required by both tasks. Try to recite poetry while juggling! To account for nonstructural interference, Kahneman (1973) proposed that all mental processes compete for a single pool of attentional resources. We call this the *resource-competition* model. Kahneman argued that attentional resources are analogous to a mental fuel that is drawn upon by virtually every mental activity. The availability of resources places a limit on the amount of mental processing that can take place at any one time.

Attentional resources are drawn upon by different mental structures in accordance with the demands that external tasks place upon them. The quantity of resources made available to a particular structure will depend on the allocation policy that is in effect. An allocation policy determines how resources are to be distributed to the structures required by competing tasks. The allocation policy is based upon the total level of resources available (the *capacity*) and the expected payoff for varying levels of performance in each task. A resource-competition model is not inconsistent with a structural model of intertask interference because the two types of models explain different situations. But how one analyzes people's ability to do several things at once does depend on whether one believes that intertask interference is primarily due to structural or to attentional resource competition.

Norman and Bobrow (1975) elaborated upon Kahneman's proposal by introducing several useful concepts. The first of these was the notion of a *performance-resource function*—a function that specifies the relationship between the level of attentional resource supplied and the performance expected on a task. A hypothetical performance-resource function is shown in Fig. 5.1 and can be used to illustrate Norman and Bobrow's ideas. An important point to remember is that Fig. 5.1 does not represent the relationship between two observables. It relates observable performance, *p,* to the conceptual but *in principle* unobservable variable, *r,* attentional resources. Symbolically, we refer to the function:

$$p = f(r). \hspace{6cm} 5.1$$

Although we cannot observe Equation 5.1 directly, we may place some restrictions on it. First, providing more resources should never hurt performance. Therefore the first derivative, f', should be nonnegative:

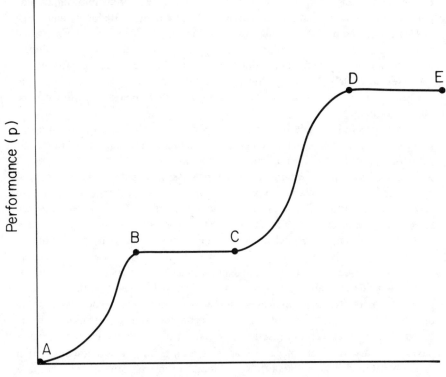

FIG. 5.1.   A performance-resource function, $p = f(r)$. Performance is resource limited in the regions A to B and C to D; it is data limited in the regions B to C and D to E.

$$f'(r) \geqslant 0. \qquad\qquad\qquad 5.2$$

Whenever f' is positive, an increase in resources will cause an increase in performance, and, conversely, a decrease in resources will cause a decrease in performance. In such cases performance is said to be *resource limited*. In Fig. 5.1, performance is resource limited from points A to B and again from C to D. Whenever f' is zero, changing the resource level will not change performance, which is said to be *data limited*.

The terms resource limited and data limited have appealing intuitive interpretations. One can easily think of tasks that seem to be resource limited (i.e., tasks in which performance is determined by the extent to which we pay attention to what we are doing). Data limitations are equally easy to envisage; most normal individuals can memorize two digits easily and could not improve performance by paying more than the minimal amount of attention required. As a more complex example, suppose that you are listening to a radio and that the transmission is masked by static. Up to a certain point, your ability to comprehend the broadcast is determined by the amount of attention you pay to it. Beyond that point, the signal-to-noise rate of the radio transmission becomes the limiting factor, and performance becomes data limited.

Data limitations are produced by the interaction between task requirements and personal capacities and thus cannot be assigned to one cause or the other. In our radio-broadcast example, we located data limitation in the radio transmitter. But two people with different degrees of high-frequency hearing loss would vary in the point at which they shifted from resource-limited performance (where they could comprehend more by paying more attention) to data-limited performance (where additional attention could not improve performance).

In spite of the heuristic value of examples, the concepts of resource and data limitation are strictly defined in terms of Equations 5.1 and 5.2 and, in the last analysis, are abstract relationships that can be represented only imperfectly in any concrete situation. The reason that the performance-resource function and its associated concepts must remain abstract is that we have no direct way of establishing a metric for r, the "amount of resources allocated."

Two indirect approaches to the measurement of resources have been attempted. One is to equate resource expenditure with a change in physiological status. Heart rate, cardiac deceleration, and dilation of the pupil of the eye have all been proposed as appropriate measures. Although these measures are interesting, the fact that they do not correlate well with each other across situations makes their conceptual status problematic.

An alternative approach, which we have taken in our own research, is to use as an index of resource allocation the extent to which one task interferes with the execution of a second standard task. Although the logic of this measurement technique does not depend on Norman and Bobrow's analysis (see, for instance, the alternative treatment by Kerr, 1973), we use their terminology.

Imagine two abstract tasks, 1 and 2, that are to be done concurrently and that do not exhibit structural interference. Performance on the first task may be plotted as a function of performance on the second. Letting p_i be performance on the ith task ($i = 1, 2$), Norman and Bobrow refer to the function:

$$p_1 = g(p_2) \qquad\qquad 5.3$$

as a *performance operating characteristic* (POC). Figure 5.2 presents an abstract POC, which can be used to illustrate some general features of performance-resource functions.

The form of a POC is determined by the competition between tasks for attentional resources. Let R be total resource capacity and let r_1 and r_2 be the resources allocated to tasks 1 and 2. The resulting performance levels are:

$$p_1 = f_1(r_1); \; p_2 = f_2(r_2), \qquad\qquad 5.4$$

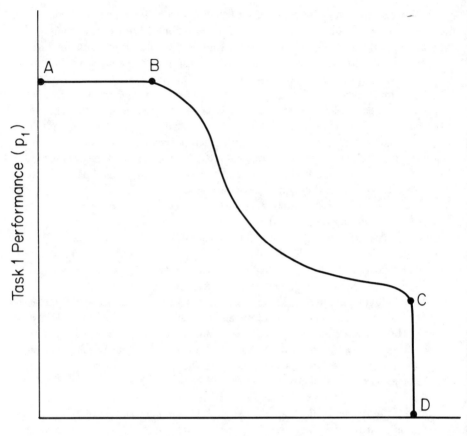

FIG. 5.2.   A performance operating characteristic (POC) plotting performance on one task as a function of performance on a simultaneously performed task.

with r_i subject to the restriction that

$$R = r_1 + r_2.$$ 5.5

Equation 5.5 represents an assumption that the participant devotes a fixed amount of mental resources to the experimental task across all single and dual task conditions. Such an assumption cannot be verified directly. Instead, it must be introduced as an axiom and tested by its implications.

Consider the horizontal section of the POC running from points A to B in Fig. 5.2. Given the assumptions of the resource-competition model, this means that task 1 is data limited at performance level $p_1{}^*$ because task-2 performance increases in the A-B interval whereas task-1 performance is constant. Inasmuch as, by assumption, performance on a fixed task cannot increase without the commitment of more resources to it, some resources must have been diverted from task 1 to task 2 without causing a drop in task-1 performance. By similar reasoning, the vertical segment of the POC, from points C to D, means that task 2 is data limited and that task 1 is resource limited in the C-D interval. Both tasks 1 and 2 must be resource limited in the B-C interval, as an increment in performance of one task is always accompanied by a decrement in performance in the other. What would happen if tasks 1 and 2 were both data limited? The POC would degenerate into a point defined by the intersection of a horizontal and vertical line.

The POC provides us with a method for determining the amount of resources required by an individual in order to reach a given level of performance on task 1, when task 1 has been designated a "primary" or most important to the performer. The experimenter specifies the external problem, establishes the desired level of performance on task 1, and then measures the resource requirements of task 1 by observing performance on the concurrent secondary task, task 2. To illustrate, consider the following experiment. A performer is asked to memorize a short list of digits (task 1) and then, while rehearsing those digits, to react to a probe signal (e.g., a light or tone [task 2]). After responding to the probe, the performer must recall the digits. Suppose that the performance-resource function for rehearsing digits is as shown in Fig. 5.3a. The number of digits one is capable of maintaining in memory increases with the resources deployed, up to the total resource capacity (R). We can replot this figure to show a family of curves: probability of correct recall as a function of resources applied to the task, with the curve parameter being the number of digits to be memorized. This is shown (for two and five digits) in Fig. 5.3b. The goal is to measure the minimum amount of resources required to memorize one, two, three, four, or five digits—points A and B (for two and five) in Fig. 5.3b. But, the abscissa of the performance-resource function refers to a hypothetical variable, r, which, in principle, is not open to direct observation.

Performance on the probe reaction-time task (task 2) may be used to obtain the needed measure. The argument is that, under an appropriate payoff arrangement, a person should devote to the secondary task only those resources that are left over from the primary task. Thus, performance on the secondary task provides a measure of the "spare capacity" left over after adequate resources have been devoted to the primary task. This procedure is valid only if the secondary task is resource limited over the range of performance under consideration.

Continuing our example, suppose that the speed of reaction to a probe is a monotonically increasing function of the resources devoted to the reaction-time task. The argument does not depend on the form of the function, only on the fact that the function satisfies the criterion for resource limitation, $f_2'(r) > 0$.

More generally, resource-competition models make only the weak assumption that overt performance is an ordinal measure of the resources allocated to a task. This has posed problems in the analysis of experiments because of the limited statistical analyses that can be justified when dealing with ordinal data. In the

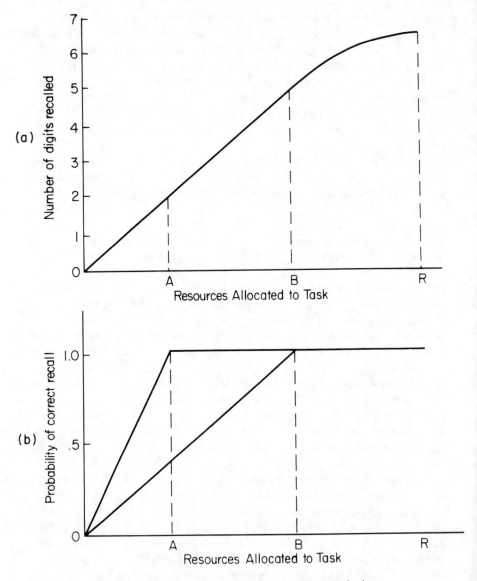

FIG. 5.3.   Performance-resource functions for digit memorization.

following sections, we present an information-theoretic reformulation of resource-competition theory that can be used to justify more powerful statistical methods.

Figure 5.4 shows two POCs that might result if the task of memorizing two digits (easy) or five digits (hard) was combined with the task of responding to a probe signal. Probability of recall is indicated on the ordinate, and speed of

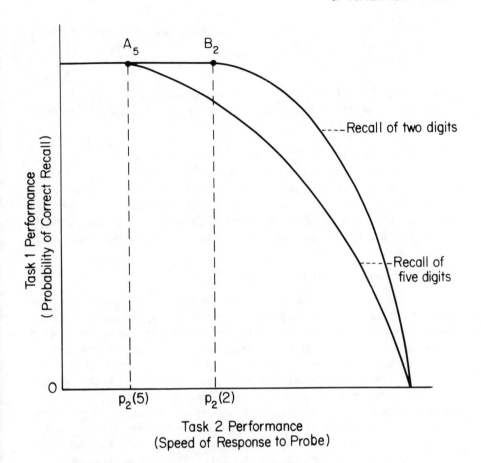

FIG. 5.4.   POC for digit recall (primary) and probe reaction time (secondary) tasks under two levels of primary task difficulty.

responding to the probe is indicated on the abscissa. Note that on both measures good performance is associated with movement away from the origin. Consider points A_2 and A_5. These are the points at which recall of two and five digits, respectively, becomes data limited. Data limitation is shown by the flatness of the POC from the data-limitation point to the ordinate. Fewer resources are required to reach the data-limitation point for the memorization of two than five digits. If subjects are instructed to devote enough resources to the memorization task so that they can recall the digits correctly, and to devote their remaining capacity to the probe task, probe responses should be faster in the two-digit than in the five-digit condition.

Task-2 performance may thus be used as a measure of task-1 resource requirements. Let $p_2(2)$ and $p_2(5)$ be task-2 performance in the two- and five-digit memorization conditions. Similarly, $r_2(2)$ and $r_2(5)$ refer to the resources allocated to task 2 in the two conditions. Resources allocated to task 2 can be defined by the equations:

$$r_2(2) = f_2^{-1} [p_2(2)]; \ r_2(5) = f_2^{-1} [p_2(5)]. \qquad 5.6$$

Inasmuch as total resource capacity, R, is split between the two tasks, Equations 5.5 and 5.6 combine to define $r_1(i)$, the amount of resources required to maintain i digits in memory, by:

$$r_1(i) = R - f_2^{-1} [p_2(i)]. \qquad 5.7$$

To what extent is this a scale? For the scale to be a linear or stronger measure of r, we would have to make (and justify) some assumptions about f_2. We discuss this in more detail later. For the present, we point out that the weak assumption that f is a performance-resource function and the much stronger assumption that R is constant over conditions are sufficient to insure that $p_2(i)$ is an ordinal scale of $r_1(i)$. That is,

$$[p_2(i) > p_2(j)] \supset [r_1(i) > r_1(j)]. \qquad 5.8$$

Quite aside from measurement-theory considerations, the paradigm that has been described contains some important and not always obvious assumptions about behavior. These have been discussed in detail by Navon and Gopher (1979) and are mentioned here only briefly. One of the most important assumptions, and one of the most difficult to justify, is that the performer is indeed operating at the point at which task-1 performance shifts from a resource to a data limitation. Experimenters attempt to insure this by instructing performers to devote enough effort to the primary task to perform it correctly and to devote their remaining effort to the secondary task. In some experiments, these instructions are supplemented by an explicit payoff scheme so that a person who wishes to maximize objective rewards will perform at the data-limiting point. Obviously, a performer can do this only if the performer and the experimenter agree, quite precisely, on the meaning of the instructions and the values of the payoffs. Secondary task instructions also implicitly assume that performers have a sophisticated knowledge of their personal performance-resource function for the task.

A second question concerns the concept of a general resource. Should one think of mental resources as commodities that are infinitely transferable from one task to another, like money, or as commodities that are very useful for some tasks and acceptable but less useful for others, like alternative sources of energy?

These issues are serious ones and should not be minimized. Initially, however, we can ignore them. Later we examine the plausibility of the assumptions and consider how our data and models might be affected by their violation.

A third issue has been raised as a problem for resource-competition theories. In many nomothetic experiments, data have been aggregated over individuals. This often amounts to the highly questionable assumption that there is negligible interindividual variation in resource capacity. Rather than regarding interindividual differences in capacity as random variation, we attempt to incorporate them within a resource-competition model.

The Easy-to-Hard Paradigm

Much of our work is based on an experimental design that we have come to call the *easy-to-hard* paradigm. Imagine that two individuals are performing an easy version of task 1 (e.g., solving easy reasoning problems). It could easily happen that two individuals who perform at the same level (virtually perfectly) on this task might differ markedly in their ability to perform a more difficult reasoning task. The easy task would not be challenging enough to reveal the difference between the two performers. However, one might be able to discriminate between the two individuals by using the secondary task technique explained in the previous section. The spare capacity of each individual would be measured during performance of the easy version of task 1. This spare capacity measure would predict performance on a more difficult version of the task.

This logic can be illustrated graphically by considering the POCs for two different individuals, A and B. The performance-resource functions are shown in Fig. 5.5 separately for performance on easy and hard versions of task 1. In the easy condition (Fig. 5.5a), both individuals are able to reach a high level of performance, and thus the easy task fails to discriminate between them. Individual differences do appear in the hard condition (Fig. 5.5b), where neither individual can reach maximum possible performance.

Now suppose that we wished to predict performance in the hard condition on the basis of performance in the easy condition. This would clearly be impossible because both individuals are performing at the same level (p^*) on the easy task. However, they may be expending different amounts of resources to achieve this level of performance. Thus, we can use performance on a secondary task to predict performance on the hard version of task 1. Although we cannot discriminate between persons A and B on the basis of unobservable performance-resource functions, we can discriminate between them on the basis of their POCs, which can be observed directly. Good performance on the secondary task should be an indication of spare capacity that could be usefully applied to the primary task if it became harder.

This is illustrated by the POCs shown in Fig. 5.6. Both A and B perform the easy version of task 1 at level p^*. However, A can achieve this performance with a smaller output of resources. Therefore, A will achieve a higher level of performance on task 2 than B.

This informal presentation of the easy-to-hard paradigm has stressed its intuitive appeal, but a closer look at the reasoning behind it reveals complexities. Individuals can differ in several characteristics that determine single and dual task performance: (1) structural parameters pertaining to performance of task 1, which determine the resources necessary to perform that task at a given level; (2)

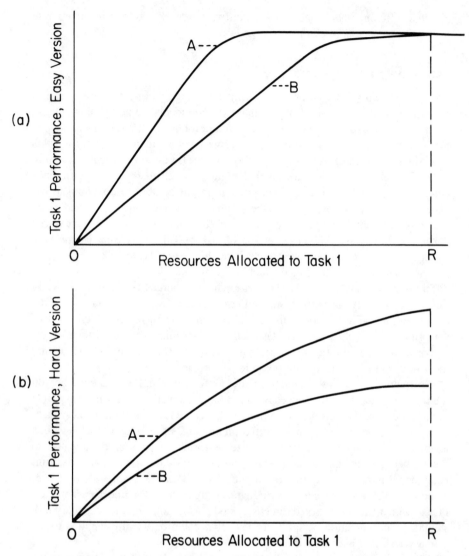

(a)

(b)

FIG. 5.5.   Performance-resource functions for two subjects (A and B) for task 1
(the primary task).

structural parameters pertaining to performance in task 2, which determine the
resources necessary to perform that task at a given level; and (3) total resource
capacity. Performance on tasks 1 and 2 in each of the single and dual task
conditions is determined by various combinations of these unobservable variables. Unfortunately, we do not know the form of the relationships between the
unobservable parameters and the performance measures.

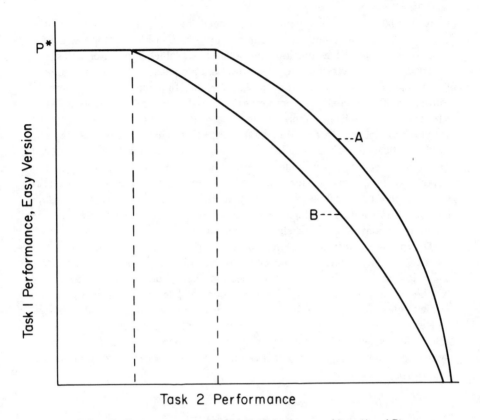

FIG. 5.6.   Performance operating characteristics for two subjects (A and B).

In the following section, we demonstrate how information theory can be used to generate specific predictions concerning the relationships between performance measures. The general argument of this section can be summarized as follows. If there is a causal relationship between a set of unobservable traits and each of a set of observable measures, then knowledge of one observable measure may provide information concerning another. In the simplest case, if the same trait determines two observable measures entirely, then one of these measures will predict the other perfectly. When the relationships between observables and unobservables becomes more complex, information theory can be used to determine whether one performance measure provides information about another.

In the easy-to-hard paradigm, the three unobservable parameters—task 1 structural parameters, task 2 structural parameters, and total capacity—determine performance in single and dual task conditions. Information theory can be used to demonstrate that performance on task 2 in the dual task condition provides information concerning performance on the difficult version of task 1 and that this information is independent of performance in any of the single task conditions. The advantage of using information theory for this purpose is that it makes no assumptions concerning the measurement properties of the performance measures or the form of the functions that relate observables to unobservables.

To say that one variable provides information concerning another is equivalent to saying that there is some function of the first measure that improves estimation of the second. The problem is then to determine that function. If such a function exists, it can be approximated *in a given set of data* by expressing one variable as a linear polynomial function of the other. This fact provides the basis for a statistical test of the model. If the unobservable causal relations postulated by the resource-allocation model are true, then certain predictive relations uncovered by the information-theoretic analysis must exist between observables. If the predictive relationships exist, then a statistically reliable linear relationship between observables should appear in any given data set. This statement can be tested using conventional correlational analysis.

The role of the information-theoretic techniques is to determine, in a precise manner, just what relations between observables are predicted by resource-allocation models. The use of information theory does not introduce any psychological content; the psychological content lies in the definition of the resource-allocation model. The role of information theory is to provide a bridge between the theoretical concepts of "structure" and "resource" and the observable performances. This is done by using information theory to provide a theoretical justification for the use of conventional linear regression methods in the analysis of observables.

A FORMAL MODEL
OF INDIVIDUAL DIFFERENCES

Definitions and Preliminary Notation

The model to be developed deals with the relations between primary and secondary task performance over four different conditions. Conditions will be indexed by the variable c, where:

$c = 0$.   The secondary task is done alone.
$c = 1$.   The primary task is done alone, at an easy level.
$c = 1+$.   The primary task is done at the easy level, and the secondary task is performed concurrently.
$c = 2$.   The primary task is done alone, at a difficult level.

As an example, suppose that the primary task was to memorize either three or seven digits and that the secondary task was to respond to a visual signal. Condition $c = 0$ would be a "probe alone" condition, in which the visual signal was presented and reaction time recorded. Condition $c = 1$ would require memorizing three digits. Condition $c = 1+$ would require memorizing three digits, and a visual probe signal might be presented during the rehearsal period. Condition $c = 2$ would involve memorizing seven digits.

An individual performer, i ($i = 1 \ldots N$), will be characterized by a triplet, (e_{1i}, e_{2i}, R_i), where e_{1i} represents the ith individual's structural efficiency at the primary task, and e_{2i} represents the individual's structural efficiency at the secondary task. R_i represents the person's attentional resource limit, or *capacity*. Collectively, the individuals in an experiment constitute a set S, where:

$$S = \{(e_{1i}, e_{2i}, R_i)\}\ i = 1 \ldots N. \qquad 5.9$$

Performance on any task t ($t = 1, 2$) requires the allocation of attentional resources to the task. Let $r_{ti}(c)$ be the amount of resources devoted to task t by individual i in condition c. By the definition of resource capacity:

$$0 \leq r_{ti}(c) \leq R_i, t = 1, 2\ i = 1 \ldots N. \qquad 5.10$$

Let $p_{ti}(c)$ be the observed performance of person i on task t in condition c. Then:

$$p_{ti}(c) = \text{Min} \{f_t[r_{ti}(c) ; e_{ti}, d], D_t(e_{ti}, d)\} \qquad 5.11$$

where $f_t\ [r_{ti}(c); e_{ti}, d]$ is the performance-resource function for an individual with task structural parameter e_{ti}, who is faced with an external task of difficulty d ($d = 1$, easy; $d = 2$, hard), and $D_t\ (e_{ti}, d)$ is the data-limit function. This function establishes maximum performance for an individual, given the structural parameter and the external level of task difficulty.

It follows from Equation 5.11 that there will be a "maximum economic investment" that a person should make in task t at a given level of difficulty and in a particular condition. Let this be $r^*_{ti}\ (c)$, where $r^*_{ti}\ (c)$ is the minimum value of $r_{ti}(c)$ that satisfies

$$f_t[r^*_{ti}(c); e_{ti}, d] = D_t\ (e_{ti}, d). \qquad 5.12$$

A person will be said to be an economic performer in condition c if and only if resources $r^*_{1i}(c)$ are invested in the primary task.

The assumption that f_t does not change over individuals and conditions, except for changes in parameters, is actually an assumption of some content. This sort of assumption is made in much psychological research. For instance, it is made in stronger form in virtually all research on learning, where individual parameters are fit to a generalized learning curve, and in psychometrics, where the factorial content of a task is assumed not to change over individuals. It might be questioned in situations in which individuals could differ in the strategy with which they approach the task.

A point that is important in later analyses is that $r^*_{ti}\ (c)$ is established within a condition by the value of e_{ti}. This is apparent from Equation 5.11.

Task Assumptions

The task assumptions deal with the resource requirements of the primary task at the easy ($d = 1$) and hard ($d = 2$) levels of difficulty and with the requirements of the secondary task at its constant level of difficulty, $d = k$:

1. All individuals reach a data-limiting point in the performance of the easy primary task.
2. All individuals are resource limited in the performance of the hard primary task.

Comment.   One of the primary tasks used in our experiments provides an illustration of these assumptions. The task required active rehearsal of either a small or large number of letter-digit pairs. When there are only a few pairs to be rehearsed, subjects report that the task can be done with less than maximum output of effort, and most perform at a very high level. However, perfect performance is usually not attained due to momentary lapses or failure to code a stimulus correctly when it is presented. If there are many pairs to be rehearsed, it is difficult to reach the last pair before the first pair is forgotten, and the effectiveness of rehearsal is closely tied to the effort put into the task.

3. All individuals reach a data-limiting point in the performance of the secondary task done alone.
4. All individuals are resource limited in the performance of the secondary task done in conjunction with the primary task.

Comment.   Assumption 3 states that if a person is able to devote all attentional resources to the secondary task, a point will be reached at which structural limitations determine performance. In our work, secondary task performance generally required a simple motor response to a visual or auditory probe. At a certain point, the reaction time (RT) to such a signal will be determined by equipment and structural, rather than resource, variables. Assumption 3 asserts that people reached this point.

Assumption 4 can be evaluated by inspecting the data. As the secondary task does not change its difficulty level, any difference in performance of an individual in the 0 and 1+ conditions will have to be associated with a change in resource allocation. If performance deteriorates from the 0 to 1+ condition then, perforce, performance in the 1+ condition must have been resource limited. This situation always arises in the experiments that we have completed on dual task performance.

5. Whenever any two tasks are done concurrently, some amount of attentional resources, Δ, will be diverted to the superordinate task of coordinating the two concurrent tasks.

Comment. Assumption 5 has been introduced to cope with the common observation that in a wide range of dual task studies primary task performance is worse in dual than single task conditions, despite instructions that primary task performance should be maintained (Kerr, 1973). Assumption 5 amounts to an assertion that individuals set aside an economically appropriate amount of resources, r^*_{1i} (c), for primary task performance but that this allocation is preempted by the obligatory high priority assigned to intertask coordination. Note that Δ is not subscripted, indicating that individual differences in intertask coordination ability will not be considered. This might appear to many to be an unrealistic assumption. Somewhat surprisingly, though, experimental attempts to identify consistent individual differences in intertask coordination have produced negative results (Hawkins, Rodriguez, & Reicher, 1979; Poltrock, Lansman, & Hunt, 1980). Presently available evidence indicates that treating Δ as a constant across subjects will not be too crude an approximation.

These assumptions lead to the following performance-resource functions, each of which is accompanied by a description.

$$p_{1i}(1) = f_1[r^*_{1i}(1), e_{1i}, 1] \qquad \text{Primary task, alone, easy condition.} \qquad 5.13$$

The performer devotes an economically appropriate amount of resources to the primary task, thus reaching the data-limiting point (see Equation 5.18).

$$p_{1i}(1+) = f_1\{[r^*_{1i}(1)-\Delta], e_{1i}, 1\} \qquad \begin{array}{l}\text{Primary task, dual, easy}\\\text{condition.}\end{array} \qquad 5.14$$

Performance is slightly below the data-limiting point due to the diversion of some resources to the coordinating task.

$$p_{1i}(2) = f_1(R_i, e_{1i}, 2) \qquad \text{Primary task, alone, hard condition.} \qquad 5.15$$

Performance is limited by the individual's resource capacity.

$$p_{2i}(0) = f_2(r^*_{2i}(0), e_{2i}, 2) \qquad \text{Secondary task, alone.} \qquad 5.16$$

The performer devotes an economically appropriate amount of resources to the secondary task and, hence, is data limited (see Equation 5.19).

$$p_{2i}(1+) = f_2\{[R_i - r^*_{1i}(1)], e_{2i}, k\} \qquad \begin{array}{l}\textit{Secondary task, dual, with}\\\textit{easy primary task.}\end{array} \qquad 5.17$$

Secondary task performance is determined by the resources remaining after an economically appropriate amount of resources has been assigned to the primary and coordination tasks. By virtue of the assumptions concerning data limitations (Assumptions 1 and 3):

$$p_{1i}(1) = D_1(e_{1i}, 1) \qquad 5.18$$

and

$$p_{2i}(0) = D_2(e_{2i}, k). \qquad 5.19$$

On occasion, we refer to a variable itself rather than to a specific value of the variable. In such cases, we write $p_t(c)$, suppressing the subscript for the individual. To refer to a set of observations for a particular task and condition we write:

$$p_t(c) = \{p_{ti}(c)\} \qquad \begin{aligned} t &= 1, 2 \\ i &= 1\ldots N \\ c &= 0, 1, 1+, 2. \end{aligned} \qquad 5.20$$

An analogous notation is used to refer to structural and resource variables e_1, e_2, and R.

Assumptions About Unobservables

The variables e_1, e_2, and R play a role analogous to the role of latent traits in psychometric theories of intelligence. In principle, they are unobservable, but they are presumed to establish the observable values. In this section, some assumptions are made about the relationship between the unobservable variables. In the following section, these are combined with the assumptions about the unobservable–observable relations expressed in Equations 5.13 through 5.17 in order to derive predictions about the relations between observables. This procedure resembles the data handling techniques used in the analysis of causal models (Bentler, 1980). The mathematics are different because we limit our assumptions about observable–unobservable relations to the concept of a performance-resource function and because we allow for the possibility of nonlinear relations. Therefore, we base our analysis on information-theoretic concepts rather than on the partitioning of covariances into components.

Summary Comments on Information Theory

This section presents some information-theoretic concepts used in this chapter. The presentation is intended to be a reminder of such concepts rather than a tutorial discussion. (Luce, 1960, provides an excellent in-depth presentation.) For ease of exposition, a simplified notation is used. It is elaborated on in the following section, which deals with the application of information theory to resource-allocation experiments.

Imagine two abstract variables, x and y, with associated sets of probabilities:

$$X = \{p\,(x = a)\} \qquad a \in \text{range of } x$$

$$Y = \{p\,(y = b)\} \qquad b \in \text{range of } y \qquad 5.21$$

The information in each of these variables is defined as:

$$H(x) = -\Sigma_a\, p(x = a) \cdot \log_2 [p\,(x = a)] \qquad 5.22$$

and similarly for $H(y)$. The set of probabilities

$$X \times Y = \{p\ (x = a\ \&\ y = b)\} \tag{5.23}$$

states the probabilities of pairs of values for x and y, and

$$H(x,\ y) = -\Sigma_a\ \Sigma_b\ p\ (x = a,\ y = b) \cdot \log_2 p(x = a,\ y = b). \tag{5.24}$$

Equation 5.23 can be used to define the sets of conditional probabilities $p(x = a|y = b)$ and $p(y = b|x = a)$, with the associated information measures $H(x|y = b)$ and $H(y|x = a)$. The average information in y, given x, is defined by:

$$H(y|x) = \Sigma_a\ p(x = a) \cdot H(y|x = a). \tag{5.25}$$

The information in a pair of observations can be expressed in terms of the information in the individual observations and the conditional probabilities as:

$$\begin{aligned} H(x,\ y) &= H(x) + H(y|x) \\ &= H(y) + H(x|y). \end{aligned} \tag{5.26}$$

The maximum value of $H(x,\ y)$ is

$$H_{\max}\ (x,\ y) = H(x) + H(y), \tag{5.27}$$

which is reached only when

$$H(y|x) = H(y)\ \text{and}\ H(x|y) = H(x). \tag{5.28}$$

This is sometimes stated in terms of the information transmitted from x to y, which is defined by:

$$\begin{aligned} T(x,\ y) &= H_{\max}(x,\ y) - H(x,\ y) \\ &= H(x) - H(x|y) \\ &= H(y) - H(y|x). \end{aligned} \tag{5.29}$$

Two variables are said to be independent if $T(x,\ y)$ is zero. This is a more general definition of independence than the more familiar one, in which the product-moment correlation is zero. The former definition rules out any relation between the two variables, whereas the latter rules out any linear relation.

Transmitted information $[T(x,\ y)]$ is bidirectional. One could speak of the information transmitted from y to x or from x to y. This is apparent in the first line of Equation 5.29, which defines $T(x,\ y)$. Predictability, however, is not symmetric because it depends on both $t(x,\ y)$ and the value of $H(x)$ and $H(y)$. This can be seen by examining the bottom two lines of Equation 5.29. The point can be illustrated with a simple example. Suppose that variable x may take the values $-1, 1, -2,$ or 2 with equal probability and that $y = x^2$. It is easy to show that in this case:

$$\begin{aligned} H(x) &= 2 \\ H(y) &= 1 \\ H(x,\ y) &= 2. \end{aligned} \tag{5.30}$$

In terms of conditional information:

$$T(x, y) = 1$$
$$H(x|y) = 1$$
$$H(y|x) = 0. \qquad 5.31$$

Thus, y is perfectly predictable from x, but not vice versa. This situation can be expected to arise in observable–unobservable relationships. Observable performance should be predictable given the values of unobservable parameters, but two or more combinations of parameters might give rise to the same observation.

Now consider the case of three variables, x, y, and z, with their associated probability distributions. If $H(x, y, z)$ is the information in the set of triplets, $\{(x, y, z)\}$, then the information transmitted from the (x, y) pair to the z variable, or vice versa, is:

$$T[(x, y), z] = H(x, y) + H(z) - H(x, y, z). \qquad 5.32$$

The conditional information transmitted from x to z or from z to x, after allowing for the information transmitted by y, is:

$$T(x, z|y) = H(x, y) + H(y, z) - H(y) - H(x, y, z). \qquad 5.33$$

The expressions for $T(y, z|x)$ and $T(x, y|z)$ are similar.

There is a particular meaning of $T(x, y)$ that should be kept in mind. If the transmitted information between a pair of variables is greater than zero, then it is possible to use knowledge of one variable to make a good estimate of the other, provided that good estimate is defined in terms of the probability distributions. To use an illustration that takes on importance later, suppose the best estimate is one that minimizes the conventional least squares loss function,

$$L = \Sigma_y \, p(y)(y - \bar{y})^2 \qquad 5.34$$

where $\bar{y}$ is the estimate of y. If $T(x, y) > 0$, then there is some function $g(x)$ such that

$$\bar{y} = g(x) \qquad 5.35$$

will, on the average, produce a lower value of L than simply using the expectation of y $[E(y)]$ as the estimate of y.

Resource-Allocation Models
Expressed in Information-Theoretic Terms

One may think of all conceivable values of the parameters, e_1, e_2, and R, as having certain a priori probabilities of occurrence, both individually $[p \, (e_{1i} = a)$, etc.] and in pairs $[p(e_{1i} = a; \, e_{2i} = b)]$ and triplets. In order to maintain a meaningful distinction between resources and structure, these are required to be statistically independent over individuals.

6. An individual's attentional resource capacity is independent of the individual's structural parameters.

In information-theoretic terms

$$T(R, e_1) = T(R, e_2) = 0. \qquad\qquad 5.36$$

This assumption defines resources as those capacities of the individual that are relevant to performance but independent of the ability to do any one task. Such a definition is at first reminiscent of g, the general ability from classic intelligence theory. At the empirical level there is a slight difference in definitions because resource capacity could be identified by nonlinear relationships between performance over different tasks, whereas g, as strictly defined in factor analytic studies, is determined by linear relations. We suspect that most intelligence theorists would regard this as a minor technical quibble, and we agree.

There is also a conceptual distinction. Resource allocation is an "energy" concept. Resources are looked upon as commodities to be parceled out in response to competing demands. As such, resource capacity might be thought of as one component of g. The concept of general intelligence itself is broader. It would have to include any structure that is involved in a variety of cognitive activities. It should also include the effectiveness of the strategies that people use in deciding how to approach a problem, including the policies that they follow in allocating resources to various activities during problem solving. Sternberg (1980) has referred to such strategies as "metacomponents."

General structures and metacomponents are part of g, but they are not attentional resources in themselves. There are probably individual differences in the efficiency of widely used structures, in the possession of different metacomponential strategies, and in resource capacity. They all would contribute to a g factor in an analysis of the correlations between intellectual tasks done one at a time. There seems to us to be no way of distinguishing between the ideas of general attentional resources and general intellectual competence so long as one deals only with statistical relationships between performance on different tasks done one at a time. The distinction between the two concepts depends on performance when tasks can compete for attention.

In order to test the model, some constraints must be stated on the relationships between observables. This is done by designating performance on the primary task alone, at the hard level of difficulty [variable $p_1(2)$] as a target variable, and expressing this variable in terms of the other observable variables. The approach regards performance-resource functions as mappings between sets of observable and unobservable variables. The information-theoretic consequences of these mappings are then examined. To aid in following the argument, Table 5.1 summarizes the mappings involved. The same information is shown graphically in Fig. 5.7, which depicts the unobservable variables e_1, e_2, and R as being connected to the observable variables by arrows, whose direction is intended to

TABLE 5.1
Summary of the Mappings Between Observable and
Unobservable Variables in the Easy-to-Hard Paradigm

Primary Task	
Equation	*Mapping*
$p_{1i}(1) = f_1[r^*_{1i}(1), e_{1i}, 1]$	$f_1: \quad E_1 \rightarrow p_1(1)$
$p_{1i}(1+) = f_1\{[r^*_{1i}(1) - \Delta]; e_{1i}, 1\}$	$f_1: \quad E_1 \rightarrow p_1(1+)$
$p_{1i}(2) = f_1(R_i, e_{1i}, 2)$	$f_1: \quad E_1 \times R \rightarrow p_1(2)$

Secondary Task	
Equation	*Mapping*
$p_{2i}(0) = f_2(r^*_{2i}, e_{2i}, k)$	$f_2: \quad E_2 \rightarrow p_2(0)$
$p_{2i}(1+) = f_2[R_i - r^*_{1i}(1), e_{2i}, k]$	$f_2: \quad E_2 \times E_1 \times R \rightarrow p_2(1+)$

illustrate causation. Unobservable variables e_1 and e_2 are connected to each other by a double-headed arrow, indicating that the model permits a statistical association between these variables without any implication of causation. Variable R stands alone because, by assumption, it is independent of the structural variables.

The method of predicting target-variable performance from performance on other variables can first be presented in an informal argument, which may be followed graphically by examining Fig. 5.7. It is clear from the figure that target-variable performance, $p_1(2)$, depends jointly on e_1 and R. Thus, any information that improves the ability to predict e_1 and R should improve prediction of target-variable performance. What sources of information can be used to estimate the two unobservables?

Suppose, for the moment, that one knew the performance-resource functions and could state a priori probabilities for all values of the unobservables. In general, a performance-resource function establishes a many:one mapping from the set of possible values of unobservable parameters into the set of possible values of an observable performance. Conversely, there is a one:many mapping from observable performance back into the unobservable parameters. This means that although one cannot determine a set of parameter values uniquely from performance, it is possible to alter one's estimate of the likelihood of a parameter value by observing performance. This, in turn, should make it possible to predict performance in a new situation, providing that the new performance depends (partly) on the same unobservable parameters. However, there will be redundancies between predictor variables. There may be two or more performance measures that yield the same, or nearly the same, information about unobservables. With these considerations in mind, let us examine ways to predict target-variable performance.

Primary Task Measures   **Secondary Task Measures**

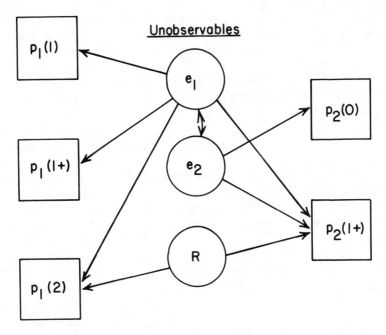

FIG. 5.7.   A diagram showing the causal connections between the three unobservable parameters, e_1, e_2, and R, and five single and dual task measures.

Performance on the easy version of the primary task [variables $p_1(1)$ and $p_1(1+)$] depends on the primary task structural parameter, e_1. This is an example of the general rule that if performance is data limited, then there is a mapping from the structural parameter for that task into performance. Thus $p_1(1)$ and $p_1(1+)$ provide information about e_1. Whether or not these two information sources are redundant depends on the value of Δ, the amount of resources devoted to coordination between tasks in a dual task condition. If Δ is zero, then $p_1(1)$ and $p_1(1+)$ are completely redundant.

Information about e_1 may also be obtained by examining secondary task performance either alone or in the dual task condition [$p_2(0)$ and $p_2(1+)$]. Consider first the case of secondary task performance alone, variable $p_2(0)$. Inasmuch as this performance is data limited, there will be a mapping onto performance from the set of possible e_2 values, making it possible to improve our estimate of the secondary task structural parameter. If there is a statistical (not causal) association between the two structural parameters, this relationship can be used to estimate the value of e_1. The logic is similar to the logic of using a measure of arm strength to estimate leg strength; there is no direct causal connection between the two measures, but knowledge of one would probably improve prediction of the other.

The case of secondary task performance in the dual task condition, variable $p_2(1+)$, is more complicated. Variable e_1 can be estimated indirectly through estimation of e_2, as described earlier. Variable $p_2(1+)$, however, is a resource-limited variable. Resources made available to the secondary task in the dual task condition will be equal to the difference between the individual's resource capacity and the resources required to bring the primary task to its data limit, the difference between R_i and r^*_{1i} $(1+)$. The latter variable is determined by e_{1i}, the individual's primary task structural parameter. Thus, secondary task performance in the dual task condition will be partly dependent on the primary task structural parameter.

Resource capacity, R, enters into the determination of only two performance variables—the target variable itself and the secondary task performance in the dual task condition. Thus, secondary task performance in the dual task condition is connected to target-variable performance by three chains of information—links through e_1 and e_2, which may be partly or wholly redundant to the links connecting target-variable performance to other predictors and a link through R, which is independent of the chains of information involving other predictor variables.

Turning again to Fig. 5.7, we see that each of these links corresponds to a path in the graph. There are paths from $p_1(1)$, $p_1(1+)$, and $p_2(1+)$ to $p_1(2)$ going though e_1. There are paths that go from $p_2(0)$ and $p_2(1+)$ to $p_1(2)$ by moving first to e_2 and then to e_1. Only $p_2(1+)$ has a path that moves to $p_1(2)$ through R. Thus, $p_2(1+)$ should make a contribution to the prediction of $p_1(2)$ that is independent of any other prediction. The information-theoretic basis for the assertions can now be given.

The performance-resource function states that the value of $p_1(2)$ is completely established (within the limits of measurement error) when the pair of parameters (e_1, R) is known. Furthermore, by the definition of a performance-resource function, any change in R will cause a change in performance, as difficult primary task performance is resource limited. The information transmitted from R to $p_1(2)$, independently of e_1, is:

$$T(R, p_1(2) \mid e_1) = H(e_1, R) + H[e_1, p_1(2)] - H(e_1) - H[e_1, R, p_1(2)]. \qquad 5.37$$

Because $p_1(2)$ is completely determined by e_1 and R:

$$H[e_1, R, p_1(2)] = H(e_1, R). \qquad 5.38$$

Substituting Equation 5.38 into 5.37:

$$\begin{aligned} T[R, p_1(2) \mid e_1] &= H[e_1, p_1(2)] - H(e_1) \\ &= H[p_1(2) \mid e_1] \\ &= \Sigma_a\, p\,(e_1 = a) \cdot H[p_1(2) \mid e_1 = a]. \end{aligned} \qquad 5.39$$

By the definition of a resource limitation, and the performance-resource function, it is true that for every pair of values R_i, R_i', $R_i \neq R_i'$,

$$f_1(R_i \mid e_{1i}, 2) \neq f_1(R_i' \mid e_{1i}', 2) \qquad 5.40$$

if $e_{1i} \neq e_{1i}'$. Thus for fixed e_1, there is a one:one mapping from R to $p_1(2)$. This means that

$$H[p_1(2) \mid e_1 = a] = H(R \mid e_1 = a). \qquad 5.41$$

By assumption 6, e_1 and R are independent. Therefore,

$$H(R \mid e_1 = a) = H(R) \qquad 5.42$$

and therefore

$$T[R, p_1(2) \mid e_1] = H(R). \qquad 5.43$$

Equation 5.43 states that unless R is known completely, there will be uncertainty in predicting the target variable regardless of how accurately we have established the value of the structural parameter e_1. Thus, it always pays to improve the prediction of R because this always reduces the uncertainty in estimating the target variable.

The situation is not quite the same with respect to e_1. By reasoning similar to the derivation of Equation 5.39:

$$
\begin{aligned}
T[e_1, p_1(2) \mid R] &= H[p_1(2) \mid R] \\
&= \Sigma_b \, p(R = b) \cdot H[p_1(2) \mid R = b].
\end{aligned}
\qquad 5.44
$$

However, the performance-resource function does not define any condition for fixed R and varying e_1. In fact, quite reasonable functions can be drawn that show $e_{1i} \neq e_{1i'}$, but for some R:

$$f_1(R = b \mid e_{1i}, 2) = f_1(R = b \mid e_{1i'}, 2). \qquad 5.45$$

In words, these equations show that if one knows the structural capacities of an individual, it is still necessary to know the amount of resources allocated in order to predict performance. On the other hand, if one knows the resource allocated, it may not be necessary to know an individial's precise structural capacity in order to make a prediction. Why is there this asymmetry between resource and structural capacity? The question requires two answers—one to establish an intuitive understanding of what the asymmetry means and another to explain how it arises.

Figure 5.8 illustrates how the asymmetry arises. The figure shows primary task performance $[p_1(2)]$ as a function of the resources committed to the primary task. Three performance-resource functions are plotted for levels a, b, and c of the primary task structural variable, e_1. Each of the performance-resource functions can be thought of as the function expected from an individual with structural variable $e_1 = a$, b, or c, as that individual varies the amount of resources committed to the primary task. Performance on that task will thus vary

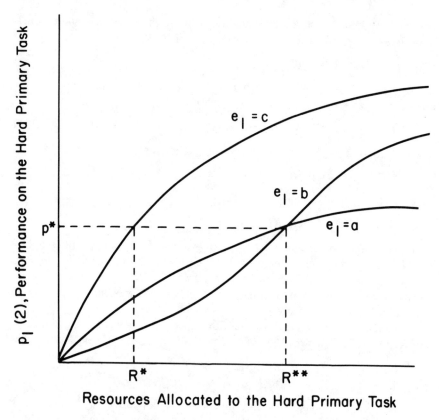

FIG. 5.8.   Performance-resource functions illustrating the point that R must be known perfectly, but e_1 may be known only partially, in estimating target variable performance.

in a manner characteristic of the individual. Hence, although two individuals may show identical performance at *some* level of resource commitment, there must also be some level at which performance differs. If such a level did not exist, then the two individuals would have identical performance-resource functions throughout the range of possible levels of resource commitment, and, by definition, they would have the same structural capacity.

Graphically, suppose that e_1 is known, so that an individual has been identified as being either on curve *a, b,* or *c* in Fig. 5.8. It would clearly be necessary to know what level of resource had been committed to the primary task before one could estimate performance. Conversely, suppose that one knew both the level of resource committed and the performance level achieved. Would one then necessarily be able to identify the structural parameter, e_1, and thus locate a person as having a particular performance-resource function? The answer to this is "it depends," and Fig. 5.8 shows why. If a person committed resource level

$R*$ to the task and showed performance level $p*$, then the performance-resource function for that person would be uniquely defined (within the set of functions shown in Fig. 5.8). If resource level $R**$ were committed, the $e_1 = c$ performance-resource function could be distinguished from those associated with $e_1 = a$ and $e_1 = b$, but the latter two functions could not be distinguished from each other.

Apart from the abstract mathematics, why are structural and resource parameters treated asymmetrically? The reason is that "structural parameters" and "data limits" are defined in terms of the relation between resource allocation and performance. Thus, although it is possible to observe performance directly and to infer resource allocation from performance on single and dual tasks of varying priority, there is no way to "observe" structural limits other than by watching the variation between performance on a specific task and resources allocated to that task. One could conceive of a theory that did offer independent definitions of structural capacities. (Indeed, some factor analytic theories of mental performance could be framed in this way.) Such theories could then, conceivably, be coordinated with models of resource allocation, but this has not yet been done.

In our own experimental work, which has been carried out strictly within the confines of the resource-allocation model, our interest is in predicting primary task performance in the hard condition, variable $p_1(2)$. As Fig. 5.8 shows, whenever performance is resource limited, one must know the level of resource allocation to a task before predicting performance, even if structural capacity is already known. However, as the figure also shows, it is sometimes necessary to know both resource allocation and structural capacity before a prediction of task performance can be made. Stating this in the information-theoretic notation, information that alters the probability that $e_1 = c$, $p(e_1 = c)$, will transmit information about the value of the target variable. Information that changes $p(e_1 = a)$ and $p(e_1 = b)$ relative to each other, but leaves unchanged the probability that the value is either a or b, will not influence the accuracy of a prediction.

The results just given generalize to the prediction of performance in any resource-limited situation. Inasmuch as information transmission is defined by a statistical relationship rather than by an interpretation of causality, prediction is possible in both directions. (The accuracy of prediction may vary.) This may also be seen by examining Fig. 5.8. If performance were to be observed at point $p*$, then resource capacity would have to be either at point $R*$ or $R**$. The results also apply to residual uncertainties. Suppose that by utilizing one set of observations one obtained an imperfect estimate of the e_is and the R value. The reasoning just given could be applied to an analysis of residual variation in the unobservables, after allowance had been made for the reduction in uncertainty due to the initial observations.

The next step is to apply the method of analysis to the easy-to-hard prediction. This is done by showing that knowledge of secondary task performance in the easy primary $(1+)$ condition provides information about an individual's resource-capacity level, R. This information is required for complete prediction of performance on the primary task in the hard primary (2) condition. Furthermore, the information needed is available only by analysis of secondary task performance in the easy primary condition. Therefore, secondary task performance in the $1+$ condition $[p_2(1+)]$ can be shown to provide a unique source of information about performance in the hard primary condition $[p_1(2)]$.

Consider first the source of the statistical relation between performance on the primary task in the easy and hard conditions without any secondary task present [variables $p_1(1)$ and $p_1(2)$]. Figure 5.7 and Table 5.1 show that this relation is due to the joint dependence of the variables on e_1, the primary task structural variable. The performance-resource function establishes a many:one mapping from $e_1(1)$ to $p_1(1)$. Hence,

$$T[e_1, p_1(1)] = H[p_1(1)] + H(e_1) - H(p_1, e_1)$$
$$= H[p_1(1)] + H(e_1) - [H(e_1) + H(p_1(1) \mid e_1)]. \qquad 5.46$$

Because $p_1(1)$ is data limited, as $H[p_1(1) \mid e_1] = 0$, Equation 5.46 reduces to:

$$T[e_1, p_1(1)] = H[p_1(1)]. \qquad 5.47$$

Thus, individual variation in observable primary task performance in the easy-alone condition can be used to gain information about individual differences in the primary task structural parameter, e_1. Whether or not this information will aid in determining primary task performance when the task becomes harder depends on the role of resource capacity in establishing primary task performance in the hard (2) condition. Information about e_1 may help in prediction, and our intuitions are that it usually will. But, as was shown in discussing Equations 5.44 and 5.45, structural information must be supplemented by information about resource capacity.

A similar argument applies to the prediction of the target variable, hard primary task performance, from performance on the secondary task alone, variable $p_2(0)$. Here the prediction involves two steps. Given observed performance, the secondary task structural parameter, e_2, can be estimated. If $T(e_1, e_2)$ is not zero (and the assumptions of the model permit this), then prediction of e_1 is possible, indirectly, through e_2. Again, our intuitions are that such information will assist in predicting the target variable, but the model does not demand that this be so.

The foregoing considerations show that primary task performance in a hard condition cannot be predicted completely either from knowledge of primary task performance alone, in an easy condition, or from knowledge of secondary task performance alone. The reason is that neither of these measures provides information about resource capacity, R, and such information is needed in predicting resource-limited performance. Some relevant information about R can be obtained, however, by considering secondary task performance done in the presence of the easy primary task, variable $p_2(1+)$. From Table 5.1, $p_2(1+)$ is a function of the secondary task structural paramater, e_2, the individual's resource capacity, R, and the level of resources used on the primary task in order to bring its level of performance up to the data limit, $r_1^*(1+)$. The variable r_1^* $(1+)$, however, is itself a function of e_1. Thus, the performance-resource function for the secondary task in the dual condition can be written:

$$p_2(1+) = f_2^* (R \mid e) \qquad\qquad 5.48$$

where

$$e = (e_1, e_2). \qquad\qquad 5.49$$

The information shared by the observable performance, $p_2(1+)$, and the theoretical variable R, can be expressed as:

$$T[p_2(1+), R \mid e] = H(R). \qquad\qquad 5.50$$

The equality is justified because resource capacity has been defined to be independent of structural capacity (i.e., independent of information associated with e). Equation 5.50 does not imply that R be perfectly predictable from knowledge of secondary task performance in the dual task condition, but it does mean that by observing secondary task performance one can improve one's guess concerning the value of R (see the analogous illustration associated with Fig. 5.8). As improving one's prediction of R will always help in predicting the target variable, the model demands that there be an association between the target, $p_1(2)$, and $p_2(1+)$. This association will be independent of any association due to joint statistical relations between these variables and the other observables.

The information-theoretic analysis can be summarized in a form that approximates conventional statistical analysis. Two variables are said to be associated if there is a statistically reliable correlation between the first variable, y, and a prediction function of the second variable, $\bar{y} = g(x)$. The foregoing arguments show that there "may exist" two functions that associate the target variable, primary task performance in the hard-alone condition [$p_1(2)$] with primary task performance in the easy-alone condition [$p_1(1)$] and secondary task performance in the secondary task alone condition [$p_2(0)$]. Call these functions $g_1[p_1(1)]$ and $g_2[p_2(0)]$. There must exist a function $g_0[p_2(1+)]$ that associates secondary task performance in the dual task condition with the target variable. Furthermore, this association is at least partially independent of the two previous and possibly nonexistent functions.

Approximation by Linear Polynomials

If the prediction functions g_0, g_1, and g_2 were known, one could simply contrast the predicted and obtained values. This would provide a strong test of the model. The problem is that there is no way to identify the prediction functions unless a task-specific model of response production is also stated. Furthermore, the strong test of the resource-competition model would also be a test of the associated response-production models.

Fortunately, there is a way to construct a test of the resource-competition model alone. This test makes use of the fact that the information-theoretic analysis has shown what predictor functions must exist, even though it has not shown what they are. Our approach has been to find arbitrary (and not psychologically interpretable) approximations to each g function. These are constructed by using the fact that if x and y are arbitrary real variables and y is a single valued function $y = g(x)$ of x, then g may be approximated to any desired level of accuracy by the linear polynomial function

$$\tilde{g}(x) = \Sigma_{v=0}^{K} a_v x^v \qquad\qquad 5.51$$

with suitably chosen K and $\{a_v\}$. At the extreme, if one has N data points (x_i, y_i) and if $x_i = x_j$ implies that $y_i = y_j$, then the relation between x and y in this data set can be stated exactly by Equation 5.51, with $K \leq N - 1$. (If the equality condition is not met, the problem may be reformulated by replacing the various ys at a given x value by their average. Fluctuation about this point is thus assumed to be due to variation in y not associated with x.)

In practice, K would not be allowed to be as high as $N - 1$, as the resulting $\{a_v\}$ would capitalize on chance fluctuations in the data. Limits on K are appropriate. One limit is simply intuition: It is hard to imagine reasonable psychological functions that would require approximations using terms higher than $K = 5$. In practice, we have used 6 and 10 as limits on K (see Tukey, 1977, for a discussion of the introduction of such arbitrary assumptions). A second limit is established by the reliability of the data. If the reliability of the predictor is only r, there is little point in choosing K to be so large that the correlation between y and $g(x)$ exceeds r.

The following method was used. Given two observables, x and y, with y to be predicted using a possibly nonlinear function of x, we calculated the multiple regression of y on the variables $x_v = x^v$, for $v = 1 \ldots K$, where K is either an arbitrarily established limit or the value of v at which the multiple regression first exceeds the reliability imposed by the data. Predictor variables were entered in order of ascending vs. Any regression weight a_v not reliably different from zero was set to zero. The .01 criterion of reliability was adopted, but it was not followed slavishly. That is, if a significance level of .02 or .03 was found, we experimented with regression equations that did or did not use the variable. Multiple regressions were calculated using only the reliable relations. At each step, the change between the multiple regression levels at the current and previous value of K was examined. If there was no large change, the process was terminated, and the resulting function was used as an approximation of g. If there was a change, we experimented with various combinations of predictor variables to determine whether or not we had uncovered a suppressor variable. (We did uncover one case of ''classical suppression'' in one of our analyses. The mathematical basis is described by Cohen & Cohen, 1975). If suppressor variables were discovered, they were included in the equation.

The linear polynomial approximation procedure may involve substantial capitalization on chance fluctuations in the data. Therefore, it was used only for a large secondary task study involving 81 subjects. To deal with smaller studies, we applied the much more arbitrary criterion of dealing only with linear relations (i.e., $K=1$) and using conventional correlational analyses. The resource-competition model provides some justification for doing so in dealing with a relation between observables that is dependent on resource capacity (R). By the definition of a performance-resource function, performance is always an increasing function of R in resource-limited situations. Hence, there should always be a positive linear term in the function relating two observables to R. If the relationship between observables is traced through one of the structural parameters, e_1 or e_2, a linear analysis introduces an additional assumption. This assumption is that the task structural parameter is unidimensional and that there is the same ordinal relationship between the structural variable and both the observable performance variables. This assumption does not seem to be unreasonable and is not required in the nonlinear analysis.

The use of a linear analysis would perhaps be least justified in examining the independence of predictions of the target variable based on different predictors. Suppose that there is some predictability in the y variable associated with a linear function of x (as in conventional correlational analysis) and that there is a further component of y that can be predicted by a linear analysis using a second predictor, z. It is possible that the additional component, which appears to be predictable only from z, might be predictable by a nonlinear association between x and y. Although this may seem to be an unlikely possibility in practice, there is nothing in either the resource-competition model or in the mathematics of approximation that guards against such a spurious result.

In summary, the technique of approximation of predictor functions by linear polynomial analysis provides a justifiable way of examining the implications of the resource-competition model. The approximation technique, however, requires precise data that can be obtained only in a large experiment. Conventional linear analysis can be justified in some cases, but it may suppress relationships that could cause one to question the model. In practice, a linear analysis was applied to smaller experiments, and a nonlinear analysis to very similar larger studies. Fortunately, the results of the two analyses were consistent.

EXPERIMENTAL RESULTS

The resource-competition model has been used to reanalyze several experiments reported in a series of studies of dual task performance (Lansman & Hunt, 1980). All of the experiments used the easy-to-hard paradigm in which performance on a difficult primary task, done alone, was predicted from various combinations of primary and secondary task performance measures. A linear analysis of two smaller experiments involving about 50 subjects each is reported first, and then a nonlinear analysis of a larger study involving 81 subjects.

The first two experiments used a verbal short-term memory task as the primary task. The sequence of events observed by the subject is shown in Table 5.2. First, several letter-digit pairs were presented to establish an initial set of paired associates to be retained in memory. Each subsequent trial contained a test phase and a study phase. During the test phase, a letter was presented with a question mark, and the subject attempted to recall the digit most recently paired with that letter. In the study phase, the same letter would be paired with a new digit. The difficulty of this task was manipulated by varying the number of letter-digit pairs involved.

This task is generally referred to as a continuous paired associates task. The present form was developed by Atkinson and Shiffrin (1968), who used it to test their buffer model of short-term memory. A similar task was used by Yntema and Meuser (1962) some years earlier. Performance on the task has been shown to be related to scores on tests of scholastic aptitude (Hunt et al., 1973) and to the performance of computer programmers (Love, 1977).

A probe reaction-time task was used as a secondary task. In dual task conditions, a probe was presented during the study phase of 75% of the trials. In one experiment, the probe signal was a set of asterisks shown immediately above the letter-digit pair. In the other, the probe was a tone presented through headphones. Subjects responded to the asterisks by pressing a key; they responded to the tone by uttering the syllable *bop* into a microphone. Paired associate and probe tasks never required a response during the same interval.

If paired associate and probe tasks compete for resources, then performance on the secondary task should decrease as the difficulty of the primary task is increased. Figure 5.9 shows probe reaction time as a function of the difficulty of

TABLE 5.2
Sequence of Events for the Paired Associate Task

Event	Display	Duration
Sequential presentation of initial pairs.	A = 7	3 sec
	B = 3	3 sec
Question. The correct answer is 3.	B = ?	Subject paced.
Rehearsal interval. Letter just queried is paired with a new number.	B = 4	3 sec
Probe. A probe may occur 500, 1000, or 1500 msec after presentation of a new pair.	(****) B = 4	Probe is presented until subject responds for a maximum of 1500 msec.
Question. The correct answer is 7.	A = ?	Question remains on screen until subject responds.
Rehearsal interval. Letter just queried is paired with a new number.	A = 5	3 sec

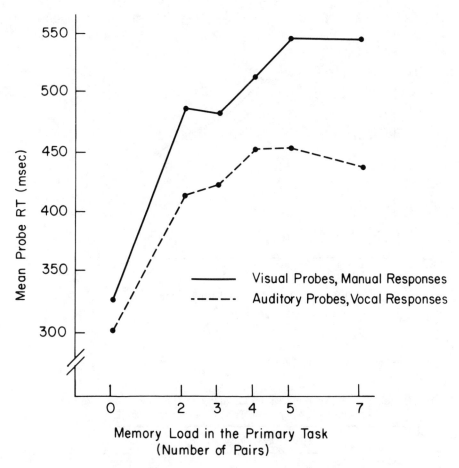

FIG. 5.9.   Mean probe RT for the visual-manual and auditory-vocal secondary tasks as a function of memory load in the paired associate primary task.

the concurrent memory task. The zero memory-load condition represents the probe task done alone. Probe RT increased sharply from the control to the dual task conditions and also increased with the number of paired associates to be rehearsed. Figure 5.10 shows performance on the paired associate task as a function of the number of pairs to be maintained in memory and of the presence and type of probe task. The presence of either type of probe task caused a slight but significant drop in paired associate recall. This pattern of interference between tasks is typical of that found in many experiments.

If our model of individual differences is correct, then we would expect performance on easy and hard versions of the primary task to be correlated because they are both influenced by e_1, the structural parameter for the primary task.

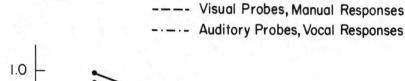

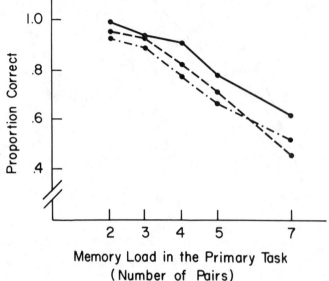

FIG. 5.10. Proportion of paired associate items correctly recalled in single and dual task conditions as a function of memory load.

TABLE 5.3
Correlations Between the Target Variable and Three Predictor Variables
in the Paired Associate Task, Experiments 1 and 2[a]

	First Order Correlations			Partial Correlations		
	Predictor Variable			Predictor Variable: Covariate		
	$p_1(1)$	$p_2(0)$	$p_2(1+)$	$p_2(1+)$ $: p_1(1)$	$p_2(1+)$ $: p_2(0)$	$p_2(1+)$ $: p_1(1), p_2(0)$
Experiment 1: Paired associates with visual probe, manual response	.52	$-.05$	$-.40$	$-.32$	$-.44$	$-.36$
Experiment 2: Paired associates with auditory probe, vocal response	.28	$-.37$	$-.39$	$-.37$	$-.28$	$-.28$

$p_1(1)$ = Accuracy in the easy paired associate task done alone.
$p_2(0)$ = RT in the probe task done alone.
$p_2(1+)$ = RT in the probe task during the easy paired associate task.

[a] Correlations greater than .27 are significant at the .05 level.

Performance on the hard primary may also be predicted by RT in the secondary task done alone due to a correlation between e_1 and e_2. However, RT to the probe in the dual task condition should improve prediction of accuracy on the hard primary task because RT in the dual task condition is influenced by resource capacity, R, as well as by e_2.

Table 5.3 summarizes the linear correlations obtained in the two experiments. Of greatest interest are the partial correlations between accuracy on the hard primary task (the target variable in our theoretical analysis) and probe RT in the dual task condition. The variable "held constant" by the partial correlation technique is either accuracy in the easy primary task done alone, probe RT in the secondary task done alone, or both of these. The partial correlations are shown in the three right-hand columns of the table. In each case, the correlation is reliably different from zero. Thus, probe RT in the dual task condition did convey information about the target variable, even after the information associated with the two single task variables was removed statistically.

Event	Display	Duration
Standard pattern (Probe could occur 500, 1000, or 1500 msec after onset of standard pattern.	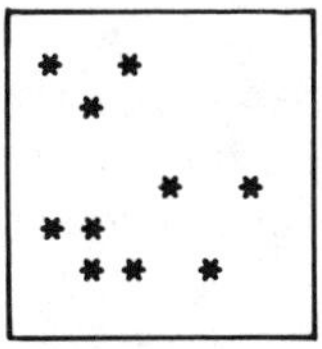	3 sec
Mask.	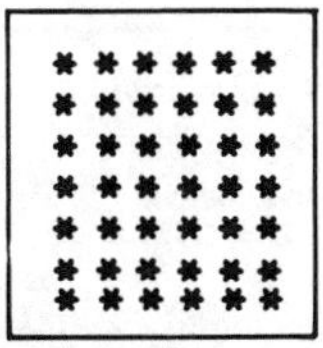	1 sec
Test pattern. Subject responds as to whether test pattern is the same or different from the standard.		Test pattern remains on screen until the subject responds.

FIG. 5.11.   Sequence of events in the spatial memory primary task.

A third experiment involved 81 subjects, selected from a wide adult age range in order to maximize individual differences. The first part of this experiment was essentially a replication of the previous work. The primary task was the continuous paired associates task, and the secondary task involved manual response to an auditory probe. The second part of the experiment involved a new primary task. Subjects were shown a random pattern of plus (+) signs on a computer display screen. This standard pattern was followed by a mask and then by a pattern of plus signs that was either identical to the standard or differed from it by the movement of a single plus. The subject's task was to indicate whether the second pattern was identical to or different from the standard. In the easy version of this task, patterns were composed of four plus signs in a three-by-three matrix. In the hard version, there were ten plus signs in a seven-by-seven matrix. As in the case of the paired associates task, probes were presented during the study phase of 75% of the trials. The exact sequence of events is shown in Fig. 5.11.

Table 5.4 shows data from the paired associates task. Presented are correlations of the target variable and performance on the hard paired associates task, with linear and nonlinear functions of several predictor variables. Of particular interest is the correlation between the target variable and performance on the secondary task in the dual condition, after the effects of the other two predictors have been held constant by partial correlation. This correlation is reliably greater than zero in both the linear and nonlinear analyses.

A glance at the table shows that there are only slight differences between the linear and nonlinear analyses. These differences would not change our conclusions in any way. This result strengthens our confidence in the linear analyses of

TABLE 5.4
Correlations Between the Target Variable and Linear and Nonlinear Functions
of Three Predictor Variables in the Paired Associate Task, Experiment 3[a]

	First Order Correlations			Partial Correlations		
	Predictor Variable			Predictor Variable: Covariate		
	$p_1(1)$	$p_2(0)$	$p_2(1+)$	$p_2(1+)$ $: p_1(1)$	$p_2(1+)$ $: p_2(0)$	$p_2(1+)$ $: p_1(1), p_2(0)$
Correlations with the variable itself	.57	$-.21$	$-.49$	$-.30$	$-.47$	$-.36$
Correlations with a nonlinear function of the variable	.60	$-.21$	$-.49$	$-.32$	$-.47$	$-.31$

$p_1(1)$ = Accuracy in the easy paired associate task done alone.
$p_2(0)$ = RT in the probe task done alone.
$p_2(1+)$ = RT in the probe task during the easy paired associate task.

[a] Correlations greater than .22 are significant at the .05 level.

the smaller experiments. Visual inspection of the form of the nonlinear analyses indicates that they all have strong linear components and that the nonlinearities are usually introduced to modulate extreme effects (e.g., to correct for excessively pessimistic predictions of recall that are associated with extremely long RTs).

A rather different picture emerged from examination of the data from the spatial memory task. Two observations led us to suspect that even the difficult version of this task was not resource limited. First, although the primary task did

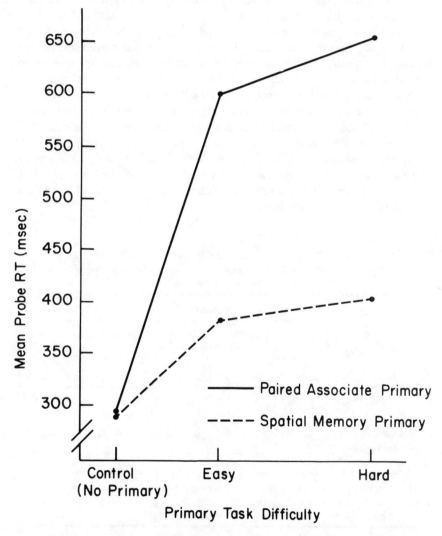

FIG. 5.12.   Mean probe RT during paired associate and spatial memory primary tasks as a function of primary task difficulty.

interfere with the secondary, the effect was much smaller than in the experiments using the paired associate primary task. Figure 5.12 compares the effects of the spatial memory and paired associate tasks on probe RT. The second observation was that subjects reported quite different strategies in attacking the two tasks. The paired associates task was almost always attacked by concentrated rehearsal of the current pairs. No such rehearsal strategy is available for the spatial memory task. Instead, subjects reported that a passive approach of simply looking at the standard patterns was most effective. If active rehearsal strategies are ineffective in the spatial memory task, then we would expect data rather than resource limitations to be important in determining performance on that task.

Table 5.5 presents the linear and nonlinear correlations for the spatial memory task. Consider first the linear analysis. No reliable partial correlation remains between RT in the dual task condition and accuracy in the hard spatial memory task, after allowing for individual variability in single task conditions. The same holds true in the nonlinear analysis. Although the nonlinear analysis is not identical to the linear analysis (because of the change in correlation between the target variable and performance in the probe alone condition), the partial correlations measuring the predictability of the target from secondary task performance in the dual condition remain low. In terms of the model, there does not seem to be a path leading to the target variable via the resource latent variable (R). This situation would arise if performance were data limited thoughout levels of difficulty of the spatial memory task.

TABLE 5.5
Correlations Between the Target Variable and Linear and Nonlinear Functions of Three Predictor Variables in the Spatial Memory Task[a]

	First Order Correlations			Partial Correlations		
	Predictor Variable			Predictor Variable: Covariate		
	$p_1(1)$	$p_2(0)$	$p_2(1+)$	$p_2(1+)$: $p_1(1)$	$p_2(1+)$: $p_2(0)$	$p_2(1+)$: $p_1(1), p_2(0)$
Correlations with the variable itself	.27	−.27	−.29	−.23	−.14	−.11
Correlations with a nonlinear function of the variable	.27	.44	−.29	−.22	−.14	−.11

$p_1(1)$ = Accuracy in the easy paired associate task done alone.
$p_2(0)$ = RT in the probe task done alone.
$p_2(1+)$ = RT in the probe task during the easy paired associate task.

[a] Correlations greater than .22 are significant at the .05 level.

CONCLUSIONS

One reason for studying individual differences in information processing is to relate these differences to variation along other cognitive and noncognitive dimensions. This is the reason for studying information processing in people whose intelligence test scores vary and for contrasting the verbal and spatial information-processing abilities of men and women. A second reason for studying information-processing ability is to generalize nomothetic models of cognition to the realm of individual differences. Such generalization both widens the scope of the nomothetic models and provides a test of their validity (Underwood, 1975). The research reported here was directed toward the second, more theoretical goal. Previously, models of competition for attentional resources have been used to explain average performance of groups of individuals in a variety of situations. By logical analysis, we have shown that a resource-competition model implies the existence of certain patterns of individual differences in single and dual task performance. Our experimental studies demonstrate that the patterns do exist.

These results have implications at several levels. The present studies of individual differences in attention can be fit into the framework established by previous theoretical studies of individual differences in information processing. The idea that individual differences in attentional capacity partially determine cognitive performance forces us to rethink our idea of what intelligence is. In addition, the analytic techniques that have been introduced here may be applicable in other studies of information-processing ability. These conceptual and methodological points are discussed in the following subsections.

Attention, Individual Differences, and Intelligence

Much recent research on information-processing ability has dealt with individual differences in memory. Examples include our own work on speed of access to information in semantic memory (Hunt, 1978; Hunt, Davidson, & Lansman, 1980), Chiang and Atkinson's (1976) study of short-term memory processes, and Underwood, Boruch, and Malmi's (1978) study of episodic memory. This emphasis on memory is hardly surprising, given the prominent role that memory plays in modern theories of cognition. But memory is certainly not the only source of individual differences in cognition. Indeed, there is a substantial body of literature on cognitive style stemming from the Gestalt view that thinking is primarily a reflection of perceptual capacity.

Modern experimental psychologists focus on memory as a source of individual differences because memory is central to their theory of cognition, whereas Gestaltists focused on individual differences in perception because perceptual processes were central to their cognitive theories. The two views are complementary rather than mutually exclusive. In this chapter, we have related the study of individual differences to another conceptualization of the mind—a conceptualization that emphasizes the role of attention and attention allocation.

The basic premise of attentional resource theory is that performance is limited by the amount of attentional resources devoted to a task, in addition to any limits imposed by task relevant processes and structures. This premise has been put forward in the experimental literature by Moray (1967), Kahneman (1973), Norman and Bobrow (1975), and others. In order to apply attentional resource theory to the study of individual differences, we assigned all task-specific structure and process variables to a single category, which we referred to as "structural parameters." We then made the assumption that performance is determined by two factors: structural parameters and attentional sources. This assumption was combined with a number of more specific assumptions concerning the conditions under which performance is determined by structural parameters alone (i.e., is data limited) or by both resources and structural parameters (i.e., is resource limited). The easy-to-hard prediction was then derived: Performance on a secondary task done concurrently with an easy version of a primary task should predict performance on a harder version of the same primary task. The easy-to-hard prediction was then verified.

This work is an example of a theory-oriented study of individual differences. The performance measures used in the study were dictated by a particular model of cognition rather than by usefulness in predicting performance in some applied setting. The purpose was not to relate variation in attentional processes to variation along some other dimension, but rather to study the interrelationships between measures assumed to reflect either structural parameters alone or structural parameters and general resources.

Introducing the concept of attention to the study of individual differences extends that study to include a rather different theoretical entity than those incorporated in many models of cognition. These models often make the distinction between structure and process (e.g., Atkinson & Shiffrin, 1968). The term "structure" generally refers to invariant information-processing mechanisms that underlie thought. These mechanisms are often compared to the circuits of a digital computer. The term "process" refers to a sequence of actions in which the structures are employed to produce some cognitive product. This is analogous to a computer program rather than to circuit elements. The concept of "attention," as used here, refers to neither a structure nor a process. Rather, attention is senn as an energy concept. There is an implied analogy to an electrical power source.

How does the energy concept fit into our thinking about thinking? The notion would be of limited interest if its relevance were restricted to the paradigms discussed here. Intuitively, though, it seems that many tasks are resource limited. That is, they are performed at a point on the performance-resource function at which an increase in resources would produce an increase in performance. Given that attentional capacity is an important limitation on individual performance of cognitive tasks, what is the relationship between attentional capacity and general cognitive competence or "intelligence?"

The concepts of intelligence and attention have previously been used in separate contexts. Intelligence is seen as a relatively permanent characteristic of the individual. Certainly we do not think of intelligence as changing from minute to minute. Attention is seen as an allocatable resource that can be parceled out according to the momentary demands of competing tasks. A person may fail to pay attention to the task at hand and, as a consequence, fail to act intelligently even though retaining the quality of being intelligent. In this chapter, we have argued that "total attentional resources" is a relatively constant individual characteristic that influences performance in many situations. How is this characteristic related to intelligence?

According to the reasoning presented here, task performance depends jointly on specific abilities and attentional capacity. These two types of individual characteristics must underlie the correlations between performance on various cognitive measures. A possible pattern of relationships can be illustrated by considering the performance-resource functions of several tasks. Expanding somewhat on our earlier notation, performance on a task (t) can be considered a function $f_t(r; s_1, s_2)$ of the resources assigned to the task (r), as modulated by the structural parameters (s_1, s_2) of the performance-resource function. Consider two additional tasks (t' and t^*) with performance-resource functions $f_{t'}(r; s_2, s_3)$ and $f_{t*}(r; s_4, s_5)$. The relationship between observable performance on the three tasks and the various unobservable structure and resource parameters are shown in Fig. 5.13. All three resource-limited tasks are connected through their common dependence on attentional capacity, and tasks t and t' are further connected by a common structural parameter.

Figure 5.13 bears an obvious resemblance to Spearman's (1927) theory of special and general intelligence. Indeed, Spearman himself suggested that g might be thought of as "mental energy." The view of attention presented here amplifies on Spearman's idea. According to this view, all resource-limited tasks will be intercorrelated with one another. Similar tasks will share additional variance because of their dependence on common structural parameters. If g can indeed be identified with attentional capacity, then it follows that tasks which load highly on g are resource limited. Some evidence has been offered that the Raven's Progressive Matrices Test, usually considered an indicator of g, is in fact resource limited (Hunt, 1980), but a good deal of further research is needed to explore this suggestion. There is an additional means by which g and attentional capacity could be linked. It could be that attentional capacity is necessary during the acquisition of certain knowledge or skills but unimportant during the measurement of these characteristics. For example, attentional capacity may be a factor in acquiring vocabulary but may not be a factor when taking a vocabulary test. If this were the case, we would expect a positive correlation between knowledge tests, where performance is not resource limited, and other tests, such

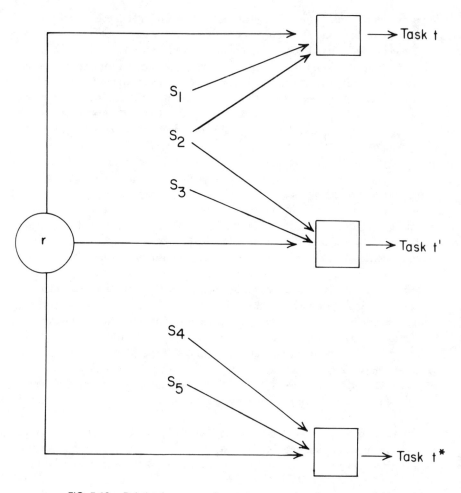

FIG. 5.13. Relation between performance, structural, and resource variables.

as the Raven's Progressive Matrices Test, where performance is resource limited.

The concept of attention may also be helpful in understanding a finding that has been something of a puzzle to those who wish to relate conventional measures of intelligence to measures of information processing. In the typical information-processing study, a theoretical model is used to interpret the relationship between performance in several experimental conditions. For example, Clark and Chase's (1972) model of sentence verification was based on reaction times to different types of sentences: true versus false, positively worded versus negatively worded, marked versus unmarked. According to their analysis, the contrast between conditions measures the duration of specific information-processing steps. In our terminology, such measures represent structural parameters because they measure structures that are used in some information-processing tasks but not others. A byproduct of the analysis of contrasts in performance over conditions is a parameter that measures the influence of any variable that has an effect in all conditions of the experiment. (In practice, the parameter is usually the intercept term in a linear regression equation.) Sternberg (1977) has referred to such terms as "wastebasket parameters." A frequent finding is that the wastebasket parameter is as highly correlated with standardized test scores as are parameters than can be identified with specific information-processing steps. From the viewpoint of attentional resource theory, such a correlation would be expected as long as both the experimental tasks and the standardized tests were resource limited.

These arguments are concerned with the correlations between cognitive tasks done singly rather than in combination. In fact, most psychometric research concerns the ability to perform one task at a time, and our concept of intelligence is generally related to maximum performance under such single task conditions. In many situations though, people are forced to handle several tasks at once. Is there a distinct ability to divide attention between multiple tasks—an ability that is distinct from the ability to do the same tasks in isolation? The ability to do several things at once has been discussed extensively in the applied literature (Damos, 1978; Fleishman, 1965; Gabriel & Burrows, 1968; Jennings & Chiles, 1977; Ogden, Levine, & Eisner, 1979), where it is sometimes referred to as "time-sharing ability." In spite of the intuitive appeal of the notion that there are people who are good (or bad) at time-sharing activities, it has been difficult to find experimental evidence for the existence of a general time-sharing factor (Hawkins et al., 1979). Failure to find such a factor may result from the lack of an appropriate model to guide the search.

Suppose that the ability to do several tasks at once depends primarily on attentional capacity. What patterns of correlations would we expect to find between tasks done singly and in combination (single and dual tasks)? The answer depends on whether the tasks to be studied are resource limited or data limited. For simplicity, consider just two tasks to be done in both single and dual-task conditions. If both tasks were resource limited when performed alone, then performance in single and dual task conditions would be determined by both attentional capacity and by the structural parameters relevant to the tasks. Thus, single and dual task performance should be highly correlated. Often, this pattern of results has been obtained in the limited research that has been done on the issue. Performance on tasks done singly predicts performance on the same tasks when performed in combination, without any need to introduce a time-sharing factor (Lansman, 1978; Poltrock et al., 1980).

Suppose, on the other hand, that performance in the single task condition is data limited but that performance in the dual task condition is resource limited. This would be the case if neither component task alone required the individual's total attentional capacity but the two tasks in combination exceeded attentional capacity. In this situation, performance on the component tasks alone would be determined by structural parameters, but performance in dual task situations would be determined by structural parameters and attentional capacity. Performance in the single task conditions would not predict performance in the dual task conditions perfectly.

The second set of conditions was assumed to have been met in the current experiments. Performance on both the secondary probe task and the easy primary tasks was assumed to be data limited, whereas performance in the dual task condition was assumed to be resource limited. Furthermore, the resource limitation was assumed to be reflected primarily in the secondary (probe) task because subjects were instructed to devote all necessary attention to the primary task. According to this reasoning, probe RT in the single task condition should not predict probe RT in the dual task condition because attentional capacity influenced the latter but not the former. This is a reasonably strong prediction because the probe task was quite reliable within conditions. (The reliability of the probe task ranged from .76 to .99 in the various conditions.) As predicted, the correlation between probe RT in single and dual task conditions was far lower than the reliabilities of the measures. (The correlations ranged from .40 to .61).

This discussion of individual differences in attentional capacity has assumed a single, completely general attentional resource. But this assumption has been seriously questioned (Navon & Gopher, 1978; Wickens, 1978). It could well be that our cognitive machinery requires a variety of mental fuels. Whether or not a task is resource limited may depend on what fuel is in short supply. The question may be resolvable by systematic study of the extent to which different tasks interfere with each other, as has been suggested by Wickens (1978), and study of the correlations among various dual task measures.

Methodological Implications

The application of information-processing models to the study of individual differences has been hampered somewhat (although investigators have not been deterred!) by a logical problem. The goal of the research is to interpret individual differences in performance in terms of the variables of cognitive process models. In most of these models, however, behavior is assumed to be only ordinally related to theoretical variables. This raises a problem in interpreting results based upon the analysis of product-moment correlations. From a strict measurement-theory point of view, the only statistics that may be computed on ordinal measurements are those that are invariant over all order-preserving transformations. Such statistics are said to be formally meaningful for ordinally represented data (Suppes & Zinnes, 1963). It is easy to show that the product-moment correlation is not formally meaningful for ordinal data. Covariances may be similarly attacked.

The measurement problem is generally ignored in the traditional psychometric approach to intelligence, and two arguments have been advanced for using correlations in spite of measurement problems. First, in spite of the logical case against correlational analysis, it does produce coherent results. Second, measurement theorists have not offered an alternative to correlational analysis (Nunnally, 1978). This second argument is not simply a know-nothing position. A serious argument can be made that the psychometric approach to intelligence involves an inductive definition of theoretical as opposed to observed variables and that, as a consequence, psychometric theories are basically descriptive rather than deductive. Correlational analysis provides an economical description of the data, and the measurement-theory argument is irrelevant.

It is clear that the atheoretical approach to measurement is not appropriate if models of individual differences are to be derived from information-processing models of cognition. Information-processing models deal with the relationships between unobservable theoretical variables. Tests of the models are only possible to the extent that a relationship between unobservables and observables is stated as part of the model. In most cases the stated relationship is ordinality. In fact, this is explicit in Norman and Bobrow's (1975) analysis of dual task performance. Norman and Bobrow quite carefully avoid assuming anything more than an ordinal relationship between performance on a task and the amount of resources committed to the task.

An analysis of information-processing models, including but not limited to analyses of resource-competition models, may lead to the prediction of fairly complex interactions between theoretical variables. The easy-to-hard prediction is a good example. In order to test these predictions the power of correlational analysis is needed. Therefore, we need some justification for correlational analysis that does not depend on the assumption that the particular values of the correlations are formally meaningful.

In this chapter, such a justification was provided by the use of the mathematical theory of information, which does not even depend on an ordinal relationship between theoretical and observed variables. The axioms of a resource-competition model were reworded into information-theoretic terms. This enabled us to prove that the easy-to-hard prediction must hold for some unknown set of functions relating performance on the various observable variables to each other. Extension of the analysis to the relation between two variables, conditional upon knowledge of the value of a third, resulted in a nonlinear analogue to partial correlations.

Information-theory analysis could only be used to assert that certain unknown functions "must exist" (if the model is correct). In order to identify these functions, we resorted to what might be considered a mathematical trick. We made use of the fact that any function of a real-valued variable can be approximated by a linear polynomial in that variable. The easy-to-hard prediction could thus be formulated in terms of relationships between linear polynomials in the observed variables and tested using standard methods of partial correlation.

The combination of information theory and linear polynomial analysis produces two things: a list of reliably established associations between variables and a list of the linear polynomial functions used to describe those associations. It is important to distinguish between the empirically derived linear polynomials and the theoretical functions they are presumed to describe. The two are not the same, and it will require further elaboration of the theory (especially with respect to performance measures on a specific task) before it would be appropriate to interpret the relationships that we observed. To illustrate, in several of our analyses we found that there was a linear relation between performances in different pairs of resource-limited tasks. This does not mean that the relation between the attentional resources allocated to each task was linear or that the within-task performance-resource functions were linear. It does mean that any more elaborate model of the performance-resource function for these tasks must account for the observed linear relationship.

The method of analysis that we have used does not depend on any assumptions that are specific to attentional resource theories. The analytic technique should be widely applicable to studies in which individual differences in performance are to be related to models of information processing in cognition.

ACKNOWLEDGMENTS

This research was supported by the Office of Naval Research, Contract # N00014-77-0225, Earl Hunt, principal investigator. We would like to thank Colene McKee for assistance in the analyses reported here, and Christopher Hertzog for assistance in discussing some of the statistical issues involved.

REFERENCES

Atkinson, R. C., & Shiffrin, R. M. Human memory: A proposed system and its control processes. In K. W. Spence & J. T. Spence (Eds.), *The psychology of learning and motivation: Advances in research and theory* (Vol. 2). New York: Academic Press, 1968.

Baddeley, A. D., & Hitch, G. Working memory. In G. H. Bower (Ed.), *The psychology of learning and motivation* (Vol. 8). New York: Academic Press, 1974.

Bentler, P. M. Multivariate analysis with latent variables: Causal modeling. *Annual Review Psychology*, 1980, *31*, 419–456.

Chiang, A., & Atkinson, R. Individual differences and inter-relationships among a select set of cognitive skills. *Memory & Cognition*, 1976, *4*, 661–672.

Clark, H., & Chase, W. On the process of comparing sentences against pictures. *Cognitive Psychology*, 1972, *3*, 472–517.

Cohen, J., & Cohen, P. *Applied multiple regressional correlation analysis for the behavioral sciences.* Hillsdale, N.J.: Lawrence Erlbaum Associates, 1975.

Damos, D. L. Residual attention as a predictor of pilot performance. *Human Factors*, 1978, *20*, 435–440.

Fleishman, E. A. The prediction of total task performance from prior practice on task components. *Human Factors*, 1965, *7*, 18–27.

Gabriel, R. F., & Burrows, A. A. Improving time-sharing performance of pilots through training. *Human Factors*, 1968, *10*, 33–40.

Hawkins, H. L., Rodriquez, E., & Reicher, G. M. *Is time-sharing a general ability?* (Tech. Rep. No. 3) University of Oregon, Center for Cognitive and Perceptual Research 1979.

Hunt, E. Mechanics of verbal ability. *Psychological Review,* 1978, *85,* 109–130.

Hunt, E. B. Intelligence as an information processing concept. *British Journal of Psychology,* 1980, *71,* 449–474.

Hunt, E. B., Davidson, J., & Lansman, M. *Individual differences in long-term memory access.* Manuscript submitted for publication, 1980.

Hunt, E., Frost, N., & Lunneborg, C. Individual differences in cognition: A new approach to intelligence. In C. Bower (Ed.), *Advances in learning and motivation* (Vol. 7). New York: Academic Press, 1973.

Hunt, E., Lunneborg, C., & Lewis, J. What does it mean to be high verbal? *Cognitive Psychology,* 1975, *7,* 194–227.

Hunt, E., & Poltrock, S. The mechanics of thought. In B. Kantowitz (Ed.), *Human information processing: Tutorials in performance and cognition.* Hillsdale, N.J.: Lawrence Erlbaum Associates, 1974.

Jennings, A. E., & Chiles, W. D. An investigation of time-sharing ability as a factor in complex performance. *Human Factors,* 1977, *19,* 535–547.

Kahneman, D. *Attention and effort.* Englewood Cliffs, N.J.: Prentice-Hall, 1973.

Kerr, B. Processing demands during mental operations. *Memory & Cognition,* 1973, *1,* 401–412.

Lansman, M. *An attentional approach to individual differences in immediate memory* (Tech. Rep. No. 1). University of Washington, Department of Psychology, June 1978.

Lansman, M., & Hunt, E. B. Individual differences in secondary task performance. *Memory & Cognition,* in press.

Love, T. *Relating individual differences in computer programming performance to human information processing abilities.* Unpublished doctoral dissertation, University of Washington, 1977.

Luce, R. D. Theory of selective information and some of its behavioral applications. In R. D. Luce (Ed.), *Developments in mathematical psychology.* Glencoe, Ill.: Free Press, 1960.

Moray, N. Where is capacity limited? A survey and a model. *Acta Psychologica,* 1967, *27,* 84–92.

Navon, D., & Gopher, D. On the economy of the human-processing system. *Psychological Review,* 1979, *86,* 214–255.

Norman, D. A., & Bobrow, D. B. On data-limited and resource-limited processes. *Cognitive Psychology,* 1975, *7,* 44–64.

Nunnally, J. C. *Psychometric theory.* New York: McGraw-Hill, 1978.

Ogden, G. D., Levine, J. M., & Eisner, E. J. Measurement of workload by secondary tasks. *Human Factors,* 1979, *21,* 529–548.

Pellegrino, J. W., & Glaser, R. Editorial: Cognitive correlates and components in the analysis of individual differences. *Intelligence,* 1979, *3,* 187–216.

Poltrock, S. E., Lansman, M., & Hunt, E. *Automatic and controlled attention processes in auditory detection* (Tech. Rep. No. 9). University of Washington, Department of Psychology, 1980.

Posner, M. I. *Chronometric explorations of mind.* Hillsdale, N.J.: Lawrence Erlbaum Associates, 1978.

Simon, H. *The science of the artificial.* Cambridge, Mass.: MIT Press, 1969.

Spearman, C. *The abilities of man.* New York: Macmillan, 1927.

Sternberg, R. J. *Intelligence, information processing, and analogical reasoning: The componential analysis of human abilities.* Hillsdale, N.J.: Lawrence Erlbaum Associates, 1977.

Sternberg, R. J. The nature of mental abilities. *American Psychologist,* 1979, *34,* 214–230.

Sternberg, R. J. Sketch of a componential subtheory of human intelligence. *Behavioral and Brain Sciences,* 1980, *3,* 573–614.

Suppes, P., & Zinnes, J. Basic measurement theory. In R. P. Luce, R. R. Bush, & E. Galanter (Eds.), *Handbook of mathematical psychology.* New York: Wiley, 1963.

Tukey, J. W. *Exploratory data analysis.* Reading, Mass.: Addison-Wesley, 1977.

Underwood, B. J. Individual differences as a crucible in theory construction. *American Psychologist*, 1975, *36*, 128–134.

Underwood, B. J., Boruch, R. F., & Malmi, R. A. Composition of episodic memory. *Journal of Experimental Psychology: General*, 1978, *107*, 393–419.

Wickens, C. D. The structure of attentional resources. In R. S. Nickerson (Ed.), *Attention and performance VIII*. Hillsdale, N.J.: Lawrence Erlbaum Associates, 1980.

Yntema, D., & Meuser, C. Keeping track of variables that have few or many states. *Journal of Experimental Psychology*, 1962, *63*, 391–395.

6 The Chronometry of Intelligence

Arthur R. Jensen
Institute of Human Learning
University of California at Berkeley

A clearly formulated hypothesis, a well-designed experiment, and a generalizable conclusion of theoretical or practical importance are all products of much analysis and cogitation. But what initiates such analysis and cogitation in the first place? The answer calls for autobiographical retrospection, and so here, of course, I can only speak for myself. By way of introduction, it might be useful to try to discern what kinds of things get me going as an investigator. Some of these general reaction tendencies that seem to be recurrent throughout my career in psychological research also quite likely account for my current fascination with the connection between reaction time and intelligence, which is mainly what this chapter is about.

In general, five things seem to arouse my research impulse. In no particular order of importance, they are:

1. In reading the psychological literature, if I repeatedly encounter what seems to be a popular or commonly accepted belief, generalization, or theory, which for some reason looks questionable to me or cries out to be debunked, I am apt to go to work on it (provided that its technical aspects as a research problem fall more or less within what I perceive as my sphere of competence or at least a compentence that I think I could acquire without an unfeasible expenditure of time and effort). Certain topics in psychology are notably rich in this vein, and the literature on intelligence may well be the richest. At least it is difficult for me to think of any other *major* topic in psychology, as treated in general textbooks, that presents what seem to me more potentially debunkable popular beliefs than the topic of intelligence. Hence, the fact that my investigative tendency is aroused by anything I perceive (for whatever reason) as an unfounded belief is

probably a factor in my attraction to intelligence as a research topic. It offers us many unfounded but popular beliefs, and some of these apparently refuse to die even in the face of decisively contradictory evidence. In such a case, one's research efforts must simply move on to more genuinely unsettled questions, in the realization that there will always be some small carp of critics who will forever cling to the belief that the earth is flat.

2. This is almost a corollary of the first point: I am aroused by findings or phenomena that would seem to contradict a common belief or explanation we had regarded as too obvious to question. The contradictory fact can be a springboard for investigations that may support a better scientific explanation. Any seemingly contradictory phenomenon must, of course, also be critically examined to rule out possible artifacts and to insure its replicability. If it stands up, we have a new lead for investigation.

3. Another quality of a phenomenon that enhances its interest for me is its being counterintuitive, surprising, or inexplicable in terms of any established principles. Once such a a phenomenon attracts my attention, of course, the first job is to establish its reality and make sure it is not just a fluke—an experimental or statistical artifact. The researcher's nightmare, it seems to me, is the risk of squandering resources on the investigation of some apparently interesting phenomenon that turns out to be merely some kind of artifact. Almost as bad but even more likely is the risk that the phenomenon, although real, is so narrowly specific to a particular laboratory procedure, measuring device, or sample so unrepresentative of the general population that it is scientifically and theoretically trivial. I seek evidence that a phenomenon is fairly "robust" before making any strong research commitment, recognizing, however, that what at first may appear to be an ephemeral or unreliable phenomenon might be turned into a robust phenomenon by improved measurements, procedures, or analytic techniques.

4. A psychological phenomenon that can be measured reliably or has potentially quantifiable properties is thereby a more attractive subject for scientific study. It is not necessarily a more important phenomenon than one that does not lend itself so readily to quantification; but the study of measurable phenomena, I believe, more surely and quickly yields objective knowledge. Similarly, I am more closely drawn to a phenomenon when it displays what appears to be a simple, regular, or "lawful" relationship to some other variable or when it shows invariance over a wide range of conditions. (The well-known serial-position effect in serial rote learning is a good example of a highly invariant phenomenon.) Invariance usually signifies that the causal mechanisms are robust, general, and probably more biologically wired in rather than experiential. A phenomenon that shows essentially the same lawfulness and invariance in different species of animals, including humans, is thereby made even more attractive; this interspecies continuity of the phenomenon suggests that it is a product of biological evolution, which I find much more interesting than any predominantly cultural phenomenon. This preference for biological rather than

cultural phenomena is merely a personal idiosyncracy to which I attach no general importance.

5. Psychology has many unsolved problems and unexplained phenomena that have been around for a very long time. There are basic, recurring questions. Unsuccessful early attempts to understand a phenomenon may lead to its abandonment as a topic of inquiry, but the basic questions that prompted investigation in the first place remain unanswered. On the other hand, there are short-lived fads in psychological research that distract from the enduring basic issues. Acquaintance with the history of the major topics of psychology affords one a perspective and context for appreciating a phenomenon. Over the years, research questions with little or no past history have seemed less and less interesting to me. Too many PhD dissertations deal with questions that have no history and, most likely, no future. A science cannot develop by a continual succession of unanswered or half-answered questions about an ever increasing multitude of phenomena. Hence, I am most attracted to the still unresolved questions in those topics that are strongly rooted in the history of our field. The nature of intelligence and the measurement of individual differences in intelligence are such topics. There are many phenomena in this domain that evince all the features of attractiveness for investigation that I have indicated. In addition, the topic of intelligence is commonly regarded as having great relevance to education and, indeed, to society and the quality of life. This is a bonus, but not the intrinsic attraction, from the standpoint of research.

DEFINITION OF INTELLIGENCE

It is a mistake to waste time arguing about the definition of intelligence, except to make sure everyone understands that the term does not refer to a "thing." Nearly everyone understands its lexical meaning—*intelligence* would be a relatively easy word in a vocabulary test, for example. Scientifically, intelligence is perhaps best characterized at present as an unclear hypothetical construct (or class of constructs) that has sprung from observations of individual differences in a class of behaviors called "abilities," specifically "mental" abilities, meaning that individual differences in performance are not mainly attributable to differences in sensory or motor functions per se. An ability is distinguished from other types of behavior by the fact that it is performance that can essentially be quantified in terms of a wholly objective or universally agreed upon standard of "goodness," quite aside from any value judgment as to the moral, social, or cultural value of the performance.

But I am content, for the time being, to let intelligence be a vague concept. In that respect it is in quite good company in the history of science. As a philosopher of science, H. A. Kramers (quoted in Elkana, 1974) has noted: "In the world of human thought generally and in physical science particularly, the most fruitful concepts are those to which it is impossible to attach a well-defined meaning [p. 52]."

Psychologists' conceptions of intelligence are bound up with their methods of measuring it. But rather than debate whether an IQ test, for example, *really* measures intelligence, we should heed Miles' (1957) advice: "The important point is not whether what we measure can appropriately be labelled 'intelligence,' but whether we have discovered something worth measuring. And this is not a matter that can be settled by an appeal to what is or is not the correct use of the word 'intelligent' [p. 157]."

NOTIONS ABOUT MEASURED INTELLIGENCE

Standardized intelligence tests, or so-called IQ tests, undoubtedly yield quite highly reliable measurements or scores. What these scores represent, besides themselves, can only be known through their correlations with other variables that are independent of the test yielding the scores in question. It is well established that IQ is substantially correlated with children's scholastic performance and with their eventual occupational status—facts that lend the IQ its popularly recognized importance. These socially important correlates of IQ, however, provide very little psychological information about what it is that the IQ tests measure, a point on which prominent psychologists still express strongly differing notions.

Consider the dispute between Albee and Hebb appearing in a recent issue of the *American Psychologist*. Albee (1980) states:

Hebb's letter makes it clear that he believes in an underlying intelligence separate from IQ test scores. He describes the IQ as an accurate reflection of this underlying intelligence. This view is not shared by many experts in measurement, who view the IQ test as a measure of prior learning of skills and knowledge, not as a measure of some underlying native ability [p. 386].

Hebb's and Albee's views clearly reflect quite different notions about what our present IQ tests measure; their dispute epitomizes two of the most opposing viewpoints.

One of the aims of scientific research is to settle such arguments. This is done best by subdividing the problem into its elemental units and formulating *strong* hypotheses about each unit. Strong hypotheses can be refuted by evidence and are therefore scientifically useful. Weak hypotheses do not compel strong conclusions, whatever the evidence shows. Strong hypotheses often seem more extreme and less reasonable than weak hypotheses, but they are surely more vulnerable to refutation, and that is their virtue. They permit us to reject empirically and decisively those elements of our notions that are false.

From Albee's previously quoted statement we find certain implicit hypotheses about what IQ tests measure. These can be stated in a weak form, which may permit anyone to escape the implications or constraints of any empirical findings and cling to a favored hypothesis. On the other hand, hypotheses can be stated in a strong form, which risks compelling empirical refutation. For example:

Hypothesis 1: What do IQ Tests Measure?

Weak Form.   The IQ test measures individual differences in prior learning of skills and knowledge.

Strong Form.   The IQ test measures individual differences *only* in prior learning of skills and knowledge.

In its weak form the hypothesis seems too obvious or trivial even to arouse one's investigative impulse, at least that of anyone familiar with, say, the content of the Stanford–Binet or Wechsler IQ tests. In contrast, the strong form of the hypothesis invites curiosity and a search for contradictory evidence. Several lines of evidence, including research on reaction time, clearly refute this hypothesis in its strong form (as I show later). If this strong hypothesis is one of the elements of Albee's (or anyone else's) belief about IQ tests, they have the benefit of knowing it is decisively refuted.

Hypothesis 2: Is IQ Inherited?

Weak Form.   The IQ test is not a measure of some underlying native ability.

Strong Form.   When correctly estimated by appropriate methods of quantitative genetics, the heritability of IQ in the general population is zero.

This hypothesis is overwhelmingly rejected by a perponderance of the evidence, including the most recent studies of IQ heritability (Plomin & De Fries, 1980).

If we try to imagine doing a factor analysis of current notions about what it is that standard IQ tests measure, the "pure" factors might be described as follows:

1. IQ tests measure prior learned *knowledge* (e.g., vocabulary, general information).
2. IQ tests measure prior learned skills or *strategies* for solving certain classes of problems (e.g., analogies, matrices, number-series completion, block designs).
3. IQ tests measure innate *learning ability*.
4. IQ tests measure innate *information-processing capacity*.
5. IQ tests measure *motivation* or willingness and effort to perform well on a certain class of tests.

Individual differences in IQ are viewed, in terms of each of these factors, as being the result of inequalities of opportunity to learn the particular knowledge or problem-solving strategies called for by the test (1 and 2) or inborn inequalities in learning ability or in information-processing capacity (3 and 4) or motivation (5).

Although I have represented these views as ''pure factors'' in the entire domain of notions about what IQ tests measure, they are more often found in various combinations, with different degrees of importance attributed to each factor.

One aim of research on intelligence at this stage is to determine, on the basis of evidence, which of these views are correct and which are incorrect or, if a number of these factors contribute to IQ variance, what is their relative importance? One would imagine that the relative importance of these factors would differ to some extent from one IQ test (or subtest) to another. Some of the factors may be more important in terms of the amount of variance accounted for in some tests, whereas others might be more important in terms of the number of different tests to which they contribute variance. What are my own hunches concerning these notions about what IQ tests measure?

We all begin researching with some background of hunches about the nature of the phenomenon of interest based on our impressions gained from previous research. We carry on new research essentially to produce evidence that will confirm or disconfirm our hunches, and this in turn gives rise to new hunches, and so on. When the confirming or disconfirming evidence is sufficiently rigorous and solid at each step in this process, the result is cumulative, systematic scientific knowledge—an increased understanding of the phenomenon. My interest in reaction time in relation to IQ can perhaps be best introduced in terms of my hunches about intelligence and about the particular notions it may be possible to confirm or disconfirm through studies of reaction time, which is now better termed *mental chronometry* because the method involves considerably more than just reaction time per se.

Some of my hunches about intelligence concern:

1. IQ as Knowledge.   I see items of knowledge or prior learned information merely as one possible *vehicle* for the measurement of intelligence, which itself is not the specific knowledge per se. If this is ture, it might be possible to measure intelligence without requiring persons to recall past learned knowledge. The amount of knowledge acquired in a given period of time with equal access to the experiences that convey the knowledge, however, may be monotonically related to intelligence. Archimedes and Einstein undoubtedly possessed quite different knowledge, but they may well have been equally intelligent.

2. IQ as Learned Cognitive Skills and Problem-Solving Strategies.   These, too, are merely reflections or indicators of intelligence, and their number and efficiency are monotonically related to intelligence, given equal opportunity. I doubt that the level of complex information processing that we ordinarily think of as cognitive *skills* or *strategies* is innate or "wired" into the brain, like a spider's ability to construct a particular form of web. Rather, skills have to be learned through certain experiences, but the ease of such learning and the complexity of the strategies that can be learned and applied in a given amount of time are directly related to intelligence. If true, it should be possible, at least in principle, to measure individual differences in intelligence by means that do not involve what we generally mean by an acquired skill or strategy.

3. IQ as Learning Ability.   Some IQ tests undoubtedly use prior learned knowledge and skills as a vehicle for the measurement of intelligence. Is intelligence, therefore, the same as learning ability, and are individual differences in IQ mainly a reflection of differences in learning ability? I once thought this was probable, but now I strongly doubt that individual differences in learning speed or retention are the same as intelligence. The "purer" we make our learning tasks and the less dependent they are on reasoning, problem solving, or transfer from prior learning, the less they correlate with IQ. Performance on laboratory rote learning tasks is a surprisingly poor indicator of IQ. Some form of *complexity* (not just difficulty) has to be added to the learning task to make it correlate substantially with IQ. It is also of interest that different species of animals that we intuitively perceive as differing markedly in intelligence (e.g., chickens, dogs, and chimpanzees) do not differ nearly as much in tests involving primarily learning and memory as in tests involving reasoning and problem solving or more complex forms of *relational* learning. Learning and memory per se seem to be a poor paradigm for understanding intelligence.

The hypothesis that IQ tests measure *only* innate learning ability and the products of prior learning (i.e., knowledge and strategies) would be disconfirmed if it could be shown that some kinds of preformance, which do not involve any past or present learning at all, are correlated with IQ.

4. IQ as Motivation, Effort, Willingness, Compliance, etc.   Motivation, in the sense of making a conscious, voluntary effort to perform well, does not seem to be an important source of variance in IQ. There are paper-and-pencil tests or other performance tasks that do not superficially look very different from some IQ tests, that can be shown to be sensitive to motivational factors by experimentally varying motivational instructions and incentives, and that show highly reliable individual differences in performance but show no correlation with IQ. Differences in IQ are not the result of some people simply trying harder than others. In fact, there is some indication that, at least under certain conditions, low scorers try harder than high scorers. Ahern and Beatty (1979) measured the degree of pupillary dilation as an indicator of effort and autonomic arousal when subjects are presented with test problems and found that: (1) pupillary dilation is directly related to level of problem difficulty (as indexed both by the objective complexity of the problem and the percentage of subjects giving the correct answer); (2) subjects with higher psychometrically measured intelligence show less pupillary dilation to problems at any given level of difficulty. (All subjects were university students.) Ahern and Beatty (1979) conclude:

> These results help to clarify the biological basis of psychometrically-defined intelligence. They suggest that more intelligent individuals do not solve a tractable cognitive problem by bringing increased activation, "mental energy" or "mental effort" to bear. On the contrary, these individuals show less task-induced activation in solving a problem of a given level of difficulty. This suggests that individuals differing in intelligence must also differ in the efficiency of those brain processes which mediate the particular cognitive task [p. 1292].

This strikes me as one of the most interesting and important findings in recent research on mental ability. I wonder how it ties in with Bastendorf's (1960) finding that the galvanic skin response (palmer conductance level), which is another indicator of autonomic arousal, is positively correlated with both age and Wechsler IQs in school children.

5. Intelligence as a Product of Biological Evolution.   Several lines of evidence lead me to believe that intelligence is a product of biological evolution: (1) differences between various animal species in what we generally think of as intelligence; (2) certain similarities and continuities between animal and human intelligence; (3) the interspecies relationship between brain size (particularly the cerebral cortex) and apparent intelligence; (4) the marked increase in brain size in the course of human evolution; and (5) the dependence of intellectual functions on the anatomic intactness and physiological state of the brain. If intelligence is a product of biological evolution, it must depend on certain physical properties of the brain, the development of which is, to a large extent, conditioned by polygenetic factors. The question, then, is to what extent do scores on IQ tests reflect this "biological intelligence"? The evidence on the heritability of IQ scores suggests that genetic factors contribute to individual differences. But another, more direct, way to determine if IQ scores reflect biological intelligence, rather than cultural acquisition, would be to look for correlations between IQ and direct measurements of anatomical properties or physiological functions of the brain. As Miles (1957), in a critical discussion of the the factor analysis of ability tests, aptly observed:

> We can be most sure of progress when links are found, not between one test and another, but between a person's test behavior and the behavior of genes and neurones. Genes and neurones, be it noted, are parts of the *body;* and, to put the matter epigrammatically, we could perhaps say that factors have a real existence, not when they are "factors of the mind" (whatever that means) but when they are *factors of the body* [p. 165].

Quantitative genetic analyses, of course, can prove that there is a biological substrate of individual differences in IQ, but more direct methods of study, at the interface of brain and behavior, are required for us to understand the mechanisms and processes that constitute this substrate. At present, there are two available techniques that leave the nervous system wholly intact and do not interfere in the least with its normal functioning, yet afford a means of analyzing the processes underlying intelligence. They are *evoked potentials* and *mental chronometry*. Both techniques yield measurements that are significantly related to IQ.

THE ROLE OF FACTOR ANALYSIS

The block designs and vocabulary subtests of the Wechsler Adult Intelligence Scale (WAIS) are correlated about .60 (corrected for attenuation) among individuals 18- to 19-years of age. These two tests look as different from each other in terms of content and task requirements as one could imagine. A fine-grained "task analysis" of each test would reveal little, if anything, in common between them. The relatively high correlation between these tests, therefore, strikes me as a highly arresting phenomenon. As interesting as the causes of individual differences on either task in itself might be, of much greater interest, I think, is the *correlation* between them. It epitomizes the central problem—the fundamental phenomenon—for a theory of ability. An adequate theory of intelligence must explain not only why people differ from each other in performance on the block designs test or on vocabulary (or any other mental test), but why there is a substantial correlation between individual differences on such widely different tests.

If the correlation between any two tests is of greater interest than the variance on either test alone, then it seems that the common factor among a large number of diverse tests should be of even greater interest—not more tractable, to be sure, but theoretically more challenging. Hence the importance of Spearman's *g* (the *general factor* of mental ability) for psychological research. I am not referring to any particular *theory* Spearman may have suggested about *g* but merely to the empirical observation that *g* best summarizes what Thurstone termed "positive manifold"—the fact that all tests of ability, however superficially diverse, are positively intercorrelated. Any *particular* test might be of greater interest than some other test for a variety of practical reasons or because it is more amenable to experimental analysis. But it is really the fact that diverse tests are intercorrelated, and therefore *g* loaded, which is the central phenomenon that a theory of intelligence must attempt to explain.

Factor analysis, then, is best viewed not as a theory in itself, nor as an explanation of anything, but as a means for most clearly highlighting phenomena worthy of scientific investigation and theoretical explanation. These phenomena are the general factor (g) and the major group factors identified by common factor analysis.

Because virtually all tests share in g, I give research priority to g. Also, the g factor comes closest to common-sense notions of intelligence. I consider g a "working definition" of intelligence. By working definition I simply mean a set of general operations by means of which different investigators can arrive at similar measurements and identify the same phenomenon for investigation, more or less regardless of the specific tests they employ, so long as the tests are diverse, numerous, and yield a large first principal factor. The g factor loosely fulfills these purposes. It permits identification of the most g-loaded tests, which can be used as reference variables in the analyses of newly devised tasks. By their simplicity or amenability to experimental manipulation and fine-grained analysis of performance, these tests may be more revealing of the nature of g than the majority of highly g loaded standard tests.

In addition, factor analysis (or at least reference tests that factor analysis has shown to be highly g loaded) provides a kind of insurance to the researcher. It insures that one is not wasting efforts on a highly specific, nongeneralizable phenomenon with little or no importance in the practical world. The tests or test items that most clearly discriminate between criterion groups of low and high intelligence selected by common-sense judgments in which there is virtually universal agreement are the very tests or items that are also the most g loaded.

It is an interesting fact, too, that a test's g loading is related to its subjectively judged "complexity," whatever that term may mean to naive observers asked to rate the complexity of test items. I have tried this with groups of students who have never heard of g or factor analysis. When asked to rate test items or homogeneous subtests (ranging in item difficulty as indexed by percentage passing) on "complexity" (the meaning of which is left to the raters), these students made ratings that showed considerable correspondence between the rated complexity of subtests and their g loading ascertained by factor analysis. For example, the Number Series Completion test (e.g., 1, 4, 3, 6, 5, —)was always rated as more complex than the Memory for Numbers test (recalling a string of numbers after one presentation), and the g loadings of these two tests (when factor analyzed among 18 other diverse tests) were .79 and .46, respectively. We have found the same direct relationship of g loadings to complexity when tests have been specially constructed to differ objectively in complexity.

Another telling point is that g is related to common-sense notions of "thinking." That is, tests' g loadings seem to reflect the degree to which people judge that the task requires "thought" or "mental effort." This coincides with the finding that very small g loadings are seen on tests of sensory and motor abilities or rote learning and memory. Even *within* any one of these domains, the first principal factor of a battery of varied tests is remarkably meager when compared to the first principal factor of a comparably sized battery of more "cognitive" tests, even though these may appear extremely diverse in the kinds of knowledge and skills they require.

Choice of Factor Model

If our interest is in the general factor of a collection of diverse tests, orthogonal rotation of factors is immediately ruled out because orthogonally rotated factors necessarily hide the general factor. This still leaves us with a choice among other factor models that allow the extraction of g. But, at least theoretically, these could result in gs that might vary from one method to another. So we are faced with the practical question of which of the available methods yields the best g. This is a question to which I have not been able to find a clear-cut or generally agreed upon answer among leading experts in factor analysis. The question calls for a thorough discussion and resolution, if possible, by the experts. Meanwhile, I can only make some pragmatic suggestions based on my own experience in applying different factor models to a variety of test data.

There are basically two aspects of the problem. First, there is the purely mathematical and statistical question of the robustness, reliability, and invariance of the extracted g involving questions such as:

1. How stable is the g for a given battery of tests across different samples (of a given N) from the same population, or across samples from different populations?
2. More important, how stable or invariant is the g for different batteries of tests (given to the same groups of subjects), and how much is the degree of invariance of g at the mercy of the particular tests in the battery?

These questions could be answered, in principle, without knowing anything at all about the specific tests that were subjected to analysis, aside from the fact that they are all truly ability tests. If they are, the intercorrelations will show positive manifold, which is the phenomenon of primary interest and which the g factor is intended to represent.

The second aspect of the problem concerns the theoretical or psychological interpretation of the extracted g. From countless previous factor analyses—from the time of Spearman up to the present day—we have gained some ideas about the psychological nature of g and about the observable features of test items that are typically the most g loaded. Some tests, such as Raven's Progressive Matrices, have become regarded as reference or marker tests for g because of their fairly consistent record of high g loadings when factor analyzed among many different test batteries. Thus, the question is: Which factor method, when applied to different test batteries and different populations, most consistently accentuates the g loadings of these reference tests that best typify our psychological notions of g?

It boils down to a choice between the following methods for representing g: (1) the first principal component; (2) the unrotated first principal factor (common factor analysis, iterated to get conforming communalities); or (3) a higher-order g (first principal factor) extracted from the intercorrelations among the obliquely rotated first-order factors. How do these alternatives compare as indices of g in terms of the criteria described in the preceding paragraphs?

The first principal component (FPC) and the first principal factor (FPF) generally differ very little in the relative magnitudes of their loadings on the various tests included in a given analysis; the Pearson correlation between the loadings is, in my experience, almost never below .95 and is typically about .97 or .98. (The Burt–Tucker congruence coefficient is even higher.) Thus, the FPC and FPF rarely lead to different conclusions when they are used merely to identify the most g loaded tests or to rank order the tests on g. Beyond this use, there are advantages and disadvantages of each model, which generally weigh in favor of the FPF. The FPC is slightly larger, accounting for more variance than is accounted for by the FPF, because it includes some fraction of each test's "uniqueness" (i.e., variance not shared by other tests in the battery) as a result of beginning the analysis with unities in the principal diagonal. This fraction of unique variance in unwanted if we are trying to get as "clean" a g as possible. The FPF, in which the analysis begins with estimated communalities (the proportion of the total variance that a given test has in common with all the other tests) in the principal diagonal, is theoretically a "cleaner" g factor. Differences between test's g loadings on the FPF invariably appear more accentuated and clean-cut than on the FPC. However, more interesting psychologically is that, even though it is not inevitable mathematically, it turns out, in fact, that the most and the least "g-ish" tests in the psychological, Spearmanian sense are the very tests on which the highest and lowest loadings on the FPF stand out most sharply, more so than on the FPC. When one or two of the reputedly best g reference tests are included in a battery, they more often have the highest loadings on the FPF, not on the FPC. Therefore, I believe the FPF better represents Spearman's g. Those advantages of the FPF outweigh the one slight advantage that the FPC possesses when the subject sample is not very large. The FPC appears less sensitive to sampling fluctuations and population differences because the FPF, unlike the FPC, depends on the estimated communalities, which are influenced by the number of factors extracted and are subject to sampling error.

I am most impressed, however, by the almost incredible robustness or stability of either the FPF or FPC across very widely differing samples taking the same battery of tests and across quite different batteries of tests given to the same sample. The g factor scores (based on the FPF) are highly correlated across quite different test batteries, provided that each battery contains a sufficient variety of tests so that no battery predominantly represents some narrow group factor or what Spearman (1927) regarded as "overlapping specifics." The six verbal subtests and the five performance subtests of the Wechsler, for example, are very different batteries. Each of the verbal tests requires the subject to give spoken answers to questions presented orally; each of the performance tests requires manipulation of some kind of puzzle or task such as block designs and object assembly. Yet g scores on the verbal and performance batteries, based on the g factors extracted separately from each battery, are correlated over .80. When different batteries are larger and even more heterogeneous in content and task requirements than the verbal or performance scales of the Wechsler, their respective separate g factors are even more highly similar. Such findings suggest that individual differences in g have some objective reality that exists independently of any particular test or any particular battery of tests. This is not to reify g as a thing. But it implies that there is some substrate of processes, independent of test content, that accounts for g and that, therefore, should be detectable and potentially measurable by means other than the usual mental tests, at least in principle.

What are the strengths and weaknesses of the extraction of g as a higher-order factor (usually second- or at most third-order) derived from the obliquely rotated first-order (or primary) factors? Theoretically, this hierarchical model should yield a g that is more invariant across different test batteries. The hierarchical g is less affected than the FPC or FPF by the overrepresentation of certain group factors in some collections of tests. For example, if the verbal tests in a battery outnumber the nonverbal tests (or greatly outweigh the nonverbal tests in total amount of true score variance), the g represented by the FPC or FPF will be somewhat "contaminated" by a verbal factor, whereas the hierarchical g is much less liable to such contamination. In brief, the hierarchical g is less influenced by variations in the particular collection of tests entering into the factor analysis, whereas g as represented by the FPC or FPF is more at the mercy of the particular collection of tests, and its degree of invariance is more dependent on good "psychometric sampling." The chief weakness of the hierarchical g is its comparative statistical unreliability. It is more susceptible to subject sampling error in the original correlations, and the error is compounded at each higher level of the hierarchy so that in samples of fewer than 100 subjects the hierarchical g may be considerably less invariant than the FPC or FPF. It boils down to weighing the risk of loss of invariance of the estimated g due either to: (1) fluctuations in psychometric sampling of the abilities domain (in which case hierarchical g is the more invariant); or (2) fluctuations in subject sampling or the use of samples from different populations (in which case FPF is the more invariant). Hierarchical g is made less risky by using very large samples; the FPF g is improved by including a greater number and diversity of tests, with no one type of test overrepresented. When these sampling conditions are reasonably well met for both tests and subjects, I have generally found that the hierarchical g and FPF g are very similar in the relative magnitudes of g loadings on the various tests, although the FPF g loadings are generally larger overall. The two types of g, based on the same test battery and subject sample, usually correlate above .80 in my experience, and experts in the mathematical basis of factor analysis tell me that the hierarchical g and the FPF g should converge as both psychometric and subject sampling are improved (i.e., sampling errors of both types are decreased).

All things considered, the FPF seems to be the preferred method for representing g and for obtaining reliable factor scores in most practical situations. Our confidence in this generalization could be improved by some elaborate studies using Monte Carlo techniques based on artificial, hypothetical "tests" of known factorial composition, from which FPF g and hierarchical g are extracted and compared for invariance under systematic variations of "psychometric" and "subject" sampling from the artificially constructed populations of "tests" and "subjects." The same could be done with real data, if the tests and subjects were sufficiently varied and numerous.

The importance of obtaining a good g factor for the measurement of individual differences in research on the chronometric analysis of intelligence is not only that g is the best working definition of intelligence and best represents the common factor of the great variety of intelligence tests, but that it minimizes variance attributable to any specific prior learned content, skills, talents, or interests—variance that is apt to be less indicative of the more basic levels of cognitive processing (and their physiological substrate) presumably assessed by chronometric techniques. The use of g factor scores or good g reference tests helps to winnow the psychometric chaff from the individual differences to be subjected to chronometric study, the principal aim of which, as I see it, is not to account for variance in any particular test or performance, but in psychometric g. The practical compromise of using only one or two g reference tests attenuates analysis, but this can be taken into account and is not a serious problem in the initial exploratory stage of this research. Ultimately, however, it will be important to demonstrate the amount of intelligence variance that can be accounted for by an optimal combination of chronometric indices, and this will depend on very adequate measurement of individual differences in g. That cannot be assured by any single test.

CHRONOMETRIC ANALYSIS OF g

It seems a reasonable hypothesis that g itself can be analyzed at *some* level. It is mainly a question of how much of the g variance can be accounted for at each level of analysis. The most implausible hypothesis is that g is an absolutely irreducible, unitary property of the brain—the bottom line of all analyses. This is not even true of the proton. Borrowing a metaphor from neurophysiology, a psychometric test score—even performance on a single test item—can be viewed as the "final common path" of a number of distinct, more elemental, processes. And conceivably, for any given item different processes (or different combinations or different weightings of the same process) can result in the same "final common path'' for different individuals or for the same individual at different times. We hypothesize a small number of processes that enter into all cognitive tests in varying degrees. Individual *differences* in test scores will be reflected in individual differences in processes, but identical test scores do not assure identical processes.

The immediate aim of chronometric analysis is to measure individual differences in performance on simple tasks that are correlated with psychometric factors (especially g, at this point) but that are much simpler and, hence, more representative of certain hypothesized elemental processes than the ''final common path'' of typical intelligence test items at a suitable level of difficulty for measuring individual differences in terms of dichotomously (i.e., ''right'' or ''wrong'') scored responses. Because of the extreme simplicity of the information-processing tasks best suited for this purpose, the correct ''final common path'' is achieved by all subjects. Hence, individual differences in these simple tasks can be measured only by speed of performance. The simpler the task, the less is the variance attributable to individual differences in prior learning of knowledge or skills.

Some of the aims and pitfalls of the chronometric analysis of ability can be seen in reference to the simplified schema shown in Fig. 6.1. All that we can observe directly are scores on various tests (A, B, C) that are all correlated with g. (Connecting lines all represent correlations.) Processes X, Y, and Z are unobservable hypothetical constructs that are *functionally* correlated with test performance. If tests A and B are highly g loaded but too complex for the contributing processes to be discerned, we may use one of them (e.g., B) as a reference test and find an analytically much simpler task (e.g., C) that affords more measurable parameters of the individual's performance and allows experimental manipulation of task parameters, such as some of the reaction-time paradigms described later. Or, C could be some more directly brain-related measurement, such as the amplitude or latency of the average evoked potential or the chemical products of brain activity.

If the target measurement C is correlated with reference test B, the analysis of C may elucidate the nature of the underlying processes common to C and B. But this is true *only* if the correlation between B and C represents a *functional* relationship between them due to common processes. Not all correlations indicate functional relationships in this sense. Figure 6.1 illustrates a functional correlation between tests A and B, which share processes X and Y, whereas the correlation between B and C is nonfunctional—it is the result of a purely genetic correlation between the genotypes y and z underlying the development of processes Y and Z, which are represented here as nonfunctionally correlated. Such purely genetic correlations come about through the common assortment of genes for different characteristics that have no intrinsic relationship to one another. The cause of the common assortment of functionally unrelated genes is related to cross-assortative mating for the particular traits. Although this is of sociological

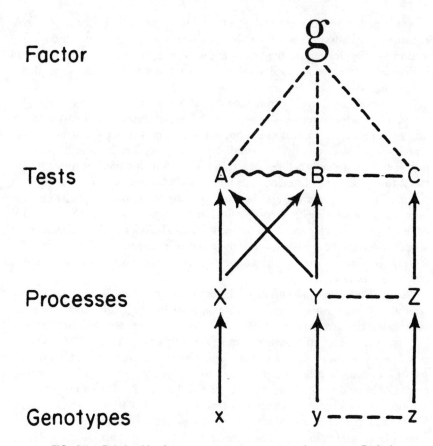

FIG. 6.1.   Relationships between *g*, tests, processes, and genotypes. Dashed lines represent correlations without functional relationships; arrows are functional correlations; wavy line is functional relationship due to mutual underlying processes.

interest, it contributes nothing to a psychological understanding of *g*. If test *C* is *g* loaded only by reason of its purely genetic correlation with other *g* loaded tests, it is a blind alley in research on *g*. Avoiding blind-alley variables that are nonfunctionally correlated with *g* (or any other cognitive reference tests of interest) becomes especially important in seeking out physical correlates of *g* that may afford clues as to its nature. Spearman (1927), for example, made a point of the fact that *g* has certain physical correlates such as height. But this point is psychologically useless because the correlation of height with *g* is, as best as we can determine, a strictly genetic correlation without any functional significance, and the same is probably true for many other physical features that are known to be correlated with IQ. The simplest method for detecting such purely genetic (or purely environmental) correlations, which are nonfunctional, is by means of a sibling study. A correlation between two variables that is found in a sample of nonsiblings but fails to appear *within* sibships is a nonfunctional correlation, which should be ignored in research on the *nature* of g (as contrasted with studies of the mere correlates of g or the practical predictive validity of g). The rationale and methodology of the sibling method for distinguishing *intrinsic* (functional) and *extrinsic* (nonfunctional) correlations have been fully explicated elsewhere (Jensen, 1980c).

Age is not essentially a psychological variable and should be completely partialed out of the correlation matrix before extracting g. The best solution is to use homogeneous age groups. This is not to say that g should not be studied in relation to age as an independent variable, but only warns that g measurements should not be *confounded* by age.

Various reaction-time paradigms have been used as the target tasks in the schema of Fig. 6.1. The first requirement in this research is to establish the target tasks' correlations with g or with two or three g reference tests.

REACTION-TIME RESEARCH
WITH THE MENTALLY RETARDED

For various historical reasons (see Jensen, 1980a), attempts to measure intelligence by means of reaction time (RT), which began with Galton in the late 1800s, were prematurely abandoned in the eraly 1900s, and the field of research on RT in relation to psychometrics lay dormant for nearly half a century. Beginning around the mid-1906s, the only research on the relationship of RT to intelligence was conducted with the mentally retarded. The results of these investigations have been comprehensively reviewed elsewhere (Baumeister & Kellas, 1968; Nettelbeck & Brewer, 1981). Unfortunately, much of this excellent research has made little impression on the general study of the nature of intelligence. Psychologists have usually viewed the retarded as a group that is so set apart from the nonretarded population that research on the retarded is believed to have little or no general theoretical implications for individual differences throughout the normal distribution of IQ above the level of retardation. Until recently, it was a common belief that although RT was correlated with IQ among the retarded, there was little, if any, relationship in the nonretarded. The demonstration of significant differences in RT between the retarded and nonretarded has been regarded as trivial or theoretically uninteresting because it was thought to indicate not so much a relationship between RT and intelligence as a difference between ''defective'' and ''normal,'' despite the fact that most of the RT research is based on mildly retarded persons (classed as cultural-familial retardation) with no signs of brain damage or sensory-motor impairment. But the defect conception of the distinction between ''retarded'' and ''normal'' as being a dichotomy or a qualitative distinction, rather than a quantitative one, is deeply ingrained in laypeople and professionals alike.

However, in my own work with retarded and nonretarded groups using exactly the same RT paradigms and procedures in both groups, we have found no phenomena in the retarded groups, either of the most severely retarded (with IQs between 15 and 50) or of the moderately retarded (IQs of 50 to 80), that are not also apparent in groups of university students. Although the retarded and superior groups differ about as much in various RT parameters (when differences are expressed in standard scores) as they differ in IQ, we have not found any differences in RT pheonmena in the range of IQs from 15 to 150 that do not appear to be a part of continuous variation in the RT parameters. The differences are systematically quantitative rather than qualitative. Also, virtually all of the important relationships reported in the literature that have been discovered between RT and IQ *within* retarded groups have recently been rediscovered in university students. For example, one of the clearest phenomena is the difference between the severely and mildly retarded (and normals) in response consistency as measured by intraindividual (intertrial) variability in RT, which is higher in low-IQ subjects. We have found the same differences to the same degree between groups of college students who differ in IQ but who are all above the average IQ of the general population. Contrasts of RT phenomena between retarded and normal groups merely magnify the differences that are observed between low- and high-IQ groups *within* relatively homogeneous segments of the total IQ distribution. One of the aims of our research in the immediate future is to determine if the various RT phenomena that discriminate among lower and higher subgroups in the IQ range (from the severely retarded to university students) will discriminate similarly between groups of the "gifted" (IQs 130–150) and the "supergifted" (IQs above 150). My hypothesis is that the same RT differences will be found between the gifted and supergifted as between the severely and the mildly retarded or between the mildly retarded and persons of average IQ. Confirmation of this hypothesis will clinch the demonstration, which is already well supported in the IQ range below the supergifted, that certain RT phenomena are systematically related to general mental ability throughout the entire measurable range of human intelligence.

Such a demonstration would not enforce the conclusion that faster RT is a cause of higher intelligence, or vice versa. In my view, individual differences in both RT (and its various parameters) and psychometric g are merely correlated because they both reflect individual differences at some sub-behavioral, neurophysiological, and electrochemical level. My hypothesis is not that RT parameters are themselves *components* (or even reflections of other *cognitive* components) of g or the kinds of cognitive activities into which performance on any specific g loaded psychometric test items may be analyzed. Thus, my proposed use of RT parameters is rather different from Sternberg's (1977) componential analysis of relatively complex cognitive tasks such as analogical reasoning. In my approach, it is wholly unimportant whether or not correlations between more elemental and more complex tasks (e.g., RT parameters and Raven

Matrices scores) make any sense *psychologically*. Chances are that the correlated chronometric variables that do make sense will prove to be the least important because they are merely instances of the same behavior that is manifested in performance on the more complex psychometric task. The important requirement for potential fruitfulness is that the elemental and complex measurements be *intrinsically* correlated, rather than just genetically or environmentally correlated, as I have previously explained. The value of more elemental measures such as RT parameters, provided they are intrinsically correlated with *g,* is not that they are themselves elements of intelligence test performance but that their comparative simplicity, their various manipulable experimental facets, and their considerable physiological sensitivity may afford a more direct (or at least a quite different) basis for hypotheses about causes of individual differences in *g* than are afforded by inferences based on more complex cognitive tasks. The position of Sternberg's *components* of complex reasoning tasks, yielded by chronometric analysis, is no less uncertain as to the *causal* underpinnings of individual differences in mental ability. It remains to be seen to what extent specifically task-derived components can account for the correlation between such highly diverse tasks as, say verbal analogies and block designs. Componential analysis, like research with other RT paradigms, is a potentially fruitful intermediate stage toward discovering the nature of *g.* At this intermediate stage, the hypothesized cognitive processes are useful psychological or computer metaphors. The true *causal* processes, however, are neurophysiological.

REACTION-TIME PARADIGMS
AND COGNITIVE PROCESSES

Reaction time has become a generic term for a number of tasks and procedural paradigms that reflect some form of cognitive processing in which the dependent variable is a time measurement. In this section, the term RT is used in this generic sense.

Several distinct RT paradigms have become important in the study of individual differences because each one reflects what seems to be some basic component of information-processing capacity, such as stimulus encoding or perceptual speed, decision time, scanning of information in short-term memory, and retrieval of highly overlearned information from long-term memory. It is hypothesized that the relatively complex items typically found in psychometric tests of general intelligence call upon all of these elemental cognitive processes in varying degrees. Therefore, independent measurements of these processes afford one means of analyzing the nature of individual differences in intelligence, or *g.* Moreover, if some substantial proportion of the true variance in psychometric *g* can eventually be accounted for by the measurement of some optimal combination of these more elemental cognitive processes, psychologists would possess a truly analytic means for the clinical assessment of intelligence and cognitive disabilities.

The three most important general advantages in all of these RT techniques are:

1. The use of time as the dependent variable makes it possible to minimize the importance of differences in prior learning, which are more apt to be reflected in traditional test scores based on the number of correct, incorrect, and omitted answers. Most of the RT tasks are so simple as to have a near-zero error rate in virtually all persons except very young children and the severely retarded. One aim of the RT methods is to eliminate or minimize individual-differences variance attributable to knowledge and acquired skills.

2. Reaction-time measurements, unlike traditional test scores, are a ratio scale with all of its well-known advantages. Various scores, indices, and parameters derived from time measurements can also have the properties of a ratio scale. Such measurements can enter into mathematical formulations with a rigor that is not possible with the usual psychometric scores. A ratio scale, with a true zero point and equal intervals, is also helpful for studies of the growth or developmental course of any trait and is practically essential for rigorous study of the precise form of the growth curve of any ability as a function of chronological age. Therefore, RT techniques are destined to become a powerful tool in the developmental psychology of cognition. Reaction time need not be norm referenced to be meaningful, as in the case of test scores, although the means of measuring RT, of course, must be standardized and calibrated, as with all physical measurements in scientific research.

3. The extreme simplicity of RT tasks makes the identical test procedure applicable over a very wide range of ability and age. Younger and older children or retarded and gifted individuals cannot be directly compared on ordinary psychometric tests because their scores are based on quite different test items, which tap different types and amounts of knowledge and acquired skills and may involve different cognitive processes.

The main disadvantages of RT techniques, even assuming they can account for a substantial proportion of g variance, are purely practical in nature. The precise measurement of RT involves fairly expensive electronic apparatus, and any apparatus may present problems not found with ordinary psychometric tests. Reaction-time measurements also appear to be much more sensitive to the subject's temporary physiological state and, hence, are less stable than the usual test scores. The correlation of RT with other variables is thereby attenuated. This greater sensitivity to physiological variables, of course, is also an advantage for certain research purposes, such as discovering a person's diurnal peak of cognitive efficiency and the effects of diet, drugs, or other experimental treatments on performance.

General Methodology of Reaction-Time Research

In exploratory research aimed at discovering RT parameters that are related to intelligence, it is probably more efficient to compare the *mean* RT measurements of criterion groups specially selected from different sectors of the IQ scale than to obtain a coefficient of correlation between RT and IQ within a single sample. The main reason for this is that most RT measurements have much lower day-to-day test-retest reliability than do psychometric tests. This instability of RT, as measured at any given time, precludes a high correlation between RT and other variables. Interestingly, it is just those parameters of the RT paradigms (such as slope of RT as a function of bits and intertrial, intraindividual variability) that show the strongest relationship to *g* that are also the most unstable from one day to the next. Day-to-day intercorrelations of the same RT parameter as low as .50 to .60 are the rule. Yet, the mean and standard deviation of RT for any given *group* remains highly constant from day to day. Subjects merely change their rank order within the group from one testing session to another. In any given testing session, however, the split-half internal consistency (odd–even trials) reliability of all RT parameters is very high (usually above .90), and it can be made as high as desired simply by increasing the number of trials. Consequently, even when the correlation between RT and IQ is quite low (usually between .20 and .40) *within* groups drawn from different segments of the IQ scale, the mean difference in RT *between* the groups is usually about the same as their mean difference in IQ, when the mean differences in RT and IQ are both expressed in standard deviation units.

The advantage of the correlation coefficient (r) is that it expresses the degree of linear relationship between two variables; r^2 indicates the proportion of variance in the one variable accounted for by its linear regression on the other. However, in most of the RT research literature, it is a mistake to pay too much attention to the size of the reported correlation between RT and IQ without careful evaluation. More often than not, the correlations are misleadingly low due to attenuation (i.e., the instability already mentioned) and the restricted "range-of-talent" in the subject samples typically used in RT research, such as the mentally retarded and college students. Considering both of these limiting factors on the correlation between RT and IQ, the typical range of r between .25 and .45, with a central tendency near .35, seems remarkably high. When these correlations are corrected for attentuation due to the day-to-day instability of RT and the restricted range of IQ in the sample, the correlations are generally boosted to the .50 to .70 range.

My own approach to establishing relationships between various RT parameters and psychometric test scores has employed a combination of methods: (1) comparison of groups selected from different segments of the IQ scale; (2) correlations between RT and test scores *within* groups; (3) repeated measurements of RT on different days to estimate stability coefficients of each of the RT parameters to be correlated with IQ, to permit correction for attentuation; and (4) the use of a psychometric reference test of intelligence, for which the distribution of scores in the general population is known, from which to estimate the effect on the obtained correlation of a restricted range of test scores in a selected sample.

EMPIRICAL FINDINGS
WITH REACTION-TIME PARADIGMS

Inspection Time

This paradigm, invented by Nettelbeck and Lally (1976), is intended to measure the speed of sensory registration or stimulus encoding. Two vertical lines 24 mm and 34 mm long and 10 mm apart, connected at the upper ends by a horizontal line, are presented tachistoscopically for durations of from 10 to 100 msec, followed by a backward masking stimulus. The shorter of the two lines appears randomly on the right or the left side on each presentation, and the subject simply states the location of the shorter line. The subject's score, termed *inspection time* (IT), is the duration of the stimulus exposure at which almost errorless (97.5% correct) performance occurs. This procedure obviates the problem of trade-off between speed and accuracy, as the level of accuracy is made constant for all subjects. There are large and reliable individual differences in IT.

Nettelbeck and Lally (1976) found correlations of $-.92$ and $-.89$ between two separate estimates of IT and IQ in 10 young adult subjects whose IQs ranged from 47 to 119 (7 subjects were below 85). A larger study by these investigators showed a correlation of $-.80$ between WAIS Performance IQs and IT in 48 subjects with IQs ranging from 57 to 138. The very wide range of IQs in these samples, of course, favors finding substantial correlations between IQ and IT.

A series of four studies reported by Brand (1979), using a similar technique, showed correlations between IQ and IT ranging between $-.31$ and $-.98$ (with a central tendency around $-.75$) in various groups that were mostly very heterogeneous in IQ, often spanning the range from retarded to gifted. The size of the IQ $\times$ IT correlation is highly related to the range of IQ in the sample. In my own lab, we have found an r of only $-.31$ between IT and scores on the Advanced Raven Matrices in university students whose IQs are all in the upper quartile of the general population.

The average IT for nonretarded young adults is about 100–150 msec, whereas it is about twice as long for mildly retarded young adults. Something other than a difference in mental age is suggested, however, because the mean IT of nonretarded children in the age range from 7 to 10 years is only slightly greater (141 msec) than for nonretarded adults (130 msec) and is much less than for mildly retarded adults (256 msec) (Nettelbeck & Lally, 1979). Although IT is correlated with psychometric g, it differs markedly from traditional g loaded tests in showing little relationship to chronological age (CA) beyond about age 7. It has not yet been determined to what extent this is a result of the correlation between psychometric g and CA reflecting experiential factors in the development of g and to what extent it is a result of the simplicity of IT not reflecting the more complex components of information processing that only become functional at later ages. Developmental studies of these various elemental components of information processing are clearly needed. It seems likely that different components will show different growth curves (Chi, 1977). Because the measurements are on a ratio scale (time), comparisons of mental growth curves will have the same scientifically desirable properties as growth curves for physical characteristics.

REACTION TIME-MOVEMENT TIME PARADIGM

The apparatus for this paradigm is called the reaction time-movement time (RT-MT) apparatus (Fig. 6.2). (It is described in more detail by Jensen & Munro, 1979.) The subject places the preferred index finger on the "home" button, a "beep" ready signal sounds for 1 second, and, after a random interval of 1 to 4 seconds, one of the green lights goes on. The subject turns off the light as rapidly as possible by touching the button adjacent to it. Reaction time is the interval, measured in milliseconds, between the light's going on and the removal of the subject's finger from the home button. Movement time (MT) is the interval between release of the home button and touching the response button that turns out the light. Different templates are placed over the whole console to expose any number of light/button alternatives from 1 to 8. In most of our research we have used 1, 2, 4, and 8 alternatives, corresponding to 0, 1, 2, and 3 bits of information. Following instructions and several practice trials, subjects are given 15 trials on each number of alternatives (60 trials in all) in a single session.

The main individual-difference parameters derived from this paradigm for each subject can be most easily described with reference to Fig. 6.3:

1. RT intercept (i.e., the intercept of the regression of RT on bits).
2. RT slope (i.e., the slope of the regression of RT on bits).
3. Total RT (i.e., the sum of all RTs over all 60 trials).
4. Mean intraindividual variability of RT: symbolized $\bar{\sigma}_i$ of RT (i.e., the subject's standard deviations of RT over each set of n, usually 15 or 30, trials at 0, 1, 2, and 3 bits, averaged over the four sets).
5. RT slope of σ_i: Intertrial or intraindividual variability (σ_i) of RT increases regularly as a function of bits, and there are reliable individual differences in the rate of increase. This is measured for each subject by the slope of the

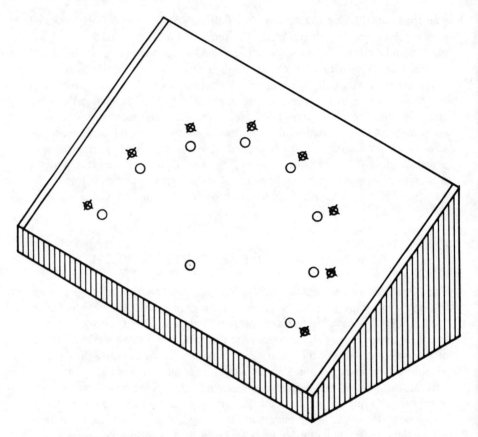

FIG. 6.2.   Subject's console of the reaction time-movement time apparatus. Push buttons are indicated by circles; green jeweled lights by circled crosses. The "home" button is in the lower center, 6 inches from each response button.

regression of σ_i on bits, where σ_i is the standard deviation of RTs over a set of n trials for each level of bits.

6. Mean median MT: The regression of MT on bits shows no significant slope in any of the samples we have tested, hence only the mean of the median MTs over all conditions (i.e., bits) is used.

7. Intraindividual variability of MT: analogous to σ_i for RT.

General Characteristics of RT-MT Data

1. Reliability and Stability.   Reliability refers to the consistency of measurements from trial to trial in a single testing session, as determined by the correlated split-half method (odd vs. even trials), boosted by the Spearman–Brown formula to estimate the reliability of subjects' mean RTs over all n trials.

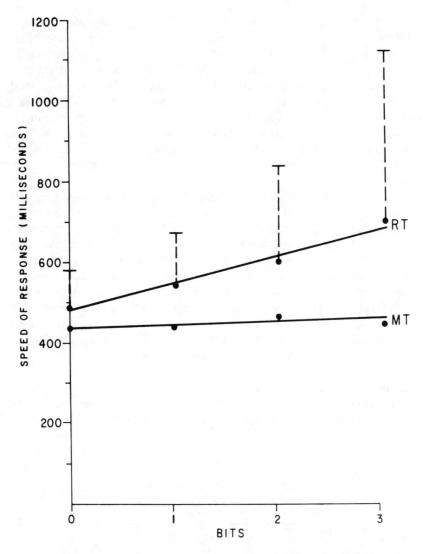

FIG. 6.3.   Mean RT and MT, as a function of bits, and mean intraindividual variability (vertical dashed lines = mean intraindividual standard deviation of RT over 15 trials), in 46 borderline retarded young adults (from Vernon, 1981).

The number (n) of trials for any one condition (bits) in our studies is usually either 15 or 30.

Stability is the Pearson r between measures obtained on different days, usually not separated by more than 1 or 2 days. The stability coefficient is the more important for evaluating the correlation between any RT or MT parameter and external variables such as chronological age or scores on psychometric tests. Reliability and stability can differ markedly for any given RT parameter. Typically, intertrial reliability is much higher than day-to-day stability. The day-to-day stability of individual measurements of RT or MT parameters is generally much lower than the stability of most standard test scores. Reliability and stability coefficients for various RT and MT measurements obtained on 100 university students are shown in Table 6.1. Because of the restriction of range in a university sample, these coefficients are probably somewhat lower than would be found in the general population, but the relative magnitudes of the reliability and stability coefficients for the various parameters probably have considerable generality.

Low stability, of course, imposes a low ceiling on the highest possible correlation (viz., the square root of the stability coefficient) that any measurement can have with any other variable. Measurements of RT parameters are apparently sensitive to a person's momentary physiological and emotional state. They fluctuate from day to day and even within a single day. This is not measurement error in the instrumental sense, but seems to be an intrinsic organismic phenomenon. All the same, it must be reckoned with in any correlational study. It is noteworthy that the RT-MT parameters that generally correlate most highly with psychometric tests of g (even when the correlations are not corrected for attenuation) also have the lowest stability coefficients. It is as if those aspects of the RT paradigm that most reflect the "higher" mental processes are the least stable.

2. *Absence of Practice Effects.*   We have found no indication of practice effects in any of the samples tested for any of the RT-MT variables, either across trials in a single session or across sessions from day to day. In one study, 10

TABLE 6.1
Reliability and Stability Coefficients
for Measurements of Various RT and MT
Parameters Obtained on 100 University
Students

Parameter	Reliability[a]	Stability[b]
RT intercept	.97	.72
RT slope	.75	.35
RT σ_i	.65	.42
Mean MT	.96	.84
MT σ_i	.81	.56

[a] Odd–even split-half reliability, Spearman–Brown boosted to 15 trials.
[b] Correlation (r) between day 1 and day 2, based on the mean of 15 trials each day.

university students were tested every other weekday for 3 weeks—60 trials in each of nine sessions. Analysis of variance showed no significant main effects for trials, sessions, or their interaction for any of the RT-MT variables used in our studies. Moreover, the matrix of covariances among trials for RT is homogeneous, that is, we cannot reject the hypothesis that all the covariances differ by more than chance from the overall average covariance of RT among trials. This suggests that the between-trials fluctuations of RT are purely random—every trial is essentially equivalent to every other trial, except for random fluctuations, and there are no order effects or systematic changes in performance over the course of practice.

These findings are consistent with the hypothesis that the RT-MT paradigm does not involve anything that could be called learning, association, or memory scanning. Certainly, the task does not involve cognitive strategies in the usual sense of the term. Whatever simple acquired skills are called for are apparently already asymptotic for all subjects when they begin the test. In the case of the severely retarded (IQs below 40), however, we have routinely given 3 to 5 minutes of demonstration and practice trials to insure the necessary skills for this task. With this condition, the actual test trials evince no practice effect.

3. Involuntary Nature of RT.   In the RT-MT paradigm, RT does not appear to be under the subject's voluntary control. For one thing, subjects cannot perceive the short time differences in the range of fluctuations in their own RTs when they are voluntarily performing at their normal "best." When asked to judge whether their RT on a given trial was faster or slower than the immediately preceding trial, their subjective judgments are no better than chance guessing. The majority of subjects feel that their RT is much faster than their MT, whereas in fact, for nonretarded subjects, RT averages 100 to 150 msec slower than MT. Most subjects are amazed that, regardless of their conscious effort, the average RT to three bits of information (i.e., eight light/button alternatives) is greater (by about 70 to 100 msec) than to zero bits (i.e., one light/button). Subjects are even more surprised that they cannot voluntarily slow down their RT in the one-bit condition to equal their RT in the three-bits condition. The least conscious intention of the subject to "relax" the effort to respond as quickly as possible results in RTs that fall beyond the normal range of RTs. Subjects' attempts to "fake" slower RTs consciously usually exceed their own "unfaked" RT by several standard deviations.

The most likely explanation of this apparent lack of voluntary control of RT within the normal range of RT variation is the fact—discovered in experiments by Libet, Alberts, Wright, and Feinstein (1965, 1971) involving direct electrical stimulation of the brain—that the speed of conscious awareness of a peripheral stimulus is about 500 msec, whereas the RTs of nonretarded subjects to three bits average faster than 500 msec and are therefore executed before the subject is even consciously aware of the stimulus. The RT is thus beyond the subject's intentional control or subjective evaluation. This finding, along with the lack of practice effects in RT, has the theoretically interesting implication that the component of psychometric g that is correlated with the RT parameters is based in the sphere of involuntary biological functions.

4. *Age Trends in RT-MT Parameters.*   We have investigated age trends in each of the RT-MT parameters in a sample of 160 normal children ranging in age from 9 to 14 years. Every RT-MT parameter (except intraindividual variability in MT) shows a highly significant and regular trend as a function of age in the direction of "better" performance with increasing age. The trends are fairly linear in the 9- to 14-year range. Data on older adolescents and college students suggest that the age trend for all RT-MT parameters becomes very negatively accelerated after puberty and is probably asymptotic at about age 15 or 16.

Perhaps the most interesting theoretical aspect of the age trends is that the *slope* of the regression of mean RT on age increases almost linearly as a function of the number of bits (light/button alternatives); the same is true for intraindividual variability (σ_i) in RT (Fig. 6.4). This is in marked contrast to MT, which although showing an age trend, shows no systematic relationship to the number of bits of information. Thus, it is the information-processing aspect of the RT-MT variables that displays the most pronounced improvements with age during the preadolescent period.

Because of the correlation between age and the more "cognitive" aspects of RT such as the linear increase in RT as a function of bits of information conveyed by the reaction stimulus, it is essential in studies with children to take age into account when computing the correlations between RT parameters and mental test scores. Both the zero-order correlations and correlations with age (in months) partialed out should always be reported. If the reliabilities of the variables are known, the zero-order correlations should be corrected for attenuation before computing the partial correlations. Our analyses clearly indicate that RT variables are significantly related to age *independently* of the ability measured by raw scores on g loaded psychometric tests such as Raven's Progressive Matrices. In addition, RT variables are significantly related to mental test scores independently of age.

5. *Relationship Between RT and MT.*   Many studies of RT have not distinguished between *decision* time (here labeled RT, i.e., the time for overt reaction to the reaction stimulus such as removing the index finger from a push button when a light goes on) and *movement* time (here labeled MT, i.e., the time needed to make an additional response such as touching another button to turn off the light). With our RT-MT apparatus, we can measure these two response times separately. The data clearly show that they do not reflect only one and the same process.

Reaction time and movement time reveal their independence in several ways. The most consistent difference, manifest in every study, is that RT always

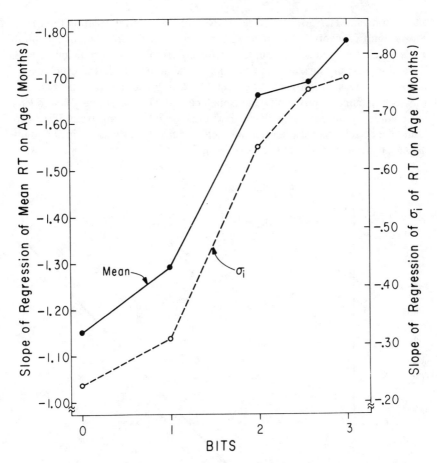

FIG. 6.4. Slope (i.e., RT decrement in msec per one month of age) of the regression of mean RT and intraindividual variability (σ_i) of RT on age, as a function of bits of information, for 160 school children aged 9 to 14 years.

increases as a function of the amount of uncertainty as to the reaction stimulus, measured as bits of information (i.e., the logarithm, to the base 2, of the number of different alternative forms, colors, or spatial locations in which the reaction stimulus can occur). Reaction time in all samples we have tested, except the severely retarded, increases as a linear function of bits of information in the array of reaction stimuli. Also, intraindividual trial-to-trial variability in RT (σ_i) increases exponentially as a function of bits. In marked contrast, neither MT nor intraindividual variability in MT varies as a function of bits. The typical relationships of RT and MT to bits is shown in Fig. 6.3.

Another important difference between RT and MT can be found in their correlations with psychometric g. Reaction-time parameters, especially σ_i, more consistently show significant correlations with psychometric g than does MT, although mean MT (i.e., MT averaged over all levels of information [bits]) also shows significant correlations with g in preadolsecent children and in both mildly and severely retarded adults. But it is a striking fact that the correlation between RT and g generally increases as a function of the number of bits to which the RT is made, whereas the correlation between MT with g does not vary in any regular way as a function of bits. Lally and Nettelbeck (1977), using a very heterogeneous sample of subjects with WAIS Performance IQs ranging from 57 to 115, found the correlation between RT and IQ to increase linearly as a function of bits in the range of one to three, as shown in Fig. 6.5. We have found the same

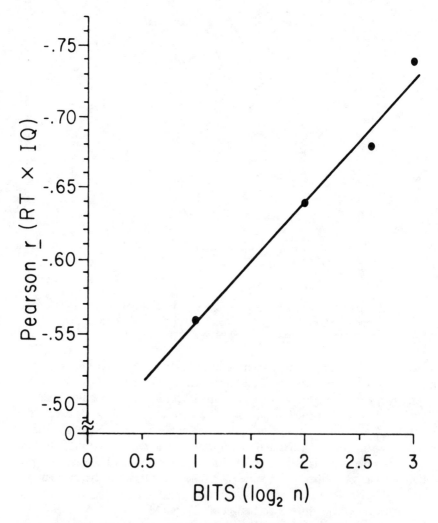

FIG. 6.5.   The correlation between RT and WAIS Performance IQ as a function of bits in the multiple-choice RT paradigm (from Lally & Nettelbeck, 1977).

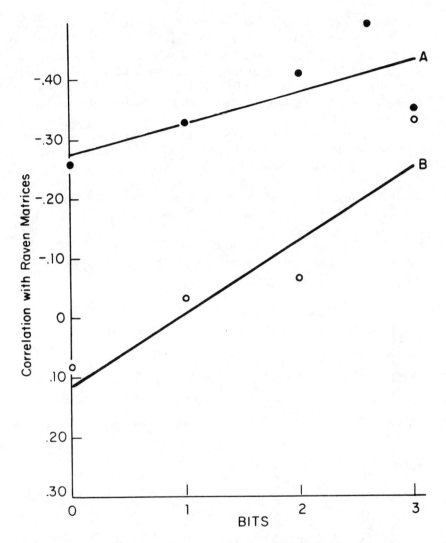

FIG. 6.6.   Correlation of Raven Matrices scores with RT as a function of bits for:
(A) female ninth graders ($N = 39$) and (B) university students ($N = 50$), who,
probably because they are more restricted in variability on g, show the smaller
correlations.

general relationship, although with smaller correlations, on unspeeded tests
(Standard and Advanced Raven Matrices) in relatively homogeneous groups of
above-average school children and university students, as shown in Fig. 6.6.

Although there is a significant positive correlation between individual differences in RT and MT, the r is usually quite low, typically $+.20$ to $+.40$ in
nonretarded samples. This suggests that RT and MT must involve different

processes or sources of variance. (The r is raised only about .10 by correction for attenuation.) Intraindividual variability (σ_i) in RT and MT generally shows a nonsignificant intercorrelation. When individual differences in RT and MT for 0, 1, 2, 2.58, and 3 bits are all intercorrelated and factor analyzed, with varimax rotation (i.e., orthogonal factors), RT and MT load quite distinctly on two different factors, again showing that they do not reflect one and the same source of individual differences.

Reaction time and movement time jointly seem to be related to intelligence level in a complex way even for 0 bit (one light/button), that is, simple RT. Reaction time is *relatively* longer than MT in higher IQ groups. The ratio of *mean RT/mean MT* (for 0 bit) in groups with different average levels of IQ is seen in Fig. 6.7. A suggested explanation of this phenomenon is that, although high-IQ subjects are faster than low-IQ subjects in both RT and MT, in high-IQ subjects the ballistic response reflected in MT is more completely or more adequately "programmed" (adding to the time that is a part of RT) before subjects take their finger off the "home" button. This could result in *relatively*

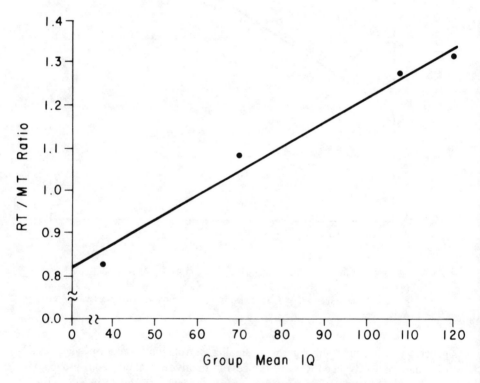

FIG. 6.7.   Ratio of mean of simple RT (zero bits) to mean MT as a function of average intelligence levels of adult criterion groups: severely retarded, borderline retarded, vocational students, and university students.

longer RTs and shorter MTs for higher-IQ subjects. This finding is at least superficially similar to what has become a rather common finding in the componential analysis of more complex cognitive tasks. For example, Sternberg (1977, 1980) and Sternberg and Rifkin (1979) have reported that when the total time for solving analogy problems is decomposed into five component processes, the time for the first-stage process (stimulus encoding) is *longer* for high scorers on a psychometric reasoning test, whereas these same subjects have *shorter* latencies than less bright subjects on the later-stage components, especially the component reflecting multiple-choice response selection. This, I believe, is one of the most important recent findings in this field; it underscores the necessity of examining separate components of performance on complex tasks if interpretable correlations between latencies and psychometric g are to be discovered. For complex cognitive tasks, at least, there is now convincing evidence that subjects of different levels of psychometric g may distribute their total time quite differently over the various processes involved in attaining the correct solution.

Something at least *analogous* to Sternberg's finding seems to be evident in the RT/MT ratio in relation to general intelligence. I emphasize analogous because there is presently no warrant for believing that the same processes are involved in the RT-MT phenomena as in Sternberg's analogical reasoning components. The latencies in the Sternberg paradigms are greater by anywhere from a factor of 10 to 20 (depending on the task and the age of the subjects), which suggests that the Sternberg components are much less "elemental" than those in the RT-MT paradigm. It would be useful theoretically to know how individual differences in the Sternberg component latencies are related to RT and MT. I venture that RT and intraindividual variability in RT would be substantially loaded (after correction for attenuation) on the general factor of Sternberg's verbal and pictorial analogical reasoning components.

Evidence that some part of the subject's total RT is taken up by the response preparation (later reflected in faster MT) was obtained on 25 college students under two conditions: (1) double response—both RT and MT responses were required in response to the reaction stimulus (i.e., our usual procedure); (2) single response—only RT was required (i.e., subjects only had to remove their index finger from the "home" button; no other response was required). On the average, RT was about 30 msec (or about 10%) faster under the single response condition, which required no ballistic movement (see Fig. 6.8). Interestingly, Hick's law concerning the increase in RT as a linear function of bits (Hick, 1952) does not depend on subjects having to make a *differential* response to the reaction stimulus. Thus, Hick's law depends essentially on the uncertainty of the reaction stimulus per se, rather than on making different responses to the various reaction stimuli. Individual differences in RT in the single and double conditions are correlated .63, .63, .56, and .57 for 0, 1, 2, and 3 bits, respectively. The single response condition results in slightly (but nonsignificantly) larger (negative) correlations of RT (and σ_i of RT) with intelligence (Raven Advanced

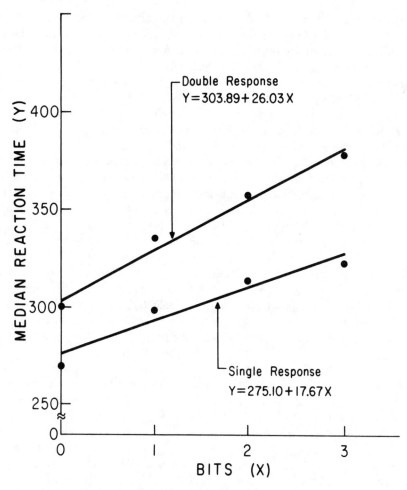

FIG. 6.8.   Median RT (in msec) as a function of bits for university students ($N =$ 25) on RT-MT apparatus under conditions requiring: (1) a differential ballistic response to the reaction stimulus (double response) and (2) removing index finger from "home" button when reaction stimulus occurs (single response).

Progressive Matrices) than the double response condition. This is at least consistent with the hypothesis that brighter subjects use relatively more of their RT in programming the ballistic MT response, and this programming slightly attenuates the correlation of RT with g. This is offered only as a speculative hypothesis.

If a longer ballistic response programming time resulted in faster MT for any given trial, as would be dictated by a direct causal hypothesis, one should expect to find a *negative* correlation between RT and MT *within* individual subjects. It turns out, however, that the within-subject correlations between RT and MT over 30 trials at each of 0, 1, 2, 2.58, and 3 bits for 162 subjects did not differ significantly from zero. At each level of bits, the correlations were normally distributed about means close to zero (rs = .008, .000, .024, $-$.007, and $-$.037). The *between*-subject correlations of RT and MT, on the other hand, are all significant beyond the .01 level, averaging close to $+$.30. One possible interpretation of these findings would be that the tendency to devote a greater proportion of the RT to programming the ballistic response is a general disposition of brighter subjects. But, there appears to be no direct single, trial-by-trial causal effect on MT because the small increment of programming time that contributes to the total RT may be relatively constant across trials and therefore would be so swamped by the much larger trial-by-trial intraindividual variability of RT and MT as to prevent any appreciable within-subject correlation between RT and MT.

6. Group Differences in RT-MT Parameters and Psychometric g.   Because of the low individual stability of some of the RT parameters and the restricted range of psychometric *g* in most study samples, the observed relationship between RT and *g* appears much less tenuous in comparisons between the mean RTs of groups differing in IQ or general intelligence (here labeled *g*), as assessed by standard tests, than in correlations between RT and *g within* any of the relatively homogeneous groups used in our studies. I am not aware of any adequate estimation of the correlation between RT parameters and *g* in a truly representative sample of the general population. I suspect, however, that such correlations properly corrected for attenuation might be substantial. The multiple correlation (R) between several optimally weighted RT-MT parameters and IQ scores might even approach the average intercorrelations among many standard tests. Figure 6.9 shows the mean RT as a function of bits in several diverse groups. All of the groups, except the most severely retarded with a mean IQ of 39, conform to Hick's law.[1] (The trend analysis reveals that data points, which are omitted for the sake of graphic clarity, do not evince any significant nonlinear trends in any of the groups with the exception of Group F.) Although some of the groups do not differ significantly at zero bits, all except the two retarded groups differ

---

[1]We have found, virtually without exception, that RT increases linearly with bits (i.e., Hick's law) (Hick, 1952; Hyman, 1953) for all individuals except the severely retarded (mostly IQs below 40). (The failure of Hick's law might also be found for preschool-aged children, but there is as yet no adequate evidence on this age group.) A possible explanation for the apparent failure of Hick's law in the retarded group is that the relationship of RT to bits is actually not linear. Rather it is a parabolic curve that asymptotes at the limit of the subject's information-processing capacity, which is less than three bits for the severely retarded. The parabolic curve, however, is statistically (and visually) indistinguishable from a linear trend in the range of zero to three bits for nonretarded subjects and the mildly retarded. (Jensen, Schafer, & Crinella, 1981, present a more detailed discussion of this hypothesis.)

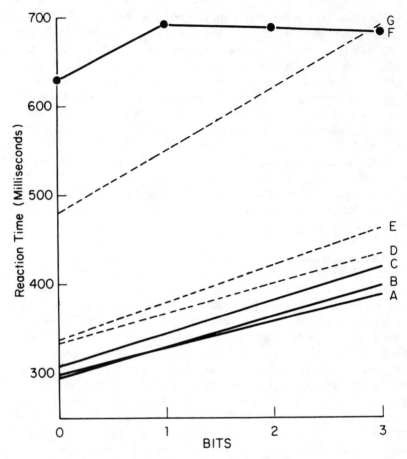

FIG. 6.9. Reaction time as a function of bits, illustrating Hick's law and differences in intercepts and slopes for diverse groups varying in age and intelligence:
(A) university students; (B) ninth-grade girls; (C) sixth graders in a high SES-high
IQ school; (D and E) white and black, respectively, male vocational college
freshmen with approximately equal scholastic aptitude scores; (F) severely mentally retarded young adults (mean IQ 39); (G) mildly retarded and borderline
young adults (mean IQ 70) (from Jensen, 1980a, p.. 697).

significantly at three bits. What may appear as small differences graphically are,
in fact, not only statistically significant but are as large, in standard deviation (σ)
units, as the average difference in IQ between the groups. For example, the
vocational college students and university students, who differ about 1σ in
scholastic aptitude scores, differ in mean RT by 1.2σ (in vocational college σ
units) and 1.9σ (in university σ units). The same groups differ by $.68\sigma$ in mean
intraindividual variability for *simple* RT (ie., one light/button or zero bits).
Borderline retarded young adults (mean IQ 70) differ from college students

(mean IQ 120) by about 6σ on Raven's Matrices and about 7σ in mean RT (based on σ of college students). If we select only the one fastest simple RT out of 15 trials produced by each subject in each group, the mean group difference of 111 msec is 1.2σ (in the retarded σ units) and 4.80σ (in the college-student σ units). In fact, the mean of the students' slowest simple RT (in 15 trials) is 32 msec faster than the retarded group's fastest RT. These results are shown in Figs. 6.10 and 6.11 when simple RTs in 15 trials for each individual are ranked from fastest to slowest (omitting the 15th rank to eliminate possible outliers).

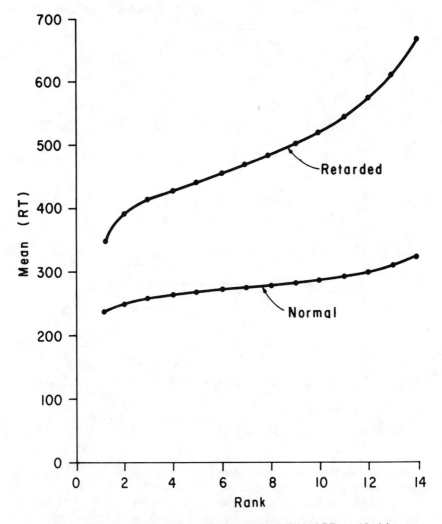

FIG. 6.10. Mean simple RT plotted after ranking individual RTs on 15 trials from the fastest to the slowest trial (omitting the 15th rank) for retarded subjects ($N = 46$) and normal university students ($N = 50$).

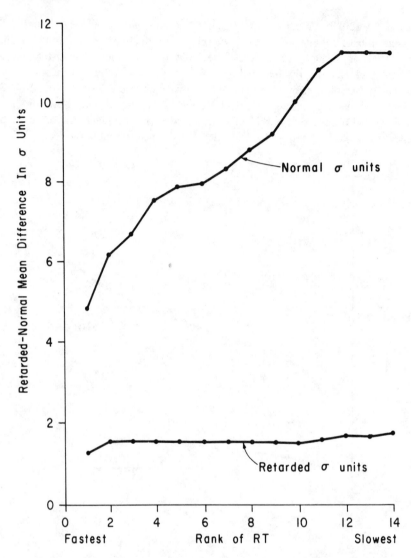

FIG. 6.11. Differences in simple RT between retarded and normal subjects, expressed in both normal and retarded σ units, when simple RTs for 15 trials are ranked from fastest to slowest.

We have found no significant sex differences in any of the RT parameters. Female university students, however, show significantly slower MTs than males, but MT was not significantly correlated with intelligence test scores in these groups of university students. Females usually appear to be less aggressive and more delicate than males in their manner of "hitting" the push buttons, which may slow their MT.

7. Relationship Between RT-MT Parameters and Psychometric g within Diverse Groups.   In the typical fairly homogeneous groups on which RT studies have been reported, correlations between RT and IQ can be generally characterized as quite low compared to the usual correlations among more complex mental tests. But in reviewing the body of literature on RT in relation to general mental ability as assessed by standard psychometric tests, I have found virtually no correlations on the "wrong" side of zero. Most *r*s are in the range from 0 to $-.50$, with a central tendency close to $-.30$. It appears that correlations are generally somewhat larger in retarded groups than in above-average groups of similar age, although there are insufficient data on the reliabilities and variances of RT within these two types of groups to warrant a definitive interpretation of this point.

My own research with the RT-MT procedure, in its initial, exploratory stage, has been aimed at discovering if there are significant correlations between *g* loaded psychometric test scores and various parameters of the RT-MT paradigm. This was not undertaken with the intention of showing that the low (but significant) correlations, if found, could "explain" *g,* but to establish reliable phenomena in need of theoretical explanation. An adequate theory of intelligence could not ignore the intuitively surprising finding that anything as content-free as the RT-MT parameters is significantly related to *g* as measured by the usual psychometric tests. And this is true even if the correlations are quite small. To obviate the most common (but probably overly superficial) explanation of the correlation between RT-MT parameters and test scores, we have always given the psychometric tests without time limit or time pressure of any kind. After being given instructions, subjects take the tests alone in a room and are required to attempt every item. In the one study of 50 university students in which we recorded each subject's total time for completing Raven's Matrices under these test conditions, without the subject's being aware of being timed, we found the correlation between Raven scores and total time to be exactly zero. It is hard to see how one could easily explain a correlation between Raven scores and RT-MT variables in terms of test-taking speed per se. Such an explanation would be rendered even more improbable by correlations between test scores and RT-MT variables that do not reflect speed per se, such as: (1) the *slope* of RT as a function of bits; (2) intraindividual variability (σ_i) of RT.

Significant relationships of RT-MT variables to scores on *g* loaded tests have been found in all of the samples we have tested. Examples from several highly diverse groups in age and general ability level are summarized below.

Severely Retarded Adults.   Jensen, Schafer, and Crinella (1981) obtained a battery of 15 diverse, individually administered, unspeeded verbal and performance tests on 54 mentally retarded adults with IQs ranging from 14 to 62 (mean = 39, s.d. = 14). The matrix of intercorrelations was subjected to a common factor analysis, and the first principal factor, which was interpreted as a good estimate of Spearman's *g* in this population, was used for calculating a *g* factor score for each subject. Average evoked potentials (AEP) to auditory stimuli (clicks) were also obtained under conditions in which the stimuli were administered either automatically at brief random intervals or were self-administered by the subject, thereby creating an expectancy. A ''neural adaptibility'' (NA) index derived from these measures represents essentially the percentage difference between the latency of the AEP under the automatic and self-stimulation conditions. Previous studies (see Jensen et al., 1981) with nonretarded subjects have shown that this NA index is positively correlated with general intelligence level.

Table 6.2 shows the correlations between g factor scores and several variables derived from the RT-MT paradigm as well as the NA measure. The slope of RT as a function of bits was not included in this study because this retarded sample did not display Hick's law. The RT-MT composite (i.e., the mean of the standard scores on the four RT-MT variables) is correlated $-.33$ ($p < .01$, one-tailed test) with NA. The RT-MT composite and NA together yield an unbiased (i.e., shrunken) multiple correlation of .54 ($p < .001$) with g factor scores. It is noteworthy that intraindividual variability (σ_i) in both RT and MT account for most of the correlation with g scores. This has also been found, although to a less pronounced degree, in mildly retarded and above-average nonretarded groups (Jensen, 1979, 1980b; Vernon, 1981). Regarding this phenomenon, Jensen et al. (1981) state:

TABLE 6.2
Correlation (r) of RT-MT Variables
and Neural Adaptability
with Psychometric g Factor Scores
in Severely Retarded Adults ($N = 54$)[a]

Variable	r
Median RT	$-.13$
Median MT	$-.19$
σ_i of RT	$-.44$[d]
σ_i of MT	$-.57$[d]
RT + MT composite[b]	$-.54$[d]
Neural adaptability (NA)[c]	$+.31$[e]

[a] From Jensen, Schafer, and Crinella, 1981.

[b] The mean (for each subject) of the standardized (z) values of the median RT, median MT, σ_i of RT, and σ_i of MT. Each of these component variables for each subject is derived from a total of 60 trials.

[c] For a detailed description of the NA index, which is derived from the latency of the average evoked potential, see Jensen et al., 1981.

[d] $p < .01$, one-tailed test.

[e] $p < .05$, one-tailed test.

Our theoretical speculation concerning the relationship between intraindividual variability and g is based on a concept of a rapidly oscillating cortical potential for response; stimuli that occur during the below-threshold phase of the wave of oscillation fail to elicit a response until the wave goes above threshold. Because the occurrence of the reaction stimulus is completely random with respect to the wave phase of cortical potential on each trial, the RT will vary from trial to trial. Individual differences in the amount of this variability are hypothesized to be the result of differences in the rate of oscillation of cortical potential, with faster oscillation producing both shorter average RT over trials and less variability from trial to trial. More rapid oscillation means that more information is processed per unit of time, with consequently faster acquisition of the types of knowledge and cognitive skills reflected in psychometric g [p. 195].

Mildly Retarded Adults.   Vernon (1981), using the RT-MT apparatus with 46 borderline retarded adults (IQ 70) in a vocational training institute, obtained correlations between Raven Standard Progressive Matrices (SPM), the Figure Copying Test (FCT), and several RT-MT variables. Table 6.3 shows the correlations of each of the RT-MT variables with the SPM and FCT and the loadings of each variable on the first principal component of all eight variables. The lower correlations for the FCT are most likely due to its having lower reliability than the SPM. The quite restricted range of psychometric g in this sample militates against high correlations in general. Yet there is considerable agreement between the pattern of correlations of SPM and FCT with the RT-MT variables. The two

TABLE 6.3
Correlations of RT and MT Variables
with Standard Progressive Matrices (STM)
and Figure Copying Test (FCT) and Loadings
on the First Principal Component (PCI)
of All the Variables in Mildly Retarded Adults
$(N = 46)^a$

Variable	SPM^b	FCT^b	PCI^c
Median RT (0 bit)	−.25	−.09	−.72
Median RT (1 bit)	−.27	−.10	−.84
Median RT (2 bits)	−.31	−.19	−.84
Median RT (3 bits)	−.06	−.01	−.66
Median MT	−.25	−.26	−.66
σ_i of RT	−.35	−.22	−.64
Raven (SPM)		+.54	+.55
Figure copying (FCT)	+.54		+.48

^{a} From Vernon (1981).

^{b} Correlations greater than .24 are significant beyond the .05 level (one-tailed test).

^{c} The first principal component accounts for 46.8% of the total variance.

columns of correlations are themselves correlated .74. The SPM and FCT are correlated .55 and .48, respectively, with the first principal component, which largely represents the RT-MT variables.

The one seeming anomaly in Table 6.3 is the near zero correlation of median RT for three bits with the mental test scores. It is the lowest correlation for both SPM and FCT. It seems anomalous because in nonretarded samples the correlation between RT and test scores usually increases going from zero to three bits. Vernon hypothesizes that, beyond a certain degree of complexity, individual differences in intelligence have a decreasing correlation with response latencies, and this point is reached somewhere between two and three bits of information for the borderline retarded. The hypothesis is not ad hoc but is consistent with the findings of near zero correlations between IQ and response latencies to relatively complex information-processing tasks requiring in excess of 1 second with non-retarded subjects (reviewed in Jensen, 1980b). It is noteworthy that these retarded subjects (none of them below about IQ 60 and averaging IQ 70) show about the same average RT to the three-bits condition as do the severe retardates with a mean IQ of 39 (described in the study by Jensen et al., 1981), although the two groups differ by about 160 msec (or 1.2σ) in RT for zero bits.

Junior High School Pupils.   Jensen and Munro (1979) obtained RT-MT data and Raven Matrices (SPM) on 39 ninth-grade girls aged 14 to 15. Dividing the sample into the high, middle, and low thirds of the distribution of SPM scores reveals the quite regular relationship of SPM level to RT and MT (Fig. 6.12). The Raven scores are correlated with RT-MT variables as follows:

RT (overall mean):		$r = -.39 \; (p < .02)$
σ_i of RT:		$r = -.31 \; (p < .05)$
slope of RT:		$r = -.30 \; (p < .06)$
MT (overall mean):		$r = -.43 \; (p < .01)$
σ_i of MT:		$r = +.07$ n.s.
RT (mean) + MT (mean):	multiple	$R = \;\;.50 \; (p < .01)$
All five RT − MT variables:	multiple	$R = \;\;.66$ (shrunken $R = .49$)

Jensen and Munro (1979) note that many of these correlations are not appreciably different from the correlations of Raven scores with other psychometric tests reported for unselected samples of school children (e.g., Peabody Picture Vocabulary Test IQ, $r = .35$, WISC Full Scale IQ in several studies, median $r = .51$).

University Students.   Jensen (1979, 1980a) presented the loadings on the first principal component (PC I) of a number of RT-MT variables along with several other variables including verbal (Terman's Concept Mastery Test) and nonverbal (Raven's Advanced Progressive Matrices) psychometric tests obtained from 50 university students. These loadings are highly similar to the loadings on the first principal factor (PF I) when iterated for six common factors with latent

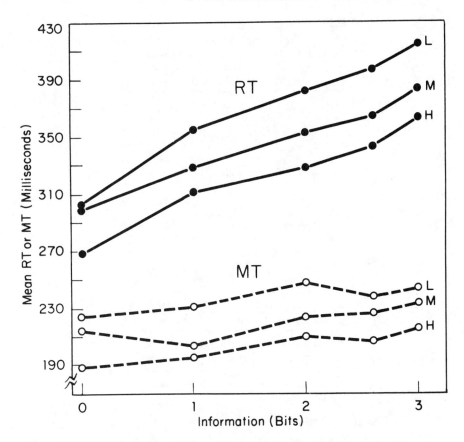

FIG. 6.12.   Mean RT and MT as a function of bits in the RT-MT paradigm for high (H), middle (M), and low (L) thirds of a sample of ninth graders on Raven's Standard Progressive Matrices (from Jensen & Munro, 1979).

roots greater than 1. My interest here is in the one most general factor of this set of variables (i.e., the one that accounts for more of the total variance than any other single factor) and in observing the manner in which the RT-MT and psychometric variables loaded on this one large factor, which both sets of variables share in common (see Table 6.4). It is not claimed that the PC I or PF I are to be interpreted as Spearman's g, but it should be noted that the Raven, which is generally considered a good g reference test, has the highest loading on this factor followed by the Concept Mastery Test (CMT), which is a high-level test of verbal reasoning ability. The Raven and CMT are intercorrelated only $+.40$ in this highly restricted college population, which represents about the top 12% of high school graduates in scholastic ability. It seems of some interest that the RT slope (RT σ_i) and RT slope of σ_i over bits all have substantial loadings on this factor—a result entirely consistent with an information-processing interpretation

TABLE 6.4
Loadings on the First Principal
Component (PCI) and First Principal Factor
(PFI) of a Number of RT-MT and
Psychometric Variables

Variable	PCI^a	PFI
1. RT intercept	+.42	+.42
2. RT slope (on bits)	−.65	−.60
3. σ_i of RT	−.50	−.50
4. Slope of RT σ_i (on bits)	−.73	−.66
5. MT mean	−.18	−.15
6. σ_i of MT	−.08	−.06
7. Serial rote learning (errors)	−.07	−.07
8. Digit span memory	+.41	+.31
9. Raven Advanced Matrices	+.73	+.78
10. Concept Mastery Test	+.57	+.53
Eysenck Personality Inventory		
11. Extraversion	−.32	−.24
12. Neuroticism	+.09	+.07
13. Lie scale	−.19	−.12
Percentage of Total Variance	20	18

^{a} For PC and PF loadings greater than .36, $p <$ .01; for loadings greater than .46, $p < .001$.

of these RT parameters. However, in a methodological critique of this analysis Carroll (1979) used a maximum liklihood factor analysis and extracted three orthogonally rotated factors, on which the Raven and CMT have their largest loadings on two different factors. The Concept Mastery Test loads .99 on a factor on which the next two largest loadings are Digit Span Memory (.44) and Raven (.34). But the Raven still has its highest loading (.53) on the factor defined by the RT slope (−.82), RT σ (−.54), and RT slope of σ_i (−.66), on which the CMT loads only .12. I view the PF I and the rotated factors as a matter of preference, each one permitting examination of the data from different perspectives. Neither analysis is compelling to the exclusion of the other.

For a definitive *statistical* test of the relationship between the RT-MT variables and each of the psychometric tests, which measure nonverbal and verbal reasoning ability or perhaps fluid and crystallized *g*, we must look at the simple correlations (Table 6.5). Because of our prior hypotheses of how each of the RT-MT variables should be related to *g* in terms of an information-processing interpretation of the independent variables, one-tailed tests of significance are called for. The Raven is more clearly related to the RT variables than is the CMT, and this should be expected if the Raven and CMT are viewed as measures of fluid and crystallized *g*, respectively. None of the RT-MT variables is signifi-

TABLE 6.5
Correlation of the RT-MT Variables,
Rote Learning, and Digit Span
with Raven's Advanced Progressive Matrices
and Terman's Concept Mastery Test (CMT)
for 50 University Students

Variable	Raven	CMT
1. RT intercept	.15	.20
2. RT slope (on bits)	$-.41^a$	.00
3. σ_i of RT	$-.35^a$	$-.08$
4. Slope of RT σ_i (on bits)	$-.32^b$	$-.25^b$
5. MT mean	$-.25^b$	$-.16$
6. σ_i of MT	.10	.02
7. Serial rote learning (errors)	$-.25^b$	$-.02$
8. Digit span memory	.22	$.44^a$
Variables 1–8: Multiple R	$.64^a$	$.56^b$

$^a p < .01.$
$^b p < .05.$

cantly correlated with either serial rote learning or digit span memory, a finding consistent with our view that the RT-MT variables in this paradigm do not involve learning or memory processes. It is noteworthy that the multiple correlations of all the experimental variables with the Raven and CMT approach the upper limit of the correlations found among standard psychometric tests in this restricted university population. These multiple correlations (which are not corrected for attentuation) suggest that a combination of tests virtually free of intellectual content are capable of predicting a substantial proportion of the psychometric ability variance among bright young adults.

8. The RT-IQ Correlation and Task Complexity. We have already seen that the correlation between RT and IQ generally increases as a function of task complexity or bits of information (Figs. 6.5 and 6.6). However, this relationship appears to hold only for relatively simple tasks such as the RT-MT paradigm in which the information-processing time is less than 1 second for nonretarded subjects. Beyond a certain information load, probably in the range of three to five bits, further increases in task complexity do not regularly show an increasing correlation between response latency and IQ. For example, Speigel and Bryant (1978) found correlations of around $-.6$ between IQ and choice RTs to cognitive tasks at three levels of complexity given to 94 sixth graders. But, task complexity was unrelated to RT. All of the tasks used by Speigel and Bryant, however, were of much greater complexity than those involving only zero to three bits of information, as shown by the fact that the range of mean RTs for these tasks was from 4500 to 8300 msec compared with a range from 250 to 500 msec for RTs to stimulus arrays ranging from zero to three bits of information.

For tasks as complex as Raven Matrices items, which take several seconds or more to solve, the mean latencies over single correctly answered items have been found to correlate near zero with psychometric intelligence (Jensen, 1980b; Snow, Marshalek, & Lohman, 1976; White, 1973). Using a geometric figure-analogies task of more intermediate complexity, Mulholland, Pellegrino, and Glaser (1980) found a significant correlation ($-.44$) between overall response latency and psychometric scores but found nonsignificant correlations between *rates* of increase in processing time as a function of task complexity and psychometric scores using the Cognitive Abilities Test. They interpret this outcome as a result of individual differences in processing strategies involving a speed-accuracy trade-off and different allocations of effort and time to different stages of task solution. They suggest, following Sternberg (1977), that abler individuals spend relatively more time on the initial stimulus encoding phase of problem solving, making for relatively greater speed in the subsequent transformations required for solution. When the information load of the reaction stimulus exceeds the subject's asymptotic capacity for one-stage processing, other stages and types of cognitive processing must come into play (e.g., chunking, rehearsal, transfer of information into short-term or intermediate memory, and retrieval). Thus, response latencies in complex tasks can reflect an amalgam of processes and could consistently show correlations with g only if the latencies of the various processes could each be measured separately and then combined in a multiple regression equation.

SHORT-TERM MEMORY SCAN PARADIGM

This technique, invented by S. Sternberg (1966), measures the speed of scanning information in short-term memory. Number sets of differing lengths (two to seven digits), presented either simultaneously or successively, are shown and then followed a few seconds later by a probe digit, which was either present or absent in the target set. Subjects respond "present" (or "yes") or "absent" (or "no") by push buttons, and the RT is measured. Reaction time increases as a linear function of set size. (Set size, not the location of the probe digit in the set, is the crucial factor as it seems the memory scanning does not terminate when the probe digit is found but is always exhau~·'ve.) Both the intercept and slope of the regression of RT (to the probe) on set ze are related to psychometric intelligence (Fig. 6.13).

Other studies show highly significant differences between retarded and nonretarded subjects in scanning rate (i.e., slope) (Dugas & Kellas, 1974; Harris & Fleer, 1974; Maisto & Jerome, 1977; Silverman, 1974). The retarded groups in these studies appear to employ the same short-term memory scanning strategies

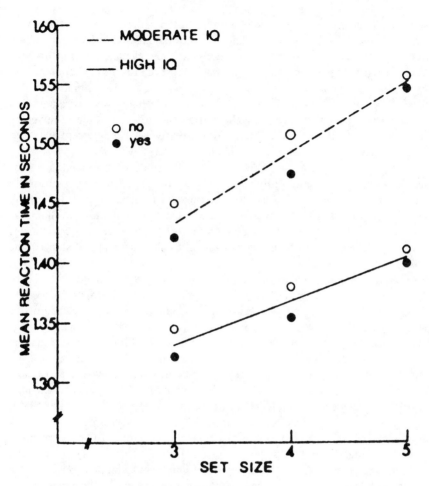

FIG. 6.13.   Mean RTs for correct "yes" and "no" (i.e., presence or absence of probe digit in target set) for moderate-IQ (95 or below, $\overline{X} = 88$) and high-IQ (115 or above, $\overline{X} = 126$) fifth and sixth grade children. The equations for the two lines are: moderate-IQ RT = 1265 + 58s and high-IQ RT = 1210 + 40s, where RT is in milliseconds and s = number of digits in the target set (from McCauley et al., 1976).

(serial and exhaustive search) as the nonretarded. Like RT in the decision-time paradigm, the short-term memory scanning rate is more related to IQ than to mental age. Children 10 to 12 years of age with IQs comparable to those of university students show about the same scanning rate as the university students (about 40 msec per digit) (cf. Chiang & Atkinson, 1976; McCauley, Dugas, Kellas, & DeVellis, 1976). This observation is consistent with other evidence on the developmental aspects of short-term memory scanning and information processing (Chi, 1977).

The parameters of this paradigm are related to intelligence even among very superior subjects. The first investigations to show significant differences in scanning rates between university students scoring in the upper and lower quartiles of the SAT Verbal were reported by Milliman, Frost, and Hunt (1972) and Hunt, Frost, and Lunneborg (1973). In a study by Snow et al., 1976, individual differences in the intercept and slope of the short-term memory scan were predicted on the basis of scores on several psychometric tests and sex of subject (university students) with multiple Rs of .88 and .70, respectively. The intercept and slope predicted SAT Verbal and SAT Quantitative scores with Rs of .54 and .21, respectively, in a group of Stanford University students representing a very restricted range of general ability. The prediction of scan parameters by the much larger R for the psychometric scores, rather than vice versa, suggests that nearly all of the scan components operate in the much more complex psychometric tests, whereas the tests involve many other information-processing components (as well as specific knowledge) not measured by the intercept and slope of the scan paradigm.

The memory scan paradigm has a sensory counterpart in the visual scan paradigm, in which a single target digit is presented first, followed by a set of digits. The subject's latency of response as to the presence or absence of the target digit in the set is a measure of visual scanning. As with memory scanning, visual scanning latency increases linearly as a function of set size. The reciprocal of the slope of this function is a measure of the *rate* of visual scanning. Chiang and Atkinson (1976) found, in a sample of 30 university students, a nonsignificant but suggestive correlation ($r = .43$) between visual and memory scanning rates. (Intercepts correlated .97.) Keating, Keniston, Manis, and Bobbitt (1980), in a similar study with school children, ages 9 to 15, were able to correct the correlation between the slopes (or scanning rates) for the visual and memory modes for attenuation, yielding a corrected r of .50 ($p < .001$). Visual and memory scanning rates in this study were significantly related to age in the expected direction, but there was no significant relationship of scanning rate to psychometric ability as measured by the California Test of Mental Maturity. In a previous study based on groups of more heterogeneous ability, Keating and Bobbitt (1978) found a significant ($p < .05$) relationship between memory scanning rates and Raven scores.

LONG-TERM MEMORY RETRIEVAL
OF SEMANTIC CODES

This paradigm, originated by Posner (1969, 1978; Posner, Boies, Eichelman, & Taylor, 1968), measures the speed with which highly overlearned information stored in long-term memory (e.g., the names of letters and numbers) can be retrieved. The procedure consists of measuring discriminative ("same" vs. "different'') RT to pairs of stimuli, which are the same (identical) or different either physically or semantically. Discrimination of a physical difference does not require access to a prior learned semantic code, whereas discrimination of semantic differences requires access to information stored in long-term memory. The difference between RT to physical identity and RT to name identity is taken as a measure of speed of access to long-term memory. A pair of letters is presented that are physically identical (e.g., *AA, aa, BB, bb*), physically different (*Aa, bB, AB*), semantically identical (*Aa, Bb*), or semantically different (*AB, aB, ab*). Under each condition (physical or semantic), subjects are required to respond "same" or "different" by corresponding push buttons, and RT is recorded. The RTs of interest are those to physical and semantic *identity* (RT on "same" push

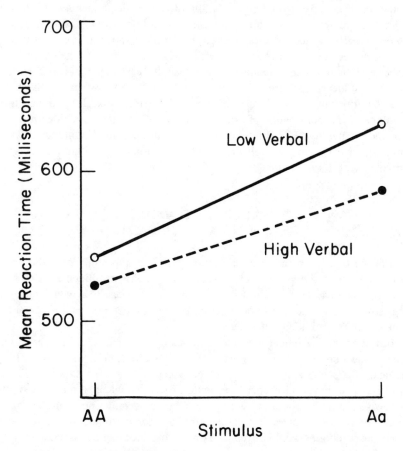

FIG. 6.14.   Time required to recognize physical (*AA*) or semantic (*Aa*) identity of letter pairs by university students who score in the upper (high) or (low) quartile on the SAT Verbal (from Hunt, 1976).

button). It takes young adult subjects an average of about 70 msec longer to respond "same" for semantic identity (*Aa*) than for physical identity (*AA*).

Hunt (1976) was the first to demonstrate a relationship between speed of accessing long-term memory, as measured by the difference in RT between *Aa* and *AA*, and scores on the SAT Verbal (Fig. 6.14). The average RT difference of 75 msec between *Aa* and *AA* (i.e., the semantic encoding time) for university students is the same as the average RT difference between zero and three bits of information in the decision time paradigm.

Goldberg, Schwartz, and Stewart (1977) have made this long-term memory paradigm more discriminating for verbal IQ by using three conditions of "same" versus "different" word pairs: (1) physical identity (*cow–cow*); (2) homophonic identity (*bare–bear*); (3) taxonomic category identity (*hand–foot; cello–violin*). All the words are so easy and highly familiar to university students that errors in responding are very few and are uncorrelated with IQ. Individual differences in this task clearly do not reflect a difference between "knowing" or "not knowing" the correct answers; rather they reflect the speed with which the information is accessed in long-term memory. The mean RTs of high- and low-scoring university students on Lorge–Thorndike Verbal IQ are shown for each of the three conditions in Fig. 6.15. Correlations of RT with Verbal IQ under each of the three conditions are: physical identity, .32; taxonomic identity, .63; *homophonic* identity, .68. This again illustrates the common finding that RTs to stimuli requiring greater complexity of information processing are more highly correlated with IQ or *g*.

RELATIONSHIPS AMONG
REACTION-TIME PARADIGMS

Each of the four RT paradigms representing different types of information processing has been shown to relate RT to psychometric intelligence. The only paradigm that involves prior knowledge as such is the access to semantic codes in long-term memory, but the prior acquired knowledge per se is probably not the main source of individual differences.

An important theoretical question is the extent to which the four paradigms measure the same or different sources of individual differences. If they all tap one and the same source of variance, except for purely task-specific or paradigm-specific variance, then we should expect that when all are entered into a stepwise multiple correlation with psychometric *g*, only one of the variables would carry all of the predictive variance. As a corollary to this, the correlations among the paradigms would be reduced to zero by partialing out psychometric *g*, unless the paradigms shared some source of variance that is unrelated to *g*. On the other hand, if the unbiased (i.e., corrected for shrinkage) stepwise multiple *R* for predicting *g* was significantly increased by the addition of variables from

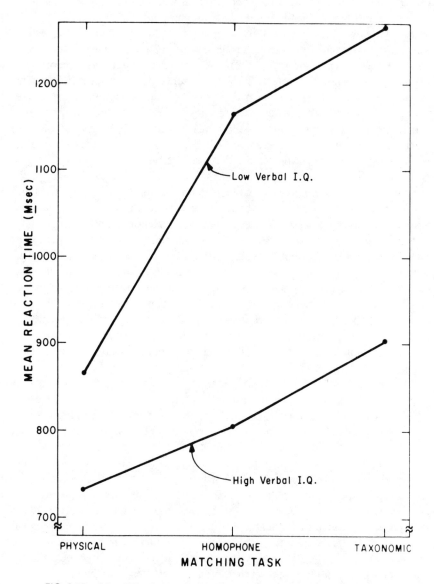

FIG. 6.15.   Mean RTs of university students of high (132) and low (89) verbal IQ in responding to identity of words under three conditions: physical, homophonic, and taxonomic matching (from Goldberg et al., 1977).

305

each RT paradigm to the regression equation, it would mean that each paradigm is tapping a different cognitive process that contributes to g.

As yet, however, we have only an inkling of the answer to this question. Much more systematic investigation is needed. A good beginning is illustrated in a study by Keating and Bobbitt (1978), who used three chronometric paradigms: (1) simple and choice RT; (2) physical and semantic letter identification; (3) memory scanning. They hypothesized various combinations of a four-step sequence of cognitive processes as operating in each of three chronometric paradigms, the steps being: (1) encoding; (2) operation; (3) binary decision; (4) response. Parameters of each chronometric paradigm can be expressed in terms of the various component processes. For example, simple RT (SRT) is $1 + 4$, choice RT (CRT) is $1 + 3 + 4$, and hence CRT $-$ SRT is 3. Keating and Bobbitt hypothesized that chronometric parameters in the three paradigms involving *similar* processes would be more highly intercorrelated than the parameters involving *dissimilar* processes. The average intercorrelations were .66 for parameters involving similar processes and .30 for dissimilar processes. The pattern of intercorrelations implies that individual differences in different parameters (e.g., intercept, slope) and in different paradigms are attributable to a general factor common to all of the parameters and paradigms as well as to group factors that are specific to each parameter and paradigm. If this is indeed the case, the only hope for accounting for any really substantial proportion of the variance in psychometric g by means of chronometric techniques would be by discovering an optimal combination of various chronometric paradigms and parameters, each independently tapping different parts of the total g variance.

This is clearly one of the next important steps in the research agenda of this field. We will be in a much better position to evaluate the potential fruitfulness of chronometric research on intelligence after we have estimated the proportion of true variance in g that can be accounted for by the RT parameters derived from all four of the basic chronometric paradigms I have described. I would not expect the RT paradigms to account for most of the true score variance in scores on any single psychometric test or a composite of just a few tests because most standard tests involve specific or group factors linked to certain kinds of past-learned knowledge and skills (vocabulary, arithmetic, information, etc.), which are strongly influenced by experiential factors in addition to reflecting biological intelligence. A very substantial proportion of the g factor variance common to a number of cognitive tests of considerable diversity, however, might be predictable from a combination of chronometric parameters derived from these fundamental paradigms. To account for most of the variance in any particular type of test (e.g., analogies, number series, matrices, etc.), it would probably be necessary to hypothesize individual differences in more complex processes or strategies. It should also be remembered that any *particular* test item measures much more of some *specific* factor (or at least a non-g factor) than g, and this is true even of items in the most g loaded tests taken as a whole (e.g., Raven's Matrices).

The few studies using two or more of the RT paradigms on the same group afford only a hint of what might be discovered in more ambitious investigations. For example, Lally and Nettelbeck (1977) found no significant correlation between inspection time (IT) and choice RT in groups of retarded and nonretarded subjects, but they did find a correlation of $-.63$ between IT and the reciprocal of *slope* (i.e., *rate* of information processing) of choice RTs to tasks involving one to three bits (2, 4, 6, and 8 choices). The multiple R for predicting WAIS Performance IQ from IT and the slope of RT in the combined retarded and nonretarded groups is .84.

In a study performed in our lab by Vernon with 25 university students, IT was found to correlate $-.31$ with Advanced Raven Matrices scores and only .10 with intraindividual variability (σ_i in choice RT—σ_i being the RT parameter most highly correlated [$-.43$] with the Raven. The multiple R of IT and σ_i with Raven scores was .51 ($p < .04$). (It should be noted that even two high-level psychometric tests of intelligence, the Advanced Raven and the Terman Concept Mastery Test, are correlated only about .50 in this restricted university population, whereas the correlations between similar verbal and nonverbal tests in the general population are commonly .70 to .80.) In this sample, IT had generally low (and mostly nonsignificant) correlations with all of the RT and MT parameters.

Only one study (Keating & Bobbitt, 1978) has reported correlations among information-processing indices derived from as many as three distinct RT paradigms: (*a*) decision speed as measured by choice RT (one bit) minus simple RT (zero bit); (*b*) long-term memory accessing time as measured by semantic minus physical identity of letter pairs; (*c*) short-term memory scanning rate as measured by the slope of RT to probe digits for set sizes of one, three, and five digits. The intercorrelations among these indices are: $r_{ab} = .35$, $r_{ac} = .26$, and $r_{bc} = .19$. It is evident that these three indices (*a*, *b*, and *c*) do not measure entirely common sources of individual differences. The multiple Rs of these variables with Raven scores among school children of average and superior intelligence in age groups 9, 13, and 17 were .59, .57, and .60, respectively. (In all age groups combined, age alone accounts for 47% of the variance in Raven scores, and the three central processing variables together account for 15%, which corresponds to a multiple R, with age partialed out, of .39.) It would have been informative to have used at least one other standard psychometric test of intelligence to see how much more it would be correlated with the Raven than the three indices of information-processing speed in combination. But the fact that each of the RT indices made a significant independent contribution to the multiple R with the Raven at least suggests that the component of information-processing speed, which is correlated with g, is not an entirely unitary component. Rather it represents different, albeit slightly intercorrelated, components involved in the different information-processing systems.

Further studies now in progress in our lab use all four of the RT paradigms that I have described and are aimed at settling, as definitively as possible, the question of unitary versus multiple sources of RT variance in g and determining the proportion of g variance that can be accounted for by an optimal combination of RT parameters derived from the four information-processing paradigms. Once these points have been firmly established, we can use the various RT paradigms and their g loaded parameters to learn more about the nature of g. The RT paradigms and parameters afford many more facets from which elemental processes and neural mechanisms can be more clearly inferred than do ordinary psychometric tests and test items, however sophisticated our statistical analyses may be.

The study of the RT correlates of g also brings us closer to the interface of brain and behavior—the point at which individual differences in intelligence must ultimately be understood. Already, very direct connections have been shown between RT and such neurophysiological phenomena as the latency and amplitude of evoked brain potentials (Jensen et al., 1981; Kutas, McCarthy, & Donchin, 1977), cardiac deceleration (Krupski, 1975; Obrist, Webb, Stutterer, & Howard, 1970; Runcie & O'Bannon, 1975; Sroufe, 1971), body temperature, high altitude anoxia, and neuroactive drugs (Woodworth & Schlosberg, 1954). All such physical correlates of RT should prove useful in developing a biologically based theory of individual differences in RT in all its aspects and thereby in the variance that these variables may explain in Spearman's g as well.

REFERENCES

Ahern, S., Beatty, J. Pupillary responses during information processing vary with Scholastic Aptitude Test scores. *Science, 1979, 205,* 1289–1292.

Albee, G. W. Open letter in response to D. O. Hebb. *American Psychologist, 1980, 35,* 386–387.

Bastendorf, W. L. *Activation level, as measured by palmar conductance, and intelligence in children.* Unpublished doctoral dissertation, Claremont Graduate School, 1960.

Baumeister, A. A., & Kellas, G. Reaction time and mental retardation. In N. R. Ellis (Ed.), *International review of research in mental retardation* (Vol. 3). New York: Academic Press, 1968.

Brand, C. *General intelligence and mental speed: Their relationship and development.* Paper presented at the NATO International Conference on Intelligence and Learning, York University, England, July 1979.

Carroll, J. B. *A first principal component does not necessarily indicate a g factor: Remarks on Jensen's data and g factor computations.* Unpublished manuscript, L. L. Thrustone Psychometric Laboratory, Univ. of North Carolina, 1979.

Chi, M. T. H. Age differences in speed of processing: A critique. *Developmental Psychology, 1977, 13,* 543–544.

Chiang, A., & Atkinson, R. C. Individual differences and interrelationships among a select set of cognitive skills. *Memory & Cognition, 1976, 4,* 661–672.

Dugas, J., & Kellas, G. Encoding and retrieval processes in normal children and retarded adolescents. *Journal of Experimental Child Psychology, 1974, 17,* 177–185.

Elkana, Y. *The discovery of the conservation of energy.* Cambridge, Mass.: Harvard University Press, 1974.

Goldberg, R. A., Schwartz, S., & Stewart, M. Individual differences in cognitive processes. *Journal of Educational Psychology*, 1977, *69*, 9-14.

Harris, G. J., & Fleer, R. E. High speed memory scanning in mental retardates: Evidence for a central processing deficit. *Journal of Experimental Child Psychology*, 1974, *14*, 452-459.

Hick, W. On the rate of gain of information. *Quarterly Journal of Experimental Psychology*, 1952, *4*, 11-26.

Hunt, E. Varieties of cognitive power. In L. B. Resnick (Ed.), *The nature of intelligence*. Hillsdale, N.J.: Lawrence Erlbaum Associates, 1976.

Hunt, E., Frost, N., & Lunneborg, C. Individual differences in cognition. In G. Bower (Ed.), *The psychology of learning and motivation: Advances in research and theory* (Vol. 7). New York: Academic Press, 1973.

Jensen, A. R. *g:* Outmoded theory of unconquered frontier? *Creative Science and Technology*, 1979, *2*, 16-29.

Jensen, A. R. *Bias in mental testing*. New York: The Free Press, 1980(a).

Jensen, A. R. Chronometric analysis of mental ability. *Journal of Social and Biological Structures*, 1980, *3*, 103-122. (b)

Jensen, A. R. Uses of sibling data in educational and psychological research. *American Educational Research Journal*, 1980, *17*, 153-170. (c)

Jensen, A. R., & Munro, E. Reaction time, movement time, and intelligence. *Intelligence*, 1979, *3*, 121-126.

Jensen, A. R., Schafer, E. W. P., & Crinella, F. M. Reaction time, evoked brain potentials, and psychometric *g* in the severely retarded. *Intelligence*, 1981, *5*, 179-197.

Keating, D. P., & Bobbitt, B. Individual and developmental differences in cognitive processing components of mental ability. *Child Development*, 1978, *49*, 155-169.

Keating, D. P., Keniston, A. H., Manis, F., & Bobbitt, B. L. Development of the search-processing parameter. *Child Development*, 1980, *51*, 39-44.

Krupski, A. Heart rate changes during a fixed reaction time task in normal and retarded adult males. *Psychophysiology*, 1975, *12*, 262-267.

Kutas, M., McCarthy, G., & Donchin, E. Augmenting mental chronometry: The P300 as a measure of stimulus evaluation time. *Science*, 1977, *197*, 792-795.

Lally, M., & Nettelbeck, T. Intelligence, reaction time, and inspection time. *American Journal of Mental Deficiency*, 1977, *82*, 273-281.

Libet, B. Cortical activation in conscious and unconscious experience. *Perspectives in Biology and Medicine*, 1965, *9*, 77-86.

Libet, B., Alberts, W. W., Wright, E. W., Jr., & Feinstein, B. Cortical and thalamic activation in conscious sensory experience. *Neurophysiology studied in man. Procedings of a symposium held in Paris at the Faculte de Sciences, 20-22 July, 1971*. Amsterdam: Excerpta Medica, 1971.

Maisto, A. A., & Jerome, M. A. Encoding and high-speed memory scanning of retarded and nonretarded adolescents. *American Journal of Mental Deficienty*, 1977, *82*, 282-286.

McCauley, C., Dugas, J., Kellas, G., & DeVellis, R. F. Effects of serial rehearsal training on memory search. *Journal of Educational Psychology*, 1976, *68*, 474-481.

Miles, T. R. Contributions to intelligence testing and the theory of intelligence. I. On defining intelligence. *British Journal of Educational Psychology*, 1957, *27*, 153-165.

Milliman, P., Frost, N., & Hunt, E. *Intelligence and search rate in short term memory*. Paper presented at the meetings of the Western Psychological Association, Portland, Oregon, April 1972.

Mulholland, T. M., Pellegrino, J. W., & Glaser, R. Components of geometric analogy solution. *Cognitive Psychology*, 1980, *12*, 252-284.

Nettelbeck, T., & Brewer, N. Studies of mental retardation and timed performance. In N. R. Ellis (Ed.), *International review of research in mental retardation* (Vol. 10). New York: Academic Press, 1981.

Nettelbeck, T., & Lally, M. Inspection time and measured intelligence. *British Journal of Psychology,* 1976, *67,* 17–22.

Nettelbeck, T., & Lally, M. Age, intelligence, and inspection time. *American Journal of Mental Deficiency,* 1979, *83,* 398–401.

Obrist, P. A., Webb, R. A., Sutterer, J. R., & Howard, J. L. The cardiac-somatic relationship: Some reformulations. *Psychophysiology,* 1970, *6,* 569–587.

Plomin, R., & DeFries, J. C. Genetics and intelligence: Recent data. *Intelligence,* 1980, *4,* 15–24.

Posner, M. I. Abstraction and the process of recognition. In G. H. Bower & J. T. Spence (Eds.), *The psychology of learning and motivation* (Vol. 3). New York: Academic Press, 1969.

Posner, M. I. *Chronometric explorations of mind.* Hillsdale, N.J.: Lawrence Erlbaum Associates, 1978.

Posner, M., Boies, S., Eichelman, W., & Taylor, R. Retention of visual and name codes of single letters. *Journal of Experimental Psychology,* 1969, *81,* 10–15.

Runcie, D., & O'Bannon, R. M. Relationship of reaction time to deceleration and variability of heart rate in nonretarded and retarded persons. *American Journal of Mental Deficiency,* 1975, *79,* 553–558.

Silverman, W. P. High speed scanning of nonalphanumeric symbols in culturally-familially retarded and nonretarded children *American Journal of Mental Deficiency,* 1974, *79,* 44–51.

Snow, R. E., Marshalek, B., & Lohman, D. F. *Correlation of selected cognitive abilities and cognitive processing parameters: An exploratory study* (Tech. Rep. No. 3). Stanford, Cal.: Stanford University, Aptitude Research Project, School of Education, December 1976.

Spearman, C. *The abilities of man.* New York: Macmillan, 1927.

Spiegel, M. R., & Bryant, N. D. Is speed of processing information related to intelligence and achievement? *Journal of Educational Psychology,* 1978, *70,* 904–910.

Sroufe, L. A. Age changes in cardiac deceleration within a fixed foreperiod reaction-time task: An index of attention. *Developmental Psychology,* 1971, *5,* 338–343.

Sternberg, R. J. *Intelligence, information processing, and anological reasoning: The componential analysis of human abilities.* Hillsdale, N.J.: Lawrence Erlbaum Associates, 1977.

Sternberg, R. J. Stalking the IQ quark. *Psychology Today,* 1979, 13, 42–54.

Sternberg, R. J., & Rifkin, B. The development of anological reasoning processes. *Journal of Experimental Child Psychology,* 1979, *27,* 195–232.

Sternberg, S. High speed scanning in human memory. *Science,* 1966, *153,* 652–654.

Vernon, P. A. Reaction time and intelligence in the mentally retarded. *Intelligence,* 1981, *5,* 31–36.

White, P. O. Individual differences in speed, accuracy, and persistence: A mathematical model for problem solving. In H. J. Eysenck (Ed.), *The measurement of intelligence.* Baltimore, Md.: Williams & Wilkins, 1973.

Woodworth, R. S., & Schlosberg, H. *Experimental psychology.* New York: Holt, Rinehart, & Winston, 1954.

7 Process Analyses of Spatial Aptitude

James W. Pellegrino
University of California at Santa Barbara

Robert Kail, Jr.
Purdue University

INTRODUCTION

Approaches to the Study of Aptitude and Intelligence

The past decade has been particularly significant with respect to the emergence of renewed interest in the psychological study of individual differences in aptitude and intelligence. A number of important volumes have appeared (e.g., Resnick, 1976; Snow, Federico, & Montague, 1980a, b; Sternberg, 1977), and all have been centrally concerned with an improved definition and understanding of the rather nebulous constructs known as aptitude and intelligence. In large part, the issues discussed in these volumes reflect a concern with developing a psychology of aptitude and intelligence in addition to the prevailing psychometry of these constructs. This reflects both pressing social and philosophical concerns relative to tests and an awareness of the possible relevance of developments in cognitive and developmental psychology for explaining what is typically assessed by psychometric instruments.

One of several possible approaches to studying the nature of intelligence and aptitude is to apply cognitive process theory and methodology to the analysis of performance on tasks that are found on various specific aptitude and general intelligence test batteries. This so-called "cognitive components" approach (Pellegrino & Glaser, 1979) does not presuppose that intelligence and aptitude are uniquely defined by the circumscribed performances required by intelligence and aptitude tests. Obviously, intelligence covers a much wider range of knowledge and skill. However, the cognitive components approach recognizes that various tests have been devised that reliably assess individual differences in cognitive

311

abilities and that these differences are predictive of success and achievement in diverse real-world settings. The question then is: What are the skills that are being assessed by such instruments and how can we understand the basis for individual variation? Thus, the goal is to treat the tasks found on aptitude and intelligence tests as "cognitive tasks" (Carroll, 1976) that can be approached and analyzed in the same way that cognitive and developmental psychologists have approached and analyzed memory search, visual scanning, sentence verification, and mental arithmetic tasks, to name just a few.

Most of the research that can be described as cognitive components analyses has been summarized in a number of papers (e.g., Carroll & Maxwell, 1979; Pellegrino & Glaser, 1979, 1980, in press; Sternberg, 1977, 1979), and it focuses primarily on inductive and deductive tasks. Relatively little has been reported on process analyses of tasks representing spatial aptitude (but see Cooper, 1980; Egan, 1979). In this chapter, we discuss research that we have pursued jointly and individually on the analysis of individual differences in spatial aptitude. Our studies represent an attempt to employ cognitive process methods for the analysis of performance differences on tasks representing common measures of spatial ability. The different studies that have been conducted can be best understood in the context of a general plan or framework for the analysis of individual differences in any cognitive aptitude or ability (see Pellegrino & Glaser, 1980, in press). Such a plan or framework is necessary for cognitive components research to yield data and theory that lead to a better understanding of spatial ability.

The initial step in a systematic analysis of individual differences in spatial aptitude (or any aptitude construct) is to identify the domain of tasks that serve to define it. This involves identifying a core or prototypical set of tasks that frequently occur across many widely used spatial-aptitude tests and that have a history of consistent association with the spatial-aptitude construct. Such an initial step delineates the task forms that should serve as the target for rational, empirical, and theoretical analysis. A multitask approach is important because an adequate understanding of individual differences in spatial ability cannot be based upon an intensive analysis of only a single task with a high loading on the spatial-aptitude factor(s). Rather, it is necessary to conduct analyses that consider the various tasks that yield correlated performance and, in so doing, specify a set of performances that define the aptitude construct. A successful process analysis of multiple tasks should provide a basis for understanding the patterns of intercorrelations among tasks. More importantly, the analysis of multiple related tasks should permit the differentiation of general and specific cognitive processes and knowledge. This differentiation can lead to a level of analysis where research can be pursued on the feasibility of process training and transfer.

Having identified the domain of tasks that define spatial aptitude, we must then develop and validate information-processing theories and models for the different tasks. The theories and models can be derived from computer-simulation programs or from empirical studies of the effects of task properties on latency, solution protocols, and error patterns. These models must contain information about multiple levels of cognitive processing, including both basic processes and strategies that control process integration and sequencing. Such a multilevel approach is necessary because individual differences may exist at different levels over the entire range and distribution of age and ability that can be considered.

The third major step in the analysis is to use the models of task performance as the basis for individual-differences analyses in each task. In this way, the utility of a model for explaining the source(s) of individual differences can be further tested and validated. Thus, we are explicitly proposing the idea that a model that serves to capture group performance must also be shown to be valid at the individual-subject level. Individual differences can be investigated in terms of the parameters of a single model or in terms of the applicability of different models for the performance of different individuals. Part of such an analysis involves the investigation of the sources of inter-age and intra-age individual differences. An approach combining developmental and individual-differences analyses is particularly important to the validation and application of task-performance models. Theories and models of task performance should be able to account for overall developmental changes in a specific aptitude as well as the sources of individual differences within separate age groups. With respect to the latter issue, there is no reason to assume that the sources of individual differences within one age group are necessarily applicable to other age groups.

The next step in the analysis is the examination of cross-task consistency in the sources of individual differences. Based upon the outcomes of the preceding stages, one can attempt to specify and test the cognitive components that are general across all task forms representative of spatial aptitude and those that may be specific to a given task form or stimulus type. Analyses of cross-task consistency are particularly important with respect to providing a basis for explaining the consistent correlational patterns found in the psychometric literature. Such analyses are also critical with respect to verifying some important implicit assumptions at the core of cognitive theory and methodology. We discuss the latter issue at the end of this chapter.

In the remainder of the chapter, we present the results of research that follow from the preceding analytic scheme. First, we briefly discuss spatial aptitude as a psychometric construct. This discussion also serves as a means for describing the various tasks that represent the spatial-aptitude domain. Then, we present data and theory on processing in both simple and complex spatial-relations and spatial-visualization tasks. Our most complete and detailed treatment of processing involves simple spatial-relations or "mental-rotation" tasks. Here, we discuss sources of individual, sex, and developmental differences in performance, as well as developmental changes in the sources of individual differences. The discussion of performance in complex spatial-relations and visualization tasks is limited to process models and sources of adult individual differences in performance. The final section of the chapter attempts an integration and interpretation of our findings and considers some issues associated with the analysis of spatial aptitude in particular and the analysis of individual differences in general.

An Overview of Spatial Aptitude

Hierarchical theories of aptitude, such as those developed by Cattell (1971) and Vernon (1965) based upon procedures of factor analysis, typically distinguish among verbal, general reasoning, and spatial-mechanical aptitude factors. In Cattell's theory, this distinction is represented by the partition among crystallized (g_c), fluid (g_f), and visualization (g_v) intelligences. Vernon's hierarchy distinguishes between a verbal-educational construct ($v:ed$) and a practical-mechanical construct ($k:m$). The latter is then further subdivided into more specific aptitudes, some of which involve common spatial-processing tasks. Recently, two reviews of factor analytic research on spatial aptitude have appeared (Lohman, 1979; McGee, 1979a). Both have reemphasized points made by Smith (1964) in an earlier review of spatial ability. First, they were clear in noting that all major factor analytic studies have identified mechanical/spatial factors that are distinct from other general and specific factors. However, both also point out that spatial aptitude is still an ill-defined construct after 70 years of psychometric research. There appears to be little agreement among major studies as to the number of distinct spatial abilities that may exist and how best to characterize each one. Lohman (1979) has provided an overview of some of the problems encountered in trying to integrate the major factor analytic work that has been done on spatial aptitude. First, identical tests appear with different names in different studies, and tests with the same name are often quite different in appearance and demands. A second problem is that subtle changes in test format and administration can have effects on the resultant factor structures (e.g., the use of solution time as opposed to number correct as the measure of performance). Finally, perhaps the most important difference relates to procedural variation in factor extraction and rotation.

To correct for some of these problems, Lohman (1979) reanalyzed the data from several major studies in an attempt to isolate a common set of spatial factors. The result of these efforts was the delineation of three distinct factors, two of which are of direct concern in this chapter. One factor was labeled *spatial orientation* and appeared to involve the ability to imagine how a stimulus or stimulus array would appear from another perspective. Typically, such tasks require individuals to reorient themselves relative to the array, as would be the case when a plane or boat shifts heading relative to some land mass. The other two factors were labeled *spatial relations* and *spatial visualization*. The spatial-relations factor appears to involve the ability to engage rapidly and accurately in mental rotation processes that are necessary for judgments about the identity of a pair of stimuli. Examples of common spatial-relations tasks are shown in Fig. 7.1. The first problem type is drawn from the Primary Mental Abilities Space Test (hereafter referred to as the PMA) and requires the individual to identify those alternatives that are identical to the standard on the left. Identity is defined in terms of rotation in the picture plane whereas mismatches involve rotation plus mirror-image reversal. The second problem type in Fig. 7.1, similar in format to the PMA, is the Cards Test from the French Reference Kit for Cognitive Factors (French, Ekstrom, & Price, 1963). The third problem type is the Cube Comparisons Test from the French Reference Kit. The individual's task is to determine if two cubes are logically consistent (same) or inconsistent (different), and this requires the 90° rotation of one or more surfaces to bring the two stimuli into congruence for a consistency check. The final problem type is taken from a test developed by Vandenberg based upon stimuli originally used by Metzler and Shepard (1974). The individual's task is to find the two stimuli that are the same as the standard on the left.

The spatial-visualization factor is defined by tests that are relatively unspeeded and more complex. Such tasks frequently require a manipulation in which there is movement among the internal parts of the stimulus configuration or the folding and unfolding of flat patterns. Examples of representative tasks are provided in Fig. 7.2. The first problem type shown in Fig. 7.2 is taken from the

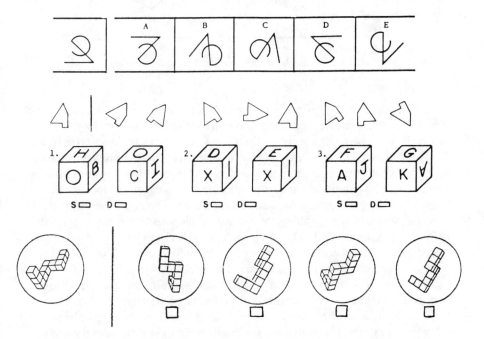

FIG. 7.1.   Examples of common spatial-relations tasks.

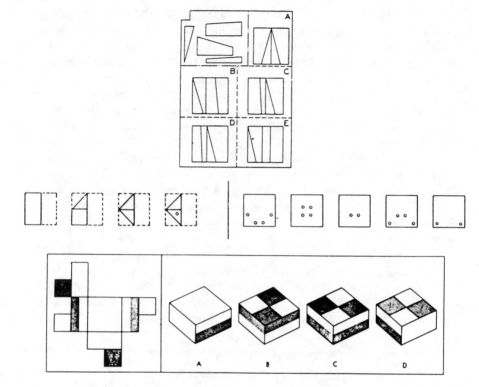

FIG. 7.2.   Examples of common spatial-visualization tasks.

Minnesota Paper Form Board Test. The individual's task is to select the completed figure that can be constructed from the set of randomly arranged pieces shown in the upper left corner of the item. The second problem type is the Punched Holes Test taken from the French Reference Kit. The problem shows a series of hypothetical folds of a square of paper followed by the punching of a single hole. The individual's task is to determine the number and location of the holes when the paper is unfolded and select the appropriate answer. The third problem type is a paper-folding or surface-development item taken from the Differential Aptitude Test. The problem contains a representation of a flat unfolded object and several complete objects. The individual's task is to select the completed object that can be made from the unfolded object.

The differences between spatial-relations and visualization tasks seem to reflect two complementary dimensions of performance (Lohman, 1979). One of these is the speed-power dimension. Individual spatial-relations problems are solved more rapidly than spatial-visualization problems, and the tests themselves are administered in a format that emphasizes speed in the former case and both speed and accuracy in the latter case. The second dimension involves stimulus complexity. A gross index of complexity is the number of individual stimulus elements or parts that must be processed. Spatial-relations problems, although varying among themselves in complexity, involve less complex stimuli than do spatial-visualization problems. This particular conception of these two dimensions as mapped onto the tasks and aptitude factors is represented in Fig. 7.3. In terms of a process analysis of spatial aptitude, the important question is whether individual differences in performance on these various tasks reflect differential contributions of the speed and accuracy of executing specific cognitive processes. The remainder of this chapter reports our initial attempts to address this question in the course of considering the components of processing that contribute to individual differences in performance on specific tasks.

PROCESS ANALYSES
OF SIMPLE SPATIAL RELATIONS

Our research on performance in simple spatial-relations tasks has primarily focused on a single task—the PMA (Thurstone & Thurstone, 1949). This test was chosen for several reasons. First, as indicated earlier, the PMA is typical of many measures of spatial aptitude in which an individual must "mentally rotate" a stimulus in the picture plane in order to differentiate it from other similar stimuli and match it against some standard. Second, the PMA loads heavily on the spatial-relations factor in factor analytic studies of the structure of intelligence (Cattell, 1971; Lohman, 1979; Smith, 1964; Thurstone, 1938). Third, the PMA

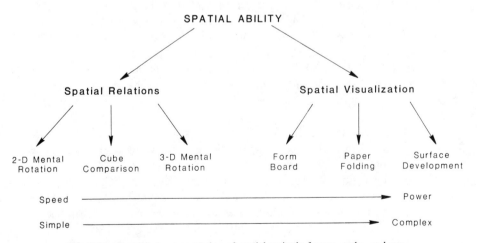

FIG. 7.3. Simplified representation of spatial-aptitude factors, tasks, and performance dimensions.

is appropriate across a relatively broad developmental range, beginning at 10 or 11 years of age and continuing through adulthood (Thurstone & Thurstone, 1949).

Performance on simple spatial-relations problems such as those found on the PMA can be related to the general model of the processes required for mental rotation problems proposed by Cooper and Shepard (1973). The process model was based upon data obtained in a paradigm that required individuals to decide, as rapidly as possible, if two stimuli presented in different visual orientations were the same. This single-trial comparison of a stimulus pair closely resembles the individual comparisons that must be made to solve PMA problems (see Fig. 7.1). An example of the application of this paradigm is a study by Cooper (1975), in which she presented two nonsense shapes that differed in orientation from 0–300°; subjects judged whether the shapes were identical or mirror images of one another. Response latencies in this task were a linearly increasing function of the difference in orientation (angular disparity) between the two shapes. Such a result has been interpreted as indicating that subjects mentally rotate the stimuli in a manner analogous to the actual physical rotation of the object. The greater the "mental distance" to be traveled, the longer it takes to solve the problem.

Cooper and Shepard (1973) presented evidence that response latency on these problems reflects four discrete stages of processing. The model that they proposed is illustrated in Fig. 7.4. The first stage of processing requires encoding of the stimuli, which involves representing the stimuli (i.e., their identity and orientation) and storing this information in working memory. The second phase of processing involves rotation of the mental representation of the nonvertical stimulus to bring it into congruence with the vertical stimulus. This phase is followed by a comparison of the stimulus representations to determine if they are identical. The outcome of the comparison leads to a positive or negative response. As shown in Fig. 7.4, only the second stage of processing (i.e., mental rotation) is affected by the orientation of the stimulus (Cooper & Shepard, 1973). Encoding, comparing, and responding take approximately the same amount of time, regardless of the orientation of the stimulus. The most controversial of these claims is the suggestion that the rate of encoding is unaffected by stimulus orientation, but supporting evidence includes:

1. Cuing subjects regarding the orientation or identity of a to-be-presented stimulus affects the intercept but not the slope of the function relating reaction time to angular disparity (Cooper & Shepard, 1973).
2. When encoding and rotation are separated experimentally by having subjects first view a stimulus briefly and then instructing them to rotate it to a particular orientation, rotation rates are quite similar to those found in other studies that measure encoding and rotation simultaneously (Cooper, 1975).

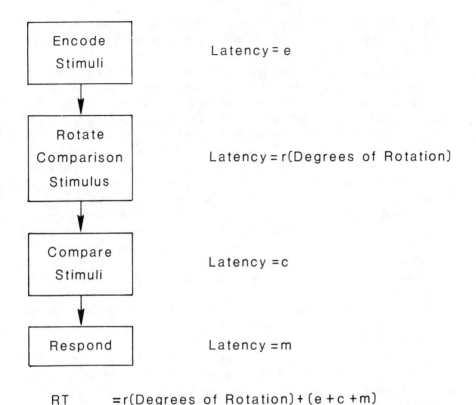

$$RT_{total} = r(\text{Degrees of Rotation}) + (e + c + m)$$

FIG. 7.4.   Representation of the Cooper and Shepard (1973) model for the solution of simple mental rotation problems.

Consequently, the overall equation for reaction time in this task is generally written as: $RT = x(r) + (e + c + m)$, where x represents the angular disparity between the stimuli being compared, and r, e, c, and m represent the times for rotation, encoding, comparison, and motor response. The slope of the function relating response time to stimulus orientation is used to estimate the rate of mental rotation, whereas the intercept provides an estimate of the total time necessary for the remaining processes that are constant over problems.

Individual Differences

The process analysis of performance on a mental rotation problem provides an obvious scheme for the analysis of individual and developmental differences in simple spatial-relations performance. If the processes involved in solving mental rotation problems can be reliably estimated for individuals, then what remains to be determined is the respective contributions of these processes to age and skill differences in this cognitive aptitude.

Individual differences in performance on a speeded test such as the PMA may well be due entirely to speed differences in the cognitive process of mental rotation. To estimate this process in its simplest form, one can determine the slope value for the rotation of familiar stimuli such as alphanumerics. The intercept of the function for processing alphanumeric stimuli is an estimate of the time to encode, compare, and respond to familiar stimuli, and it, too, may be related to individual differences in reference test performance. A potentially important aspect of performance on a test such as the PMA may involve the capacity to encode, compare, and rotate unfamiliar stimuli that lack representations and labels in permanent memory. Previous studies have shown that it takes longer to rotate unfamiliar stimuli such as PMA characters than to rotate familiar alphanumerics. Similarly, there is a higher intercept for processing unfamiliar stimuli of the PMA type. Thus, it is necessary to consider the additional times associated with encoding, comparing, and rotating unfamiliar stimuli as potentially important aspects of skill differences on a reference test such as the PMA. All of these aspects of processing were considered in a study conducted by Pellegrino, Mumaw, Kail, and Carter (1979).

The Pellegrino et al. (1979) analysis of spatial relations and mental rotation performance involved the testing of 99 adults (46 males and 53 females) who represented the entire range of performance on the PMA Spatial-Relations Test. This included low scores near 0 and high scores at the upper limit of 70. The sample had a deliberately disproportionate representation in the tails of the distribution, although the total distribution of skill preserved the general characteristics of normality. Each subject was tested individually in experimental sessions involving the presentation of over 275 stimulus pairs. The pairs represented actual PMA stimuli or asymmetric alphanumerics. Each trial involved the presentation of an upright PMA character or alphanumeric and a comparison stimulus rotated 0–150° from upright. "Same" and "different" judgment trials were intermixed, as were the different stimulus types. A total of eight different PMA characters and eight different alphanumerics were used to create the stimulus set.

The overall performance data for "same" judgment trials are shown in Fig. 7.5. As can be seen, alphanumeric stimuli had both a smaller slope and intercept value than the PMA stimuli. Both functions represented in Fig. 7.5 clearly show that there is a relatively constant increase in the time to solve an item as the degree of angular disparity between the standard and comparison stimulus increases. Error rates on both types of stimuli were relatively low, with an overall error rate of .03 for alphanumerics and .09 for PMA characters.

Individual subject data showed the same linear trends exhibited in the group mean data. Least squares regression lines were obtained for both stimulus types, and these were used to provide individual subject estimates of the four basic

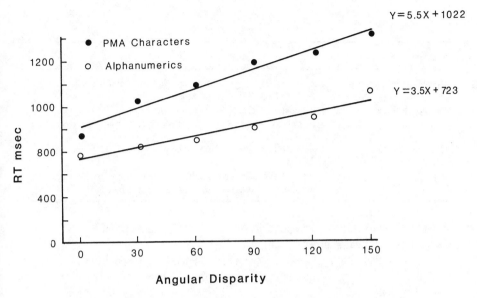

FIG. 7.5.   Mental rotation latency data as a function of stimulus type and angular disparity of stimulus pair.

processing components. An important issue relative to these process estimates is their reliability. Table 7.1 shows both the pattern of intercorrelations among the parameters and their individual split-half reliabilities (along the diagonal). As might be expected, the highest correlations are between measures that are assumed to share some commonality of processing operations. Thus, the intercept for alphanumeric stimuli is highly correlated with the intercept for PMA stimuli, and there is less shared variance between slope and intercept measures. The correlations, even when corrected for attenuation, are not at the level where one

TABLE 7.1
Parameter Intercorrelations and Reliabilities

	Alphanumeric Intercept	PMA Intercept	Alphanumeric Slope	PMA Slope
Alphanumeric intercept	$(.82)^a$	$.77^a$	$.22^b$	.14
PMA intercept		$(.84)^a$	$.52^a$	$.32^c$
Alphanumeric slope			$(.87)^a$	$.72^a$
PMA slope				$(.82)^a$

$^a p < .001.$
$^b p < .05.$
$^c p < .01.$

TABLE 7.2
Parameter Descriptions

Parameter Label	Process and Operational Definition
Alphanumeric intercept	Time to encode, compare, and respond to alphanumeric stimuli; intercept of alphanumeric linear function.
Intercept difference	Additional time to encode and compare unfamiliar PMA stimuli; intercept of PMA linear function minus intercept of alphanumeric linear function.
Alphanumeric slope	Time to rotate alphanumeric stimuli; slope of alphanumeric linear function.
Slope difference	Additional time to rotate unfamiliar PMA stimuli; slope of PMA linear function minus slope of alphanumeric linear function.

should assume that the two slope measures nor the two intercept measures assess completely identical sources of variance.

The slope and intercept measures were used to derive four specific parameters that formed the basis of the analysis of individual differences. These are described in Table 7.2, and they represent: (1) the time to encode, compare, and respond to familiar stimuli; (2) the additional time for encoding and comparing unfamiliar PMA stimuli; (3) the time to rotate familiar alphanumeric stimuli; and (4) the additional time for rotating unfamiliar PMA stimuli. As can be seen in Table 7.3, the simple correlations show that PMA test performance is most highly correlated with the speed of the mental rotation process for familiar stimuli and the processes associated with encoding and comparing unfamiliar stimuli (i.e., the intercept difference parameter). The multiple regression analysis shows that the slope difference parameter (i.e., the additional time to

TABLE 7.3
Correlational Results with PMA as Criterion

Predictor	Simple r	Multiple Regression F	β
Error rate	$-.18$	2.37	$-.15$
Alphanumeric intercept	$-.24$	2.83	$-.15$
Intercept difference	$-.41^a$	4.90^b	$-.24$
Alphanumeric slope	$-.42^a$	5.11^b	$-.26$
Slope difference	$-.14$	4.67^b	$-.20$

$$R = .57$$
$$R^2 = .32$$

[a] $p < .01$.
[b] $p < .05$.

rotate unfamiliar PMA stimuli) is also a significant predictor of PMA performance. Two additional points must be made relative to the results of the multiple regression analysis. First, the least important latency parameter for predicting performance is the intercept for alphanumeric stimuli. Such a result is of interest because this parameter accounts for approximately 50% of the total time to solve a typical rotation item. Second, errors are generally low on both PMA and alphanumeric rotation problems, and individual differences in error rates on experimental items are not related to skill differences on the PMA. Thus, differences in speed rather than accuracy seem to account for spatial aptitude differences as measured by the PMA. The particular speed differences that account for aptitude differences involve a basic mental rotation process and the speed of encoding, comparing, and rotating unfamiliar stimuli. Estimates of these components yield a multiple R of .57 when PMA performance is the criterion.

Although the simple and multiple correlation analyses are informative, they involve sets of assumptions about linear combinations of processing components that may be inappropriate. In essence, there may be a variety of ways in which individuals can achieve moderate to high scores on aptitude tests by trading off one process against another. In an attempt to look at such a possibility, as well as to get a more graphic representation of the differences among our subjects, a series of cluster and scaling analyses were conducted. The first analysis involved the clustering of individuals on the basis of their similarities over the four basic processing parameters. The 99 subjects could be reasonably divided into 12 separate groups. Table 7.4 identifies and orders the groups with respect to mean performance on the PMA. Additional data are provided on error rates on experi-

TABLE 7.4
Group Characteristics in the 2-Dimensional Mental
Rotation Study

Group	Mean PMA	Mean Error Rate	Males	Females
A	53.4	14.0	9	4
B	49.9	10.6	2	5
C	48.7	11.6	7	2
D	47.7	6.0	3	6
E	43.7	9.7	4	2
F	42.8	6.0	4	1
G	40.7	13.4	1	6
H	40.0	21.7	2	3
I	39.0	10.0	3	5
J	37.8	7.1	3	5
K	31.2	12.0	4	1
L	27.7	12.0	4	11

mental items and the total N in each group as well as on the distribution of males and females. The similarities among the groups were analyzed by using INDSCAL, and a clear picture emerged with respect to the group relationships and dimensions. Each of the three dimensions represented a speed continuum for: (1) the rotation of familiar alphanumerics; (2) the additional rotation time for unfamiliar PMA stimuli; and (3) the additional time to encode and compare unfamiliar PMA stimuli. Figure 7.6 shows the group patterning for each pair of dimensions and the results of a group-cluster analysis. The separate figures have been drawn so that the upper right quadrant represents above average speed on both dimensions; the lower left quadrant represents below average speed on both dimensions.

The combined cluster and multidimensional scaling analyses clearly indicate that the groups with the highest average PMA performance consistently appear in the upper right quadrant (groups A–E); the groups with the lowest average PMA performance consistently appear in the lower and/or leftmost quadrants (groups J–L). The four groups with intermediate levels of performance (groups F–I) form two different clusters that are average on some dimensions and above or below average on others. Some of the differences among groups also seem to be linked to sex differences as well as possible speed-accuracy trade-offs as evidenced by high or low error rates on the experimental items. Most importantly, the analyses indicate that superior performance on the spatial-aptitude measure is generally associated with greater speed in all the different components of processing. Intermediate performance typically involves weakness in one or perhaps two components. The source of the difficulty can vary over individuals and groups. Poor performance seems to involve extreme weakness in two or all three major processing components.

The regression analysis, cluster analysis, and multidimensional scaling data that were obtained by Pellegrino et al. (1979) suggest some of the important

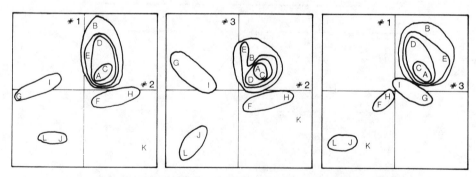

FIG. 7.6. Multidimensional scaling representations of groups differing in latency parameters and PMA performance. Dimension 1 represents additional time to encode and compare unfamiliar stimuli. Dimension 2 represents additional time to rotate unfamiliar stimuli. Dimension 3 represents time to rotate familiar stimuli.

processing components that contribute to overall individual differences in performance on spatial-relations tasks such as the PMA. The data also indicate that there may be a variety of ways in which individuals can achieve low, moderate, and high scores on such tests. A number of issues remain to be addressed with respect to the group and individual differences that were found, particularly with regard to the encoding, comparison, and rotation of the unfamiliar PMA stimuli. One issue is why such stimuli take longer to rotate and show greater variability with respect to the duration of the rotation process. Related to this is the question of why some individuals have such difficulty in processing these stimuli. One hypothesis is that for unfamiliar stimuli, and perhaps also for familiar stimuli, rotation may be a composite of several processes rather than an holistic analogue process as some have postulated (e.g., Shepard, 1975). The solution of even a simple mental rotation problem may involve repetitive processing of a series of separate stimulus elements. Such an assumption can begin to explain why alphanumerics, which may be holistically processed given the availability of a long-term memory representation, are rotated more rapidly than PMA stimuli. The latter may often require stimulus fractionation prior to rotation. Individuals who show particularly long latencies for rotating such stimuli may be forced to execute a rotation process several times because of their inability to achieve a sufficiently stable internal representation that can be operated on holistically. Similarly, the additional time to encode and compare unfamiliar PMA stimuli may be due to the need to execute a comparison process for each separate stimulus element that is rotated. What we are suggesting is that individual differences in spatial ability may emanate from fundamental representational and "visual memory" skills that affect the total time and course of item processing. We consider this possibility in greater detail in the context of other individual difference data to be presented subsequently.

Sex Differences

Sex differences are found on many psychometric measures of spatial aptitude, including spatial-relations tests such as the PMA (McGee, 1979b; Thurstone, 1958). The typical finding is that females score lower than males, and such a trend was also evident in the data just reported on individual differences in PMA performance. Much of the research on sex differences in spatial aptitude has focused on several biological factors that might account for these differences. One possibility that has been considered is that sex differences in spatial aptitude may be attributable to a sex-linked recessive gene (e.g., Bock & Kolakowski, 1973; Boles, 1980). Another possibility relates to androgyny and sex differences in the gonadal hormones such as estrogen and testosterone. An hypothesized quadratic relationship between testosterone levels and spatial ability in adults has recently been verified by Cantoni (1981). One reason for exploring a possible hormonal basis for sex differences in spatial ability is evidence that reliable test differences do not appear until early adolescence and then are maintained throughout adulthood (Maccoby & Jacklin, 1974). Other research has investigated differences in lateralization of the cerebral hemispheres as a basis for sex differences in spatial aptitude (Harris, 1978; Kail & Siegel, 1978).

Only recently, however, have investigators attempted to identify the specific cognitive processes that are implicated in sex differences in spatial aptitude. For example Metzler and Shepard (1974), reported a series of experiments in which subjects processed pairs of abstract three-dimensional objects, of the type shown in Fig. 7.1, that differed in orientation by up to 180°. Women tended to have steeper slopes (i.e., slower mental rotation), but the effects were not significant. In one experiment, women also had nonsignificantly greater intercepts and error rates. Interpretation of these findings, however, is complicated by the fact that subjects in the experiments were selected on the basis of their high scores on two psychometric measures of spatial ability.

Tapley and Bryden (1977) conducted several experiments similar to those of Metzler and Shepard (1974). Two of these involved concrete rather than abstract three-dimensional stimuli. In both studies, women had nonsignificantly larger intercepts and, in one, women were less accurate. In a third experiment, the Metzler–Shepard abstract stimuli were used. Women had significantly steeper slopes than men and had nonsignificantly greater intercepts. Differences in accuracy favoring males emerged in one analysis of the error data but not in the second.

In these studies, we see trends rather than definitive patterns. For the abstract three-dimensional stimuli, women generally had steeper slopes and, less frequently, larger intercepts and error rates. For the realistic three-dimensional stimuli, sex differences seem to be limited to a small difference in the intercept. Perhaps the most revealing aspect of these two studies, then, is the finding that sex differences in spatial ability may be dependent on the type of stimuli presented, with sex differences more likely with unfamiliar stimuli. To evaluate this possibility, Kail, Carter, and Pellegrino (1979) tested a different and totally random sample of 51 men and 53 women in the paradigm described in the previous section, in which pairs of PMA characters and alphanumeric symbols that differed in orientation by 0–150° were presented.

As before, the principal data of interest are the slopes and intercepts of the functions relating response times on correct responses to the difference in stimulus orientation. However, two ancillary findings should be mentioned first. Errors were infrequent for both males (6%) and females (5%). Also, although errors increased as a function of the difference in orientation, this increase was comparable for men and women. In short, men and women were both capable of performing the task.

Equally important was the finding that the latency data were quite linear for both men and women. Linear functions fit to the group data account for 90–97% of the variance in latencies. When functions were calculated for individuals, latencies from men on alphanumeric stimuli were fit slightly more accurately by the linear model than were latencies on PMA characters (r^2s of .75 and .72), whereas the reverse was true of females (r^2s of .66 and .77). More important, however, is the fact that the linear model accounts for a large proportion of the variance in subjects' response times, which suggests that both men and women were solving the problems using the processes described by Cooper and Shepard (1973).

Of greater interest are the findings for the slopes and intercepts. The intercepts for men and women were quite similar on both the alphanumeric stimuli (760 msec vs. 814) and the PMA characters (1064 msec vs. 1101). This suggests that males and females executed encoding, comparison, and response processes at comparable rates, although because the intercept is a composite measure, a sex difference in only one of these processes might not be evident in our data. An intercept difference parameter also fails to show any evidence of a sex difference.

Turning now to the slope parameter, males mentally rotated stimuli more rapidly than did females. Further, the sex difference, although reliable for both types of stimuli, was greater for PMA characters (4.61 msec/deg vs. 6.66) than for alphanumeric stimuli (2.93 msec/deg vs. 3.88). Thus, not only was there a sex difference in the time to rotate familiar stimuli, but there was also a sex difference in the additional time needed to rotate unfamiliar PMA stimuli. Analysis of individual differences in slopes within each sex shed considerable light on the nature of the sex difference in the means for slopes. Figure 7.7 shows the distribution of slope values within each sex. For men, the distributions for both alphanumeric and PMA stimuli were generally normal, with some positive skew. For women, the distribution of alphanumeric slopes differed significantly from normality due to considerable positive skew. A similar pattern, in extreme form, was found in the women's distribution of slopes for PMA stimuli. The distribution was clearly bimodal: One mode, 3.5 msec/deg, approximates the male mode of 4.5 msec/deg. The second mode, 8.5 msec/deg, was essentially outside the range of the male distribution. Stated another way, 70% of the women had slopes in the range of the male distribution, whereas 30% fell outside that distribution.

Thus, the findings of Kail, Carter, and Pellegrino (1979) implicate a single component of spatial processing—the rate of mental rotation—as the major locus of sex differences in performance on a prototypic measure of simple spatial relations (see also Petrusic, Varro, & Jamieson, 1979). Men mentally rotated stimuli, especially unfamiliar ones, at a much faster rate than women did. Furthermore, this sex difference in average rate of mental rotation was attributable to greater variability among women. In all other aspects of processing—including the ability to perform the task (error data), the extent to which their data conformed to the predictions of the Cooper and Shepard (1973) model (r^2 values), and the estimates of encoding, comparison, and response processes—men and women were quite alike. The Kail, Carter, and Pellegrino (1979) analysis of sex

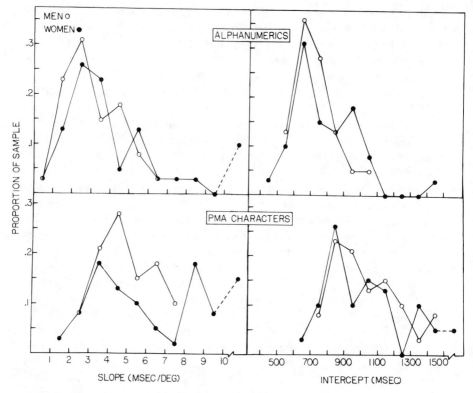

FIG. 7.7.   Frequency distributions of slopes and intercepts on alphanumeric and PMA stimuli plotted separately for men and women. From Kail, Carter, and Pellegrino (1979).

differences also serves to emphasize two other points. First, the majority of the variance in performance was associated with individual differences rather than with a sex difference per se. This is most obvious in the comparison of the slope distributions. Second, finding a sex difference in the rate of mental rotation such that certain women seem to execute this process more slowly than others does not constitute an explanation of the effect. One possibility is that individuals exhibiting longer times execute a rotation process several times and/or behave more cautiously in responding. Given that there are important differences in the rate of mental rotation, it remains to be determined if they are associated with identifiable differences in the strategy or process sequence for performing the task.

Developmental Change

There is a large body of literature in developmental psychology on spatial perspective taking that originated with Piaget and Inhelder's (1956) work on the "three mountains" task. In this problem, a child is shown a model depicting three mountains, each with a distinctive object at the summit. The child is asked to imagine how the mountains appear to a doll, who is placed in several positions around the model. The child responds by selecting the photograph that depicts the doll's view.

Piaget and Inhelder (1956) found that prior to 7 or 8 years of age, children selected photographs corresponding to their own view of the mountains rather than to the view of the doll. Beginning at 7 or 8 years, children realize that the doll's view differs from their own, but they often select an incorrect photograph because they relate the doll's position to one mountain rather than to the entire group. Not until 9 or 10 years of age do children consistently select the appropriate photograph. According to Piaget and Inhelder (1956), this demonstrates the knowledge that: "to each position of the observer there corresponds a particular set of left–right, before–behind relations between the objects constituting the group of mountains. These are governed by the projections and sections appropriate to the visual plane of the observer [p. 241]."

The literature stemming from Piaget and Inhelder's (1956) findings has attempted to reveal conditions that would facilitate young children's ability to coordinate perspectives (e.g., Liben, 1978); to determine the relations between perspective taking in which an array is stationary and the observer moves versus rotation problems in which a stationary observer anticipates the appearance of an array after it moves (e.g., Huttenlocher & Presson, 1973); and research concerning rotation and perspective-taking skill in large-scale spaces (e.g., Hardwick, McIntyre, & Pick, 1976). Common to much of this research is an emphasis on spatial processing in young children. According to the Piagetian account, the critical developmental changes occur between 4 and 10 years of age, so adolescents and adults typically are not studied, and, when they are, it is primarily to provide a baseline against which to assess the performance of the younger children of interest. Yet, the fact that there are consistent individual differences in spatial aptitude among adolescents and adults suggests that, although all children may acquire the rudiments of spatial processing by middle childhood, development in this realm continues, with individuals ultimately attaining different levels of skill.

To investigate the development of spatial processing in late childhood and adolescence, we (Kail, Pellegrino, & Carter, 1980) tested 37 8-year-olds, 22 9-year-olds, 44 11-year-olds, and 58 19-year-olds using the general procedures described previously. That is, two versions of a stimulus—a standard and a comparison—were presented on each trial, and the comparison stimulus was rotated 0–150° from the standard. Subjects determined if the standard and comparison stimuli would be identical or mirror images (i.e., reflections) if the standard and comparison stimuli were to appear at the same orientation. On 72 trials, the stimuli were pairs of alphanumeric symbols; on 72, they were characters from the PMA.

As was the case in our study of sex differences (Kail, Carter, & Pellegrino, 1979), the error data and r^2 values, although not the parameters of primary consideration, are of more than passing interest. Errors were infrequent at all age levels, with values of 6%, 8%, 4%, and 5% for 8-, 9-, 11-, and 19-year-olds, respectively. Consistent with the Piagetian position, by middle childhood children are quite capable of anticipating the appearance of an object that is to be rotated. Similar developmental invariance was generally the case for r^2 values as well. The r^2 values for alphanumerics based on group data were .91, .87, .91, and .94 for 8-, 9-, 11-, and 19-year-olds, respectively; corresponding values for PMA characters were .80, .97, .90, and .96. The r^2 values were smaller when derived from functions fit to individuals' data. Mean r^2s ranged from .68 to .78, with the exception of the 8-year-olds' mean r^2 for PMA characters, which was .52. Thus, with the exception of this one instance, the linear fit was quite good for individuals, indicating that their performance was consistent with the expectations of the Cooper and Shepard (1973) model.

Developmental changes in the parameters of primary interest are depicted in Fig. 7.8, and three features of these data are noteworthy. First, there was a regular developmental change in rate of mental rotation from approximately 7 msec/deg among 8- and 9-year-olds to somewhat less than 4 msec/deg for 19-year-olds. Second, unfamiliar stimuli were rotated approximately 2.5 msec/deg more slowly than alphanumerics by all groups except 8-year-olds, for whom

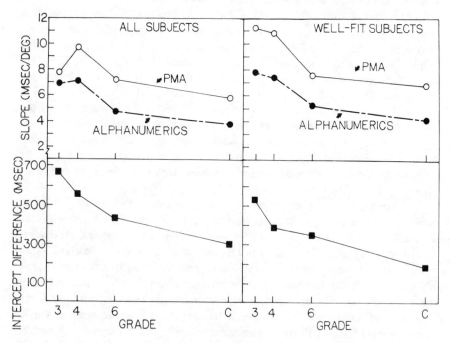

FIG. 7.8.   Mean parameter values for individual subjects plotted as a function of age. From Kail, Pellegrino, and Carter (1980).

interpretation of the parameters is problematic due to the smaller r^2 values. Finally, the difference between the intercepts (i.e., PMA intercept–alphanumeric intercept) also declines systematically over development. Assuming that the response-time component of these two intercepts is the same, then this decline reflects a developmental change in the speed with which unfamiliar stimuli are encoded and compared.

These findings were based on slopes and intercepts computed for all individuals. However, at each age level, there were some individuals whose r^2 values were not significant. In these cases, interpretation of the slope and intercept parameters is not straightforward. Consequently, we repeated the analyses including only individuals with significant r^2 values for both types of stimuli. The percentage of individuals who met this criterion increased developmentally, with values of 38%, 50%, 50%, and 59%, for 8-, 9-, 11-, and 19-year-olds, respectively. However, the pattern of results is remarkably similar to that found when we analyzed the data for all individuals: The mean slope declines with development, as does the mean difference between intercepts. The difference between slopes, in contrast, is essentially constant developmentally, changing less than 1 msec/deg between 8 and 19 years of age.

What factors account for the developmental change observed in the various parameters? Age differences in the slope parameter might reflect a developmental shift toward a more efficient alogorithm for mentally rotating stimuli (a suggestion we examine in detail in the next section). Regarding the greater speed with which older individuals encoded and compared stimuli (i.e., the intercept difference), note that encoding of an alphanumeric stimulus presumably involves the activation of information already stored in long-term memory, whereas encoding of PMA characters involves generating such a pattern anew for each trial. Thus, the age differences may reflect the greater speed with which older individuals construct such internal representations of unfamiliar stimuli.

To this point, we have focused exclusively on change in the average speed with which individual processes are executed at different ages. An important related issue concerns the development of individual differences in spatial skill. We have been particularly interested in: (1) the magnitude of within-age individual variation in the different processing parameters; and (2) whether such within-age individual variation is associated with psychometric performance differences.

Evidence regarding the first of these issues comes from the Kail et al. (1980) study discussed previously. The standard deviations for each of the parameters were comparable for 9-, 11-, and 19-year-olds (8-year-olds are not considered here because of the interpretive problems associated with the low r^2 values). Yet, this similarity is somewhat misleading due to the large developmental changes in the means associated with these standard deviations. A more insightful view of the range of individual variation is provided by the following analysis. We compared the performance of a hypothetical individual in the 5th percentile of his or her age group (i.e., $X + 2$ s.d., because superior performance is associated with smaller parameter values) with that of a person in the 50th percentile. Such comparisons were made for three parameters: the intercept for alphanumeric stimuli, the intercept difference (i.e., PMA intercept–alphanumeric intercept), and the slope for PMA stimuli. The results are shown in Fig. 7.9 in which the parameter values for the hypothetical 5th-percentile person are expressed as a percentage of the value for the 50th-percentile individual (i.e., the group mean).

First, consider the alphanumeric intercept. Values for the 5th percentile are approximately 50% greater than the mean, for all age groups. The intercept difference shows similar developmental invariance, but the 5th-percentile values are more than twice as large as the mean. Quite a different pattern is found for the slope parameter. Among 8-year-olds, the 5th-percentile value is nearly 70% larger than the mean, but, among adults, the value is approximately 110% larger. In short, among young children, the additional time to encode and compare unfamiliar stimuli is the source of greatest individual variation; among adults, these processes plus the rate of mental rotation are equally large sources of

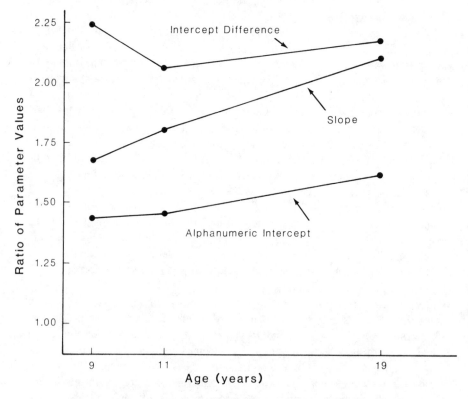

FIG. 7.9.   Parameter values for a hypothetical 5th-percentile individual expressed as multiples of corresponding values for a 50th-percentile individual at each age level.

TABLE 7.5
Correlations Between Parameters
and PMA Scores

Predictor	9-Year-Olds	13-Year-Olds
Slope	$-.23$ $(-.31)^a$	$-.40^b$ $(-.57)$
Intercept	$-.42^b$ $(-.53)$	$-.45^b$ $(-.57)$

[a] Values in parentheses are adjusted for reliability of measures.
[b] $p < .05$.

individual differences. Rate of encoding and comparing alphanumeric stimuli and responding has the smallest range of individual variation at all ages.

In a subsequent study (Kail, Carter, & Pazak, 1979), it was shown that individual differences in these parameters are systematically and differentially related to differences in psychometric test performance. Slope and intercept parameters were estimated for an additional 26 9-year-olds and 42 13-year-olds who were first tested on the PMA Spatial Relations Test, then were given 100 trials in which pairs of PMA stimuli were presented, which differed in orientation by 0–135° in 15° increments. Raw and corrected correlations are depicted in Table 7.5. Consistent with the findings presented in Fig. 7.9, the intercept parameter was significantly correlated with PMA performance for both younger and older children, whereas the slope was correlated only for the older group. Thus, some as yet undetermined combination of speed in encoding, comparison, and response processes is associated with superior spatial skill for both children and adolescents. Presumably, this result is attributable to the special demands of encoding and comparing unfamiliar stimuli, as is the case for adults. In contrast, rate of mental rotation is linked to psychometrically measured ability only for adolescents and adults. It would appear that individual differences in spatial aptitude are initially associated with basic encoding and comparison processes, that such differences persist over development, and that the differences are then accompanied by additional differences in the speed of mentally rotating or transforming the information that has been encoded. These developmental changes in the sources of individual differences are coincident with overall developmental trends indicating general improvement in the encoding, comparison, and rotation of unfamiliar stimuli. Thus, it seems that the overall developmental improvement in mental rotation speed is not uniform over individuals, and thus it may become a primary basis of individual differences in adolescents and adults.

Alternative Process Models

The research described thus far has been based entirely upon the aforementioned Cooper and Shepard (1973) model. Generally, the model has proven quite satisfactory in the sense that it accounts for substantial proportions of variance when applied either to group or individual data. However, in each case, the Cooper and Shepard (1973) model was applied only to judgments for identical pairs; when applied to judgments based on mirror-image pairs, the model encounters difficulties that have led us to revise it.

Data from a study by Carter, Pazak, and Kail (1981) indicate the nature of the problem. In this experiment, 9- and 13-year-olds and adults were shown pairs of PMA stimuli that differed in orientation by 0–135°. Mean latency as a function of the difference in orientation is depicted in Fig. 7.10 for all three age groups. The salient feature in all sets of data is an interaction between orientation and response. On identical pairs, latencies increased as a function of the difference in orientation; on mirror-image pairs, the increase was more gradual and not as regular.

We first fit the Cooper and Shepard (1973) model to the group data in Fig. 7.10 with three parameters: the slope, the intercept for judgments on identical pairs, and the difference between the intercepts for identical and mirror-image pairs, which reflects the time needed to change the response index from "same" to "different." This model accounted for 87%, 87%, and 85% of the variance in latency data for 9- and 13-year-olds and adults, respectively. Although accounting for highly significant proportions of variance, this model is less than completely satisfactory because it predicts that the slope for identical and mirror-image pairs should be the same, but in all three sets of data the slope is greater for identical pairs.

Our efforts to modify the Cooper and Shepard (1973) model were guided by two considerations. First, some individuals reported that after rotating mirror-image pairs to a common orientation, they did not immediately respond "dif-

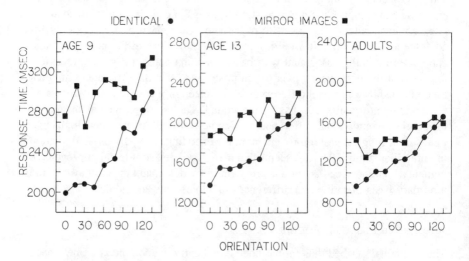

FIG. 7.10. Mean latency data for "same" and "different" judgment items as a function of age and angular disparity.

ferent.'' Instead, they would attempt to discover some other way in which rotation (in the picture plane) would result in identical stimuli. Second, on tasks like the present one in which individuals are encouraged to respond rapidly, subjects often impose deadlines on themselves (e.g., Ollman & Billington, 1972). If the self-imposed deadline is reached, processing in halted, and the individual responds on the basis of processing completed prior to the deadline.

Modifying the Cooper and Shepard (1973) model to reflect these notions resulted in the simple ''deadline'' model depicted in Fig. 7.11. This model differs from that of Cooper and Shepard in its description of processing of mirror-image pairs. On such pairs, subjects continue processing until they reach a deadline, at which point they respond ''different.'' Thus, the model includes three parameters: the slope and intercept from the Cooper and Shepard (1973) model plus a deadline value.

The deadline model accounted for 86%, 82%, and 80% of the variance in latency for the three age groups. Hence, it does not fare as well as the Cooper and Shepard model in terms of the proportion of variance it explains. Further, the deadline model predicts flat latency functions for mirror-image pairs, which clearly is not the case for the data in Fig. 7.10.

One possibility is that the group data in Fig. 7.10 reflect a mixture of individuals using the two algorithms. That is, if both algorithms were used by a substantial number of individuals at each age level, then latencies on mirror-image pairs would increase as a function of orientation, but not as rapidly as on identical pairs. We evaluated this possibility by fitting both models to individual's data. The percentage of individuals at the three age levels who were best fit with the Cooper and Shepard model were 38, 35, and 44. Comparable percentages for the deadline model were 15, 24, and 25. Finally, 26, 21, and 13% were fit equally well by the two models. Thus, there were consistent individual differences at each age level in the algorithms used to solve problems like those on the PMA, but there was no evidence of developmental change in the preferred algorithm.

One other outcome of this experiment is noteworthy. Some adults' data resembled the group data in Fig. 7.10 in that latencies increased linearly for both identical and mirror-image pairs, but more rapidly for identical pairs. A single change in the deadline model makes it compatible with such results at both the individual subject and group level, as well as with typical findings for mental rotation of familiar alphanumeric symbols. The latter type of stimuli produce equivalent slopes for both identical and mirror-image pairs (Carpenter & Eisenberg, 1978; Cooper & Shepard, 1973). The change is illustrated in Fig. 7.11 and involves a more elaborate comparison process—one in the spirit of models proposed by Atkinson and Juola (1974) and Kreuger (1978). Put simply, the comparison process can now have three outcomes: (1) pairs can be judged as identical, in which case processing ceases with a ''same'' response; (2) pairs can be judged as different, in which case processing terminates with a ''different'' response; or (3) pairs can be judged as indeterminate, in which case processing

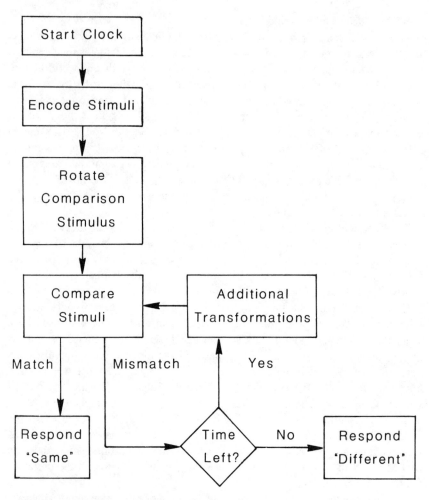

Pure Deadline Model

FIG. 7.11.   Representations of the pure deadline and modified deadline process models for mental rotation performance.

iterates. Thus, this model is, in effect, a compromise between the previous two, with the iterative processing of the deadline model presumed to occur on some but not all trials. The advantage of such a model at the outset is that the slope of the latency function for mirror-image pairs can vary from being identical to the slope for identical pairs (the outcome when no pairs are judged indeterminate) to perfectly flat (the outcome when all pairs are judged indeterminate). This "modified deadline" model emerged as the preferred model for 18% of the adults but not for 9- or 13-year-olds. The model also provides the "best" fit to the overall group mean data shown in Fig. 7.10. The latter result, however, is artifactual

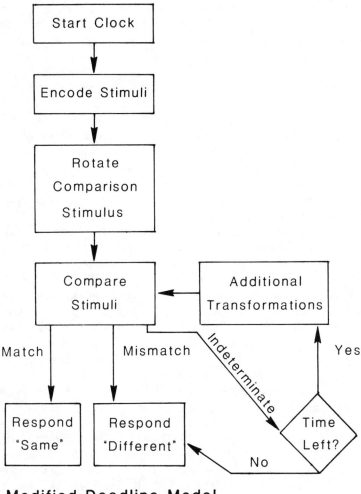

Modified Deadline Model

FIG. 7.11.   (*Continued*)

because the modified deadline model is not the preferred model at the individual subject level. This anomaly illustrates the need for evaluating process models at the individual subject level in addition to evaluations at the group mean level.

It must be emphasized that the presence of model or strategy differences as another possible source of individual differences does not call into question the data and interpretations of individual, sex, and developmental differences presented in previous sections. The model differences pertain to the sequence of processing operations that may occur for different judgment trials. The slope and intercept values obtained for "same" judgment trials remain unaffected by the need to include the assumption of a comparison process that can lead to indeterminate outcomes or a response deadline. What remains to be determined is whether individual differences in reference test performance are systematically related to the presence (and values) of such processes in addition to the demonstrated relationships to encoding, comparison, and rotation speed.

One final comment is also required relative to the presence of a more complex comparison process with an accompanying response deadline. We have implied that the need to consider such a set of processes and their probability of influencing different judgment-latency data is a function of stimulus familiarity or complexity. When two stimuli are being compared, one of which has been mentally transformed, there may exist various levels of uncertainty about the failure to establish their identity. When the stimuli are familiar, as is the case for alphanumerics, there is little or no question. An R and $Я$ do not correspond. The likelihood that the mental rotation process is at fault is generally low. However, this is not the case when dealing with unfamiliar, nonlabelable stimuli such as the PMA characters. When two stimuli fail to correspond following rotation, the individual may question the adequacy of the rotation process and attempt to execute it again. If all attempts to achieve congruence fail and the deadline is reached, then the individual responds negatively. The implication of this analysis is that the difference between "same" and "different" judgment slopes should systematically increase as one moves along a continuum of stimulus familiarity and/or complexity. Evidence for this type of orderly progression is provided by some of our adult data. A set of 42 subjects who received an equivalent number of same and different judgment trials on both alphanumeric and PMA stimuli provided the following overall mean slope values: alphanumeric "same" = 3.49; alphanumeric "Different" = 3.04; PMA "same" = 5.42; PMA "different" = 3.39. These data confirm previous studies showing little in the way of a slope difference for alphanumeric "same" and "different" judgment trials and a substantial slope difference for PMA "same" and "different" judgment trials. These results lead to two further predictions that are borne out in our analysis of complex spatial-relations tasks that follow: (1) the slope difference for "same" and "different" judgment trials should be even larger than that obtained for PMA stimuli; (2) aspects of different judgment processing will become increasingly important in understanding individual differences.

PROCESS ANALYSES
OF COMPLEX SPATIAL RELATIONS

Studies of different spatial-relations tasks have highlighted important similarities and differences in performance that are related to stimulus complexity. This is most readily illustrated by the data shown in Fig. 7.12, which contrasts performance observed in the rotation of simple alphanumeric stimuli with that obtained

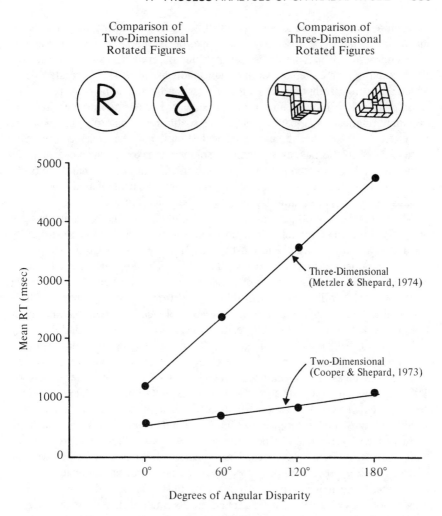

FIG. 7.12. Prototypical latency data for simple and complex mental rotation problems. From Pellegrino and Glaser (1979).

for the rotation of more complex, three-dimensional block configurations. Both stimulus types produce systematic linear increases in solution latency as a function of angular disparity of the stimulus pair. In both cases, the slope has been generally interpreted as an index of the rate of mental rotation. The important differences between stimuli rest in the greater intercept and slope values that are observed. These differences far exceed any differences we have previously reported for the contrast between alphanumeric and PMA stimuli. The higher intercept obtained for the three-dimensional block configurations can be readily interpreted in terms of longer encoding and comparison times associated with these more complex, abstract stimuli. What is of greater concern, however, is the magnitude of the slope difference. The slope for the three-dimensional stimulus is several orders of magnitude greater than that observed for alphanumerics (or PMA stimuli). There are several important implications of such a result, one of which relates to assumptions about the processes reflected in the slope (e.g., Just & Carpenter, 1976). We return to this issue later. For our present purposes, the important implication is that the solution of spatial-relations problems involving the rotation of complex three-dimensional stimuli may be considerably more difficult (i.e., if the latency of problem solution is taken as an index of difficulty). In terms of a speed-power continuum, it certainly seems that these problems may represent a significant shift toward involvement of both speed and accuracy of process execution as aspects of individual differences.

The available data on performance in this complex spatial-relations task are relatively limited and do not permit strong conclusions relative to task difficulty and individual differences. The most thorough analysis of performance in this task was reported by Metzler and Shepard (1974). The emphasis in their studies was on analyzing a small number of subjects who were preselected for their high levels of spatial ability (i.e., their ability to perform the task). Even so, there appeared to be substantial differences between subjects in certain parameters of task performance, as noted earlier relative to sex differences. Similarly, Tapley and Bryden (1978) obtained evidence of differences among individuals in processing parameters and error rates. However, no attempt was made to link performance measures to aptitude differences as measured by reference tests. The one major attempt to do so was a study by Egan (1978), which examined the performance of Naval pilot and flight officer candidates. His data indicated significant individual differences in both speed and accuracy measures that were correlated with reference test performance as well as achievement and performance scores in training courses. Unfortunately, his range of ability was restricted, and his processing measures tended to be somewhat unreliable.

Another issue that is typically ignored in most studies dealing with mental rotation of these complex, three-dimensional stimuli is the contrast between performance on same–different judgment trials. The data for "different" judgment trials are seldom reported, partly because they tend to be "less reliable." We suspect that the linear trend observed for "same" judgments is neither as obvious nor of the same magnitude for "different" judgments. However, such a result would be important given our earlier discussion of "different" judgment processing for unfamiliar and complex stimuli. An indeterminate comparison process and the imposition of a response deadline are perhaps most likely to occur when individuals must compare these stimuli. The reasons for increased uncertainty about the mismatch between two stimuli include the fact that complementary stimuli are used to create "different" judgment pairs and rotation about any of the three major axes is a possibility.

In an attempt to examine performance on complex spatial-relations problems, Pellegrino and Mumaw (1980) conducted a study of individual differences that systematically explored these issues. The subjects were 56 college students (27 males and 29 females) who represented the entire range of spatial ability as measured by a battery of reference tests. One of the reference tests was modeled after the one developed by Vandenberg (see Fig. 7.1), which used stimuli of the type generated by Metzler and Shepard (1974). But rather than following the format used by Vandenberg, our test contained problems that represented individual stimulus pairs. For each pair, the subject marked an answer sheet indicating whether the stimuli were the same or different. A total of 72 pairs was presented with a total time limit of 6 minutes. No individuals completed all problems within the time period, and the average score (after correction for guessing) was 33.7 with a range of 11 to 69. The subjects were then individually tested in an experiment that included 168 separate trials. On each trial, a pair of stimuli was presented, and the subject's task was to respond "same" or "different" as rapidly and accurately as possible. The 168 trials represented eight different block configurations, rotation about the X, Y, or Z axes, and rotation values that ranged from 0 to 180° in 30° increments. Equal numbers of same–different judgment trials were used.

The individual subjects differed substantially in terms of both their latency and accuracy data. Rather than reporting overall means for the entire sample, we have chosen to illustrate performance in the tasks in terms of the top and bottom quartiles of our distribution of subjects based upon their performance on the paper-and-pencil reference test. Figure 7.13 shows the relevant latency and accuracy data that were obtained for these extreme groups. The points plotted in Fig. 7.13 represent group means. As can be seen, both groups showed the typical pattern for "same" judgments with a highly significant linear trend. The least squares regression lines are also shown, and the r^2 value for each group was above .97. Also apparent in the figure is the substantial difference between the two groups in the slope of the linear function. The ratio of slopes is 2.25:1, whereas the ratio of "same" judgment intercepts is 1.27:1. Another important aspect of the data involves performance on "different" judgment trials. For both groups of subjects the linear trend was significant, $r^2 = .89$, albeit providing a less adequate fit than was the case for "same" judgments. The slope for "different" judgments is substantially shallower than the slope for "same" judgments, and the ratio of different-to-same judgment slopes is roughly equivalent for both groups ($\approx .65$). When the two skill groups are compared with respect to "different" judgment performance, the ratio of slopes is 2.42:1, and the ratio of intercepts is 1.75:1.

The mean data indicate several measures of performance that differentiate the upper and lower skill groups. However, both groups show the predicted pattern whereby the slope for "different" judgment trials is significantly shallower, with convergence of the two functions at the 180° value. These results support the assumption that there is a significant probability that the comparison process on "different" judgment trials yields an indeterminate outcome leading to subsequent processing that finally terminates when a response deadline is reached.

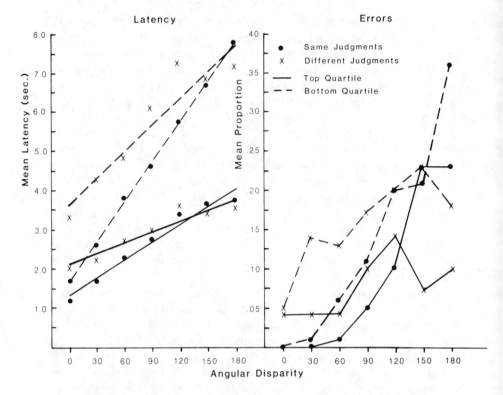

FIG. 7.13.   Mean latency and error data for "same" and "different" judgment
items for top and bottom quartile subjects.

When such a modified deadline model is fit to the same–different judgment data
for each group, the values obtained for the probability of an indeterminate outcome and the deadline were .37 and 3326 msec for the skilled subjects and .32
and 7668 msec for the less skilled subjects. The r^2 and RMSD values were .95
and 180 for the skilled subjects and .97 and 335 for the less skilled subjects.

Another measure of performance shown in Fig. 7.13 is error rate. Within each
group, the probability of error significantly increased as a function of angular
disparity on "same" judgment trials. The most marked increase appears following the 90° rotation value, and there appears to be a difference between the
groups in the likelihood of error at high rotation values. The "different" judgment trials show less of a relationship between error rate and angular disparity
and a larger overall difference between the two skill groups. The shallower
error-rate function for "different" judgment trials in both groups is also in
accord with the assumptions of a response deadline. If a deadline is reached on a
significant number of "different" judgment trials and if the subject employs a
response rule of different for such cases, then errors should be more uniform over

rotation values. If the subject employs a guessing strategy, then errors should also be uniform but equivalent to or higher than the values observed for "same" judgment trials.

Linear functions were also fit to individual subject latency data and, as expected, the fits were more variable but still highly significant. Table 7.6 provides illustrative individual subject data by again contrasting the top and bottom skill groups, whose mean performance was just illustrated. Means and standard deviations are shown, and it is apparent that there is considerably more variation within the lower skill group than within the skilled group for almost every measure of performance. The major exception involves the r^2 values obtained for linear fits to both "same" and "different" judgment latency data. Error data are also illustrated in the Table, and it appears that the less skilled individuals have more difficulty with "different" than "same" judgment pairs and that the greatest difference between skill groups is for such pairs.

The superior fit of the modified deadline model at the group level was not an artifact of averaging over subjects. The data of each subject within the top and bottom quartiles were fit by the original Cooper and Shepard (1973) model, the simple deadline model, and the modified deadline model. For all subjects, the simple deadline model provided the poorest fit to the data. In the top quartile group, 13 of 14 individuals were best fit by the modified deadline model with the increase in r^2 ranging from .02 to .19 and an average r^2 of .84. The remaining subject's data were fit equally well by the Cooper and Shepard model and the modified deadline model. A similar pattern was found within the bottom quartile group, with 12 of 14 individuals showing a best fit for the modified deadline model. The increase in r^2 ranged from .01 to .21, and the average r^2 was .86. Of the remaining two subjects, one showed no difference in the fits of the Cooper and Shepard and modified deadline model, whereas the other showed a slight superiority of the Cooper and Shepard model. Thus, the individual subject data

TABLE 7.6
Characteristics of Individual Subject Performance

		Mean		Standard Deviation	
		Top Quartile	Bottom Quartile	Top Quartile	Bottom Quartile
Slope	Same	15.03	33.80	5.16	25.85
	Different	9.43	22.78	4.28	18.93
Intercept	Same	1313	1666	283	543
	Different	2064	3618	388	2138
r^2	Same	.88	.89	.12	.12
	Different	.77	.67	.13	.22
Errors	Same	.09	.14	.08	.06
	Different	.07	.17	.04	.12

support the modeling at the group level, in contrast to what was observed earlier in modeling performance on simple spatial-relations problems.

The data of all subjects were used for a complete analysis of individual differences. Slope and intercept values for "same" and "different" judgment trials were determined as well as error rates on both trial types. Table 7.7 shows the pattern of intercorrelations as well as reliability data (along the diagonal). The reliabilities were high for all measures except the "same" judgment intercept. The conclusions that emerge from this pattern are: (1) errors on same–different judgment trials are only partially related; (2) the intercept for "same" judgment trials assesses components of performance that are largely unrelated to the other latency measures; (3) the components of processing required on "different" judgment trials are highly related to the processes assessed by the slope for "same" judgment trials; and (4) greater processing speed is associated with higher errors (i.e., there is a slight speed-accuracy trade-off across individuals).

Each of the latency and error measures was used in simple and multiple regression analyses with reference test performance as the criterion. The results of these analyses are shown in Table 7.8. As might be expected given the data already presented, the slope-same, slope-different, and intercept-different parameters all showed approximately the same significant simple correlation with reference test scores. However, when entered in the multiple regression analysis, only the slope-different measure was significant. The "same" judgment intercept showed a marginal simple correlation with the reference test but a highly significant contribution in the multiple regression. Finally, the overall speed-accuracy trade-off produced nonsignificant simple correlations between error rates and reference test performance. However, the multiple regression analysis indicated that "different" judgment errors were also significantly related to reference test performance. The overall multiple R was quite high. The results of the simple and multiple regression analyses are consistent with the more global contrast between top and bottom quartile subjects shown earlier.

TABLE 7.7
Parameter Intercorrelations and Reliabilities

	Slope Same	Slope Different	Intercept Same	Intercept Different	Errors Same	Errors Different
Slope same	$(.90)^a$	$.82^a$	$-.23$	$.74^a$	$-.25$	$-.22$
Slope different		$(.82)^a$	$-.14$	$.60^a$	$-.30^b$	$-.32^b$
Intercept same			$(.44)^b$	$.05$	$.19$	$.24$
Intercept different				$(.94)^a$	$-.27^b$	$-.11$
Errors same					$(.83)^a$	$.45^c$
Errors different						$(.81)^a$

$^a p < .001.$
$^b p < .05.$
$^c p < .01.$

TABLE 7.8
Correlational Results with Three-Dimensional
Rotation Test as Criterion

Predictor	Simple r	Multiple Regression	
		F	β
Slope same	$-.53^a$	<1	$-.12$
Slope different	$-.57^a$	11.09^b	$-.54$
Intercept same	$-.25$	7.76^b	$-.28$
Intercept different	$-.54^a$	1.35	$-.17$
Errors same	$-.03$	<1	$-.06$
Errors different	$-.23$	11.72^b	$-.36$
		$R = .79$	
		$R^2 = .63$	

$^a p < .001.$
$^b p < .01.$

The analysis of individual differences supports two general predictions relative to performance in complex spatial-relations tasks. First, individual differences are a result of both speed and accuracy of processing. This is consistent with the assumption that a speed-power continuum is appropriate not only for the contrast between spatial-relations and visualization tasks but also within the domain of spatial-relations tasks. Not only do three-dimensional mental rotation problems take longer to solve, but they are more difficult, and this difficulty contributes to differences among individuals in reference test scores. The second general prediction is that in more complex spatial-processing tasks, individual differences are also related to the special processing demands associated with making "different" judgments. The exact nature of these processing demands remains to be specified, but it appears to involve criteria and confidence relative to detecting differences between stimuli.

The results that we have obtained for sources of individual differences in task performance are in general agreement with those previously reported by Egan (1978). The identification of slope and intercept differences suggests possible components of processing that may serve to differentiate individuals. However, the major problem with such data is that they are relatively crude with respect to precise models of task performance. We have avoided the assumption that the slope measure for "same" judgment trials assesses only mental rotation speed, whereas the intercept assesses encoding, comparison, and motor response speed. The reason for doing so relates to some logical problems associated with such assumptions. The nature of the problem is best illustrated by again referring to the contrast between simple and complex mental rotation data as shown in Fig. 7.12. If the slope of both functions is interpreted as an index of mental rotation speed, then, logically, we cannot be referring to the same psychological process if process invariance is also to be maintained as an assumption. There are at least two possible interpretations of the very substantial slope difference that exists. One is that the process of mental rotation can assume a very wide range of values and that it is dependent on the nature of the information being operated on. Using the analogy between mental and physical rotation, heavier and/or larger objects are more difficult to move and thus are moved more slowly through physical space given some constant force ($f = ma$). Thus, perhaps mental rotation is similar to physical rotation, and three-dimensional stimuli are "mentally heavier" and more difficult to move through psychological space. Such an explanation begs the question, however. Leaving such analogies aside, perhaps it is to be concluded that basic or elementary cognitive processes such as mental rotation are not invariant but contextually determined.

An alternative explanation of the substantial slope differences that are found for simple and complex spatial-relations problems is that the slope obtained for processing complex stimuli is a composite of several processes or represents several iterations of the same process. This alternative receives support in the analysis of performance conducted by Just and Carpenter (1976). They examined eye-movement patterns and fixation durations in the solution of three-dimensional rotation problems. Their data led them to suggest a more complex model of performance than the one postulated for the solution of simple spatial-relation tasks. The basic processes specified in their model include encoding, search, rotation, comparison, confirmation, and response. The slope of the function for "same" judgments is a composite of several processes, each of which increases in duration as a function of angular disparity. These include search and a combined rotation and comparison process. The intercept of the function for "same" judgments seems to reflect encoding, confirmation, and response processes. In their subsequent eye-movement analysis of performance on simple spatial-relations tasks (Carpenter & Just, 1978), they were able to confirm the validity of the Cooper and Shepard (1973) model and show that estimates of the basic rotation and comparison components were equivalent for the two types of stimuli. Thus, there does appear to be invariance in the duration of the mental rotation process, at least as determined for a small sample of individuals who are capable of performing mental rotation tasks.

Ideally, the process analysis of individual differences in spatial-relations tasks, particularly complex spatial relations, should involve the estimation of individual rather than conglomerate process values. To do so in complex spatial-relations tasks requires the use of different problem types that vary in their process composition. Such a design permits the use of subtractive logic to estimate each process and to decompose the slope measure into separate components. We provide an illustration of such an analytic strategy in the next section on spatial visualization. At present, this type of task decomposition has not been done for complex spatial-relations performance. Nevertheless, our analyses suggest that substantial individual differences exist in the speed and accuracy of encoding, search, rotation, and comparison processes. This conclusion is based upon the slope, intercept, and error differences that have been observed and appropriate possible interpretations of the individual processes that contribute to such measures.

PROCESS ANALYSES
OF SPATIAL VISUALIZATION

The tasks associated with spatial visualization have received considerably less attention than spatial-relations tasks. Relatively little has been done to develop and validate information-processing theories and models for such tasks. There are two major exceptions, and these include the early work of Shepard and Feng (1972) and our own recent work (Mumaw, Pellegrino, & Glaser, 1980). Shepard and Feng (1972) studied performance in a mental paper-folding or surface-development task (an example of such a task was shown earlier in Fig. 7.2). In the Shepard and Feng (1972) study, individuals were presented with a representation of a flat, unfolded cube. Two of the surfaces had marked edges, and the task was to decide if these marked edges would be adjacent when the pattern was folded to form the cube. The items that were used varied in number of 90° folds that were required to bring the two marked edges together. Items were also classified by the number of surfaces that had to be carried along with each fold (i.e., the number of surfaces that had to be moved mentally to complete each new fold). Ten different stimulus values were obtained, and decision times for items showed a general linear trend consistent with the total number of folds and surfaces that had to be processed to solve a problem. Shepard and Feng (1972) were not explicit about a model of performance for this task. Thus, the component processes and their sequencing are not well understood at present, and no systematic process analysis of individual differences has been conducted.

The specific performance that Mumaw et al. (1980) analyzed was the solution of Paper Form Board items. These items are found on a variety of spatial-ability batteries and are most commonly associated with the visualization factor of general spatial ability. Such tasks typically emphasize a combination of both speed and accuracy of spatial-information processing (an example of such a task was shown earlier in Fig. 7.2). The example was selected from the Minnesota Paper Form Board Test, and it requires the individual to match a series of completed figures against an array of individual stimulus elements or pieces. Thus, a series of same–different judgments must be executed to solve the problem. Items on form board tests vary in the number of pieces that must be processed, the similarity of the pieces, and the number of mismatched pieces. Mumaw et al. (1980) developed a laboratory task that emulated the problems and processing required by psychometric test items. The experimental item form that was created involved individual stimulus pairs that consisted of a complete figure and an array of individual pieces. The stimuli that they used were both selected from psychometric tests and constructed so that they would permit the evaluation of several models of performance.

A possible process model for performance on an item from the experimental tasks is shown in Fig. 7.14. According to this model, it is assumed that there is an initial encoding of one of the pieces followed by a search for a potentially corresponding piece. Given the identification of a possible match, there is rotation to bring the two stimuli into congruence so that a comparison process can be executed. If the two pieces correspond and all pieces have been examined, then a positive response is executed. If all pieces have not been examined, then the entire process recycles for examination of another stimulus element. There are three required processes and two optional processes that depend on the nature of the stimulus type. The example problem shown in Fig. 7.14 is one that presumably requires all five processes. The search process is required because the pieces are randomly arranged and have been displaced relative to each other, given their position in the completed figure. The rotation process is required because each piece has also been rotated in the picture plane in addition to being spatially displaced. Both rotation and displacement characterize items on psychometric tests. The appropriate general reaction-time equation for such items is also shown

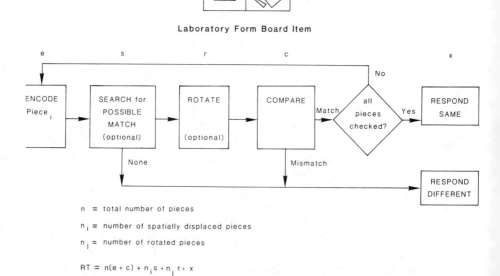

Laboratory Form Board Item

n = total number of pieces

n_i = number of spatially displaced pieces

n_j = number of rotated pieces

$$RT = n(e + c) + n_i s + n_j r + x$$

FIG. 7.14.   Example of a form board item and a process model for its solution.

in Fig. 7.14. By varying the number of pieces for a given stimulus pair, we would expect to obtain a linear function for reaction time. The slope of that function would represent encoding, comparison, search, and rotation. The intercept would represent preparation-response time.

In order to test the viability of this model as well as to separate the different processing parameters, Mumaw et al. (1980) designed several types of stimuli. The different stimulus types are shown in Fig. 7.15 together with initial assumptions about the processes required for item solution. At the top is shown the prototypical case where individual stimulus elements have been both rotated and displaced in the picture plane. This condition should require execution of all five processes. The second stimulus type is one that involves only rotation. This condition should require four of the five processes and may also require a search process. The third stimulus type involves the physical displacement of elements but without any rotation. Thus, this condition should only require four of the five processes. The fourth involves neither rotation nor displacement of stimulus

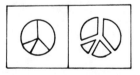

Rotated & Displaced

Encoding, Search, Rotation, Comparison, Response

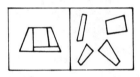

Rotated

Encoding, (Search), Rotation, Comparison, Response

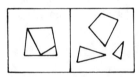

Displaced

Encoding, Search, Comparison, Response

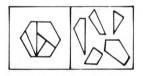

Separated

Encoding, Comparison, Response

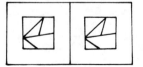

Wholistic

Encoding, Comparison, Response

FIG. 7.15. Examples of different item types used in the study of form board performance.

elements. This condition is designed to assess stimulus-element encoding and comparison. The final stimulus type is a wholistic presentation condition that provides a base line for encoding, comparison, and response.

The different assumptions about item processing were tested in an experiment conducted with 34 college students who varied in spatial ability as measured by a battery of reference tests. Included in the battery was the revised Minnesota Paper Form Board Test. The subjects were presented 300 separate stimulus pairs representing both positive and negative trial types. The positive trials included the five different problem types shown in Fig. 7.15. The number of stimulus elements for a given problem type ranged from two to six. Similar manipulations were employed for negative trials, and items were made incorrect by having either one mismatched element in the array or all mismatched elements.

We first focus on the latency results obtained for the positive trials. These data are shown in the left-hand panel of Fig. 7.16. The data for both the rotated and rotated and displaced problem types have been combined because they did not differ. The linear functions shown in the figure represent the least squares regression lines for each of the four problem types. As can be seen, performance in each condition was consistent with a simple additive model. As expected, the condition with the steepest slope was the one requiring search and rotation in addition to encoding, comparison, and response. The next steepest slope occurred in the condition that required only search in addition to encoding, comparison, and response. The shallowest significant slope occurred in the separated condition, which presumably required only encoding, comparison, and response.

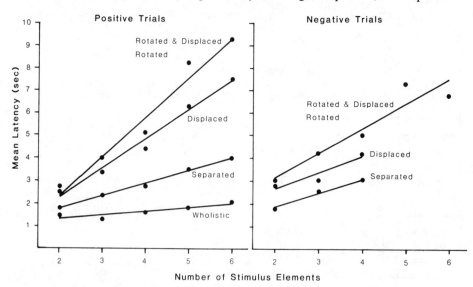

FIG. 7.16.   Mean latency data for positive and negative trials as a function of item type and number of stimulus elements.

Finally the base-line wholistic condition showed a basically flat function, as expected.

The adequacy of the model shown in Fig. 7.14 and the assumptions about processing for each problem type were tested by fitting the data from all conditions simultaneously (Table 7.9). When group mean data were used, the overall fit of the model was quite good. The values obtained for each of the individual parameters were plausible, and there were no major deviations from the model. Model fitting was also done for each individual subject. Almost all subjects had r^2 values above .90, and only three subjects had poor model fits. Thus, the model was not only representative of the group data, but it also provided a good characterization of the performance of each individual.

The latency data for negative trials complement the data for positive trials and allow us to determine if task performance is consistent with the use of a self-terminating processing strategy. An examination of the model shown in Fig. 7.14 reveals that when there is a mismatched stimulus element, the individual may exit from further processing and immediately execute a negative response. This can occur if no potential match is found during search or if the comparison process indicates a mismatch. If individuals use such a self-terminating processing strategy, then the functions relating reaction time to number of stimulus elements should be flatter than in the case of positive trials, where exhaustive processing of all elements is required.

The actual latency data for negative trials are shown in the right-hand panel of Fig. 7.16. The least squares regression lines for each problem type are also illustrated. Certain points are not represented because of unreliability due to an extremely high error rate. The latency data are consistent with the assumptions of a self-terminating processing strategy. The slopes of the least squares regression lines are less than the corresponding functions for positive trials. The results of jointly fitting both positive and negative trial data are shown in Table 7.9. The overall model fit remains quite good, and the parameter estimates do not change substantially. In addition, the value of the negation parameter is consistent with

TABLE 7.9
Results of Model Fitting for Positive and Negative Trials

Positive Trials (N = 25)	Positive and Negative Trials (N = 41)
R^2 = .965	R^2 = .94
RMSD = 461	RMSD = 545
Parameters	Parameters
Encode and compare = 538	Encode and compare = 556
Rotate = 255	Rotate = 299
Search = 687	Search = 689
Preparation-Response = 760	Preparation-Response = 624
	Index reset (negation) = 859

previous values for such a component. Finally, model fitting that assumes exhaustive processing provided a poorer fit and also produced an unacceptable negative value for the negation parameter.

The error data for both positive and negative trials were also systematic and of considerable importance relative to individual differences. The error data for positive trials are shown in the left-hand section of Fig. 7.17. As can be seen, positive trial errors were related to the presence of the rotation component. There was a significant increase in overall errors as a function of the number of times that the rotation process needed to be executed. The other processing components, with the possible exception of search, did not systematically contribute to errors for positive trial types. Individual subjects differed substantially in error rates, with an overall range of 0–23% for all positive trial types. For the problem types involving rotation, the range was 0–43% errors.

Of particular interest is the different patterning of error data for the negative trial types. The highest error rates were obtained for the conditions that did not require rotation. This is not to say, however, that the presence of rotation did not lead to errors. Rather, errors were highest when the ratio of matched to mismatched pieces was high and when processing could proceed rapidly because of the absence of a rotation component. It appears as if individuals may have processed elements superficially for comparison purposes and thereby failed to

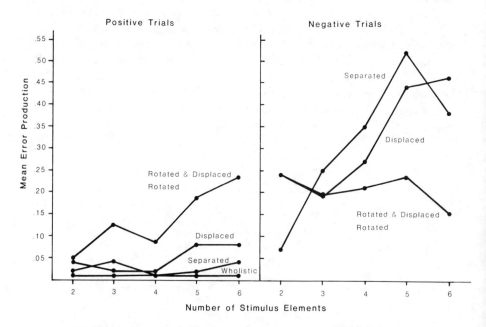

FIG. 7.17.   Mean error data for positive and negative trials as a function of item type and number of stimulus elements.

detect differences in size and shape for globally corresponding elements. The individual subject error rates on the negative trials ranged from 8–55%.

The error data for the positive and negative trials support the notion of different mechanisms contributing to incorrect final decisions. In the case of positive trials, errors seem to result from the inability to determine the correspondence between two stimulus elements that must be rotated into actual congruence. Thus, either rotation is incorrectly executed or the resultant representation following rotation is imprecise, leading to a rejection of a matching element. Errors resulting from execution of the rotation process also appear in the negative trials, where there is a tendency to accept the match between two similar but nonidentical pieces that are in different orientations. However, the largest error rates were obtained for pairs of stimulus elements that have the same orientation, a similar but nonidentical shape, and occur in the context of a larger number of matching pieces. Such a pattern supports the interpretation that individuals may be using a global stimulus-comparison process that often leads to errors. With respect to individual differences, there may be two separate aspects of incorrect performance—the encoding and comparison process and the rotation process. Evidence for such an assumption was provided by the lack of correlation between subjects' error rates on positive and negative trial items. The overall correlation across subjects was zero. However, both error rates were significantly correlated with overall performance on the reference test.

The analysis of individual differences in spatial-visualization ability utilized both latency and accuracy data. An individual subject's positive trial latency data were used to estimate the four basic processing parameters of the general model. In addition, error rates for both positive and negative trial types were determined for each subject. The latency-parameter intercorrelations and split-half reliabilities (along the diagonal) are shown in Table 7.10. The only significant correlation between parameters involved the encoding and comparison measure

TABLE 7.10
Parameter Intercorrelations and Reliabilities

	Encode and Compare	Search	Rotation	Preparation Response	Same Error	Different Error
Encode and compare	$(.77)^a$	.07	$.52^b$	−.33	.26	−.28
Search		$(.83)^a$	.30	−.33	.20	.43
Rotation			$(.54)^c$	−.34	.06	−.15
Preparation-Response				$(.65)^b$	−.04	−.07
Same error					$(.88)^a$	.00
Different error						$(.91)^a$

[a] $p < .001$.
[b] $p < .01$.
[c] $p < .05$.

and the rotation measure. Parameter reliabilities were greatest for the encoding and comparison and search measures. The four latency parameters and the two error parameters were then entered into a multiple regression analysis with performance on the Minnesota Paper Form Board as the criterion variable. The results of both simple and multiple regression analyses are shown in Table 7.11. The simple correlations show that reference test performance is significantly correlated with "same" and "different" judgment errors and the value for the search parameter. The multiple regression analysis shows that the overall level of prediction was quite high, especially given the reliability of the reference test scores, which is in the mid to upper 70s. Three of the predictors were significant. With respect to the latency parameters, the combined encoding and comparison parameter was now also shown to be related to spatial-visualization skill. Skilled individuals are faster at encoding and comparison of stimulus elements, and they are also faster at searching through an array to find a potentially corresponding stimulus element. With respect to accuracy measures, skilled individuals make fewer errors on problems involving rotation, and they also are more accurate in detecting mismatches between similar stimuli.

The data thus support a conclusion that skill in a visualization task such as the form board is related to the speed and quality of the stimulus representation that is achieved. A more precise representation of individual stimulus elements may permit both a more rapid search for a corresponding stimulus element and a faster and more accurate decision about correspondence between two target stimuli. Such an interpretation of spatial ability is also consistent with some of our other research indicating that skilled individuals are more adept at encoding unfamiliar stimuli. In the previously discussed research involving mental rotation tasks,

TABLE 7.11
Correlational Results with Minnesota Paper Form
Board as Criterion

| | | Multiple Regression | |
Predictor	Simple r	F	β
Encode and compare	−.27	3.87	−.27
Search	−.42[a]	<1	−.10
Rotation	−.17	—	—
Preparation-Response	.13	—	—
Positive trial errors	−.58[b]	14.40[b]	−.49
Negative trial errors	−.44[a]	10.53[b]	−.48
		$R = .78^b$	
		$R^2 = .61$	

[a] $p < .05$.
[b] $p < .01$.

skilled individuals were found to be faster at encoding and comparing unfamiliar stimuli of the type found on psychometric tests. Skilled individuals were also found to be faster in rotating such unfamiliar stimuli. One possible interpretation of facility in encoding and comparison speed is that more precise and stable representations are initially formed. Such high quality representations then enhance the speed and accuracy of subsequent processing. In spatial-relations or rotation tasks, this would primarily appear as speed differences in executing simple and complex rotation processes. In more complex visualization tasks such as the form board, this could appear as differences in both the speed and accuracy of executing several different components of processing, each of which must be executed several times in an iterative manner.

In summary, we have shown that it is possible to construct and validate a process model for performance in a spatial-visualization task that reliably assesses individual differences in spatial ability. The model not only provides a good characterization of group performance, but it also captures the performance of individual subjects. The component process parameter values estimated from individual subject model fitting, together with individual subject error patterns, captured a significant proportion of the variance in reference test performance. The latency and error components related to skill differences are suggestive of more fundamental differences in representational processes. The speed and quality of visual stimulus representation may underlie speed and accuracy differences in components of processing in both simple spatial-relations and more complex spatial-visualization tasks. Several issues remain to be explored in our own data, including the possibility that subjects differed in their strategy for task execution as a function of representational and memory demands imposed by different types of stimuli (e.g., those that could be labeled vs. those that could not) and the total number of stimulus elements to be processed. Finally, we must emphasize that the particular task we have modeled is only one example of a constellation of visualization tasks that need to be similarly studied.

GENERAL ISSUES

Relations Among Tasks and Processes

Our primary concern in this chapter has been the description of research that focuses on the process analysis of spatial aptitude as defined by psychometric tests. A general framework for aptitude analysis provided the schema for organizing and presenting our findings. That schema also serves as a basis for briefly summarizing and discussing the major implications of our efforts to date.

The domain of spatial aptitude was described in terms of the sets of tasks that define two major subfactors or specific aptitude constructs. The spatial-relations and spatial-visualization factors, although significantly related, seem to emphasize somewhat different aspects of spatial information-processing skill. This has been characterized in terms of a speed-power continuum that coincides with a continuum involving simple to complex tasks and stimuli (Lohman, 1979). These continua reflect an intuitive, rational analysis of major factor analytic results and the psychometric tasks that produce them. The intuitive analysis is supported, however, by several aspects of our data and those of others. First, if we look only at the time to solve typical problems representative of simple spatial relations, complex spatial relations, and form board tasks, there are clear and substantial differences. The time to evaluate the identity of a pair of stimuli drawn from the PMA is approximately 1.5 seconds, whereas the times for similar judgments for complex spatial relations and form board stimuli are 3.0 and 6.0 seconds, respectively. A similar ordering of tasks emerges if we examine the overall level of accuracy on these different types of problems. The latency and error differences that exist among problem types can be readily mapped back onto differences in the process models that characterize performance on each problem type. The model for simple spatial relations involves fewer processes than those assumed for complex spatial relations and form board tasks. Not only are there differences among tasks in the number of processes that need to be executed, but there are also differences in the number of times a given process must be executed. This is seen in the contrast between simple and complex spatial relations and also in the contrast between complex spatial relations and form board tasks. Thus, the total time and likelihood of a correct response are systematic functions of the number and type of processing operations to be performed. This relationship is expected because the models that were postulated and then verified were designed to reflect the apparent complexity of each task.

The speed-power continuum is also supported by data on individual differences in the performance of each task. The primary sources of individual, sex, and developmental differences in simple spatial-relations tasks were speed of processing measures. Both speed and accuracy measures were important in complex spatial-relations performance. Accuracy measures were even more important in accounting for individual differences in form board performance. We suspect that more complex spatial-visualization tasks would show that differences in accuracy rather than speed were critical. Thus, our individual-difference data support the idea that speed and power or accuracy of processing are separate sources of individual differences. This argument has also been advanced by Egan (1978), based upon patterns of intercorrelations involving speed and accuracy measures. Our own individual-difference data support the conclusions of Egan by showing low correlations between speed and accuracy measures obtained within the same task.

Although task differences and a general speed-power continuum have been supported, it must be remembered that these are highly related sets of tasks. Our analyses were primarily designed to determine the common processes underlying their interrelationships. The strategy for doing so involved developing, validating, and applying cognitive process models for performance on a representative set of spatial-aptitude tasks. It is important that we briefly review what has been learned about each task before attempting to discuss their interrelationships. In the case of performance on simple spatial-relations tasks, we have shown that extant (and modified) process models can be applied to the analysis of individual, sex, and developmental differences. The results are quite consistent in showing that substantial speed differences exist in the encoding and comparison of unfamiliar stimuli and in the execution of a rotation or transformation process that operates on the internal stimulus representation. Adult individual differences exist in all these components of processing, and individual differences mirror overall developmental trends. The limited analyses of age changes in sources of individual differences further suggest that individual differences initially relate to encoding and comparison processes and that the rotation process subsequently becomes an increasingly important source of individual differences. A further potential source, which needs further analysis, involves the strategy for task execution as reflected by the contrast between "same" and "different" judgment performance. Systematic individual differences may also exist in the speed and criteria for judging the mismatch between stimuli in different orientations.

The differences in encoding, comparison, and rotation that exist for simple spatial-relations tasks are of even greater magnitude in complex tasks. The complexity and abstractness of the stimuli leads to substantial errors on these problems that are also related to individual differences in reference test scores. The particular errors that seem most important for differentiating among individuals involve the processes associated with making different judgments. Latency data for different judgment performance also contribute to predicting individual differences in reference test performance. A more sophisticated analysis of individual differences in terms of specific processing components and strategies for task execution is now required. The current data, when interpreted in terms of a model such as the one proposed by Just and Carpenter (1976), would imply that individuals experience considerable difficulty in establishing the correspondences between the common segments of these complex stimuli, leading to several iterations through a sequence of processes, and often culminating in an incorrect evaluation or guess.

The spatial-visualization task that was examined also showed substantial differences among individuals in both speed and accuracy measures. A general process model for performance on form board problems provided an adequate initial representation of task performance at both the group and individual subject level. The speed of encoding and comparison and search processes estimated for individual subjects is related to individual differences in reference test performance together with differences in error rates on same–different judgment items. The error patterns seemed to indicate that comparison following rotation leads to errors, particularly for some less skilled individuals. Other less skilled individuals show a high preponderance of errors on "different" judgment problems that do not involve rotation. The interpretation of these errors is in terms of a superficial encoding or representation that is inadequate for precise comparisons of stimulus elements. Individual differences may also exist in the strategy or process sequence for task execution, and these differences remain to be explored.

The process models and individual-difference data obtained in all three tasks can be considered together to formulate a preliminary answer to the question of what constitutes general spatial aptitude. By looking across all three tasks, one might initially conclude that spatial aptitude is associated with the ability to establish sufficiently precise and stable internal representations of unfamiliar visual stimuli that can be subsequently transformed or operated on with a minimal information loss. In all three spatial-aptitude tasks, speed of encoding and comparison was significantly related to skill. In the more complex tasks, accuracy of encoding and comparison was also significantly related to skill. Thus, individuals who are high in spatial aptitude are faster at representing unfamiliar visual stimuli, and what is ultimately represented is more precise. Differences in representation, most likely quality differences, may also give rise to other speed differences such as the superior rotation and search rates exhibited in the different tasks. Problems of representation are most apparent in the more complex tasks that involve the representation and processing of stimuli having several interrelated elements. If we assume that stimulus representation and processing involve a visual short-term or working memory, then skill differences may be a function of coding and capacity within such a memory system. Differences between the spatial-relations and spatial-visualization tasks (factors) may reflect a difference in emphasis on coding versus transformation processes within this system. Another difference between the two factors may involve single versus sequential transformations and the ability to coordinate and monitor the latter.

Commonalities among spatial-aptitude tasks and factors can also be approached by considering the common processes specified within the models for task performance. The models for spatial-relations and visualization tasks all include encoding, rotation, comparison, decision, and response processes. The more complex tasks include an additional search process. Thus, there would appear to be a process basis for establishing overall performance correlations among the three tasks. However, differences exist among tasks in the complexity of the process sequence for task solution. The processes that are executed only once in simple spatial-relations tasks are necessary but not sufficient to account for performance on complex spatial-relations and visualization tasks. Nevertheless, we should be able to establish correspondences across tasks at the individual process level. An important step in the analysis of spatial aptitude is the analysis of consistencies across tasks in measures of performance. Such an analysis provides a further means of validating assumptions about processing in each task and about common processes across tasks.

In a previous section, we considered differences between spatial-relations tasks as reflected by intercept and slope differences for "same" judgment trials (see Fig. 7.12). The predominant interpretation of these measures of performance involves encoding, comparison, and response processes for the intercept and rotation processes for the slope. A logical difficulty arises when the substantial differences in slope values are considered. It does not seem plausible that the same process could assume such enormously different values. Either the process is not the same, or other processes also contribute to the slope measure for the more complex stimuli. Performance analyses by Just and Carpenter (1976; Carpenter & Just, 1978) help resolve the problem by showing that the slope measure for complex stimulus processing is a composite of different processes and that values obtained for the rotation component are consistent over simple and complex spatial-relations tasks. Thus, establishing process commonality depends on the ability to estimate individual processes for individual subjects and then showing consistency within and between individuals over tasks.

Two further examples can be provided on the use of individual-difference data to examine consistency across tasks in measures of mental rotation performance. The first involves data that we have already presented on performance in spatial-relations tasks. Our subjects were required to solve problems involving familiar alphanumerics and unfamiliar PMA stimuli. Slope and intercept measures were obtained for each stimulus type. Under the assumption that the slope reflects rate of mental rotation, whereas the intercept reflects encoding, comparison, and response processes, high correlations between corresponding measures would be expected. Such correlations were obtained (see Table 7.1), but the values indicated that the slope and intercept measures were not measuring exactly the same processes. A failure to find significant and high correlations for corresponding measures could have called into serious question our basic processing assumptions for one or both stimulus types. The second example involves expectations if we correlate slope and intercept measures from simple and complex spatial-relations tasks. The general expectation, given our previous discussion of the multiprocess nature of the slope for the complex task, is that the correlations should drop. This expectation is borne out in data available for 56 subjects who performed both sets of tasks. The correlations of the slope measures did not exceed .56. However, it must be noted that a highly significant relation still exists, and this, too, is expected. The intercept measures were also significantly correlated across tasks but again at a lower level. The correlations of the intercept for three-dimensional stimuli with intercepts for alphanumerics and PMA stimuli were .31 and .44, respectively.

The analysis of process commonalities across tasks through the use of individual-difference data is particularly important in the refinement of models of processing for sets of related tasks. The typical procedure in modeling performance on a given task is to designate some latency measure (e.g., slope, intercept, or a difference score) as an index of process x. A similar task is then modeled, and, in an effort to achieve consistency of language, the same elementary process x is labeled and estimated in the new task. It may in fact turn out that the times associated with x are similar for the two tasks, or the times may be widely different. The latter occurred in the case of spatial-relations tasks. Whether x is actually the same process can only be determined by reliably estimating it at the individual subject level and showing that there is at least relative consistency in the values obtained for x by different individuals. The magnitude of the obtained correlation indicates whether the measures of performance that are being considered reflect a complete, partial, or nonexistent process commonality.

Our analyses of spatial aptitude are far from complete, given the general framework outlined in the introduction. Additional tasks within the spatial-visualization domain require analysis and modeling. The models that we currently have for spatial-relations and visualization tasks require refinement, and intensive analyses are needed to determine the underlying bases of the individual differences that have been observed. A systematic analysis of process commonality across tasks also needs to be attempted. Nevertheless, we feel that we have made reasonable progress toward understanding individual differences in spatial aptitude. Such an understanding is essential if individual differences in aptitude are to be useful for purposes of creating adaptive instructional environments that facilitate the course of learning and skill acquisition. Spatial aptitude is not highly related to typical academic achievement, which is better predicted by verbal and quantitative aptitude and intelligence measures. However, spatial-aptitude measures are correlated with achievement and success in a variety of technical training courses and environments (e.g., courses in engineering design and graphics and mechanical drawing). If we wish to optimize instruction and achievement in these types of practical competencies, then we need to have a better way to assess and understand the spatial-processing skills that individuals bring to the instructional setting and the impact that these skills can have on instructional design and skill acquisition.

Individual Differences and Cognitive Theory

The research reported here, like that of Hunt, Frost, and Lunneborg (1973) and Sternberg (1977), represents a belated response to Cronbach's (1957) well-known plea for a rapprochement between the two disciplines of scientific psychology. We think that our research demonstrates three important ways in which cognitive theory can achieve both greater precision and greater breadth through the consideration of individual differences. First, an old lesson—but one that each generation of experimental psychologists seems to learn anew—is that evaluating theories and models with group data is a risky endeavor. The pattern observed in such data can often be a hybrid that is not found in any one individual's data. This point was well illustrated in the learning literature when contrasting conclusions were reached from forward learning curves based on group data and backwards learning curves that adjusted for individual differences in rate of learning (Estes, 1964; Hayes, 1953). In our research on processing of simple spatial relations, a similar situation arose in which the model that best described the group data (the modified deadline model) was not an accurate model of most individuals' data. Because of cases like these, we feel that individuals' data should be seen as the principal evidence with which cognitive models are evaluated, not merely as supplementary evidence as is currently the general practice.

There is a second way in which earnest consideration of individual differences can enhance cognitive theory. Given group means from various conditions in an experiment, the goal of the typical cognitive theorist is to find the model that best describes the data, where "best describes" is usually defined in terms of the fewest free parameters and the smallest unexplained variance. However, most cognitive psychologists never seriously consider the possibility that the most appropriate model might vary from person to person. Put another way, the notion that there might be multiple equally appropriate models of performance on a given task simply is not part of the zeitgeist of contemporary cognitive psychology. We question the wisdom of attempting to identify the definitive cognitive theory for performance on a given task. Our findings, as well as those of Sternberg (1977), suggest that analyses of most tasks will reveal multiple possible models or classes of models, many or all of which may characterize the performance of at least some individuals on the task.

The third way in which the study of individual differences can affect cognitive theory is by forcing greater precision in the description and measurement of individual cognitive processes. Current cognitive psychology embraces assumptions about a core set of elementary information processes that serve as the building blocks for all cognitive activity (e.g., Chase, 1978; Simon, 1976). Psychologists currently use the same limited set of process labels to describe performance on a wide range of simple and complex tasks. Examples include encoding, search, retrieval, decision, rotation, comparison, inference, and response. Thus, we appear to have a very powerful and general set of basic processing components. Unfortunately, little has been done to support or document its generality and existence. Data on the duration and existence of specific mental processes come from independent studies, using different stimuli, with different groups of individuals. All that appears to be common is the labels and the assumption that the processes are the same across tasks, subjects, etc. Individual-difference data can and must play an important role in validating some of our very basic assumptions about human cognition (e.g., process invariance). Underwood (1975) referred to the study of individual differences in cognitive processes as a "crucible in theory construction." By studying individual differences in cognitive processes, we can begin to verify some general assumptions about cognitive processing and at the same time open up possibilities for identifying elementary processes and higher level strategies that contribute to general theory development.

Finally, consider the impact of cognitive theory on our understanding of individual differences. The first benefit is perhaps obvious, but it should be mentioned. For most of the 20th century, research on individual differences in cognition has been the exclusive domain of factor analytic theorists. A shortcoming of factor analysis—and hence of almost all research on individual differences until recently—is that it fails to identify the processes underlying cognition as well as individual differences in these processes (McNemar, 1964). Thus, 'for example, finding that two spatial tests load heavily on the same factor tells us only that people who do well on one test generally excel on the other; it does not indicate the processes that are used to solve problems appearing on either test. The infusion of cognitive theory (and methods) has made it possible, for the first time, to indicate the processes underlying individual differences in intelligence.

One immediate outcome of this process-based analysis of individual differences has been to reveal the number of distinct ways in which people solve problems. In our research, as well as in that of Hunt et al. (1973) and Sternberg (1977), there are instances in which different individuals solve a problem using the same algorithm but vary in the speed and/or accuracy with which they execute the components of that algorithm. In other cases, individuals differ in the emphasis that they place on executing the different components of the algorithm. Finally, in still other cases, individuals rely on different algorithms to solve the same problem. In our opinion, this demonstrates that a process-based description of individual differences can be considerably richer than is possible by relying solely on factor analysis and derivative methods.

ACKNOWLEDGMENTS

The research described in this chapter was supported in part by funds provided to the first author as part of ARPA Contract No. N00014-79-C-0215, by funds provided to the second author by NIMH Grant 1 R03 MH 34173-01, and by a faculty grant from the Purdue Research Foundation. The authors wish to acknowledge the extensive contributions and assistance of Randy Mumaw and Philip Carter in this research.

REFERENCES

Atkinson, R. C., & Juola, J. F. Search and decision processes in recognition memory. In D. H. Krantz, R. C. Atkinson, & P. Suppes (Eds.), *Contemporary developments in mathematical psychology*. San Francisco: Freeman, 1974.

Bock, R. D., & Kolakowski, D. Further evidence of sex-linked major gene influence on human spatial visualizing ability. *American Journal of Human Genetics*, 1973, *25*, 1–14.

Boles, D. B. X-linkage of spatial ability: A critical review. *Child Development*, 1980, *51*, 625–635.

Cantoni, V. J. *The relationship between testosterone levels and spatial abilities in humans.* Unpublished masters thesis, University of California at Santa Barbara, 1981.

Carpenter, P. A., & Eisenberg, P. Mental rotation and the frame of reference in blind and sighted individuals. *Perception & Psychophysics*, 1978, *23*, 117–124.

Carpenter, P. A., & Just, M. A. Eye fixations during mental rotation. In J. Senders, R. Monty, & D. Fisher (Eds.), *Eye movements and psychological processes II*. Hillsdale, N.J.: Lawrence Erlbaum Associates, 1978.

Carroll, J. B. Psychometric tests as cognitive tasks: A new "structure of intellect." In L. B. Resnick (Ed.), *The nature of intelligence*. Hillsdale, N.J.: Lawrence Erlbaum Associates, 1976.

Carroll, J. B., & Maxwell, S. E. Individual differences in cognitive abilities. In M. R. Rosenzweig & L. W. Porter (Eds.), *Annual review of psychology* (Vol. 30). Palo Alto, Cal.: Annual Reviews, 1979.

Carter, P., Pazak, B., & Kail, R. *Developmental change in spatial information processing*. Unpublished manuscript, Purdue University, 1981.

Cattell, R. B. *Abilities: Their structure, growth and action*. Boston: Houghton Mifflin, 1971.

Chase, W. G. Elementary information processes. In W. K. Estes (Ed.), *Handbook of learning and cognitive processes* (Vol. 5). Hillsdale, N.J.: Lawrence Erlbaum Associates, 1978.

Cooper, L. A. Mental transformations of random two-dimensional shapes. *Cognitive Psychology*, 1975, *7*, 20–43.

Cooper, L. A. Spatial information processing: Strategies for research. In R. E. Snow, P-A. Federico, & W. E. Montague (Eds.), *Aptitude, learning, and instruction (Vol. 1): Cognitive process analyses of aptitude*. Hillsdale, N.J.: Lawrence Erlbaum Associates, 1980.

Cooper, L. A., & Shepard, R. N. Chronometric studies of the rotation of mental images. In W. G. Chase (Ed.), *Visual information processing*. New York: Academic Press, 1973.

Cronbach, L. J. The two disciplines of scientific psychology. *American Psychologist*, 1957, *12*, 671–684.

Egan, D. E. *Characterizing spatial ability: Different mental processes reflected in accuracy and latency scores* (Research Rep. No. 1224). Pensacola, Fl.: Naval Aerospace Medical Research Laboratory, August 1978.

Egan, D. E. Testing based on understanding: Implications from studies of spatial ability. *Intelligence*, 1979, *3*, 1–15.

Estes, W. K. All-or-none processes in learning and retention. *American Psychologist*, 1964, *19*, 16–25.

French, J. W. Ekstrom, R. B., & Price, L. A. *Kit of reference tests for cognitive factors*. Princeton, N.J.: Educational Testing Service, 1963.

Hardwick, D. A., McIntyre, C. W., & Pick, H. L. The content and manipulation of cognitive maps in children and adults. *Monographs of the Society for Research in Child Development*, 1976, *41*, Serial No. 166.

Harris, L. J. Sex differences in spatial ability: Possible environmental, genetic, and neurological factors. In M. Kinsbourne (Ed.), *Hemispheric asymmetries of function*. New York: Cambridge University Press, 1978.

Hayes, K. J. The backward curve: A method for the study of learning. *Psychological Review*, 1953, *60*, 269–275.

Hunt, E. B., Frost, N., & Lunneborg, C. L. Individual differences in cognition: A new approach to intelligence. In G. Bower (Ed.), *The psychology of learning and motivation* (Vol. 6). New York: Academic Press, 1973.

Huttenlocher, J., & Presson, C. C. Mental rotation and the perspective problem. *Cognitive Psychology*, 1973, *4*, 277–299.

Just, M. A., & Carpenter, P. A. Eye fixations and cognitive processes. *Cognitive Psychology*, 1976, *8*, 441–480.

Kail, R., Carter, P., & Pazak, B. *Development of individual differences in spatial ability*. Paper presented at the annual meeting of the Psychonomic Society, Phoenix, November 1979.

Kail, R., Carter, P., & Pellegrino, J. The locus of sex differences in spatial ability. *Perception & Psychophysics*, 1979, *26*, 182–186.

Kail, R., Pellegrino, J., & Carter, P. Developmental changes in mental rotation. *Journal of Experimental Child Psychology*, 1980, *29*, 102–116.

Kail, R. V., & Siegel, A. W. Sex and hemispheric differences in the recall of verbal and spatial information. *Cortex*, 1978, *14*, 557–563.

Kreuger, L. E. A theory of perceptual matching. *Psychological Review*, 1978, *85*, 278–304.

Liben, L. S. Perspective-taking skills in young children: Seeing the world through rose-colored glasses. *Developmental Psychology*, 1978, *14*, 87–92.

Lohman, D. F. *Spatial ability: A review and reanalysis of the correlational literature* (Tech. Rep. No. 8). Stanford, Cal.: Aptitude Research Project, School of Education, Stanford University, 1979.

Maccoby, E. E., & Jacklin, C. N. *The psychology of sex differences.* Stanford, Cal.: Stanford University Press, 1974.

McGee, M. G. Human spatial abilities: Psychometric studies and environmental, genetic, hormonal, and neurological influences. *Psychological Bulletin*, 1979, *86*(5), 889–918. (a)

McGee, M. G. *Human spatial abilities: Sources of sex differences.* New York: Praeger, 1979. (b)

McNemar, Q. Lost: Our intelligence? Why? *American Psychologist*, 1964, *19*, 871–882.

Metzler, J., & Shepard, R. N. Transformational studies of the internal representations of three-dimensional objects. In R. Solso (Ed.), *Theories in cognitive psychology: The Loyola Symposium.* Hillsdale, N.J.: Lawrence Erlbaum Associates, 1974.

Mumaw, R. J., Pellegrino, J. W., & Glaser, R. *Some puzzling aspects of spatial ability.* Paper presented at annual meetings of the Psychonomic Society, St. Louis, Mo., November 1980.

Ollman, R. T., & Billington, M. J. The deadline model for simple reaction times. *Cognitive Psychology*, 1972, *3*, 311–336.

Pellegrino, J. W., & Glaser, R. Cognitive components and correlates in the analysis of individual differences. *Intelligence*, 1979, *3*, 187–214.

Pellegrino, J. W., & Glaser, R. Components of inductive reasoning. In R. E. Snow, P-A. Federico, & W. E. Montague (Eds.), *Aptitude, learning, and instruction (Vol. 1): Cognitive process analyses of aptitude.* Hillsdale, N.J.: Lawrence Erlbaum Associates, 1980.

Pellegrino, J. W., & Glaser, R. Analyzing aptitudes for learning: Inductive reasoning. In R. Glaser (Ed.), *Advances in instructional psychology* (Vol. 2). Hillsdale, N.J.: Lawrence Erlbaum Associates, in press.

Pellegrino, J. W., & Mumaw, R. J. *Multicomponent models of spatial ability.* Unpublished manuscript, University of California at Santa Barbara, 1980.

Pellegrino, J. W., Mumaw, R. J., Kail, R. V., & Carter, P. *Different slopes for different folks: Analyses of spatial ability.* Paper presented at the annual meeting of the Psychonomic Society, Phoenix, November 1979.

Petrusic, W. M., Varro, L., & Jamieson, D. G. Mental rotation validation of two spatial ability tests. *Psychological Research*, 1978, *40*, 139–148.

Piaget, J., & Inhelder, B. *The child's conception of space.* London: Routledge & Kegan Paul, 1956.

Resnick, L. B. (Ed.). *The nature of intelligence.* Hillsdale, N.J.: Lawrence Erlbaum Associates, 1976.

Shepard, R. N. Form, formation, and transformation of internal representations. In R. L. Solso (Ed.), *Information processing and cognition: The Loyola Symposium.* Hillsdale, N.J.: Lawrence Erlbaum Associates, 1975.

Shepard, R. N., & Feng, C. A chronometric study of mental paper folding. *Cognitive Psychology*, 1972, *3*, 228–243.

Simon, H. A. Identifying basic abilities underlying intelligent performance of complex tasks. In L. B. Resnick (Eds.), *The nature of intelligence.* Hillsdale, N.J.: Lawrence Erlbaum Associates, 1976.

Smith, I. *Spatial ability: Its educational and social significance.* London: University of London Press, 1964.

Snow, R. E., Federico, P-A., & Montague, W. E. *Aptitude, learning, and instruction (Vol. 1): Cognitive process analyses of aptitude.* Hillsdale, N.J.: Lawrence Erlbaum Associates, 1980. (a)

Snow, R. E., Federico, P-A., & Montague, W. E. *Aptitude, learning, and instruction (Vol. 2): Cognitive process analyses of learning and problem solving.* Hillsdale, N.J.: Lawrence Erlbaum Associates, 1980. (a)

Sternberg, R. *Intelligence, information processing, and analogical reasoning.* Hillsdale, N.J.: Lawrence Erlbaum Associates, 1977.

Sternberg, R. J. The nature of mental abilities. *American Psychologist,* 1979, *34,* 214–230.

Tapley, S. M., & Bryden, M. P. An investigation of sex differences in spatial ability: Mental rotation of three-dimensional objects. *Canadian Journal of Psychology,* 1977, *31,* 122–130.

Thurstone, L. L. *Primary mental abilities.* Chicago: University of Chicago Press, 1938.

Thurstone, L. L., & Thurstone, T. G. *Manual for the SRA primary mental abilities.* Chicago: Science Research Associates, 1949.

Thurstone, T. G. *Manual for the SRA primary mental abilities.* Chicago: Science Research Associates, 1958.

Underwood, B. J. Individual differences as a crucible in theory construction. *American Psychologist,* 1975, *30,* 128–134.

Vernon, P. E. Ability factors and environmental influences. *American Psychologist,* 1965, *20,* 723–733.

8 Problem Solving as Search and Understanding

Peter Polson
University of Colorado

Robin Jeffries
Carnegie-Mellon University

INTRODUCTION

Puzzlelike problems have been widely used in the study of problem-solving processes. They possess several qualities that make them desirable for this purpose: (1) they are concise—the information needed to solve them can usually be provided in a single page of text; (2) no extensive training procedures are needed; (3) they come in a range of difficulty levels—in fact, it is often possible to realize a wide range of difficulty using only variants from a single problem family; (4) they supply different types of information (e.g., transformation puzzles, which are solved by specifying a sequence of moves ending at a goal state, provide the experimenter with a substantial amount of information about the solution attempt, rather than simply whether or not the subject solved the problem); (5) they have a high, intrinsic interest for subjects.

For these and other reasons, puzzles have captured the interest of a variety of theorists in the last few years. Performance models have been considered for water-jug problems (Atwood, Masson, & Polson, 1980; Atwood & Polson, 1976), missionaries-cannibals problems (Greeno, 1974; Jeffries, Polson, Razran, & Atwood, 1977; Simon & Reed, 1976; Thomas, 1974), and the Tower of Hanoi puzzle (Egan, 1973; Karat, in press; Simon, 1975). These puzzles have also been used to study other issues of interest such as learning (Anzai & Simon, 1979) and transfer (Jeffries, 1978; McDaniel, 1980). Insights gained from work on these and similar tasks form the basis of much of what is currently known about problem solving (Ernst & Newell, 1969; Greeno, 1978; Simon, 1978).

Puzzle tasks similar to the ones just mentioned have been employed as components of tests designed to measure intelligence. The same features that make them useful vehicles for research (i.e., their intrinsically high interest value; their ability to tap problem solving skills without requiring large amounts of specific knowledge) make them suitable measures of individual differences in problem solving skills. However, the focus of the work described here is not on the role of such puzzles as measures of intelligence. Rather, our general strategy has been to model the commonalities in the problem-solving processes used in this class of tasks across both problems and subjects. We feel that we have captured the common processes used by a variety of solvers on a range of problems and, to a lesser extent, the characteristics of particular problems that lead to deviations from these standard procedures. Missing is a description of how differences among solvers can be accounted for in this framework. An understanding of the modal strategies used to solve such problems and of how the properties of the task itself influence the solution have taken priority in this research effort over investigations of variations in how those strategies are applied.

This chapter describes the work we have done in modeling performance on transformation problems. Greeno (1978) defines a transformation problem as a task in which the subject is given well-specified initial and goal states and must discover a sequence of legal moves that transforms the initial state into the goal state. Transformation problems include water-jug problems, the Tower of Hanoi puzzle, various kinds of mathematics problems, theorem proving tasks, and common-sense reasoning problems like "How do I get to Timbuktu?" (McCarthy, 1959). Research using such tasks has been a focus of modern work on problem solving. The objective of this chapter is to review our work in this area, which has employed such tasks to study problem solving, learning, and transfer.

Our theoretical framework characterizes problem solving in such task environments as a mixture of understanding and search. Problem solvers use task-specific strategies to the extent that they have derived an understanding of the underlying structure of the task from either the problem description or from information acquired through experience with the same or similar problems. Otherwise, solvers use general search strategies—predominantly means–ends analysis and the selection of moves that lead to new states.

Whether a problem solver uses problem-specific strategies or must revert to more general search strategies depends on both the structure of the problem and the solver's experience with related tasks. The puzzles we have used and the conditions under which they have been presented vary greatly in the degree to which an understanding of the structure of the problem is possible. We first discuss problems for which little understanding was evidenced. The water-jug and missionaries-cannibals problems are solved by naive subjects primarily by means–ends and memory driven search. For other problems, subjects derive a partial understanding directly from the problem description. The Tower of Hanoi and Hobbits, Orcs, and Gold (a problem derived from missionaries-cannibals) have this property. Finally, we describe work on learning and transfer, where the understanding of the problem's structure evolves from experience with similar tasks. This work has used the water-jug and missionaries-cannibals problems. But before presenting the specific experiments, a brief discussion of work on understanding in problem solving and a description of our theoretical and empirical methodology are given.

Understanding

There are two views of understanding as applied to problem solving. Hayes and Simon (1976a) describe understanding as a process that extracts relevant information from the problem description in order to pass it on to a general problem-solving mechanism. The understanding process constructs representations of the initial state, goal state, salient intermediate states, and the process by which legal moves are generated. This information then guides the process of solving the problem.

Another perspective on understanding is presented by Greeno (1977), whose views are motivated by the work of Gestalt psychologists (e.g., Wertheimer, 1959). For Greeno, understanding is the process of constructing a representation of the structure underlying the problem to be solved. He discusses the notion of the quality of understanding by developing three criteria for understanding: (1) the structure generated by the understanding process should correctly represent the underlying structure of the problem; (2) the elements of this structure should be connected and have a coherent organization; and (3) the elements of the representation should be well integrated with other knowledge possessed by the solver. Similar views of the understanding process have been articulated by Moore and Newell (1974). We feel that Greeno's characterization of problem solving as a process of understanding is an apt description of the behavior of expert problem solvers in any domain.

However, we believe that novices have a very limited understanding of any novel problem, and this limited understanding manifests itself in two ways: (1) search processes dominate much of their problem-solving behavior; and (2) their understanding is both shallow and fragmented. This shallowness is evidenced by the absence of successful plans. Planning requires, at a minimum, a partial understanding of the structure of a task. It is often difficult to gain an understanding of a task's structure from either the problem description or from local exploration of problem states and their immediate successors. Often, such structural knowledge can only be derived from experience with a class of tasks.

The fragmentary nature of novices' understanding is exhibited through the inconsistencies with which various criteria are used to select moves. Novices are often able to derive criteria for choosing among moves. However, because they lack an underlying structure for the problem, novices are unable to select among conflicting criteria or integrate them into a coherent structure for making decisions. Thus, fragmentary and shallow understanding leads to trial-and-error behavior and the use of general search strategies such as means–ends analysis or choosing moves leading to arbitrary new states.

Theoretical and Empirical Methodology

The theories we have developed to describe problem-solving behavior have been formalized as stochastic models in the form of computer programs. We believe that the construction of such models, although admittedly an onerous task, results in theories that are more precise and testable. Unlike a theory presented as descriptive prose, a process model of a task requires the concrete specification of the actions and decisions that a solver performs. Consider, for example, the selection of potential moves. A less specific theory might merely state that a move is selected for consideration, whereas the computer formalism forces us to decide the order in which moves are chosen. We can do this at different levels of detail, however. We can specify an order, which becomes a testable tenet of the theory. Alternatively, we can introduce a free parameter that represents the likelihood of a given move being selected.

Free parameters can be interpreted in one of several ways. One can see them as statements of ignorance and/or simplification. For example, the memory encoding parameter of our models is the condensation of a great deal of research about memory storage and retrieval into a single parameter that represents the likelihood that a given state will be remembered when appropriate. Because memory for states is not of central interest to us, we condense some complex concepts into a simplified process governed by (in this case) a single parameter. In other cases, our ignorance of the underlying processes leads to a similar introduction of parameters.

The second use of free parameters is to eliminate individual-difference variance. This is because our interest has been on the common processes used by the majority of problem solvers. A free parameter can be used in situations where we might expect large individual differences to exist in how the process was performed when those differences are not of primary interest. Note that this implicitly assumes that the basic processes used by all subjects are the same except that they differ in the speed, efficiency, consistency, etc., with which they are performed.

A third use of stochastic parameters occurs when the process under consideration is assumed to be truly random. This may be because the controlling event is external to the organism (e.g., presentation order, which could be randomized, might control the order of move consideration) or simply a random internal process. In such a case, the parameter is not free to vary, but its value is chosen consistent with the most plausible underlying distribution (usually equiprobability).

The precision with which the model must be specified enables us to obtain, by the manipulation of the free parameters, quantitative estimates of performance on specific tasks. The model is validated to the extent that it predicts the quantitative performance of subjects, using parameter estimates that are psychologically plausible and that vary across conditions only when it is reasonable to assume a change in the processes involved. This contrasts with less precisely specified models, which at best can make claims about the relative difficulty of different experimental conditions.

In addition to being testable as a whole, many of the model's individual assumptions can be tested separately. With an explicit postulate such as "moves are selected in this specific order," experiments can be designed to isolate one process from the others and verify it separately. Furthermore, the explicitness of these assumptions frequently leads the model to make concrete predictions in areas where a less specific model may be mute. These predictions are not always verified, but the activity of testing and modifying the model should lead closer and closer to a correct description of the process.

The complexity of these models becomes in some sense the strongest argument for their usefulness. All of our models are complex enough, that we find it difficult to determine the consequence of a potential experimental manipulation without running the actual simulations. We have frequently assumed that a model would predict A easier than B, when in fact the actual prediction was reversed. Post hoc, it is usually easy to see what features of the model led to the observed ordering, but, without the simulations, we would not have taken those aspects into account properly. In other situations, we have correctly inferred a difference between groups, but the simulation has shown that the magnitude of the difference is much smaller than we would have expected. Such simulation results have helped steer us away from the statistical problems of distinguishing a small difference from no difference. Without the quantitative predictions from the simulation, such specificity in our empirical work would not have been possible.

Two kinds of evidence are used to show that a particular simulation model is an adequate account of performance in a given experimental paradigm. First, traditional indices of goodness of fit are used. These models contain free parameters that are manipulated to produce a "best" fit to the data. Observed and predicted means and variances for several descriptive statistics are then compared. In addition, correlations between observed and predicted state-to-state transition matrices are presented. These matrices tabulate the number of moves made to and from each possible state of the problem. Because of the large number of possible transitions, these correlations and the percentage-of-variance-explained statistics derived from them represent sensitive measures of the fit of the model to the data. A simulation program is written to generate actual trial-by-trial performance data for each experimental condition. The program calculates a set of descriptive statistics from the simulated data that is equivalent to that obtained from the observed data. Comparisons are typically made between observed performance and the simulated data of 250 statistical subjects, thus giving a great deal of stability to the predicted quantities.

The other method of evaluating models involves demonstrating that the theory makes adequate predictions about variations in problem difficulty and other experimental manipulations. Two things are meant by adequate predictions. First, the theory must fit the data from each of the individual experimental conditions. Second, the parameters required to fit data from individual conditions must have sensible relationships. For example, experimental manipulations that should have no effect on the underlying processes, yet should affect problem difficulty, must be fit with one set of parameters.

The same general procedures have been used in all of our experiments. All studies were run under computer control. In every condition, the current state and other information, which varied from experiment to experiment, were displayed on a CRT. This information could include the goal to be achieved or the possible moves from the current state. Subjects indicated a move by pressing buttons on a keyboard connected to the computer. Included among the buttons were provisions for subjects to edit a response before the computer actually performed the move they entered. If a valid move was entered, the display was changed in the fashion appropriate for that move. Illegal moves resulted in a warning message and a return to the representation of the current state. Large numbers of subjects were run in each experimental condition in order to generate enough data to make stable comparisons between theory and data for individual cells of an experiment. Inasmuch as the objective of many of the experiments was to show that the model could give a consistent account of performance across different experimental conditions, a much larger number of subjects was required in each cell than would be needed simply to show that these manipulations produced significant differences in performance.

PROBLEM SOLVING AS SEARCH

This section describes models for water-jug and river-crossing problems in which means–ends search is the dominant problem-solving mechanism. Both the theoretical framework and the experiments that were designed to test the framework are described. The success of these models encouraged an attempt to extend them to other environments. But, the shortcomings of these simple models in other problem domains led us to the view that problem solving is determined by the interaction of a solver's partial understanding of the problem and general search strategies.

The Theoretical Framework

The theoretical framework underlying the Atwood and Polson (1976) and the Jeffries, Polson, Razran & Atwood (1977) models assumes that move selection in a transformation problem involves the interaction of evaluation processes and memory processes. Evaluation processes describe how means–ends heuristics and information retrieved from long-term memory are employed to evaluate a move under consideration. Memory processes, derived from a simplified version of a multistore memory model, describe how information used in the move-selection process is stored and retrieved. A three-stage process model integrates the information from the memory and evaluation processes and leads to the selection of the next move. It is assumed that subjects use only information about the current state and its immediate successors to select the next move.

Evaluation Processes.   There are five aspects of the evaluation processes: (1) state evaluation; (2) the acceptability criterion; (3) optimal move selection; (4) a noticing order; and (5) an illegal move filter.

The models derived from this framework incorporate an evaluation function that gives a figure of merit, a numerical value, for any state of the problem. The function is intended to characterize the solver's perception of the distance of the current state from the goal. A move is evaluated by comparing the evaluation of the current state (e_i) with the evaluation of the state resulting from the move under consideration (e_j). We assume that the evaluation function is used to classify moves as either acceptable or unacceptable. Moves that lead to a significant improvement in the evaluation function are classified as acceptable. The solver is indifferent to small differences, and such moves are also acceptable. (The value of the difference required for a move to be judged as similar is termed the acceptability criterion.) All other moves are classified as unacceptable. The evaluation function, the acceptability criterion, and the process of comparing the evaluation of the current state with the evaluation of the resulting state make up the means–ends process.

Since each move selection process continues until an acceptable candidate move is found, in general fewer moves will need to be examined if the most likely candidates are considered first. In many tasks, it is possible to rank order the desirability of various moves independent of the state they are related to. If this is the case, we assume that moves are considered in the order of their desirability. Desirability is derived from considerations of means–ends heuristics and other specialized properties of the particular problem. If the desirability of a move depends on the current state or the resulting state in some idiosyncratic fashion, we assume that moves are considered in a random order.

The move selection processes generate moves for consideration independently of their legality. All physically possible moves are evaluated, even if they violate other restrictions of the problem. Illegal moves are detected only after a move has been proposed for execution. This detection process is fallible, and the probability of successfully detecting an illegal move depends on the precise characteristics of the resulting illegal state.

Memory Processes.   The memory structure and storage and retrieval processes can be described by a simplified version of a multistore model of memory

(Bower, 1975; Kintsch & Polson, 1979). During the move-selection processes, information about the current state and its successors is stored in short-term memory. Information about states visited during previous episodes is stored in long-term memory; this information is used by both the evaluation and move-selection processes.

During the first stage of the move-selection processes, the framework assumes that the solver computes and stores in short-term memory information about the move under consideration, the resulting state, its evaluation, and other characteristics of that state. Accurate information about at most r moves can be stored in short-term memory. A solver is unable to store accurate information about all of the various successors if the current state has more than r successors.

Representations of states actually entered during the course of problem solving are stored in long-term memory. A simple all-or-none model is assumed for the storage process. The representation of a state that has been entered is stored in long-term memory with probability s. We assume that there is no forgetting and that information that has been stored can always be successfully retrieved. In other words, "old" states can always be recognized; "new" states are those that have never been entered or for which a representation has not been stored during some previous entry.

The Move-Selection Processes.   A complex three-stage process is used to integrate the information from the evaluation processes and the memory processes in order to select a move. Each stage incorporates a serial self-terminating process in which different criteria are used to evaluate successors of the current state. Once a move is selected, the process terminates, and the subject attempts to execute that move. If all moves have been evaluated during one stage and no move selected, the subject goes on to the next stage. The order in which moves are chosen for evaluation is determined by the noticing order if there is one, or it is random.

The following decision rules are used by the solver during Stage I of the process (Atwood & Polson, 1976):

1. An unacceptable move is never taken.
2. The move leading to the immediately preceding state is never taken.
3. A move leading to the goal state is always taken.
4. An acceptable move leading to a "new" state is taken with probability α.
5. An acceptable move leading to an "old" state is taken with probability β [p. 197].

These decision rules describe how moves that satisfy the means–ends criteria are evaluated. Means–ends moves that lead to new states are taken with a fairly high probability, α. Moves that satisfy the means–ends criterion, but lead to old states, are taken with a lower probability, β.

During Stage II, a solver again serially evaluates the successors of the current state in the order specified by the noticing order. The first move that leads to a new state is taken. Stage III is entered only if there are no new successors to the current state. There are two move-selection processes that may be executed during Stage III. If the current state has more than r successors, the information necessary to select an optimal move will have been lost from short-term memory; it is assumed that the solver randomly selects any of the successors of the current state. If the current state has r or fewer successors, accurate information about these states and the moves leading to them remains in short-term memory. In this case, the solver selects the move that leads to the best value of the evaluation function with probability α. Otherwise, a random move is selected.

The Water-Jug Task

The water-jug task was selected for the original series of experiments for three reasons. First, the initial situation, goal, and legal moves are easily understood by subjects. Furthermore, subjects can facilely perform the mental operations necessary to calculate the consequences of a move. The theoretical framework just outlined assumes that solvers have a low-level understanding of the basic elements of the problem, including a characterization of the initial, intermediate, and final states and the basic operations that define legal moves. Second, the water-jug task environment allows the definition of whole families of problems with different structures and presumably varying sources of difficulty. Thus, it is possible to evaluate a model for this task by using a variety of problems with different structures. Third, the structure of the water-jug task permits a stringent test of the means–ends assumptions.

Our water-jug problems are similar to those used by Luchins (1942) in his experiments on set. The task involves three jugs (A, B, C) of varying sizes; for example, (8, 5, 3) indicates that the A jug has a capacity of eight units, the B jug five units, and the C jug three units. Initially, the largest jug is full, and the two smaller jugs are empty. The subject's task is to determine a series of moves that divides the contents of the largest jug evenly between jugs A and B. Legal moves are defined by two pouring operations. Water is either transferred from a jug until that jug is empty or the jug being poured into is filled. Water cannot be added or deleted during the course of solving the problem.

Graphs of the (8, 5, 3) and (24, 21, 3) problems are shown in Fig. 8.1. Other problems used in these studies had similar structures. All had the same configuration of states at the top of the graph and two different solution paths. They differed in the lengths of the solution paths and other characteristics to be discussed later. The letters shown in the figure are state labels: S is the start state, R and L are the initial states on the left and right solution paths, T is the transition state between the two solution paths, and G is the goal state. All moves shown as connecting two states are reversible. There are two reversible moves from S

(A) (8,5,3)

(B) (24,21,3)

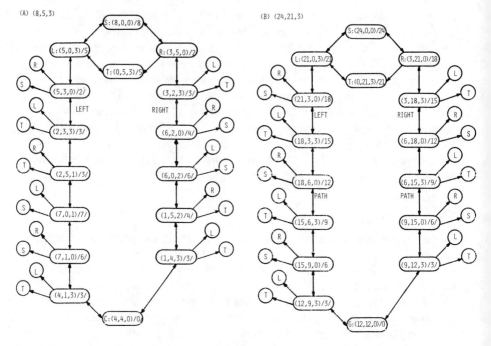

FIG. 8.1. Graphs of the possible states and legal moves for both the (8, 5, 3) (panel A) and the (24, 21, 3) water-jug problems (panel B). For each state, the three numbers in parentheses are the current contents of jugs A, B, and C respectively (from Atwood & Polson, 1976).

leading to states R and L, respectively. From states R and L there are three reversible moves: one forward move, a move to the transition state, and a backward move to the start state. From the remaining states of the problem, there are always four possible moves: a reversible forward move, a reversible backward move, and irreversible moves up to two of the four states at the top of the graph (S, T, R, L). These irreversible moves are errors, and the subject's tendency to take certain irreversible moves causes much of the difficulty in a water-jug problem.

The state-evaluation process or evaluation function is given by:

$$e_i = [C_i(A) - G(A)] + [C_i(B) - G(B)] \qquad\qquad 8.1$$

where $C_i(A)$ is the number of units of water in jug A for the ith state and $G(A)$ is the number of units in A specified by the goal; similar quantities are defined for jug B. Equation 8.1 is defined such that moves perceived as being closer to the goal have smaller values. Thus, if the value of Equation 8.1 for the state resulting from the move currently under evaluation is significantly larger than the evaluation of the current state, the subject perceives that the move under consideration leads to a state that is "further away" from the goal state, and the move is considered unacceptable. Recall that only acceptable moves are considered during the first stage of the move-selection process.

There are other aspects of the evaluation process for the water-jug model. There is no error filter in this model. We have never attempted to model the process that leads to errors on this problem, even though approximately 10% of the moves were illegal. Moves are selected in a random order by the model. This is justified by the fact that it is not possible to describe the effects of any given move (e.g., pouring the contents of A into B) consistently. The effects of such a move are completely dependent on the current state.

We review three experiments that provide support for the model of the water-jug task developed from the theoretical framework just described. The first experiment provides a test of the means–ends process incorporated into the framework. The second validates the model by showing that it can describe performance from water-jug problems that differ widely in difficulty. The third experiment is a test of the assumption that subjects do not plan in this task and that they only consider information about the successors of the current state in the process of selecting moves.

Experiment 1 reported by Atwood and Polson (1976) provides a test of the means–ends heuristic incorporated into the model and Equation 8.1. This experiment compared performance on two problems: (8, 5, 3) and (24, 21, 3). The graphs of these problems are nearly identical, but they have quite different patterns of acceptable and unacceptable moves as defined by Equation 8.1 and the means–ends heuristics (see Fig. 8.1). For two of the states in the (8, 5, 3) problem, the correct forward move is classified by the evaluation function as being unacceptable. Furthermore, from a majority of the states in this problem, there are acceptable incorrect moves leading back to one of the four states at the top of the graph. For the (24, 21, 3) problem, there are no unacceptable correct moves, and the correct forward move is the only acceptable move for all but two of the states in the entire problem. The model predicts that subjects solving the (8, 5, 3) problem should find this problem far more difficult than the (24, 21, 3) problem because the move-selection heuristics incorporated into Stage I can cause them to take moves back to the initial states of the problem and prevent them from taking the correct forward move from two of the states.

Table 8.1 gives means and standard deviations of the number of legal moves to solution along with predictions derived from the model by simulation. Atwood and Polson (1976) concluded that the pattern of acceptable and unacceptable moves was the primary determinant of move choices in the water-jug problem, not the graph structure. The results are clear as shown in the table. The (24, 21, 3) problem was almost trivial for these subjects, whereas the (8, 5, 3) problem was quite difficult to solve. Thus, the means–ends heuristic is clearly a major determinant of move selection in these problems.

In a second experiment, Atwood and Polson evaluated their model by testing its ability to account for performance on four water-jug problems that vary widely in difficulty. All four problems had the same general structure shown in

TABLE 8.1
Observed and Predicted Mean Legal Moves
and Standard Deviations
for Two Water-Jug Problems
(Adapted from Atwood & Polson, 1976,
p. 204, Table 3)

	Legal Moves	
Problem	Observed	Predicted
(8, 5, 3)		
Mean	24.90	23.69
SD	14.75	15.31
(24, 21, 3)		
Mean	12.03	11.84
SD	7.44	6.66

Fig. 8.1. The problems used were (8, 5, 3), (12, 7, 4), (14, 9, 5), and (16, 10, 3). These problems differed in the lengths of their right and left paths, the number of correct forward moves that were classified as unacceptable by the means–ends heuristic, and the number of acceptable moves that lead back to one of the four states at the start of the problem. Problems ranged in difficulty from the (8, 5, 3) problem, which had right and left solution-path lengths of 7 and 8 respectively, to the (16, 10, 3) problem with solution-path lengths of 11 and 14. There was a large difference in the lengths of the solution paths for the (12, 7, 4) problem with the right solution path being 7 moves long and the left solution path being 14 moves long. The number of correct forward moves that were classified as unacceptable by the means–ends heuristic was, in general, a function of the length of the solution path, as was the number of acceptable moves that cause the subject to back track to a state at or near the start of a problem.

The observed performance measures along with predicted values obtained by simulation are shown in Table 8.2. Included are the observed and predicted values for the mean number of moves to solution. If subjects failed to solve the problem within 100 moves, they were given an arbitrary score of 100 moves. Also displayed are the observed and predicted proportions of solution types—the proportion of subjects who solve the problem by traversing the right solution path, the left solution path, and those that failed to solve in 100 trials. The predictions shown in Table 8.2 were obtained using a single set of parameters to account for performance in all experimental conditions. We feel that the results shown in the table clearly demonstrate that the model is capable of providing an accurate account of changes in problem structure that lead to wide variations in performance.

Although Atwood and Polson (1976) showed that a model derived from the framework is able to make accurate predictions about problem-solving perfor-

TABLE 8.2
Observed and Predicted[a] Performance Statistics for Four Water-Jug Problems
(Adapted from Atwood & Polson, 1976, p. 208, Table 5)

	Problem			
	(8, 5, 3)	(12, 7, 4)	(14, 9, 5)	(16, 10, 3)
	Legal Moves			
Mean	34.23 (31.90)	49.90 (43.59)	64.15 (62.01)	68.12 (68.60)
SD	27.21 (30.18)	27.11 (35.90)	25.88 (33.64)	22.92 (32.23)
	Proportions Using Each Solution Path			
Right path	.64 (.50)	.77 (.60)	.46 (.25)	.32 (.23)
Left path	.18 (.36)	.00 (.11)	.08 (.23)	.28 (.16)
Nonsolver	.18 (.14)	.23 (.29)	.46 (.52)	.40 (.61)

[a] Predictions in parentheses.

mance across a range of water-jug tasks, neither of the aforementioned experiments directly tested the assumption that subjects use only information about the current problem state and its immediate successors to select a move. Earlier proposals concerning problem-solving processes in transformation problems asserted that move selection involved the planning and execution of multistep move sequences (Egan & Greeno, 1974; Greeno, 1974; Thomas, 1974). Atwood et al. (1980) report experiments that attempt to test the no-planning assumption incorporated into the framework described here. They showed that various assumptions about possible planning mechanisms in the water-jug task would lead to predicted patterns of performance that were quite different than those observed. Further, they showed that there were ways that subjects could discover the primary cause of difficulty in this problem and gain a limited understanding of the problem's underlying structure. Recall that two of the four moves on each step of both solution paths are irreversible moves that lead to one of the four states at the top of the graph. There are several ways that subjects could discover characteristics of these irreversible moves and learn to avoid them once they have encoded the identity of the four critical states in long-term memory. Avoiding moves that lead back to the top of the graph and moves that lead to the immediately preceding state would enable the subject to solve any of these problems at or near the minimum number of moves. Atwood et al. (1980) evaluated the possibility that subjects could develop the understanding necessary to plan on water-jug problems. They compared the performance of subjects in control conditions with those in experimental conditions who were provided information that would presumably facilitate the planning process.

Experiment 2 of Atwood et al. (1980) tested the conjecture that subjects are attempting to use more complex move-selection processes (e.g., forward planning) but are unable to do so reliably because of resource limitations. One interpretation of Atwood and Polson's (1976) results is that requiring a subject to calculate the consequences of each move mentally, as well as to select the next move, uses most of the subject's processing and memory resources. Thus, a subject is unable to execute more complex move-selection processes consistently. This experiment compares performance of subjects in control conditions with subjects in move-availability and memory conditions. In the control conditions, subjects were provided only with the goal and the current state of the problem; they had to calculate the consequences of each possible move. This was the procedure used by Atwood and Polson (1976). Subjects in the move-availability conditions were given the current state, all possible successors of the current state, and the move necessary to reach each successor. Subjects in the memory conditions were provided with the same information given to the subjects in the move-availability conditions (i.e., all successors of the current state and the move required to reach each successor) plus information showing which successors of the current state they had entered previously. There were 12 groups in the experiment: control, move-availability, and memory conditions with four different problems for each of the three conditions. The water-jug problems were similar to those used previously and ranged widely in difficulty.

The observed and predicted mean legal moves to solution from Experiment 2 in Atwood et al. (1980) are shown in Fig. 8.2. An analysis of the legal moves to solution showed significant differences among the four problems and among the three conditions, but the interaction was not significant. Atwood et al. were able to obtain excellent fits to the data from all 12 experimental conditions with a priori shifts in some parameter values, with common values for α and s in all conditions, and by manipulating the single remaining free parameter, β, the probability of making an acceptable move to a previously visited state. For example, the best-fitting value for the parameter r, the number of successors that could be perfectly retained in short-term memory, was found to be 3 for the control condition. Atwood et al. argued that the value for r in the move-availability and memory conditions would equal 4 (the maximum possible value) because a large amount of the information that the subjects had to retain in short-term memory was now presented on the display in the experimental conditions. Furthermore, they argued that the good fits to the data from all experimental conditions and the fact that only a single free parameter had to be manipulated gave strong support to the argument that the model was a good account of performance in control conditions and that, with the plausible auxiliary assumptions, it could account for the data from move-availability and memory conditions.

In addition, Atwood et al. developed an insight model of a possible understanding process that they incorporated into the simulation model. They assumed that with probability p the solver would discover the underlying structure of the water-jug problem in an insightful fashion. This insight process was assumed to

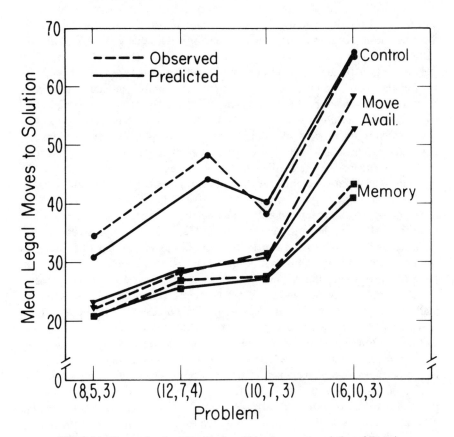

FIG. 8.2.   Observed and predicted values of legal moves to solution of Experiment 2 in Atwood et al. (1980).

occur in an all-or-none manner. After gaining insight, solvers would avoid all moves that looped them to the top of the graph and would only take forward moves. They found it necessary to set their insight-learning parameter to a very low value ($p = .015$) in order to obtain acceptable fits between the data from the memory conditions and predicted performance from the insight model. Attempts to fit the data with more substantial values of the insight parameter (.05 or .10) led the model to predict the problems would be solved far faster than actual subjects did. Atwood et al. concluded that these results substantiate the claim that subjects use only local information in solving such problems.

River-Crossing Tasks

Jeffries, Polson, Razran, & Atwood (1977) sought to extend the framework presented here to account for performance on various isomorphs of the missionaries-cannibals problem. Their objectives were to provide additional support for the theoretical paradigm outlined earlier and at the same time attempt to disprove the conjectures concerning planning processes that several investigators had concluded underlie performance in river-crossing problems (Greeno, 1974; Reed, Ernst, & Banerji, 1974; Thomas, 1974). Our study used isomorphic variants of the following problem. Three missionaries and three cannibals have to cross a river in a boat that holds only two travellers. The problem is complicated by the fact that missionaries can never be outnumbered by cannibals at any point during the ferrying process. We employed four isomorphic versions each involving different characters and giving different motivations to the outnumbering restriction. Figure 8.3 shows the graph of both legal and illegal states for the problem. The legal problem states are shown as rectangles. Illegal states, in which the outnumbering restriction is violated, are shown as ovals. M stands for missionaries; C stands for cannibals. The numbers are state identifiers.

Jeffries, Polson, Razran, & Atwood (1977) made several additions and modifications to the Atwood and Polson (1976) model in order to fit the data from river-crossing problems. All of their changes were confined to the evaluation processes. Recall that the evaluation processes are the way the model represents the subject's understanding of the problem. The most significant change made to the framework was the addition of a process to account for illegal moves. The move-selection processes of the model consider all physically possible moves from any state. Moves that are illegal because they violate the outnumbering restriction are included in this initial move-selection process. Legality of a proposed move is evaluated after it has been selected for execution. This evaluation process, termed the error filter, was assumed to be fallible, and the probability of successfully detecting an illegal move was a function of the perceptual characteristics of the state and, thus, the saliency of the rule violation.

The next change was to incorporate a different evaluation function into the model. The function used was:

$$e_i = aC_i + bM_i + cP_i \qquad\qquad 8.2$$

where C_i is the number of cannibals on the goal bank for state i, M_i is the number of missionaries, P_i is the number of missionary-cannibal pairs, and a, b, and c are positive constants. A similar concept of an acceptability criterion was incorporated into this model. Acceptable moves were those that did not significantly decrease the value of e_i.

Jeffries et al. also incorporated a fixed noticing order. In the missionaries-cannibals problem, the desirability of the move can be determined independently of the configuration of travelers in a state. The rank ordering for moves that they incorporated into the model was as follows: a pair, two missionaries, two cannibals, one missionary, or one cannibal. It was assumed that the preference ordering reversed when returning from the goal bank to the start bank. The noticing order was derived from two considerations that govern move selections in this problem. The first is that the outnumbering restriction is most easily satisfied by

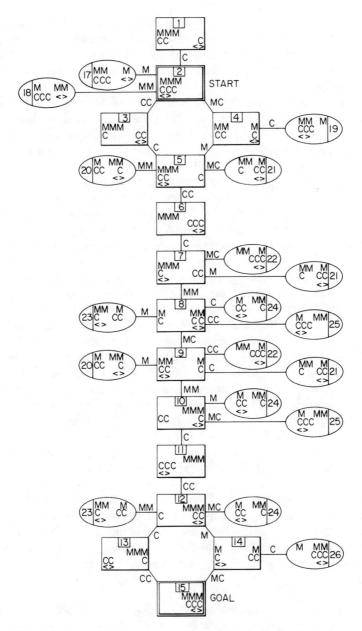

FIG. 8.3. Graph of possible moves and legal and illegal states for (3, 2) version of the missionaries-cannibals problem.

moving a pair of travelers on each move. If this move is physically possible and legal, the problem solver is always assured that the resulting state is also legal. The second criterion involves means–ends considerations. One would always want to take as many travelers from start to goal bank as possible and return as few as possible.

Four groups of 60 subjects each solved one of four different isomorphs of the missionaries-cannibals problems. Jeffries et al. found no differences in the number of legal moves to solution or in the profiles of the mean number of times subjects entered various legal states of the problem. In addition, the legal move data were similar to those obtained from other studies using missionaries-cannibals problems. However, there were significant differences in the number and patterns of illegal moves. For all isomorphs, the largest number of illegal moves were made at states 5 and 8, but the relative numbers of illegal moves made in these two states varied as a function of isomorph.

Jeffries et al. were able to develop models that gave excellent fits to the data from the four isomorphs. The observed and predicted means and standard deviations of legal and illegal moves are shown in Table 8.3.[1] Four models were derived from the general framework having the additions described in the preceding paragraphs. Certain components of the evaluation structure were varied as a function of isomorph. The same noticing order was used in all four conditions as well as the same evaluation function with common values of the weights a, b, and c. The patterns of illegal moves were fit by manipulating the values of the illegal move-rejection parameters for each of the four isomorphs. The model turned out to predict similar patterns of legal moves for a range of weights in the evaluation function and illegal move-filter parameters. This invariance in the pattern of legal moves was found by Jeffries et al. and in other studies of missionaries-cannibals.

The data from river-crossing problems were fit by making some additions and modifications to the original Atwood and Polson (1976) model for water-jug problems. Most of these changes involve the manner in which moves are evaluated (e.g., noticing order, evaluation function). We interpret these modifications as incorporating into the model the fragmentary and frequently incorrect understanding that solvers have of this problem. In domains where more understanding occurs, we found it more productive to model this understanding explicitly rather than incorporate it into various processes of the original framework.

---

[1] After the publication of Jeffries, Polson, Razran & Atwood (1977), we discovered a "bug" in the simulation model that affected the number of backward moves a solver would take. After correcting this error, the simulation for the hobbits-orcs isomorph was rerun. In the corrected simulation, the ad hoc assumption that state 6 was unacceptable was dropped. With minor parameter changes, the model fits the data even better, accounting for 96% of the variance of legal and illegal moves. (The previous model accounted for 94% of the variance.) All subsequent simulations using this framework include the corrected model.

TABLE 8.3
Observed and Predicted[a] Means and Standard Deviations for Legal and Illegal Moves
to Solve Four Isomorphs of the Missionaries-Cannibals Problem
(Adapted from Jeffries, Polson, Razran, and Atwood, 1977, p. 430, Table 1)

	Isomorph			
	Hobbits-Orcs	Elves-Men I	Elves-Men II	Silver-Gold
Legal Moves				
Mean	18.62 (17.75)	18.97 (18.19)	18.67 (17.86)	20.27 (19.59)
SD	10.54 (9.05)	11.05 (10.84)	9.35 (11.11)	11.77 (15.03)
Illegal Moves				
Mean	2.75 (2.51)	5.42 (4.88)	5.50 (5.72)	6.65 (6.32)
SD	2.38 (1.88)	7.16 (3.63)	5.74 (4.48)	5.77 (5.83)

[a] Predictions in parentheses.

PROBLEM SOLVING
AS PARTIAL UNDERSTANDING

The framework from which the models for water-jug and river-crossing problems
were derived has no mechanisms for planning or generating subgoals. It was
assumed that solvers used only local information when solving these problems,
because of their limited understanding of the problem's overall structure. For
naive subjects at least, water-jug and river-crossing problems have no obvious
subgoals. The problem instructions, which simply describe the goal state, the
start state, and the rules for legal moves, evidently give subjects no insights into
the global structure of these tasks. Obviously, this is not true in general. The
claim to be explored in this section is that solvers do plan in situations where they
have at least a partial understanding of the structure of the problem.

Hobbits, Orcs, and Gold

Karat, Polson, Jeffries, and Razran (1978) conjectured that subjects may set up
and manipulate subgoals when they attempt to solve a problem with obvious
subcomponents. They combined the hobbits-orcs isomorph of the river-crossing
problem with the additional concurrent task of ferrying some bags of gold across
the river, one bag at a time. Four different versions of the basic problem, which
we call hobbits, orcs, and gold, were constructed. The number of bags of gold
could be either three or six. Orthogonal to that, half of the versions introduced a
complication: If all three orcs and all the bags of gold are ever left alone on either
side of the river, the orcs steal the gold. This introduces two potential detours
into the problem.

This family of problems has several interesting characteristics. It factors into
two obvious subproblems: (1) ferrying the gold across the river; (2) ferrying the

travelers across. The gold problem is trivial, whereas ferrying the travelers across has been shown to be solved by means–ends driven search. Also, the addition of the complication of the orcs stealing the gold produces an interaction between the two subproblems, whose resolution may not be apparent to someone who does not understand the underlying structure of the missionaries-cannibals problem. Figure 8.4 diagrams the problem states of the three-bag interaction version of the problem.

Karat et al. distinguished among three sets of solution paths and the problem-solving strategies associated with each of them. The gold-first strategy involves using some combination of travelers to ferry the gold across the river first and then moving the travelers across. This takes one across the top of the graph in Fig. 8.4 and then down the right-hand side. In the no-interaction versions, one can travel straight down the right-hand side of the graph; in the interaction versions, this requires a detour. The second strategy, travelers first, requires one first to solve the travelers subproblem and then ferry the gold across. In Fig. 8.4, this moves one down the left-hand side and then across the bottom of the graph. Again note that a detour is required to solve the interaction versions. The final strategy is to solve both problems concurrently (combined strategy); such a solution path moves one diagonally across Fig. 8.4. Note that either of the two sequential strategies, gold first or travelers first, defines a longer than minimum solution path. Moreover, in the interaction versions, solvers are required to detour around an illegal state. The combined strategy solution paths are of minimum length and avoid the detour in the interaction versions.

In the empirical results, two types of solution paths are observed: gold first and combined. Subjects are classified as gold-first solvers if they make a series of moves that results in all the gold being carried across before reaching state 6 of the missionaries-cannibals problem (see Figs. 8.3 and 8.4). The solvers not meeting this criterion are classified as combined solvers. In several replications and variations using these problems, only one subject showed any evidence of using the travelers-first strategy.

This criterion for distinguishing gold-first from combined solvers motivates the use of both three- and six-bag versions of the problem. One can consider stochastic models of the type previously described as analogous to a random walk through the problem space, constrained to move from the upper left to the lower right corner of the problem graph. A model with no planning processes should predict that the likelihood of any path is a function of how directly it heads toward the goal state. Such a random-walk model might produce a sequence that ferried three bags of gold fairly frequently. A sequence involving six bags of gold, however, should occur much less often. On the other hand, for a model with an explicit ferrying process, the length of the ferrying sequence should make no difference in the frequency of its occurrence.

Karat et al. (1978) compared groups of subjects solving one of the four versions of the hobbits, orcs, and gold problem. The empirical results are shown

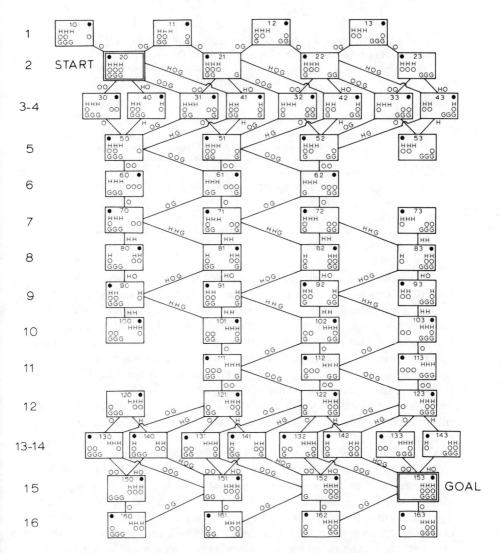

FIG. 8.4. Problem graph of the legal states of the three-bag, interaction version of the hobbits, orcs, and gold problem. H stands for a hobbit; O stands for an orc; G stands for a bag of gold; • is the position of the boat.

in Table 8.4. The six bags of gold versions were more difficult than the three-bags versions. The interaction versions of the problem were more difficult than the no-interaction versions. If we calculate statistics conditionally on solution type (combined or gold first), a better understanding of the results emerges. These results are shown in Table 8.5.

TABLE 8.4

Observed and Predicted[a] Means and Standard Deviations for
Legal Moves and Correlations Between Observed and
Predicted Move Choices for Four Versions of the Hobbits,
Orcs, and Gold Problem

	Condition			
	3-Bag: No Interaction	*3-Bag: Interaction*	*6-Bag: No Interaction*	*6-Bag: Interaction*
Legal Moves				
Mean	22.3 (20.9)	27.0 (28.4)	24.6 (26.5)	31.1 (29.2)
SD	11.8 (13.7)	16.0 (16.4)	9.4 (10.1)	15.9 (15.8)
Correlation	.93	.89	.92	.87

[a] Predictions in parentheses.

The number of gold-first solvers varies across conditions from 50% in the three-bag interaction version of the problem to 31% in the six-bag interaction version. There were no differences in moves to solution between interaction and no-interaction versions of the problems for the combined solvers. In the no-interaction versions, the gold-first solvers took approximately the combined numbers of moves subjects take to solve the two problems separately. The subjects who used the gold-first strategy in the interaction versions of the problem had a great deal of difficulty detouring around the illegal state that the interaction generates. They took many more moves to solve the problem than either the combined solvers on the same problem or the gold-first solvers on the no-interaction versions.

We first attempted to fit the data with a straightforward extension of the Jeffries et al. model. The model was modified by simply defining a noticing order for the 10 possible moves from each state. The best fits were obtained by adopting a generalized means–ends criterion for the noticing order. The first three moves involve combining one bag of gold with: (1) a pair; (2) two hobbits; (3) two orcs. Moves 4 through 6 include the same traveler sequence, but without any gold. The remaining moves were: (7) a hobbit with a bag of gold; (8) an orc with a bag of gold; (9) a hobbit; and (10) an orc. This model gave a reasonable account of the behavior of the combined solvers. However, it had two shortcomings. First, it was unable to predict the necessary percentage of gold-first solvers. Second, the model had a difficult time detouring around the illegal state in the interaction version of the problem.

Inasmuch as the noticing order going from the goal bank back to the start bank is the reverse of the noticing order just presented, the model could not execute an efficient detour around the illegal state. The top two moves on the noticing order did not involve moving a bag of gold; therefore, the model had a tendency to

TABLE 8.5

Observed and Predicted[a] Means and Standard Deviations for Legal Moves as a Function of Solution Path Choice and Percentages of Solvers Selecting the Gold-first Solution Path for Four Versions of the Hobbits, Orcs, and Gold Problem

	3 Bag:No Interaction		3-Bag:Interaction		6-Bag:No Interaction		6-Bag:Interaction	
	Combined	Gold-first	Combined	Gold-first	Combined	Gold-first	Combined	Gold-first
Legal Moves								
Mean	19.5 (18.9)	26.1 (23.8)	17.5 (18.4)	36.5 (38.3)	21.0 (21.8)	29.3 (31.8)	23.8 (21.4)	57.3 (45.3)
SD	9.6 (12.8)	14.0 (14.6)	7.9 (8.6)	16.6 (18.8)	8.9 (6.5)	7.8 (12.0)	10.3 (7.0)	20.2 (21.2)
%Gold-first	41% (40%)		50% (53%)		44% (42%)		31% (36%)	

[a] Predictions in parentheses.

return to the start bank without taking a bag of gold, a move that is necessary to get around the illegal state. Furthermore, once it had succeeded in getting a bag of gold back across the river, the moves at the top of the noticing order on the next move all included gold. Thus, the model would tend to get trapped in the upper right-hand corner of the graph (see Fig. 8.4) and oscillate.

To account for these two aspects of the data successfully, a new model was constructed that includes two assumptions about the type of understanding that occurs in this problem. First, the model understands that the two subproblems are independent and can be treated separately. Second, the idea of ferrying the remaining bags of gold across the river is discovered in an insightful fashion and is modeled by a simple all-or-none model of the insight process.

The model assumes that the solver treats the two subproblems separately: Flags are kept in working memory that indicate which, if either, of the two subproblems is solved. First, the solver attempts to deal with the gold subproblem. If it is not yet solved, with probability f the solver decides to ferry the remaining bags of gold across the river. The ferry strategy involves a repetition of the last legal move carrying a bag of gold when traveling from the start to the goal bank. If the solver decides not to ferry, a decision is still required as to whether gold should be taken on this move. Gold will be moved with probability g if the move is from the start bank and with probability h if the move is from the goal bank. g will be a high probability, whereas h will be low. Once a decision to move gold or not has been made, the simulation calls on the Jeffries et al. model to select hobbits and orcs to be moved, that move is combined with the gold choice, and the move is executed.

The model claims that understanding and search in this problem factor perfectly. The search processes involving the gold subproblem are trivial. Choices of moves involving travelers are made by the Jeffries et al. model, which is called as a subroutine, with the same parameters used in both models. Observed and predicted means and standard deviations for moves to solution for the no-interaction conditions are shown in Tables 8.4 and 8.5. The model fits the data well. It can correctly account for the percentage of subjects who used the gold-first strategy. Correlations between observed and predicted state to state transition frequencies for the no-interaction conditions range from .91 to .94.

Two modifications were made to the model to account for the data from the interaction conditions. First, a temporary change in the probability of moving gold is introduced whenever the solver is trapped in the upper right-hand corner of the graph. The model realizes it is trapped once it considers the move into the illegal state that permits the gold to be stolen. It immediately takes one bag of gold back across the river. Next, the probability of moving gold at all is drastically reduced for the next two or three moves. At the end of this sequence, when the solver has detoured around the illegal state, the same processes described for the no-interaction version are used to complete the solution to the problem. These modifications describe solvers' understanding of the fact that it is necessary to take at least one bag of gold back across the river and keep it there for several moves until the illegal state is detoured.

The second modification to the model incorporates the realization of some subjects that they could avoid the difficulty introduced by the interaction if they ferried all but one of the bags of gold across the river and then solved the travelers subproblem. The ferrying process is the same for both the interaction and no-interaction versions of the model. However, if a solver has not decided to ferry but has moved all but one of the bags of gold across the river, the probability of moving a bag of gold is greatly decreased until most of the travelers have crossed the river.

With these additions, the model also accounts for the results in the interaction conditions. The same parameter values are used to fill all four conditions in the experiment. The model's results for the interaction conditions are also shown in Tables 8.4 and 8.5. The percentage of gold-first solvers is well accounted for, and the state-to-state transition frequencies correlations range from .85 to .91.

These results demonstrate that problem solving in these sorts of tasks can be characterized as a subtle mixture of understanding and search. They suggest that subjects will exploit all of the information that can be derived from the description of the problem and from experience with various subproblems encountered during the solution. The model contains a detailed and deterministic description of the aspects of the problem grasped by all subjects. The Jeffries et al. model proves to be a good description of the default means–ends search process that was used to select moves in situations where little understanding occurs.

Tower of Hanoi

A transformation problem with a very different flavor from water-jug and river-crossing problems is the Tower of Hanoi. This problem has a number of interesting structural and perceptual properties. The problem solution is hierarchically structured, with each version containing all smaller variants as subproblems. Moreover, even a naive subject can infer a great deal from only the start state, goal state, and problem rules about possible subgoals and reasonable courses of action. The problem involves some number of graduated disks (three to six in the experiments reported here), which are initially stacked on one of three pegs. The task is to transfer the disks to another peg (the goal peg). The rules of the problem specify that the disks are to be moved one at a time, with the restriction that a larger disk may never be placed on top of a smaller one.

The Tower of Hanoi has been one of the most extensively studied transformation problems. It has been used to study transfer (Hayes & Simon, 1976a) and the understanding of written instructions (Hayes & Simon, 1976b). Simon (1975) has presented an analysis of the kinds of strategies that could be used to solve such problems in a minimal number of moves. The Tower of Hanoi was one of the tasks given to GPS in Ernst and Newell's (1969) study of problem solving

and generality. Anzai and Simon (1979) studied the learning processes of a
subject who repeatedly solved the Tower problem and rapidly gained a complete
understanding of a general strategy sufficient to solve all such problems.

The problem graph of the three-disk problem is presented in Fig. 8.5; a
schematic of the five-disk problem is presented in Fig. 8.6. Figure 8.5 shows all
possible legal configurations of disks for the three-disk problem. Lines connecting each node represent the legal moves. There are 27 states for this problem. In
general, there are 3^N possible states in the N-disk Tower of Hanoi problem; the
minimal number of moves to solution is $2^N - 1$. Figure 8.6 abstracts the legal
moves for the five-disk problem by treating each three-disk problem as a single
move. Thus, each triangle in Fig. 8.6 could be expanded into a replica of Fig. 8.5
with additions of disks 4 and 5 and other changes in labeling.

The recursive characteristics of this problem are apparent in the illustrations.
First, the three-disk problem graph consists of three two-disk problem graphs
connected by moves of the largest disk. Second, the five-disk problem can be
broken down into three four-disk problems connected by moves of the largest

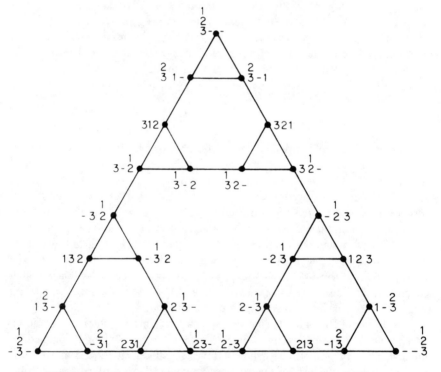

FIG. 8.5. Problem graph of the legal moves and states for the three-disk Tower
of Hanoi problem. Disks are represented by the numbers 1, 2, and 3, with 1 being
the smallest disk. (from Karat, in press)

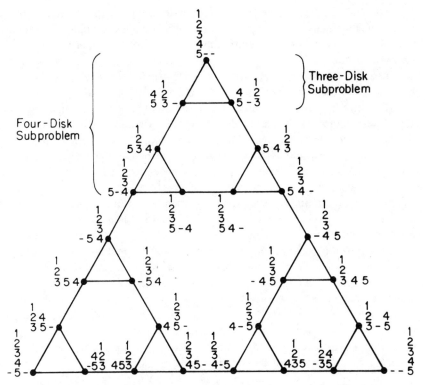

FIG. 8.6.   A schematic problem graph of the five-disk Tower of Hanoi problem where each three-disk subproblem is represented as a single move. Disks are represented by the numbers 1 to 5. (from Karat, in press)

disk, and each four-disk problem can be similarly broken down into three-disk subproblems. In general, the graph of any N-disk Tower of Hanoi problem is composed of three $(N - 1)$-disk problem graphs connected by moves of the largest disk. This property of the problem permits an elegant, recursive characterization of the solution in terms of solutions to the smaller problems of which it is composed.

Karat (in press) has developed a model that accounts for the behavior of subjects solving Tower of Hanoi problems (both legal moves and move latencies). The model is based on the assumption that subjects have some limited understanding of how to go about solving the problem but are not able to generate a complete solution plan. Solution of the problem involves a mixture of understanding and search, similar to that observed in the hobbits, orcs, and gold problem. Karat describes the model as a hierarchical production system. The productions making up the model are grouped into three subsystems referred to as the *execute, propose,* and *evaluate* subsystems.

Productions in the execute subsystem monitor the contents of working memory for the presence of information about approved moves that must be executed. If such a move is in working memory, the execute subsystem causes the move to be taken. If no move is currently in working memory, the propose subsystem is activated. This subsystem consists of rules for generating moves given information about the current state. There are two subsets of such rules, which correspond to situations where the solver does or does not have an understanding of an appropriate course of action. In the former, configurational properties of the situation cause specific moves to be deterministically selected; in the latter, moves that are consistent with a means–ends criterion are stochastically selected. The evaluate subsystem examines proposed moves for legality.

This model is intended to account for the performance of subjects who have had minimal pretraining on other versions of the task. With this small amount of experience, subjects appear to acquire information about both the local and global attributes of the problem.

The local information is derived from two simple heuristics. The first is that it is never useful to move the same disk on two successive moves because the same result could have always been accomplished in a single move. Because of the structure of the task, this leads to the realization that the smallest disk (disk 1) should be moved on odd-numbered moves, whereas some other disk should be moved on even-numbered moves. The second heuristic is to avoid undoing the effects of moves recently made. This heuristic, combined with the realization about alternating moves of the smallest disk, leads to solving the problem by repetition of the following four-move pattern: (1) move the smallest disk; (2) move disk 2 to the only available peg; (3) put disk 1 on disk 2; (4) move the only possible other disk. Any other move sequence leads to the undoing of a recently accomplished state; in particular, if disk 1 is not replaced on top of disk 2, the effects of moving disk 2 must be undone. Note that in this sequence, where the smallest disk is to be moved in step 1 is not specified. Additional heuristics are required to select among the two possible moves at this point.

Solvers also appear to acquire an understanding of some of the major subgoals in the solution to this problem. They realize that the movement of the largest disk is the most constrained. Therefore, once it is placed on the goal peg, it is important that it not be moved again. Once the largest disk is on the goal peg, the second largest disk becomes the critical disk, and so on.

The model assumes that the solver uses means–ends driven search in situations where the foregoing heuristics do not lead to the choice of a unique move (i.e., in the move of disk 1 in step 1). When a single execution of the four-step cycle leads to the solution of the current subgoal, the correct move of disk 1 is selected. Otherwise, with probability p_1, the move that leads closer to the goal according to a means–ends criterion is chosen. The means–ends criterion is also occasionally applied to the move of disk 1 in step 3. This move is often counter to a means–ends strategy. Most of the time (probability p_2), a solver will make the move dictated by the avoid loops heuristic; however, occasionally this process fails, and the other move of disk 1, which is consistent with a means–ends rule, is chosen.

To make the workings of this model clearer, a short description of how it solves three-, four-, and five-disk Tower of Hanoi problems follows. The three-disk problem is trivial for both subjects and the model. It first moves disks 1 and 2 out of the way of the largest disk; then it moves the largest disk over to the goal peg, thus accomplishing its current subgoal; and finally it moves disks 1 and 2 on top of disk 3.

The four-disk problem is more difficult. The model begins by establishing the subgoal of moving disk 4 to the goal peg. It now decides to move disk 1, but the solution to the subgoal is far enough away that it cannot determine which move to take. Since for the four-disk problem, the correct initial move is counter to the means-ends strategy, the correct move will be chosen with probability $(1 - p_1)$. If the correct first move is chosen, the model has a high probability of solving the problem in a minimum path. The only errors made will be failures of the avoid loops rule, but these occur infrequently. If the wrong first move is chosen, the model wanders through the problem graph until it manages to accomplish the current subgoal. The remainder of the problem, which is equivalent to a three-disk problem, is solved in a near minimum path as before.

Note that the model does not divide the four-disk problem into two three-disk subproblems with an intervening move of the largest disk. However, once the largest disk is moved to the goal peg, the model is able to treat the remainder of the problem exactly as if it were a three-disk problem (which it is).

The five-disk problem presents even more difficulties for the model. It essentially wanders through the problem graph until the first subgoal is accomplished. It then solves the remainder of the problem exactly as it solved the four-disk problem.

Karat (in press) reports an experiment in which he recorded both move choices and latencies for four groups of subjects solving a series of pretraining problems followed by a five-disk problem. The groups varied in the nature of their pretraining. The first group had a single three-disk training problem. The second group had six three-disk training problems, defined by the various possible combinations of the start and goal peg. The third group had three three-disk problems followed by three four-disk problems. The fourth group had one three-disk training problem followed by two five-disk problems. Subjects' performance on the final five-disk problem was very similar for groups 2–4, even though group 4 had two five-disk problems during pretraining.

The model fits the data very well. It accounts nicely for the relative difficulties of the three-, four-, and five-disk problems. Moreover, its predictions about the relative difficulties of the two halves of the five-disk problem are supported. Table 8.6 shows the observed and predicted moves to solution for groups 3 and 4 on the five-disk problem and its various subproblems. Not only does the model

TABLE 8.6
Observed and Predicted Mean Legal Moves
to Solve Five-disk Tower of Hanoi, Selected Subproblems,
and Training Problems (adapted from Karat, in press)

	Observed		Predicted
	Group 3	Group 4	
Full five-disk problem	47.4	46.3	46.0
First four-disk subproblem	29.2	26.7	27.2
Second four-disk subproblem	18.2	19.6	18.8
Third three-disk subproblem	10.8	12.3	11.8
Final three-disk subproblem	7.3	7.3	7.0
Final four-disk training problem	17.6	—	
Final three-disk training problem	7.5	—	

match the subjects' overall data, but its predictions that the final four-disk and three-disk subproblems are solved exactly the same as in isolation are borne out. The mean number of moves to solve the final four-disk and three-disk subproblems within the five-disk problem are indistinguishable from the number of moves required to solve the three-disk and four-disk training problems.

River-Crossing Problems Revisited

Schmalhofer, Polson, and Karat (in preparation) have developed a model for river-crossing problems from the same framework that motivated Karat's (in press) model for the Tower of Hanoi problem. The components of this framework are: (1) the model is formalized as a production system; (2) there are productions that describe a solver's understanding of the structure of the problem and of the deterministic move choices that are the results of this understanding; (3) there are productions that describe general search processes (e.g., means-ends analysis) as they manifest themselves in this particular task environment; (4) the production system can be partitioned into execute, propose, and evaluate subsystems.

The propose subsystem of the Schmalhofer et al. model generates up to three potential moves from the current state for the evaluate subsystem to consider. These moves are either selected randomly from the possible moves, or they are selected to be consistent with a strategy of keeping the travelers balanced. Which selection criterion is used varies from move to move. Once the set of moves is selected, they are stored in a means–ends order before being passed to the evaluate subsystem.

The evaluate subsystem evaluates each of the selected moves. With some probability, a move will be taken if it is acceptable according to the current criterion; otherwise, the evaluation process will continue to a deeper level. First, a proposed move may be taken without any evaluation. At the second level, the model tests to see if the move returns to the just previously visited state or to another particularly salient state (e.g., the start state). If it does, the move is rejected; otherwise, the move may be accepted, or the analysis may continue. In the final level of analysis, the move is evaluated to see if it satisfies the means-ends criterion or if it would undo a desirable configuration. The model recognizes that having the missionaries all on the goal bank is highly desirable. At this level of evaluation, it will reject any move that returns missionaries to the start bank once all missionaries have been moved to the goal bank.

In the execute subsystem, the move is evaluated for legality and for whether it returns to an already visited state. Both of these processes are fallible. The representation of the resulting state is then stored in long-term memory.

The Schmalhofer et al. model provides a more useful characterization of the relationship between search and understanding components in the solution of river-crossing problems than did the earlier model. In attempting to extend the Jeffries et al. model to more complex river-crossing problems, we found that aspects of subjects' understanding of the problem were being introduced into the model in baroque and ad hoc ways. The propose, evaluate, execute framework makes the distinction between understanding and search processes clearer. In addition, other problems can easily be incorporated into this theory, as well as notions about learning and transfer.

Table 8.7 presents observed and predicted means and standard deviations for legal and illegal moves and correlations between observed and predicted state-to-state transition frequencies for an experiment that compared three versions of the hobbits-orcs problem. A single set of parameters was used to fit all three problems. The resulting fits are quite reasonable.

TABLE 8.7
Observed and Predicted[a] Means and Standard Deviations
for Legal and Illegal Moves and Correlations
Between Observed and Predicted Move Choices
for Three Versions of the Missionaries-Cannibals Problem

	Problem		
	(3,2)	*(4,3)*	*(5,3)*
Legal Moves			
Mean	16.55 (17.34)	18.90 (18.45)	28.25 (27.37)
SD	6.85 (7.72)	12.48 (9.51)	17.67 (15.28)
Illegal Moves			
Mean	3.73 (2.86)	3.13 (2.69)	5.63 (5.24)
SD	5.47 (3.09)	3.60 (2.77)	6.23 (4.73)
Correlations			
Legal Moves	.97	.91	.93
Illegal Moves	.91	.90	.91

[a] Predictions in parentheses.

COMPLETE UNDERSTANDING:
LEARNING AND TRANSFER

We have characterized the performance of naive subjects solving transformation problems as a mixture of search and understanding. We now consider the performance of subjects who have acquired a fairly complete understanding of a problem through learning. We focus on what is learned in such tasks rather than on a detailed description of the mechanisms underlying the learning process. This section examines the kind of understanding a subject acquires through experience and how the conditions of acquisition can affect that understanding. First, we consider a problem in which the understanding necessary for a minimum path solution is acquired in an insightful, all-or-none manner. Then, we explore what is learned when subjects repeatedly solve a river-crossing problem. Finally, we show that river-crossing problems can be used fruitfully to investigate educational issues such as differences between discovery and expository learning.

These experiments make extensive use of versions of the missionaries-cannibals problem. The experiments utilize problems involving ferrying n missionaries and n cannibals in a boat that holds k travelers, with the usual restriction that the cannibals can never outnumber the missionaries on either bank of the river. We denote such a river-crossing problem by the tuple (n, k).

The set of problems used in these studies can be solved by one of two general strategies. The first is a repetitive solution in which two pairs of travelers are taken across the river, the boat returns with one pair and the cycle repeats until all the travelers have been transferred to the goal bank. Any river-crossing problem involving a boat that holds at least four travelers can be solved with this strategy. Examples include $(4, 4)$, $(5, 4)$, $(6, 4)$, $(8, 4)$, and $(8, 5)$. We call such problems four-in-the-boat problems and refer to this move sequence as the *pairs strategy*. All river crossing problems can also be solved by a second strategy: (1) take the orcs across the river; (2) interchange the positions of the hobbits and the orcs; (3) ferry the remaining orcs back across the river. We refer to this strategy as the *orcs-switch-orcs strategy*.

The more complex river-crossing problems have multiple, empirically distinguishable solutions. To evaluate what has been learned during the training process, we examine subjects' performance on novel problems that have several distinct solutions. It is possible to evaluate how various training problem procedures and instructions affect what is learned by observing changes in the distribution of subjects using various solutions to a particular transfer problem.

Four-in-the-Boat Problems

In some problem-solving situations, the understanding of a problem can be characterized as an insight process. A subject's discovery of the pairs strategy when solving a four-in-the-boat problem is an example of such a process. The acquisition and transfer of the pairs strategy in such problems were investigated in the series of experiments reported by Jeffries, Polson, Razran, and Tinsley (1977), Jeffries, Polson, and Tinsley (1978), and Jeffries and Polson (in preparation).

Jeffries, Polson, Razran, and Tinsley (1977) investigated acquisition of the pairs strategy by having subjects in different conditions solve four-in-the-boat problems that had varying length solution paths. Various groups solved either (4, 4), (5, 4), or (6, 4) problems. Jeffries et al. distinguished three kinds of solutions involving utilization of the pairs path. Subjects were considered to have discovered the pairs strategy if they made a sequence of short latency moves that involved taking two pairs of travelers from the start to the goal bank and returning with one pair, but made no illegal moves during the sequence. The sequence had to terminate at the solution state. A computer program did the actual classification of solution strategies.

A *preplanner* was an individual who exhibited perfect mastery of the pairs strategy from the first move of the problem. An *insight planner* exhibited an initial sequence of trial-and-error behavior but made a sudden transition to short latency moves that were on the pairs path. A *gradual planner* showed the same pattern of move choices as an insight planner but a different pattern of move latencies. After starting the sequence of moves on the pairs path, the gradual planner showed a gradual reduction in the latency of moves.

Jeffries et al. (1977) found that 13% of the subjects, independent of the problem solved, used the pairs strategy from the very start (preplanners). They also found that the probability of discovering the pairs solution, if it was not employed initially, was a function of the length of the solution path. The distribution of the percentage of subjects in each condition who used the various strategies is shown in Table 8.8.

The behavior of subjects who have discovered the pairs strategy is not consistent with that of subjects solving other types of river-crossing problems, nor is it consistent with the predictions of the Jeffries et al. (1977) model. Because paired moves are at the top of the noticing order, the model predicts that some of the moves will be consistent with the pairs strategy. What the model cannot predict is a long sequence of such moves. Taking a pair back is a low probability move for a subject.

Jeffries, Polson, Razran, and Tinsley (1977) argued that discovery of the pairs strategy was a learning process not within the scope of the model. Rather, this discovery was an example of the type of sequence-induction processes that are part of the learning-by-doing mechanisms discussed by Anzai and Simon (1979). Regularities in the move sequence can be detected and extrapolated by subjects. Successful discovery of such a sequence radically changes the subjects' understanding of the problem and the resulting problem-solving behavior. Jeffries et al. (1978) further evaluated the conjecture that discovery of the pairs strategy was an example of insightful learning and that the insight changed the subjects'

TABLE 8.8
Classification of Subjects by Type of Plan
and Mean Legal Moves for Each Plan Type
of Subjects Solving Three
Four-in-the-boat Problems

	Problem		
	(4, 4)	*(5, 4)*	*(6, 4)*
Percent classified as[a]			
Preplanners	14%	11%	14%
Insight Planners	38%	42%	48%
Gradual Planners	0%	16%	29%
Nonplanners	48%	32%	10%
Legal moves			
Preplanners	5.0	7.0	9.0
Insight Planners	6.3	9.0	11.3
Gradual Planners	—	15.6	12.5
Nonplanners	8.4	13.3	20.8

[a] Percentages may not add to 100% due to rounding error.

understanding of the four-in-the-boat problem. If the insight hypothesis is correct, once a subject discovers the pairs strategy, the strategy should transfer
perfectly to a second problem.

The training procedure involved having subjects in three groups solving either
the (4, 4), (5, 4), or (6, 4) problem. Subjects were then given the (6, 4) problem
to solve. Data from experiments using isomorphs of the (3, 2) problem have
shown that there was surprisingly little improvement in subjects' performance
after a single solution (Reed et al., 1974). In contrast, Jeffries et al. (1978)
found that 91% of their subjects who discovered the pairs strategy on the first
problem used it exclusively on the second problem. This supported their claim
that subjects understood the strategy and its applicability to new problems.

Learning and Transfer
in Other River-Crossing Problems

Next we describe situations in which the learning process occurs over several
repetitions of the training problem. Jeffries (1978, 1979) focused on two questions. The first was what an individual learns by solving a sequential problem
until reaching a strict performance criterion. Jeffries was particularly interested
in whether subjects' understanding could be characterized as the abstraction of
the general structure underlying solution or whether the subject simply
memorizes the sequence of moves. She evaluated these two possibilities by

having subjects solve a novel problem. The transfer problem was so structured that different strategies acquired during training would manifest themselves as empirically distinguishable behaviors during solution of the transfer problem.

A second closely related issue examined by Jeffries concerns how information acquired during training will be applied to solution of the transfer task. The answer, of course, depends on what is learned and on the nature of the understanding that results from the training process. One can view a transfer task as a problem-solving situation in which the task is to discover how previously acquired knowledge can be applied in a novel situation. Currently, very little is understood about how individuals solve transfer problems. In fact, problems that are structurally identical can be perceived by subjects as completely unrelated, if the problem descriptions are baroque enough (e.g., compare the descriptions of the Tower of Hanoi and the Tea Ceremony in Hayes & Simon, 1974).

Jeffries used three versions of the hobbits-orcs problems in her experiment: (3, 2), (5, 3), and (6, 4). All of these problems can be solved by the orcs-switch-orcs strategy. In addition, the pairs strategy can be used to solve the (6, 4) problem. Two water-jug problems were also used, the (24, 21, 3) and (8, 5, 3) problems (from Atwood & Polson, 1976). Recall that the (24, 21, 3) problem can be solved using a pure means–ends strategy and is a trivial problem for naive subjects. The solution of the (8, 5, 3) problem requires violations of the means–ends strategy and is consequently more difficult.

Jeffries' motivations for selecting these two types of problems came from the fact that similar process models have been used to account for performance of naive subjects on both water-jug and river-crossing problems. The strategy-transformation model of Neches and Hayes (1978) and Neches (1979) suggests that extensive experience with a process should lead to better integrated, more efficient realizations of the process when it is employed on another task. Thus, she conjectured that there could be positive transfer between water-jug and river-crossing problems because trained subjects would use a more sophisticated variant of the common process.

The experiment involved eight groups of subjects. A common procedure was used in all experimental conditions. Subjects solved training problems to a criterion of three consecutive, minimum path, errorless solutions. They were then transferred to another training problem or to the final test task. The final problem was solved once.

The eight groups were: (1–2) control groups given only a test problem, either (6, 4) or (5, 3); (3–4) groups trained on the (24, 21, 3) water-jug problem following by one of the two test problems, either (6, 4) or (5, 3); (5–6) groups trained on the (8, 5, 3) water-jug problem followed by one of the two test problems; (7–8) groups trained on the (3, 2) river-crossing problem and then transferred to one of the two test problems. The data on the first trial of the second problem were used to evaluate performance on the test problems after being trained on a single river-crossing problem. Subjects were trained on this new problem until they reached the learning criterion. They were then transferred to the other test problem. Thus, these last two groups provided data for two comparisons: transfer performance after training on a single problem and then performance after training on a second river-crossing task.

Two sorts of analyses were carried out on the data from the test problems. The first involved characterizing subjects' performance in terms of mean number of legal moves to solve the test problems. The results for the various groups are shown in Table 8.9. Asterisks indicate those groups that were significantly different from their appropriate control. The results for the (5, 3) problem show that training on one or more river-crossing problems led to significant improvements in performance on the test task. The results for the (6, 4) transfer problem show little or no improvement as a function of training. This was due to the fact that even naive subjects solved this problem in nearly a minimal number of moves, using the pairs strategy.

Moves to solution as a dependent measure are not very illuminating for a sequential problem of any complexity. For these problems, there are solutions having widely differing structures. An analysis of the two test problems, (5, 3) and (6, 4), was performed, and a set of templates that describe possible solution strategies was developed.

A computer program was written that matched subjects' move sequences against the templates representing each strategy. If the subject made more than three errors (e.g., illegal moves) or took more than 18 legal moves to solve the problem, none of the templates would match, and the subject was considered to have used some sort of trial-and-error process. Thus, all of the strategy templates assume that utilization of the strategy would enable the subject to solve the problem in a near minimal number of moves, making at most one or two errors.

TABLE 8.9
Mean Legal Moves to Solve Two
Missionaries-Cannibals Problems
as a Function of Training Condition
(Adapted from Jeffries, 1978)

	Test Problem	
Training Problem	(5, 3)	(6, 4)
None	31.5	11.2
(24, 21, 3)	31.3	11.5
(8, 5, 3)	26.4	11.9
(3, 2)	16.4*	10.4
(3, 2) & (5, 3)	—	9.5
(3, 2) & (6, 4)	16.1*	—

*differs significantly ($p < .01$) from the appropriate control.

Each template described one or more move sequences consistent with the underlying strategy. A template was considered to fit if there were no more than two deviations from one of the move sequences specified by the template.

Five different strategies and their associated move templates were identified. For two strategies, simple and sophisticated memorized moves, the transfer solution is a transformation of a move sequence that solved the training problem. Simple memorized moves involve the utilization of the identical move sequence that solved the training problem. This leads to a dead end after five or six moves because the move sequence for the training problem cannot be continued in the test problem. Sophisticated memorized moves involve some transformation of the sequence used to solve the training problem into a move sequence that can be used to solve the test problem. The best illustration of such a transformation is the transformation of the solution to the (3, 2) problem into a solution to the (6, 4) problem. In this case, sophisticated memorized moves involve doubling the numbers of both kinds of travelers from each move of the (3, 2) problem.

The majority of the subjects trained on hobbits-orcs problems used some variation of the general orcs-switch-orcs strategy in order to solve the test problem. A detailed description of the strategy is as follows: First, ferry almost all of the orcs across the river. Next, move the hobbits so that there are equal numbers of hobbits and orcs on the goal bank. Now, move a pair of travelers from the goal bank back to the start bank. Then, move all of the hobbits remaining on the start bank to the goal bank, moving orcs back to the start bank as needed. This completes the intermediate stage of exchanging the positions of the hobbits and orcs. The final stage is simply to ferry back to the goal bank all the orcs that were returned to the start bank.

The next strategy, means–ends, is a sort of catchall. It includes those sequences of moves that are consistent with a generalized means–ends strategy in that a maximum number of travelers are moved from the start to the goal bank and a minimum number are returned. There is a large amount of overlap between the means–ends strategy and some paths in the orcs-switch-orcs strategy. Means–ends was used as a default description for any rapid and efficient solution to a problem that is not better described by one of the more specific strategies outlined earlier. Finally, the pairs strategy, which is only applicable in the (6, 4) problem, involves bringing two pairs of travelers from the start to the goal bank, returning with a pair, and cycling that move sequence until the problem is solved.

The results of the strategy-classification procedure are shown in Table 8.10. First, note that for the untrained subjects, all of the solution strategies except pairs on the (6, 4) problem have low base rates. Second, observe that the distribution of strategies used by subjects pretrained on a water-jug problem is very similar to the observed distributions for subjects who received no pretraining. There is some suggestion of an additional increase in the utilization of the means–end strategy for subjects pretrained on the (8, 5, 3) water-jug problem. However, this may be an artifact. A significantly larger number of subjects were

TABLE 8.10
Percentages of Subjects Conforming to Each Strategy Template
on Two Missionaries-Cannibals Test Problems as a Function of Training Problem
(Adapted from Jeffries, 1978)

Training Condition	Test Problem	Simple Memorized Moves	Sophisticated Memorized Moves	Orcs-Switch-Orcs	Means-Ends	Pairs	None
None	(5, 3)	0	5	6	3	—	87
	(6, 4)	0	0	0	3	60	38
(24, 21, 3)	(5, 3)	0	0	3	7	—	90
	(6, 4)	0	0	4	8	80	6
(8, 5, 3)	(5, 3)	0	0	3	13	—	85
	(6, 4)	0	0	3	17	70	10
(3, 2)	(5, 3)	8	5	58	10	—	20
	(6, 4)	0	13	58	15	13	3
(3, 2) & (6, 4)	(5, 3)	3	8	56	8	—	28
(3, 2) & (5, 3)	(6, 4)	0	0	78	10	3	10

replaced in this condition because they failed to reach criterion on both training task and test problem in the time allotted.

Examination of the bottom half of Table 8.10 shows that training on hobbits-orcs problems had a dramatic effect on transfer performance. A majority of the trained subjects use the orcs-switch-orcs strategy. Another interesting point comes from the comparison of the transfer performance of the two groups that received a single (3, 2) training problem. Note that the distribution of strategies used to solve the transfer problems is very similar for both (5, 3) and (6, 4) problems, even though the overt manifestations are quite different for these two tasks. In addition, observe that there is a dramatic reduction in the use of the pairs strategy in the (6, 4) problem. Naive subjects almost exclusively use this strategy to solve the (6, 4) problem.

The results give credence to the claim that subjects acquire an understanding of the structure of problems that are solvable by the orcs-switch-orcs strategy from exposure to a single realization of the strategy. Further, this understanding is derived from memory for the actual sequence of moves used to solve the (3, 2) problem, rather than from an abstract understanding of the orcs-switch-orcs strategy. A significant portion of the subjects showed patterns of solution performance that could be directly identified with the solution to the training problem (i.e., simple and sophisticated memorized move strategies).

The fact that training on the water-jug problems had little effect on performance of the testing problems either in terms of moves to solution or in changes to strategies suggests that there is very little, if any, in the way of generalized transfer from one transformation problem to another. The training procedure used in the Jeffries experiment seems to have led to a narrow kind of understanding, in the sense that subjects showed great facility in transferring from one variation of a river-crossing problem to another, but little or no facility from practice with another transformation problem like the water-jug task.

Discovery Versus Expository Learning

McDaniel (1980) used the training procedures and transfer performance evaluation processes that were developed by Jeffries in order to study a question that has been of central interest to educators and psychologists for many years: What differences, if any, exist between discovery and expository learning? Many claims have been made to the effect that discovery learning promotes deeper understanding of a class of problems (Bruner, 1961; Kendler, 1966; Suchman, 1961); equally strong counterproposals have been put forward claiming that expository training produces a deeper level of understanding (Ausubel, 1964).

There is a large body of literature that attempts to settle the question of the superiority of expository or discovery learning. McDaniel's review of this literature brought to light several interesting facts. First, much of the research in this problem has used puzzles equivalent in complexity to river-crossing problems. Second, many of the training procedures used in these experiments resulted in low levels of performance on the transfer tasks that were used to evaluate the efficacy of the various training procedures; strong conclusions are made about the superiority of discovery or expository learning based on data that show low levels of performance for all groups. When data from naive controls are available, reservations concerning the absolute effectiveness of any of the training procedures become stronger. Finally, none of the studies that McDaniel reviewed used sophisticated techniques to evaluate what was learned. Thus, McDaniel sought an experimental situation that would lead to high levels of transfer performance by training subjects—one that would enable him to operationalize precisely what was meant by superior, more insightful, or flexible performance.

All of McDaniel's subjects were trained on the (5, 3) problem to a criterion of three consecutive, minimum path, errorless solutions. Half the subjects in each training condition were then transferred to the (8, 4) problem and the remainder to the (8, 5) problem. All three of these problems can be solved by different variations of the general orcs-switch-orcs strategy. In addition, the (8, 4) problem can be solved using the pairs strategy; the (8, 5) problem also has a pairs solution, but it is not minimum path. Furthermore, adaptation of the orcs-switch-orcs solution for the (5, 3) problem to the (8, 4) problem is a nontrivial task in itself. McDaniel argued that questions concerning the superiority and flexibility of the knowledge gained in a given training condition should translate into the efficiency with which a subject receiving a specific type of training could construct a solution to a test problem.

McDaniel's basic procedures were identical to those used by Jeffries. Half of McDaniel's subjects were trained using a discovery or, in McDaniel's terms, "bottom–up" training procedure. In these conditions, subjects were simply given the rules for the problem. Subjects in the expository ("top–down") conditions were given a brief, quite abstract, description of the general orcs-switch-orcs strategy.

Analysis of the training phase showed an almost 2:1 superiority in terms of number of problem repetitions to reach criterion for those subjects receiving the expository instructions. Analyses of the solution paths chosen by subjects during repeated solutions to the training problem showed that this superiority occurred because top–down subjects more rapidly acquired various components of the general orcs-switch-orcs strategy than did bottom–up subjects. Bottom–up subjects explored a number of alternative incorrect solutions before finally discovering the orcs-switch-orcs strategy. In particular, they had a great deal of difficulty in discovering that they had to take almost all of the orcs across the river as their initial sequence of moves.

McDaniel found that there were no differences in performance for bottom–up and top–down trained subjects in terms of legal moves to solution and other such measures on the transfer task. Thus, questions concerning the efficacy and flexibility of knowledge acquired during training were recast in terms of the kinds of strategies that various groups of subjects used on the initial solution to the transfer problem.

McDaniel identified six different solution strategies: three variations of the general orcs-switch-orcs schema; two mixed strategies in which, during the first or last half of the problem, the move sequence was consistent with orcs-switch-orcs and a pairs solution path was used to traverse the remaining segment of the problem; and a pure pairs strategy.

Examination of Table 8.11 shows that the performance of the two groups was very similar. A significant percentage of subjects in the top–down groups used the orcs-switch-orcs-1 strategy, in which the initial sequence of moves involved only orcs. Otherwise, there is no evidence at all that the discovery learning

TABLE 8.11
Percentages of Subjects Conforming to Each Strategy Template
on Two Missionaries-Cannibals Test Problems as a Function of Type of Training
(Adapted from McDaniel, 1980)[a]

Test Problem	Training Condition	Orcs-Switch-Orcs-1	Orcs-Switch-Orcs-2	Orcs-Switch-Orcs-3	Orcs-Switch-Orcs/Pair	Pair/Orcs-Switch-Orcs	Pair	None
					Strategy			
(8, 4)	Bottom-up	38	13	10	30	0	3	8
	Top-down	53	3	5	20	5	3	10
(8, 5)	Bottom-up	33	38	18	0	0	3	10
	Top-down	53	30	3	0	0	5	10

[a] Rows may not add up to 100% because of rounding error.

procedure leads to any greater flexibility or wider set of intuitions about the structure of the problem. McDaniel concluded that the two procedures were equivalent in terms of what was learned and the flexibility of the knowledge acquired. However, there were large differences in the effectiveness and efficiency of the two training procedures. The top–down group took half the number of problem repetitions to reach the same criterion of performance on both transfer and training problems.

CONCLUSIONS

This chapter has chronicled the development of our thinking about the processes used to solve puzzles from a view of problem solving as means–ends driven search to problem solving as partial understanding. Our original work was derived from Ernst and Newell's (1969) demonstration that GPS could solve a range of problems, from simple puzzles like water-jug and river-crossing problems to calculus and logic problems. Newell and Simon (1972) and Hayes and Simon (1976b) further articulated this basic paradigm. The paradigm assumes that there is a set of general problem-solving mechanisms that guide search through problem spaces. An understanding process encodes information for the solution of a particular problem in a form that can be used by these mechanisms (Hayes & Simon, 1976b). Our early work (Atwood & Polson, 1976; Jeffries, Polson, Razran, & Atwood, 1977) conforms to this paradigm.

Atwood and Polson (1976) and Jeffries, Polson, Razran, & Atwood (1977) showed that very similar three-stage process models could account for problem-solving behavior in two different tasks. The theoretical framework assumed that subjects' problem-solving behavior involved an interaction between means–ends driven search processes and information acquired during the course of attempting to solve the problem. Furthermore, we were able to obtain evidence in favor of some of the subprocesses that were incorporated into the model (e.g., the means–ends driven search component in the model for the water-jug task, Atwood & Polson, 1976). However, we have never found any direct evidence that other processes, such as the control structure incorporated into the three-stage model, were correct descriptions of the processes used to solve these problems.

Our newer models, which are formalized as production systems, incorporate three ideas about problem-solving processes. First, the naive subject has a fragmentary, superficial understanding of the structure of the problem and of strategies for selecting good moves. Second, the problem-solving process can be partitioned into subprocesses that propose moves, evaluate proposed moves, and execute approved moves. Third, we can partition the productions making up each of the subsystems into those that represent the solver's understanding of the task and those that represent search processes, which are executed when solvers find themselves in a situation in which their limited understanding leaves them with no basis for selection of a move.

Although we are reasonably confident that our original theoretical framework could have been extended to deal with the Tower of Hanoi and the more complex river-crossing problems, we rejected this course of action for three reasons. First, our initial framework did not clearly differentiate between the solver's partial understanding of the task environment and the general search mechanisms used to solve a class of problems. The evaluation function, the noticing order, and other aspects of the model confounded general problem-solving mechanisms and task-specific information. The lack of a clean separation in the theory between the solver's understanding of the task and the search component was not a desirable characteristic. Second, we had no evidence for the complex serial control structure that was part of the framework. Neisser (1976) has criticized such models on the grounds that the human information-processing system is more flexible. This is a reasonable criticism and is one of the major motivations for the development of production-system models of various cognitive processes (Anderson, 1976). Third, the most important reason for development of the new framework is that our original theoretical framework had no principled way to describe the effects of learning. Current theoretical work on a cognitive theory of learning (e.g., Anderson, Kline, & Beasley, 1978) partially characterizes learning as the acquisition of new productions. We feel that this is a reasonable mechanism for the acquisition of new knowledge in puzzlelike problems. As a subject gains experience with these tasks, he or she begins to acquire fragments of information about their structure. These are then integrated into a coherent description of the underlying structure of the task.

We feel that the study of puzzlelike tasks has made, and will continue to make, fundamental contributions to our understanding of problem-solving mechanisms and cognitive processes in general. How adults solve puzzlelike problems is the basis for much modern work on problem solving; we feel it represents one of the real triumphs of modern psychology. Our work is just one small part of the ongoing developments. The understanding of these tasks is rich and detailed. However, we feel that developments in understanding how such problems are solved no longer are a central area of research on problem-solving mechanisms. The theoretical basis provided by research using puzzles has caused the frontier to expand to textbook-level problems such as Larkin's (1977) work in physics problem solving and Greeno, Magone, and Chaiklin's (1979) work in geometry.

Intelligence differences ought to manifest themselves most directly as differences in learning a task. In our experiments on learning and transfer, there were indeed large differences across subjects in the generality of what was learned and the rate at which it was acquired. We do not, however, have any data that shed light on how these variations are related to intelligence. Gathering such data would clearly be a productive research endeavor. But, in order to understand the relationship of intelligence variables to learning, it may first be necessary to explicate the basic mechanisms that underlie the learning process.

One of the curious omissions of cognitive psychology is that until very recently there has been no cognitive theory of learning, and a cognitive theory of transfer is still in its earliest stages. We feel that puzzlelike tasks are an ideal environment in which to study basic learning processes. Anzai and Simon (1979) have used the Tower of Hanoi as a task environment to study the transition of a subject from a state of partial understanding to complete understanding of the problem. We are in the initial phases of a project to develop quantitative models of the acquisition process used in the Jeffries (1978) and McDaniel (1980) dissertations.

Results by Anzai and Simon (1979) and Neches and Hayes (1978) have demonstrated the intimate relationship between learning mechanisms and problem-solving processes. These authors argue that learning occurs in the context of attempting to solve a novel problem. Problem-solving mechanisms cause the solver to acquire information about the structure of the task, which is incorporated into a more sophisticated problem-solving process, which enables the solver to acquire additional information, and so on, until the solver eventually masters the task. Learning mechanisms encode information about the consequences of particular moves, discover structure underlying the sequencing of moves, and induce information about the structure underlying the task.

We feel that studies using puzzlelike tasks have fundamental contributions to make to the understanding of transfer mechanisms. Our understanding of transfer has advanced very little beyond Woodworth's (1938) "common elements" explanation of successful transfer. The education literature is filled with studies in which training manipulations failed to show any significant effects on performance on the target task. McDaniel (1980) found that much of the literature discussing the relative merits of discovery versus expository learning is based on low levels of performance in all conditions. Moreover, current educational technology is not very successful in producing transfer from the classroom to applied situations, where knowledge learned takes on additional relevance.

Two of the frontiers for research in cognition in the 1980s will be the development of theories of learning and transfer. Puzzlelike problems are ideal tools to begin the study of these processes. The behavior of naive subjects in a variety of experimental paradigms is well understood. These tasks are complex enough to provide rigorous tests of the kinds of mechanisms that have been proposed for a cognitive theory of learning (e.g., Anderson et al., 1978).

ACKNOWLEDGMENTS

This research was undertaken within the Institute for the Study of Intellectual Behavior, University of Colorado, and is Publication No. 98 of the Institute. This work was supported in part by NSF Grants BNS 72-02084 and BNS 77-06779 and was performed using the facilities of the Computer Laboratory for Instruction in Psychological Research, which is supported in part by the University of Colorado.

The work described in this review is the joint effort of many people. We wish to acknowledge Michael Atwood, Michael Masson, John Karat, Franz Schmalhofer, Lydia Razran Hooke, Daniel Ketchum, Jane Harmel Massey, Mark McDaniel, Martha Tinsley, and Peggy Beecher-Deighan for their contributions to the work described herein.

REFERENCES

Anderson, J. R. *Language, memory, and thought.* Hillsdale, N.J.: Lawrence Erlbaum Associates, 1976.

Anderson, J. R., Kline, P. J., & Beasley, C. M. *A theory of the acquisition of cognitive skills* (ONR Tech. Rep. 77-1). New Haven, Conn.: Yale University, 1978.

Anzai, Y., & Simon, H. A. The theory of learning by doing. *Psychological Review,* 1979, *86,* 124–140.

Atwood, M. E., Masson, M. E. J., & Polson, P. G. Further explorations with a process model for water jug problems. *Memory & Cognition,* 1980, *8,* 182–192.

Atwood, M. E., & Polson, P. G. A process model for water jug problems. *Cognitive Psychology,* 1976, *8,* 191–216.

Ausubel, D. P. Some psychological and educational limitations of learning by discovery. *Arithmetic Teacher,* 1964, *11,* 290–302.

Bower, G. H. Cognitive psychology: An introduction. In W. K. Estes (Ed.), *Handbook of learning and cognitive processes* (Vol. 1). Hillsdale, N.J.: Lawrence Erlbaum Associates, 1975.

Bruner, J. S. The act of discovery. *Harvard Educational Review,* 1961, *31,* 21–32.

Egan, D. E. *The structure of experience acquired while learning to solve a class of problems.* Unpublished doctoral dissertation, University of Michigan, 1973.

Egan, D. E., & Greeno, J. G. Theory of rule induction: Knowledge acquired in concept learning, serial pattern learning, and problem solving. In L. W. Gregg (Ed.), *Knowledge and cognition.* Hillsdale, N.J.: Lawrence Erlbaum Associations, 1974.

Ernst, G. W., & Newell, A. *GPS: A case study in generality and problem-solving.* New York: Academic Press, 1969.

Greeno, J. G. Hobbits and orcs: Acquisition of a sequential concept. *Cognitive Psychology,* 1974, *6,* 270–292.

Greeno, J. G. Process of understanding. In N. J. Castellan, D. B. Pisoni, & G. R. Potts (Eds.), *Cognitive theory: Volume II.* Hillsdale, N.J.: Lawrence Erlbaum Associates, 1977.

Greeno, J. G. Natures of problem-solving abilities. In W. K. Estes (Ed.), *Handbook of learning and cognitive processes* (Vol. 5). Hillsdale, N.J.: Lawrence Erlbaum Associates, 1978.

Greeno, J. G., Magone, M. E., & Chaiklin, S. Theory of construction and set in problem solving. *Memory & Cognition,* 1979, *7,* 445–461.

Hayes, J. R., & Simon, H. A. Understanding written problem instructions. In L. W. Gregg (Ed.), *Knowledge and cognition.* Hillsdale, N.J.: Lawrence Erlbaum Associates, 1974.

Hayes, J. R., & Simon, H. A. Understanding complex task instructions. In D. Klahr (Ed.), *Cognition and instruction.* Hillsdale, N.J.: Lawrence Erlbaum Associates, 1976. (a)

Hayes, J. R., & Simon, H. A. The understanding process: Problem isomorphs. *Cognitive Psychology,* 1976, *8,* 165–190. (b)

Jeffries, R. M. *The acquisition of expertise on missionaries-cannibals and water jug problems.* Unpublished doctoral dissertation, University of Colorado, 1978.

Jeffries, R. *The acquisition of expertise on simple puzzles.* Paper presented at the meeting of the American Educational Research Association, San Francisco, April 1979.

Jeffries, R., & Polson, P. G. *Planning in river crossing problems.* Manuscript in preparation.

Jeffries, R., Polson, P. G., Razran, L., & Atwood, M. E. A process model for missionaries-cannibals and other river crossing problems. *Cognitive Psychology,* 1977, *9,* 412–440.

Jeffries, R., Polson, P. G., Razran, L., & Tinsley, M. *Detecting plans from data: Best laid plans that go astray.* Paper presented at the meeting of the Psychonomics Society, Washington, D.C., November 1977.

Jeffries, R., Polson, P. G., & Tinsley, M. *Planning in the missionaries-cannibals problem.* Paper presented at the meeting of the Rocky Mountain Psychological Association, Denver, April 1978.

Karat, J. A model of problem solving with incomplete constraints knowledge. *Cognitive Psychology,* in press.

Karat, J., Polson, P. G., Jeffries, R., & Razran, L. *The generation and execution of subgoals.* Paper presented at the meeting of the Psychonomics Society, San Antonio, Tex., November 1978.

Kendler, H. H. Reflections on the conference. In L. S. Shulman & E. R. Keislar (Eds.), *Learning by discovery: A critical appraisal.* Chicago: Rand McNally, 1966.

Kintsch, W., & Polson, P. G. On nominal and functional serial position curves: Implications for short-term memory models? *Psychological Review,* 1979, *86,* 407–413.

Larkin, J. H. *Skilled problem solving in physics: A hierarchical planning model.* Unpublished manuscript, Group in Science and Mathematics Education, University of California, Berkeley, 1977.

Luchins, A. S. Mechanization in problem solving. *Psychological Monographs,* 1942, *54*(6, Whole No. 248).

McCarthy, J. Programs with common sense. In D. Blake & A. Uttely (Eds.), *Proceedings of the symposium on the mechanization of thought processes.* London: H. M. Stationery Office, 1959.

McDaniel, M. A. *Bottom-up and top-down acquisition of expertise on river crossing problems: A study of knowledge acquisition.* Unpublished doctoral dissertation, University of Colorado, 1980.

Moore, J., & Newell, A. How can Merlin understand? In L. W. Gregg (Ed.), *Knowledge and cognition.* Hillsdale, N.J.: Lawrence Erlbaum Associates, 1974.

Neches, R. *Promoting self-discovery of improved strategies* (CIP #298). Pittsburgh: Carnegie-Mellon University, Psychology Department, 1979.

Neches, R., & Hayes, J. R. Progress towards a taxonomy of strategy transformations. In A. M. Lesgold, J. W. Pellegrino, S. Fokkema, & R. Glaser (Eds.), *Cognitive psychology and instruction.* New York: Plenum, 1978.

Neisser, U. *Cognition and reality.* San Francisco: W. H. Freeman, 1976.

Newell, A., & Simon, H. A. *Human problem solving.* Englewood Cliffs, N.J.: Prentice-Hall, 1972.

Reed, S. K., Ernst, G. W., & Banerji, R. The role of analogy in transfer between similar problem states. *Cognitive Psychology,* 1974, *6,* 436–450.

Schmalhofer, F., Polson, P. G., & Karat, J. *A mixed strategy model for river crossing problems.* Manuscript in preparation.

Simon, H. A. The functional equivalence of problem solving skills. *Cognitive Psychology,* 1975, *7,* 268–288.

Simon, H. A. Information processing theories of human problem solving. In W. K. Estes (Ed.), *Handbook of learning and cognitive processes* (Vol. 5). Hillsdale, N.J.: Lawrence Erlbaum Associates, 1978.

Simon, H. A., & Reed, S. K. Modelling strategy shifts in a problem solving task. *Cognitive Psychology,* 1976, *8,* 86–97.

Suchman, J. R. Inquiry training: Building skills for autonomous discovery. *Palmer Quarterly of Behavioral Development,* 1961, *7,* 147–169.

Thomas, J. C., Jr. An analysis of behavior in the hobbits-orcs problem. *Cognitive Psychology,* 1974, *6,* 257–269.

Wertheimer, M. *Productive thinking.* New York: Harper & Row, 1959.

Woodworth, R. S. *Experimental psychology.* New York: Holt, 1938.

9 A Componential Approach to Intellectual Development

Robert J. Sternberg
Yale University

The question of "what develops" is probably the most central one in developmental psychology. Most theoretical and empirical works in developmental psychology attempt to deal with this question in greater or lesser degree, and, indeed, the form a particular investigation takes is in large part shaped by the investigator's presuppositions as to the sources of intellectual development. Many aspects of behavior change with age, but only some of them help elucidate the basic mechanisms responsible for developmental change.[1]

In this chapter, I propose one approach to addressing, although not, of course, to answering in full, the question of what develops in human intelligence. The approach, which I call the "componential approach," attempts to understand intellectual development in terms of changes in the availability, accessibility, and ease of execution of a variety of kinds of information-processing components.[2] Obviously, this approach is only one of a number of alternatives that provide frameworks for understanding how intelligence develops. In an historical perspective, the approach may be viewed as one of a number of current information-processing approaches for understanding intellectual development; in this perspective, information-processing approaches can be contrasted with alterna-

---

[1] Some alternative contemporary approaches to the question of what develops in thinking, in general, are presented in a recent book edited by Siegler (1978); alternative approaches to the question of what develops in intelligence, in particular, are presented in a recent chapter by Sternberg and Powell (in press).

[2] A recent description of the componential approach to understanding human intelligence can be found in Sternberg (1980e; see also Sternberg, 1977, 1978, 1979b). Examples of the application of componential analysis to the study of intellectual development are described in this article.

413

tive psychometric and Piagetian approaches, among others. No claim is made, however, that the present approach is in some sense the correct one or even that the information-processing paradigm provides the right way to understand intellectual development. To the contrary, a detailed review of alternative approaches to the development of intelligence has convinced me that alternative viewpoints (e.g., psychometric, Piagetian, and information-processing) are for the most part complementary rather than mutually exclusive. In addition, they can be used to greater benefit in combination than in isolation (Sternberg & Powell, in press).

The proposals in this chapter are presented in five main parts. In the first, the main terms used in discussing intellectual development are defined and briefly illustrated. In the second, it is shown how the components of information processing represented by these terms develop in a variety of task contexts as people grow older. In the third, some speculations are presented as to possible mechanisms by which observed changes in behavior may take place with age. In the fourth, the constructs of the proposed componential approach are related to constructs in alternative approaches to intellectual development and are found to be highly compatible with them. In the fifth and final part, it is claimed that at least some aspects of intelligence may be viewed as continuous throughout a person's life span.

THE COMPONENTIAL FRAMEWORK

The basic construct in the componential framework for understanding human intelligence is the *component*. A component is an elementary information process that operates on internal representations of objects or symbols (Sternberg, 1977; see also Newell & Simon, 1972). The component may translate a sensory input into a conceptual representation, transform one conceptual representation into another, or translate a conceptual representation into a motor output. What is considered to be "elementary" is viewed as a property of the level of theorizing one attempts, rather than of the human mind. A given component may or may not be elementary, depending on the theoretical context in which it is presented.

Each component has three important properties associated with it: duration, difficulty (i.e., probability of being performed incorrectly), and probability of execution. In order to estimate these properties, one needs to select appropriate dependent variables (e.g., response latencies for duration, error rates for difficulty, and response-choice probabilities for probability of execution).

I have referred to five kinds of components, with each kind performing a different function (Sternberg, 1980e). *Metacomponents* are higher-order control processes that are used for executive planning and decision making in problem solving. Deciding what problem or problems to solve or deciding how to solve the problem(s) are examples of metacomponential decisions. *Performance com-*

ponents are processes that are used in the execution of a problem-solving strategy. The actual working through of the problem one has decided to solve in the way one has decided to solve it is done via a set of performance components. *Acquisition* (or storage) *components* are processes used in learning new information. Rehearsing new information in order to transfer a trace of it into long-term memory would be an example of an acquisition component in action. *Retention* (or retrieval) *components* are processes used in accessing previously stored knowledge. Searching through long-term memory to find a particular fact needed at a given moment would be an example of a retention component in action. *Transfer components* are processes used in generalization, that is, in carrying over knowledge from one task context to another. The realization that a newly learned aphorism (e.g., "Out of sight, out of mind") is incompatible with a previously learned aphorism (e.g., "Absence makes the heart grow fonder") would be an example of one (or possibly more than one) transfer component in action. In what follows, I become more specific about what the set of each kind of component includes and about how these components develop with age.[3]

LOCI OF INTELLECTUAL DEVELOPMENT

Scope of Inquiry

In identifying loci of intellectual development, it is necessary to use some sensibly circumscribed task domain as the basis for studying intelligent functioning. In the account to follow, I draw heavily (although not exclusively) upon my own research in the realm of reasoning. A substantial base of prior research indicates that reasoning processes are central to intelligent functioning (Piaget, 1972; Reitman, 1965; Spearman, 1927; Terman & Merrill, 1973; Thurstone, 1938; see also Sternberg & Powell, in press) and that understanding of reasoning processes can serve as a useful start toward a more general theory of intelligence (see Sternberg, 1977, 1979b, 1980e). I wish to emphasize at the outset, however, that no claim is being made that reasoning processes account for all or even most of what constitutes intelligence. To the contrary, I believe that intelligence, broadly defined, must take into account a wide variety of cognitive processes and

---

[3]Although I have found this particular taxonomy of components to be theoretically and practically useful, I present it as only one of the many ways in which one might subdivide components of intelligent information processing. Related views that have influenced my own conceptualizations include those of Brown (1978), Butterfield and Belmont (1977), Campione and Brown (1979), Flavell (in press), and Markman (in press) on what I call "metacomponents;" Jensen (1979), Miller, Galanter, and Pribram (1960), Newell and Simon (1972), Pellegrino and Glaser (1979, 1980), and Snow (1979) on what I call "performance components;" and Atkinson and Shiffrin (1968) and Bower (1972) on what I call "acquisition," "retention," and "transfer" components.

their interactions, as well as the motivational processes that drive the cognitive ones (see Sternberg, 1981b, 1981d; Zigler, 1969, 1971). Alternative entrees into the realm of intelligent functioning may be sought through the study of problem solving (e.g., Beilin, 1969; Brainerd, 1973, 1974; Inhelder & Piaget, 1958; Klahr, 1978; Klahr & Wallace, 1973, 1976; Siegler, 1976, 1978), verbal comprehension (e.g., Hunt, 1978; Keating & Bobbitt, 1978; Keating, Keniston, Manis, & Bobbitt, 1980; Powell & Sternberg, 1981; Werner & Kaplan, 1952), number ability (e.g., Gelman & Gallistel, 1978; Groen & Parkman, 1972; Resnick & Ford, 1981; Suppes & Groen, 1967; Woods, Resnick, & Groen, 1975), spatial ability (e.g., Huttenlocher & Presson, 1973; Kail, Pellegrino, & Carter, 1980; Marmor, 1975, 1977; Shepard & Metzler, 1971), and memory (Brown, 1978; Butterfield & Belmont, 1977; Campione & Brown, 1979; Flavell, 1977, in press; Markman, in press). Moreover, the approach I take to reasoning is only one of the many that are possible (see, e.g., Achenbach, 1970, 1971; Gallagher & Wright, 1979; Levinson & Carpenter, 1974; Osherson, 1974, 1975; Pellegrino & Glaser, 1980; Trabasso, 1975, for related but distinguishable approaches). Nevertheless, like at least some others, I believe that alternative approaches to studying intelligent behavior are leading us to highly overlapping sets of macroscopic principles of cognitive development (e.g., Brown, 1978; Brown & DeLoache, 1978; Sternberg, 1980e; Sternberg & Powell, in press), if not always to the same microscopic principles that in some cases are probably domain specific. Hence, I present this analysis as one first pass at the identification of loci of intellectual development, recognizing that other analyses are possible, but believing that others would overlap in major respects.

The task domain for the developmental research upon which I draw heavily here includes pictorial analogies (Sternberg & Rifkin, 1979) and verbal analogies (Sternberg & Nigro, 1980) in the realm of inductive reasoning and linear syllogisms (Sternberg, 1980a) and logical connectives (Sternberg, 1979a) in the domain of deductive reasoning. All but the pictorial analogies require a substantial measure of language comprehension for task solution; hence, one can view verbal comprehension abilities as being tapped as well.

In the pictorial analogies experiment (Sternberg & Rifkin, 1979, Experiment 2), between 15 and 21 parochial school children (in each of grades 2, 4, and 6) and college-level adults were timed as they solved analogies consisting of schematic figures of people (people pieces) varying in four binary attributes: height (short-tall), garment color (black-white), sex (male-female), and weight (thin-fat). Subjects were told to choose as their answer the one of two options that was the same as and different from the third analogy term in the same way that the second term was the same as and different from the first term. A typical analogy is presented in Fig. 9.1. Analogies were presented in 24 test booklets, each containing 16 analogies. Items within each of the booklets were homogeneous in terms of the number of attributes that varied from the first

A   B   C   I   2

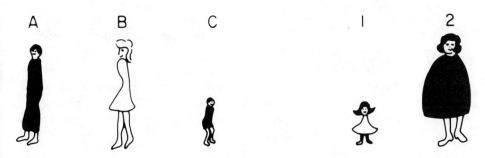

FIG. 9.1. An example of a people piece pictorial analogy. Analogies vary on
four binary attributes: height (tall–short), garment color (black–white), sex
(male–female), and weight (fat–thin).

term to the second, from the first term to the third, and between the two answer
options. Inasmuch as identities of actual values on attributes varied across
analogies, however, no two analogies were identical. Subjects were given 64
seconds to work on each booklet. The main dependent variable, solution latency
for items correctly answered, was computed by dividing 64 by the number of items
correctly completed in a given booklet. Response time was hypothesized to equal
the sum of the amounts of time spent on each of a set of performance components
(to be described later). A simple linear model predicted response time as the sum
across the different information-processing components of the number of times
each component was executed (as an independent variable) multiplied by the
duration of that component (as an estimated parameter). Parameter estimation
was done by multiple regression, predicting response times from independent
variables representing structural aspects of the analogy items, namely, the
number of attributes varied from the first term to the second term, from the first
term to the third term, and from the preferred to the nonpreferred answer option.

    Subjects in the verbal analogy experiment were 20 students in each of grades
3, 6, 9, and college. The college students were Yale undergraduates; the other
subjects were public school students from a middle-class suburb of New Haven.
All subjects received the same 180 verbal analogies. Vocabulary level was restricted to grade 3 or below according to the Thorndike–Lorge norms. The 180
analogies were cross-classified in two different ways. Of the 180 items, 36 were
classified into each of the following semantic relations: synonym (e.g., *UNDER :
BENEATH :: PAIN : [pleasure, doctor, feeling, hurt]*); antonym (e.g., *START :
FINISH :: FAR : [near, away, travel, farther]*); functional (e.g., *SHOES : FEET ::
HAT : [head, bucket, clothes, cap]*); linear ordering (e.g., *YESTERDAY :
TODAY :: BEFORE : [now, when, after, time]*); and category membership (e.g.,
NOON : TIME :: WEST : [direction, subset, east, northwest]). Crossed with this
classification were 60 items presented in each of three formats. The formats
differed in the relative numbers of terms in the analogy stem versus the number in

the analogy options. Specifically, the number of terms in the analogy stem could be either three, two, or one. The remaining terms were in the options. Consider an example of each format:

1. *NARROW : WIDE :: QUESTION : (trial) (statement) (answer) (ask).*
2. *WIN : LOSE :: (dislike : hate) (ear : hear) (enjoy : like) (above : below).*
3. *WEAK : (sick :: circle : shape) (strong :: poor : rich) (small :: garden : grow) (health :: solid : firm).*

Each option appeared on a separate line of print. Numbers of answer options varied from two to four and were equally represented across semantic relations and item formats. Furthermore, the answer options were balanced over the five verbal relations. Subjects were timed in their latency for solution of each item. Items were presented tachistoscopically via a portable tachistoscope with an attached centisecond clock. Again, a simple linear model was used to predict response time as the sum across performance components of the number of times each component was executed multiplied by the duration of that component. The three formats provided the means for separating independent variables used to estimate parameters representing the latencies of the various components.

In the linear syllogisms experiment, between 24 and 26 children in each of grades 3, 5, 7, 9, 11 of a school district in a suburb of New Haven were tested on their ability to solve linear syllogisms. Stimuli were two-term series problems (e.g., *John is taller than Bill. Who is shortest? John, Bill.*) and three-term series problems (e.g., *John is taller than Mary. Mary is taller than Pete. Who is tallest? John, Pete, Mary.*).[4] The eight types of two-term series problems varied dichotomously along three dimensions: (1) whether the premise adjective was marked (e.g., *shorter*) or unmarked (e.g., *taller*); (2) whether the question adjective was marked or unmarked; and (3) whether the premise was affirmative or negative. The 32 types of three-term series problems varied dichotomously along five dimensions: (1) whether the first premise adjective was marked or unmarked; (2) whether the second premise adjective was marked or unmarked; (3) whether the question adjective was marked or unmarked; (4) whether the premises were affirmative or negative; and (5) whether the correct answer was in the first or second premise. All terms of the problems were boys' or girls' names, and connecting adjectives were the pairs *taller-shorter* and *better-worse* (where *worse* was the marked form). Order of terms in the answer options was random. Problems were administered via a homemade, portable

---

[4]For the two-term series problems, the ungrammatical superlative was used in the question for consistency with the three-term series problems. This procedure is standard in experiments of this kind (see Clark, 1969).

tachistoscope with attached centisecond clock. The main dependent variable was response time. The previously described independent variables were theorized to serve as sources of increased latency in problem solution and, thus, formed the basis for parameter estimation in a linear model.

In the experiment on logical connectives, a total of 224 subjects in grades 2, 4, 6, 8, high school, and college solved problems requiring comprehension or reasoning with the logical connectives *and, or, if-then, only if,* and *if and only if,* as well as the terms *is* and *is not.* Elementary and secondary school students were from a suburb of New Haven; college students were Yale undergraduates. Two different tasks—encoding and combination—were presented in crossed fashion via two different content vehicles—fruits (apple, banana) and shapes (circle, square). Props for the tasks included a box, a towel to cover the box, and two objects (either an artificial apple and banana or a cardboard circle and square covered with silver paper).

In the encoding task, each problem consisted of two sentences printed on poster board and also read aloud that described the contents of the box, namely, a premise and a conclusion drawn from that premise. The subjects' task was to evaluate the validity of the conclusion. Premises were constructed on the basis of six logical relationships expressed by seven different logical connectives as described earlier. Typical premises were *There is a circle in the box* and *there is a square in the box* and If *there is a banana in the box,* then *there is an apple in the box.* Four conclusions were presented (in random order) for each premise, corresponding to the 2^2 possibilities that each of the two items (e.g., apple and banana) either was or was not in the box. Typical conclusions were *There is only a square in the box and nothing else* and *There is not a banana in the box and there is not an apple in the box.* Inasmuch as there were seven different premise connectives and four different conclusions, there were a total of 28 different encoding problems for each content.

In the combination task, each problem consisted of three sentences describing the contents of the box, namely, a major premise, a minor premise, and a conclusion. Only conjunction, disjunction, conditionality, and biconditionality were used for the major premise because the other relationships studied do not apply to pairs of items. Major premises in the combination task were identical in format to the single premises in the encoding task. There were four possible minor premises, again corresponding to each of the 2^2 possibilities that each item was or was not in the box. There were five different logical connectives in the major premises and eight possible pairings between minor premises and conclusions, yielding a total of 40 different combination problems for each content. The dependent variable in this experiment was the subject's response of true, maybe true and maybe false, or false to each conclusion (cf. Taplin, Staudenmayer, & Taddonio, 1974). An analysis of subjects' patterns of responses to each of the possible conclusions for each premise (encoding task) or pair of premises (combination task) enabled me to infer subjects' truth tables in responding. For example, suppose one is presented with the following problem and gives the following pattern of responses:

The apple is in the box or the banana is in the box.

   Can one conclude that:
There is only an apple in the box and nothing else? . . . "Maybe"
There is only a banana in the box and nothing else? . . . "Maybe"
There is an apple in the box and there is a banana in the box? . . . "False"
There is not an apple in the box and there is not a banana in the box? . . . "False"

One could infer uniquely that the subject's truth table is that of "exclusive *or.*" Had the third response been "Maybe," the truth table would have been that of "inclusive *or.*" In general, it was possible to infer the truth table uniquely (assuming a consistent truth table existed) from patterns of responses such as these.

Having reviewed the scope of the tasks that receive primary consideration in the analysis to follow, I turn now to a discussion of intellectual development from a componential point of view.

Metacomponents

I have proposed six metacomponents that I believe are critical in understanding intelligence and its development (Sternberg, 1980e). I list these metacomponents here and give illustrations of how they develop.

   1. Recognition of Just What the Problem Is that Needs to be Solved.   Anyone who has done research with young children knows that half the battle is getting the children to understand what is being asked of them. Their problem is often not in actually solving a problem, but in figuring out just what the problem is that needs to be solved (see, e.g., Flavell, 1977). A major feature distinguishing retarded from normal persons is the need of retarded persons to be instructed very explicitly and completely as to the nature of the particular task they are solving and how it should be performed (Butterfield, Wambold, & Belmont, 1973; Campione & Brown, 1977, 1979). The importance of figuring out the nature of the problem is not limited to children and retarded persons. Resnick and Glaser (1976) have argued that intelligence is in large part the ability to learn in the absence of direct or complete instruction. Indeed, distractors on intelligence tests are frequently chosen so as to be the right answers to the wrong problems.

   Unfortunately, in research with young children, one can never be certain whether failure to understand a task is due to inadequacies in the instructions given to the children or to the inability of the children to understand the task, no matter how it might be posed. For example, in our logical-connectives work, we were unable to get second graders to understand the more difficult combination task, no matter how we rephrased the instructions. But perhaps we just failed to hit upon the right channel of communication. A diagnostically more useful sign is when children of a certain age systematically misunderstand rather than utterly fail to understand a task. Examples of such systematic misunderstandings can be found in our analogies work. In the pictorial analogies experiment, for example, certain second graders consistently circled as correct one or the other of the first two analogy terms rather than one or the other of the last two terms that constituted the answer options. We were puzzled by this systematic misunderstanding until we put together three facts: (1) we were testing children in a Jewish parochial school; (2) the children normally did their lessons in English in the morning and in Hebrew in the afternoon; and (3) we happened to be doing our testing in the afternoon. Apparently, some of these young children perseverated in their normal afternoon right-to-left visual scanning, even in a task presented in English where it was explicitly stated that the options were at the right. In the verbal analogies experiment, some of the younger children (third and sixth grades) used association rather heavily in solving analogy items, despite the fact that the task was presented as an analogical reasoning task. Achenbach (1970, 1971) has devised a test, the Children's Associative Responding Test (CART), that enables one to determine the extent to which a given child relies on association between words rather than logical reasoning in the solution of analogies.

In our experiments, the terms of the problem are presented explicitly and (we hope) clearly; the question is whether these terms are understood sufficiently to allow satisfactory performance on the problems. I believe that a more important aspect of problem recognition is that in which the terms of the problem are presented incompletely, inadequately, or possibly not at all. This sense of problem recognition is the one addressed in Resnick and Glaser's (1976) definition of intelligence in terms of the ability to function well with incomplete or inadequate instruction; it is also addressed by Flavell's (in press) and Markman's (1977, 1979, in press) work on comprehension monitoring. This comprehension-monitoring work shows that young children are often unaware even that instructions are incomplete and useless for figuring out how to solve a given task.

The level of definition with which a problem is presented can be reduced one step further still to the point where the child's task is to find a problem rather than to understand a problem presented either explicitly (as in the case of the analogical reasoning studies) or implicitly (as in the case of the comprehension-monitoring studies). It has been proposed that problem finding may constitute a fifth "stage" following formal operations (Arlin, 1975), although problem finding may also be viewed as an intrinsic part of later formal operations (Inhelder & Piaget, 1958). I believe that the seeking out of novel and interesting problems is an important aspect of intelligence but that it is by no means limited to formal operational or postformal operational thinking. I explicate my own views further later on (see section on the continuity of intelligence).

2. Selection of Lower-Order Components. An individual must select a set of lower-order (performance, acquisition, retention, or transfer) components to use in the solution of a given task. Selection of a nonoptimal set of components can result in incorrect or inefficient task performance. In some instances, choice of components will be partially attributable to differential availability or accessibility of various components. For example, young children may lack certain components that are necessary or desirable for the accomplishment of particular tasks, or they may not yet execute these components in a way that is efficient enough to facilitate task solution.

Two examples of the development of component selection can be found in our studies of analogical reasoning. These examples involve the use of mapping and associative components in the solution of analogies.

A performance component of particular interest in reasoning by analogy is *mapping,* which requires an individual to link the first half of the analogy to the second half by conceiving the higher-order relation between two lower-order relations, one linking the first term of the analogy to the second and the other linking the third term of the analogy to the fourth. The ability to conceive a second-order relation between relations is of particular interest to developmental theorists because, in Piaget's theory of intellectual development, this ability marks the transition between concrete and formal operational thinking (Inhelder & Piaget, 1958). One might therefore expect concrete operational children to have great difficulty mapping higher-order relations, or to be unable to map at all. Mapping was one of the parameters estimated in the pictorial analogies study. Estimated latencies of this component were .72 second, .57 second, and .33 second at the grade 4, grade 6, and adult levels, respectively. The parameter could not be estimated at all at the grade 2 level, however. The independent variable used to estimate the mapping parameter (number of attribute values changed from the first analogy term to the third analogy term) was simply not a source of incremental latency in the solution of analogies by these children. This result could mean two things. First, it could mean that second graders always map in a fixed amount of time, regardless of the difficulty of the mapping with which they are presented. This explanation of the finding seems implausible, although not totally impossible. It would suggest that no matter how nearly or distantly related the first two terms are to the second two terms, the time to map the relation is the same at the second-grade level. Second, it could mean that second graders for the most part simply don't map higher-order relations—that they find some way of solving the pictorial analogies that bypasses the need for mapping altogether. In fact, the data we collected regarding subjects' strategies and the data of other individuals seem to support this latter view: The youngest children simply did not map. The older children were able to map, and the rate at which they did so decreased with age, as might be expected. Although one might normally expect a considerable number of fourth graders as well to have difficulty in mapping, the fact that the children in this study were upper-middle-class to upper-class children from a Jewish parochial school might suggest that, on the average, the development of these children was more precocious than that of typical children.

This finding on the relatively late appearance of mapping in children's repertoires of component skills has been replicated in a number of different ways by different investigators using different languages to describe what I believe to be essentially the same finding. Piaget, with Montangero and Billeter (1977), has collected data suggesting three stages in the development of analogical reasoning. The first, extending through the concrete operational period, seems to be marked by an inability to discern second-order relations in analogies. The second stage, marking the transition between concrete and formal operations, is characterized by a preliminary or tentative level of ability to discern second-order relations. The third stage, characteristic of formal operational children, is marked by the full ability to understand second-order relations. Lunzer (1965) presented children of ages 9 to 17+ with verbal analogies taking a number of different forms. Some had one term missing and others had two terms missing; which particular term or terms were missing varied from one analogy to another. Lunzer found that children had great difficulty with even the simplest analogies at 9 years of age and did not show successful performance until the age of 11. Lunzer concluded that even the simplest analogies require recognition of higher-order relations that are not discernible to children who are not yet formal operational. Levinson and Carpenter (1974) presented verbal analogies (e.g., *bird* is to *air* as *fish* is to _____) and quasi-analogies (e.g., *A bird uses air; a fish uses* _____) to 9-, 12-, and 15-year-old children. The standard analogies required recognition of the higher-order analogical relationship; the quasi-analogies essentially supplied this relationship. The investigators found that whereas 9-year-olds could answer significantly more quasi-analogies than analogies correctly, 12- and 15-year-olds answered approximately equal numbers of each kind of item correctly. Moreover, whereas performance on the standard analogies increased monotonically across age levels, performance on the quasi-analogies did not increase. Gallagher and Wright (1979) have done research comparing the relative abilities of children in grades 4 to 6 to provide what these investigators have called "symmetrical" versus "asymmetrical" explanations of analogy solutions. Symmetrical explanations show awareness of the higher-order relation linking the first relation to the second; asymmetrical explanations do not. These authors found percentages of symmetrical explanations to increase with age. To summarize, then, there is ample evidence of a change with age in component selection in analogical reasoning. Concrete operational children presumably cannot select mapping because it is not yet available. Transitional children do select mapping, at least in many instances, but the mapping component is probably inaccessible and executed inefficaciously. Formal operational children select mapping when needed and used it efficaciously.

Another performance component of special interest in analogical reasoning is an associative one. In our own investigation of children's solution of verbal analogies, we found that younger children were more likely to guide their solution of analogies by use of word association, whereas older children were more likely to solve the analogies strictly on the basis of inductive reasoning. It is instructive, in this regard, to compare correlations between response time for analogy solution on the one hand and either an associative component or an inference component on the other. The associative component is alogical, involving only associative relatedness of the last word in the analogy stem to the first word in each analogy option; the inference component is logical, involving discovery of the relation between the first two terms of an analogy. Correlations between associative relatedness and response time were .50, .45, .08, and −.02 at grades 3, 6, 9, and adulthood, respectively. Correlations between inference difficulty and response time were .12, .27, .64, and .73 at grades 3, 6, 9, and adulthood, respectively. The patterns of correlations show a clear trend with age away from the use of association and toward the use of logical inference.

Again, there is ample evidence for these basic findings in the research of others. The pioneering studies on the role of word association in analogy solution were conducted by Achenbach (1970, 1971), who found that use of word association decreases with age. But at any given age level, there was wide variation in the extent to which children used word association as a means for choosing one of several answer options. Moreover, the extent to which children use word association serves as a moderator variable in predicting classroom performance: Correlations between performance on IQ tests and school achievement were substantially lower for children who relied primarily on word association for analogy solution than for children who relied primarily on reasoning. Gentile, Tedesco-Stratton, David, Lund, and Agunanne (1977) further investigated children's associative responding, using Achenbach's CART. They found that associative priming can have a marked effect on test scores, leading children either toward or away from correct solutions. In summary, then, there is a clear developmental trend away from the use of an associative component in analogical reasoning and toward the use of reasoning components. At any given age, there are individual differences in the use of word association, and Achenbach's results suggest that analogies predict scholastic performance well only for children who solve them by reasoning. This finding is reasonable because it is only for these children that the analogy tests measure what they were designed to measure.

3. Selection of a Strategy for Combining Lower-Order Components.   In itself, a set of performance (or other) components is insufficient to perform a task. One also needs to sequence these components in a way that permits task solution, to decide how nearly exhaustively each component will be performed, and to decide which components to execute serially and which to execute in parallel. In an analogies task, for example, alternative possible strategies for problem solving differ in terms of which components are exhaustive and which are self-terminating. Consider again two examples from the research on pictorial and verbal analogies. Each example deals with the tendency of children to become more nearly exhaustive in their information processing with increasing age (see also Brown & DeLoache, 1978; Sternberg & Powell, in press), although each deals with a different sense of exhaustive versus self-terminating processing.

We have investigated a rather large number of different strategies for the solution of pictorial analogies (Sternberg, 1977; Sternberg & Rifkin, 1979), and the strategies that we have examined do not by any means account for all of the possibilities (see, e.g., Evans, 1968; Mulholland, Pellegrino, & Glaser, 1980). Three of these strategies are of particular interest in the present context, however. Flow charts representing these three strategies are pictured in Fig. 9.2.

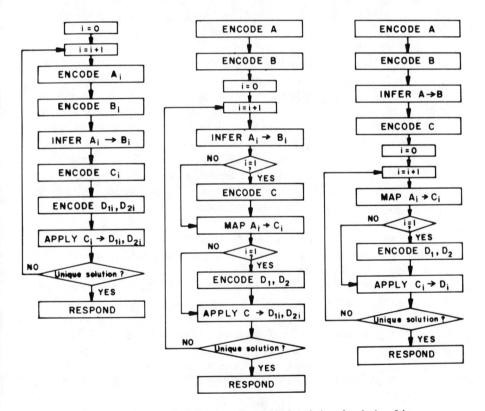

FIG. 9.2. Flow charts depicting strategies used in the solution of analogies of the form $A : B :: C : (D_1, D_2)$. The left panel shows the strategy used by second graders in solving pictorial analogies with integral attributes; the middle panel shows the strategy used by fourth graders in solving pictorial analogies with integral attributes; the right panel shows the strategy used by sixth graders and adults in solving pictorial analogies with integral attributes.

The first strategy (Fig. 9.2, far left) is a fully self-terminating one, which I have referred to as Model IVM in the past (Sternberg & Rifkin, 1979). In this strategy, subjects encode and compare the minimal possible number of attribute values. For example, consider how subjects using this strategy might solve the pictorial analogy in Fig. 9.1. First, subjects initialize an attribute counter to zero and then increment it by one, thereby readying themselves to view a first attribute. Suppose subjects decide to start by encoding sex of the figure. They encode the sex of the first analogy figure and then the sex of the second analogy figure. Next, they infer the relation between the sexes of the first two figures, in this case realizing that sex changes from male to female. Then, subjects encode the sex of the third figure and then the fourth and fifth figures (the answer options). They can now apply from the third analogy term to each of the answer options the rule inferred from the first analogy term to the second, seeking to find an option that differs in sex from the third analogy term. Unfortunately, a unique solution cannot be found on the basis of this attribute because both of the answer options are female in sex. Hence, it is necessary to return to the beginning of the "self-terminating" loop, selecting another attribute and running it through the loop. Suppose subjects select height this time. Once they have iterated execution of the loop, they will find that only one of the two options is the same height as the third figure, as required by the constraints of the analogy. Hence, they will be able to choose a unique solution and thus to respond. Had the subjects selected height as the first attribute to examine, self-termination in solution would have been possible after examination of just this single attribute of the analogy. In general, the order in which attributes are chosen for examination can have a major effect upon solution latency in execution of a self-terminating strategy because certain attributes can be used to disconfirm the wrong option or options, whereas other attributes cannot.

The second strategy (Fig. 9.2, middle) is an intermediate strategy in which encoding of analogy terms is exhaustive in the sense that subjects encode all of the attributes they can find in their first examination of each analogy term, up to some unspecified criterion for stopping encoding. In the first term of the sample analogy, subjects would encode that the figure is of the male sex, is wearing black clothing, is tall, and is thin. All other performance components are self-terminating, however, as in the first strategy. The self-terminating loop starts later in the problem than is the case with the first strategy, reflecting the exhaustive encoding of the first two analogy terms. (Other encodings are also outside the loop.) I have referred to this strategy as Model IV in past writings (Sternberg, 1977; Sternberg & Rifkin, 1979).

The third strategy (Fig. 9.2, far right) is also an intermediate one in which inference of the relation between the first two analogy terms as well as encoding of each analogy term is exhaustive. In the example, subjects would encode all of the attribute values for the first two terms and then infer that sex changes from male to female, clothing color changes from black to white, height stays the same at tall, and weight stays the same at thin. Mapping and application, as in the two previous models, are self-terminating. Here, the self-terminating loop starts even later in the problem than it does in the previous strategy, reflecting the smaller scope of the self-terminating performance components. I have referred to this strategy as Model III in past writings (Sternberg, 1977; Sternberg & Rifkin, 1979).

These three models are of particular interest in the present context because they represent the developmental shift that occurs in the solution of at least some pictorial analogies (those with integral attributes; see Garner, 1974; Sternberg & Rifkin, 1979). The first model is used by most second graders; the second model is used by most fourth graders; and the third model is used by most sixth graders and adults. These conclusions are based upon the fitting of alternative strategy models to the latency data and the selection of one model as generally ''best'' on the basis of a number of statistical and psychological criteria (see Sternberg & Rifkin, 1979). In the present instance, squared correlations between predicted and observed latencies were .82, .80, .86, and .89 at grades 2, 4, 6, and adult-hood, respectively.

The shift in strategy from grade 2 to adulthood represents a tendency for individuals to become more nearly exhaustive in their information processing as they grow older. But why should subjects become more nearly exhaustive with increasing age? One highly practical reason appears to be that greater use of exhaustive information processing is associated with (and probably leads to) higher accuracy in solution. When error rates for analogy solution using pictorial analogies just like the ones in the study described here were modeled on the basis of the performance components in the model for adults, it was found that among adults almost all errors were due to inaccurate execution of performance components executed with self-termination (Sternberg, 1977). And indeed, in the present developmental data, error rates decreased substantially with age, perhaps reflecting in part the shift in strategy. These error rates were .15, .10, .07, and .02 at grades 2, 4, 6, and adulthood, respectively.

Qualitative trends in the latency data for children solving our verbal analogies made it clear from the start that there was a shift in strategy for analogy solution with increasing age. Figure 9.3 shows these trends, plotting response time against the number of terms missing in each analogy (see the description of our verbal analogies paradigm presented earlier). In order to ascertain the nature of the strategy shift, we compared alternative models for verbal analogy solution at different age levels.

We considered four alternative models for analogy solution. Consider three sample analogies and how they would be solved under each of these alternative models (as proposed by Sternberg & Nigro, 1980):

1. *NARROW : WIDE :: QUESTION : (trial) (statement) (answer) (ask).*
2. *WIN : LOSE :: (dislike : hate) (ear : hear) (enjoy : like) (above : below).*
3. *WEAK : (sick :: circle : shape) (strong :: poor : rich) (small :: garden : grow) (health :: solid : firm).*

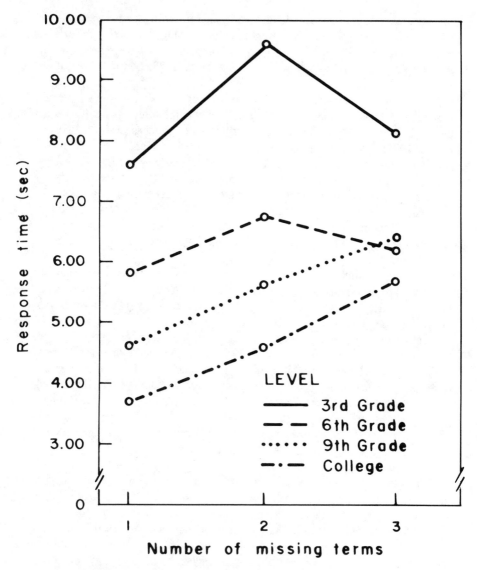

FIG. 9.3.   Mean response times on verbal analogies for each item format at each grade level.

The first model (Model A) posits that information processing is fully exhaustive with respect to all of the answer options. Subjects scan each option in the order presented and then select the best one. Thus, the time to solve an item will depend on the number of answer options, but not on the placement of the correct option within a given option set. In each of these sample problems, therefore, scanning of each of the four answer options would precede the selection of one answer as best.

The second model (Model B) posits that information processing is fully self-terminating and ordered with respect to all of the answer options. Subjects scan each option in the order presented until they reach an option that is deemed acceptable. They then select this option without further consultation of the remaining options. Because the keyed options were the third, fourth, and second in each of the respective analogy items, the number of options to be scanned would be three, four, and two in the three analogies, respectively (assuming termination of responding at the keyed response).

The third model (Model C) also posits that information processing is fully self-terminating, but the order of option examination is hypothesized to be associatively guided. This means that subjects scan the options in order of the level of word association of the first (or only) word in each option to the last word in the analogy stem. Level of association is assumed to have been computed during a preencoding of analogy terms. In the first example, the answer option having the highest association value to the last word of the stem (*QUESTION*) is *answer*. This also happens to be the keyed response. Hence, solution of this item is assumed to take place after the scanning of just one option. In the second example, *above* is only weakly associated with the last term in the stem (*LOSE*), and therefore the correct answer option is not reached until later (actually, the third pass). In the third example, the correct option is again the one in which the first word of the option (*strong*) has the highest association value to the last (and here only) term of the stem (*WEAK*) so that only one pass through a single option is necessary.

The fourth model (Model D) is a mixture of Models A and C. It posits that search through the answer options is exhaustive if subjects are able to hold all of the terms of the analogy in working memory, but it is self-terminating with associative guiding of response search if the subjects are unable to hold all of these terms in working memory. We assumed, following Pascual-Leone (1970) and Case (1974a, 1974b), that working-memory capacity, or M-space, increases with age and further speculated (*after* looking at the data) that third and sixth graders were likely to encounter difficulties in storing all of the terms in the third analogy format in working memory, whereas ninth graders and adults were not. We believed that this third format in particular was potentially difficult because of the very large number of terms in the analogy that needed to be stored in working memory.

The data indicated that third and sixth graders used Model D in their analogy solution, whereas ninth graders and adults used Model A. Multiple correlations between the two best predictors of the preferred model at each level and response times were .85 for third graders, .88 for sixth graders, .89 for ninth graders, and .92 for adults. Thus, subjects changed from a self-terminating to an exhaustive strategy for scanning answer options with increasing age. The tendency to become more nearly exhaustive thus applies across terms of an analogy as well as within the attributes of an analogy term.

The change in strategy accounted for the qualitative shifts observed in the data presented in Fig. 9.3. Third and sixth graders took longer on the second item type than on the first because of the increase in the number of analogy terms to be processed exhaustively, but they took less time on the third type than on the second because the increased number of terms in this case was processed with self-termination. Ninth graders and adults showed a linear increase in response time with increasing numbers of terms because of their use of exhaustive information processing for each item type, resulting in increased response time as the number of analogy terms increased.

In these examples, the data of interest were embedded within strategy changes that occurred during the course of intellectual development. In most instances, interactions between age and strategy provide the data of greatest theoretical interest because a primary goal of developmental research is to ascertain qualitative changes in performance with age. Sometimes, however, constancies in strategy over age can be of as great or greater theoretical interest.

Consider, for example, Bryant and Trabasso's (1971) pioneering work on the role of memory in transitive inference. These investigators suggested that differences in performance on transitive inference problems between preoperational and concrete operational children reflected not the acquisition of new reasoning components and strategies, but rather the acquisition of sufficient memory capability to implement components and strategies of reasoning that were already potentially available, if still somewhat inaccessible. Subsequent research by Trabasso and his colleagues has further substantiated and elaborated the initial finding (Riley, 1976; Riley & Trabasso, 1974; Trabasso & Riley, 1975; Trabasso, Riley, & Wilson, 1975). In my own experiment on linear syllogistic reasoning described earlier, I, too, found no significant change in children's strategies for solving linear syllogisms, at least over the age range from grade 3 upward: Subjects of all ages used essentially the same efficient strategy for solving linear syllogisms—one employing a set of performance components operating on a combination of linguistic and spatial representations for information (see also Sternberg, 1980c, 1980d; Sternberg & Weil, 1980).

Consider as a second example the case of pictorial analogies. The strategy changes described earlier apply to pictures with integral (not clearly separable) attributes. The large majority of objects in the world are in fact composed of integral attributes, and even words are probably encoded integrally; usually one does not think about each separate attribute of an object represented by a word when one encodes that word. However, if pictures are constructed so that their attributes are encoded separately rather than these attributes being integrated, then subjects of all ages use the same strategy for solving these analogies that second graders use for solving pictorial analogies with integral attributes: The subjects are maximally self-terminating, encoding and comparing just the minimum possible number of attributes. The use of this strategy may derive from the ease with which each attribute in the individual terms of such an analogy can be processed in isolation from every other attribute.

4. Selection of One or More Representations or Organizations for Information. A given component is often able to operate upon any one of a number of different possible representations or organizations for information. The choice of representation or organization can facilitate or impede the efficacy with which the component operates. So closely intertwined are components, strategies, and representations that it is difficult to discuss any of them sensibly without discussing all of them together.

An example of this close intertwining can be seen in the case of solutions to the pictorial analogies. Representation of the attributes separably is associated with the use of a fully self-terminating strategy that does not employ the mapping component. This generalization is true for all ages of subjects and for pictorial analogies with both integral (Fig. 9.1), and separable attributes. It would be difficult to assign any single direction of causality, at least in our present state of knowledge: Whether the particular way of representing information leads to a choice of performance components that in turn leads to a choice of strategy, whether the choice of strategy leads to a choice of performance components that in turn leads to a choice of representation, or whether any other permutation is uniquely correct, is simply impossible to say at this point. But it can be said with confidence that the choice of components, strategy, and representation are closely intertwined, and any one choice can be understood only incompletely in isolation.

A second example of representational development can be seen in the development of truth-table representations for various logical connectives. At one extreme, the representation of what is probably the simplest connective, *and,* did not change in the grade 2 to college age range: Subjects of all ages represented *and* with its correct logical truth table. At the other extreme, representation of the most difficult connective we studied, *if and only if,* was never correct (for most subjects) at any age: Even the oldest subjects interpreted it as a unidirectional conditional relation rather than as a bidirectional biconditional relation. Of particular interest, however, were subjects' truth-table representations of *or.* This connective has two "correct" meanings. The exclusive meaning of *or,* "one or the other but not both," is commonly used in everyday parlance; the inclusive meaning of *or,* "one or the other and possibly both," is commonly used in formal logic. Table 9.1 shows model fits (expressed as badnesses of fit in terms of root-mean-square deviations of observed from predicted values) for each of the two truth-table patterns representing these different meanings of *or.* Data are group average results for the encoding and combination tasks administered to subjects in the grade 2 to college range. The important trend is the shift from using *or* in an inclusive sense at the younger age levels to using *or* in an

TABLE 9.1
Model Fits for the Logical Connective "Or"

Grade Level	Interpretation	
	Inclusive	Exclusive
Encoding Task		
2	.26	.69
4	.31	.39
6	.41	.22
8	.35	.17
High school	.36	.18
College	.42	.10
Combination Task		
2[a]	—	—
4	.40	.54
6	.43	.65
8	.40	.38
High school	.54	.20
College	.64	.09

Note: Model fits are expressed in terms of root-mean-square deviations of observed from predicted response patterns.

[a] Data for this condition were unreliable.

exclusive sense at the older age levels (see also Paris, 1973). The switch-over occurs earlier in the encoding task than in the combination task, and this tendency toward an earlier switch-over in truth tables was general across the other connectives as well. It suggests the possibility that children use less recently acquired meanings for logical connectives when confronted with a more difficult (combination) task, perhaps because they have not yet established the new meaning well enough to use it in a task that severely taxes their intellectual resources. In any case, subjects of all ages studied here interpreted *or* correctly, switching from the logical meaning of *or* to the everyday meaning as they grew older.

5. Decision Regarding Allocation of Componential Resources. Problem solvers sometimes encounter various barriers to their efforts. Some of these barriers are external, such as the total time made available for problem solution; others are internal, such as the amount of processing capacity one has to bring to bear upon a problem. The problem solver must decide how many resources to bring to bear upon a problem and then decide how to allocate the resources that are in fact brought to bear upon the problem.

Although none of my published research has directly addressed the issue of resource allocation, its importance has nevertheless come to the fore. Consider, for example, the solution of pictorial analogies with separable attributes (Sternberg & Rifkin, 1979, Experiment 1) such as hat color (black–white), footwear (shoes–boots), handgear (umbrella–briefcase), and suit pattern (striped–polka-dot). Figure 9.4 shows distributions of performance-component times for the solution of these analogies. Plotted in the figure are composite time, encoding time, response time, and inference-application time. This last time, referring to the sum of the times to infer the relation between the first two analogy terms and to apply this relation between the last two terms, was estimated in the experiment as a confounded parameter. The major result is that whereas response time (including confounded metacomponential times) decreases monotonically with age and inference-application time also decreases and then levels off (the slight increase at the end is statistically nonsignificant), encoding time first decreases and then increases (significantly). Why might encoding time first decrease and then increase? One possibility is that the initial decrease represents straightforward development in encoding facility and that this development levels off at around the fourth grade; thereafter, the increase in encoding time represents a decision on the part of the subject to spend relatively more time encoding stimuli so as to be able to spend relatively less time in operating upon these encodings later. The idea would be to obtain a relatively good fix on the nature of the stimulus so that later one would not have to keep reencoding different aspects of the stimulus, or even the same ones. The viability of this hypothesis is supported by data obtained with adults solving pictorial analogies: Better reasoners tend to spend relatively more time encoding the stimulus terms than do poorer reasoners, but they spend relatively less time operating upon these encodings (as in inference, mapping, and application). The result is a net savings in overall solution latency (Sternberg, 1977). A parallel might be drawn to a lending library: Slower and more careful cataloging of books (encoding of analogy terms) requires a greater initial time investment, but this investment is more than repaid by the more rapid and efficient borrowing and lending (inference, mapping, application, etc.) that can later take place because of the more efficient retrieval of sought-after volumes.

This finding dovetails with other findings in the developmental literature. Siegler (1978) has found that a major source of improved performance on his balance-scale (and other) tasks in older children can be attributed to more thorough encoding of the stimulus situation on the part of the older children. And in solving physics problems, experts also seem to spend relatively more time encoding the terms of problems than do novices, but relatively less time operating upon these encodings. Moreover, there are major qualitative differences in the sophistication with which problems are encoded by the experts versus the novices (Chi, Feltovich, & Glaser, in press; Larkin, McDermott, Simon, & Simon, 1980).

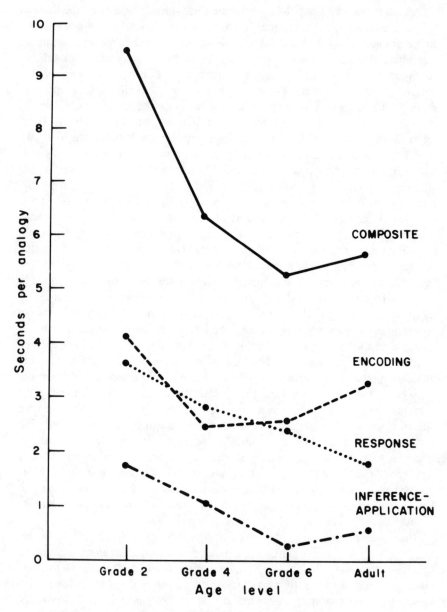

FIG. 9.4.   Composite and component latencies of correct responses to pictorial analogies with separable attributes.

We have also found a closely related result in a study of reasoning with complex analogies (multiple terms missing) in adulthood. In extracting metacomponential latencies from overall latency data in a complex analogical reasoning task, Bill Salter and I found that better reasoners tend to spend relatively more time than poorer reasoners in global planning for an entire set of problems, but they spend relatively less time in local planning for each individual problem in the set (see Sternberg, in 1981a).

6. Solution Monitoring. As individuals proceed through a problem, they must keep track of what they have already done, what they are currently doing, and what they still need to do; the relative importance of these three items may differ across problems. Moreover, if things are not proceeding as expected, an accounting of one's progress may be needed, and the possibility of a change in goals may even need to be considered. Often, new, more realistic goals must be formulated as a person realizes that the old goals cannot be reached. In a sense, solution monitoring may be viewed as a "metametacomponent" because it is needed to keep track of the operations of the metacomponents as well as of the other kinds of components. I would be most unenthusiastic, however, about supporting the notion of a clearly demarcated distinction between or among levels of metacomponents.

The use of solution monitoring in even the reasoning of very young children can be seen in the metacomponential decision of children as young as the third-grade level to use a justification component in the solution of verbal analogies. The component continues to be used until adulthood. This performance component is elicited upon the recognition by a subject that none of the presented answer options in a multiple-choice analogy provides an ideal completion for the given problem. In such an event, the subject may have to justify one of the presented options as nonideal, but superior to the alternatives. The justification component is something of a "catchall" in that it includes in its latency any reexecution of previously executed performance components that may be attempted in an effort to see whether a mistaken intermediate result has been responsible for the subject's failure to find an optimal solution. The decision to use this component reflects an awareness on the part of the subject that things are not going quite right: The path to solution has reached a dead end, and some route must be found that will yield an ideal answer, or else an answer must be selected that is acceptable, if nonideal.

That younger children are often less apt at solution monitoring than are older children is seen in the tendency of some of the second graders in the pictorial analogies experiment to circle one of the two analogy terms at the left rather than at the right of the problem. Almost all of the second graders were able to solve most analogies successfully, given that they understood what to do. The insensitivity of these subjects to the fact that right-to-left solution almost never yielded a suitable solution, much less a suitable analogy, can be viewed as a failure of these subjects to monitor their solution processes adequately.

The importance of solution monitoring in intelligent performance has been recognized by a number of investigators studying metacognitive skills. In the memory domain, it has been shown that if retarded subjects can be taught to rehearse and to monitor their rehearsal, their memory performance can be brought up to normal or near normal levels (Belmont & Butterfield, 1971; see also Brown, 1978). In the domain of verbal comprehension, Markman's (1977, 1979) research showing the failure of younger children to monitor their comprehension adequately is an example of a failure in solution monitoring. And in the numerical domain, the implementation of Gelman and Gallistel's (1978) one-one principle requires solution monitoring. The principle states that items in an array must be ticked off such that one and only one tick is used for each item. Implementation of this principle is hypothesized to involve coordinating two component processes: partitioning and tagging. Partitioning is the step-by-step maintenance of two categories of items—those to be counted and those that have already been counted; items need to be transferred one at a time from the first category to the second. Tagging is the elicitation from long-term memory of distinct tags to be assigned to each object. These two processes working in conjunction represent a kind of solution monitoring whereby children (and adults) can keep track of their progress in counting members of a set of objects.

In summary, I have proposed six metacomponents that I believe play a key role in intellectual development. My reading of my own research as well as that of others leads me to believe that these metacomponents are rather general across executions of a variety of tasks and that a fairly diverse set of developmental findings can be explained, at some level, metacomponentially.

In order for the metacomponential construct to be construct validated, there must be some way of isolating metacomponents from task performance. Bill Salter and I have proposed one way of doing so in the context of an analogical reasoning task (see Sternberg, 1981a). I present our task and method briefly as one example of how metacomponents can be isolated: The general principles of task decomposition seem relevant to tasks other than analogies.

Subjects were presented with analogies in which from one to three analogy terms were missing and in which the positions of the missing terms varied from one problem to another. Either two or three alternative answer options were substituted for each missing term. In this respect, the problems were like those used by Lunzer (1965) to study the development of analogical reasoning processes. An example of such a problem is: *man : skin :: (dog, tree) : (bark, cat)*, where the correct answers are *tree* and *bark*. Possible missing terms were the first, second, third, fourth, first and third, first and fourth, second and third, second and fourth, third and fourth, and second and third and fourth. Our particular interest in this work (done with adults) was to isolate two forms of strategy planning, which we referred to as "global planning" and "local planning."

Global planning refers to the formation of a macrostrategy that applies to a set of problems, regardless of the particular characteristics of a particular problem that is a member of a given set. The need for global planning can be largely a function of the context in which a set of problems is presented. We manipulated the amount of global planning required by presenting sets of analogies in two conditions, one mixed and the other blocked. In the mixed condition, each analogy within a given set of 10 items appeared in one of the different formats previously described (different sets of missing terms). Subjects in this condition were presumed to need considerable global planning to deal with the fact that problems within a given problem set were constantly shifting in nature. Regardless of the particular item type encountered at a particular time, this item context is not conducive to the rapid or automatic planning of a global strategy. In the blocked condition, all analogies within a given set of 10 items had the same format (i.e., were the same with respect to the positions of the missing terms). Subjects in this condition were presumed to need less global planning because all items within a given set were of the same structural format. Once a strategy was planned, it could be followed for all problems with minimal or no revision.

Local planning refers to the formation of a microstrategy that will be sufficient for solving a particular problem within a given set. Whereas global planning is assumed to be highly sensitive to the context of the surrounding problems, local planning is assumed to be context insensitive, applying to each item individually. It consists of the specific planning operations that are needed for a given item (e.g., tailoring the global plan to a specific item). We manipulated the amount of local planning required by presenting analogies in the various formats described earlier. More difficult formats were assumed to require more local planning; less difficult formats were assumed to require less local planning. Difficulty of a format was defined in terms of a strategic complexity index measuring the number of performance components that were disrupted by the construction of the item. Performance components were isolated separately. A simple linear model including the two aspects of strategy planning plus the performance components (lumped together into one "macrocomponent") and a regression constant accounted for .97 of the variance in the latency data. Most interesting was the fact that more intelligent subjects (as indicated by IQ test scores) spent relatively *more* time than did less intelligent subjects in global planning, with relatively less time in local planning. Apparently, careful global planning, like careful stimulus encoding, pays off its dividends later in facilitated execution of performance components.

Performance Components

On the whole, performance components tend to be more limited in the task domains to which they apply than do metacomponents, but there is nevertheless a considerable range of applicability: Performance components such as encoding and response are general across a wide range of tasks (although it is not clear at this point that they are the *same* psychological component in each task, and, most likely, there are several variants of each); performance components such as inference, mapping, application, and justification (as described earlier) are common to classes of tasks, in this case, inductive reasoning tasks (and these components do appear to be the same across at least several induction tasks; see Sternberg & Gardner, in press); and some performance components are essentially task specific and of little psychological interest. I have recently proposed that it is possible to classify tasks hierarchically according to their complexity as indexed by the numbers and identities of the performance components used in their solution (Sternberg, 1979b, 1981d).

I have also suggested recently that performance components tend to organize themselves into stages of task solution that seem to be fairly general across tasks (Sternberg, 1981d). These stages include encoding of stimuli, combination of or comparison between stimuli, and response. In the analogies tasks, for example, I have separated encoding and response components (each of which may be viewed as constituting its own stage) and inference, mapping, application, and justification components (each of which requires some kind of comparison between stimuli). In the linear syllogisms task, I have again identified encoding and response components (each of which may be divided into subcomponents; see Sternberg, 1980d) that form their own stages and other performance components that require combination and comparison of information (marking, negation, pivot search, response search, and noncongruence; see Sternberg, 1980d). Although I have not proposed a process model for the logical connectives task, performance on this task can be sensibly decomposed into stages of encoding of single premises, combination of the major and minor premises (where needed), and response.

1. Encoding Components. Qualitative and quantitative changes in encoding seem to constitute a major source of intellectual development. I have already discussed many of the ways in which encoding develops in the context of metacomponential decisions about encoding: (1) it tends to become more nearly exhaustive with increasing age (see also Brown & DeLoache, 1978; Siegler, 1978; Vurpillot, 1968); (2) it tends to be executed more slowly per encoded attribute with increasing age; and (3) it often operates on different representations of information with increasing age. The change in the rate at which encoding is executed in timed tasks, such as the analogies and linear syllogisms, tends to be fairly large in magnitude. And most of the difficulty in at least one complex deductive task, reasoning with logical connectives, turns out to be due to difficulty in encoding the connectives rather than difficulty in combining (reasoning with) them. Table 9.2 shows error rates for encoding and encoding plus combination in our logical connectives study. It is apparent that at every age level encoding accounts for the bulk of item difficulty. The incremental difficulty of combination of the premises is relatively small. This conclusion is consistent with that of previous investigators who have studied the development of reasoning

TABLE 9.2
Overall Error Rates for Logical Connectives

Grade Level	Task	
	Encoding	Combination
2	.90	.92
4	.76	.83
6	.67	.76
8	.44	.69
High school	.47	.56
College	.33	.43
Mean	.59	.70

with logical connectives (e.g., Taplin et al., 1974; but see Staudenmayer & Bourne, 1977, for an alternative formulation of the theoretical problem).

2. Combination and Comparison Components.   Whereas encoding seems to be a critical source of intellectual development in almost all of the tasks I and at least some others have studied, the importance of development in combination and comparison components is much more variable. Development in these components is of considerable importance in analogical reasoning, where mapping does not begin to appear until the transition into formal operations and where logical comparison components seem to replace associative comparison components with increasing age. In transitive inference tasks, there are not very large decreases in the latencies of combination and comparison components with increasing age, but it is surprising how little qualitative change there is. As noted earlier, there is a striking consistency across ages in strategy, and many of the differences in performance that have been attributed in the past to combination or comparison components now seem better attributed to failures in encoding due to memory limitations. In the previously discussed logical connectives task, most of the difficulty appears to be in encoding rather than in combination of premise information. I do not mean to denigrate the importance of these components: One need only investigate complex problem solving (e.g., Klahr, 1978; Klahr & Wallace, 1976) to see the great importance combination and comparison components can have on intelligent functioning. Thus, the importance of these components seems to be largely a function of the kind of task being studied.

3. Response Component.   In my own research as well as that of others studying quite different kinds of intellectual abilities (e.g., Kail et al., 1980; Keating & Bobbitt, 1978), substantial decreases have been observed in the latencies of components represented by the intercept of the regression equation used to estimate parameters. In some cases, this intercept has explicitly confounded encoding and response times (e.g., Keating & Bobbitt, 1978), but in other cases it has not. I am inclined to attribute the large decreases in response-component time over age, as well as the high correlations between response-component time and IQ that have been observed within age (e.g., Mulholland et al., 1980; Sternberg, 1977) to the confounding of metacomponent with response-component latency. Presumably, latency for executing at least some metacomponents is constant across the various item types that form the data points of the regression and, hence, becomes part of the regression constant that is normally labeled "response."

To summarize, performance components are potentially important sources of intellectual development, but a joint analysis of their role with that of the metacomponents leads me to believe that metacomponential development is much more fundamental and that many of the changes that are observed in performance-component availability, accessibility, latency, difficulty, and probability of execution can best be understood at the metacomponential level. Changes in metacomponential functioning lead almost inevitably to changes in the functioning of the performance components, but one can understand the latter changes only by looking for their metacomponential sources.

Acquisition, Retention, and Transfer Components

Werner and Kaplan (1952) proposed that:

> the child acquires the meaning of words principally in two ways. One is by explicit reference either verbal or objective; he learns to understand verbal symbols through the adult's direct naming of objects or through verbal definition. The second way is through implicit or contextual reference; the meaning of the word is grasped in the course of conversation, i.e., it is inferred from the cues of the verbal context [p. 3].

Our approach to the acquisition, retention, and transfer of information is loosely based on that of Werner and Kaplan (1952). Unfortunately, our research into the components of acquisition, retention, and transfer is at so inchoate a stage that it is possible to present only the bare outline of a theory, plus a description of the research Janet Powell and I are using to test it. The task being used to test the theory is similar to one employed by Heim (1970) (see Powell and Sternberg, 1981). All subjects in our study (high school students to date) received a set of 33 brief reading passages such as might be found in newspapers, magazines, novels, or textbooks. Embedded within these passages were from one to four very low-frequency words, which could be repeated from zero to four times either within or between passages, but not both. An example of such a passage is the following:

Two ill-dressed people—the one a tired woman of middle years and the other a tense young man—sat around a fire where the common meal was almost ready. The mother, Tanith, peered at her son through the oam of the bubbling stew. It had been a long time since his last ceilidh and Tobar had changed greatly; where once he had seemed all legs and clumsy joints, he now was well-formed and in control of his hard, young body. As they ate, Tobar told of his past year, re-creating for Tanith how he had wandered long and far in his quest to gain the skills he would need to be permitted to rejoin the company. Then all too soon, their brief ceilidh over, Tobar walked over to touch his mother's arm and quickly left.

Subjects were divided into two experimental and two control groups. In the first experimental group, subjects were asked to provide ratings regarding the low-frequency words and their surrounding contexts. These ratings were of various aspects of the passage (described later) that were hypothesized to affect subjects' ability to learn the meanings of the new words. When a given word occurred more than once in a given passage, subjects were also asked to provide separate ratings for each token occurrence. In the second experimental group, subjects were asked to state the main idea of the passage and to define as best they could each of the underlined (low-frequency) words. When a single word appeared twice in a passage, they only needed to define the word once, but if a given word appeared again in a later passage, subjects had to redefine the word later on. Subjects were allowed to view the passage they had just read at the time they defined the word, but they were not allowed to look back at previous passages. Subjects in a first control group were asked to read each of the passages and to provide a title for each passage. The subjects in this group thus had to understand at some level the contents of the passage in order to perform the task, but their attention was drawn to aspects of the passage that were irrelevant to understanding the low-frequency words. Finally, subjects in a second control group never saw the passage at all. All subjects received a pretest and a retest that contained passages very much like those in the main part of the study.

Our major concern in this study was with isolating variables that might affect the operations of acquisition, retention, and transfer components. Some of the variables we believe to have affected these operations, for which ratings were collected, were the following:

1. *Multiple occurrences of the target information.* Higher acquisition, retention, and transfer of information from one context to another were expected when information was presented more than once. Thus, the more times a new and originally unfamiliar word is seen, the more likely a person is to acquire, retain, or transfer its meaning.

2. *Variability in contexts for presentation of target information.* Different contexts are likely to highlight different aspects of a given word's meaning. Fuller definitions and therefore higher acquisition, retention, and transfer of

word meanings are expected when subjects make use of the variability of multiple contexts.

3. *Relevance or importance of target information to the overall situation.* Some kinds of information about a given situation are central to the understanding and making of decisions about it, whereas other kinds of information are only of minor importance. Similarly, some words are essential to understanding a given sentence or passage, whereas others are much less important. Higher acquisition, retention, and transfer of information are expected for those aspects of a situation that are more central to its overall thrust, and unfamiliar words that are central to the meaning of a passage are more likely to be learned.

4. *Helpfulness of surrounding context to the understanding of target information.* Different types of contexts may be more or less helpful to the inference of a target word's meaning. Higher acquisition, retention, and transfer are expected in those cases where context is more facilitative than where it is less so.

5. *Location of helpful information with respect to the target.* The recency of occurrence of helpful information is important in acquisition, retention, and transfer of definitions for new words, and other locational variables also have an effect on these components. For instance, subjects are more likely to utilize context that comes before an unfamiliar word than context that follows the word.

6. *Helpfulness of stored information to understanding of target information.* Previously stored information can facilitate acquisition, retention, and transfer of information. For example, the knowledge one has of background information about a situation or topic and whether or not an unfamiliar word is related to an already acquired concept can facilitate the learning of the new word. Higher acquisition, retention, and transfer of the meanings of new words are expected in those situations in which already existing concepts and frameworks can be brought to bear upon the new learning situation.

The idea in this research is to model the quality of definitions of words presented in context on the basis of these structural variables. Obviously, these do not constitute a complete list of variables that affect learning, but they seem to serve as a beginning. Acquisition components are based upon modeling of the quality of definitions of words presented for the first time. Transfer components are based upon modeling of improvement in the quality of definitions of words from earlier presentations of the words to later presentations. Retention components are based upon modeling of performance in a final definitions test presented outside the context of the reading passages. In each case, the independent variables listed are the same; only the context of the modeling changes. As of this writing, almost all of the data for this experiment have been collected, but they have not yet been analyzed. Hence, it is not yet possible to say what weights these and possibly other variables might have in predicting the quality of definitions.

MECHANISMS FOR
INTELLECTUAL DEVELOPMENT

Interrelations Among Kinds of Components

In order to understand the proposed mechanisms for intellectual development, it is necessary first to understand how the different kinds of components described earlier interrelate. My speculations regarding the interrelations among the functionally different kinds of components are shown in Fig. 9.5. The different kinds of components are closely interrelated.

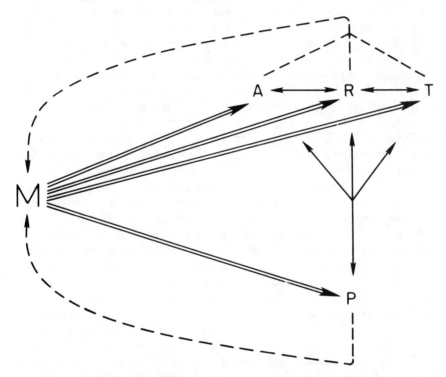

FIG. 9.5.   Interrelations among components serving different functions. "M" refers to a set of metacomponents, "A" to a set of acquisition components, "R" to a set of retention components, "T" to a set of transfer components, and "P" to a set of performance components. Direct activation of one kind of component by another is represented by double solid arrows. Indirect activation of one kind of component by another is represented by single solid arrows. Direct feedback from one kind of component to another is represented by single broken arrows. Indirect feedback from one kind of component to another proceeds from and to the same components, as does indirect activation, and so is shown by the single solid arrows.

Four kinds of interrelations need to be considered. Direct activation of one kind of component by another, referring to the immediate passage of control from one kind of component to another, is represented by double solid arrows. Indirect activation of one kind of component by another, referring to the mediate passage of control from one kind of component to another via a third kind of component, is represented by single solid arrows. Direct feedback from one kind of component to another, referring to the immediate passage of information from one kind of component to another, is represented by single broken arrows. Indirect feedback from one kind of component to another, referring to the mediate passage of information from one kind of component to another via a third kind of component, is represented by single solid arrows (following, as it does, the same paths as indirect activation).

In the proposed system, only metacomponents can directly activate and receive feedback from each other kind of component. Thus, all control to the system passes directly from the metacomponents, and all information from the system passes directly to the metacomponents. The other kinds of components can activate and receive information from each other indirectly; in every case, mediation must be supplied by the metacomponents. For example, acquisition of information affects retention of information and various kinds of transformations (performances) upon that information, but only via the link of the three kinds of components to the metacomponents. Information from the acquisition components is filtered to the other kinds of components through the metacomponents.

Consider some examples of how the system might function in the solution of an analogy problem. As soon as one decides upon a certain tentative strategy for solving the analogy, activation of that strategy can pass directly from the metacomponent responsible for deciding upon a strategy to the performance component responsible for executing the first step of the strategy, and, subsequently, activation can pass to the successive performance components needed to execute the strategy. Feedback will return from the performance components indicating how successfully the strategy is working. If monitoring of this feedback indicates lack of success, control may pass to the metacomponent that is "empowered" to select a new strategy; if no successful change in strategy can be realized, the solution monitoring metacomponent may change the goal altogether (e.g., deciding to find an answer option that is a high associate of the last term in the stem rather than logically related to it in the same way that the second term was related to the first).

As a given strategy is being executed, new information may be acquired about how to solve analogies in general. This information is also fed back to the metacomponents, either to be acted upon or ignored. New information that seems useful is more likely to be directed back from the relevant metacomponents to the relevant retention components for retention in long-term memory. What is acquired does not directly influence what is retained, hence "practice does not necessarily make perfect": Some people may be unable to profit from their experience because of inadequacies in metacomponential information processing. Similarly, what is retained does not directly influence what is later transferred. The chances of information being transferred to a later context will be largely dependent on the form in which the metacomponents decided to store the information for later access. Acquired information also does not directly affect transformations (performances) upon that information. The results of acquisition (or retention or transfer) must first be fed back into the metacomponents, which in effect decide what information will filter back indirectly from one type of component to another.

The metacomponents are able to process only a limited amount of information at a given time. In a difficult task, especially a new and novel one, the amount of information being fed back to the metacomponents may exceed their capacity to act upon it. In this case, the metacomponents become overloaded, and valuable information that cannot be processed may simply be wasted. The total information-handling capacity of the metacomponents of a given system will thus be an important limiting aspect of that system. Similarly, capacity to allocate attentional resources so as to minimize the probability of bottlenecks will be part of what determines the effective capacity of the system (see also Hunt, 1980).

Figure 9.5 does not show interrelations among various individual members of each single functional kind of component. These interrelations can be easily described in words, however. Metacomponents are able to activate and communicate with each other directly. It seems likely that the solution-monitoring metacomponent controls the intercommunication and interactivation among the other metacomponents, and there is a certain sense in which this particular metacomponent might be viewed as a metametacomponent, as mentioned earlier. Other kinds of components are not able to activate or communicate with each other directly. But components of a given kind can activate and communicate indirectly with other components of the same kind. Indirect communication and activation proceed through the metacomponents, which can direct information or activation from one component to another component of the same kind.

Interrelations Among Components and Intellectual Development

The system of interrelations among kinds of components just described implicitly contains several bases for intellectual change. In this section, at least some of these bases for change are made explicit.

First, the components of acquisition, retention, and transfer provide the mechanisms for a steadily developing knowledge base. Increments in the knowledge base, in turn, allow for more sophisticated forms of acquisition, retention, and transfer, and possibly for greater ease in execution of performance components. For example, some transfer components may act by relating new knowledge to old knowledge. As the base of old knowledge becomes deeper and broader, the possibilities for relating new knowledge to old knowledge, and thus for incorporating that new knowledge into the existing knowledge base, increase. There is thus the possibility of an unending feedback loop: The components lead to an increased knowledge base, which leads to more effective use of the components, which leads to further increases in the knowledge base, and so on.

Second, the self-monitoring metacomponents can, in effect, learn from their own mistakes. Early on, allocation of metacomponential resources to varying tasks or kinds of components may be less than optimal, with a resulting loss of valuable feedback information. Self-monitoring should eventually result in improved allocation of metacomponential resources, particularly to the self-monitoring of the metacomponents. Thus, self-monitoring by the metacomponents results in improved allocation of metacomponential resources to the self-monitoring of the metacomponents, which in turn leads to improved self-monitoring, and so on. Here, too, there exists the possibility of an unending feedback loop that is internal to the metacomponents themselves.

Finally, indirect feedback from kinds of components other than metacomponents to each other and direct feedback to the metacomponents should result in improved effectiveness of performance. Acquisition components, for example, can provide valuable information to performance components (via the metacomponents) concerning how to perform a task, and the performance components, in turn, can provide feedback to the acquisition components (via the metacomponents) concerning what else needs to be learned in order to perform the task optimally. Thus, other kinds of components can also generate unending feedback loops in which performance improves as a result of interactions between the kinds of components or between multiple components of the same kind.

There can be no doubt that in the present conceptual scheme, the metacomponents form the major basis for the development of intelligence. All activation and feedback are filtered through these elements. If they do not perform their function well, then it won't matter very much what the other kinds of components do. It is for this reason that the metacomponents are viewed as truly central in understanding the nature and development of intelligence.

INTERRELATIONS BETWEEN COMPONENTIAL MECHANISMS FOR INTELLECTUAL DEVELOPMENT AND THOSE IN OTHER APPROACHES TO INTELLIGENCE

The componential approach to intellectual development that has been described here is one of several alternative information-processing approaches that might be considered. Because this approach, like others, uses its own language, its concepts might be communicated more effectively in comparison to the claims of other approaches, both within the information-processing tradition and outside it.

In this way, I attempt to show that although various alternative approaches have all made their own unique contributions to developmental theory, these contributions are largely compatible with each other. This compatibility is sometimes hidden by differences in the languages in which the approaches and their theoretical contributions are expressed.

Information-Processing Approaches

Information-processing approaches to intellectual development share the positing of some kind of elementary information process as a fundamental unit of behavior (see Newell & Simon, 1972). It is assumed that all behavior of a human information-processing system can be understood in part as a result of the combination of these elementary processes. The various approaches differ in the units they have posited as being central to understanding behavior. I consider here some of the alternative units that have been presented, and how they relate to the component construct and the theory built upon it. (See also Sternberg & Powell, in press, for a more detailed description of these units and of research on intellectual development that has been done with each as its basis.)

1. The TOTE. Miller, Galanter, and Pribram (1960) proposed as the fundamental unit of intelligent behavior the TOTE (Test-Operate-Test-Exit). Each unit of behavior starts with a test of the present outcome against the desired outcome. If the result of the test is congruent with the desired outcome (called an "Image"), an Exit is made. If not, another operation is performed in order to make the result of the next test conform as closely as possible to the Image. If the result of the next test is congruent with the Image, an Exit is made. Otherwise, still another operation is performed, and so on down the line until the Test result corresponds to the Image (which may have been modified along the way in order to make it conform more closely to the demands of reality). An individual TOTE, a hierarchy of TOTEs, or a sequence of TOTEs (which may include hierarchies) executed in order to realize an Image is what I earlier referred to as a Plan.

The loci of intellectual development are suggested implicitly by Miller et al.'s (1960) account of the TOTE and its derivative concepts. Intellectual development in the TOTE system can be viewed as resulting from the formation of Plans that are successively more: (1) horizontally elongated, in that the number of TOTEs needed to reach the Image from an initial state increases, allowing one to undertake Plans that require successively more steps to actualize: (2) vertically elaborated, in that the hierarchical structure of the Plan involves more different levels of processing than do the simpler Plans more likely to be executed by younger children, and upon which the more elaborated Plans are likely to have been built; (3) numerous, in that one learns new kinds of routines that can be used to attain new Images constructed as one grows older; and (4) efficient, or otherwise generally efficacious, in that older Plans are supplemented or possibly replaced by newer Plans that attain Images with greater facility than did the older Plans.

The TOTE and its derivative concepts are wholly compatible with the component and its derivative concepts. A TOTE would be viewed in my own system as a substrategy consisting of two comparison components (the Tests), one encoding or combination component (the Operation), and a Response component (the Exit). A Plan is what I have referred to as a strategy, and an Image is the goal state the strategy is meant to realize. Miller et al. do not distinguish between higher-order types of metacomponential constructs, on the one hand, and lower-order types of componential constructs, on the other. Instead, they (1960) propose that:

> a central notion of the method followed in these pages is that the operational components of TOTE units may themselves be TOTE units. That is to say, the TOTE pattern describes both strategic and tactical units of behavior. Thus the operational phase of a higher-order TOTE might itself consist of a string of other TOTE units, and each of these, in turn, may contain still other strings of TOTEs, and so on [p. 32].

Thus, their preference (and at one time, mine; see Sternberg, 1977) is to use a single kind of unit to accomplish both executive and nonexecutive information processing. I suspect the difference in conceptualizations is largely a linguistic one: I introduced a higher-level kind of component because I found, like Miller et al. (1960), that: ''retaining the same pattern of description for the higher, more strategic units as for the lower, more tactical units may be confusing,'' at least ''on first acquaintance [p. 32].''

2. The Production.   A production is a condition-action sequence. If a certain condition is met, then a certain action is performed. Sequences of ordered productions are called production systems.

The executive for a production system is hypothesized to make its way down the ordered list of productions until one of the conditions is met. The action corresponding to that condition is executed, and control is returned to the top of the list. The executive then makes its way down the list again, trying to satisfy a condition. When it does so, an action is executed, control returns to the top, etc. The production construct was popularized in psychology by Newell and Simon (1972) (see also Newell, 1973) and has been used extensively in developmental theorizing by Anderson (1976), Klahr and Wallace (1976), and others. The rules for production systems may be elaborated as required. Anderson (1976), for example, has suggested rules for strengthening and weakening productions, and Hunt and Poltrock (1974) have suggested that productions may be probabilistically ordered so that the exact order in which the list of productions is scanned may differ across scannings of the list.

Cognitive development is assumed to occur through the operation of self-modifying production systems. (See Klahr, 1979, for a review of the literature on such production systems.) The basic idea is that the action in a condition-action sequence is to build a new production. Anderson, Kline, and Beasley (1980) have proposed four transition mechanisms by which modification could occur. A designation production is one that simply has as its action the instructions to build a new production of a certain kind. A strengthening mechanism increases the probability that a production will be activated. A generalization mechanism weakens the specific conditions that activate a production so that the production is more likely to be executed under a broader variety of circumstances. And a discrimination mechanism strengthens the specifications for activation of a production so that the production will be activated only when more specific conditions are met than was originally the case. Notice that a critical assumption underlying these last three mechanisms is that productions have differential strengths that affect the likelihood of being executed if they are reached. A rough analogy would be to the eliciting conditions necessary to fire a neuron in the nervous system. Intellectual development thus is a continuing matter throughout one's lifetime, and it is largely a matter of learning, which can alter the productions constituting a production system and thus the person's ways of solving various problems.

The production can easily be mapped into componential terms. The test of the condition is analogous to a comparison component (or a Test in TOTE terminology). The action that is contingent upon meeting the condition is analogous to an encoding or combination component, or possibly even to another comparison component, where the comparison is between two new pieces of information rather than between a new and an old piece of information (or an Operation, in TOTE terminology), unless the action is a terminal one, in which case it is analogous to a response (or an Exit in TOTE terminology). The componential system does not specify any one particular operating system in which components are to be embedded. Were components to be embedded in the context of a production system, then they would best be viewed as productions of various kinds. I have preferred to embed them in the context of a flow-chart system, in which a flow chart constitutes a strategy (Plan) comprising components (TOTEs). Thus, there is no necessary incompatibility between productions and components. A production implies a certain kind of operating system; a component does not. It has been a matter of my own (and other componential investigators') preference to embed components in a flow-chart system rather than in a production system; others might choose differently in future research.

3. The Scheme. The notion of a "scheme" proposed by Pascual-Leone (1970) and elaborated by Case (1974a, 1974b, 1978) is viewed as "neo-Piagetian," drawing as it does on the basic Piagetian notion of the "schema." What these investigators have done, however, is to specify the notion of a scheme more precisely than has Piaget.

There are three basic kinds of schemes—figurative, operative, and executive. Figurative schemes, according to Case (1974b), are "internal representations of items of information with which a subject is familiar, or of perceptual configurations which he can recognize [p. 545]." If, for example, a subject described a photograph as depicting a picture of his or her house, one could say that the subject assimilated the sensory input to a figurative "house scheme." Operative schemes, according to Case (1974b), are "internal representations of functions (rules), which can be applied to one set of figurative schemes, in order to generate a new set [p. 545]." If, for example, a subject looked at two different photographs of a house and judged them to be depicting the "same" house, one would describe the subject as applying an operative scheme representing a "sameness" function to the figurative schemes representing the features of each of the two photographs. Executive schemes, according to Case (1974b), are "internal representations of procedures which can be applied in the face of particular problem situations, in an attempt to reach particular objectives [p. 546]." These schemes are to a large extent responsible for determining which figurative and operative schemes a subject activates in a particular problem situation. The figurative and operative schemes just suggested in the comparison of two photographs, for example, would presumably be activated only if they were part of some larger executive scheme that required the particular comparison.

Whether or not a subject actually solves a particular problem is assumed to depend on four basic factors. The first is the repertoire of schemes that a subject brings to the problem. The second is the maximum number of schemes that the subject's psychological system is capable of activating at any one time. The maximum mental effort a subject can apply to a problem is referred to as "M-power" and is assumed to vary both within and between age groups. M-power is viewed as at least one source of individual differences within and between age levels in overall general ability (g); it is assumed to increase linearly with age. The third factor is a subject's tendency to utilize the full M-power that is available; some subjects are assumed to be more willing than others to apply full M-power, and, in general, subjects differ in the proportion of M-power they typically exploit. Finally, a fourth factor is the relative weights assigned to cues from the perceptual field on the one hand and to cues from all other sources (e.g., task instructions) on the other.

Case (1974b) describes several ways in which new schemes may be acquired and, hence, intellectual development may occur. First, new schemes can be acquired by modification of old schemes. Second, new schemes can be acquired by the combination or consolidation of multiple old schemes. These two ways of acquiring new schemes can be further subdivided, resulting in multiple means by which intellectual growth can occur.

These various types of schemes can be mapped into componential terms. Figurative schemes are unitized internal representations, roughly equivalent to what Miller (1956) has called "chunks." Operative schemes are roughly equivalent to lower-order components (performance, acquisition, retention, transfer), or to what Inhelder and Piaget (1958) have referred to as "transformations" and what Newell and Simon (1972) have referred to as "elementary information processes." Executive schemes are equivalent to strategies as formulated by higher-order metacomponents, or to what Miller et al. (1960) have referred to as "Plans" and what Newell and Simon (1972) have referred to as "executive programs."

An interesting feature of the system of Pascual-Leone and Case is the set of factors assumed to determine whether or not a given problem is actually solved. Again, these limiting factors can be mapped into componential terms. First, the repertoire of schemes is simply a repertoire of strategies, which is assumed to increase with age. Second, what is referred to as M-power in the scheme system is referred to as processing capacity or channel capacity in the componential system and most other information-processing systems. Third, the subject's tendency to utilize full M-power would be viewed as a motivational variable in the componential and most other information-processing systems. I believe that motivational variables receive far too little attention in information-processing psychology, however. Hence, the inclusion of this motivational factor is most auspicious in a theory of intellectual development (see Sternberg, 1981b). Finally, componential analysis weights the various kinds of inputs to the information-processing system through parameter estimates. These estimates tell how important each kind of information is in reaching a final solution to a given problem.

4. The Rule (or Principle).   Rules (Siegler, 1981) and principles (Gelman & Gallistel, 1978) form the final unit that I consider here. According to Siegler (1981): "The basic assumption underlying the rule-assessment approach is that cognitive development can be characterized in large part as the acquisition of increasingly powerful rules for solving problems [p. 3]." Rules or principles emphasize knowledge rather than process as the basic unit of development. What Siegler refers to as a rule, however, is virtually identical to what I have referred to as a strategy, or Miller et al. (1960) have referred to as a Plan. As children grow older, the complexity of their rules increases, generally because earlier rules fail to take into account all of the relevant information in a given problem. The rules of older children tend to reflect more thorough encoding and more nearly exhaustive information processing than do the rules of younger children; as mentioned earlier, a parallel pattern of results has obtained in my own investigations of strategy development in reasoning tasks.

The Psychometric Approach

In most psychometric investigations of intellectual development, the basic unit of analysis has been the factor. The paradigm in which this unit has been defined and used is usually referred to as the "psychometric" one, but it is also sometimes called the "differential" or the "factorial" paradigm. Factors are obtained by "factor analyzing" a matrix of intercorrelations (or covariances) between scores on tests of measures of ability. Factor analysis tends to group into single factors observable sources of individual-differences variation that are highly correlated with each other and to group into different factors observable sources of variation that are only modestly correlated or wholly uncorrelated with each other. These new groupings are each proposed to represent unitary, latent sources of individual-differences variation at some level of analysis. Theorists would generally agree that other levels of analysis would be possible as well, in which factors would either be further subdivided or further combined.

What, exactly, is a factor? There is no single, agreed-upon answer to this question. Thurstone (1947) noted that "factors may be called by different names, such as 'causes,' 'faculties,' 'parameters,' 'functional unities,' 'abilities,' or 'independent measurements' [p. 56]." Royce (1963) added to this list: "dimensions, determinants, . . . and taxonomic categories [p. 522]," and Cattell (1971) has referred to factors as "source traits."

Factor theorists have differed with respect to the particular factors purported to be basic to intelligence. For example, Spearman (1927) suggested that intelligence comprises one general factor that is common to all of the tasks that are used in the assessment of intelligence and as many specific factors as there are tasks; Holzinger (1938) suggested the need for a third kind of factor, a group factor common to some but not all of the tasks used to assess intelligence; Thurstone (1938) proposed that intelligence is best understood in terms of multiple factors, or primary mental abilities as he called them; Guilford (1967) has proposed a theory encompassing 120 factors formed by crossing five operations, six products, and four contents. The concept of a hierarchical theory can be traced back at least to Burt (1940), and more sophisticated hierarchical theories have been proposed by Jensen (1970), Vernon (1971), and others. Detailed reviews of these and other theories can be found in Brody and Brody (1976), Butcher (1970), and Cronbach (1970).

There are several possible sources of intellectual development in the factorial conception of human intelligence. These include (1) changes in number of factors with age (Garrett, 1938, 1946; Garrett, Bryan, & Perl, 1935); (2) changes in the relevance or weights of factors in human intelligence with age (Hofstaetter, 1954; Stott & Ball, 1965); (3) changes in the content (names) of factors within a given factor structure with age (McCall, Eichorn, & Hogarty, 1977; McCall, Hogarty, & Hurlburt, 1972); and (4) changes in factor scores of fixed factors with age (Bayley, 1933, 1970; Dearborn & Rothney, 1941; Honzik, 1938; Sontag, Baker, & Nelson, 1958). A discussion of these various sources of development and the evidence supporting them can be found in Sternberg and Powell (in press).

Factors represent "underlying" sources of individual differences, including the individual differences generated by differences among individuals in the components they use and the efficacy with which they use these components in their information processing. Whereas components are usually isolated by extracting between-stimulus sources of variance, factors are usually isolated by extracting between-subject sources of variance. Hence, a given factor might contain variance attributable to the actions of several different components if use of these components is correlated across subjects. Suppose, for example, that each of three metacomponents was required to solve all of the problems in a battery of tests, that each of two performance components was required to solve a subset of the problems, and that a single acquisition component was required to solve a single type of problem. Then, the metacomponents might together form a general factor, the performance components might form a group factor, and the acquisition component might form a factor specific to a single test. Moreover, common contents and modes of presentation of test items (e.g., visual or auditory) might also be confounded in these factors. If all items are presented visually, then response to visual mode of presentation will be a general source of individual-differences variance that might enter the general factor, along with the variance attributable to the metacomponents. Note that components, like factors, are subject to confoundings. In the case of components, the confoundings are attributable to shared variance across stimulus types. If all items in a set are presented visually, for example, then the global constant will include, in addition to, say, response latency, any added latency attributable to the visual mode of presentation.

I do not believe there is any meaningful sense in which one can refer to either components or factors as "more basic": Each extracts a different kind of variance, and each can be mapped onto the other. Hence, components and factors are compatible, elucidating different aspects of a single global phenomenon. (For a detailed account of how psychometric theories of intelligence can be conceptualized componentially, see Sternberg, 1980b, 1980e.)

The Piagetian Approach

Piaget (1972) has defined intelligence as "the most highly developed form of mental adaptation [p. 7]." He has further noted that "if intelligence is adaptation, it is desirable before anything else to define the latter [p. 7]." Piaget does so by defining adaptation as "an equilibrium between the action of the organism on the environment and vice versa [p. 7]" or, more specifically, as "an equilibrium between assimilation and accommodation, which amounts to the same as an equilibrium of interaction between subject and object [p. 8]."

After defining "adaptation" as an equilibrium between assimilation and accommodation, it becomes necessary to define these latter terms. Piaget (1972) defines assimilation as "the action of the organism on surrounding objects, in so far as this action depends on previous behavior involving the same or similar objects. . . . Mental assimilation is thus the incorporation of objects into patterns of behavior [pp. 7-8].'' In assimilation, then, an individual incorporates an object (whether concrete or abstract) into an existing cognitive structure, if necessary adapting the perceived properties of the object to fit the structure. Conversely, in accommodation "the environment acts on the organism . . . , it being understood that the individual never suffers the impact of surrounding stimuli as such, but they simply modify the assimilatory cycle by accommodating him to themselves [p. 8].'' In accommodation, then, the individual reverses priorities, adapting properties of the cognitive structure as needed to fit the object. Intellectual development is largely attributable to the fittings and refittings of objects to cognitive structures called schemata, and of schemata to objects, that occur as the result of assimilation and accommodation, respectively.

After defining assimilation and accommodation, one last definition is still necessary, that of "schema." Piaget never defines just what a *schema* is in any single, all-encompassing definition (Flavell, 1963); Flavell's definition of a schema as "a cognitive structure which has reference to a class of similar action sequences, these sequences of necessity being strong, bounded totalities in which the constituent behavioral elements are tightly interrelated [pp. 52-53]'' would seem to define the term as well, if as abstractly, as any definition I have found. Sucking, prehension, sight, and intuitive qualitative correspondence are examples of Piagetian schemata (Flavell, 1963).

That Piagetian theory is compatible with information-processing theory is shown by the fact that Rumelhart and Norman (1978) have proposed two modes of knowledge acquisition in information-processing language that correspond almost exactly to assimilation and accommodation. *Accretion* is the assimilation of new information to existing knowledge structures, and *restructuring* is the reorganization of existing knowledge structures to accommodate new information that does not fit into the knowledge structures that are available. In terms of the componential system for understanding acquisition, retention, and transfer, assimilation and accommodation would seem to cross-cut it. For example, in transferring information from one context to another on the basis of contextual cues, one may decide that the new information can be incorporated into existing cognitive structures or representations, or, alternatively, that the existing structures or representations have to be modified to incorporate the new information. Modification of these structures can then result in what might be viewed as backward transfer, whereby old information is re-viewed in terms of the new.

To summarize, alternative approaches to intellectual development seem to be largely compatible with each other. Their compatibility is sometimes obscured by differences in the languages in which they are presented. Compatibility is not, of course, tantamount to identity: Each system makes unique contributions by highlighting aspects of intellectual development that other systems may slight or ignore. But these unique contributions become clearer when they are distinguished from mere linguistic differences among the systems.

THE DEVELOPMENTAL CONTINUITY
OF INTELLIGENCE

A review of the abundant literature supplying correlations between scores from intelligence tests administered in infancy and scores from intelligence tests administered in later childhood and adulthood reveals a consistent dearth of impressive correlations between scores on the infant tests and scores on the tests administered to older children and adults (see, e.g., Bayley, 1955, 1970; Broman, Nichols, & Kennedy, 1975; McCall, Hogarty, & Hurlburt, 1972). The lack of a substantial relationship between infant and later intelligence test scores has led many investigators to conclude that infant intelligence (almost certainly during the first year of life and probably during much of the second year as well) is different in kind from intelligence in postinfancy.

Some recent data have led me to speculate that at least some significant aspects of intelligence may in fact be continuous over the life span (Sternberg, 1981c). These findings concern novelty-seeking and novelty-finding behavior in children and adults.

Lewis and Brooks-Gunn (1981) have found that "habituating to redundant and recovering to novel stimuli at 3 months of age . . . predict later intellectual functioning at 24 months better than 3-month global intelligence or object permanence scores. In terms of information processing skills, recovery predicted later intelligence test scores better than habituation [p. 131]." Thus, inferred increased exploration of novel stimuli following habituation to non-novel stimuli proved to be indicative of later intelligence; scores on the infant "intelligence tests," however, were not indicative of later intelligence. This interesting finding was replicated in two independent samples of subjects.

Fagan and McGrath (1981) used a recognition-memory paradigm quite different in kind from the habituation-recovery paradigm of Lewis and Brooks-Gunn. Fagan and McGrath initially tested children at ages ranging from 4 to 7 months. The main finding of the study was that: "variations in early recognition memory as indexed by preferences for visual novelty both reflect and predict variations in intellectual functioning" later on, namely, at 4 and 7 years of age.

During the past few years, I have been pursuing the idea that intelligence in postinfancy may in part be understood as the ability to acquire and reason with new conceptual systems (Sternberg, 1981a). On the basis of a recent review of different conceptual systems for understanding intelligence that has convinced me of the importance of motivation in intelligence (broadly defined) (Sternberg, 1981b; see also Zigler, 1971, for a strong statement supporting this view), I would supplement the aforementioned cognitive notion with the motivational notion that intelligence (broadly defined) is also in part one's interest in, seeking, and finding novel and interesting conceptual systems in which to think. Thus, I view intelligence as not only the ability to learn and reason with *new concepts* (as well as one's interest in such concepts) but, more importantly, as the ability to learn and reason with (and one's interest in) *new kinds of concepts*. What makes a person more or less intelligent is not so much the ability to learn or think within already familiar conceptual systems, but the ability to learn and think within new conceptual systems, which can then be brought to bear upon already existing knowledge structures. Thus, an intelligent person must first seek out and find a new (and useful) conceptual system, then learn it, then reason within it, and finally apply it analogically to old problems that were previously seen in terms of formerly acquired conceptual systems. This point of view is consistent with that of Claparède (1917), according to whom intelligence is a mental adaptation to new circumstances. It is also consistent with the views of Piaget (1972), according to whom intelligence "tends towards an all-embracing equilibrium by aiming at the assimilation of the whole of reality and the accommodation to it of action, which it thereby frees from its dependence on the initial *hic* and *nunc* [p. 9]." The view is also compatible with views of psychologists whose orientation is not particularly developmental. Psychometricians who have stressed the role of creative thinking in intelligence (e.g., Guilford, 1967) have in effect argued for the importance of behavior with and toward novelty in intelligent performance. And computer simulators who have attempted to model intelligent thinking have found that the handling of novelty is important in an intelligent machine system. Schank (1980), for example, has suggested that in understanding intelligence, "what people do in brand new situations is what is of importance. . . . The ability to make generalizations from completely new situations that are useful for future needs is what intelligence is all about [p. 13]." To summarize, then, more intelligent people tend to be those who seek to broaden their perspectives on problems and who succeed in doing so.

I have studied the performance of adults on two "novel" tasks that require kinds of strategy formation outside the usual run of experience. In one task, subjects have to make projections about future states of objects on the basis of partial and sometimes misleading information about the present states of objects; in the other task, subjects have to solve analogies presented in somewhat bizarre formats (e.g., with multiple answer options for the first, second, and third terms, and only the fourth term given). A more detailed description of these tasks is given in Sternberg (1981a). The major finding of interest for present purposes is that, in both experiments, latencies to solve problems were more highly correlated with performance on standard intelligence tests than were latencies on the more entrenched kinds of response-time tasks that most investigators, including myself, have studied in the past. Correlations of latencies from the projection and analogy tasks with scores on intelligence tests were in the .4 to .8 range. We thereby obtained some empirical support for the notion that ability to perform well on novel tasks might be a key aspect of intelligence. Intelligence tests, although perhaps not directly measuring solution of novel kinds of problems, probably measure, at least in part, people's past interest in, learning about, and reasoning with tasks that at one time were novel but that have since become more standard parts of many people's task repertoires.

The proposed notion of intelligence in part as the seeking, finding, learning, and solving of novel problems and aspects of problems seems to dovetail nicely with the findings of Lewis and Brooks-Gunn (1981) and Fagan and McGrath (1981). The total package of results is consistent with the notion that attitude toward and performance on novel tasks or aspects of tasks is an important part of intelligence, from infancy onward. Obviously, the way in which measurement operations are conducted for assessing behavior will differ greatly across age levels. Both our own results and those of the authors of these articles suggest that converging operations for measurement of the behaviors of interest are both possible and feasible. I am therefore prepared to suggest that attitude toward and performance on novel tasks or aspects of tasks form the basis for at least one developmental continuity in intelligence.

How can this view be reconciled with the massive evidence suggesting that scores on infant intelligence tests do not correlate appreciably with scores on tests of intelligence administered later? Reconciliation is possible in terms of the particular aspects of intelligence one chooses to measure. Sensory-motor intelligence is no doubt a major part of infantile development, but it is also without a doubt only a fairly minor part of postinfantile development. There is not now, and never has been, any reason to expect high correlations between tests of sensory-motor abilities, on the one hand, and tests of more cognitive abilities, on the other. Indeed, the two kinds of tests do not even correlate highly *within* age level, as Galton (1883) discovered years ago and as others have found out again and again. The problem has been to find some aspect or aspects of intelligence that are present in both infants and older people *and* that can be measured in both. The greatest stumbling block has been in finding measurable aspects of infant behavior that would continue to be important sources of individual differences in intelligence later on. The studies I have cited by Lewis and Brooks-Gunn and by Fagan and McGrath seem to have found such sources of individual differences, and I have tried to provide at least a tentative and sketchy theoretical framework in which these sources of development and individual differences can be understood.

ACKNOWLEDGMENTS

Portions of this chapter were presented in a symposium on new approaches to cognitive development, Society for Research in Child Development, San Francisco, March 1979. I am grateful to Jacquelyn Hawkins and Daniel Kaye for comments on an earlier version of this manuscript.

REFERENCES

Achenbach, T. M. The children's associative responding test: A possible alternative to group IQ tests. *Journal of Educational Psychology,* 1970, *61,* 340–348.

Achenbach, T. M. The children's associative responding test: A two-year followup. *Developmental Psychology,* 1971, *5,* 477–483.

Anderson, J. R. *Language, memory, and thought.* Hillsdale, N.J.: Lawrence Erlbaum Associates, 1976.

Anderson, J. R., Kline, P. J., & Beasley, C. M., Jr. Complex learning processes. In R. E. Snow, P.-A. Federico, & W. Montague (Eds.), *Aptitude, learning, and instruction: Cognitive process analyses of learning and problem solving* (Vol. 2). Hillsdale, N.J.: Lawrence Erlbaum Associates, 1980.

Arlin, P. K. Cognitive development in adulthood: A fifth stage? *Developmental Psychology,* 1975, *11,* 602–606.

Atkinson, R. C., & Shiffrin, R. M. Human memory: A proposed system and its control processes. In K. W. Spence & J. T. Spence (Eds.), *The psychology of learning and motivation* (Vol. 2). New York: Academic Press, 1968.

Bayley, N. Mental growth during the first three years: A developmental study of 61 children by repeated tests. *Genetic Psychology Monographs,* 1933, *14,* 1–92.

Bayley, N. On the growth of intelligence. *American Psychologist,* 1955, *10,* 805–818.

Bayley, N. Development of mental abilities. In P. H. Mussen (Ed.), *Carmichael's manual of child psychology.* New York: Wiley, 1970.

Beilin, H. Stimulus and cognitive transformation in conservation. In D. Elkind & J. H. Flavell (Eds.), *Studies in cognitive development: Essays in honor of Jean Piaget.* London: Oxford University Press, 1969.

Belmont, J. M., & Butterfield, E. C. Learning strategies as determinants of memory deficiencies. *Cognitive Psychology,* 1971, *2,* 411–420.

Bower, G. H. Stimulus-sampling theory of encoding variability. In A. W. Melton & E. Martin (Eds.), *Coding processes in human memory.* Washington, D.C.: Winston, 1972.

Brainerd, C. J. Order of acquisition of transitivity conservation and class-inclusion of length and weight. *Developmental Psychology,* 1973, *8,* 105–116.

Brainerd, C. J. Neo-Piagetian training experiments revisited: Is there any support for the cognitive-developmental stage hypothesis? *Cognition,* 1974, *2,* 349–370.

Brody, E. B., & Brody, N. *Intelligence: Nature, determinants, and consequences.* New York: Academic Press, 1976.

Broman, S. H., Nichols, P. L., & Kennedy, W. A. *Preschool IQ: Prenatal and early developmental correlates.* Hillsdale, N.J.: Lawrence Erlbaum Associates, 1975.

Brown, A. L. Knowing when, where, and how to remember: A problem of metacognition. In R. Glaser (Ed.), *Advances in instructional psychology* (Vol. 1). Hillsdale, N.J.: Lawrence Erlbaum Associates, 1978.

Brown, A. L., & DeLoache, J. S. Skills, plans, and self-regulation. In R. Siegler (Ed.), *Children's thinking: What develops?* Hillsdale, N.J.: Lawrence Erlbaum Associates, 1978.

Bryant, P. E., & Trabasso, T. Transitive inferences and memory in young children. *Nature,* 1971, *232,* 456–458.

Burt, C. *The factors of the mind.* London: University of London Press, 1940.

Butcher, H. J. *Human intelligence: Its nature and assessment.* London: Methuen, 1970.

Butterfield, E. C., & Belmont, J. M. Assessing and improving the executive cognitive functions of mentally retarded people. In I. Bialer & M. Sternlicht (Eds.), *Psychological issues in mental retardation.* New York: Psychological Dimensions, 1977.

Butterfield, E. C., Wambold, C., & Belmont, J. M. On the theory and practice of improving short-term memory. *American Journal of Mental Deficiency,* 1973, *77,* 654–669.

Campione, J. C., & Brown, A. L. Memory and metamemory development in educable retarded children. In R. V. Kail, Jr., & J. W. Hagen (Eds.), *Perspectives on the development of memory and cognition*. Hillsdale, N.J.: Lawrence Erlbaum Associates, 1977.

Campione, J. C., & Brown, A. L. Toward a theory of intelligence: Contributions from research with retarded children. In R. J. Sternberg & D. K. Detterman (Eds.), *Human intelligence: Perspectives on its theory and measurement*. Norwood, N.J.: Ablex, 1979.

Case, R. Mental strategies, mental capacity, and instruction: A neo-Piagetian investigation. *Journal of Experimental Child Psychology*, 1974, *18*, 372–397. (a)

Case, R. Structures and strictures: Some functional limitations on the course of cognitive growth. *Cognitive Psychology*, 1974, *6*, 544–573. (b)

Case, R. Intellectual development from birth to adulthood: A neo-Piagetian interpretation. In R. Siegler (Ed.), *Children's thinking: What develops?* Hillsdale, N.J.: Lawrence Erlbaum Associates, 1978.

Cattell, R. B. *Abilities: Their structure, growth, and action*. Boston: Houghton Mifflin, 1971.

Chi, M. T. H., Feltovich, P. J., & Glaser, R. Representation of physics knowledge by experts and novices. *Cognitive Science*, in press.

Claparède, E. La psychologie de l'intelligence. *Scientia*, 1917, *22*, 253–268.

Clark, H. H. Linguistic processes in deductive reasoning. *Psychological Review*, 1969, *76*, 387–404.

Cronbach, L. J. *Essentials of psychological testing* (3rd ed.). New York: Harper & Row, 1970.

Dearborn, W. F., & Rothney, J. *Predicting the child's development*. Cambridge, Mass.: Science-Art, 1941.

Evans, T. G. A program for the solution of geometric-analogy intelligence test questions. In M. Minsky (Ed.), *Semantic information processing*. Cambridge, Mass.: MIT Press, 1968.

Fagan, J. F., III, & McGrath, S. K. Infant recognition memory and later intelligence. *Intelligence*, 1981, *5*, 121–130.

Flavell, J. H. *The developmental psychology of Jean Piaget*. New York: Van Nostrand, 1963.

Flavell, J. H. *Cognitive development*. Englewood Cliffs, N.J.: Prentice-Hall, 1977.

Flavell, J. H. Cognitive monitoring. In S. Yussen (Ed.), *The growth of insight in the child*. New York: Academic Press, in press.

Gallagher, J. M., & Wright, R. J. Piaget and the study of analogy: Structural analysis of items. In J. Magary (Ed.), *Piaget and the helping professions*. (Vol. 8). Los Angeles: University of Southern California Press, 1979.

Galton, F. *Inquiry into human faculty and its development*. London: Macmillan, 1883.

Garner, W. R. *The processing of information and structure*. Hillsdale, N.J.: Lawrence Erlbaum Associates, 1974.

Garrett, H. E. Differentiable mental traits. *Psychological Record*, 1938, *2*, 259–298.

Garrett, H. E. A developmental theory of intelligence. *American Psychologist*, 1946, *1*, 372–378.

Garrett, H. E., Bryan, A. I., & Perl, R. The age factor in mental organization. *Archives of Psychology*, 1935, *176*, 1–31.

Gelman, R., & Gallistel, C. R. *The child's understanding of number*. Cambridge, Mass.: Harvard University Press, 1978.

Gentile, J. R., Tedesco-Stratton, L., Davis, E., Lund, N. J., & Agunanne, B. A. Associative responding versus analogical reasoning by children. *Intelligence*, 1977, *1*, 369–380.

Groen, G. J., & Parkman, J. M. A chronometric analysis of simple addition. *Psychological Review*, 1972, *79*, 329–343.

Guilford, J. P. *The nature of human intelligence*. New York: McGraw-Hill, 1967.

Heim, A. *Intelligence and personality: Their assessment and relationship*. Harmondsworth, England: Penguin, 1970.

Hofstaetter, P. R. The changing composition of intelligence: A study of the t-technique. *Journal of Genetic Psychology*, 1954, *85*, 159–164.

Holzinger, K. J. Relationships between three multiple orthogonal factors and four bifactors. *Journal of Educational Psychology,* 1938, *29,* 513–519.

Honzik, M. P. The constancy of mental test performance during the preschool period. *Journal of Genetic Psychology,* 1938, *52,* 285–302.

Hunt, E. B. Mechanics of verbal ability. *Psychological Review,* 1978, *85,* 109–130.

Hunt, E. B. Intelligence as an information-processing concept. *British Journal of Psychology,* 1980, *71,* 449–474.

Hunt, E. B., & Poltrock, S. Mechanics of thought. In B. Kantowitz (Ed.), *Human information processing: Tutorials in performance and cognition.* Hillsdale, N.J.: Lawrence Erlbaum Associates, 1974.

Huttenlocher, J., & Presson, C. C. Mental rotation and the perspective problem. *Cognitive Psychology,* 1973, *4,* 277–299.

Inhelder, B., & Piaget, J. *The growth of logical thinking from childhood to adolescence.* New York: Basic Books, 1958.

Jensen, A. R. Hierarchical theories of mental ability. In W. B. Dockrell (Ed.), *On intelligence.* Toronto: The Ontario Institute for Studies in Education, 1970.

Jensen, A. R. g: Outmoded theory or unconquered frontier? *Creative Science and Technology,* 1979, *2,* 16–29.

Kail, R., Pellegrino, J., & Carter, P. Developmental changes in mental rotation. *Journal of Experimental Child Psychology,* 1980, *29,* 102–116.

Keating, D. P., & Bobbitt, B. L. Individual and developmental differences in cognitive-processing components of mental ability. *Child Development,* 1978, *49,* 155–167.

Keating, D. P., Keniston, A. H., Manis, F. R., & Bobbitt, B. L. Development of the search-processing parameter. *Child Development,* 1980, *51,* 39–44.

Klahr, D. Goal formation, planning, and learning by pre-school problem solvers or: "My socks are in the dryer." In R. Siegler (Ed.), *Children's thinking: What develops?* Hillsdale, N.J.: Lawrence Erlbaum Associates, 1978.

Klahr, D. *Problem solving and planning by preschool children.* Paper presented at the meeting of the Society for Research in Child Development, San Francisco, March 1979.

Klahr, D., & Wallace, J. G. The role of quantification operators in the development of conservation of quantity. *Cognitive Psychology,* 1973, *4,* 301–327.

Klahr, D., & Wallace, J. G. *Cognitive development: An information processing view.* Hillsdale, N.J.: Lawrence Erlbaum Associates, 1976.

Larkin, J., McDermott, J., Simon, D., & Simon, H. Expert and novice performance in solving physics problems. *Science,* 1980, *208,* 1335–1342.

Levinson, P. J., & Carpenter, R. L. An analysis of analogical reasoning in children. *Child Development,* 1974, *45,* 857–861.

Lewis, M., & Brooks-Gunn, J. Visual attention at three months as a predictor of cognitive functioning at two years of age. *Intelligence,* 1981, *5,* 131–140.

Lunzer, E. A. Problems of formal reasoning in test situations. In P. H. Mussen (Ed.), European research in cognitive development. *Monographs of the Society for Research in Child Development,* 1965, *30*(2, Serial No. 100), 19–46.

Markman, E. M. Realizing that you don't understand: A preliminary investigation. *Child Development,* 1977, *48,* 986–992.

Markman, E. M. Realizing that you don't understand: Elementary school children's awareness of inconsistencies. *Child Development,* 1979, *50,* 643–655.

Markman, E. M. Comprehension monitoring. In S. Yussen (Ed.), *The growth of insight in the child.* New York: Academic Press, in press.

Marmor, G. S. Development of kinetic images: When does the child first represent movement in mental images? *Cognitive Psychology,* 1975, *7,* 548–559.

Marmor, G. S. Mental rotation and number conservation: Are they related? *Developmental Psychology,* 1977, *13,* 320–325.

McCall, R. B., Eichorn, D. J., & Hogarty, P. S. Transitions in early mental development. *Monograph of the Society for Research in Child Development*, 1977, No. 171.

McCall, R. B., Hogarty, P. S., & Hurlburt, N. Transitions in infant sensorimotor development and the prediction of childhood IQ. *American Psychologist*, 1972, *27*, 728–748.

Miller, G. A. The magical number seven plus or minus two: Some limits on our capacity for processing information. *Psychological Review*, 1956, *63*, 81–97.

Miller, G. A., Galanter, E., & Pribram, K. H. *Plans and the structure of behavior*. New York: Holt, Rinehart & Winston, 1960.

Mulholland, T. M., Pellegrino, J. W., & Glaser, R. Components of geometric analogy solution. *Cognitive Psychology*, 1980, *12*, 252–284.

Newell, A. Production systems: Models of control structures. In W. G. Chase (Ed.), *Visual information processing*. New York: Academic Press, 1973.

Newell, A., & Simon, H. A. *Human problem solving*. Englewood Cliffs, N.J.: Prentice-Hall, 1972.

Osherson, D. N. *Logical abilities in children* (Vol. 2): *Logical inference: Underlying operations*. Hillsdale, N.J.: Lawrence Erlbaum Associates, 1974.

Osherson, D. N. *Logical abilities in children* (Vol. 3): *Reasoning in adolescence: Deductive inference*. Hillsdale, N.J.: Lawrence Erlbaum Associates, 1975.

Paris, S. G. Comprehension of language connectives and propositional logical relationships. *Journal of Experimental Child Psychology*, 1973, *16*, 278–291.

Pascual-Leone, J. A mathematical model for the transition rule in Piaget's developmental stages. *Acta Psychologica*, 1970, *63*, 301–345.

Pellegrino, J. W., & Glaser, R. Cognitive correlates and components in the analysis of individual differences. In R. J. Sternberg & D. K. Detterman (Eds.), *Human intelligence: Perspectives on its theory and measurement*. Norwood, N.J.: Ablex, 1979.

Pellegrino, J. W., & Glaser, R. Components of inductive reasoning. In R. E. Snow, P.-A. Federico, & W. Montague (Eds.), *Aptitude, learning, and instruction: Cognitive process analyses of learning and problem solving* (Vol. 2). Hillsdale, N.J.: Lawrence Erlbaum Associates, 1980.

Piaget, J. *The psychology of intelligence*. Totowa, N.J.: Littlefield, Adams, 1972.

Piaget, J. (with Montangero, J., & Billeter, J.). Les correlats. *L'Abstraction réflèchissante*. Paris: Presses Universitaires de France, 1977.

Powell, J. S., & Sternberg, R. J. *Acquisition of vocabulary from context*. Manuscript submitted for publication, 1981.

Reitman, W. *Cognition and thought*. New York: Wiley, 1965.

Resnick, L. B., & Ford, W. W. *The psychology of mathematics for instruction*. Hillsdale, N.J.: Lawrence Erlbaum Associates, 1981.

Resnick, L. B., & Glaser, R. Problem solving and intelligence. In L. B. Resnick (Ed.), *The nature of intelligence*. Hillsdale, N.J.: Lawrence Erlbaum Associates, 1976.

Riley, C. A. The representation of comparative relations and the transitive inference task. *Journal of Experimental Child Psychology*, 1976, *22*, 1–22.

Riley, C. A., & Trabasso, T. Comparatives, logical structures, and encoding in a transitive inference task. *Journal of Experimental Child Psychology*, 1974, *17*, 187–203.

Royce, J. R. Factors as theoretical constructs. *American Psychologist*, 1963, *18*, 522–527.

Rumelhart, D. E., & Norman, D. A. Accretion, tuning, and restructuring: Three modes of learning. In J. W. Cotton & R. L. Klatzky (Eds.), *Semantic factors in cognition*. Hillsdale, N.J.: Lawrence Erlbaum Associates, 1978.

Schank, R. How much intelligence is there in artificial intelligence? *Intelligence*, 1980, *4*, 1–14.

Shepard, R. N., & Metzler, J. Mental rotation of three-dimensional objects. *Science*, 1971, *171*, 701–703.

Siegler, R. S. Three aspects of cognitive development. *Cognitive Psychology*, 1976, *4*, 481–520.

Siegler, R. S. The origins of scientific reasoning. In R. S. Siegler (Ed.), *Children's thinking: What develops?* Hillsdale, N.J.: Lawrence Erlbaum Associates, 1978.

Siegler, R. S. Developmental sequences between and within concepts. *Monograph of the Society for Research in Child Development*, 1981, *46*(2, Whole No. 189).

Snow, R. E. Theory and method for research on aptitude processes. In R. J. Sternberg & D. K. Detterman (Eds.), *Human intelligence: Perspectives on its theory and measurement*. Norwood, N.J.: Ablex, 1979.

Sontag, L. W., Baker, C. T., & Nelson, V. L. Mental growth and personality development: A longitudinal study. *Monograph of the Society for Research in Child Development*, 1958, *23*(2, Whole No. 68).

Spearman, C. *The abilities of man*. London: Macmillan, 1927.

Staudenmayer, H., & Bourne, L. E., Jr. Learning to interpret conditional sentences: A developmental study. *Developmental Psychology*, 1977, *13*, 616–623.

Sternberg, R. J. *Intelligence, information processing, and analogical reasoning: The componential analysis of human abilities*. Hillsdale, N.J.: Lawrence Erlbaum Associates, 1977.

Sternberg, R. J. Componential investigations of human intelligence. In A. Lesgold, J. Pellegrino, S. Fokkema, & R. Glaser (Eds.), *Cognitive psychology and instruction*. New York: Plenum, 1978.

Sternberg, R. J. Developmental patterns in the encoding and combination of logical connectives. *Journal of Experimental Child Psychology*, 1979, *28*, 469–498. (a)

Sternberg, R. J. The nature of mental abilities. *American Psychologist*, 1979, *34*, 214–230. (b)

Sternberg, R. J. The development of linear syllogistic reasoning. *Journal of Experimental Child Psychology*, 1980, *29*, 340–356. (a)

Sternberg, R. J. Factor theories of intelligence are all right almost. *Educational Researcher*, 1980, *9*, 6–13,18. (b)

Sternberg, R. J. A proposed resolution of curious conflicts in the literature on linear syllogisms. In R. Nickerson (Ed.), *Attention and performance VIII*. Hillsdale, N.J.: Lawrence Erlbaum Associates, 1980. (c)

Sternberg, R. J. Representation and process in linear syllogistic reasoning. *Journal of Experimental Psychology: General*, 1980, *109*, 119–159. (d)

Sternberg, R. J. Sketch of a componential subtheory of human intelligence. *Behavioral and Brain Sciences*, 1980, *3*, 573–584. (e)

Sternberg, R. J. Intelligence and nonentrenchment. *Journal of Educational Psychology*, 1981, *73*, 1–16. (a)

Sternberg, R. J. The nature of intelligence. *New York University Education Quarterly*, 1981, *12*, 3, 10–17. (b)

Sternberg, R. J. Novelty-seeking, novelty-finding, and the developmental continuity of intelligence. *Intelligence*, 1981, *5*, 149–155. (c)

Sternberg, R. J. Toward a unified componential theory of human intelligence: I. Fluid abilities. In M. Friedman, J. Das, & N. O'Connor (Eds.), *Intelligence and learning*. New York: Plenum, 1981. (d)

Sternberg, R. J., & Gardner, M. K. A componential interpretation of the general factor in human intelligence. In H. J. Eysenck (Ed.), *A model for intelligence*. New York: Springer, in press.

Sternberg, R. J., & Nigro, G. Developmental patterns in the solution of verbal analogies. *Child Development*, 1980, *51*, 27–38.

Sternberg, R. J., & Powell, J. S. The development of intelligence. In P. Mussen (Ed.), *Carmichael's handbook of child psychology* (3rd ed.). New York: Wiley, in press.

Sternberg, R. J., & Rifkin, B. The development of analogical reasoning processes. *Journal of Experimental Child Psychology*, 1979, *27*, 195–232.

Sternberg, R. J., & Weil, E. M. An aptitude-strategy interaction in linear syllogistic reasoning. *Journal of Educational Psychology*, 1980, *72*, 226–234.

Stott, L. H., & Ball, R. S. Infant and preschool mental tests. *Monograph of the Society for Research in Child Development*, 1965, *30*(3, Whole No. 101).

Suppes, P., & Groen, G. Some counting models for first-grade performance data on simple addition facts. In J. M. Scandura (Ed.), *Research in mathematics education.* Washington, D.C.: National Council of Teachers of Mathematics, 1967.

Taplin, J. E., Staudenmayer, H., & Taddonio, J. L. Developmental changes in conditional reasoning: Linguistic or logical? *Journal of Experimental Child Psychology,* 1974, *17,* 360–373.

Terman, L. M., & Merrill, M. A. *Stanford-Binet intelligence scale: Manual for the third revision.* Boston: Houghton Mifflin, 1973.

Thurstone, L. L. *Primary mental abilities.* Chicago: University of Chicago Press, 1938.

Thurstone, L. L. *Multiple factor analysis.* Chicago: University of Chicago Press, 1947.

Trabasso, T. Representation, memory, and reasoning: How do we make transitive inferences? In A. D. Pick (Ed.), *Minnesota symposia on child psychology* (Vol. 9). Minneapolis: University of Minnesota Press, 1975.

Trabasso, T., & Riley, C. A. On the construction and use of representations involving linear order. In R. L. Solso (Ed.), *Information processing and cognition: The Loyola Symposium.* Hillsdale, N.J.: Lawrence Erlbaum Associates, 1975.

Trabasso, T., Riley, C. A., & Wilson, E. G. The representation of linear order and spatial strategies in reasoning: A developmental study. In R. Falmagne (Ed.), *Reasoning: Representation and process.* Hillsdale, N.J.: Lawrence Erlbaum Associates, 1975.

Vernon, P. E. *The structure of human abilities.* London: Methuen, 1971.

Vurpillot, E. The development of scanning strategies and their relation to visual differentiation. *Journal of Experimental Child Psychology,* 1968, *6,* 632–650.

Werner, H., & Kaplan, E. The acquisition of word meanings: A developmental study. *Monograph of the Society for Research in Child Development,* 1952, No. 51.

Woods, S. S., Resnick, L. B., & Groen, G. J. An experimental test of five process models for subtraction. *Journal of Educational Psychology,* 1975, *67,* 17–21.

Zigler, E. Developmental versus difference theories of mental retardation and the problem of motivation. *American Journal of Mental Deficiency,* 1969, *73,* 536–556.

Zigler, E. The retarded child as a whole person. In H. E. Adams & W. K. Boardman, III (Eds.), *Advances in experimental clinical psychology* (Vol. 1). New York: Pergamon Press, 1971.

Author Index

Numbers in *italics* indicate pages with bibliographic information.

Subject Index